THE WORLD'S RELIGIONS

THE WORLD'S RELIGIONS
A CONTEMPORARY READER

ARVIND SHARMA

editor

Fortress Press / Minneapolis

THE WORLD'S RELIGIONS
A Contemporary Reader

The World's Religions After September 11, by Arvind Sharma, was originally published in hard cover by Praeger, an imprint of ABC-CLIO, LLC, Santa Barbara, CA. Copyright © 2009 by Arvind Sharma. *Part of the Problem, Part of the Solution*, by Arvind Sharma, was originally published in hard cover by Praeger, an imprint of ABC-CLIO, LLC, Santa Barbara, CA. Copyright © 2008 by Arvind Sharma. Paperback edition by arrangement with ABC-CLIO, LLC, Santa Barbara, CA.

"Eco-Justice Ethics" by Dieter Hessel is reprinted with permission from the author.

Cover photo credit: B. Tanaka / Photographer's Choice / Getty Images
Cover design: Laurie Ingram
Book design: The HK Scriptorium, Inc.

Library of Congress Cataloging-in-Publication Data

Sharma, Arvind.
  The world's religions : a contemporary reader / Arvind Sharma.
     p. cm.
  Includes bibliographical references and index.
  ISBN 978-0-8006-9746-4 (alk. paper)
  1. Religion and sociology. 2. Religions. I. Title.
  BL60.S5285 2010
  200.9'0511—dc22   2010027421

The paper used in this publication meets the minimum requirements of American National Standard for Information Sciences—Permanence of Paper for Printed Library Materials, ANSI Z329.48-1984.

Manufactured in the U.S.A.

16 15 14 13 12 11   1 2 3 4 5 6 7 8 9 10

Contents

Foreword   ix
    John Hick

General Introduction   xi

PART 1
Religion and Conflict: Terror, War, and Peace

Introduction   1

Religion and Terror: A Post-9/11 Analysis   3
    Stephen Healey

Religion, Identity, and Violence   13
    Rabbi David Rosen

The Bhagavadgītā and War: Some Early Anticipations of the Gandhian
    Interpretation of the Bhagavadgītā   23
    Arvind Sharma

The Violent Bear It Away: Christian Reflections on Just War   27
    William R. O'Neill

A Jain Perspective on Nonviolence and Warfare   33
    Padmanabh S. Jaini

The Approach of Muslim Turks to Religious Terror   43
    Ramazan Bicer

The Concept of Peace and Security in Islam   53
    Muhammad Hammad Lakhvi

Perspectives on the Conflict in the Middle East   56
    Rabbi Dow Marmur, Seyyed Hossein Nasr, Gregory Baum, Karen Armstrong

Contents

The Golden Rule and World Peace   70
Patricia A. Keefe

World Religions and World Peace: Toward a New Partnership   75
Brian D. Lepard

PART 2
Religion and Human Rights: The Worth of Persons

Introduction   81

Religion and an Implicit Fundamental Human Right   83
James Kellenberger

Religion and Human Rights   89
Shirin Ebadi

What Gives a Person Worth?: A Zoroastrian View   95
Nikan H. Khatibi

Religion, Violence, and Human Rights: A Hindu Perspective   97
Arvind Sharma

Confucian Contributions to the Universal Declaration of Human Rights:
A Historical and Philosophical Perspective   102
Sumner B. Twiss

A Bahá'í Perspective on the Universal Declaration of Human Rights
by the World's Religions   115
Brian D. Lepard

World's Religions, Human Rights, and Same-Sex Marriage   118
Brent Hawkes, Janet Epp Buckingham, Douglas Elliott, Margaret Somerville

Religion and Human Rights: A Historical and Contemporary Assessment   136
Krishna Kanth Tigiripalli, Lalitha Kumari Kadarla

PART 3
Religion and Women: Respecting Gender

Introduction   143

Women in World Religions: Discrimination, Liberation, and Backlash   145
Rosemary Radford Ruether

Women and Human Rights: The Status of Women in the *Smṛti* Texts of Hinduism   152
Abha Singh

Women's Interfaith Initiatives in the United States after 9/11   161
Kathryn Lohre

Turning War Inside Out: New Perspectives for the Nuclear Age   167
Marcia Sichol

PART 4
Religion and the Environment: Science and Ethics

Introduction   171

Religion and Science   173
  Huston Smith

Incarnation and the Environment   178
  Mary Ann Buckley

Eco-Justice Ethics: A Brief Overview   182
  Dieter T. Hessel

PART 5
Religion and Diversity: Embracing Pluralism

Introduction   189

Pluralism as a Way of Dealing with Religious Diversity   191
  Caitlin Crowley

Orientalist Feminism and Islamophobia/Iranophobia   194
  Roksana Bahramitash

Along a Path Less Traveled: A Plurality of Religious Ultimates?   198
  Arvind Sharma

Religion Is About How You Behave: The Essential Virtue Is Compassion 203
  Karen Armstrong

Religious Tolerance and Peace-Building in a World of Diversity   206
  Issa Kirarira

PART 6
Religion and Transformation: Interreligious Dialogue

Introduction   213

Promotion of Interreligious Dialogue   215
  Mihai Valentin Vladimirescu

Interreligious Dialogue Attentive to Western Enlightenment   222
  Gregory Baum

Movement and Institution: Necessary Elements of Sustaining the Interfaith Vision 230
  David A. Leslie

Buddhism Meets Hinduism: Interaction and Influence in India   234
  Arvind Sharma

Fundamentalism and Interfaith Dialogue   241
  Harvey Cox Jr.

Contents

Toward a Culture of Peace   251
Fabrice Blée

PART 7
Religion and the Twenty-First Century: Toward a Global Spirituality

Introduction   257

Religion Is Central to Human Affairs: Part of the Problem, Part of the Solution   259
Didiji

Redefining Humanity and Civilization   265
Nadine Sultana d'Osman Han

Religion in an Age of Anxiety   273
Seyyed Hossein Nasr

Religion and Media   284
Satguru Bodhinatha Veylanswami

Lessons from Hinduism for the World after 9/11   296
Ashok Vohra

The Future of Mankind: The Bhagavadgītā Doctrine   303
T. N. Achuta Rao

This Magdalene Moment   310
Joanna Manning

CaoDai: A Way to Harmony   315
Hum D. Bui

The Glory of the Divine Feminine   318
Her Holiness Sai Maa Lakshmi Devi

Religion, Fundamental Questions, and Human Society   321
Vinesh Saxena

Beyond Religion: A Holistic Spirituality   324
Mabel Aranha

APPENDICES
Primary Documents

1. United Nations Universal Declaration of Human Rights—December 10, 1948   333
2. Universal Declaration of Human Rights by the World's Religions—
December 10, 1998   337

Notes   341
Glossary   363
Index   367

FOREWORD

John Hick

Until recently, most of us in the west thought of religion in what we can now see to be unjustifiably restrictive terms. For the typical western reader, religion meant the Christian religion, or more expansively the monotheistic religions, thus including Judaism and Islam. But today we can see this is much too narrow. This limited knowledge often functioned polemically to establish the superiority of Christianity or at least most of monotheism. But we also have to take into account the nontheistic religions of the east, including not only Buddhism but also Daoism and Confucianism. This new realization needs to be supported by new teaching material, which Fortress Press has now provided in the form of this volume. It distinguishes between major and minor religions and treats them accordingly. Judicious selection from these religions' literature give the reader an accurate account of each of these faiths in both its best and its worst features.

It is also of interest that these extractions enable one to see the varying criteria by which each faith judges both itself and others. In some cases these are mutually compatible; in others, not. It is important to be able to identify these criteria, and it can be a useful exercise to ask the student to do this. A further useful exercise can be to ask the student to identify elements within each faith which that faith does not itself recognize as good or bad, but which nevertheless are so under its own criteria. For the reader new to this subject it will be encouraging to know something of what Dr. Sharma has done in the past. His many publications have required a detailed knowledge of each of the world's religions—major, minor, eastern and western. He has also engaged in comparative studies which have brought to light previously unnoticed points of both similarity and difference. He is therefore a guide to be trusted.

General Introduction

History is never contemporary, for the contemporary is perpetually slipping into history, but with some license one may refer to the immediate past as contemporary history. This point possesses some additional justification when the field to which it is applied is that of the world's religions because so much has happened in such a small time in the recent past, so far as this world's religions are concerned. To grasp this point one needs to realize that what may be called the "secular hypothesis" dominated the worldview not only of academia and the media but also the world of politicians and bureaucrats not that long ago. The belief was so widespread as to have been left virtually unarticulated, that religion as a factor in human affairs was either destined to oblivion, as the Communists would have us believe, or destined to retreat into the private realm, as liberal ideology, characterized by capitalism, would have us imagine. Not many cared about the world's religions at the turn of the century, when secularization, hand in hand with globalization, seemed to be proceeding apace, converting the world into both one market and one marketplace of ideas, promising homogeneity as a unifying force for humanity, destined to erode religious diversity as all of us became more like each other. The Iranian Revolution of 1979 could then be treated like a retrogressive hiccup of tradition in this forward march of modernity.

And then something happened. It happened, to be precise, on the 11th of September, 2001, which made a trainwreck of this expectation. An event happened, literally out of the blue, which proved to be a gamechanger, as they say. One wonders how many readers of this anthology remember the day; for those who do, the events are ineffaceable from modern memory, for those who do not they are inseparable from modern history. The foundations of the paradigm on which the modern world rested may also be said to have collapsed, with the collapse of New York City's twin towers under aerial assault.

What was referred to above as the secular hypothesis was a paradigm characterized by a subtle economic determinism and an equally subtle Western exceptionalism. It held that economic forces were destined to determine the future of humanity, the question of whether they were going to be capitalistic or communistic had already virtually been settled with the end of the Cold War. It could now be said out aloud what was hitherto muttered sotto voce, that the West's immediate past was the world's not so distant future, a future in which the secularity of modernity was set to prevail over the tradition of religiosity as manifested by the world's religions, which seemed engaged in fighting desperate rearguard battles before being overcome by the forces of modernity. But all that changed after September 11, 2001. But not necessarily for the better for our world's religions.

That the destruction of lives and property which occurred on September 11 occurred in the name of a religion produced two important consequences for the world's religions: *that* the world's religions were now in the spotlight, and *that* they were there in a *negative* spotlight, as if a beam of darkness rather than light had been focused on them.

This anthology is an attempt to come to terms with the spotlight now being turned on the world's religions with a special message: Yes, the world's religions are back in the spotlight as the thesis of the inevitable longterm secularization of the world and the marginalization of the world's religions is called into question but *no*, unlike the impression left by the events of September 11, religions are not necessarily a negative force in human affairs. The world's religions are important not because they are a destructive force; they are important because they are a *force* in human affairs (long neglected) which may be harnessed for either good or evil.

Any attempt to harness religion as a positive force must involve the recognition that religion is a *nonrational force* in human affairs. The age of Enlightenment has many achievements to its credit, but in one respect its modern legacy is rather lamentable. By looking at all of life with the binary grid of the *rational* and the *irrational*, it took a toll on the *nonrational* dimension of life, which includes the emotive side of life all the way from family relations to one's relationship with the divine. In order to make these fit into its binary perspective, the age tended to assimilate the *non*rational to the irrational, thus leading to the neglect of the emotional and transcendental dimensions of life, a neglect which has come to haunt modern civilization. As we now reintegrate religion into our worldview, we might wish to distinguish carefully among three terms: fundamentalism, orthodoxy, and fanaticism. Fundamentalism is a religious tradition's reaction to a perceived loss of power in the public square. Orthodoxy is a religious tradition's response to a perceived loss of piety in the public square. Fanaticism consists of being blinded by the intensity of the luminosity of one's own tradition by standing too close to it, instead of seeing the whole world transfigured in its light. These phenomena sometimes mimic one another but need to be identified correctly so that the proper corrective can be set in play in the form of their exposure to political pluralism, social pluralism, and religious pluralism respectively.

It was stated earlier that religion could be harnessed not only for good but also evil. This theme is explored in the early chapters of part 1, wherein the relationship of religion to conflict and terror is analyzed, as also its relation to war, and therefore, by extension, peace. For it must not be overlooked, as many modern works which chronicle the darker side of religion tend to, that religion has *also* been a positive factor in human affairs. Judaism introduced the world to the concept of ethical monotheism; Christianity put an end to the gory gladiatorial spectacles of the Roman world; Islam put an end to female infanticide in Arabia. Hinduism has promoted religious toleration; Buddhism has similarly promoted nonviolence; and Sikhism, active charity. In China, Confucianism gave to moderation an emotional force which it has only recently acquired in the West, and Taoism provides a philosophy which is being drawn upon to undergird modern ecological considerations.

That it will be this positive side of religion (and not the negative) which will play a role in securing human flourishing (rather than undermining it) is highlighted in part 2, which focuses on the relationship of religion and human rights. This attempt to positively associate religion with human rights can be traced back to the Project on Religion and Human Rights. The seeds planted by the project in 1993 have now produced a virtually global harvest of constructive engagement between religion and human rights. Nowhere is it more visible than in the field of gender, as is obvious from part 3. The inclusion of the perspective of gender paves the way for broadening the discussion to include the discussion, in part 4, of religion and the environment, given the growth and consolidation of ecofeminism.

In the next three parts of the book, the perspective is more inward-looking, as the issues the world's religions face as such come into focus. Part 5 thus deals with religion and diversity. It emphasizes the need to face pluralism, for if there is anything which obviously characterizes the world of religion, it is not merely the diversity represented by the different religious traditions but also the internal diversity which characterizes these traditions. But how then is such vibrant diversity to be precisely dealt with? An attempt is made to provide the answer in part 6 in terms of encouraging dialogue, as is obvious from the full rubric of this part of the book: "Religion and Transformation: Interreligious Dialogue."

In the final part—namely, part 7—this contemporary reader looks to the future. Many readers will perhaps feel enticed, and perhaps even rewarded, by the various chapters included in this part. Modern discourse on religion has witnessed the emergence of a significant contrast, perhaps even an antithesis in this respect, between *religion* and *spirituality*. Numerous surveys have documented a rise in the number of people who are eager to describe themselves as "spiritual" and reluctant to describe themselves as "religious." Normally, the "spiritual" is considered one dimension of religion, alongside the doctrinal, the mythical, the ritual, and so on. These surveys, however, point in a different direction. The layperson, as distinguished from the academic, increasingly identifies religion with the authoritarianism and rigidity associated with religion as an institution and rejects this form of religion in favour of "spirituality," which has come to stand for a freedom to search for the meaning of life on one's own terms and without being necessarily bound to any one single tradition in doing so. This part deals with the more evocative of the two terms, namely, *spirituality*, and tries to describe the contours of the various developments occurring in this area that are likely to play an important role in the future.

Although the various parts of the book have been outlined above, the book must be viewed as greater than the sum of the parts, for it points, as a whole, to two vital areas of human concern which are likely to persist. The first has to do with the nature of the human condition. Modern thinking has moved as far as possible in regarding the human being as a *secular* human being; just as the earlier ages had moved as far as possible in regarding the human being as a *religious* human being. Any fresh thinking on the human condition after September 11 must learn to do justice to both these dimensions of the human condition, as it is clear that excessive movement in one direction tends to create a countervailing force in the other.

The second has to do with how humanity is going to proceed to settle its differences. Interestingly, humanity has done a fairly good job of settling its difference within national boundaries, as illustrated by the effectiveness with which law and order is maintained within a nation, alongside a democratic political structure. The events of September 11 are the most dramatic illustration, since World War II, of its failure to do so across national (and perhaps also civilizational) borders. These two issues may be said to provide the fundamental template of the book, as constituting the two ends of its spine as it were. These issues are going to remain with us for a long time. They were thrown into high relief by the events of September 11. This book represents a disciplined "groping" for a solution to these problems in its aftermath.

PART 1

RELIGION AND CONFLICT

Terror, War, and Peace

INTRODUCTION

World's religions in relation to violence cover a whole spectrum of options, ranging all the way from militarism at the one end to pacifism on the other. This part tries to represent this range and to highlight the concept of a just war, a concept toward which, in some form or another, most of the world's religions tend to gravitate.

Readers might well feel particularly drawn to two pieces in this section. One is the panel discussion on the conflict in the Middle East, in which each side presents its position with remarkable force and clarity without casting aspersions on the others. The other is the discussion on Bhagavadgītā. As is well known, the setting of Bhagavadgītā is explicitly martial, yet the text has hardly ever been used to promote war, and an attempt has been made to address this paradox.

RELIGION AND TERROR

A Post-9/11 Analysis

Stephen Healey

In the nineteenth century, Horace Bushnell wrote that

> Men undertake to be spiritual, and they become ascetic; or, endeavoring to hold a liberal view of the comforts and pleasures of society, they are soon buried in the world, and slaves to its fashions; or, holding a scrupulous watch to keep out every particular sin, they become legal, and fall out of liberty; or, charmed with the noble and heavenly liberty, they run to negligence and irresponsible living; so the earnest become violent, the fervent fanatical and censorious, the gentle waver, the firm turn bigots, the liberal grow lax, the benevolent ostentatious. Poor human infirmity can hold nothing steady.[1]

Bushnell's Christian account has much to commend it. Since the terrifying acts of September 11, 2001, the relationship of religion and politics—especially purported failures and dangers of Islam—has dominated scholarly and popular discussions. From the ashes of this catastrophe, Islamophobia, an irrational fear of things Muslim, has taken on new urgency. In the last few years, scores of books have been written either denouncing or defending Islam.[2] Authors have insisted that the West and Islam are at war. In the same broad strokes, Islam has been heralded as a religion of peace. When authored by Westerners these claims are often couched in, but not sufficiently critical of, the prevalent Western view that all religions should honor the separation of church and state. When authored by non-Western Muslims, these claims generally reject church-state separation as a secular system devoid of theology, instead of viewing it as an ecclesiology.[3] Beguiled by assumptions entailed within this ecclesiology, Islam's detractors have more often misunderstood than understood the religion, and Islam's defenders have more often misrepresented than represented it. The ecclesiological-theological, and not merely secular, dimension of church-state separation has often gone unrecognized. In the post-9/11 era, renewed conversation and critical theological thinking about religion, politics, violence, and peace is mandated for everyone who wishes to see a peaceful world. In work of this sort, comparative analyses of the major religions that treat social, political, economic, and cultural contexts will be most fruitful. Since the post-9/11 era is fraught with violence, ethical concern to understand and uproot violent tendencies is also a crucial starting point.

3

Two recently published books—Sam Harris's *The End of Faith* and an edited volume titled *World Religions and Democracy*, by Larry Diamond, Marc Plattner, and Philip Costopoulos—are especially worth considering in this respect.[4] Harris reflects ethically on the capacity of religious faith to precipitate acts of madness, and Diamond, Plattner, and Costopoulos examine the capacity of world religions to support development of large-scale social systems, especially democratic politics. On the face of it, the conclusions the authors draw are diametrically opposed. Harris argues that faith is poisonous to the prospect of civility, decency, and peace. Faith, he argues, is identical to irrationalism.[5] In his view, even religious tolerance and liberalism are dangerous, because they conceal the fanaticism lurking in all kinds of religious faith.[6] On the other hand, Diamond, Plattner, and Costopoulos argue that the world religions have multivalent resources that can be marshaled to nondemocratic and dangerous or to democratic and constructive ends.[7] Understanding conditions in which particular religions support democracy and yearn for peace, and those in which they might legitimate oppressiveness and hostility, is more complex than Harris's account acknowledges.

Key differences in the approaches of Harris and Diamond, Plattner, and Costopoulos, however, make synthesizing these works profitable. The two works together suggest important views for thinking about religion and terror in the post-9/11 age. The social-historical and empirical work of Diamond, Plattner, and Costopoulos can be used to broaden Harris's ethical-analytical treatment of religions, and the moral dimensions of Harris's analysis can be used to enrich that of Diamond, Plattner, and Costopoulos. Troubling aspects of Harris's moral analysis (Harris, for example, defends the use of torture as morally equivalent to collateral damage in war) can be addressed by democratic safeguards suggested in the other work.[8] Both Harris and Diamond, Plattner, and Costopoulos raise issues about religiously associated violence and peace, interreligious dialogue, and current politics that are worth pondering in the post-9/11 era.

THE END OF FAITH?

Harris's main contention in *The End of Faith* is that religious belief is generally malicious and that religions insulate themselves from critical scrutiny by advancing claims that disallow rational analysis. Faith, defined by Harris as irrational assent, provides this insulation. Is there a God? God only knows! Harris denies that reason can answer this question. Instead of rational warrant, religions introduce the ministry of unfeasible certitude. Harris portrays this certitude as a cartoon he believes predominates in the minds of most believers. There is a God; this God revealed a book; he used especially good men as absolute examples; he gives reasons to kill neighbors when they harbor false notions of God (i.e., views that differ from this or that book, or this or that prophet). Harris suggests that religious faith exploits people's gullibility, overrides their basic capacity for sympathy, and leads them to believe incredible (even murderous) assertions. This is downright dangerous, he contends. Our beliefs, no matter how crazy, control our choices.[9] If a group believes that its neighbors are infidels whom God will punish in an eternal lake of fire, that group is likely to see violence toward these neighbors as justified. If a group believes its neighbors are worthy of love, it will love them. The religions, however, admix low and high views of neighbors and provide numerous examples of righteous warriors killing infidels. Human credulousness is easily provoked to a low view of the neighbor; thus, religions breed intolerance and foster violence. Harris points to history to show that this is more or less how it works. His catalog of evidence supporting this idea should give pause to believers and nonbelievers alike.

According to Harris, liberalism seeks to correct this penchant for religious violence. But it develops a view of religious belief, a metabelief, that Harris argues leads toward the abyss of religiously motivated global-scale destruction. Liberal tolerance, on Harris's reading, insists that religiously motivated choices should always be honored.[10] This essentially leads to winking at insanity. To make this point, Harris describes bizarre belief-based practices. For example, Harris grieves,

> The rioting in Nigeria over the 2002 Miss World Pageant claimed over two hundred lives: innocent men and women were butchered with machetes or burned alive simply to keep that troubled place free of women in bikinis.[11]

But Muslims, Harris shows, are not alone in holding silly ideas.

> We should be humbled, perhaps to the point of spontaneous genuflection, by the knowledge that the ancient Greeks began to lay their Olympian myths to rest several hundred years before the birth of Christ, whereas we have the likes of Bill Moyers convening earnest gatherings of scholars for the high purpose of determining just how the book of Genesis can be reconciled with life in the modern world.[12]

Jesus wept, Harris sighs. Come now, he argues, if something is clearly erroneous, whether it is a religious creed that motivates people to harm their neighbors or one that espouses pure nonsense, it should be judged rather than tolerated. It is unethical not to judge crazy or harmful ideas, because such ideas lead people to dangerous and harmful actions. However sharply Harris makes his points, they are often leavened with humor and wit, and he is motivated by desire to see the world at peace. Without irony, he claims to have written the book "very much in the spirit of a prayer."[13] His prayer, put simply, is that people will start thinking and as a result will stop killing in the name of incredible beliefs.

Harris's criticism of religious faith is more or less ecumenical. All religions that inspire unreasonable thinking, those that make a virtue of irrational faith, come under fire. Especially prominent in his analysis, however, are Islam and Christianity. He gives special attention to the failings (witch burnings, torture ordeals for heretics, anti-Semitism, jihad, to name a few) of these two religions.[14] The evidence, though well-known, is arranged with dark humor to prosecute the case that faith itself is to blame for insane actions of Christians and Muslims. However dangerous these faith orientations are, Harris thinks they nonetheless address real human spiritual needs that science cannot satisfy.[15] The problem is not that religions address needs, but how religions conceive irrational faith as an answer to them. Instead of faith, the current moment requires ethics and spirituality that are aligned to truths about the world and self known through science. Harris presents this mixture of resources as a rational means to address spiritual needs.

Harris's analysis leads him to be *certain* that many religious believers are wrong about important matters. Against the faithful certitude of believers, Harris does not introduce hand-wringing liberal doubt or relativism. Instead, he introduces certitude of his own by combining the convictions that science tells us what reality is like, that we should not harm sentient creatures (unless dictated by very compelling ethical reasons, such as self-defense), and that we can learn about the nature of our own consciousness through spirituality and meditation. Harris is receptive to Buddhism as a source of genuinely rational spiritual insight. Indeed, the final chapter in Harris's book, titled "Experiments in Consciousness," is the most constructive one. In this chapter, he holds that meditation helps the practitioner distinguish between thinking and consciousness. That, he says, is a key assumption of mysticism, which is rational, in contrast to irrational faith.

Though the issues Harris raises are essential, the constructive point of view he offers will not support development of institutions that will bear pressures in the post-9/11 era. To discover these, Harris's narrow view of religious faith must be complemented by socially informed study of the world religions.

WORLD RELIGIONS AND DEMOCRACY?

Whereas Harris sees the destructive potential of faith, others look to the world religions for their civilization-building potential. The essays collected in *World Religions and Democracy,* many first published from 1995 to 2004 in the *Journal of Democracy,* sponsored by the International Forum for Democratic Studies of the National Endowment for Democracy, examine whether the world religions are congenial to the development of democracy. Alongside articles by academic heavyweights such as Peter Berger, Bernard Lewis, Francis Fukuyama, and other significant academics, the volume contains essays by the spiritual leader His Holiness the Dalai Lama and Burma's human rights activist Aung San Suu Kyi. Though authored by a diverse group, the articles are fairly well integrated. Those interested in the plight of democracy in our hyperreligious world will find that these articles challenge and complement the findings of Harris. Whereas Harris focuses on religious beliefs and their implications for action, the authors in *World Religions and Democracy* give more attention to religious institutions and social-historical context.

Diamond, Plattner, and Costopoulos have grouped nineteen chapters into sections on the Eastern Religions, Judaism and Christianity, and Islam. A conceptual framework for the book is set forth in the introduction, by Philip Costopoulos, and within the first article, by Alfred Stepan. The essays are dense with sheer detail and thoughtful analysis. The discussion that follows will illuminate areas in which Harris's criticism of faith can profitably be engaged from broader social and historical perspectives.

In *World Religions and Democracy,* the conceptual framework raises the concept of "twin tolerations," which presumes the differentiation of "religious and political authority."[16] In short, the idea of twin tolerations (one for each fallen tower?) means that religions should not have the constitutional right to set public policy for democratically elected governments, and that individuals and groups should have the unrestricted right to express their values publicly, so long as they do not "impinge on the liberties of other citizens or violate democracy and the law."[17] However, the authors reject the idea that twin tolerations can be honored only through one model of church-state relations.

As such, they critically examine assumptions about this relationship.

Stepan explores how religions have actually interacted with political systems along these lines. He convincingly shows that the idealized separation of church and state so often heralded by Americans is at variance with the historical reality in Western Europe. Five members of the European Union, for example, have established churches, and those that do not nonetheless often divert significant public funds to church agencies. Germans, for example, generally elect to pay *Kirchensteuer* (Church tax), because significant social benefits (the right to be baptized, married, or buried in a church, and to be afforded access to church-based hospitals, for example) accrue primarily to those who pay it. In the EU, only Portugal prohibits political parties from using religious affiliations and symbols. Additionally, an idealized language of church-state separation inhibits understanding of Eastern Orthodoxy, Confucianism, or Islam. In sum, "From the viewpoint of empirical democratic practice . . . the concept of secularism must be radically rethought."[18]

Based upon this study of European democracies, Stepan refutes three commonly held positions. All of the essays in the volume accept these basic premises. First, religions are not reducible to single essences that can be judged, thumbs up or thumbs down. The same religion might well support diverse, even antithetical, objectives, including some that are laudatory (democracy and love, for example) and others that are horrific (antidemocracy or mindless violence, for example). Second, Stepan questions whether the social and religious conditions that prevailed at democracy's origin are necessary to export it to another society. He pointedly questions the idea (propounded by noted political scientist Samuel Huntington, and accepted by many) that societies informed by Eastern Orthodoxy, Confucianism, and Islam will remain uncongenial to democracy. Third, eliminating religion from public and political discussions is shown to be pointless, since religiously based practice is a common part of the world's most established democracies. These perspectives provide a valuable foundation to examine the implications of the world religions in the post-9/11 era.

Harris recognizes the pluralistic nature of religions, and he knows that religions have inspired great people to do great things and base people to do base things. He claims that the latter predominate by a wide margin. Whereas Diamond, Plattner, and Costopoulos work with the assumption that religions are multivalent, Harris focuses on faith and views it univocally. He holds that faith always requires suspension of reason and entails certitude about ridiculous creeds. He is aware of significant theologians (Paul Tillich, for example) who see matters with significantly greater nuance, but he does not engage their work because, in his view, the common believer gives shape to history. The common believer, Harris is convinced, is most likely a fanatic duped by unreason. Against a theological orientation, Harris's turn of mind is sociological; but his argument is a series of theological judgments. Thus, he develops an admixture of sociologically and theologically inclined perspectives. In short, Harris's *theology* is judgmental, too quickly dismissive, and thus unlikely to support the aims he has in mind.

The substantial notes to *The End of Faith* do not engage significant findings of religious studies scholarship. Too bad, because the devil, as they say, is in the details. For example, Abdou Filali-Ansary, who contributed three articles to *World Religions and Democracy,* points out that the influential work of Jamal-Eddin Al-Afghani (1838–97) has led many Arab and non-Arab Muslims to treat the word *secular* as more or less equivalent to *atheism* and *godlessness.*[19] This explanation illuminates Muslim resistance to secular democracy, but Harris's analysis does not ponder the issues deeply or broadly enough to get to this level. In his view, which he shares with Samuel Huntington, the West and Islam are at war.[20] Instead of broad-based analysis, Harris relies heavily upon his analytical schema (faith is ruinous; meditative reason is emancipatory), even when the data he presents suggests otherwise. For example, in a lengthy footnote, he states,

Attentive readers will have noticed that I have been very hard on religions of faith—Judaism, Christianity, Islam, and even Hinduism—and have not said much that is derogatory of Buddhism. This is not an accident. While Buddhism has also been a source of ignorance and occasional violence, it is not a religion of faith, or a religion at all, in the Western sense. *There are millions of Buddhists who do not seem to know this, and they can be found in temples throughout Southeast Asia, and even the West, praying to Buddha as though he were a numinous incarnation of Santa Claus.*[21]

Harris's preconceived (and essentialist) understanding of Buddhism leads him to obscure it.[22] More thorough acknowledgment of the social history of Buddhism would suggest that the simple lens used against the so-called faith-based religions and then used to praise Buddhism distorts the historical realities both of what Harris affirms and of what he denies. Harris lauds an idealized, nonexistent version of Buddhism, which is at variance with most Buddhist practice in the world. The essays by the Dalai Lama and Aung San Suu Kyi in *World Religions* provide examples of how to think about Buddhism as a living reality that is embedded in time, space, and culture. In contrast, Harris's focus on one particular definition of faith distorts the historical realities of the religions he surveys.

Harris believes that religious liberalism leads to suspension of judgment about foolish and dangerous creeds, when we should be willing, ultimately, to judge grotesque foolishness, even if it is dressed up in the pontifical vestment and florid calligraphy honored by a billion believers. Serious theology, in his view, is a mind game that ignores the predominant (and crude) dimensions of faith-based religions. This aspect of Harris's thought is not convincing, because serious theology and religious liberalism have more power to challenge foolishness than nonreligious naturalism does, even if the latter is augmented by spirituality and meditation. Harris's hope for peace is profoundly limited by the tenor and substance of his analysis. Diamond and coauthors show more ably how to engage in analysis of religious propensity to justify harmful practices while remaining open to their contributions.

Harris has noted that Western religions tend to be historically focused and action-oriented. In the histories of Judaism, Christianity, and Islam, it is undeniable that this orientation has been expressed in militant fashion. It is also true, therefore, that the basic texts of these religions contain theological justifications for war and violence.[23] Should a fanatic wish to justify his or her choices by citing chapter and verse, each of these traditions provides an ample store of references. Harris documents without attempting to understand these tendencies. As a result, he is curiously blind to the fact that his justification of war and torture is essentially analogous to what he condemns in Christianity and Islam. Harris gives no significant attention to wider histories and broader social possibilities entailed by these religions. Were he to do so, the question of ecclesiology would be a profitable beginning place. In this context, Peter Berger's brief article, titled "Christianity: The Global Picture," draws attention to the importance of social differentiation afforded by the church as an institution.[24] The article by Hahm Chaibong, titled "The Ironies of Confucianism," provides a fascinating discussion of Confucian values, statecraft, and economics. In short, Hahm argues that Confucian values show strong correlation to economic development and growth, but these same values have not provided significant resistance to absolutist governments. Confucianism's main loci are family and state, and thus it lacks "a realm of awareness or action over against the realm controlled by the state."[25] Harris's proposal may eliminate the capacity to build civil society and thus undermines a source of dissent against governments and a resource to challenge fanaticism. This is not to suggest that Harris should engage in detailed analysis of Confucianism but rather that his critical approach to the Western religions could be augmented by a richer understanding of their social potential.

None of the authors of *World Religions and Democracy* is an apologist for any religious tradition. Further, they are fully aware of the horrors cataloged by Harris. Yet the authors also rightly hold that the potential benefits of religious ideas, communities, and institutions must be weighed against their risks in a context in which religions inevitably exist. Religious communities are here to stay, and they will continue to represent promise and peril because they will guide the choices of billions of people. The best strategy is to work with urgency tempered by patience to encourage their long-term transformation. That process, almost surely, will entail religions engaging in self-criticism. Diamond, Plattner, and Costopoulos set forth examples of religious communities doing just that. Nothing Harris offers will encourage self-critique by religious groups.

Religious traditions need not speak in the idiom of liberalism, but they will need to cultivate their own deepest capacity to inspire tolerance and denounce fanaticism. In one of Harris's more heartfelt criticisms of religious faith, he points out that human beings did not require a prophet to teach them to be sympathetic to one another.[26] Harris believes that when human beings see someone suffer, they suffer along with them unless a religious tradition blunts this capacity. He believes that sympathy is rooted in human nature, which innately understands the golden rule. However true this is in intimate settings (small communities, for example), or in ad hoc settings that spontaneously partake in the intimacy of these conditions (seeing a family in the hospital worry about a sick child, for example), most societal experiences are constituted by impersonal relationships. Globalization is increasing the scope of these impersonal relationships. By their very nature, these impersonal relationships are not and cannot be founded upon sympathy; instead they need to be grounded in principle and abstraction. Prophets did not teach principle and abstraction of this sort, but they did expound religious visions that fueled later societal developments of universalistic significance.

Taken together, Harris and the authors of *World Religions and Democracy* raise questions that religious communities will need to address in the post-9/11 era. Harris's suggestion that religious fanaticism could lead to massive destruction is correct. The terror of 9/11 is a wake-up call to renew the task of theology as a public mode of inquiry. The broad-based analyses in *World Religions and Democracy* support this suggestion as well. In particular, the following recommendations for the post-9/11 era can be derived from synthesizing the works of Harris and Diamond et al. and processing implications of the post-9/11 era.

CONCLUSIONS FOR THE POST-9/11 ERA

In the post-9/11 era, religious traditions must be engaged as multivalent moral institutions capable of inspiring good and evil. To use the term *religion* as an analogue for "good" or "evil" is irresponsible. In addition to being positive resources within civilizations, religions have been sources of profound malice. Nor should there be doubt that religions continue to harbor these potentials. The pressure of teleological pursuit (the need for decisiveness and urgent action) has led members of every religion to challenge, alter, and engage in ad hoc reinterpretation of basic principles that they deem to be absolute. The appearance of doctrinal permanence is usually preserved through theological sleight of hand even as the principles are being fundamentally altered.[27] Some of these compromises have reduced religious malignancy, but others have led to its development.[28] It is an essential task to identify, then reduce or eliminate these tendencies. Harris's work contains examples of compromise that a theological-ethical analysis might well question. He supports the nonviolent tendencies of Jainism and Buddhism, yet he denies that pacifism is a viable political strategy.[29] Further, he criticizes Christians for persecuting witches (with the strappado, for example), but on the other hand suggests it would be justifiable under certain circumstance to use the strappado against a terrorist.[30] Religious ethical analysis in the post-9/11 era will require examining how religious principles interact with particular social and historical settings to justify some courses of action and discredit others. Such an examination will require making judgments for some religious points of view and against others.[31] This is not the task of one person, but a conversation for communities to inform policies of institutions. This conversation cannot rely upon Harris's judgmental idiom, since no participant will possess enough truth to justify the arrogant assertion of his or her point of view or the callous dismissal of other points of view.[32]

In the post-9/11 era, the capacity to engage in interreligious dialogue must be developed among believers of every religion. At this time, few believers are adequately equipped to engage in interreligious dialogue. Most religious communities have expended enormous energy instilling the basics of their own perspectives, but they have expended almost none teaching about other points of view.[33] Harris is correct to suggest that religious claims are not exempt from the canons of reason, argument, and debate.[34] Some positions of faith, at least the most dangerous extremes, can be shown to be unreasonable through dialogue. Conversations of this sort are important. Harris's criticism is flawed where it renders dialogue impossible, but his view that religious positions require defense is correct.[35] Interreligious dialogue and theology will not bring religiously associated violence to an end, but both are indispensable pursuits in our time. Because they will shape the choices people make, both dialogue and theology have political import. The article by the Dalai Lama in *World Religions and Democracy* demonstrates that a religious leader can benefit from fresh perspectives.[36] However, to engage in fruitful interreligious dialogue, everyday believers will need to learn how to recognize, challenge, and modify malignant tendencies in their own religions, and to engage with others in discussion about this. All religions possess resources to recognize enduring principles, accommodate change, and engage in self-correction, but too few of these resources have been made broadly available. In our time, these potencies will need to be fully utilized. In short, rethinking religions in this manner will require theological analysis combined with broad awareness of the social histories of religions. Communities will do well to train specialists and to equip everyday believers in the area of interreligious dialogue.

In the post-9/11 era, renewed attention must be given to the relationship between Islam and the West. A good starting point is to view the post-9/11 era as analogous to the post–Cold War era. A dimension of the analysis ought to question this us/them rhetorical construction. In the new post–Cold War era, "Islam" often is used as a dyadic other that replaces "Communism." If aggregate concepts are used, careful historical analysis is necessary to understand the influence of these entities.[37] All religions have at times inspired terror and violence; Harris's declaration that Islam is especially bloodthirsty is unwarranted.[38] It is true that terror attacks currently waged by Muslim terrorists capture news headlines, but this should be understood in a historical perspective. Most Muslims quietly (some vocally) find terrorist acts un-Islamic, but many Muslims also share the anger that motivates them.[39] Huntington correctly identifies the need to develop a post–Cold War *conflict* paradigm, even though the paradigm he suggests is significantly flawed.[40] The collapse of Soviet Communism and the turn of China to a market-style economy have raised questions in the minds of many Muslims about political economies that have prevailed in the Islamic countries of the Middle East and North Africa, most of which have been Islamic socialisms, dictatorships, monarchies, or an unhappy mixture of these. Leaders in these regimes have emulated Machiavelli more than Muhammad to exploit the construction of faith, world, and identity particular to Islam in order to solidify political power.[41] In the post–Cold War world, the deepest assumptions that prevailed in these regimes and in the minds of their citizens are undergoing rapid change. Whether democracy will prevail in the Middle East and North Africa—the U.S. presence in Iraq is not auspicious—is unclear.[42] But current acts of Muslim terrorists ought to be viewed as the surface-level reaction to an immense ethos shift of which the actors are only dimly aware.[43] The intellectual maps of "the world" that

have guided these actors are being dramatically altered, and what the world will become—to put it in other terms, whether Allah will emerge as the victor—is unclear. This ethos shift contributes to deep anxiety, which couples with the youthful demographic of the Arab world and the Islamic notion of divine sovereignty that seems thwarted by recent events, to promote conditions conducive to profound resentment and, for the fanatically inclined, terrorism.[44]

In the post-9/11 era, the role of theology originally promoted by sectarian ecclesiological practices and then later accorded to it by political liberalism must be rethought.[45] In the post-9/11 era, which is the post–Cold War era, the intellectual basis of political liberalism is also changing. The words of and actions sponsored by U.S. politicians show that anxiety about these profound changes is not limited to Muslims. Political liberalism renders politically (and as a normative ecclesiology) the sectarian Protestant account of the relationship of church and state. In this view, the epistemologies of faith on the one side and of politics on the other are viewed as completely separate matters.[46] Faith is viewed as a matter of speculation and opinion or unassailable heartfelt conviction. Harris is correct to criticize the notion that faith is merely private: as he says, "It is time that we recognized that belief is not a private matter."[47] When faith is held strictly separate from other cultural spheres, over time it becomes irrelevant and idiosyncratic. Further, when politics is viewed as a matter of self-evidence, the many normative, religious, and doctrinal dimensions of politics become opaque. To examine the separation of church and state, theological analysis will be necessary, because the separation itself entails many issues that are essentially theological in character. Theology must be renewed as a matter of public, and not simply ecclesial, reflection. This renewal will in turn mean that political science as a discipline will need to be intellectually reconceived, as the strictly secular object of political science is a fiction of political liberalism.

In the post-9/11 era, an important task of theological and comparative religious reflection, then, is to develop principles for dealing with religiously inspired terror. Terror is not simply a concern of political science. Religious communities can and should propose solutions to states that are dealing with terror. Further, they ought to denounce terrorist acts committed in their name; the practice of excommunication may seem a quaint residue of the past, but now is the time to renew it. The post-9/11 era has altered the moral landscape, and standard ethical and legal replies to moral questions are not sufficient. Harris's justification of torture lacks moral basis, but he is correct to encourage articulation of new principles and strategies. The acts of 9/11 contribute urgency to the suggestion that globalization is altering the significance and power of nation-states.[48] The acts of 9/11 were committed by individuals whose creed justifies, even sanctifies, acts of violence against perceived oppressors and idolaters.[49] Nation-states and international agencies will continue to supply police who find and bring terrorists to justice. The nature of justice remains somewhat open, however, since rogue individuals can affect the plight of millions of people. Also open is the question of strategies to employ against terrorists in various religious, political, and legal contexts. Without open, public reflection on these questions, the prevailing spirit of anxiety will foster extremist replies, even by those who mean well.

In the post-9/11 era, Max Weber's empirically based insight that religious strategies often lead to unintended results is worth recalling in the context of religion, terror, and dialogue. Efforts that aim to reduce religiously associated violence may actually increase it, similar to how Protestant attitudes of this-worldly asceticism had the unintended effect of stimulating wealth production. In the case noted by Weber, dualism was at work: the early Protestants feared the temptations of luxury, since they viewed luxuriousness as a tool of the devil. In seeking to avoid luxury, they created conditions that favored promoting it. In considerations of religion and violence, it seems wise to formulate less dualistic accounts, understanding that a certain level of violence and conflict are inevitable. Instead of seeking to rid the world of religious violence and conflict, it is better to seek ways to manage it and minimize its destructive potentials. This notion of conflict is a key assumption of democratic theory that has distal roots in Protestant theology. Formulating institutions that recognize the inevitability of struggle is prefigured in Protestant ecclesiologies.

The post-9/11 era apparently will be highly religious, and neither secularism nor scientism is likely to replace religious communities in the near or distant future. Thus, in the post-9/11 world, the role of religious institutions and democratic safeguards for them and against them are invaluable societal resources. It has become commonplace to observe that religion has not dwindled in significance as predicted by the so-called secularization thesis of early twentieth-century social theorists. According to that theory, the advance of modernity would lead to the decline of religion. In a vein similar to that of the great Enlightenment philosophe Voltaire, whose witty dictum was that humanity would not be free until the last king was strangled with the entrails of the last priest, these theorists foresaw a day in which religionless modernity (democracy, urbanity, capitalism, and science) would prevail. In the fully modern, hyperreligious world of today, however, religions show remarkable vitality. In addition to their power to heal, religions possess shocking destructive potential. If anything, to take a phrase from philosopher Jürgen Habermas, it is the "philosophical discourse of modernity" that has declined.[50] An implication of this is that Niebuhrian realism should prevail.[51] The world's religions are aspects of the power struggle that dominates all of life, and this power struggle is an ineradicable part of historical existence. Christianity, Islam, and the other world religions provide adherents something to live for, something to die for, and, under certain conditions, something to kill for. This way of putting it raises the issue of peace and violence in religions and begs for careful analysis. In that respect, the post-9/11 era—an era that began in 1989—will require renewed attention to theology, which itself will need to be transformed. In a theological idiom, willingness to criticize and be criticized must be cultivated. Whether the future ushers in a new dark age, an age of global renaissance, or a combination of these depends upon how well religious communities and individuals accomplish these acts of self-critique and conversation.

Acknowledgment

Originally published in *International Journal on World Peace* by Stephen Healey as "Religion and Terror: A Post-9/11 Analysis," 24, no. 3 (September 2005): 3–22; reprinted with permission of the *International Journal on World Peace*.

RELIGION, IDENTITY, AND VIOLENCE

Rabbi David Rosen

I am reminded of a story of this gentleman who survived a flood in Jonestown, Pennsylvania. The media, of course, was very interested. He was the sole survivor, and they came up to him and put these microphones and cameras in front of him, and then people invited him to come and speak, and he got paid very nice honoraria for presenting on "How I Survived the Flood in Jonestown, Pennsylvania." After earning a good living and living quite a good life, he leaves this earthly abode, and he's met at the Pearly Gates by St. Peter, or the angel Gabriel, whichever version you prefer. He is told that in order to introduce himself, he is invited to give a talk to the residents, and the title will be posted up on the notice board. So the man said, "Fine, I'll give a talk on how I survived the flood in Jonestown, Pennsylvania." So the angel Gabriel said, "Are you sure that's what you want to talk about?" He said, "Listen here, Gabriel, I made a good living down there talking about this. That's my topic." So the angel Gabriel said, "Very well, but you should know that Noah is in the audience." So sometimes, speaking on these topics to those who are academics and practitioners in this field, I feel a little bit as if I'm speaking with Noah in the audience. But I hope there will be some dimensions of my comments which will be useful and interesting.

The late Pope John Paul II said that "violence in the name of religion is not religion." Similarly, the declaration of the religious leaders of the Holy Land declared that violence in the name of religion is the desecration of religion itself. And then there were many, I imagine, who have already spoken at this conference, but one hears very frequently from scholars and representatives of different religious traditions that explain that violence in the name of religion is the hijacking of religion, and what we see today in areas of so-called religious conflicts are, of course, nothing of this sort. They are essentially territorial conflicts, or conflicts of other vested interests that exploit religion to their own particular ends. And there seems to be a lot of good sense and fairness in that analysis.

But all these comments still beg the question: Why is it that religion is so easily exploited in this manner? And the people can actually—many even within John Paul II's own church—strongly disagree that violence is automatically against religion. In fact, they're not even sure that he would necessarily have agreed with such a blanket usage, because, after all, the majority of our traditions at some stage are going to legitimate violence in the form of self-defense. And then comes the big question: What is self-defense? The vast majority of individuals who provide any kind of religious sanction in any context of any conflict never believe that they are doing something wrong by that. They'll find the rationales in order to be able to defend themselves.

So what is it that lends itself to this rather easy manipulation of religion for vile intents? Well, part of the answer, of course, lies within the power structure. There's this wonderful moment in the very famous eleventh-century book that some of you will be familiar with, written by Rabbi Yehudah Halevi, one of the great poets of Jewish Spain. And in his magnum opus—his philosophical magnum opus—which is known as the *Book of Kuzari, King of the Khazars*—there's a dialogue between the rabbi and the king, at the end of which the king converts to Judaism. The subtitle of the book is very significant, and shows that he is living after the golden age, because it's called *An Apology for a Despised People.* There are two occasions, however, in this dialogue, which is an apologia for Judaism, when the rabbi is caught out and he doesn't have an answer. And of course, this is Yehudah Halevi's way of acknowledging a problem. And the one that I wanted to mention is when the rabbi says to the king, "You know, we Jews were not like the Christians and Muslims. The Christians talk about love, but look how they hate and kill and all the violence. And the Muslims, they talk about justice, but look how unjust they are and how much oppression there is. We Jews, we don't do that sort of thing." "Oh," says the king, "Of course you don't do that sort of thing. You don't have the power to do that sort of thing. They have the power to do it." And of course, this is a very important moment in the book, because it is Halevi's critique of power, preceding Lord Acton by quite a few centuries. And certainly, this is a problematic dimension of religion, when it supports or is part and parcel of power structures. But that doesn't really go far enough in explaining the problem. The problem is complex, obviously. I believe, nevertheless, that at its heart, it concerns the whole question of the relationship between religion and identity, something that many important sociologists, or ethologists, have written about.

And of course, identity is what gives meaning to our lives, our understanding of who we are. Religion seeks, therefore, to infuse those components of our identity with purpose, with meaning, with direction—who I am as an individual, who I am as a member of a family, who I am as part of a community, what the purpose of my existence as part of a people is, as part of a community; indeed, in relation to humanity and society at large. These are the building blocks of our psychospiritual welfare, and we disregard them at our peril. Indeed, many social scientists have written very eloquently—many popular ones, you'll remember the writings of Alvin Toffler—of the whole question of drug culture and physical abuse and various cultic activities as a reflection within our society of a search for meaning, on the part of those who are either deracinated or are bored and lacking stimulation, and of this important need for an individual to feel a sense of purpose for their identity. In other words, the idea that because identities can be abused—which I'll come to in a moment—we can somehow eliminate them is fundamentally fallacious. We have this essential need to understand who we are, and religion invests this self-understanding with purpose.

Now, in understanding who I am, by definition I understand who I am not. So identity not only tells me what my own value is or what I am; but it enables me to understand what separates me from others. Now this can be used in a constructive way, or it can be used in a destructive way. It can be used in a manner in which I seek to enrich the other and enrich society, or in a manner in which I isolate myself from society—the image of a spiral might be helpful here. Our identities are circles within circles, from the smaller to the larger, and the more secure we feel in the wider circle—something that many scholars have pointed out—the more, therefore, we will be able to relate to it. So if my own particular identity feels comfortable in the wider circle of the society of which I am a part, the more likely I am to play into it and enrich it. If I feel threatened by that society, if I feel unwelcome within it, then I am more likely to isolate myself. And therefore, identities, when they are under siege, are inward looking. And because religion seeks to give meaning to identity, in those communities that are under siege, religion tends to assume an inward-looking approach. In fact, in fairness, if you look at the great prophets of Israel, you can see two very different models. There's the model of challenging the people to be righteous and just, condemning them for ignoring the orphan, the widow, the stranger, the Other, even for their own ethnocentricity, like the prophet Amos. "Are you, the children of Israel, not, unto me, like the children of Ethiopians?" Do I care a damn about your own ethnic origin? Do you think you're the only ones I care about? "Did I not bring out the Philistines out of Caphtor and the Arameans out of Kir?" Challenging the dangers of insularity, or ethnocentricity, or lack of concern for the marginalized and impoverished make the prophets of Israel stand out with grandeur. But that is always done when the people are secure in their lands. They never challenge the people when those prophetic texts refer to their brethren and sisters in exile. When they are in exile, when they are feeling vulnerable or wounded, and they don't know what the future holds for them there, the role of the prophet becomes essentially one of nurturing their identity, giving them a sense of hope. It is by definition introspective, sometimes even insular.

So religion has these different dimensions to it. And the degree to which it is used in a constructive way requires a great deal of security, first of all, within the personality, herself or himself, to be able to move beyond their own perceptions. But it also requires, in a broader context, the securer context, the securer environment, in which people feel comfortable and welcome and therefore capable of relating to it. So, all too often, we find in situations of conflict that religion, instead of encouraging people to move beyond their own trauma and own fears, tends not only to support it but even to exacerbate it and feed on it. Often, as we are all familiar with the relationship between the inferiority complex and the superiority complex, where identities feel they are demeaned outside, then the natural recourse is not only to affirm that one's identity is better but in the process to demean the other and even to denigrate the other. The historian Richard Hoftstadter describes this image as "a perfect model of malice." And that, of course, is where the real danger of the abuse of religion lies, where it is so easily to be portrayed as the battle to reinforce my own sense of identity, the battle between the godly and the godless, seeing myself and my own as the righteous against the evil on the other side. And therefore, you see situations in which religion provided the nurturing quality that can be so easily exploited to be a demonizing force. The need for that can, of course, go to a great deal of extreme.

I would say that when religion becomes violent in any form, or when it is used to justify violence, it is reflecting some kind of trauma and/or alienation. When people feel alienated from their broader context, they are likely to turn to religion in the particular models which I have tried to identify, in relation to identity, nurturing that identity, demonizing, denigrating the other. What we call, often unscientifically, fundamentalism, or, more correctly, religious extremism, tends to be a reflection of that alienation on the part of people, alienation because of economic, social and political reasons, historical reasons, but above all, psychological reasons. That alienation reflects a sense that, even unconsciously, within those who perpetrate these violent acts, that they are unwelcome in the broader context, that they are disparaged, that they are looked down upon, and this creates this inverse response, in which they see themselves as engaged in battle for the sake of God, against the godless, and in league against their interests. In these cases, we see a very problematic tendency in the way religion is expressed and articulated. Very often, this attitude is most problematic of all for people within their own community, who are seen as greater threat to this Manichean, simplistic worldview.

But while religions can be so easily abused in this way, to nurture identities under siege, they do have potential, obviously, to move us beyond the limitations of one's own particular identity—the spiral image, again, to be able to play into the wider context, and to bring people beyond the limits of their own particular concerns and preoccupation with their own community, because all religions affirm this universal dimension of our identities. They all teach principles that bond us and bind us beyond our specific confines. But as I said, to be able to articulate that requires a great deal of confidence—confidence both within one's own identity and confidence in one's place within the broader context, in which one's identity finds itself.

Therefore, one of the most crucial aspects in facilitating a mentality—religious mentality—that is not inclined to violence, that is not alienated, is ipso facto to make that identity feel welcome. This seems to me to be the wonderful metaphor of the father of all of our Abrahamic traditions, Abraham. The metaphor of Abraham within the Muslim, Christian, and Jewish traditions, of course, is the symbol of this important quality, hospitality, not adequately appreciated. You will recall the passage in Genesis where Abraham is sitting at the entrance to his tent waiting for strangers, to be able to offer them hospitality. According to the midrashic Jewish homiletical tradition, all four tent flaps were raised during the day so Abraham would not miss any wayfarer coming from any particular direction. And you'll remember the biblical text. He sees three men, and he runs up immediately to call them to bring them into his tent to offer them hospitality, refreshment, and to be able to wash their feet and give them some rest on their journey. And these characters are referred to as men. What's really interesting is, in the next chapter of Genesis, two of them go on to Sodom and Gomorrah to warn Lot and his family against the impending destruction of those cities. And there it starts off the chapter, "And two angels came to Sodom." And one of the great Hasidic masters asked why are they only referred to as angels when they go to Sodom, but to Abraham, of all people, they are just referred to as men. And the answer is because Abraham did not need to be told they were angels, because Abraham saw the angel in every human being. In other words, the affirmation of the identity of every human being created in the divine image is the way we truly express Abrahamic hospitality.

This is the power and the importance of the interfaith encounter. The interfaith encounter and dialogue stands opposed to those within our respective communities who seek to affirm an exclusive and insular perception of the world and prefer this Manichean dialectic, as a means of being able to preserve power to deal with their own insecurities, in the face of what they perceive as a hostile world. And therefore, in a sense, there is a very important dimension, just to the very fact that such a gathering like this takes place, that we are able to show those within our own communities that one can affirm one's particularity at the same time within the universal context. And thus those who often disparage the interfaith conversation as just being conversation don't understand the importance of this psychological dimension as it relates to identity and the wider society. It is the real challenge of our times. It is indeed the prophetic challenge, but it is the challenge today, more than ever before, to be able to maintain our particularity that gives a solid foundation to our understandings within our respective traditions of truth and of meaning and purpose, to whom we are and why we are, within a context that can affirm, and appreciate the Other, as the blessing of diversity as part and parcel of the creation at large. If God creates us in all our diversity and relates to us in different ways, then it seems compelling to be able to appreciate that there must be diverse ways of relating to God.

But beyond that is the other important dimension, a dimension which becomes no less significant, perhaps even more, in terms of combating violence, and that is the need to be able to bring this message, and to bring the importance of this psychological dimension or spiritual dimension, to the attention of those who are in positions of political leadership and responsibility. And this is not an easy thing to do. There has been a tendency on the part of politicians to see religion precisely as part of the problem and therefore to have nothing to do whatsoever with it, as something which seeks to overcome violent conflicts, and that has been the case in the Middle East.

An illustration of this was seen on the lawn of the White House when the famous handshake took place between Yitzhak Rabin and Yasser Arafat. There was no identifiable Palestinian Muslim religious figure there. There was no identifiable Israeli Jewish religious figure. The implication, conscious or unconscious, of the Oslo Peace Process was, "You religious people keep far away, because you only make problems. You only mess things up." And you would understand why that perception may be there when you see some of the terrible things done in the name of religion. But it is a fundamental fallacy, because it fails to understand how profound the religious dimension is to the identities of the peoples involved. In our context, similar, as I mentioned, to a vast majority of conflicts in the world, it is not in essence a religious conflict. It is a territorial and national conflict. But the religious dimension cannot be ignored because it relates to the identities of the people who are involved and therefore can easily be exploited, and be exploited mercilessly.

In fact, what we've seen in the last six years has been a kind of religionization of the conflict. If you don't want religion to be part of the problem, then you have to make it part of the solution. Simply to disregard it is a fatal and tragic error. And indeed, the message was conveyed by the peace process that this initiative was inimical to the interests of the most fervently, passionately observant within both communities. I'm not entering here into questions of judgment or equivalencies. But whether it was the carnage of the innocent by Hamas suicide-homicides or whether it was the murder of innocent Muslims who worshiped at the Ibrahimi Mosque at the Cave of Patriarchs or the assassination of Yitzhak Rabin by Yigal Amir—all those acts of violence were done with a conviction on the part of the perpetrators that that's what God wanted, that that process was against God's interests. And if one doesn't want to leave that space open for the extremists to be able to capture it and exploit it because of the needs of their own perception of their threatened identity, then one has to make sure that the moderate voices occupy that place. Therefore, it's not only the responsibility of religious leadership. It's the responsibility of political leadership to engage

those voices, to empower them to support those political initiatives.

There was an initiative we took that many of you know about—some of you here have heard me speak about it—that took place in Alexandria in 2002, where we brought together for the first time ever the religious leaders of the Holy Land, and that's both wonderful and pathetic. It's pathetic that they've never ever been brought together before. What was wonderful was that we managed to do it. But we managed to do it in no small measure because two enemies, who've probably never agreed on anything, agreed on the text of this declaration, namely, Yasser Arafat and Ariel Sharon. Both had an interest, after September 11, in being seen to be on the side of good religion against bad religion. And we couldn't have held this initiative without the involvement of President Mubarak, who until then had been very, very hostile toward any kind of engagement with religious institutions. Now, that declaration didn't lead too far, because violence continued on a political level. But nevertheless, it does reflect something very important. It reflects the essential need for religion that relates to the identities of people involved in situations of conflict to be engaged constructively, if one is to overcome the violence that all too easily exploits and abuses religion. Political processes require political initiatives. But political processes that relate to the identities of the people cannot simply succeed on their own. They have to have the support of what one might call a psychospiritual dimension that provides the glue, the cement, without which they cannot hold together.

In summary, if we don't want religion to be the problem of identities, we have to make sure that religion is part and parcel of the solution in relation to identities in conflict. Our sages in the Talmud referred to Torah, which is sometimes used to mean specifically the five books of Moses but more often than not to mean Judaism at large. They refer to it both as the elixir of life and the elixir of death. It depends on how it's used, and how it's used depends substantially on the context in which people find themselves. But today, in our globalized world, where every area of conflict has ramifications beyond its local context, and especially the conflict in my neck of the woods that I've referred to as a lighting conductor for so many complexities and so many issues, and therefore there is all the more reason that we need to address it seriously. In summation I believe that the constructive engagement of religion is essential for the resolution of conflicts, to ensure that the spiritual dimension that nurtures the identities of people, even when they're caught up in conflict, can be a source of blessing and not a curse.

QUESTIONS AND ANSWERS
FOR THE AUTHOR

Question: My question deals with translation of what you have said so well, so elegantly, and what has certainly been in my heart and, I'm sure, many other people's hearts too. Presently, I know one of the things that I deal with, in trying to get these sorts of ideas out, in terms of gaining purpose, and those who have purpose aren't wandering around like nomads being caught up by any other person who has a negative purpose in mind. The thing is, translating those ideas, or I should say, expressing them to the common folk who are the victims, who are the ones caught up in the machine, who are the ones caught up in the systemic misuse of spiritual power. . . . And the thing is, it is a difficult task to engage the people. How can we, especially those attending the conference who have this in heart, maintain the courage that it takes to engage the folk, because there are others who are willing to engage them, as you know, toward negative ends. The thing is to really engage folk, to really hold their pain, walk with them and talk with them, and to indeed see the angel in them. That takes work.

Answer: Absolutely. And you have, I'm sure, much more wisdom than I have in this regard. Your own comments reflect your understanding of that and, to some extent, reflect the—I wouldn't say disingenuity in my comments—that's not fair—but, to some extent, the easier path that I tread. I tread the path, to some extent, of foreign policy, rather than of home affairs, because my role is basically

to be ambassador for Judaism to the religions of the world. So I'm seeking to overcome that when I engage the Other, and therefore, my call that I was issuing, basically reflecting my commitment, is to be able to see the divine image in the Other, who is not part of your community. But in a way, you're absolutely right. In a way, that's often easier to do, than to do it within the context of your own community. And certainly I, as an Orthodox rabbi engaged in interfaith relations, until recently, was a very rare bird, and often subject to a great deal of criticism within my own community. An organization of which I am a founder is called Rabbis for Human Rights, which is focused primarily on Palestinian human rights, out of a conviction that this is, first of all, what our religion teaches, because every human being is created in the divine image, but also of the conviction that human rights is an indivisible concept. If you allow it to be disregarded in one place, it will come back to haunt you in another. When I've been criticized within my own community, it's hardly ever been because I care about Arab human rights. It's because I work together with Reform rabbis, and this organization includes rabbis from the different streams of Judaism. And therefore, that reflects, in a way, some of the internecine nonsense that we have to deal with when we try to move people beyond the particular positions they are at. As you correctly say, and there is a parallel to what I'm saying, we're asked to have a lot of compassion and a lot of understanding and a lot of patience, and I'm not sure if I have enough. There is a challenge within our own communities. We have to be able to reach out in constructive ways. And you're absolutely right— if you'll forgive me again for just echoing your comments—the real word is translation. I often say that even if I'm speaking Hebrew all day, I'm speaking half a dozen different languages, because I have to relate to people where they are. We've managed to move our rabbinic establishment in Israel in an incredible way. We now have structures for dialogue with the Catholic Church, with the Anglican community. We've had two world congresses of sheikhs and rabbis from the Muslim and Jewish world. And some people in this room have even been present at some of those encounters, and it's managed to involve a spectrum, not only of the Orthodox establishment, but elements even of ultraorthodoxy within Jewish life. The vast majority who participated at these congresses have been imams and rabbis who've never before met a person of another faith. And this has been a great achievement. But in order to get them there, you have to speak a different language, exactly as you say. Therefore, I speak so many different languages, all at the same time. Some people might think this is disingenuous, but in fact, it's the way you've got to go if you want to engage them constructively. So, in the final analysis in this rather long, convoluted response to your question, I have no other answer other than the great gift that the Almighty has given us. Not for nothing is he referred to in Islam as Ar Rahman Ar Rahim. In fact, in Hebrew we also refer to him as Ha Rahmanan, the most merciful one, the compassionate one. To be merciful and compassionate is, of course, exactly what Jesus of Nazareth taught. And of course the religions of the East teach the essence of compassion and of regard for all. So this is our common legacy. My basic message, however, is that when people feel really wounded, it's much more difficult for them to be compassionate. And, therefore, the answer is, again, by treating them with more compassion, one can get them to be more compassionate. This is very difficult. This requires a lot of patience. It requires a lot of devotion. But in the end, compassion and love are what overcome the alienation and the sense of woundedness.

Question: I was thinking as you were speaking about the little I know about the different religious groups in Israel. Maybe you can speak to how when the question relates to the fact that there are some who seem permanently threatened and others who don't, and so on, if that makes sense.

Answer: It's the subject of a whole day's seminar. But let me just say this: As difficult as it is for people from other communities to appreciate, everybody in our neck of the woods sees himself or herself as the victim. And everybody sees themselves as wounded by the Other. They all see themselves in different paradigms. Palestinians see themselves as vulnerable in the face of Israeli power and might. For Israelis, Palestinians are a fifth column both hostile and threatening. The Arab world sees itself as vulnerable and disrespected on the part of Western power and globalization, consumerization, imperialism, whatever, all those different things. Therefore, everybody sees themselves as the victim, everybody sees themselves as vulnerable, and everybody is waiting for the other to take initiative, and for a gesture to come from the other. That is why the role of third-party counselor who can really engage the trust of both sides is so important. That is why this initiative in Alexandria—that was actually taken by a man who I should have given credit for, and now I will, Lord George Carey, the then archbishop of Canterbury—was so important. He was able to gain the trust of the different parties involved and therefore able to bring them together. And this is actually what the international community should be doing much more to resolve the conflict there. They should be working harder together to gain the trust of all sides. Now, of course, these paradigms which I spoke of purely in terms of national and political terms relate to the religious identities, because we all carry with us our respective religious baggage and history, and we all interpret history according to our own sense of victimhood. And of course, the Christian communities in the Holy Land don't see themselves as part of the large, powerful Christian communities in the world, let alone the Christian communities in history. On the contrary, they see themselves as being the greatest victims of that kind of mentality and that particular approach. So everybody therefore reads history according to their own particular perspective. And there are even the internal feuds between them. I mentioned, I made reference to, internal Jewish tensions. But that pales into insignificance between some of the tensions between different Christian communities in the Holy Land and their historical attachments there. If you've been to the Holy Sepulcher, you'd be fully aware of that. Woe betide if a person from one Christian community steps over into the tile that borders the area of another Christian community at a time of religious worship, where they have their particular rights to conduct their worship at that time and place. This leads to fisticuffs. In fact there were two bustups, physical violence, between Franciscan monks and Greek Orthodox priests last year over these particular questions. Now they look ridiculous to us. But they're not ridiculous to them, because for them, these are issues that relate to their identity. They see themselves as preserving this historical attachment that gives meaning and purpose to who they are. And, therefore, to get over this abuse of their identity, we need to be able to offer them much more compassion and understanding. That's very difficult when you're feeling abused yourself. You're bringing with yourself your own historical roots and your own problems. That's why it's important to be able to have the outside parties, the counseling forces. The problem happens that people, because they are bound up with the identities of the different communities caught in conflict, that they naturally want to be empathic with their own sisters and brothers of a particular community, and that's the way it should be. Unfortunately, however, in being empathic, they often feel there is a need to somehow be insensitive—that is, lack empathy—for the Other caught up in the conflict. And that is the seed of the cycle of violence, in which we get into this vicious zero-sum mentality, instead of a win-win mentality. What we need in our part of the world is a little more empathy and understanding for all sides caught up. And if we have a little more empathy and understanding and positive engagement, in ways in which one can contribute constructively, it could make a lot of difference. I must say—it's important to let you know for those who are unfamiliar—we have a great deal of interfaith activity in the Holy Land. You know there are within Israel seven million citizens, of whom a million are Arabs, the vast majority of them Muslims. We have, in the Interreligious Coordinating Council in Israel, some seventy organizations which are devoted to promoting relations between Muslims, Christians, and Jews in different ways, in different dimensions. There's a lot of very positive activity. And then there are the organizations that go across the conflict in relation to the West Bank and Gaza in different ways—philanthropic, educational, social, as well as political. The more we would have support from outside for those specific engagements that bring people together and work together over those divides, the more healing can be brought to bear. Unfortunately, what tends to be the case is people exclusively supporting parties and positions that think that somehow they're defending the interests of their community by undermining or by disrespecting or by showing a lack of empathy for the needs of the Other.

Question: Considering everything you said, would you believe that, at this point, we need more of a therapeutic plan before a peace plan? And that ultimately, the step to a peace process is a therapeutic process? Now how can religion help us in devising a plan of therapeutic recovery? That we really need to (do is to) bring people who have been victimized into a period of recovery that would lead them to the safe space within that creates the peace within, that helps them to become peacemakers.

Answer: Yes, I think that's exactly right. But in practice, we don't have the time to do it in this particular way, because every time you start doing this necessary therapeutic process, we will be undermined by political events, which immediately throws us back. And, again, getting back to my earlier comments, building requires much more systematic effort than destroying. It's so easy to be able to destroy in one moment what takes a long time to be able to build. So any therapeutic initiative has to be in tandem with a political initiative for it to have any chance of succeeding, and that's my call from here, to somebody who will carry through to whoever can be able to contribute, as I seek to carry through myself whenever I have the opportunity of contacts to political leadership. I don't think that religious leadership in our part of the world can be the spearhead, because religious leadership—institutional leadership—that relates to the identities tends to be, in our part of the world, appointed by the political authorities, and therefore subject to, if not in some cases subjugated by, political authorities. But if the politicians can understand the importance of this point that you have grasped, then they can understand the need to be able to have any kind of political initiative, the parallel initiative, that provides what I've called the psychospiritual glue, which you more elegantly call the therapeutic dimension, without which no political process will hold together.

Question: Thank you, Rabbi. Brilliant, by the way. I think I got to get my dictionary out to check some of those words that you were using before. I want to bring it to a more mystical question about the Torah itself being the elixir or the Tree of Life or the Tree of Death, which in the Zohar is also the Tree of Knowledge for good and bad. In my awareness, the Tree of Life represents the world of all good, and when Adam and Eve sinned against the Creator, they did so by eating from the Tree of Knowledge of Good and Bad. And in my awareness, the Torah contains 613 commandments, half of which—248—are good, and the remaining is knowledge of bad. So the Torah itself represents what is knowledge of good and bad, and represents this world of duality that we live in, where we struggle with our neighbors, instead of having love, which is more like the world of all good. And just to bring in this part of the question, part of the problem, from the religious aspect, with Torah is that the religious Jews can quote the Torah as saying, "This land is ours," as it says in Torah. It really adds a difficult dimension to the struggle when those beliefs are so strong. And what I wanted to ask you is: Do you see that the Jewish people can move past Torah as not being the ultimate way to connect with God, to move past the Word, and to return to that state that is inherent in each individual that represents our direct connection with the Creator?

Answer: With the vastly different interpretations of the Jewish sources, you do have different approaches which may, some would say, have come under more Gnostic influences, that would see more of a dualism than uniformity. I'm not sure that it's necessary or so helpful now to be able to go into the question of interpretation of the question of good and evil. But with regard to the most important question that you have raised, and it is

really related to the gentleman before, who used the question of translation. . . . Because if I'm going to succeed in arguing the cause to somebody who is rooted within tradition that sees scripture not simply as a cultural legacy but as the ipsissima verba or the literal word of God, I can't talk to that individual in cultural terms, or in terms of the evolution of religion. I therefore have to argue my case on the basis precisely of the commandments. For the benefit of everybody here, the question he was referring to was the positive commandments and the restrictive commandments in the five books of Moses. In other words, a commandment that tells you not to put a stumbling rock in front of a blind person, that is a restrictive commandment and therefore referred to as a negative commandment. But I wouldn't say it implies any inherent negativity of course. I would see therefore the positive injunction simply articulated in a negative way, to behave positively toward those who are handicapped. But generally, for such person who is coming from a position of Orthodox commitment, I have to be able to argue in his or her language, in his or her terms. And therefore, when people, for example, say to me, "How can you be both Jewish and democratic? Isn't there a contradiction between being a Jewish state and being a democratic state?" I say to them that, in my opinion, there's no contradiction, but the alternative would be a total contradiction, because at the heart of Judaism is the affirmation that every human being is created in the divine image, and therefore the democratic system is the system that seeks to maximize it. And therefore, if Judaism, if a Jewish state is not a democratic state, then it is not a true Jewish state, because it has undermined its fundamental principle with regard to the dignity of the individual. So what I'm doing is essentially interpreting, arguing, from within the context of their points of reference. Now, to ask them to go beyond Torah is basically asking them to question the divine authority of that revelation. I'll get nowhere in doing that. What I need to do is to make it clear to them that Torah affirms the dignity of each and every human person. And I would use the paradigms as I've tried to use today, whether it's the narrative of Abraham, whether it's the text, whether it's the Great Rule, or love your neighbor as yourself, which is sometimes interpreted restrictively. I would call on those resources that would emphasize its universal application. And I would therefore argue precisely in that context, that even if Torah does mandate the land—not even, the Torah does mandate the land—but mandating the land never gives you the right to use it to justify any kind of suspension of your moral responsibility toward the Other. And therefore, if you are going to be able to live in the land and at the same time be true to Torah, this must demand territorial compromise, because to hold on to as much land as possible, that involves a denial of the dignity of others and leads to a continued cycle of conflict that threatens you as well as threatening the Other, is against the most fundamental principles of Torah. So I have to find that language of argument.

Question: I want to bring to your attention the commonality between Islam, Christians, and Jews—the Abrahamic religions. For 1,400 years, we were partners. We worked together. Even Prophet Muhammad, when he took Christians and Jews under his arm when the Romans were trying to wipe them out. In the last fifty years, unfortunately, we are suffering on account of circumstances. We have many things common in our religion, and many things we all have the same. Our beliefs, our similarity, is very much practiced the same. We can marry each other without a change of religion. There are so many things, that we can eat with each other. We can even share our kosher food. Then why can't we today—Qur'an says to dialogue—and why can't we dialogue, from both sides, between the Muslims, Jews, and the Christians, and make this world paradise, because a double-headed monster in the future is going to come and wipe all of us out?

Answer: Thank you very much. I assume your question is rhetorical, and is purely reiterating my own comments, because, of course, I totally agree with you. What I sought to present is that it's precisely our fears in relation to our own identities that prevent us from behaving in the way we should.

Question: I'm Jean Donovan and I'm a Catholic theologian from Duquesne University in Pittsburgh, and my question to you is: Have we paid attention or sought out the goodwill of people that stand by and don't know how to help? I think of my daughter. She's seventeen and she reads the newspaper every day and, honestly, she truly cares about what's going on in the Middle East, and I had a whole class surrounded by young people that were wondering if they're going to have a life, and sometimes I say to myself, "How did we get to this point?" But, for the young people in the world or for ordinary folks in their towns and villages who wish us all well, who want a world of peace, I wonder whether fine people like you that are dialoguing on such high levels need to bring in ordinary people so that they can show the support that you need in order to finish the work that you are doing.

Answer: That's why I made reference to the ICCI and the plethora of organizations where grassroots people are engaged. All these different organizations are trying to work to make things better. That was also why I issued an appeal to all good people who care about others elsewhere to try and seek to support such initiatives and activities precisely where they do bring people together. One can go onto the Web site and find those. I mean, the ICCI is easy to remember—icci.org—and that's an umbrella organization. But I'm afraid I have no more wisdom than that. I'm sure you have as much as I do.

The Bhagavadgītā and War

Some Early Anticipations of the Gandhian Interpretation of the Bhagavadgītā

Arvind Sharma

Gandhi in Dialogue

I propose to tackle this topic in three parts. First, I shall narrate an actual piece of dialogue between Mahatma Gandhi and one Dr. Kagawa, who has been identified as "a student of religion." Having presented that piece of dialogue, we shall next analyze it to identify the basic features of the Gandhian interpretation of the Gītā. Having done that, we shall finally see if the Gandhian frame of reference toward the Gītā has any precedents within the Hindu tradition.

We turn now to the first part of the chapter and recount the dialogue between Mahatma Gandhi and Dr. Kagawa that was reported on January 21, 1939, in the *Harijan*. It runs as follows:

Dr. Kagawa: I am told you recite the Bhagavadgītā daily?

Gandhiji: Yes, we finish the entire Gītā reading once every week.

Dr. Kagawa: But at the end of the Gītā Krishna recommends violence.

Gandhiji: I do not think so. I am also fighting. I should not be fighting effectively if I were fighting violently. The message of the Gītā is to be found in the second chapter of the Gītā where Krishna speaks of the balanced state of mind, of mental equipoise. In 19 verses at the close of the 2nd chapter of the Gītā, Krishna explains how this state can be achieved. It can be achieved, he tells us, after killing all your passions. It is not possible to kill your brother after having killed all your passions. I should like to see that man dealing death—who has no passions, who is indifferent to pleasure and pain, who is undisturbed by the storms that trouble mortal man. The whole thing is described in language of beauty that is unsurpassed. These verses show that the fight Krishna speaks of is a spiritual fight.

Dr. Kagawa: To the common mind it sounds as though it was actual fighting.

Gandhiji: You must read the whole thing dispassionately in its true context. After the first mention of fighting, there is no mention of fighting at all.[1] The rest is a spiritual discourse.

Dr. Kagawa: Has anybody interpreted it like you?

Gandhiji: Yes. The fight is there, but the fight as it is going on within. The Pandavas and Kauravas are the forces of good and evil within. The war is the war between Jekyll and Hyde, God and Satan, going on in the human breast. The internal evidence in support of this interpretation is there in the work itself and in the Mahābhārata of which the Gītā is a minute part. It is not a history of war between two families, but the history of man—the history of the spiritual struggle of man. I have sound reasons for my interpretation.

Dr. Kagawa: That is why I say it is your interpretation.

Gandhiji: But that is nothing. The question is whether it is a reasonable interpretation, whether it carries conviction. If it does, it does not matter whether it is mine or X.Y.Z.'s. If it does not, it has no value even if it is mine.[2]

BHAGAVADGĪTĀ: THE GANDHIAN INTERPRETATION IN OUTLINE

A close review of this dialogue reveals that Mahatma Gandhi changed his response during the conversation from a historical to a rational one. The key question asked by Dr. Kagawa was: has anybody interpreted the Gītā like you? Mahatma Gandhi began by saying yes, but then instead of citing any name of such a predecessor he started to explain how and why the Gītā should be understood allegorically. Dr. Kagawa, recognizing Mahatma Gandhi's failure to cite a precedent to his interpretation then remarked: "That is why I say it is your interpretation." Again failing to cite a precedent, Mahatma Gandhi appealed to the merit of the interpretation itself, rather than its author, as a worthy criterion of its value. So the question raised by Dr. Kagawa remained unanswered in a sense. Let us now try to answer it by asking the original question: has anybody interpreted the Gītā like Mahatma Gandhi before Mahatma Gandhi? Before an answer to the question is attempted, it is helpful to realize that on the basis of Mahatma Gandhi's dialogue with Dr. Kagawa, Mahatma Gandhi's interpretation seems to have two major components:

1. The Gītā teaches nonviolence.
2. The Gītā is to be taken allegorically and not historically.

No one denies that the Gītā refers to fighting—the question is whether this fight refers to a spiritual struggle in the heart of man or to actual warfare on a battlefield. Thus Dr. Kagawa's question—has anyone interpreted the Gītā like "you"—breaks down into two distinct though allied questions:

1. Has anyone interpreted the Gītā as preaching nonviolence before Mahatma Gandhi?
2. Has anyone interpreted the Gītā allegorically before Mahatma Gandhi?

ANSWERS TO THE QUESTIONS

The answer to the first question seems to be that no one appears to have claimed, as Mahatma Gandhi did, that the Gītā preached nonviolence explicitly. It may be argued that the message is implicit in the Gītā itself, and this is what Mahatma Gandhi did, but no one seems to have claimed this prior to Mahatma Gandhi. Having said this, however, it may now be pointed out that there are some hints in ancient Hindu literature that, although not reaching the point of articulation achieved in Mahatma Gandhi, seem to be headed in that direction. To see this, it is important to realize that one of the reasons why Mahatma Gandhi thought that the message of the Gītā was nonviolence was that, according to him, that was the message of the Mahābhārata itself, of which, as he said, "the Gītā is a minute part."[3] Thus he wrote while remarking on the message of the Gītā:

> The author of the Mahābhārata has not established the necessity of physical warfare; on the contrary he has proved its futility. He has made the victors shed tears of sorrow and repentance and has left them nothing but a legacy of miseries.[4]

In this context certain passages of the Bhāgavata Purāṇa make interesting reading. Indeed, "It is usually said that the Bhāgavata Purāṇa begins where the Mahābhārata ends, seeking to correct a story which tells of gambling, dishonouring of women and a devastating war which ends in a pyrrhic victory."[5] In the fifth chapter of the first canto we actually find Vyāsa, the putative author of the Mahābhārata, being criticized by Nārada:

> It was a great error on your part to have enjoined terrible acts (acts involving destruction of life) in the name of religion on men who are naturally addicted to such acts. Misguided by these precepts of yours (in the Mahābhārata) the ordinary man of the world would believe such acts to be pious and would refuse to honour the teachings that prohibit such action.[6]

In other words, Nārada complained that the justification of violence involved in the Mahābhārata and especially in the Gītā could have disastrous consequences in general, and urged sage Vyāsa to compose a devotional work to offset this effect, namely the Bhāgavata Purāṇa. Thus we find that even as far back as tenth century C.E., the date usually assigned to the Bhāgavata Purāṇa, there was a certain uneasiness in certain Hindu minds with the violent nature of the Mahābhārata episode. The ancient thinker writing in the name of Nārada, to be sure, took a different tack than Mahatma Gandhi—he wanted a new work to turn people's minds toward the worship of Lord Kṛṣṇa and away from the terrible war and its justification. Mahatma Gandhi thought that the work itself implied condemnation of violence. But both the pseudonymous Nārada and the famous Mahatma were grappling with the same issue: the violent nature of the Mahābhāratan narrative and its reconciliation with higher spiritual ends. The Gandhian solution, though, must be regarded as unique, for Nārada explicitly recognized the violence involved in the Mahābhārata and condemned it, but Mahatma Gandhi commended it as a warning to others. This difference in attitude between using it as a warning rather than as an example allowed him to claim, as none had done, that the real message of the Mahābhārata and the Gītā was nonviolence.

How then do we answer the first question: Did anyone interpret the Gītā as preaching nonviolence before Mahatma Gandhi did so? The answer seems to be that no one interpreted the Gītā the way it was interpreted by Mahatma Gandhi before him, even though it may be argued that the message of nonviolence is implied in the Mahābhārata itself, and even though we detect previous undercurrents of dissatisfaction with the violence involved therein. No one before Mahatma Gandhi seems to have clearly and unambiguously stated the message of the Bhagavadgītā—and indeed of the Mahābhārata—to have been nonviolence. Now the second question: Did anyone interpret the Gītā allegorically before Mahatma Gandhi? The answer to this second question can be given in the affirmative in view of certain facts that have come to light in the course of an examination of Abhinavagupta's commentary on the Bhagavadgītā, known as the Gītārthasamgraha. Before this evidence is presented, however, it seems useful to emphasize that Mahatma Gandhi's claim that the Gītā preached nonviolence rests heavily on the antecedent claim that the Gītā must be interpreted allegorically. Mahatma Gandhi was himself fully conscious of this fact, as is clear from the prefatory note with which he commences his Gujarati commentary called *Anasakti Yoga* on the *Bhagavadgītā*.[7] The remarks translate thus:

> No knowledge is to be found without seeking, no tranquility without travail, no happiness except through tribulation. Every seeker has, at one time or another, to pass through a conflict of duties, a heart-churning.[8]

Having thus provided a spiritual rather than a historical orientation, Mahatma Gandhi translates the first verse of the Gītā and then follows it up with the following annotation:

> The human body is the battlefield where the eternal duel between Right and Wrong goes on. Therefore it is capable of being turned into the gateway to Freedom. It is born in sin and becomes the seed-bed of sin. Hence

it is also called the field of Kuru. The Kauravas represent the forces of Evil, the Pandavas the forces of Good. Who is there that has not experienced the daily conflict within himself between the forces of Evil and the forces of Good?[9]

Thus Mahatma Gandhi equates the Kurukṣetra, the battlefield where the Mahābhārata war was fought, with the human body, the Kauravas with the forces of evil in the person, and the Pāṇḍavas with the forces of good. Fresh evidence, as pointed out earlier, suggests that the tradition of such an allegorical interpretation of the Gītā seems to go back at least as far as the tenth century C.E.

The reasons for making this claim are as follows. Abhinavagupta is a name with which many if not most students of Indian culture are familiar; he is well-known for his commentaries on such well-known works of Hindu prosody and dramatics as Ānandavardhana's *Dhvanyāloka* and Bharata's Nāṭyaśātra.[10] He is also a well-known exponent of the system of Kāśmīra Śaivism known as Trika.[11] His dates are not known with complete certainty, but he is believed to have been born between 950 and 960 C.E. and is thus assigned to the tenth century C.E.[12] He also wrote a commentary on the Bhagavadgītā, hitherto untranslated.[13] In this commentary, in his gloss on the first verse of the Bhagavadgītā, after making his own remarks, Abhinavagupta refers to a tradition of interpreting the Gītā in which the Kurukṣetra is equated with the human body, very much in the way Mahatma Gandhi did.[14] The relevant passage runs as follows:

> Herein some speak of an alternative interpretation. [They explain the word *kurukṣetra* as] the field of the Kurus: Kurūṇām = karaṇānām—organs of sense; kṣetra (field) = that which favours, that is, the field of the

senses is the favourer of all the properties of transmigration as being that which helps to bring them about (i.e. the human body). Whereas *dharmakṣetra* (the field of *dharma*) is to be understood from the sentence, "This is the highest *dharma*; to see the soul by means of Yoga," namely, as being the body of the [aspirant for whom the Gītā is] intended, a body which offers salvation by its attainment of *apavarga* through the abandonment of everything opposed to *dharma*. [So that the question asked by king Dhṛtarāṣṭra may be paraphrased thus:] Standing in that [battle] where passion and detachment, anger and forbearance, etc., have come together in mutual conflict, for the senses, etc., always aim at the injury of the body—what have my ignorant volitions, comparable to ignorant men, accomplished, and what have (my) wise (volitions), the Pāṇḍavas, comparable to men of knowledge, accomplished? That is to say, who has defeated whom?[15]

Conclusion

The parallels between these remarks on the first verse of the Bhagavadgītā recorded in the tenth century C.E. and the remarks made by Mahatma Gandhi in the twentieth century C.E. are quite obvious. This enables us to offer the conclusion that, whereas Mahatma Gandhi was certainly original in regarding the message of the Bhagavadgītā to be that of *ahiṁsā*, he was certainly not the first to think up the allegorical interpretation on which he based his opinion.[16] To conclude: although the claim by Mahatma Gandhi that the Gītā preaches nonviolence seems to be unprecedented, the allegorical interpretation of the Gītā on which it is based is not unprecedented in ancient Hindu exegetical tradition that grew up around the Bhagavadgītā.[17]

THE VIOLENT BEAR IT AWAY

Christian Reflections on Just War

William R. O'Neill

In a world riven by religious terror and casual slaughter, what shall we say of the *justum bellum*? Is the very notion now a *contradictio in adjecto* in late or postmodernity—war having finally become, in Karl von Clausewitz's words, "theoretically limitless"?[1] Or, as Michael Walzer urges, Is war still a "rule-governed activity, a world of permissions and prohibitions—a moral world," even "in the midst of hell"?[2] The norms of just war, after all, remain a stubborn inheritance, an "overlapping consensus" of permissions and prohibitions enshrined in international positive law (i.e., the Geneva Conventions and Protocols).[3] But just how are we to make sense of such a consensus?

Several distinct yet overlapping methodological perspectives emerge. We might, following Grotius, assume that the just-war norms derive from the "manifest and clear" dictates of natural reason (e.g., the "secular religion" of human rights and duties).[4] And yet one wonders. Can the Augustinian-Thomistic tradition so readily be trimmed of theological reference? Must an overlapping consensus of differing narrative traditions "bracket" religious belief? Or do scriptural or theological warrants rather support a "reiteratively particularist" consensus in Walzer's words—one logically dependent upon our distinctive religious narratives?[5]

In this chapter, I will propose a via media between these rival schools of thought, arguing that distinctive religious attitudes and beliefs play a constitutive role in the (1) justification, (2) modality, and (3) interpretation of the *justum bellum*. Yet the resulting consensus, I argue, rests less on the contingent iteration of particular traditions than on the family resemblance of well-formed narratives.

JUSTIFICATION

Christians after Constantine drew on their Greco-Roman and biblical heritage, working multiple variations on the theme of the *justum bellum*. Codified in the *Corpus Juris Canonici,* Ambrose's and Augustine's early speculations were later grounded in Thomistic natural law and refined by the Spanish Scholastics. Still further variations emerged in the seventeenth century, with the doctrine's progressive disenchantment. In the prolegomena of his magisterial *De Jure Belli ac Pacis* (1625), Grotius writes that the precepts of natural law retain their validity "*etiamsi daremus non esse Deum* [even were God not to exist]."[6] For Grotius, to be sure, the impious gambit "cannot be conceded"; yet for his successors, the speculative hypothesis soon became "a thesis." For Pufendorf, Burlamaqui, and Vattel "the self-evidence of natural law" left God a supernumerary in creation.[7]

Under the spell of modernity's disenchantment, Grotius's heirs regard the validity of the just-war norms as logically independent of the ethical substance of the traditions that "hand them on" (including, a fortiori, "the broad tradition of just war in Western culture").[8] Distinctive religious attitudes and beliefs, as in the "autonomy school" of Christian ethics, serve rather a paraenetic or hortatory function, inspiring us to do what morally (rationally) we are required to do. But such beliefs do not alter the logical force of the *ad bellum* or *in bello* criteria. Consensus, in Walzer's felicitous terms, is "thin," or narrative-independent, as in President Bush Senior's assertion that the Gulf War was "not a Christian war, a Muslim war, or a Jewish war, but a just war."

Yet it seems modernity's final disenchantment is of itself.[9] Not only are the norms of just war dishonored in the breach, but the rationalist foundations of the *justum bellum* have ceased to be perspicuous. Reason is more parsimonious than Grotius believed. Indeed, it is precisely with respect to such foundations that the putative consensus breaks down. James Childress, for instance, proposes a "prima facie duty of nonmaleficence—the duty not to harm or kill others"; the U.S. bishops argue in a similar vein in their "Peace Pastoral."[10] James Turner Johnson demurs: "The concept of a just war" begins not with a "presumption against war" but rather with "a presumption against *injustice* focused on the need for responsible use of force in response to wrongdoing."[11]

Such internal *différance* may well support a rival interpretation of the consensus, specifically, that of a merely contingent overlap of "thick" narrative traditions.[12] Intercommunal agreement, that is, rests not on the "manifest and clear" precepts of natural reason, but, in Walzer's words, on the "reiteratively particularist" convergence of normative practices.[13] Thus Christians and Muslims may agree on the *in bello* norm of noncombatant immunity, but their agreement is not foreordained by natural law.

Curiously, Francisco Suárez argued in an analogous manner, distinguishing the merely contingent agreement of states from the *jus gentium* proper, the "rational basis" of which

> consists in the fact that the human race, into howsoever many different peoples and kingdoms it may be divided, always preserves a certain unity, not only as a species, but also a moral and political unity (as it were) enjoined by the natural precept of mutual love and mercy; a precept which applies to all, even to strangers of every nation.[14]

The latter, or "second kind of jus gentium," conversely,

> embodies certain precepts, usages, or modes of living, which do not, in themselves and directly, relate to all mankind; neither do they have for their immediate end (so to speak) the harmonious fellowship and intercourse of all nations with respect to one another. On the contrary, these usages are established in each state by a process of government that is suited to the respective courts of each. Nevertheless, they are of such a nature that, in the possession of similar usages or laws, almost all nations agree with one another; or at least they resemble one another, at times in a generic manner, and at times specifically, so to speak.[15]

We cannot, alas, keep "our metaphysics warm" by invoking Suárez's "natural precept of mutual love and mercy." Yet, with a nod to Suárez, we may seek a pragmatic via media between a freestanding, "thin" rationalist interpretation and a "thick," narrative-dependent overlap. For we may distinguish two modes of narrative dependence: although a "reiteratively particularist" interpretation exhibits strong narrative dependence, a weaker narrative dependence permits us to affirm both (1) that the grammar of the just war is "empty" if not embodied or schematized in our particular traditions and (2) that our traditions are themselves "blind" if not internally disciplined by such narrative grammar. (In Kant's Second Critique, the synthetic role of a schema is played by the type of pure, practical judgments, i.e., a realm or kingdom of ends. By analogy, the ideal of a well-formed narrative schematizes the depth grammar of claim-rights, e.g., in the *ad bellum* and *in bello* norms.[16])

The overlapping consensus of the *justum bellum* rests, then, not in a freestanding (i.e., logically and epistemically autonomous) set of "secular" norms, but rather in the "family resemblance" of rhetorical practices.[17] The *ad bellum* and *in bello* norms exhibit a *concrete* universality such that distinctive religious beliefs may provide for their *ultimate* justification—and, as we shall see, motive force and interpretation—even as our particular religious narratives are "well-formed" precisely inasmuch as they embody (or schematize) the norms.

In short, such a weak narrative dependence allows us to identify, pragmatically, performative contradictions in denying just cause or noncombatant immunity, while grounding such norms in a theological doctrine of the natural law as, in Aquinas's words, our "share in the divine reason itself," our "participation in the Eternal law."[18] Consider the practical import of religious "grounding reasons" in the Augustian-Thomistic tradition of the *justum bellum*.

War, for Augustine, was a tragic necessity, the consequence—and remedy—of fallen nature. The "love of enemies" admits "of no exceptions," yet the "kindly harshness" of charity does not "exclude wars of mercy waged by the good." Inspired by the "severity which compassion itself dictates," such "wars of mercy" presumed that those inflicting punishment had "first overcome hate in their hearts." Neither Ambrose nor Augustine permitted violent *self*-defense; only defense of the innocent neighbor could satisfy the stringent claims of charity.[19] Thomas Aquinas recognized the normative primacy accorded *caritas* in forming justice, posing the *quaestio* in the *Summa Theologiae* II-II, Q. 40, "whether it is *always* sinful to wage war?" Harking back to their Thomistic heritage, the Renaissance Spanish schoolmen Francisco de Vitoria and Francisco Suárez fashioned the just-war tradition

as we know it today in the law of nations or international law—law ordained, in Vitoria's words, to "the common good of all," including that of one's enemies.

In the Augustinian-Thomistic tradition, we begin, then, not with simple premises or prima facie presumptions underlying "the concept of a just war," but rather with a grammar embedded in a complex web of belief consisting of nested values, ideals, tales, and tropes. Thus, in modern Roman Catholic social teaching, the religiously inspired ideal of the *bonum commune* integrates the "prima facie" rules of nonmaleficence and justice in what we might call, following Sen, a "consequentially sensitive" redemption of basic human rights. *Justice,* extended beyond strategic national interest, recognizes the basic security rights of citizen and noncitizen alike (their claim to *nonmaleficence*). For it is precisely the grave, systemic violation of such claims, for example, in genocide or mass atrocity, that renders a just war "just." But just so, terrestrial peace (*tranquilitas ordinis*) presumes more than mere nonmaleficence. Duties correlative to basic human rights, including social, economic, and cultural rights, generate structural imperatives of provision and protection—the set of institutional arrangements constituting, for John XXIII, the universal common good.

Other religious traditions, such as Jewish or Muslim, "do likewise," embodying the just-war norms in their distinctive narratives and casuistry, for example, in notions of divine obedience.[20] Such a narrative rapprochement thus permits us to speak of their family resemblance, which as such remains fluid and open-textured. For we interpret and apply the just-war norms of the *jus gentium* as an overlapping consensus, not a grand meta-narrative. Family resemblance is not reified; yet neither is it infinitely malleable. Tacit prejudices distort our use, and, as Gadamer reminds us, notable among such prejudices is the "prejudice against prejudice" itself, the "foundationalist" prejudice that just-war norms function as a freestanding, impartial decision-procedure.[21]

Proceeding *more geometrico*, the use of just-war norms would be independent (logically and epistemically) of their particular narrative embodiment (or schematization). Yet, as we argued previously, the rules of just war are hermeneutically underdetermined. Grammar without narrative *is* empty. But such hermeneutical naïveté may blind us to misuse—distortions arising less from formal incoherence (of the *ad bellum* or *in bello* criteria per se) than interpretive inadequacy. Just as the devil quotes Scripture, so we may speak of just war with a Hobbesian inflection.

Hobbes, indeed, does just that. In Hobbes's militant rhetoric, of course, the "state of nature"—no longer naturally pacific—is aptly "called war, as is of every man against every man." And in that inglorious "tract of time" we call history, "wherein the will to contend by battle is sufficiently known," we have but *one* right, that of "self-defense"—the very right Ambrose and Augustine denied.[22] Violent self-preservation, no longer a "stain upon our love for neighbor" in Ambrose's words, is our natural right, writ large upon the "artificial person" of the state.

Neither does Leviathan sacrifice this right, even if it is tempered by the rule of international law. Hobbesian "realism" legislates for general self-preservation in the form of laws of nature, the force of which depends upon general compliance. In a state of partial compliance, governed by weak international law, "reason" will abide by the laws of nature, and of the *justum bellum,* if, and to the degree, they promote self-preservation. There are, in this sense, theoretical limits to Hobbesian realism, underwritten by realism itself. And so, the "violent bear it away"—not merely by abjuring the norms of just war, but by incorporating (schematizing) them within the realist narrative.[23]

President George W. Bush's defense of our war in Iraq, for instance, seems less "a synthesis of idealist and realist elements," in Johnson's words, than a bricolage "from many contexts"—a rhetorical locus beholden more to Machiavelli's "armed prophets" than to Augustine's "kindly harshness."[24] Now, with the eclipse of Christian narrative's "ontology of peace," proportionality, and, by implication, reasonable hope of success and last resort, are ordered, not to the "common good,"

including the good of enemy civilians, as a "final end," but rather to the limited aims of strategic self-interest.[25] American exceptionalism, not the universal *bonum commune,* legitimates "preventive war" in U.S. strategic doctrine.[26] So too, we shall see, the *in bello* norm of discrimination is trumped by "political necessity."

MODALITY

In such a locus, the *justum bellum* becomes, as the rhetoricians say, a "self-consuming artifact." For it is not only the use of just-war norms that political realism distorts, but their form and force. In accordance with the Geneva Conventions, norms prohibiting torture are general in form, applying to all agents, and nonderogative—claims against torture oblige categorically. Signatory to the relevant Conventions, the United States holds Saddam Hussein's human rights violations as (the remaining) *casus belli.* How, then, to account for George W. Bush's brief for torture, abrogating these very accords? Hobbes, again, is instructive.

Even for Hobbes, the laws of nature "dictate peace." Yet such laws, though "immutable and eternal," obtain only notionally prior to Leviathan. "The laws of nature oblige *in foro interno* only," says Hobbes. "And whatsoever laws bind *in foro interno* may be broken." Indeed, "every man, ought to endeavor peace, as far as he has hope of obtaining it; and when he cannot obtain it, that he may seek, and use, all helps, and advantages of war." Even Hobbes, then, does not banish the rules of war, but so empties them of force that they become nugatory.[27]

Still subtler variations are worked on this theme. Thus we may recognize ordinary "permissions and prohibitions," but only within limits and not "in the midst of hell." Only a "supreme emergency" warrants a teleological suspension of the ethical. *In extremis* only do we permit torture, renditions, and the like. But with (post)modern terror, the extreme becomes quotidian, supreme emergency naturalized. Our Hobbesian logic is thus circumscribed within a "moral world," and to preserve this world, we betray the very tenets that make it moral. Realism is, in effect, moralized, and in such "utopian" realism, the "absorption of politics by the language and imperatives of war," says Jean Bethke Elshtain, becomes "a permanent rhetorical condition."[28]

INTERPRETATION

In the previous sections, I have argued that we must look to the "thick" uses of just war, attending precisely to the family resemblance—or distortions—introduced by the many (narrative) contexts at play in public, political reasoning. Yet distinctive religious beliefs never displace such reasoning in complex, pluralist polities where civility and reciprocity prevail. Our religious teaching, stories, and tropes do not typically dictate specific policies; rather, they rein in our *hybris,* permitting us to imagine otherwise, for example, in seeing systematic distortions in our just-war rhetoric.

The Augustinian sense of even legitimate warfare as tragic thus recalls the stringent demands of *caritas,* even to one's enemies, a theme echoed in Pope John Paul II's lament for Iraq that "War is never just another means that one can choose to employ for settling differences between nations. . . . War is not always inevitable. It is always a defeat for humanity."[29] At the heart of Christian narrative, after all, is suffering innocence, crucified love. The polemics of "focused brutality" and "self-confident relentlessness" are never warranted by claims of American exceptionalism, of lost innocence after September 11. *That* innocence, as H. Richard Niebuhr once wrote, was "slain from the foundations of the world."[30] And if the cross speaks of innocent suffering, it does so sans qualification: not only Americans figure in the calculus of innocence betrayed, but all those "crucified on many an obscure hill," including the innocent Afghani civilians killed as collateral damage, the Iraqi children malnourished, the families displaced.[31] Innocence, of course, is never policy, but the metaphor of crucifixion extends our gaze to every cross and every obscure hill, whether in New York or Afghanistan or Iraq.

Reinscribing the *justum bellum* in Christian narrative thus serves to remind us of the original uses (section 1) and form and force (section 2) of the *ad bellum* and *in bello* norms. Indeed, religious *différance* casts the Christian churches (and *pari passu,* synagogues, mosques, et al.) in a critical role; theirs must remain a hermeneutics of suspicion in assessing the state's use of just-war rhetoric. And it is against this backdrop, I believe, that we best interpret the "moral reality" of Christian pacifism: first with respect to public reason or deliberation and then with respect to personal discernment. Were pacifism merely rule-governed behavior, its opposition to just war is patent: in Childress's words, the "duty of nonmaleficence—the duty not to harm or kill others" is not prima facie, but absolute. Yet as Lisa Cahill has shown in an incisive critique, Christian pacifism is rather a "way of discipleship," guided by radical fidelity to the gospel. To be sure, its maxims preclude violence; yet the leitmotif of discipleship, of "loving your enemy," is decisive.[32]

Where Machiavelli (whose infamy is exceeded only by his emulation) bequeaths us an armed peace in which there is no "place" for shalom, the pacifist bears witness to precisely such a place or locus. And this witness, precisely as such, plays its role in public reasoning. Christian pacifists may concede, with Augustine, that the *tranquilitas ordinis* of earthly peace falls short of the biblical ideal of shalom. But Christian narrative is never bracketed (as in modernity's disenchantment), even if it is, at best, only partially translated into public *reasons.* What remains is witness. And though witness is not simply argument, it is, as Rawls himself recognized on reading Martin Luther King Jr., no less relevant to argument—that is, to public *reasoning.* For the regulative ideal of shalom, of "love of enemies," remains the locus of deliberation—even if disciples, pacifist *or* just-war, differ as to its implications, *hic et nunc.*

Pacifism, then, is no mere exercise of private piety. Neither can we regard the state as simply fallen or "immoral" as in Reinhold Niebuhr's Christian realism. Public reason, though disciplined by pluralism—and thus the virtues of civility and reciprocity—is not, for that reason, disenchanted. We cannot bracket "mutual love and mercy," as if the City of God and earthly cities were not only distinct (as for Augustine), but entirely separate. Still, there is a surplus of religious meaning. We remain citizens of two kingdoms, and hence of differing, but not opposed, moral rubrics (e.g., Niebuhr's love and justice).

Christian narrative, one might say, sublates natural law; grounding public reasons, yet providing, as well, for existential discernment. In an illuminating essay, Karl Rahner distinguishes "essentialist" ethics—what I have treated here as the generalizable grammar of just-war norms—from "formal, existential ethics," wherein we discern the particular call of God for the disciple as "*individuum ineffabile,* whom God has called by name, a name which is and can only be unique."[33] Obedience to the "grammar" of our narrative traditions frames our existential obedience; yet the "natural precept of mutual love and mercy" does not exhaust it. Whether one should fight, as in the *justum bellum,* or refrain from fighting, as in the Christian pacifist tradition, would here be assimilated to discernment—that is, obedience to the concrete, particular will of God. Yet the state, as I argued previously, is not simply the individual writ large. The state is not an *individuum ineffabile,* and precisely so, falls under different moral rubrics: the state can never claim divine sanction for its warmaking; at best, obedience to the divine will would be mediated through generalized *political* norms of the just war.[34]

Conclusion

"Christian realism" for Niebuhr remains a paradox, but Niebuhr's paradox lacks the saving subtlety of Kierkegaard's irony. In times of terror, realism is quickly moralized in the polemics of "focused brutality" and "self-confident relentlessness." Lance Morrow thus urges us to "relearn why human nature has equipped us all with a weapon (abhorred in decent peacetime societies) called hatred."[35] Rage has found a voice, seductive as it is potent. And yet, for the Christian, it is Calvary's silence that enfleshes the great command, "Love your enemy." For Christians, this is the very touchstone of discipleship. Christians are summoned to seek those things that "make for peace," to embody, personally and collectively, the "gospel of peace." The hermeneutics of hatred is not, after all, something we Americans must relearn. It is a weapon we have wielded often and well in the past. Perhaps we must rather relearn, in Augustine's words, that for those called Christian, "love of enemy admits of no exceptions," and that those inflicting punishment must "first overcome hate in their hearts." A hard lesson, to be sure, after September 11, but enmity cannot be a fitting memorial to our grief. Nature, graced even in tragedy, has equipped us with other, better weapons. If September 11's tragedy has taught us anything, perhaps it is to imagine otherwise: in the words of Dorothy Day, whom Machiavelli would deride as an unarmed prophet: "Yes we go on talking about love. St. Paul writes about it, and there are Father Zossima's unforgettable words in the Brothers Karamazov, 'Love in practice is a harsh and dreadful thing compared to love in dreams.' What does the modern world know of love, with its light touching of the surface of love? It has never reached down into the depths, to the misery and pain and glory of love which endures to death and beyond it. We have not yet begun to learn about love. Now is the time to begin, to start afresh, to use this divine weapon."[36]

A JAIN PERSPECTIVE ON NONVIOLENCE AND WARFARE

Padmanabh S. Jaini

September 11 is not an isolated event. It has a long history in the past: from the last century, in which most of us were born, the horrendous events that history has recorded—the First World War, and then the Second World War and the fifty odd million people who perished in that war, the Holocaust, the atom bomb, the partition of India, the colonial powers and the fight against them in Asia, Africa, in North Africa, the rise of Mao and Communism and the slaughter of several million there, and the rise of Stalin before him. And so one after another, these events accumulate and produce a Vietnam, a Pol Pot in Cambodia, the Taliban in Afghanistan, Iraq, and recently what we see in Lebanon, and only yesterday what we saw on campus here. This seems to be a perennial problem: we cannot live without bloodshed, without going after our enemies. But most of the warfare is undertaken under the aegis of some church, some holy place, some holy order, some organization that protected, favored, assured that there would be no evil consequences to you because you are right in doing it.

And yet, one can speak of Jainism and of Buddhism—they are in many ways similar—that there is another way of looking at what is happening. The Jains and the Buddhists will be a little different from the other world religions. These are the two religions of India—and Jainism is a little older than Buddhism, historically speaking. Mahavira, the teacher of the Jains, and Gautama, the Buddha, are contemporaries, from 600 to 500 B.C.E., in that range. They never mentioned the name of any God as a creator. There was no discussion on when the world was created, who created it, why was it created, or whether there was a fall from paradise, for whatever reason. We do not know how, but all of a sudden, without any prior discussion in the earlier Vedic literature, an atheistic movement appears on the horizon. There are no doubt theories of creation, or of re-creation, in the Vedic texts. The Jains and the Buddhists went forward straight ahead, assuming as if you already knew the reasons for not believing in a creator. That pretty much leaves us with the idea that there is no creation, but we have to figure out by ourselves what we are!

In the world of today we have Christianity, Islam, and Judaism, three religions that spring from the same monotheistic faith. They have a definite answer to this: they believe that we live only once as human beings and will never be reborn as humans. After this life, we will either end in heaven above or hell below, and forever, a consequence of a good or evil life lived on this earth.

33

Now, the alternative to this theistic belief would be a total rejection of any life after death. According to this belief we live but only once; nothing after this happens. Your life ends here, "dust to dust" as the poet says. But the poet also says "this was not spoken of the soul." If that is the case, then there has to be a third alternative. That alternative would be an affirmation of life after death, but not only leading necessarily to a heaven or a hell, as the monotheistic religions believe. Heaven there must be for the virtuous few and hell for those unfortunate evil people, fewer still. In the monotheistic system, souls do not progress further from hell or heaven. One certainly does not come back on this earth as a human being, or any other being at all, because animals are not considered to have souls, in the sense of being reborn in heaven or hell. The alternative of "this is the only life and here it ends" is a totally materialistic doctrine. We have thus these two options, one saying yes, there is life after death, but in heaven or hell; the other professing end of life at death. The third alternative is of Jains and Buddhists, who maintain that the world is altogether without a beginning. Nobody created and nothing has been created. But life in some form, human or nonhuman, has existed eternally and will remain so through endless times. Any suggestion that human life has a beginning in time, a certain number of years, as some theologians would profess, would be arbitrary, to say the least. The Jains and the Buddhists have declared that all forms of life, as human beings, animals, the plants, as well as those beings in heaven or hell—they also do exist—inhabiting the entire world, have been in some form or another in existence from times without a beginning, and will remain so through endless times, continuously moving from one existence to another. This forms a sort of recycling of life, a cycle of rebirths for each sentient being, from one body to another.

What follows from this is the first principle that there was never a time when the soul was free of body, some form of carnation. Soul and body are totally fused together, mixed together in such a way that they are inseparable. But nobody mixed them, saying, "Go mix." The Jain metaphor for such a mixture is that of gold hidden in the ore in the rocks, which is pure gold. Nobody took out a piece of pure gold and said, "Go to that rock there." It is there now, and it has been there at all times. But you can go and dig it up. You can apply the chemicals required, and you can purify it. Then it can become pure, and there would be no reason for it to become impure again. Not all gold is discoverable. There's no guarantee that all gold is discoverable, nor that all discovered gold will attain equal purity or perfection.

But there are certain rules that apply here. This is only a metaphor, but this will help you understand how the Jains view the entire human existence, the animal existence, and also the vegetable existence. In a way, others don't see it at all, that each and every leaf of grass, each and every animal you can think of, every insect you can think of . . . is like that "hidden" gold. You can think of any number of beings with two senses, three senses, four senses, and the five senses. Within the five senses, you have beings with intelligence, including certain animals and of course, the entire world of human beings. And there are also the heavenly and hellish beings. All these share one thing. Everyone is an embodied person. The soul is attached to a body. And this body, this material body, is somehow joined with this nonmaterial, spiritual element, which is called a soul, characterized by consciousness. You can never find consciousness independent of matter. But you can find matter without consciousness. The idea of a "pure" soul without any body at all, and yet conscious and active, is an exception to the rule, conjured up by those who believe in a Creator God. The Jains allow no such exception, not a single being, however exalted.

Such a God, Ishvara, The Lord, is further believed to be eternally pure *sadā śuddha* and hence able to save those who are bound to this world of suffering. Such a being does not exist. We are all in this bondage. But some of us, if not all of us, can strive to break this, through the process of purifying (like chemical to the impure gold), and proceed to the path that leads to freedom. This will be a total freedom from bondage to the body, to the senses, and the limitations that come with it, and all the passions that go with it. The hunger and thirst and everything else will cease, and then a time may come when this consciousness will have reached such a point—freedom of, freedom from, all the wants—that this consciousness can—and here we're probably involved in a leap of faith, so to say, that we will escape from this body connection forever, once and for all. And we will remain in the infinite glory of omniscience and peace, never to return, like the purified piece of gold.

This is the sum total, so to say, of how the bondage is and how the freedom from bondage takes place. For at least the technical terms are words such as—all Indians use the same words—*saṁsāra*, which means the recycle of going on and on and on, and *mokṣa*, which literally means a release, emancipation from this body. Jains would say that in the worldly life, at the time of death, impelled by desires, our soul grasps some body, some material thing. It will animate it and proceed to the next existence. And this movement is dominated by what we have done, or continue to do. All volitional acts, called karma, are preserved like so many memories. The memories of the world are stored in our mind. The words are stored by a certain mechanism called memory. And this memory comes and goes. You add some memory and you take away some memory. You forget your old phone number. You pick up your new phone numbers. You pick up new words and other words remain dormant inside.

Seemingly, there's a karmic impression, with the volitions that we have producing some kind of an impression. When that particular volition is very strong, it will produce strong impressions. When the volition is very low, it will create a different kind of impression. Such as, say, if you were to make a mark on water, and a mark will be made, but it will soon disappear. Or if you go and cut part of a tree with an arrow, saying "John loves Jane," so that this gets inscribed on the tree. That will remain for a long time and then fall out next season. And then, you may cut something with a chisel on the stone. It will remain for a very long time. Volitions are seen like that, that they leave a stamp. Our angers and our thirsts and our passions and our

hatreds and our ambitions and our compassions— good things also—these things will make a mark somewhere in a way which we cannot explain how. The Jains have chosen the word *karma—karma* means basically what you do. So what you do really has a way of staying there for some time, for a longer time, and building up, so to say. And if it stays a longer time, it will take more time than one life, this one. So it will continue with you when you leave this body and pick up another. The time taken in leaving one body and picking up another is a fraction of a second. There's no time lag, that you wait somewhere in a waiting hall. The soul has this particular ability to pick up immediately, because that is the way it has been conditioned. But even when the soul is free from this body, there is the subtle body of karma, with which it then picks up another body. And so the process goes on.

But there are two things happening. We are inheriting something now from the past. I have inherited my body, my senses, the way I am, and so forth—the whole mechanism of the body. And what I am doing now is adding to something that is already there. I am losing something as I go, and I also add something. So in sum total there will always be something abiding there. And this particular thing is what is "me" at this moment, as a result of my wandering into these various states of being, from human, animal, human, and so forth.

Jainism is a word about which I should probably say something. It began with the mendicants who left the household life and thought about these things. They analyzed what is the way—very detailed descriptions are found in the Jain texts— as to how to take control of ourselves? What are the driving forces within us? And they analyzed right from the vegetable life, observing a "leaf of grass" grasping water and seeing how ants go on busily from one ant to another picking up piece by piece, going here and going there. And of course, they could see the other animals and human beings. They arrived at four driving forces called *saṁjñās. Jwña* means to know. It is cognition, gnosis. So *saṁjñās* are the basic instincts. And there are four basic instincts in all beings, regardless of what they are. From the lowest form of being, a leaf of grass, up to fully grown up human beings or animals.

The first thing is food, *āhāra*. Constantly, we are looking out for food. Animals are running around seeking nothing but food. The lower species are working most of their time hunting for food and digesting it, and so on. So food is the biggest thing, and as human beings started living in the caves or whatever we have, in society as human beings, it is for food that they then come out and then they go. So the world is constantly reappearing the way it is now. Do not think we have not been here like this before! In the beginningless past, all sorts of possibilities have existed. So the first instinct is for *āhāra*. We begin to understand that a being is alive because it's craving for food. And this particular instinct is so strong that nature has provided; we see how the newborn animals can find where milk is and go automatically to that place. And so this one therefore is the major preoccupation of all beings, regardless of whether they are two-sense or five-sense animals and human beings.

The second instinct is the mating, *maithuna,* procreation if you want to call it that. It is a dominant factor, with the food comes this one. And it is hunting after the mate or hunting after the partner, with procreation and other things being added to that. Procreation, however, is not driving us all the time; we know that now.

But the basic drive is to get food and to get mating available. And it is in this that Jains perceive what kinds of passions are working. Little food is enough for sustenance. Animals can only eat so much. And yet they all have desires for more than the available food. We can hold a lot and gobble it up, eat it up. Our desires for food are a billion more times than what our body actually needs. And since everybody wants that food, there's scarcity of food. Because our desires are far more, there is not enough of anything for anybody. And the same thing occurs with mating also. Although one need not have more than one, or one time to procreate, so to say, there's a fight that goes on among the animal world and even among men. Greed is such that it cannot be satisfied.

And this produces what then? Because the source material is not enough, it produces the third *saṁjñā*. It doesn't come after, but they are all together. It is fear, *bhaya saṁjñā*; that is, fear of the other. This fellow wants my food. I want this, and this fellow also wants it and therefore I must dominate this person. And it is this fear of the other, that my needs will be somehow taken away by the other person, that this fear drives on to the fourth want, and that is the most deadly one, according to the Jain texts, which is the sole source of many evils existing now.

Thus the desire to dominate, the desire to obtain mastery of everything, all sources of food and all sources of mating, and other things added up. It is this desire to dominate, to hoard the whole thing in hand, to have all the oil in your hand, all the raw material in your hand. This is called the fourth deadly drive. It's called *parigraha saṁjñā*. What does *parigraha* mean? Multiplied possessions. *Parigraha* is all around. I'm surrounded by food, surrounded by everything so that my hands are so extended and nobody can touch it. Animals cannot indulge much in *parigraha saṁjñā* because they have no pockets to carry. We build up pockets. Right now I have about ten pockets on me. It is the idea that you can store things. Animals also have *parigrahas.* They also know how to store. Ants gather and bees gather. Animals have ways of storing something. Stealing here and putting there. If you observe the films made by David Attenborough, I think you've seen how the birds and the bees and all those little things do it. But there is a limit to them, because they cannot carry on them more than what they can. But they can't make clothes for them to put on so they can add up the pockets, so to say. *Parigraha* is surrounding yourself with possessions. It is this particular instinct in which the human beings have been extraordinarily inventive, to increase *parigraha,* and to hold on to it in some way.

That is how the wars take place. The deadliest, our instinct to fight and to dominate, are all part of this, and that is called *hiṁsā.* I have given this example elsewhere, how this *parigraha* is dominating in such a way that it has been affected by technology. Because technology makes it possible to make storehouses, to make all other things in such a way that you can make them compact, keep things and everything, almost like the CDs now. Just imagine how much they can just control in one disk.

I shall provide Mahatma Gandhi's example, because you cannot talk of *ahiṁsā* without mentioning Mahatma Gandhi, and this is a small example. In the days when Mahatma Gandhi was writing for his *Navajivan* [name of a journal edited by him] and other things, he used to correspond with people. And in those days, postcards were available, a postcard for a penny each. And he would never use any other paper but postcards, one postcard after another, serially, number two, three, like that. And after it is written, you don't have to buy a stamp. It all came with one go. One day he received a very abusive letter, a letter of four pages, with a pin attached to it to hold it. And it abused Gandhi for various reasons. So Gandhi read it, and he picked up this pin. He used to carry a pincushion, in which he put it so it could be used again. So he wrote one card, one letter of that one-line card to that gentleman, saying—he saved that pin—"Your point is well taken." I'm giving this to contrast the pin with the advanced technology, although there's a technology in the pin also, which can be used a hundred times. But new technology is staples. Imagine now. For staples, you need staples themselves, a machine to carry the staples, you need a thumb, you need to press it. And you need so many more things. And the staples are useless later on. I'm just giving you the amount of waste that comes with the comfort that is provided. This is a small amount. And now you can multiply this into the atomic weapons and the things that have come in with atomic weapons, that you cannot store them and there's danger there. The basic instinct is the same—to overpower others, to control the means of having food and water and, well, everything else.

For those who are probably not aware of who the Jains are, let me say a few words. The word *Jina* has the root *ji*—you apply a certain suffix and now it becomes—*Jina*, "he who is a conqueror of oneself." That word is never used for a person who wins a war on the battlefield. It is only applied to the spiritual victors in that sense. And Mahavira is called a *Jina*, just as Buddha is called a Buddha, meaning one who is enlightened, from the root *budh*. And so the followers of this *Jina* are called *Jaina*, a secondary form. And from that you get the world Jainism. Originally, the word applied only to those mendicant followers who followed Mahavira's path of total renunciation of all or most of our wants. They would not commit themselves nor cause anybody to commit any violence to any being. And they will not promote anything that will make violence possible. And it is in this way that Jainism began, with a large group of mendicants who left the household life, left all the activities, subsisted on the least possible amount needed for food and water and shelter, and led a very frugal life, sustained by the laypeople able to support them.

So there's a bicameral system. We've got the followers of *Jina,* who are actively engaged in meditation, and then there are laypeople following those similar rules in some minor ways, and in this way, they help each other. So the monks will help the laypeople keep their practices, and the laypeople will support them by providing the food and shelter that is needed. And it's in this way, how the minimal can produce spiritual existence, that the Jain community has been living—a smaller community compared to others. I think the followers of Jainism are only more than the Zoroastrians among the ancient world religions I'm talking about. I'm talking about the modern period, or the medieval period. There are not more than, I was told, about five million Jains, maybe seven. But my point here is that the number has not prevented them from leading a life that is consistent with the life of the mendicants. In other words, the mendicancy is to be understood not simply as living in a monastery. The monastic life elsewhere (in the West) is a different one. The monastic life is a boarding school life. You live in one place, you eat in one place, and you do not go out. You spend your whole life there, like a nunnery or monastery. Not the Jain monks. They must walk, barefoot, in India. They are all celibate, and they must not eat from sunset to sunrise, for life. And imagine the kind of living, that at the same time, *ahāra* and *maithuna*—those two drives have been taken care of by minimizing them on one hand and removing them altogether. No fear and no *parigraha*. And monks in India have no pockets at all. No food can be saved or stored for tomorrow. And in this way, the Jain community of mendicants and the lay followers have sustained each other.

The layperson also has vows, restricted ones or minor ones. Well, how does a Jain layperson achieve his goals, living in this world? The mendicants have left it, and they are making spiritual progress in their own way. For those who are living in this world, as we do, how will they achieve this? And here I'm coming to *ahiṁsā*, which will take me to the favorite subject of the day, warfare, in a short while. To practice *ahiṁsā* means not only refraining from inflicting injury on others but also renouncing the very will toward attachment and aversion that initiates such wants. A Jain therefore examines in minute detail the intentions that lie behind ordinary activities that constitute the daily life of the householder—earning a livelihood, raising a family, and supporting the mendicants. Not to entertain even the thought of injury would be a tall order for one who must deal every day with a world that is prone to violence.

A householder's activities, however, could be examined to see whether they were free from what the Jains call *saṅkalpaja hiṁsā* [*Saṅkalpaja* = intentional]: harm intentionally planned and carried out; organized violence, as one used in warfare. But more than that, *saṅkalpaja hiṁsā* would be, for example, the intention with which a hunter might stalk his prey, or someone who goes fishing will make a similar effort. Such willful violence has to be renounced before one can be considered a follower of *Jina*. And the Jain texts are replete with sermons rejecting all violence perpetrated for sport, or in sacrifices, whether sacred or familial. Adopting a proper means of livelihood becomes extremely important for a conscientious Jain. There are not many of them, mind you. Nevertheless, there are models and examples. Since the chosen occupation determines the degree to which violence can be restricted, the Jain texts have drawn up a long list of professions that are unsuitable for a Jain layperson. Certain Jain texts forbid, for example, animal husbandry and trade in alcohol or animal by-products, leaving room for only such professions as commerce, arts and crafts, and clerical and administrative occupations. In all these activities, some harm to the lowest forms of life is inevitable, but Jains engage in them if they behave with scrupulous honesty. Injury done while engaged in such activities was considered—and this is the second thing—*ārambhaja-hiṁsā*, occupational violence. A doctor must perform an operation. But this violence cannot be helped, but could be minimized by choosing a profession like business, which is free from causing harm, as indeed Jains have traditionally done. There are a great many of them in commerce and industry.

Now, of course, Jains do not prefer military service much. Larger questions facing modern society such as national defense, weaponry of mass destruction, limiting populations of wild animals and insect pests, the use of toxic chemicals, the morality of capital punishment, the use of animals in medical research, and other social concerns that perforce involve violence were not addressed by the Jains in the past. But nowadays these are asked and they must perforce find answers to them. But one thing that I will say for certain, that the Jains have been able to continue down through the ages the practice of nonviolence, adjusting themselves to the situation in such a way that they could minimize the violence and yet carry on leading a holy life as they understood it.

Vegetarian food is the first thing that comes to my mind, and you could say that a Jain is a vegetarian. A nonvegetarian can become a Jain, but soon he or she will be vegetarian too. But of course, those who are following vegetarianism without being a Jain, we also count them as Jains. For those, especially in the West, who are used to associating the practice of nonviolence with such larger movements as advocacy of civil rights, the Jain preoccupation with eating vegetarian food and protecting domestic animals may seem rather trivial. But the privileged position enjoyed by being such a small minority may appear to have given the Jain community a unique niche in Indian society. So it was able to concentrate all of its missionary zeal on reforming the dietary habits of other Indians. Since meat could not be procured without cruelty, partaking in the meat of animals in fact harms oneself by creating a latent effect in the mind of the meat-eater. They accept items of dairy products. They did not have a conflict with the Jain logic on this point, but dairy was justified because milking a cow or a goat did not involve any harm to the animal itself.

Most Jains advocate kindness, in some form or another, to animals. Other religions might advocate kindness to animals either because they also are creatures of God, according to their theology, or because they are the embodiment of the same spirit as us human beings, as Vedantins might explain, that all life is coming from the same source. But this has not deterred the adherents of some of these religions from sacrificing animals for ritual purposes, nor prevented the advocates of other religions from rationalizing animal slaughter in order to sustain the higher life of humans. When you look to the number of cattle that were slaughtered mercilessly in the wake of the Mad Cow Disease, or Mad Man Disease, whatever you call it, and nobody shed a tear about them. They were raised to die anyway. But the point is, the Jains felt that there was a great, great violence being done to the animals.

Notwithstanding the practical difficulties for all people to procure strictly vegetarian food, the Jains have continued to argue that animal slaughter can never be tolerated under any circumstances. We may recall here the words of the Jina Mahavira, the Great Hero. His real worldly name is Vardhamana, but he is better known by his title Mahavira, the Great Hero—just as Buddha's real name is Gautama Siddhartha, but he's known as Buddha. These are the words of Mahavira, in translation: "No being in the world is to be harmed by a spiritually inclined person, whether knowingly or unknowingly. All beings wish to live, and no being wishes to die." A true Jain, therefore, consciously refrains from harming any being, however small.

The Jains here share the belief that *himsā* is a cause of transmigration. Either you have the model of nothing after this; heaven and hell, and nothing after that; or the infinitely beginningless recycling of life. There's nothing possible in between. It would be completely arbitrary to say fifteen lives ago or twenty lives ago. But that begs the question again. No creator, no creations, and therefore, we are as we are, in some form or other, from beginningless times. Sometimes we have been animals too, or even worse. For this reason, a being who today is an animal might once have been a human being, or by exercising moral powers, that same animal may be reborn in the future as a human being. In the course of transmigration, there is no spiritual progress possible during a lifetime spent in heaven or hell, states which the Jains consider noneternal, but of long duration. Nobody goes to heaven forever. You must come down. Similarly with hell. Short time there, short time here. Nothing eternal. The cycle is eternal. You can see yourself now. The dimension you have, each soul has, and we are moving in a parallel fashion. Within the virtually infinite variety of animal life-forms, however, it is possible for a soul to progress from one animal to another animal until by some force, it would be able to cut asunder. It belongs to the animal realm and it wants a human existence.

Jains thus consider human existence to be the gravitational center of the rebirth process, and assume that all other life forms have to be reborn in a human state in order to achieve spiritual liberation. The Jains seem to be unique in believing that all higher animals possess five senses, like an elephant or a tiger, for example, which would include all domestic animals as well as wild animals that could be trained, and must therefore be allowed to naturally wander through their destinies without interruption by human violence. And I'm going to tell you a story here that tells you what kind of stories were the staple food once upon a time for Jain children.

You can think of a story here that can be seen on the TVs. A beautiful story about an elephant, narrated in the Jain scriptures, illustrates the moral capacity ascribed to higher animals by the

Jains. This is a tale about an elephant. Elephants are notable for their long memory. They're huge, but they're vegetarian. That gives them a special place in the mythologies of the Hindus, Buddhists, and the Jains as well. This is the tale of an elephant, which, in his very next rebirth, was reborn as Prince Megha and became an eminent Jain monk under Mahavira. And Mahavira is telling the past story of this particular man: "Look here, this was you in the past." This elephant was the leader of a large herd. You can call it Jumbo the Elephant if you want, to make it a story for children. This elephant was the leader of a large herd that was caught in a huge forest fire. All the animals of the forest ran from their haunts and gathered around the lakes so that the entire area was jammed with beings, both large and small. After standing there for quite some time, the elephant—imagine the crowded place where all the beings are there because there's fire going on all around—after standing there for quite some time, the elephant lifted his leg to scratch himself, and immediately a small hare landed to occupy the spot vacated by his raised foot. Rather than trampling the helpless animal, however, the elephant's mind was filled with great compassion for the plight of his fellow creature. Indeed, his concern for the hare's welfare was so intense that he's said to have cut off forever his associations with future animal destinies. The elephant stood with one leg raised for more than three days until the fire abated and the hare was able to leave. By then, however, the elephant's whole leg had gone numb. And, unable to set down his foot, he toppled over. While maintaining his purity of mind, he finally died and was reborn as Prince Megha, the son of the King Shrenika, the ruler of Magadha, who becomes then a monk and joins the mendicants and follows the spiritual path. This is the attitude, therefore: Thou shall not kill an animal because there is life there capable of rising to human existence. And if you are also not following the required human spiritual life, you may go back to the animal life, which has countless animal species, whereas human life is only one species. But in remembering this story, one must distinguish between what the Jains consider

superstitious belief in the holiness of animals, such as the proverbial sacred cows of Hindus, because the Jains don't worship cows. Jains don't dip in the Ganges. Jains don't do such things.

Warfare has been defined as organized violence carried out by political units against each other, and peace as the absence of organized violence. The lawgivers and all Indians have divided such wars into two main categories: permitted wars and obligatory wars, the latter being further qualified as just wars, or *dharma yuddha*. In all these cases, it is claimed by the leaders that war becomes just only because it is ordained by God himself and that human beings are merely exercising the will of the divinity. Mythical stories from the canons of old can be cited in support of this position. And we know that how in the *Gītā*, Arjuna, the great warrior, had been told by the Lord Krishna, who is an *avatara* of Vishnu, *hato vā prapsyasi svargam,* "that if you are killed in this battlefield, you will go to heaven"; *jitvā vā bhoksyase mahīm*, and if you live, you'll enjoy this earth. Therefore, rise and fight. Now, one can add all sorts of commentaries on this. The basic thing I am talking about here is that all religions have promised that there'd be heaven available for anyone who dies as a martyr in the war, the battlefield. The Jains are an exception to this; this is why I want to read this story.

And this is a story which is based on the sacred texts. And this story appears in the canonical *Bhagavatī Sutra,* which purports to preserve the words of the last *tīrthaṅkara* Mahavira. There, Mahavira is asked about the war between the king of Magadha and some independent kings, which it is now agreed was a historical event, a war in which 84,000 people died. Mahavira's disciples specifically wanted to know whether it was true that all those men would have been reborn in heaven because they had perished on the battlefield. Whether the Jihadist believe in the birth in heaven immediately and therefore they are induced to do that, that also is something that comes to my mind. In answer to this question, Mahavira declared that only one man out of this large army was reborn in heaven, and only one reborn as a man. All the rest ended up either in hell or in the animal realms. Contrary to the widely held belief that death on the battlefield is almost equal to holy martyrdom, the Jain answer as put in the mouth of Mahavira shows extraordinary courage of conviction that death, accompanied by hatred and violence, can never be salutary and must therefore lead to unwholesome rebirths. And then, the story goes, the man who ended up in heaven was a Jain man. The world doesn't know his name. It is Varuna, who had taken the laypeoples' minor vows before he was drafted by his king and sent to the front. Prior to his departure, Varuna vowed that he would never be the first to strike anyone. He would always wait until he was struck first before attacking. Armed with bow and arrow, he took his chariot into battle and came face to face with his adversary. Varuna declared that he would not take the first shot and called on his opponent to shoot. Only after his opponent's arrow was already in deadly flight did he let fly his own arrow. His enemy was killed instantly, but Varuna himself lay mortally wounded. Realizing that his death was imminent, Varuna took his chariot off and sat on the ground, and holding his hands together in veneration to his teacher Mahavira, he said—and these are the words, quoted—"Salutations to Mahavira, wherever he may be, who administered to me the layman's precepts. Now the time has come for me to face my death; making Jina Mahavira my witness, I undertake the total renunciation of all forms of violence, both gross and subtle, body mind and speech. I remain steadfast in maintaining absolute detachment from this body." Saying this, he pulled out the arrow, and, his mind at peace, died instantly, and was reborn in heaven. This is how you go to heaven.

The second man, a friend of this warrior, was himself severely wounded in the battle. He wanted to follow Varuna and witnessed his peaceful death. He died soon afterward, wishing to be like him, and was reborn as a human being. Whatever the moral of this story, the Jains are clear in their belief that wholesome rebirth is assured only to those who die a peaceful death and who renounce all hostility and violence. Without achieving these qualities, no amount of valor on the battlefield guarantees even

true death and victory, let alone improving one's spiritual life.

The image of the Jains throughout their long history has been associated with the doctrine of *ahiṁsā*. And the Jains themselves identify with the observance of the practice in their day-to-day life. The fact that human contemporary society, where materialism is all-pervasive even in India, Jain mendicants, who scrupulously adhere to their old vows of nonviolence and nonpossession, still number (in a small community of about six or seven millions Jains) over 12,000 mendicants. Half of them are nuns. A very large number indeed, considering the very small size of the Jaina community, testifies to the continued dedication to the ideal of *ahiṁsā*. Without such total dedication, *ahiṁsā* itself would remain either a fond memory of a lost golden age or an unachievable future goal. Lay Jains as well abhor all forms of intentional violence and reduce the necessary amounts of violence associated with their occupations to an absolute minimum. This does not mean that Jains are total pacifists. However, a lay person, as we said above, is given the option of countering an armed adversary in kind, with the reminder that it's proper for a Jain not to be the first to strike. The combatant would also cultivate in mind the Jain doctrine of multiple perspectives, an attitude which allows the Jain to recognize the validity of his adversary's point of view as well. By enabling him to recognize the idea of common ground between himself and his opponent, a Jain would therefore be able to avoid confrontation and try reconciliation and resort to warfare only out of dire necessity, with the understanding that there's no heaven after violence. The Jains appear to have outlined a path of nonviolence that would allow the lay adherents to conduct his daily life with human dignity, while permitting him to cope with the problems of the world in which violence is all-pervasive. The Jains would be the first to admit, in accordance with their own doctrine of *syādvāda*, or qualified assertion, that other religions too discuss some of these same issues. But what distinguishes the Jain conception of nonviolence from that found in other world religions is that it is truly a personal way of religious discipline. It forbids the taking of all life; however, that might be justified or excused in other religions, and warns that nothing short of animal rebirth or hell awaits those who kill or who die while entertaining thoughts of violence. This perspective, however, does allow the Jain to sacrifice even his own life by performing what is called *sallekhanā,* or peacefully reducing intake of food when the time of death arrives. In this way, the soul may remain unaffected by attachment and aversion and may meet its corporeal death in perfect peace with itself and the world. Indeed, the holy life is truly consummated when a Jain dies reciting the words of the religion's most solemn prayer: "I ask pardon of all creatures; may all of them pardon me; may I have friendship with all beings; and hostility towards none." Thank you very much.

QUESTIONS AND ANSWERS FOR THE AUTHOR

Jaini: Since nobody asked a question, I have brought this to read and I will read it for you. This is not a Jain speaking here. But this has the same message. This is by the great Irish poet Yeats.

> Things fall apart; the centre cannot hold;
> Mere anarchy is loosed upon the world,
> The best lack all conviction, while the worst
> Are full of passionate intensity.

I think he's also giving voice to the same feeling that we are seeing: "The center does not hold." That's the center, that's what we want. Not going to the extremes. I think this is the theme we've seen all over the world. Thank you very much.

THE APPROACH OF MUSLIM TURKS TO RELIGIOUS TERROR

Ramazan Bicer

DEFINITION OF TERROR

Terrorism is an expression of conflict. It operates within a political construct in which one or both parties refuse to recognize the other's legitimacy. In fact, one goal of a legitimate political entity, when it is fighting a political movement seeking legitimacy, is to disallow negotiation. "Terrorism" and "terrorist" are thus significant legal constructs. Successfully labeling a group, a movement, or even a state as terrorist denies its political legitimacy. It can then be dealt with as a merely criminal organization. One doesn't negotiate with criminals; one simply brings them to justice. We know from history that the attempt to criminalize authentic political movements has often failed. Terrorist conflicts end up being just as much about negotiation as any legal war is. Many terrorist entities have been awarded political legitimacy, often after a long conflict, and often by the very parties that sought to destroy them.[1]

Terror is a kind of dissension; in Islamic terminology, it is called *fitnah.* Dictionaries give various meanings for *fitnah:* temptation, misguidance, commotion, sedition, confusion, affliction, torture, and strife.[2] Among the juridical meanings, of immediate concern, are seditious speeches that

attack a government's legitimacy and that deny believers the right to practice their faith.[3] Simultaneously, the correct meaning of *fitnah* here is aggression that seeks to eliminate freedom of belief.[4] Freedom of expression should not be used to justify corrupt views and influences that violate Islamic principles. Such offensive speech and conduct may be penalized, although the precedents of the Prophet's four immediate political successors suggest that punishment should be severe only if the conduct in question amounts to blatant disbelief. Although Islam forbids the use of coercion by those seeking to spread the faith, it also takes measures to protect Muslims against aggression that would deny them their own freedom.

Terrorism is a complex phenomenon. Therefore, it is not easy to describe clearly. Terrorism, which possesses a global dimension today, does not possess a single definition. There is no prevailing consensus on what terrorism includes and excludes. The meaning of terror depends on the time and place, such that a so-called terrorist act could be regarded at one place and time as a struggle for freedom yet proclaimed a terrorist act at another.[5] Acts considered terrorist in nature in some countries may be considered only political crimes in others. Was not Gandhi hastily labeled a terrorist by the United Kingdom, and Mandela imprisoned for years? Even UNESCO has awarded some of its peace prizes to those who were once called terrorists.[6]

REASONS FOR TERRORISM

In fact, terror does not exist and survive without external support. Major factors that shed light on and nurture the phenomenon of terrorism in a given country can be broadly placed in four categories. They can be listed as follows:

- Economic reasons
- Sociocultural reasons
- Educational reasons
- Religious reasons [7]

Socioeconomic and Cultural Reasons

Emile Durkheim's dictum that "social events/phenomena can only be explained by social events/phenomena"[8] helps us to solve the problem here. Terrorism as a social phenomenon has many dimensions and aspects to it.

Social change involves every kind of change in society, and in its institutions and organizations. Social division involves the departure of society from its national culture to the maximum extent. Societies are constantly changing. If social change makes the institutions in society unable to perform their activities and causes defects in the system, then change results in division.

A major reason for social change is urbanization. Urbanization involves a rapid change of lifestyles and cultures in society as a whole, but city life is not the only source of violence. Nonetheless, uneven opportunities, unequal levels of income, and different life patterns in urban and rural areas, and likewise differences within city areas caused by insufficient urbanization planning, have fed tendencies toward violence in society in the case of Turkey.[9]

According to research on reasons behind the rise of terror in Turkey, economic conditions and matters of education appear as primary factors.

Research clearly indicates that most members of what may be perceived as Turkish terror organizations come from layers of society with low income and education. A noticeable observation is that individuals, and groups of individuals, with higher education and income are infrequently participants in such organizations.[10]

Financial problems affect people not only materially but also psychologically. That is why terror organizations exploit disparities in income and social equity in a society. It is used as material for propaganda and as a tool of exploitation. Consequently, uneducated and ignorant people are easily subject to manipulation.[11]

According to research on terrorism, militant actions in terror operations are mostly performed by people of low income and education. The main item of propaganda for Communism is poverty. Communist ideologists exploit the economic conditions of the people. For instance, a militant gave his personal reason for being impressed by the leftist organizations as follows: "I could not own anything I wanted in my childhood and youth because of having a very poor family. While the young people of my age were having fun in summer holidays, my family and I were obliged to go to Cukurova to work under the scorching heat in cotton fields for the summer. I had to work while studying. The condition I was in caused me to get interested in the approach to those organizations."[12]

Another member, who joined a terrorist group because of hard living conditions, and not due to ideological beliefs, proclaims: "I went to somewhere far from home because of economical difficulties. I did not have any occupation. That's why I started to work as a building constructions worker. It was impossible to make a living with the amount of money I earned."

Despite many positive consequences, rapid development in economic and social life can produce inharmonious and destabilizing effects on a group of young people in their most sensitive period of development. A lack or insufficiency of basic institutions for dealing with such problems among young people is unfortunately aggravating the situation. A system cannot work properly if economic development and growth are not supplemented by social integration.

Educational Reasons

These terrorists are people who grew up in Muslim families before our eyes. We thought they were Muslims. What kind of process have they undergone, such that they turned out to be terrorists? Aren't we all guilty? Our guilt is the guilt of a nation. It is the guilt of an inadequate educational system. A real Muslim, who understands Islam in every aspect, cannot be a terrorist. It is hard for a man to remain a Muslim if he gets involved in terror. Religion disapproves of using manslaughter to reach a goal.

Education begins within the family and continues in school, at the workplace, and so on. Political parties, civil associations, nonprofit organizations, mass media, and other social organizations are part of this educational process. If one neglects the role played by nonschool educational processes, one cannot penetrate into the reasons why some join a terrorist group or participate in terrorist acts. As a matter of fact, leaders of terrorist groups in Turkey generally either never had or discontinued their higher education. They are not uneducated.[13] If the number of higher-educated people who are involved in terrorist acts is relatively high, then this is a warning that the education system should be examined. Therefore, one might argue that student movements should be taken seriously into account, in order to understand the possible relationship between them and the violence occurring in Turkish society.[14]

Education has the power to thoroughly change the thoughts and minds of individuals and society. Education gives opportunity to shape people according to a set of goals, even if all of the goals cannot be attained. Philosophers such as Herbert Spencer believe that education makes people become more reasonable, more decent, and less greedy. The psychologist Gustave Le Bone asserts that education is an act of constructing and understanding relations of reason and result and not a matter of only memorizing and being able to

repeat material. It is unfortunately true that education in Turkey brings people up as civil servant individuals, bound to desks at which the students are expected to sit rather than act, create, and produce. As a result, a person henceforward rising to a leading position at a high rank in, for example, government services, will be incapable of comprehending necessary democratic aspects of social management and, further, real-life problems in his or her society.[15]

Peace in society depends on thoroughly tested and positive education being imparted to its members. Briefly, the better and the more sufficient and affirmative the education is, the more useful the educated individuals are to the society, or vice versa. The role and duty of families, schools, institutions, and media are to cultivate character, leading people to serve society. The role of a society's government is to make this education possible, at the same time supervising and controlling it. A basic feature of education today is mere parroting, making students memorize without directing them to think.

A leading member of the MLAPA (Marxist-Leninist Armed Propaganda Association), having participated in 184 operations involving 117 murders, states the following about his life: "I joined leftist groups at the age of 17, when at high school. Because the people around me were in different political groups, I felt obliged to take part in one of these. At the time, I believed that the method for correcting defects in the social structure was the revolution of proletarians, aiming directly at dominant government control as in the Marxist-Leninist doctrines." The former general secretary of a terrorist group also says the following: "We were interested in social issues, as we were youngest leaving the childhood behind. We were not satisfied with what we learned from our families or people we lived with in our environment. The communists made use of this period of our youth, manipulating our inexperience and excitements, weakening religious and national senses into annihilation through time. They tried to substitute nationalism and national morality with internationalism and proletarian morality."[16]

Clearly, relative weakness of a country's inner structure provides an opportunity for interests prone to make use of terrorism.

The problem of terrorism will be solved once economic and educational problems are solved; these are, as pointed out earlier, the main reasons behind terrorist acts in Turkey. It should be kept in mind that counterviolence is not a historically proven solution to stop terrorism, because violence always gives birth to violence. In addition, the continuation of the possibility of violence is also violence.[17]

Religious Reasons

First of all, we may mention the existence of various religious opinions, and lack of tolerance is one among them. Thus, many think that they can deliver religious judgments on the basis of God's will. However, almost all of those who use this religious message miss the main point; namely, that no one has the ability to know the exact will of God. We also cannot disregard the fact that some religious leaders lead their followers astray. Clearly, ordinary people consider these men as religious leaders; people tend to think that the views of their leaders reflect the judgment of God. Consequently, the worldly opinions of these leaders come to be taken as constituting the essence of religion. Another important reason for intolerance is fanaticism existing in the subconscious of many people. This fanaticism cannot bear to endure the existence of other opinions. Thus it produces people who stand against God and also produces people who behave harshly and violently against their fellow men.

It should be explained that Muslims couldn't possibly be terrorists. The Qur'an says, "Killing one is the same as killing all" (5:32). Ibn Abbas, a companion of the Prophet, says, "A killer of a man will stay in hell for eternity."[18] This judgment is also true for unbelievers. This means that any person in Islam is subject to the same worldly judgment as an unbeliever. That is, the killer of a human being is equivalent to an atheist and thus someone who does not accept Allah and the Prophet. Now, if this

is fundamental to religion, then it should be taught through education. This is not done. After September 11, we saw that Muslims tended to indulge in convolutions. Does it always have to be the "others" who are guilty? Does it always have to be that they want us to be the bagman? Why is there no culture of self-criticism in Islam? Now, it is necessary to correct the statement that "Islam does not have a culture of self-criticism." There is self-criticism in Islam. Muslims question everything, except for the holy messages. To my knowledge, such self-criticism does not appear to exist in other religions: "If you are not right, we will do this to you." Scholars and ethnologists have discussed and debated Islamic issues so many times that these discussions fill countless volumes. Anybody may criticize another in Islam. These criticisms have been met with sensible tolerance. For example, Ghazali wrote a *tahafut* (a critique on a philosopher's incoherence of teaching). Subsequently, another scholar was free to reply to this. Had there been an Islamic state at the time, these people would have been severely punished. However, no offense was involved, and the respondent did not come to grief: "There are many different thoughts."[19]

The Sources of Religious Terror

Nevertheless, a most arresting and unexpected development has taken place during recent years; namely, the emergence of the theological justification of terrorism, a phenomenon that makes it possible to label terror "holy" or "sacred." Put another way, it is *jihad*. Some radical religious groups use the term *jihad* to describe a sacred and holy war.

Jihad in Arabic is both a verb and a noun. Its singular past tense verb is *jahada* or *jahadat*. The singular active participle of *jihad* is *mujahid* or *mujahida*. The verb *juhd* means exertion. Another related word is *ijtihad*, which means to struggle hard or assiduously.

Jihad is simply the process of exerting one's best in some form of struggle and resistance to realize a particular goal. In other words, *jihad* is the struggle against, or resistance to, something with the goal in mind. The meaning of the word is independent of the nature of the effort or the intended goal.

As a term, *jihad* is used by the Qur'an to indicate striving against something, as, for instance, in the following passage: "And We have enjoined on man goodness to parents, but if they *jahadaka* [do *jihad* against you] to make you associate [a god] with Me, of which you have no knowledge [being a god], do not obey them. To Me is your return [O people!], so I shall inform you of your past deeds" (XXIX:8).

Additionally, the Qur'an defines *jihad* as a system of checks and balances, as a way that Allah set up for one group of people to act as a check on another. When one person or group oversteps the limits and violates the rights of others, Muslims have the right and the duty to intervene and bring them back in line. There are several verses of the Qur'an that describe *jihad* in this manner, such as "And did not Allah check one set of people by means of another, the earth would indeed be full of mischief; but Allah is full of Bounty to all the worlds" (2:251).

The term *jihad* has acquired a number of meanings, which include the effort to lead a good life, to make society more moral and just, and to spread Islam through preaching, teaching, or armed struggle. Such a definition has virtually no validity in Islam and is derived almost entirely from the apologetic works of nineteenth- and twentieth-century Muslim modernists. To maintain that *jihad* means "the effort to lead a good life" is pathetic and laughable. In all the literature concerning *jihad*—whether militant or internal *jihad*—the fundamental idea is to disconnect oneself from the world, to die to the world, whether bodily (as in battle) or spiritually (as in internal *jihad*). The semantic priorities of *jihad* in Islam are here exactly reversed from the point of view of historical and religious realities: the armed struggle—aggressive conquest—came first, and then additional meanings became attached to the term.[20]

Historically speaking, *Kharijites,* a well-known Islamic sect, gave primary importance to this idea when they spread pernicious views and doctrines against Islam. They were not exercising legitimate freedom of expression in pursuit of either truth or knowledge, but were bent on destruction and abuse. Their activities threatened to disintegrate their community. The *Kharijites* acted in concert and had enough power to jeopardize the security of the nascent Islamic state.

Thus, ancient authority on *jihad* has modern force. For example, the thirteenth-century Mamluk scholar Ibn Taymiyyah reached out through the centuries to mold today's radical Islamist thinking about *jihad*. Carole Hillenbrand explains why Ibn Taymiyyah's ideas have been embraced enthusiastically by modern Islamic reform movements: To him, *jihad,* both spiritually and physically, is a force within Islam that can create a society dedicated to God's service. But although stressing the prototypical religious importance of the Prophet's career for those who wish to wage *jihad,* Ibn Taymiyyah is sufficiently a man of his own age to draw parallels between Muhammad's time and contemporary events. Ibn Taymiyyah sees the Muslim world assailed by external enemies of all kinds, and the only solution is to fight *jihad* so that "the whole of religion may belong to God."[21] There are several important insights here. First, the mid-thirteenth century was a time of danger and crisis for Islam. The danger was not simply from external enemies—in the *Dar al'Harb*—but from enemies within—in the *Dar al'Islam* itself.[22] Second, *jihad* is the path to renewal in Islam, but that renewal requires both armed struggle and spiritual struggle. Third, no one is exempt from the struggle when Islam is threatened at its very heart. Finally, this collective *jihad* is in itself a form of celebration, creating a current of collective piety that in effect moves history forward.

A detailed exposition of *jihad* is given by the Ottoman Hanafite legist Ebu's Su'ud (d. 1574). His views reveal the conservative nature of the Islamic legal tradition and how little the theory of *jihad* changed over the centuries. Indeed, there is very little difference in content and structure between Islamic law books composed in the tenth century and those composed in the nineteenth. According to Ebu's Su'ud, *jihad* is not incumbent on every individual but on the Muslim community as a whole.[23] Fighting should be continual and should last until the end of time. It follows, therefore, that peace with the infidel is impossible, although a Muslim ruler or commander may make a temporary truce, if it is to the benefit of the Muslim community to do so. Such a truce is not, however, legally binding. Hillenbrand is saying many things here. First, the implication is that Islamic law, especially in terms of *jihad,* has not really evolved over the centuries. Second, centrality is accorded to perpetual struggle: it is a condition of the religious life. Third, its existential rules for living—the heart of Islam's ethos—do not apply to relations with the infidel. This is not the radical ideology of Islamists. Such is the very nature of Islam.[24]

Many of the books and ideas of the classical period involve *jihad* and importance of *jihad.* All of the books are especially interested in their times. The authors mean to take care of their people, and consequently these books define the term *jihad* strategically in accordance with their times, their adversaries, and associates. So *jihad* is, more often than not, defined politically.

It is clear that, at the same time, the definition and understanding of classical Muslim scholars do not transcend their historical contexts and events.

It is clear that, according to the views regarding *jihad* found in classical books, the normal state of affairs, and peaceful relations between the Islamic and non-Islamic states, are contingent on the acceptance of Islam by the non-Islamic states, and on their payment of annual tributes to the Islamic state.

Contemporary Understanding of Jihad

Radical movements striving for the purification of Islam and the establishment of a purely Islamic society have proclaimed *jihad* against their opponents, both Muslim and non-Muslim, throughout the history of Islam, although this is a particularly marked feature of the eighteenth and nineteenth centuries. In order to justify the struggle against their Muslim adversaries, they brand them as unbelievers for their neglect in enforcing the strict rules of Islam.

In the case of some intellectuals, the colonial experience affected their outlook on *jihad.* Some would argue, in view of the military superiority of the colonizer, that *jihad* was not obligatory anymore, on the strength of Qur'an (2:195). Others, however, elaborated new interpretations of the doctrine of *jihad.*[25]

Contemporary *jihad* theory begins from the time when overt military resistance to Western incursions ceased and the need arose to radically redefine the meaning of *jihad,* either for apologetic reasons or because the definition was no longer relevant to new circumstances. By the early twentieth century, most of the Muslims world was ruled over by Europeans, who imposed their laws and norms upon Muslim societies. In some cases the Europeans ruled directly (as in India and Algeria); in others they ruled through proxies (as in Morocco, Tunisia, and Iran) or through local elites that were clearly subservient to their dictates.[26]

Historical reasons required a redefinition of *jihad.* Most Muslim scholars now exhibit new thinking about *jihad.* Besides these powerful writings themselves, a major factor in the success of the movement may be attributed to the very method Said Nursi (1878–1960) chose, which may be summarized in two phrases: "manevi *jihad*" (that is, "*jihad* of the word" or "nonphysical *jihad*") and "positive action." Nursi considered the true enemies in this age of science, reason, and civilization to be materialism and atheism, and their source, materialist philosophy.

He combatted and "utterly defeated" these with the reasoned proofs offered in *Risale-i Nur.* He also strengthened the belief of Muslims and raised it to a new level of sophistication. *Risale-i Nur* thus served as a most effective barrier against the corruption of society initiated by these enemies. Nursi insisted that his students avoid any use of force and disruptive action in order to be able to pursue this *jihad* of the word. Through positive action, and the maintenance of public order and security, the damage caused by the forces of unbelief could be repaired by the healing truths of the Qur'an. And this is the way they have followed.[27]

Moreover, in Nursi's view, the essential enemy of the Muslims in this age was not the outside enemy but the enemy within, in the form of ignorance, poverty, and conflict—the antithesis of Islam. These pitiless enemies and their consequences had brought about the Islamic world's decline, and prevented Muslims from performing the duty of upholding the Word of God.[28]

As far as the *jihad* against poverty is concerned, he first defined poverty as the material and technical backwardness of Muslim communities. He also included need, hunger, and want in his examination of poverty. Nursi always stressed hard work and thrift. The third enemy was conflict. Nursi asked Muslims to cooperate with all other religious groups to avoid conflict. He identified ignorance as one of the key sources of conflict and suggests education and constant exchange with all groups as a way of overcoming suspicion in society.

Nursi regarded such words as *dissension*, *disorder*, and *enmity* as synonyms of conflict and offered a general solution by translating religious ideas into everyday life practices to build a more just society. According to Nursi, it was ignorance that brought about the decline of the Muslim world. He called upon all Muslims to withdraw from the darkness of ignorance, poverty, and conflict through self-contemplation. *Jihad*, for Nursi, means to kill the inner enemy and to do good work to please God.[29]

Another contemporary Islamic scholar, Mawdudi, advised Muslims "not to establish secret organizations in order to spread Islam, and not to appeal for the use of force or violence in order to change the conditions. Such methods are detrimental to both religion and society. Call people to Islam openly. Be broad-minded and try to change the hearts and minds of people. Make people approve of you by your morality and virtue."[30]

According to those who share the thinking of Bruno Etienne, the term *jihad,* heavily referred to in Western media, is reduced to a single meaning. However, the term *Guerre Sainte* has other meanings in theological and hermeneutic senses; for example:

1. The war made to spread Islam.
2. The war waged against Muslims who deviated from Islam later on, as atheists or *mushriks* (idol worshipers).
3. Defensive wars.[31]

According to Etienne, *jihad* in general means to struggle to attain religious and moral excellence. In addition, lately Muslim scholars have warned people not to engage in activities that may be defined as "terrorist."[32]

Some radical Islamist approaches, like those of Al Qaeda and Taliban ideology, might seem archaic or even unacceptable to most Muslims. Ibn Taymiyyah here has done a disservice to today's Islamist cause. Again, as Hillenbrand explains: his implacable diatribes against all kinds of innovations in Islam—against mystical practices, philosophy, theology, and veneration of tombs—are all motivated by his desire that the true religion should not resemble in any way the practices of non-Muslims.[33] Ibn Taymiyyah's interpretation of *jihad* in effect has created a historical precedent for approaching non-Muslim innovation solely in terms of its potential theological impact on Islam. Thus, some radical Islamists today judge Western technology on theological grounds as potentially corrupting, as exemplified by the Taliban's rejection of TV. Mohammed and original Islam, in contrast, welcomed innovations of all kinds, whole-heartedly adopting such as were useful.

MUSLIM TURKS AND RELIGIOUS TERROR

There is today a prevailing view that the world is witnessing a resurgence of Islam. It is therefore important to determine whether this view is justified or well-founded. In order to do so, an understanding of what Islamic resurgence means is needed. Is it a revival of Islamic teachings, or is it a radical religious movement that aims at making Islam the basis of temporal power through the establishment of a theocracy? Or is it both at the same time?[34] If this is a reasonable and plausible characterization of the causes and motives of Islamic resurgence today, then it suggests that the problem it reflects is not so much one that concerns the rest of the world but Islamic society itself. Nor is it a new problem.

Before going in detail, it is better to give some historical information about the role of religious people in Turkish society. The Ottoman religious elite could offer no effective response either to European intervention or to the determination of the state elite to create a secular national state. The religious elite in effect consisted of subordinate functionaries of the state, committed to the authority of a regime, which for centuries had been a warrior state and protector of Muslim peoples. Throughout the nineteenth century, Ottoman sultans continued to stress their credentials as caliphs and defenders of Islam. With their base of power crushed by the liquidation of the Janissaries in 1826, and ambivalent about reform because of their desire to see a revitalization of Muslim life, the *ulama* were unable to resist the program of the state intelligentsia. Whatever the opinion of the *ulama,* and whatever the shock to the feelings of masses of Turkish Muslims, the voice of the Westernized political establishment was the only one heard at the foundation of the Turkish modernization.

Thus, from its inception, the Turkish republic was aggressively committed to a cultural revolution and to state-sponsored economic development. The heritage of strong state control as well as nineteenth-century circumstances induced the country's political elite to implement Western-type reforms and to subordinate the religious establishment, allowing the state elite to pursue policies of economic and cultural development. These processes seem to have broken inherited institutional patterns and created a more differentiated and pluralistic society.[35]

Another consideration in assessing the credibility and prospects of the current movements of militant Islam is the effectiveness of Islam as a political ideology. In the recent past (since the nineteenth century), Islam as a political ideology was tried briefly as a defense against the onslaught of the West and was quickly abandoned in favor of borrowed secular ideals of nationalism, progress, and modernity.[36]

Religion is a fact of life. Thus, even when the first human being came into being, he always felt the need to worship a superior power. The fact is that religions change according to people's cultures, traditions, and understandings. In this

manner, in such a state as ours, in which Islam is the common belief, there are bound to be some misinterpretations and misunderstandings about religion. However, when we search the roots of radical ideas, we may find the Middle East countries to be their source.

Radical thoughts are easily adopted by the people of underdeveloped countries, who are economically weak. The people of such countries could easily rebel against the existing administration, as they have lost their confidence in the government institutions, but they find themselves demoralized because of political and economic pressures.

Although radical Islamic thoughts are opposed to the Turkish culture, they have been adopted by some marginal Turkish groups through Iran's influence. Geographical closeness could be considered the reason for the diffusion of Iran-originated religious thoughts in Turkey. Islamic policies became a topic of discussion for the first time after the revolution in Iran, and unfortunately Iran became a role model for reactionary Muslims in many countries.

However, Iranian Shiite Islam and Turkish Sunnite Islam differ in many ways. Essentially, Islamic scholars are convinced that Turkey is a country in which Islam is lived freely. On the other hand, Iran always sees Shiism as its most important government institution. Thus, Muslims in Iran are in many ways stricter in following their religion than Muslims in Turkey are. Generally speaking, Islam is not a religion of wars and bloodshed, but a religion of tolerance, eternal love, and peace. The translations of the works that identify Islam with revolution, blood, and wars have affected some groups in Turkey. The Qur'an says, "The one who killed another is as guilty as if he killed all, the one who saved another's life is as precious as he gave life to all" (5:32).

The vast majority of the Turkish people are opposed to terrorism. According to research carried out in Turkey, the Turkish people are against terrorism and violence.[37] It is known that most Turkish people are Muslim. In any case, according to Islamic thought, "nobody can be killed unjustly" (5:32).

For this reason, Muslims, Christians, and Jewish people have been all living together in the same region without conflict. In other words, in Turkey they have lived together peacefully for ages in the same neighborhoods and still do so. As a matter of fact, mosques, churches, and synagogues have existed side by side through centuries in Istanbul and in other Anatolian cities. The people in Turkey have lived in this way through history, although they believe in different religions. No one is accused or denounced for his or her belief.

The fact is that terrorism has no religion; it means that all terrorists are criminals, regardless of who they are, or what cause they claim to serve.

For this reason, all moderate Muslims in Turkey condemned the terrorist attacks in November 2003 on the British embassy, HSBC, and on synagogues in Istanbul. Among the people who died in these unfortunate events were Muslims; actually, a greater portion of the lives lost were Muslim, which further shows to the world and the Turkish public that the terrorists who carried out these attacks were not trying to serve the cause of Islam or the Muslims.

Consequently, the shopkeepers and businessmen in the districts of Istanbul who were attacked by terrorists reopened their shops and offices the next day, as a reaction to the terrorist attack. By doing so, they declared and proved that they are not afraid of terrorists and that they are actively opposing terrorism.

Turkey and Turkish people suffered a lot for a very long time from terrorism, especially in the eastern part of Turkey. More than thirty thousand people and military personnel have been killed by terrorists. This is one of the reasons why the Turkish public is so sensitive toward the subject of terrorism. Turkish people who have experienced terrorism in this bitter way condemn and reject terrorism of all sorts, including the fatal attacks on the synagogues, the British embassy, and HSBC headquarters.

Generally, Muslims, and in particular religious people from Turkey, have been associated with various terrorist attacks and organizations in the world media, and as a result of this, Western societies misunderstand Muslim people and sometimes incorrectly identify Muslims with terrorists. These misunderstandings and incorrect views about Muslims in the Western public arise because of the way in which the media represents Muslims to the world. The media is reluctant to investigate the issues and the events, and their reluctance to pursue the truth of news stories results in incorrect, if not fictitious, news coverage and reports. This creates grave misunderstandings and misrepresentations, which further create prejudices about Muslim people in the West, as a result of which various discriminative behavior patterns emerge in Western societies with regard to Muslims.

It is a fact that some terrorists present themselves as Muslims, but what they have done is incompatible with the principles of Islam. Islam, just like other major religions of the world, has many different branches and sects. Some heretical branches or sects might preach terrorism to their followers, but orthodox Islam opposes "the killing of a person unjustly," and hence opposes terrorism. Terrorists who present themselves as Muslims live isolated from everybody; their thoughts and mentality do not coincide with reality. At the same time, according to those terrorists, "dissimulation" (*taqiya*) is the most important belief.[38] Radical thoughts like these may be found in any religion or movement. Although this is definitely incorrect according to Islam, people with such radical tendencies might be found among the followers of any religion.

We should think very deeply about the Muslim terrorists. Is religious anxiety its source? Terrorism as a phenomenon is a complex entity. Like other forms of violence, there is no single reason why people engage in acts of terrorism and no simple solution to the problems this poses. But if we wish to move beyond vengeance and seek a solution, we must try to understand and effectively address the conditions that give rise to terrorism and help it grow. In our search for a solution, there is no doubt that economic and political development play a critical role. They do not constitute the whole answer, but they are an important part of it.[39]

Finally, one of the leading Muslim organizations, along with several other Muslim outfits owing allegiance to different sects and ideologies in India, issued a "fatwa" against terrorism at the Anti-Terrorism Global Peace Conference. But Islam is a religion of peace and security. In its eyes, rioting, breach of peace, bloodshed, killing of innocent persons, and plundering are the most inhuman crimes irrespective of where they are practiced. At this event, delegates from various Islamic sects, numbering around 10,000, were administered an Islamic pledge to stay away from terror.[40]

We can be sure that the Turkish people are opposed to terrorism like the fatwa. It would be unjust to claim that any existing terrorist group originated in Turkey.

THE CONCEPT OF PEACE AND SECURITY IN ISLAM

Muhammad Hammad Lakhvi

The literal meaning of the word *Islam* is "peace and security," which means that Islam attaches utmost significance to harmony, peace, and the smooth running of society. Islam seeks to bring about peace in society. It gives it first priority, and it ranks foremost among the aspirations of that religion. It seems appropriate, in this context, to cite as evidence the fact that one of the names of Allah is "The Peace," which denotes that he, the Almighty, is the source of and cause for peace. Moreover, the salutation customarily exchanged among Muslims takes the following form: "May the peace and blessings of Allah be with you." Muslims use appropriate words to invoke the blessings and mercy of the Almighty when they enter the mosques, and they complete their prayers by turning their heads to the right and then to the left, saying each time, "Peace and mercy of Allah be upon you." Muslims also invoke for each other the mercy and blessings of Allah after one sneezes. Furthermore, there are many verses of the Holy Qur'an that speak of peace and encourage people to be peaceful. Allah Almighty says in the Qur'an:

> And Allah calls to the home of peace and guides whom He wills to the right path.[1]

God also says about his virtuous servants as follows:

> For them is the abode of peace with their Lord.[2]

The Almighty also informs us in the Qur'an that the greeting of the believers in the hereafter is "peace," as is mentioned in the following verse:

> Their salutation on the day when they shall meet Him will be "Peace."[3]

The angels will also salute the believers in Paradise with the word "peace" according to the Qur'an, which says:

> The angels enter unto them from every gate (saying), Peace be unto you because ye persevered. Ah, passing sweet will be the sequel of the (Heavenly) Home.[4]

Islam has its own aims and objectives as well as a specific moral value system, but Islam's commitment to a society without any bigotry of race, color, or creed is absolute. Islam is devoted to the protection of the lives and properties of all the members

53

of the society. Life and property of citizens are regarded as sacred in Islam, and the murder of one person is held tantamount to the massacre of all human beings. The Holy Qur'an says:

> If anyone killed a person not in retaliation of murder, or (and) to spread mischief in the land, it would be as if he killed all the mankind.[5]

On the other hand, the attempt to save one human life is said to be equal in value to saving all human beings.

> And if anyone saved a life, it would be as he saved the life of all mankind.[6]

Islam respects the inviolability of the human soul and does not tolerate humiliation; nor does it acquiesce in aggression. It emphasizes harmony, peace, and mutual security. All the human beings living in an Islamic society have equal rights so far as the protection of their lives and properties is concerned. Their lives are supposed to be a benediction for each other. The Prophet (peace and blessings be upon him) was reported to have said, "The best among people is he who benefits them the most."[7]

The Prophet (peace and blessings be upon him) was also reported to have said, "A (true) Muslim is the one who avoids harming Muslims with his tongue and hands, and a (true) believer is the one on whose part Muslims fear no aggression."[8]

Islam protects and provides shelter to the lives of all the people. It outlaws any kind of violation, aggression, and intervention in this respect, and safeguards and guarantees the peace and security of the society.

A key factor in securing peace and security in the world is justice, which should apply to all the fields of life. Islam gives special attention to this important principle. The Qur'an and Sunnah contain many provisions commanding Muslims to practice justice toward friends and enemies alike. Allah says:

> Allah doth command you to render back your Trusts to those to whom they are due; And when ye judge between man and man, that ye judge with justice.[9]

He also says, "Whenever ye speak, speak justly, even if a relative is concerned."[10]

Further, the Prophet (peace and blessings be upon him) reports that Allah Almighty said, "O my servants! I have forbidden injustice for Myself and forbade it also for you. So avoid being unjust to one another."[11]

Every kind of injustice, individual or collective, is prohibited and forbidden in Islam, as it comes in the way of securing peace and security of the society. Keeping in view all these aspects, it becomes clear that Islam is the religion of peace and safety, and there is no room therein for violence or aggression. Islam does not care for even its righteous personalities when it comes to disturbing peace. One example seems appropriate to be cited here from a very important phase of Muslim history. The second Caliph of Islam, Umar-e-Farooq, nominated a six-member committee before his martyrdom, to elect his successor of the Caliphate. He was then himself seriously injured as the result of an assassination attack. He then ordered that a decision be reached by the committee within three days after his death. Nobody had the right to disagree once the decision was made, and anyone dissenting on this point was to be put to death. It should be noted that all these six personalities were the most pious and best people among the Muslims of that time and were the cream of the nation in all respects. The reason he ordered death as punishment was to protect the peace and smooth running of society, for any one of these leading personalities could, by their actions, create pandemonium and commotion in society. This illustrates that Islam attaches so much importance to the peace and harmony of the society that it does not hesitate even to put its leading personalities to death in order to secure peace. Islam thus gives topmost priority to maintaining peace in society and would stop at nothing to achieve this goal.

Islam sets great store by the inviolability of the person of the individual in society. Any kind of aggression or oppression is not allowed at any cost. Upheaval, turmoil, tumult, or any kind of disruption in the society is unbearable in the eyes of Islam. Any aggression or use of force, individually or collectively, is strictly prohibited, if the society is running smoothly with peace and security.

If, however, internal and external factors cause a disturbance in the society, then they must be opposed with force. Islam tries to crush all such forces as could disturb a society's peace. This view finds its expression in the institution within Islam called *jihad*. Islamic *jihad* exhorts one to struggle with all of one's power against all kinds of invaders and is a tool for maintaining and guaranteeing peace and security in society. *Jihad* does not mean that one can perform an act of aggression or to attempt any other kind of violence. Any violence that disturbs the serenity and peace of the society is not considered permissible within Islam. *Jihad* is just to oppose or combat those forces that disturb peace in society. *Jihad* is not necessary if a society is not threatened in any way. This institution of *jihad* has thus been strictly established as a way of securing peace and security of the society. Islam recognizes the use of force as lawful and just only for self-defense, in resisting aggression, and for freeing people from tyranny. The struggle and efforts to maintain peace would be better understood if the Qur'anic concept of permissibility of *jihad* were kept in mind.

Thus, there are three major situations in which Islam accepts the right to use force, situations in which *jihad* can be set in motion. First of all, Islam gives permission to its followers to fight when they are suppressed or maltreated or have been victimized. Hence, the Qur'an says, "Sanction is given unto those who fight because they have been wronged; and Allah is indeed able to give them victory."[12]

Second, the permission of *jihad* or fighting is given for self-defense in the event of any kind of invasion. This principle of war in Islam is expressed in the Qur'an: "Fight in the way of Allah against those who fight against you, but begin not hostilities."[13]

Third, Islam also dictates that fighting is a legitimate means for defending the rights of the oppressed. The Qur'an says:

And why should ye not fight in the cause of Allah and of those who, being weak, are ill treated (and oppressed)? Whose cry is: Our Lord! Rescue us from this town whose people are oppressors; and raise for us from thee one who will protect; and raise for us from thee one who will help. Those who believe fight in the cause of Allah, and those who reject Faith fight in the cause of evil: So, fight ye against the friends of Satan: feeble indeed is the cunning of Satan.[14]

In all three cases, it is not the followers of Islam who are the cause of turmoil but the invader and the intruder. Therefore, the institution of *jihad* has to come into force to safeguard and secure the peace of society. It also does not mean that, once a *jihad* has started, that one can indulge in violence according to one's own wishes. Islam dictates that Muslims ought to make peace with their enemy if the latter has stopped its aggression and accepted peace based on justice and honoring the rights of the oppressed. Allah Almighty thus says, "And if they incline to peace, incline thou also to it, and trust in Allah. Lo! He is the Hearer, the Knower."[15]

Islam therefore takes a dynamic view of peace. It is committed to peace and lays down the conditions under which disruption of peace calls for necessary action to restore it.

PERSPECTIVES ON THE CONFLICT IN THE MIDDLE EAST

Rabbi Dow Marmur

Seyyed Hossein Nasr

Gregory Baum

Karen Armstrong

RABBI DOW MARMUR

The starting point of my remarks is a quotation from a Christian, from the Protestant Bible scholar Walter Brueggemann: "Place is space which has historical meanings." He makes this fundamental distinction between place and space.

> Place is space which has historical meanings, where some things have happened which are now remembered and which provide continuity and identity across generations. Place is space in which important words have been spoken, which have established identity, defined vocation, and envisioned destiny. Place is space in which vows have been exchanged, promises have been made, and demands have been issued.

I would like to suggest to you that from the beginning of its history, the land of Israel has been the place of the Jewish people. And the modern state of Israel is only the current manifestation.

The Jews have occupied many spaces—this so-called diaspora. They've never broken the link with the place. That's why worshipers in every synagogue face Jerusalem to this very day, as worshipers in mosques face Mecca. The feasts and fasts are celebrated according to the calendar and the seasons in the land of Israel. And the land of Israel, together with the people of Israel, and the faith of Israel, constitute the triangle we call Judaism. And though during much of the time of its history, the land component has been dormant as it were, it was only so geographically. Theologically, it has always stayed alive. And there have always been Jews, albeit a few, in the land of Israel. So to assume this is a new phenomenon, that Zionism is the force by which this situation has emerged, is, I think, to misunderstand Jewish history.

Before the emergence of modern Zionism, pious Jews believed they had to wait until the Messiah would come. What modernists did is that they decided to walk toward the Messiah and regard the passive waiting as the opium of the weaklings. Those who wished to assimilate disagreed with them, but then were proven, particularly in Germany, terribly wrong. The space Jews have occupied in so many places has proven ominously inhospitable. And when alternatives were offered, Jews in modern times nevertheless decided that, despite the temptation of other countries, they would concentrate on the land which was part of their Jewish consciousness. The Holocaust didn't give rise to the state of Israel. But of course, the Holocaust made it apparent to the world what happens to a people that only has space at the discretion of others rather than place that is their own. So the emergence of the state of Israel is perceived in the Jewish consciousness today as a triumph, because now, we say, it is always possible for Jews to have place, so that when a space becomes precarious, and God knows it does, there is somewhere to go.

But we are also aware of the fact that this has been achieved with tragedy, a double tragedy. The tragedies that came about after the destruction of most of European Jewry, and the tragedy that it was brought about because people who had lived there, namely the Palestinians, many of them were displaced. Partition seemed to be the answer at the time. The Arabs didn't accept it. And the rest we know. Now, of course, it might have been neater and easier if Jews never returned to the land of Israel. Some of our problems would not be there. But the question the Jews ask themselves is: would that be a model answer? After all that has happened to the people, would not having a place to turn to as their own be the answer? We also have to be aware, from a Jewish point of view, that they read pronouncements—by no means of all Muslims, but some Muslims—including their neighbors, who say, "We will only be satisfied when the Jews go elsewhere." That's the view of the country of Iran. That's the view of the Hamas government of the Palestinians. So I'd like to suggest to you that it's not the occupation of 1967 that has created the problems. There were riots in the 1920s and 1930s. And even if tomorrow the Israelis vacate all the territories, it doesn't mean that the day after there's going to be peace and harmony, because the history before 1967 shows otherwise. Now let me also say this: I belong to those Jews who are totally opposed to the occupation of the territories conquered in 1967. I believe that it is wrong, not only because of what it does to the occupied, but what it does to the occupiers, in the way it compromises Jewish teachings and Jewish values. So I ally myself with those who, even now, without going back on the history—whose fault that partition didn't take place?—I ally myself

with those who say the two-state solution seems to be the answer.

Now, we are talking in the context of religion after September 11. And I don't have to tell you that that situation has exacerbated what's going on in the Middle East and has turned the old enmity into that global war on terror, with the irrhetoric and the mismanagement and all that goes with it. And so I belong to those who in that situation are looking for dialogue. And I'm delighted to be here and to speak, in the hope that we will be able to identify more in the Muslim world, more women and men, who're prepared to dialogue with us. I'm even naïve enough to believe that the recent Lebanon war gives us new opportunities because it has shown to governments, including the government of Israel, that the use of power in itself, that military might in itself, doesn't solve anything. And perhaps more diplomacy and a genuine desire to see the other's point of view may. Prayer before politics may become a viable option. Historical and theological considerations may take precedence over political expediency. But that can be done only if there are partners in dialogue on all sides.

Now you'll tell me and I'll know it, that fanaticism is more prominent in the religious world today, in all the monotheistic religions. We have an expert on the subject in Karen Armstrong. So what I would like to suggest in order to further that dialogue, we probably need the Christian catalysts. My experience of being involved in Muslim-Jewish dialogue for many, many years is that it is extremely difficult. And to the extent that it was at all possible, it has often been facilitated by Christian mediators, or catalysts, what have you.

Now so far, we know that no overarching solution under whatever name has been successful. Therefore, I think what religious dialogue is looking for is what they used to call confidence-building measures, namely, small steps, where religious communities come together and try to create a climate of opinion that, in the end, those in power, often divorced from what happens among the people, will have to take note and do something about it. For it's becoming increasingly clear to women and men in all walks of life, whether their special interest is war and peace, ecology, gender equality, or economics, that the desire to dominate in the end destroys dominator and dominated alike. Only cooperation, coexistence, and the determination to seek fulfillment with others, rather than power over others, can save the planet, including the slice of it we call the Middle East. Religion—that is, you and I—has a vital role to play in this historic task. If we don't, our message of peace and love of all God's creatures will ring as hollow as cynics and opponents say it does. Thank you.

SEYYED HOSSEIN NASR

In a few minutes, it's hardly possible to address an issue that's as vast as the Middle East, in the light of religion, this being a congress on religion, and not in the impact of the price of oil and other matters. Many points that were mentioned by the previous speaker need to be thought of in relation to how those very concepts are conceived by the Palestinians and other Muslims and also Arab Christians. First of all, the Palestinians do not forget the nineteen-hundred-year hiatus between the time when the Jewish people lived in the land of Israel and the second phase of living in the land of Israel. And during that long time, there were people who lived on that land, and therefore, it's not a question of a people without a land and a land without a people, but two people warring for the same land. And much of the theology of it—because theology under tanks and F-16s takes on a very special character—has been actually mutilated and distorted since 1948. If there's going to be any serious discourse—and there are Jews in Israel and there are Jews in this country, as well as Muslims both here and in the Arab East, who are interested in deeper understanding—these issues must come to the fore. If one presents only one point of view, there's no dialogue, there's no discourse, and we're wasting our time.

Let me begin with one of the most important myths—I don't mean myth in the sense of Mircea Eliade, but myth as a substitute for reality, because true myth is reality—one of the most famous myths, is that the Middle East has always been in turmoil. That's nonsense. The relation between

France, Germany, and England has been more in turmoil during the last four hundred years than the Middle East. Why do we not look at our history? Before the French cut up Lebanon in order to have a foothold, with the pretext of wanting to protecting the Maronites, Lebanon was part of the Ottoman Empire. And for centuries ever since the crusaders left, Palestine and Israel, for the most part—I don't say completely—Jews, Christians, and Muslims lived in relative peace. It was much easier to have a picnic between Jews and Muslims in Jerusalem four hundred years ago than it was between French and German neighbors in Strasbourg or some place like that. First of all, this has to be made clear—that the tremendous contention we have today has not always been there. It was created on the basis of certain actions that have been taken by powers going back to the colonial period before the twentieth century. Jews have lived with Muslims—I'm an Iranian, I've had a lot of Jewish friends since I was a child and they speak Persian as well as I do and they listen to Persian music like I do and they cook Persian food perhaps even better than my wife—well, not quite—but almost as good. And this idea that there's always been contention is really false. When the Jews were expelled from Andalusia in 1492, they were expelled along with the Muslims, and most of them settled in the Islamic world. And their situation and their history cannot at all be compared with what happened to Judaism for the next five hundred years in Europe, even before we get to Hitler. Hitler is just the last phase of many other factors; nobody wants to talk about [what went on before that], but I think that the discussion of these things has to be resuscitated.

Next I want to mention something perhaps provocative, the idea that everything always has to do with oil in the Middle East. If Abraham had been told by God to give part of Burma to the Jewish people, and all the oil wells had been discovered in Southeast Asia, the Middle East would be as peaceful a place as anywhere else on the earth. It would not be what it is today. This is the important issue: the West wanting the oil of the Middle East. Unfortunately, most of the money paid for the oil is not spent appropriately, which makes things much,

much more difficult. I hope you understand the allusion that I'm making—that is, the need to have certain governments in the Middle East who spend most of the money that they receive for the oil back in the West. Otherwise, they'll become known as dictators and terrorists, and they get toppled very quickly. Second, of course, there's the question of the land, the land which is holy to Judaism and to Islam and to Christianity. It is these issues that must be kept in mind. There's nothing innately warlike in the Middle East, nor is it the fault of the family of religions of Abraham. How many times have you read in the last few decades that there is something wrong with Abrahamic religions? "Look at the people fighting together in Middle East." No one says that about Hinduism and Buddhism in Sri Lanka, where they're killing each other off. That is a question of contention over a piece of land and over power that goes along with it. As I've said, if the oil wells had been discovered in Southeast Asia rather than in West Asia, we would have had the same situation there. So I want to defend Abrahamic faiths, first of all, all three of them. It is not their fault that these contentions are carried out in their names. But it happens that these interests for both oil and land are turned to where all the three Abrahamic religions are present.

I want to mention another point. Present relations between Islam, Christianity, and Judaism are not ideal, but nor are they as bad as some people think, if you take the whole of the global situation into consideration. What exacerbates this relationship is not only those internal contentions of which I spoke, but also two very, very important factors which we need to remember in all honesty. First, invasion always causes reaction, and the Islamic world has been invaded in one form or another for the last few centuries. The invasion of Iraq and Afghanistan is only the last phase. No one denies the great tragedy of September 11, with which this conference began. Three thousand Americans, including over 100 Muslims, lost their lives in that tragedy. But over 100,000 Muslims have lost their lives since then as a result of that tragedy. Over 100,000. Nobody talks about that. That's irrelevant. Because if 100,000 mosquitoes have been killed, it

doesn't make the papers exactly. That's the situation in which we live, and that causes a reaction. And it is not the opposition of the Islamic world to the West that is causing problems, even by the most extreme Muslims. It is their opposition to the interests of the West in the Islamic world, which does not always accord with the interests of the Islamic peoples. There is no Islamic country that has interests in the Gulf of Mexico. It's not a question of equivalence whatsoever.

And let me also mention this because it is causing a tragedy globally—the War on Terror. The greatest war that should be fought against terror is against our destruction of the environment. We've ten to twenty years left before we destroy ourselves completely. We're terrorizing the environment. We're killing off the world of nature. To forget about all of that reality, and then anyone one doesn't like, to give him the title "terrorist" and start fighting against him, is not going to get us anywhere. We must pay attention to the roots of what brings terrorism about and why it is that certain people are willing to give up their lives. What ideology is it? What worldview is it? These issues have to be confronted, and the people of religion should be the very first to do this. I always say a window of opportunity existed for three weeks after September 11, when Americans were asking the deep question "Why?" Suddenly, after three weeks, all the windows closed and this became a taboo question. Nobody has the right to ask that question anymore. The fact that I do it is because I'm not a media person nor am I afraid of not getting full professorship. But other people are afraid. Even professors are afraid to speak, whose duty it is to do so. I don't know what the situation is in Canada, but certainly in the United States. And there goes along with this a virulent—I mentioned that the other day—an aggressive, missionary activity which has become exacerbated with the military presence of the so-called alliance of the willing or whatever it is, with United States at the center and England next to it and other smaller countries next to them, that constitute the alliance of the willing. One finds along with the military presence a very virulent missionary activity which only causes extremism. We also see that in Hindu India, not only in the Islamic world. We see it in Hindu India, except there it doesn't have military power behind it. I said jokingly the other day that if we had Bulgarian Orthodoxy preaching in Egypt, it would never cause a reaction. There's no military power behind Bulgaria, and the Bulgarian missionaries would be human beings living there like St. Francis of Assisi, who went to Tunisia in the thirteenth century. But today, this is not the case at all, and we have a kind of aggressive impingement upon the Islamic world, which is causing so many of the reactions that people in the West are trying to solve, without paying attention to the forces that cause those reactions, that to which we have to pay attention.

Finally, the last point, because each of us has only a few minutes. In contrast to the idea of the rabbi friend, I do believe there should be direct Jewish-Muslim dialogue. I've been a pioneer in ecumenical discussions before most of you in this room were born. I was president of the Harvard Islamic Society in my early twenties, the very first Islamic society on an American campus established in the '50s, when I was invited to participate in Morocco in a Muslim-Christian dialogue. And I participated a lot in the so-called trilogue—this word is a bastard word in the English language, but everybody understands it to mean a dialogue of the three Abrahamic religions, because anyway, in the 1960s, an attempt was made by the then Pope just a few months before the 1967 war to have a very secret meeting between leading Jewish figures, including Teddy Kollek, who was then the mayor of Jerusalem, and Muslims and Catholics and a few Protestants. And he brought people like Gershom Scholem—a very great Jewish figure—to that meeting. Most people were somewhat afraid to go, but I went. And you had sharpshooters from ceilings and so forth and so on. The Catholic Church was trying to become the mediator for dialogue between Muslims and Jewish people. Unfortunately, that fizzled out. It didn't work out. But since then, there have been some dialogues. And I think in the same way that Jews and Christians need to have a dialogue without the presence of Muslims, and Christians and Muslims without Judaism, because they all have their own particular theological problems; there's nothing more important than a direct Muslim-Jewish dialogue. It's remarkable how similar the two religions are, from the meat they eat to the burial of their dead, and everything in between. And that, I think, is a very important step, despite the tragedies that happened in the last month or two—all the civilian killing in Lebanon, and, to a lesser extent, in Israel, all of these tragedies. Dialogue is in fact still going on in a very secret way. And I think for an international conference on religion, it is very important to emphasize that this is needed as much as the other kinds of dialogue and within the matrix of more general dialogue between the three children of Abraham. Thank you.

Gregory Baum

I would make three remarks. The first one: the present conflict is to a large extent the result of policies devised by Western powers. Here, I must disagree a little with my friend Rabbi Marmur. The Zionist movement started at the end of the nineteenth century. It was, at that time, supported by a minority of Jews. The Orthodox said, "No, we are a people in a religious sense, but not in a political sense." The Jewish middle classes in Western Europe were assimilating, and they wanted to be good citizens of their country, and they thought that to be a good Jew meant to testify to justice and seeking the truth. The socialist Jews, both in Eastern Europe and the West, wanted to transform society. There was little sympathy for Zionism. This can be documented. It was only after the Holocaust that the majority of Jews and the great majority of Western peoples believed that the Jews needed a house against death, and therefore, they supported the state of Israel.

Second, the history of the Arab people has also been shaped by Western political policies. If you look at the history of colonialism, it began in Algeria in the 1830s, Tunisia, Morocco, Libya, Egypt, faraway India, and then, after the First World War, the colonial mandates of Palestine, Lebanon, Syria, and Iraq. No wonder that the Arabs considered the creation of Israel as part of the wave of colonization that had come down on them, especially since it was the British imperial government that made the Balfour Declaration in 1917. The alternative interpretation of history by Arabs and by Israel is due to the impact of Western powers. I make this remark because many of the conflicts in the world have been generated by Western policies, especially by the colonial conquest of Asia, Africa, and the Americas.

I want to mention a second difficulty. Another enormous difficulty is that Israel and Palestine belong to different cultural spheres. Israel has become a Western society, industrially developed, familiar with capitalism, advanced in the sciences, having a large middle class, and enjoying a European standard of living. By contrast, the Palestinians belong to a much poorer, more traditional society with a communal inheritance and cultural values at odds with Western modernity. The Israeli-Palestinian encounter is, in a certain sense, a conflict between two worlds, often called the developed and the developing world. Westerners are not impressed by countries with a Muslim majority because they do so very little to remedy the widespread poverty. And conversely, Arabs and many Asian people think that the cultural experiment of Western nations has become materialistic, dominated by market values, and bereft of ethical norms. The difference in cultural vision makes an understanding between Israelis and Palestinians difficult.

The third remark. There will be no peace in the Middle East as long as Palestine is occupied by the state of Israel. Military occupation of other countries has always produced counterinsurgency and acts of violence. Occupation produces arrogance and cruelty in the occupier and resistance, rage, and violence in the occupied. In Europe, the model for this is the British conquest of Ireland and the British settlements in the northern part of that island. Here, arrogance, cruelty, and exclusion on the one hand, and resistance, rage, and violence on the other. This has gone on for generations. According to an article in yesterday's *Le Devoir*,

the peace agreement is again being questioned in Northern Ireland. I believe it is common sense to recognize that there can be no peace in the Middle East as long as the occupation of Palestine lasts. As long as it lasts, there'll be continued acts of violence among the occupied people, foolish and criminal acts of terrorism which serve no political purpose, which kill and maim innocent people, and which provoke military retaliation.

The next remark. There are Jews in Israel and America who oppose the occupation and illegal settlements on Palestinian territory. And we heard that Rabbi Marmur, too, agrees that the occupation has to stop. The Christians who have been involved in Jewish-Christian dialogue and have wrestled against Christian anti-Semitism are often put on the e-mail lists of Jewish peace and human rights groups in Israel and North America. These Christians admire Judaism and recognize the spiritual richness of Jewish traditions, religious and secular. I receive almost daily messages and articles written by Jewish human rights activists in Israel. These men and women are Jewish Israelis who love their country and want Israel to thrive. At the same time, they are opposed to the occupation of Palestine and the Jewish settlements on the conquered territories. They criticize the expansionist policies of their government. They want Israel to respect the resolutions of the United Nations and to return to the 1967 borders. And they support the Palestinian right to self-determination. These activists think of themselves as reformed Zionists or post-Zionists. They want to live in peace, friendship, and cooperation with their neighbors.

The voices of these people are hardly ever heard. The press coverage of terrorism gives them no space. They are easy to find on the Internet. If you were to Google and look for Gush-Shalom, a radical peace movement in Israel, and then you click "links," you'll find a long list of Jewish human rights organizations in Israel and in America opposed to the occupation and the settlements. They refute the argument of the Israeli government that it had no trustworthy Palestinian partner with whom to negotiate. Here is just an example. The Web site of the Rabbis for Human Rights in Israel presented a list of the human rights violations in the occupied territories. It mentions expropriation of land, demolition of houses, uprooting of trees, confiscation of identity cards to remove rights of residents, the use of torture to obtain information, demeaning and humiliating Palestinians, double standard in judging the violence committed by the occupied and the occupier, excessive force used by the military, sometimes shooting to kill, imprisonment without trial. You find this on their Web site. Another example: in an article in *Haaretz,* an Israeli newspaper, of September 4, 2006, an article written by Danny Rubenstein calls for a commission to investigate human rights violations and the oppressive conditions in the occupied territories, which have been getting worse over the years. He writes: "During the past two months, July and August, 251 Palestinians were killed in Gaza and the West Bank, all of them by Israeli Defense Force fire. About half of them were civilians, including women, children, and the elderly. More Palestinians than Israelis were killed during the war in Lebanon, even though the Palestinians did not participate in the war." Now these are examples. If you're interested, you go to the Internet and you can find Jewish descriptions of a group called PAJU, uniting Jews and Palestinians in the common name of peace, the end of the occupation and the closure of the illegal settlements. You can find their platform on the Internet.

These groups complain that the large Jewish organizations in America accuse critics of the Israeli government as anti-Semitic and call Jews critical of Israel "self-hating Jews." Reading newspapers and reviews, I have the impression that, after the bombing of Lebanon, this strategy no longer works. Jews, Muslims, and Christians believe in the God of Abraham. We all depend on God's mercy. We all pray that God may lead us to reconciliation. And because we believe in God, we will not despair, but live in hope. Thank you.

KAREN ARMSTRONG

We've had some very eloquent and passionate discussions of the history of this conflict. I myself have become a historian, and I'm aware of the real complexity of these historical issues, which are not always understood by people who take violent, aggressive positions either for or against, on one side or the other, in the West. And I think there's been now a history of pain in this region for a hundred years and history is part of each side's identity. It has become a narrative of pain, and the historical gives it, in the full sense of the word, mythical significance. But what we're going to do now, because this summer we've seen the conflict rising to appalling levels. . . . Nobody can be happy with what has happened this summer. And this conflict was originally a secular conflict on both sides. Zionism was initially a secular movement, a rebellion against religious Judaism, and opposed by most Orthodox rabbis. And the Palestinian movement was also secular. The PLO consisted of Christians as well as Muslims and therefore the secular option was almost essential for it. But, over the years, unfortunately, this conflict has been allowed to fester and go on. It has been sacralized on both sides with a species of what we call fundamentalist religion and has become a symbol, something more, something greater than itself. And this also pertains in the West, where people look at the thing with mythical spectacles, instead of seeing things as they are.

Fundamentalist movements almost always have a symbolic issue that seems to reflect everything that's gone wrong in the world. In the United States, among the Christian Right, that issue is abortion or evolution. These issues are not discussed scientifically. They are each surrounded with a nimbus of evil. They seem to sum up everything that has gone wrong in the modern world, and the murderous, aggressive, soulless aspects of modernity. Now, in the Jewish world, the state of Israel, either for or against, has been at the root of every single fundamentalist movement. Some Jewish fundamentalists are passionately for the state of Israel, the secular state of Israel which they see as sacred. Others see the state of Israel as at best a neutral value. And some even see it as evil, because it is secularizing in their view an important religious symbol in Judaism. In the Muslim world too, the situation of the Palestinians has become a symbol of everything that has gone wrong in the modern world—the sense of powerlessness among Muslims, the sense of frustration. The knowledge that thousands of people could be displaced, while the world stood by and did nothing. The issue has, therefore, become larger than itself and is now surrounded with an aura of absolute wrong. And finally, among Christians in the United States, the state of Israel has become symbolic too. As you know, the Christian Right believes the Jews must be in their land before Jesus can return. So they are passionate supporters of the state of Israel. But it is also a very anti-Semitic ideology because when antichrist appears and inaugurates the last day, he's going to slaughter all the Jews who refuse baptism in the land.

So it's very difficult for any of us to see these issues correctly. And I've traveled around the United States, and I'm sometimes appalled by the ignorance. People say to me, "Well, where did Palestinians come from?"—and these are university professors. And I said, "Palestine, of course," and they look absolutely astonished. Now, the peace will be made here, I think, in the West. I think the West has a huge responsibility. I agree with all that's been said about the West's contribution to this, especially the contribution of Great Britain to this conflict. But we have to understand that whatever happened in the past, there are now two peoples in that land. The Jewish state is there. It is de facto. But the Palestinian movement is there, de facto. Palestinians are not going to go away. And we know from our religious traditions that however holy a land can be, if there's no justice, there's no real holiness. This goes right back to the Psalms, the ancient Psalms of Israel, which said that unless there was *tseddeq* (justice) in the land, there could be no *shalom*, no peace, no holiness. And that is the challenge for us today.

I think we have to see that fundamentalist movements—I don't like that term, but we've only got a few minutes—fundamentalist movements are all rooted in fear of annihilation. The Jewish people have experienced near annihilation in Europe. The Palestinian people constantly have a sense of annihilation, a sense that they'd be wiped off the map. And when these movements are attacked—this is a historical fact—they always become more extreme. So going to war to make peace or attacking extremist movements will be counterproductive. It will only lead to more extremity. Policies have to work. You can have very, very principled policies, but if they're not working, then they're useless. And certainly, you'd be hard put to say that whatever policies are being adopted in the Middle East, are they working? No. And this cycle of war is increasing the problem. It increases the sense of extremism. Osama bin Laden, for example, who had no interest whatever, I believe, in the Palestinian problem originally, knows his audience and knows this is a symbolic issue and he uses it to demonstrate his good credentials. We must find a solution. There'll be no peace in the world unless there is a peace solution for Palestine.

And this is a religious question. It may be a secular conflict, but we need a change of heart—all of us, not just pointing our finger at the other, but all of us. The great prophets of Israel made it clear that, when Israel was threatened with annihilation way back in the eighth, seventh, sixth centuries B.C.E., it was no good just blaming the enemy. The prophets of Israel said, "Look to your own behavior. Look to your own heart." Jesus said, "Don't look at the splinter in your neighbor's eye and neglect the beam in your own." Always self-criticism. And that means all of us have to engage in that, including the Western countries, and examine our own predispositions toward one side or the other, because the thing is getting out of hand and is threatening world peace.

Second, when I spoke on the first night of the conference, I mentioned the golden rule: "Don't do to others what you would not have done to you." If politicians observed this rule, the world would be a better place. And that's not a simple thing to do. You have to look carefully at your own history of pain and then say, "Do you want to inflict this on anybody else?" We've all now been experiencing terrorism and violence and hatred and danger and fear. Do we want, even in a passive way, to inflict this on anybody else? We need to start to think again.

One of the other great religious principles is to see things as they are, not how you feel they ought to be, but as they really are. So you need to have dispassionate, fair, impartial reporting of events in the Middle East, which is not always done—maybe, I don't know about Canada so much. But certainly, in the United Kingdom and the United States, the reporting is not always fair. So we need to see things as they are because we cannot hope to bring peace to the world unless we sort out this problem, and that means absolute respect for all the parties involved, and an acknowledgment that we Westerners carry a responsibility for what has happened. And we bear a great responsibility to help these people to live together in peace. Thank you.

QUESTIONS AND ANSWERS FOR THE AUTHORS

Question: I spent the war in Lebanon in Tibet, of all places. I was reminded, while the violence was going on, that anger, rage, and violence are not the only possibility by means of which we can respond to occupation. And that has led me to think about the question that goes beyond looking at the issue of justice—Who is right? Who is wrong? Who did this? Who did that?—we also have to discuss how our religions equip us to respond to the challenges of what happens. A presentation that says "Jews occupy and we understand the rage of the other side" is by nature one-sided. We have to look at the question, In what way do all our religions bring out the best in us? What type of religious response do they condition? I cannot speak for Islam—let someone else do that. I'll only share a brief point regarding Jewish responses to bus bombings. The usual Jewish response has been, a bus explodes, we blame the others, we'll go get them. When a bus exploded in an ultraorthodox Jewish community, the communal response was to say, "What have we done wrong? What is God telling us? How can we be transformed?" If all of us can galvanize our forces, not to blame, not to seek justice, but to seek the kind of self-transformation through religious response, we may be able to bring out the best in our traditions.

Question: My question is to Ms. Armstrong. My name is Abram Allen. I'm from Paducah, Kentucky, U.S.A. I wish I could recall my namesake here, Abraham, to moderate what we consider tonight, for what we're experiencing in the Middle East is a struggle for truth possession, that is, the aggressor's right and defender's truth.

Armstrong: Is there a subject, any subject at all?

Question: Is there any subject that can possess truth?

Armstrong: This might be a little deep for me. I think we always have to understand that our understanding is partial and always conditioned by how we've been brought up, by our sympathies—our national sympathies, our cultural sympathies. And I don't believe, for example, that any one religious maxim or doctrine ever has the entire truth about God, because God is transcendent. And certainly, I don't like the idea of possession, because it suggests my truth and not anybody else's truth. Truth is not possessed. I don't like the idea of possessing truth. I don't like the idea of truth ever being summed up in a single maxim. We're always striving to achieve greater insight into truth. And I think in this situation, we have not always been looking for truth. We've been looking for proof-texts and justifications.

Nasr: Very quickly, Christ said, "I am the Way, the Life and the Truth," so no religious person as a Christian can negate the possibility of truth with a capital *T*. And in Islam, one of the names of God is Al-Haqq, the truth. And since everything is created by God, truth manifests itself on all levels of reality, which does not mean there are not different interpretations and different perspectives on something which is true. I don't think it is at all possible to have a serious religious engagement without accepting the truth on some level. But that does not mean my subjective appraisal of something that's true is the truth as such. Ms. Armstrong quoted a verse which really is a saying of the Prophet of Islam: "Oh Lord, show us things as they really are," which is a prayer of the Prophet to be shown things as they really are. It doesn't mean in human experience there are no things that reveal themselves as they really are; it means that we usually have a slanted, subjective perspective which prevents us from seeing things as they really are. But there are things as they really are, and that's where the truth lies.

Marmur: Just a comment. In Jewish tradition, God's seal is truth. Human beings cannot attain it. Our problem is, we settle for certainty, and certainty includes everything else. And we then go blindfolded into the world and make any kind of dialogue impossible. Please note that the four presenters today, there's really a lot of consensus here. There's a lot of agreement. We could sit down and spend hours and come to that kind of agreement. It is when we believe with certainty that what we are saying is the only thing possible that we get into trouble.

Question: Just a short question on the role of the media in misrepresenting Middle Eastern religion. We always get the impression that Arabic Islam is different from Islam elsewhere. There's this idea that the media is playing up the misrepresentation of religion in the media in relation to the Middle Eastern conflict. I was wondering if anybody would like to take that up, because we really get the impression that religion in the Middle East is different. . . . A Christian in the Middle East is different than he is here. A Muslim is different in Lebanon than he would be in Tunisia. We get this impression. . . . I personally think the media is being irresponsible in presenting religion.

Baum: I agree with you that the media misrepresents religion very often. That is, the media in a capitalist society, newspapers have to survive, and therefore they have to sell their newspapers, and therefore don't blame them if they say we need sensation in order to sell our newspapers. Isn't that the market virtue? It's the system that demands that they constantly think of market principles. And therefore if there's violence between religions, it is immediately reported. If a hundred rabbis and imams meet in Morocco for peaceful conversation and to find a common ground, this is never mentioned. The same is true of the reporting on

religion, certainly on Islam. The caricature that Muslims and Islam are suffering at this time is scandalous. There's research done on this. Professor Rachad Antonius has done research on this. He has looked at television, the newspapers, and so on. This is quite scandalous, the distortion of Islam that's taking place. But this is true of Judaism and Christianity too. It is the sensation that matters, the bizarre aspects of religion that make the newspapers. But upon reflection, it's very [dangerous].

Nasr: A very quick comment. What he said is completely right, but the needs of the market do not seem to apply to Judaism and Christianity. They only apply to Islam. Because of the political correctness which is now very dominant, no newspaper in the United States would dare criticize Judaism or Christianity or African-Americans. The only open field is Muslims and Arabs. So it's not only a question of the market. It's something else that is involved.

Armstrong: I would agree with that. We've just seen this disgraceful business of the Danish cartoons. The newspaper had refused a caricature of Jesus earlier but was quite happy to go ahead. . . . This I've been aware of for years, and it's what got me into all this in the first place, because it strikes me that once you start thinking routinely in a distorted way about a people, you are heading for a great darkness. We saw that in the 1930s in Europe, and I've been very concerned about the matter that Professor Nasr has just explained so well.

Question: My question is more philosophical, and it's addressed to all the panelists. I'd like to thank all of you for your contributions here tonight. In your respective opinions, what is the importance of the challenge of different groups of people who interpret their sacred texts as well as their understanding of their own national identities in essentialist ways; that is, ways that are often interpreting texts and notions of identities in literalist ways but end up excluding others?

Nasr: I know where you're coming from. Once you said "essentialist," that means postmodernism, which refutes the possibility of any innate truth to

65

any text. Texts are related to power structures, and once you interpret something as having an essence, you in a sense have absolutized it and that is what postmodern philosophy is against. Now, I'm not going to debate with you and Derrida about this matter. What I want to say is that those who are literalists in their interpretation of their scriptures are not necessarily the same people who are violent, who are terrorists and the like. Literalism is a way of defense when one's religious identity is being diluted. In traditional Christianity, as well as traditional Islam and Judaism, you had over the centuries commentators who were literalists, those who were mystical, those who were theological, those who were philosophical. You have all kinds of comments about the Qur'an, the Torah, the Bible, and so forth and so on. What has happened today is quite something else, to which she [Armstrong] drew attention. And that is that you have a kind of literalism which is based on the fear of extinction, and therefore poses itself as the antipode of all this postmodern textual study that goes on in Western universities and has been going on in America in the last two or three decades.

Baum: I too have little sympathy for certain postmodern trends. There's no access to truth. There're just different stories, different spins. Each person looks at the matter from a different point of view. There's no truth. I mean, this is used by Holocaust deniers. They say that, "Yes, many people think there was a Holocaust. I think I can give another interpretation. This never really happened. The Jews were put into hotels and they didn't really suffer." So I'm extremely nervous about the idea that you can't really find historical truth. I mean, I don't want to give a lecture against postmodern thought at this time, but I think it's worth saying that this is very dangerous territory.

Armstrong: Just to give you a quick story. A couple of years ago, I was giving a lecture, and a policeman came up to me and told me that a young man had read my book on the Buddha and had marked it heavily on an airplane journey, and had then gone, as a result of that, and killed his parents and then killed himself. Now, this is what can be done with any text. When I told this story to somebody, their response was, "Thank goodness the young man didn't pick up a copy of the Bible, because then it probably could have been a massacre." But if you can do something like that with Buddha—nonviolent, compassionate Buddha—it's what you bring to these texts that count. And in previous years, before the invention of printing, before everybody put out their own Bible, people listened to their texts. And they didn't just pick out their favorite bits here and there and sling them together to create their own religions. They had to take the whole and listen to it and had an entirely different relationship with scripture. But now we're all making our own religions. And furthermore, it's amazing how many Western people feel that they are absolute authorities on the Qur'an. [They consider it an] absolutely violent text, and you say, "Hello, what about the book of Joshua? Or the book of Revelation?" They don't like that either. They don't see it. So I think we have to really think to try to get back to what we mean by a sacred text, how complicated it is, that it does not give us simple answers to hugely complex questions.

Question: What does overpopulation have to do with this problem? Armstrong told us back in Mississippi that the Palestinians have about twice as many children as the Israelis, so that's why I'm asking.

Armstrong: I think what you may be referring to is the demographic problem. Rabbi, is this not a problem that people are concerned about in Israel? That they will soon have a Palestinian majority and the country will be oppressed by a [former] minority? I think that's what you are referring to. But I don't think you meant this is overpopulation. The Palestinians do tend to have more children than Israelis, and many Israelis are concerned about this. But the issue is an issue of justice rather than just demographics, I think.

Question: This is a question that came from a point that Karen Armstrong raised, but I suppose anyone can comment on it. You said that all fundamentalism comes out of fear. Could you comment on what is the fear of Christian fundamentalism? What feeds the fear of annihilation in Christian fundamentalism?

Armstrong: Even in the United States, there are Christians in what we would call "small-town" America who feel colonized by the, to them, alien ethos of Harvard, Yale, or Washington and feel that the modern liberal voice is drowning out what they regard as true faith, and they feel that their whole faith is in jeopardy. Most fundamentalism— and this includes fundamentalism in the United States—begins with what is perceived to be an attack by an aggressive secularism or an aggressive liberalism. That's what happened in the churches at the beginning of the twentieth century, when the liberals started vilifying the conservatives and they became more conservative and started to fight back to defend what they regard as the true faith. In the course of defending it, however, you inevitably start getting distortions, because people start getting defensive. But that's what it is.

Question: At other conferences, I've heard that the imbalance of power is one of the obstacles to negotiation and dialogue. I wonder if someone could speak to that. It comes in part from the belief that Israel has United States with it, and therefore there's an imbalance.

Baum: Yes, I think it is obviously true that sometimes our newspapers speak as though Israel and Palestine are two equal quantities, and they are in conflict. This is not true at all. Israel is very powerful and has powerful arms, and Palestine is very weak in arms. Even the suicide bombers. . . . They wouldn't do this if they had tanks. They do it obviously because they don't have weapons. The question is quite right. The policy of the United States could have been to promote dialogue and promote negotiation and demand some kind of settlement. But the United States policy, certainly of the present administration, has been to support Israel in its expansionist policies. So I do think there's a great deal of inequality.

Nasr: Every dialogue presumes either a person or an organization behind the dialogue. And every

dialogue, even concerning the price of oil in OPEC, not only grand religious or political issues, is always unequal if one side is much more powerful than the other. The reason that a country like Iran—I don't think it wants to, but here people say that it wants to—wants to have the nuclear bomb is because those countries which do, when they sit around the table, cause the whole tenor of discussion to be very different. They dominate over those who don't, even if the discussion were to concern mining tin in Indonesia or something like that. So there's no doubt about it that the lack of equality or parity in power structures affects very much the result of any dialogue and for any subject.

Question: You are a distinguished panel of experts in the history on your land. My question is simple and difficult. I am a follower of Gandhi and I also believe in Bhagavadgītā, where Krishna had acknowledged a just war. My question is based on the premise which has already been discussed by the panel: How can this panel challenge yourself to bring the two parties on the discussion table for a dialogue? Otherwise, this is a fruitless discussion, because this is not going to reach the parties which are going to be deciding.

Armstrong: I think there is an avoidance of this issue among the powers that be. You're constantly hearing President Bush saying this Palestinian problem is not a cause of the rising tide of extremism in the world, not the source of all our difficulties. Mr. Blair, to his shame, says the same. I think there needs to be more recognition that this is a major problem, and I think that the Western powers should inaugurate a really unbiased dialogue. But it's difficult. In Northern Ireland, it took us years. You have to be prepared to talk to everybody. "We don't talk to terrorists," and so on. This is all very well. But in Northern Ireland, people were talking to terrorists—the so-called terrorists, the IRA—subrosa. And it was these discussions that eventually led them to the extraordinary moment when they were all sitting around the table together. So I think there needs to be more real taking into cognizance the other point of view. The United States, for example, needs to have a much more unbiased attitude, and to see that, and to really try to understand what some of the Palestinians and some of their supporters are trying to say, often in an aggressive way. Look at the underlying content of the rhetoric.

Nasr: Time is running out very quickly, but I see a gentleman asked what we as panelists can do. I think the best we can do next time is for Professor Sharma to get suicide bombers and drivers and pilots of F-16s from Israel together and we'll talk to both of them. But before we get there, I believe that the expression of truth on another level itself has unforeseen consequences. That is something in the nature of reality. Of course, of the people in this room, none of them is going to make major decisions for the United States or Canada or the Arab world or Israel. But, nevertheless, like a wave that ripples along, there's a ripple effect, and that's the best that we can hope for. Otherwise, we have to follow the advice which remains in my ear when, in 1957, the great French Orientalist and Catholic thinker, Louis Massignon, made a remarkable comment. This being Montreal, I'll quote it first in French and then in English—Il a dit, "C'est trop tard pour les congrès; ce qui est important maintenant, c'est la prière du coeur." That is, "It's too late for congresses. Now, the only thing that counts is the prayer of the heart." We take that advice to heart or do the best that we can in the hope that this will gradually reach a wider audience.

Baum: I mean, the panelists can do something. I'm a member of a church. Churches take public positions, and therefore I belong to circles and groups in churches that try to influence the policies that the church adopts. And this could have an influence on public opinion and eventually even affect the government.

Question: I'm Daniel Helminiak from the University of West Georgia in the United States, and I'm embarrassed to make this point. For the sake of seeing what's really happening. . . . I've heard these stories. Is there any factuality to it? What can you say about it, even for the level of true believers in the White House, this issue about the Apocalypse

and wanting to bring it on because of the return of Christ, in the States?

Nasr: Very quickly, this is a heresy, from the point of traditional Catholicism or Protestantism. I'm not a Christian. I'm a Muslim. But allow me to say that even from the point of Islam, to try to force God's hand, to try to force God's will is a great sin. All the three monotheisms believe in a messianic event at the end of the world, but have said that only God knows when that will occur. So I see this as nothing more than a politicization of a very profound and important Christian doctrine.

Baum: I agree with this. Whether these rumors are true I don't know. I don't have any connection with the White House at all. But there are certainly authors in the United States who write books on these things. There's no doubt about this. How far they influence policy, this I cannot say.

Armstrong: I think this reflects a mood. I think President Bush comes from a sort of fundamentalist background. He depends upon that kind of constituency. The whole package of Christian Right ideas is very congenial to the administration. Whether he actually believes that he is the president who is going to lead us to rapture remains to be seen. But you're right. This is a heresy. The point is, however, whether this hard-line rapture theology is right or not, diluted versions of it come down among believers, and this also affects the mood to which the administration is responding.

Nasr: The question of leading us to rapture or rupture. . . .

Question: I wish I could pass on the same message which I gave in this conference about ahimsa, nonabsolutism and nonattachment, and you panelists can take this message further out and take this message for further nonviolence and bring about peace and justice everywhere. I would like to make a last announcement over here that we have a concert in the next room, and we're going to have a concert on interfaith dance. I hope all of you can join us. Thank you.

Question: My name is Lyndon Harris. I was the priest in charge of St. Paul's Chapel, which is right across from the World Trade Center site. We ran relief operation there after the attacks on September 11 and also spent a lot of time on the site doing blessings and prayers on body bags and, Dr. Armstrong, I remember with great fondness you were with us. I'm now working with an organization called the Garden of Forgiveness. It's based on the original Garden of Forgiveness in Beirut, Lebanon, and we want to advance the cause of forgiveness around the world. And we want to invite every community to plant your own Garden of Forgiveness, because we believe that forgiveness is a way for us to break the cycle of violence, retribution, revenge and a way to redress, in some measure, the motivating factors behind terrorism, the shame and all of that. I wonder if each of you would have a minute to make a comment about the role forgiveness can play in breaking the cycle of violence and helping us move on toward creating the future.

Baum: I assure you this is terribly important, but forgiveness doesn't dispense you from restitution.

Question: Neither does it exclude or preclude justice.

Baum: Yes, that's right. In other words, forgiveness doesn't dispense you from restitution. And so I think this cannot be used. . . . I mean, forgiveness can be used ideologically as a way to maneuver people away from making just claims. So I think I'm all for forgiveness, but I'm worried about the ideological use of it.

Nasr: In Islam, of course, one of the names of God is the forgiver, Al-Ghafur, and in most parts of the Islamic world, Muslims use the invocation of Al-Ghafur everyday. Yet some of them forget that this must be applied also to life. God forgives us. And if we are his vice regents on earth, we have the duty to forgive others to the extent that we can. And I think that that works on an individual basis, rather on a social, collective basis. That is the problem. Most societies have not practiced forgiveness as a collectivity during most of their history. But if individuals have and do, especially in the present situation we are in, I think that they can play a very important role.

Armstrong: I think the Garden of Forgiveness is a wonderful idea. I'd just like to take the line from the Lord's Prayer: "Forgive us our trespasses, as we forgive those who trespass against us." Remember, we've trespassed too, so that when we're forgiving others, we are not doing so in a position of absolute righteousness and graciously handing out forgiveness, but that we realize our own culpability, that it usually takes two to tango, two to reach a hideous conflict—more than two—and that as we forgive others, we would recognize our own part in creating the situation of pain and suffering and cruelty.

THE GOLDEN RULE AND WORLD PEACE

Patricia A. Keefe

OVERVIEW OF THE GOLDEN RULE IN HUMAN HISTORY

The golden rule, though phrased in various ways in the major religions of the world, is an aspect of each and expresses a commonality of relationship: "'Do to others as you want others to do to you' and its expression in all of the world's religions is part of our planet's common language, shared by persons with differing but overlapping conceptions of morality. Only a principle so flexible can serve as a moral ladder for all humankind."[1]

There is a well-known poster that contains the golden rule as stated in the major religions of the world. The core meaning has to do with what some call "the ethic of reciprocity." How do these basic ethical formulations relate to a peaceable kingdom on our earth? How does the failure of world religions and their members to abide by the golden rule result in violent conflict and war? Whatever else can be said, the golden rule is not so much an answer to the world's needs as it is an ethical question often not addressed in contexts in which it would be useful for resolving conflict. In this section, the formulations found in Confucian, Jewish, Christian, and Hindu expressions will be explored in some detail.

CONFUCIAN GOLDEN RULE

Confucius (551–479 B.C.E.) is said to have provided the first recorded statement of the golden rule.[2] During a time of political corruption, war, disintegrating society, and declining personal standards, Confucius synthesized and added to traditional Chinese teachings in an effort to reestablish social and political order on a firm foundation. The cornerstone of his edifice was excellence of character, expressed especially in the basic relationships of society, family, political relationships, and friends. Mencius (371–289 B.C.E.) and Chu Hsi (1130–1200 C.E.) were the major Chinese philosophers who developed the Confucian golden rule. Practice of the golden rule sometimes involves an explicit imaginative role reversal, putting oneself in the other person's situation.

Elements of the Confucian understanding of the golden rule are the following:

1. In comparing self and other, the agent imagines him- or herself in the situation of the recipient. One assumes that others also get hungry and thirsty, desire to succeed, and so on.
2. Though our empathetic understanding of

another is not perfect, we do have an intuitive grasp of others.

3. The agent sees the recipient in terms of a relational pattern: father/son and so on.

4. Comparing is a matter of heart and mind. Separation of these two is un-Chinese. Comparing is a creative, artistic activity. Understanding another is as much an art as a science.

5. In order to elicit the appropriate feeling for a challenging situation, the agent may need to construct an analogy between the immediate situation and one that spontaneously elicits the appropriate feeling. In order to adequately identify with a stranger's situation, the agent may need to take a preliminary step, to bring to mind his or her sympathy for some person closer to the agent.

6. The agent identifies with concrete aspects of the recipient's situation. The agent may need to be able to empathize with the patriotism of the agent if another country is involved.

7. There is a scientific dimension to understanding others. Scientific component of understanding is prominent in Chinese tradition.

8. We can see the recipient in terms of the Way (tao) without explicit comparison. One can find the Way in oneself and in the other person. Mencius: "A noble man steeps himself in the Way (tao) because he wishes to find it in himself. When he finds it in himself, he will be at ease in it; when he is at ease in it, he can draw deeply upon it; when he can draw deeply upon it, he finds its source wherever he turns."[3]

For Chang Tsai (1020–1077 c.e.), "Heaven is my father and Earth is my mother. . . . All people are my brothers and sisters."[4]

JEWISH GOLDEN RULE

Rabbi Hillel (active 30 b.c.e.–10 c.e.) was key in the formulation of the golden rule. Upon being asked for a summary of the Torah, he replied: "What is hateful to you, do not do to your neighbor, this is the whole Torah, while the rest is commentary thereon. Go and learn it." The story of Nathan to King David, to illustrate what David had done to take to himself the wife of Uriah, illustrates the golden rule. David acknowledged that the judgment he had made on the rich man, who in Nathan's story had taken the most precious lamb of the poor man for himself, applied by implication to his own action.[5]

Rabbi Arthur Waskow in a recent book, *The Tent of Abraham,* builds on the story of Abraham and his two sons, Isaac and Ishmael. These two brothers were at enmity due to the story of Abraham, Sarah, and the mother of Ishmael, Hagar. At the funeral of Abraham, these two long-standing enemies came together. Waskow notes that the Palestinians and Israelis continue to look past each other as did Isaac and Ishmael until the death of their father. Waskow suggests that only by recognizing that the land over which they are fighting is the land of Abraham for both will they ever stop warring. They are not yet able to stand in the other's shoes, as required by the golden rule. "Both peoples sit unwilling to imagine that there might be a land of Abraham in which his two descendant peoples are entitled to be present, side by side, not dissolved into one but each with its own identity and self . . . each with its own self-determination, each complementary to the other."[6] Waskow is really talking about the golden rule and applying it to this most horrendous of conflicts. Imagination to look differently is what the Confucians understood.

CHRISTIANITY AND THE GOLDEN RULE

The expression of the golden rule in Christianity follows upon the insights of the Jewish religion; Jesus's expression of the golden rule is a strong statement. The flexibility of a rule that remains widely accessible and reasonable while conveying a high standard can be understood as engaging the hearer/reader in a movement through several levels of interpretation.

1. The Golden Rule of Prudence: do to others as you want others to do to you . . . with realistic attention to the consequences of your

choices for the long-term welfare of your recipient. This rule must be distinguished from a pseudo–golden rule of self-interest: do to others as you want others to do to you . . . with an eye to avoiding punishment and gaining rewards for yourself.

2. The Golden Rule of Neighborly Love: do to others as you want others to do to you . . . as an expression of consideration and fairness among neighbors, where the scope of the term *neighbor* extends to all without regard to ethnic or religious differences. Because the neighbor can be the enemy, however, fulfilling a "conventional ethic of fairness" can require extraordinary love, which involves the next level.

3. The Golden Rule of Fatherly Love: Do to others as you want others to do to you . . . imitating the divine paradigm.[7]

When the interior is uncovered, the golden rule takes on a deeper interiority: Look into your own heart. Discover what causes pain. Refuse to inflict this pain on anyone else. Are we as focused on the interior as our culture is on exploring the universe? Don't deny the truth of others. Dogmatism can be a kind of idolatry.[8]

Golden Rule in Hinduism

"Let no man do to another that which would be repugnant to himself."[9] "Knowing how painful it is to himself, a person should never do to others which he dislikes when done to him by others."[10] "A person should not himself do that act which, if done by another, would call down his censure."[11] "One should never do that to another which one regards as injurious to one's own self."[12] More advanced according to Erik Erikson is: "No one is a believer until he loves for his brother what he loves for himself," which is usually attributed to Islam.[13] In the Upanishads, Erikson finds the most unconditional commitment: "He who sees all beings in his own self and his own self in all beings."[14]

"The Hindu identification of the spiritual self of the agent with the spiritual self of the recipient

of the agent's action provides a basis for golden rule thinking."[15]

Is the Golden Rule Based Solely on Individual Actions with no Impact on International Relations?

The golden rule is first and foremost a principle in the philosophy of living, expressing a personal standard for the conduct of one-to-one relationships.

> If there is righteousness in the heart, there will be harmony in the home. If there is harmony in the home, the nation will be well governed. If the nation is well governed there will be peace in the world.[16]

Political reforms do not necessarily work for a regeneration of righteousness in the hearts of individuals, but "primary leverage occurs at the level of the individual and unless individuals cooperate ideas for reform won't happen."[17] If the limitation of a radical ethics of relationship lies in its inability to cope with systems, its strength is in honoring the way relationships transcend social systems.

Sensitive application of the rule takes into account those indirectly affected by one's actions. If the golden rule is to be a truly universal principle, then there must be threads of consistency linking moral judgments about personal problems with ethical judgments about social, economic, and political affairs.

What the rule does for systems is to prompt questions that imply norms for systems; for example, "Does a national government go beyond intelligent patriotism to assert sovereignty without regard for planetary responsibilities?"

I am primarily interested in the life of the rule, how the rule moves, how its various meanings weave into one another, and how working with it promotes growth. Presenting the golden rule as a principle with emotional, intellectual, and spiritual significance has become, in part, a way to recover a more adequate conception of what it means to be human and a way to move beyond theories of morality that undervalue any one of these dimensions. "So long as the development of religious consciousness functions to deepen, not discard, the concept of the universal family of God, the golden rule with its universal applicability will continue to symbolize the moral expression of religious consciousness."[18]

THE GOLDEN RULE EXEMPLIFIED IN THE PRACTICE OF THE NONVIOLENT PEACEFORCE

An idea that came together at the Hague Appeal for Peace in May 1999 was for the formulation of a nonviolent peace army, or *Shanti Sena,* in Gandhi's terms. After this meeting, research was conducted on the feasibility of third-party nonviolent intervention, and structural development was undertaken. In November and December 2002, representatives of forty-five member organizations from around the world, committed to nonviolence, came together in New Delhi, India, to launch the Nonviolent Peaceforce. These representatives chose the international governing council for the Peaceforce and selected, from among proposals from groups in three different conflict areas, the proposal from Sri Lanka.

Thereafter, recruitment of the field team and training took place in collaboration with partner organizations in Sri Lanka. Training involved practice of nonviolent strategies that have been developed through the centuries. These practices include the following:

1. Accompaniment
2. Monitoring
3. International presence
4. Interpositioning

Recruits learn about nonviolence from leaders in movements in every part of the world, including Gandhi, Martin Luther King, Thich Nhat Hanh, and others. Teachings of these and other nonviolent leaders reflect the golden rule. Martin Luther King explained how we can love our enemy, a key aspect of nonviolence: "We must not seek to defeat or humiliate the enemy but to win his

friendship and understanding. . . . Every word and deed must contribute to an understanding with the enemy and release those vast reservoirs of goodwill which have been blocked by impenetrable walls of hate. . . . Returning hate for hate multiplies hate, adding deeper darkness to a night already devoid of stars. Darkness cannot drive out darkness; only light can do that . . . Hate multiplies hate, violence multiplies violence, and toughness multiplies toughness in a descending spiral of destruction."[19]

King's words reflect the golden rule in that loving one's enemies requires that one stand in that person's shoes. King recognizes that there is "some good in the worst of us and some evil in the best of us."[20]

Gandhi wrote: "Passive resistance is an all-sided sword: it can be used anyhow; it blesses him who uses it and him against whom it is used. Without drawing a drop of blood it produces far-reaching results. It never rusts and cannot be stolen."[21] Further: "It is the acid test of non-violent conflict that in the end there is no rancour left behind, and in the end the enemies are converted into friends. That was my experience in South Africa with General Smuts. He started with being my bitterest opponent and critic. Today he is my warmest friend."[22]

Gandhi's statements reflect the basic premises of the golden rule. His grasp of nonviolence was based on deep inner awareness that all of us have the same humanity.

Thich Nhat Hahn, a Buddhist monk, writes of mindfulness as the way of nonviolent living: "Nonviolence can be born only from the insight of non-duality, of interbeing. This is the insight that everything is interconnected and nothing can exist by itself alone. Doing violence to others is doing violence to yourself. If you do not have the insight of non-duality, you will still be violent. You will still want to punish, to suppress, and to destroy, but once you have penetrated the reality of non-duality, you will smile at both the flower and garbage in you, you will embrace both. This insight is the ground for your non-violent action."[23] These articulations of nonviolence reflect the deeper meanings of the golden rule. These are understandings of nonviolence that form the basis of training for the Nonviolent Peaceforce field teams.

In 2005, reporter Chris Richards visited Sri Lanka, where Nonviolent Peaceforce field teams were working. His description of one incident:

> What would you do? There is a gang of young men surrounding your car—banging on your doors, your windows and your roof. You do not know how many there are, but when you saw them as you drove by before, there looked to be 20 or 30. Some were drunk. All looked angry—and they were angry with you. This is the time for self-preservation. There's nothing stopping you from driving off to leave it all behind. Except that you're a peace keeper; a peace builder. It's something you believe in to your core. So you wind down the window and talk with them. They say that you have undermined them—stopped a project close to their hearts. They think you are spying on them. They are not prepared to listen . . . except you think that if you stay and engage with them you can transform the situation and defuse their violence. . . . This is the assessment that Peters Nywanda and Atif Hameed make when they get out of their car to talk with the group.[24]

Five days later as Richards drives with Atif past the area, four of the young men who attacked the car earlier wave and smile. Richards concluded: "What is happening in this city could never have been achieved through violence."[25]

In 2006, Atif Hameed of Pakistan and Sreeram Cahulia of India, both veteran field team members in Sri Lanka, joined in an assignment to the Philippines to assess the violent situation in Mindanao. They, whose countries are at loggerheads, show the power of nonviolence, reaching the common humanity of each other and those in the area of conflict.

CONCLUSION

The golden rule has not died. In fact it has developed beyond its original conception and now has a deeper foundation through the work of nonviolent leaders and practitioners. In the Nonviolent Peaceforce, a global organization with now ninety-five member organizations from all over the globe, the wisdom of nonviolence in the world's religions comes to bear on concrete problems and specific conflicts. The golden rule is not just an abstraction. It is as real as the anger of the gang in Sri Lanka and the nonviolent action of the Nonviolent Peaceforce team based on the common humanity of all involved. It is as real as the nonviolent actors in the U.S. Civil Rights movement who faced angry crowds, water hoses, and death with the strength of nonviolence.

WORLD RELIGIONS AND WORLD PEACE

Toward a New Partnership

Brian D. Lepard

In this essay, I will explore how world religions can become a force for peace in the world rather than a cause of division and war. I will first review the history of religion-based violence and conflict. I will then examine the contribution that world religions can make, based on their peace-inducing teachings, to the mitigation and resolution of conflict. I will suggest that world religions and world peace need to form a new partnership, in which peacemaking efforts can benefit from certain unique perspectives on peace gleaned from the scriptures of the major world religions.

RELIGION AND CONFLICT IN THE WORLD TODAY

First of all, there is no need to recount the tragic and disgraceful history of wars and conflicts instigated, pursued, and escalated under the banner of religion and religious ideologies—a history that regrettably persists in the twenty-first century. We need look no further than the Middle East, not to mention many other regions of the world, to perceive the destructive effects of religious prejudices and hatreds. Moreover, even where entreaties by religious leaders and adherents to fight rival religions or secular ideologies do not result in outright

war, they create in too many regions today a tense and electrified atmosphere of what we might call pre-conflict, in which at any moment a misguided act of terrorism or an isolated attack on an individual could spark a new religion-inspired conflagration.

In centuries past, religion was such a volatile instigator of war that religious wars led to the first calls for the creation of a secular international law based on respect for sovereignty and the freedom of countries, if not individuals, to follow the religion of their choice. This was, for example, the outcome of the Thirty Years' War, which resulted in the Peace of Westphalia of 1648, regarded by many scholars as the inauguration of the modern-day state system and of contemporary international law. As a result of this pathetic history, many secular observers believe that peace, and respect for international law, can only be achieved by keeping the world religions at bay.

HOW CAN WORLD RELIGIONS BECOME A FORCE FOR WORLD PEACE?

In this chapter I suggest by contrast that the world religions can and must become wholehearted supporters of world peace and in fact that a durable and profound world peace cannot be achieved without respect for and adherence to fundamental moral teachings shared by all religions. Religion-inspired conflict is based on religious prejudice and fanaticism, which defy the essential teachings of the world religions themselves, as articulated in their most revered scriptures. If we look at these teachings, we see many commonalities that offer moral hope in a divided and traumatized world. I review some of these commonalities in my recent book, *Hope for a Global Ethic: Shared Principles in Religious Scriptures.*[1] In particular, we find in the world's great scriptures a unique and multilayered conception of peace that can make a positive contribution to resolving all conflicts peacefully, whether or not they are religious in origin.

COMMON MORAL PRINCIPLES IN WORLD SCRIPTURES RELATING TO PEACE

What are some of these common principles that can serve as the foundation for a new conception of peace?

The Spiritual Nature of Human Beings

A first is the common religious teaching that all human beings have a spiritual nature and have the capacity to acquire spiritual qualities. For example, according to the Hebrew scriptures, we are all created in the image of God. Buddhist scriptures counsel us, "Even as a mother watches over and protects her child, her only child, so with a boundless mind should one cherish all living beings, radiating friendliness over the entire world, above, below, and all around without limit."[2] Jesus teaches us, "Be perfect, therefore, even as your heavenly Father is perfect."[3] According to the Qur'an, the reason God has created us is so that we can cultivate good relations with one another, especially those different from us: "O mankind, We have created you male and female, and appointed you races and tribes, that you may know one another. Surely the noblest among you in the sight of God is the most godfearing of you."[4] And Bahá'u'lláh counsels humanity, "O friends! Be not careless of the

virtues with which ye have been endowed, neither be neglectful of your high destiny."[5]

By virtue of this spiritual nature not only do we have an obligation to respect others as spiritual beings but we ourselves have the capacity to rise above animalistic urges, including the desire for blood or revenge, and treat others with compassion, kindness, and justice. Unlike materialistic theories that view humans as just another form of animal, inebriated with the desire for power and with lust and greed—a view that sees war as inevitable and unavoidable—this spiritual conception of humanity's purpose sees war as a product of humanity's failure to rise to the spiritual heights of which it is fully capable, which, indeed, is the divine will for humanity.

This teaching thus makes it a moral imperative that we pursue peace and the eradication of unjust wars. It can give us the resolve to keep trying because of a recognition of humanity's divine potentialities and a shared belief that we are not mere animals, consigned to a life of competition and combat either for limited resources or for power, glory, or other materialistic values.

The Unity of the Human Family

A second unique spiritual teaching of the world's religions is that all human beings are, first and foremost, members of one human family, a family that morally ought to strive day and night to become ever more united, both materially and spiritually. Thus, for example, the Bhagavadgītā, of Hinduism, asserts that the "whole world" is "united" and affirms that if we achieve true enlightenment we will be one with all beings.[6] The Hebrew scriptures ask, "Have we not all one Father? Did not one God create us?"[7] Buddhist scriptures affirm that we should love all other beings in the entire world, free from ill will or hatred.[8] The Analects of Confucius teaches that we are all brothers and sisters.[9] Through the story of the Good Samaritan, Jesus asserts that we are all spiritual neighbors who should love one another. The Qur'an announces that all humanity was created of a "single soul."[10] The Bahá'í writings declare, too, that "all peoples and nations are of one family, the children of one Father, and should be to one another as brothers and sisters!"[11]

In short, according to the scriptures, we are neither mere individualistic automatons intended to pursue our self-interests nor simple appendages of our communities, whether religious, local, or national. Rather, we are fundamentally members of a single world-embracing family. At the same time, the scriptures elevate to a moral value the diversity of thoughts, opinions, beliefs, and aspirations that characterize the human family. They see this diversity as an evidence of the divine good pleasure and a value we ought to cherish rather than lament or oppose in the interest of creating an artificial homogeneity of thought and belief. For example, the Qur'an declares that the variety of our "tongues and hues" is a sign of God.[12]

This teaching of the unity of the human family has a number of implications for peacemaking. For example, it counsels us to make peace with others because they are fellow family members. No one is an enemy. Furthermore, the goal is not mere toleration of others we view as fundamentally different from ourselves; it is to achieve a profound level of mutual understanding. Belief in the unity of the human family, coupled with recognition of humanity's spiritual character, implies, too, that we ought to be simultaneously optimistic and pragmatic about peace-building efforts. We ought to reject the pessimism that can infect purely secular approaches. The teaching of the unity of the human family furthermore can fortify our resolve to keep trying to settle seemingly intractable conflicts rather than to give up.

Peace as a Moral Imperative

Third, all the world's revered scriptures uphold peace as a moral imperative. It is not some vague social good, to be aimed at where possible. Rather, the promotion of peace, at both the interpersonal and international levels, is the raison d'être of our social lives on this earthly plane of existence. For example, the Bhagavadgītā instructs us to practice nonviolence and harmlessness (*ahimsa*). The

Hebrew scriptures teach us to "seek amity and pursue it."[13] Buddhist scriptures counsel us to purify ourselves from anger and to promote peace. Confucian writings condemn cruelty, arrogance, and vengeance while praising social peace. In the New Testament, Jesus announces, "Blessed are the peacemakers, for they will be called children of God."[14] Thus, we are all called upon to be engaged as peacemakers. The Qur'an declares that it is "a Book Manifest whereby God guides whosoever follows His good pleasure in the ways of peace."[15] And the Bahá'í writings teach, "When a thought of war comes, oppose it by a stronger thought of peace. A thought of hatred must be destroyed by a more powerful thought of love."[16]

A DYNAMIC CONCEPTION OF PEACE

Fourth, however, the religious scriptures articulate a dynamic conception of peace rather than a static notion of peace as the mere absence of overt conflict. This includes seeing peace as intimately intertwined with justice, with the elimination of extremes of wealth and poverty, and with the practice of open-minded consultation. This dynamic vision of peace is sorely needed today, because we are often tempted to see war and peace in black-and-white terms—like a light switch that simply is turned on or off. We are tempted to define peace simply as the absence of war and to be willing to trade off virtually any other values to achieve it.

I will elaborate on each of these points in more detail.

Peace and Justice

With respect to justice, all the scriptures affirm that peace and justice go hand in hand and that true peace must encompass a just ordering of society, including the punishment of wrongdoers. For example, the Bhagavadgītā extols both "harmlessness" and "uprightness." The Hebrew scriptures affirm that the "work of righteousness shall be peace, And the effect of righteousness, calm and confidence forever."[17] Buddhist scriptures recognize that sometimes the use of force may be necessary to achieve justice and prevent unjust wars. Confucian writings also endorse "uprightness" along with peace and indicate that we should respond to wrongdoing with justice rather than kindness.[18] The New Testament also repeatedly emphasizes the imperative of justice alongside peace, as does the Qur'an. And the Bahá'í writings assert that peace must be "based on righteousness and justice."[19]

Regrettably, today, as in times past, such as the events leading up to World War II, we witness attempts to appease gross human rights violators in the name of achieving peace. But the scriptures indicate that long-lasting peace includes justice and respect for human rights, which are an integral element of peace—that, indeed, peace without justice and human rights is an illusionary peace, morally as well as practically.

Peace and the Elimination of Poverty

Further, recent events make clear that attempts to impose or create peace without economic justice in particular are doomed to end in disaster. A failure to address the injustice of millions living in abject poverty while others benefit from enormous riches inevitably leads to chronic frustration and anger that can easily bubble to the surface and result in war or terrorism.

Religious scriptures categorically reject the materialism that is insinuating itself into global culture, led by the West, which is only destined to create more dissatisfaction. They call upon us not only to pursue spiritual values rather than material goods in our own lives but to take effective action to help the less fortunate. For example, Hindu scriptures extol the virtues of generosity and detachment from material things. The Hebrew scriptures, the Buddhist scriptures, and Confucian writings all require that we give to the needy as a strong moral obligation. In the New Testament, Jesus advises us to "give to everyone who begs from you, and do not refuse anyone who wants to borrow from you."[20] The Qur'an teaches us to provide sustenance to the "needy, the orphan, the captive" because of love for God and not expectation of appreciation or any personal benefit."[21] And

Bahá'u'lláh advises us to "be a treasure to the poor, an admonisher to the rich, an answerer to the cry of the needy."[22]

Of course, this compelling principle in the scriptures calling upon us to assist the needy does not imply that the mere existence of poverty excuses conflict or terrorism. But there is no doubt that it creates justified grievances that must be remedied in order for a lasting peace to be built. The right to economic justice and development is another facet, then, of peace with justice.

Peace and Open-Minded Consultation

According to the world's religious scriptures, open-minded consultation is also an essential element of peace. Open-minded consultation is a process by which we solve problems through freely expressing our own views with an attitude of courtesy and respect while inviting and seeking to learn from the views of others, ultimately with the goal of reaching a unified consensus. All the scriptures endorse open-minded consultation instead of conflict. For example, the Hebrew scriptures teach that magistrates should "not be partial in judgment," but instead "hear out low and high alike."[23] Buddhist scriptures recount the parable of the blind men and the elephant, teaching that we can only apprehend truth in all its fullness through open-minded consultation as opposed to engaging in useless argumentation.

Confucian writings indicate that everyone else can be a teacher for us and that we must seek out the opinions of others with a humble attitude. The New Testament likewise praises consultation and a process of mutual learning and encouragement.[24] The Qur'an also exhorts us to practice open-minded consultation, affirming, "Take counsel with them in the affair; and when thou art resolved, put thy trust in God."[25] The Bahá'í writings affirm, "Take ye counsel together in all matters, inasmuch as consultation is the lamp of guidance which leadeth the way, and is the bestower of understanding."[26]

Again, too often today we strive for the illusion of a peace based on a fragile truce, a peace that is false because the parties involved are not able or willing to talk with one another. This kind of peace through mutual bare toleration inevitably breeds renewed tensions, and ultimately new conflicts. If individuals, nations, or peoples experiencing tension with one another can begin to engage in open-minded dialogue, inspired by recognition of their common humanity, they can better avoid conflict. And in the aftermath of conflict, they can pursue through consultation a long-lasting peace. Moreover, we have learned that consultation must involve all elements of society, including historically marginalized groups and individuals such as women. A peace among leaders alone that does not nurture the full participation of ordinary citizens is likely to be transient and ephemeral.

THE LIMITED USE OF FORCE

Finally, as intimated by the title of this section, the world's great scriptures also teach us that sometimes the use of force may be justified, and even necessary, to promote justice and peace. This view of the use of force is consistent with the scriptures' recognition that peace and justice are two sides of the same coin; true peace cannot exist without justice, and justice may require the use of some kind of force. In this connection, the concept of just war appears in all the scriptures.

Obviously, when abused, just-war theory has served as ideological fuel for the kinds of atrocious interreligious conflicts I described at the outset of this chapter. But the scriptures themselves indicate the primacy of peaceful methods of dispute resolution and impose strict limitations on the use of force, limitations that render it more in the nature of a police operation than what we traditionally have called war. Indeed, these limitations correspond closely with emerging standards of just war under international law, including those that appear in the Charter of the United Nations. It is critical to emphasize, too, that the scriptures, as a general rule, emphatically declare that religious prejudice is morally inexcusable and can never justify war between members of different religions.

Let me give here just a few examples of these scriptural warrants for the limited, and pure-minded, use of force to achieve peace, justice, and the protection of others. The Hebrew scriptures authorize certain limited wars, but also provide some of the world's first protections for innocent combatants, and indicate that war must be used as a last resort. Buddhist scriptures likewise authorize wars to promote justice after all peaceful attempts at resolution have failed. According to Buddhist scriptures, the Buddha affirmed, "All warfare in which man tries to slay his brother is lamentable, but [the Buddha] does not teach that those who go to war in a righteous cause after having exhausted all means to preserve the peace are blameworthy. He must be blamed who is the cause of war."[27]

Confucian texts authorize wars to liberate people oppressed by tyrants, and arguably only such wars. As we are aware, Christian doctrine has evolved a concept of just war grounded in biblical teachings involving love and justice. The Qur'an prohibits aggressive war but allows wars in self-defense and wars to protect the innocent from oppression. Finally, the Bahá'í writings, while outlawing "holy war" based on religion, imply that in some cases war may be necessary as a last resort to inhibit an aggressor or protect human rights victims, and that the world needs to establish a system of collective security for these purposes.[28]

As noted earlier, in our praiseworthy quest for peace today we often are tempted to insist on peace at any price and regard the use of force as inherently morally reprehensible or forbidden. The scriptures can serve as a correction to these myopic well-intentioned views. The scriptures teach us that, regrettably, in a world in which tyrants and human rights violations are ubiquitous, the use of force may be the only way to forestall conflict, stop it once it has occurred, or rescue imperiled human rights victims. This is an important teaching of the scriptures. But the scriptures also emphasize that the use of force, which importantly can take forms far short of what we think of as war, must be carefully regulated and calibrated.

Some scriptures imply that ideally, where possible, legitimate uses of force should be supervised by global institutions that operate under a principle of open-minded consultation. These checks and balances help ensure that the use of force is morally justified and appropriately limited. These shared ethical principles in the scriptures point to the imperative of adhering to, but also where necessary reforming, similar rules and limitations that have found their way into contemporary international law. These include rules in the U.N. Charter, which allows military action only in self-defense or where it has been authorized by the U.N. Security Council.[29]

CONCLUSION

To conclude, despite the sordid record of religious instigation of war, any successful effort to achieve durable peace in the world must take into account and draw inspiration from the shared teachings concerning peace and the just use of force in the scriptures of the world religions. We thus need a new partnership between world religions and world peace. If members of religious communities around the globe can work together to perceive and act on these common principles, the world may yet avoid the resurgence of hatred and violence that seems to be on the immediate horizon.

RELIGION AND HUMAN RIGHTS

The Worth of Persons

INTRODUCTION

Readers might be intrigued in this section by the fact that the various religions offer their own particular reasons, in which they might well differ, for upholding the worth of the human being in general. This phenomenon has sometimes been referred to as that of overlapping consensus and helps explain how different religions, despite their differences, may find it possible to support similar positions on human rights.

A practical observation supports this theoretical position. When the basis for human rights is discussed by the representatives of various religions, it can lead to long arguments; but when the same group of representatives is presented with actual instances and asked to decide whether they do or do not constitute violations of human rights, then agreement is rapidly forthcoming.

Some readers may feel particularly drawn in this section to the panel discussion on world's religions, human rights, and same-sex marriage in view of its contemporary relevance. This selection captures the contours of the debate as it unfolded in Canada and is quite relevant to the unfolding debate on the same topic in the United States.

Religion and an Implicit Fundamental Human Right

James Kellenberger

It is a platitude that horrendous things have been done in the name of religion. Individuals belonging to one religion are forced to convert to another. Torture is done in the name of religion. Nations go to war with each side calling upon God's help in defeating the other. Examples could be multiplied, but the point is not in contention. The terrible events of September 11, 2001, did not create the perception, held by many, that religion is a home for aggression and violence, although those events may have awakened it in some and strengthened it in many more.

On the other side, religion can also be a force for good. The presence of the different major religions in the world, their social influence, and their presence in individual lives have often been a force for good. This observation, too, is platitudinous. In addition to personal spiritual development, religions provide support for stable families, they support relief organizations, and so on. In what follows I intend to focus on a particular way that the religions of the world can be a force for good. They can be a force for good by affirming human rights and vivifying our sense of general human rights. My exact thesis is that a fundamental human right is implicit in the world religions.

It has been observed that talk of rights emerged only comparatively recently in human history, much more recently than the advent of religions such as Hinduism or Buddhism, or even Judaism, Christianity, or Islam.[1] This may not be quite right. In the Revised Standard Version, Deut 21:17, the "right of the first-born" to a double portion is spoken of. In the Tanakh, the point is phrased as "the birthright is his due." One might say here that what is spoken of is not a general right, a right that a human being has as a human, or a natural right. Consider, however, the reflections of St. Thomas Aquinas on what would come to be called the Dominion Theory. This is the idea, considered by some to be biblical, that God has given human beings dominion over all the other creatures of the earth. Aquinas says in the *Summa* that "it matters not how man behaves to animals because God has subjected all things to man's power."[2] Aquinas does not use an expression that can be translated as "a right," but he is using the concept of a right, and here it is a general or human right that human beings have by virtue of being human beings. I cite Aquinas here not to affirm the right of human beings to treat animals as they please but to show that the idea of a general human right was deployed by Aquinas in the thirteenth century, and that, if Aquinas is right, such a right is affirmed in the Bible. Similarly, Khaled Abou El Fadl argues that the idea of rights and the idea of duties are both well established in the premodern Islamic juristic tradition: he cites a jurist who, in the century before Aquinas, discussed the "rights of human beings" and maintained they could not be "dismissed" except by the person concerned.[3]

However, while these reflections might soften whatever resistance we feel to the idea that human rights are to be found in early religious traditions, my argument does not depend on references to rights in passages of scripture or on there being a religious or theological affirmation of rights in any of the religious traditions. The argument that I am going to develop allows (1) that we will search long for an explicit scriptural affirmation of general human rights in the world religions; (2) that many or all the religions do not do much to uphold such rights as those relating to the status of women and religious freedom; (3) that an affirmation of human rights, as in the Declaration of Human Rights by the World's Religions, if it is going to have any authority, must be endorsed by as many people as possible; and (4) that even if the world's religions came to agree that there are human rights, there still would be disagreement on just how they should be understood.[4]

What I want to show is that a fundamental human right is implicit in the world religions. In order to see that this is so, we should start with a consideration of an ethical principle that is found in the various religious traditions. In a Christian expression, it is, "As you wish that men would do to you, do so to them" (Luke 6:31). In a general expression that John Hick gives, it is "that it is good to benefit others and evil to harm them." Hick finds an expression of this principle in the various religious traditions of the world. In the Hindu tradition, in the *Mahābhārata,* we find this: "One should never do that to another which one regards as injurious to one's own self. This, in brief, is the Rule of Righteousness." In the Buddhist tradition, we find it in the teaching of Gautama Buddha in the *Sutta Nipata:* "As a mother cares for her son, all her days, so towards all living beings a man's mind should be all-embracing." In the Analects of Confucianism, we have this statement: "Do not do to others what you would not like yourself." In the *hadith* of Islam, we find these words of Muhammad: "No man is a true believer unless he desires for his brother what he desires for himself." In Judaism, in the *Babylonian Talmud,* we find this: "What is hateful to yourself do not do to your fellow man." Hick finds similar expressions in Jainism and Zoroastrianism.[5] For Hick, these are various expressions of the golden rule, which he finds is universal among the religions of the world, in a positive or negative statement. While we might debate the extent to which the different religious traditions agree on how we should treat our fellow human beings as ourselves, and on whether every follower in each of the various religions understands "brother" and "fellow human being" to be inclusive of those beyond one's own religion, still I think we can allow that Hick is right that the golden rule in some expression is to be found in all the religious traditions.

Second, we should acknowledge that embodied in this ethical principle is the perception or the avowal that we human beings are in a relationship to one another. We see this most clearly in several of the formulations. In the Buddhist expression, we are told that our minds should embrace others, all living beings, as a mother cares for her son. We should see our relationship to others as like a mother-child relationship, in which we should care for others as a mother cares for her child. In the expression from the *hadith,* we should desire for our brothers what we desire for ourselves. The idea that the others are our brothers affirms a relationship between each of us and the others in which concern is appropriate. Another example that Hick goes on to cite is the second commandment of Christianity: "You shall love your neighbor as yourself" (Matt 22:39). Here too, a relationship between one and each is being affirmed, that of neighbor to neighbor.

The third step is to recognize that relationships can be respected and lived up to, or they can be violated. In this way, relationships have a moral aspect. Take the relationship in the Buddhist expression, the relationship of a mother to her child. When a mother nurtures, cares for, and instructs her child, she fulfills her relationship to her child. When she fails to do these things, she does not act as a mother should; she thereby morally fails her child, and she does so because she violates her relationship to her child. Underlying these various expressions of the ethical principle of the golden rule is the postulation of a morally demanding relationship that each has to each, as morally demanding as the relationship of a mother to her child, or of a brother to a brother.

The next step is to acknowledge that, if we violate this posited relationship, each has to each, we do not give what we owe to others, what is appropriate to and due to them as the persons they are, what they have a right to as persons to whom we are related in this posited relationship. And this right, as one that flows from nothing more than their humanity as persons, is a genuine human right. The analogy between the relationship of each to each that underlies the golden rule in its various expressions and the relationship between a mother and her child, or between a brother and a brother, remains close. But it is only an analogy. When a mother withholds from her child the nurturing and care required by her relationship to her child, she withholds what her child has a right to. She violates the right her child has to a mother's care and support. This right, however, is not a human right. It does not flow from the child's basic humanity. It flows from the relationship the child has to his or her mother. If the mother does not give to children not her own the care and support she gives to her own child, she does not violate her mother-child relationship to them or violate their right to her parental attention, for they have no such right. The relationship posited by the golden rule, by contrast, is a relationship between each and each, and when we violate it, we violate a right that others have that does flow from their simply being human beings, for it is their being human beings that makes them our brothers or neighbors. The Buddha says, "*As* a mother cares for her son, all her days, *so* towards all living beings a man's

mind should be all-embracing." Affirmed here, on my reading, is an analogy, a close analogy, but not an identity.

In violating the relationship of each to each that is posited by the golden rule, we do not treat others as they deserve to be treated as brothers or neighbors. We violate the worth they have as brothers or neighbors by virtue of which they are in this relationship. This construction, then, requires that human beings have a kind of inherent worth, which makes them worthy of compassion or of being treated as neighbors, and which makes compassion or being treated as neighbors their due or their right. Different religions may bring forward different glosses on the inherent worth of human persons: for Christianity, we are in the image of God; for Buddhism, we are potential Buddhas. These different glosses, however, do not deny that the inherent worth of our neighbors or brothers that informs and creates this relationship attaches to their humanity. It is not something that they have come to merit through virtuous action, for if it were, then only some would qualify as our brothers or neighbors. The Buddhist formulation is instructive on this point. A mother cares for her child because her child is her child, not because her child has earned her love and care by being good. A mother cares for her child, and ought to, irrespective of the child's moral character. Analogously, the Buddhist formulation tells us we should be compassionate toward all living beings, irrespective of their earned merit. The idea here is opposed to the notion that human beings are not themselves worthy of compassion or love, but we should nevertheless endeavor to emulate God's love for God's wretched and unworthy creatures, and to the notion that we should endeavor to show compassion or love precisely and only because we are commanded to do so or only because it helps us on the path to Buddhahood.

On this reasoning, then, the religions of the world, in affirming the ethical principle of the golden rule, couched in the language of universal brotherhood or the language of all being neighbors or some cognate language, implicitly affirms the basic human right of each person to be treated as a human person with inherent worth, as a brother or a neighbor. What, though, does this fundamental right entail? Does it carry in its train the other human rights, such as the right to life and liberty, the right to freedom of movement, the right to freedom of expression, the right to work, and the right to education, all of which are named in the United Nations Universal Declaration of Human Rights and in A Universal Declaration of Human Rights by the World's Religions? Perhaps so. The test is whether we deny the right of persons to be treated as fellow human beings with inherent worth, as brothers or neighbors, when we deny them freedom of expression or work or education, and so on. Abstractly, the test is easy to state. Seeing whether a proposed specific right concretely passes the test may be a more difficult matter. Do only immunities, such as the right not to be tortured, pass the test, or do entitlements, such as the right to work, also pass the test? And in which cultural understanding will, say, the right to work pass the test? Allowing that the right to work passes the test, what kind of work do human beings have a right to? What labor-place conditions do human beings have a right to work in? For what level of compensation? Do I have the right to expect others to provide me with work or only the right not to be prevented from working? Do I have the right to move to any country I please? James Fredericks, in the context of reflection on Buddhist understanding of human rights, asks, "Do Han Chinese people have a right to residence in Tibet?" Tibetan Buddhists, he observes, deny any such right.[6] If this test is passed, however, the answer to another question is clear, I think. That question is, Who has the obligation to see that the rights just considered are met? The answer is, we all do.

Just here there may arise the question, What is the relationship between rights and obligations? For some, if there is an obligation, there is a right, and if there is a right there is an obligation. So if I have an obligation to help you, then you have a right to my help; and if you have a right to my help, then I have an obligation to help you. Damien Keown is among those who accept this symmetry.[7] Others, however, deny this symmetry. Perhaps all rights

entail obligations, but not all obligations entail rights, they hold. John Stuart Mill thought this. He held that when we have an "imperfect obligation," that is, an obligation such that, although "the act is obligatory, the particular occasions of performing it are left to our choice," as he thought was the case with "charity or beneficence," then there is no right that correlates with the obligation.[8] Joel Feinberg and Craig Ihara agree with Mill. In fact, they both cite the example of charity.[9] As they see it, we have an obligation to practice charity, but no particular person has a right to our charity. The same would hold for whatever obligation we have to provide education or work for others. I suggest, however, that Mill and company may have too narrow a view of rights. Many human rights are understood to be "in rem rights," such as the right to an education and the right to work. An in rem right is one that all who are able are called upon to fulfill.[10] The right to charity, like the right to an education and the right to work, may also be such an in rem right. If our neighbor or our brother, or our fellow being, has an in rem right to education or to work, or to various other things we can help to provide, then we all ought to help provide it. The reasoning I have presented, citing the golden rule and its posited relationship of each to each, in effect establishes the in rem right of each person to be treated as a neighbor or brother and allows that at least many of the human rights in its train are in rem rights.

However, this is not to say how each of us is equally required to meet that obligation, for, as far as this point carries, what individuals are called upon to do to meet their obligation may vary from person to person. Furthermore, our universal obligation to help meet the rights of others could, in many cases, conflict with obligations that are more pressing morally, and such obligations would then be superior. Thus, for those in severe straits, the obligation to care for one's own family may override their obligation to help provide education for those in need of education worldwide. This of course does not mean that they or others with conflicting obligations have no obligation to meet the rights of persons worldwide to be provided with an education, and so too for other human rights.

An overridden obligation does not cease to be an obligation.

Allow me to enter three caveats at this point. (1) While Christianity speaks of our neighbors, whom we should love as ourselves, and Islam speaks of our brothers, for whom we should desire what we desire for ourselves, Buddhism speaks of our minds being all-embracing toward all beings, all sentient beings, not just human beings. (2) Allowing that there is this test for human rights, we do not ipso facto rule it out that there could be other tests and sufficient grounds for human rights, such as an essential contribution to welfare or the demands of cooperative living, or even the demands of a social contract, although aspects of social-contract thinking may be in tension with religious sensibilities. (3) In arguing that this fundamental human right is implicit in religious traditions, I am not arguing that the individualistic culture of human rights is implicit in religious traditions. I am not arguing that within each religion are the seeds of a culture in which individuals are encouraged to assert their individual rights against others in an adversarial fashion.

Some have expressed the concern that positing or recognizing rights will give rise to such an adversarial mentality. As they see it, rights do not fit with the requirements of a religious morality. Craig Ihara has argued that rights cannot be introduced into "classical Buddhism," with its focus on Dharma and duty, without radically transforming it.[11] It must be allowed that "rights" thinking opens the potential for individuals to assert their rights against others in an adversarial manner. But the same potential is there for a moral system of duties. One who recognizes the general moral duty to help other persons can emphasize the duty that others have to help him as against the duty that he has to help others. This adverse potential exists whether the duty is "the duty to help others" or "the duty *to others* to help them." As Ihara sees it, it is a duty *to other persons* that will correlate with rights (so that, if the duty is not fulfilled, an injury is done to those persons, which a violation of a right requires).[12] By contrast, the duties that exist in classical Buddhism, he argues, can be understood as the first

sort, duties that are not to other persons. If I am right, however, it does not matter which kind of duty informs Buddhist morality. Both kinds present the same adverse potential that Ihara and others find accompanying rights.

Ihara is not alone in observing that an adversarial mentality runs counter to Buddhist ethics.[13] The same could be said for Christian ethics, and the ethics of every major religion that keeps central the ethics of the golden rule. But we should be clear that recognizing the fundamental right of persons to be treated as brothers or neighbors, and whatever further human rights are in its train, does *not* require us to assert our right to what is our due against our neighbors' rights. In fact, it forbids it to the extent that doing so is not treating others as brothers or neighbors.

Beyond what we have seen so far, there is a dimension of the fundamental right of persons to be treated as brothers or neighbors that owes much to the religious understanding that surrounds it. This right extends to our interior action. Our minds should embrace others as a mother cares for her child. We should desire for our brothers what we desire for ourselves. We should love our neighbors as ourselves. A part of what we owe to our brothers or neighbors is caring, right desire, love. Most often human rights are understood in terms of exterior action, as requiring us to do something or to refrain from doing something in the realm of overt action. The fundamental human right that the thesis of this paper argues is implicit in religion is the right of persons to be treated as brothers or neighbors, including their right to our care or compassion or love.

When Jesus is asked, "Who is my neighbor?" he replies with the story of the Good Samaritan. The story not only answers the question posed to Jesus but also brings to light what one must do to be a neighbor. The Samaritan helps the man who has fallen among robbers by binding up his wounds, taking him to an inn, and paying others to take care of him in his absence. But, moreover, Jesus says that when the Samaritan saw the man stripped and half-dead by the roadside, he had compassion. And in the story, the Samaritan is the passerby who showed mercy for the man in need. Compassion and mercy are the interior side of the Samaritan's action. Abou El Fadl says in his article on the human-rights commitment in modern Islam that, if he is right, "Dignity and justice need compassion and mercy."[14]

For some, this implication for interior action may seem to be grounds for saying that there is no such human right implicit in religion, for, they would say, morality and moral rights do not extend to our affective attitudes toward others. Their argument might go this way: "We may be required to help others, and they may even have a right to our help; but we do not have to like them, let alone love them. Perhaps religion can require this of us, but morality cannot, and hence, since human rights are in the moral domain, there is no such human right."[15] This argument is very far from conclusive, however. For one thing, it is less than clear that morality never makes demands on our interior actions. Wrong motives can affect the morality of our actions, a point Kant understood very well. We at times recognize insensitivity to the feelings of others as a moral fault. A husband's or wife's lack of affection can be a moral failure. Anger is counted a vice. Second, allowing that there is a widespread tendency to regard the demands of morality as limited to our overt actions, this is not to say that this is the most profound understanding of morality. It may be that religion can help to expand such a moral understanding and in this way be a further force for good in our world.

Religion and Human Rights

Shirin Ebadi

At the outset, I'd like to seize the opportunity to express my deepest sorrow over the recent events in Lebanon and to express my condolence to the relatives of the victims from both sides of the war. In every war, the real losers are the people. There are only arms dealers and salesmen that reap the benefits of wars. These arms dealers have reaped billions of dollars in benefits as a result of this recent war that destroyed the beautiful country in Lebanon and led to huge civilian loss from both sides of the war.

Dear colleagues, an understanding of different cultures is the path, the way for peace, and I'd like to seize this opportunity to thank all those who facilitated holding the meeting in this beautiful city and everyone at McGill University.

When we look at the world map and different countries, we realize that many countries across the Muslim world are accused of severe violations of human rights. This begs a fundamental question: Is Islam truly incompatible with human rights? The question therefore is: Are Islamic countries capable of being democratic or not? Some Muslims hold to the belief that Islam is fundamentally incompatible with democracy, for democracy connotes a majority rule by the will of the majority. That majority, too, can at times be wrong. The

followers of this belief do not have the tolerance to hold themselves open to other systems of thoughts and beliefs and choose to regard the realities of the world and the rise of their predecessors. This group of people does not believe that the elected authorities by the people, including members of Parliament, have a lot of rights in creating laws. They believe that the maximum responsibility of the Parliament lies in identifying divine laws and legislating in accordance, and nothing more. In other words, they believe that the Parliament does not have the right to make laws separate from divine laws. The unfavorable situation of democratization and democracy in some Islamic countries is the result of such thinking. And of course, to this group, Islam is only the interpretation of the religion that government offers and any other interpretation offered by other individuals or groups is considered as invalid. With this thinking, anyone who opposes government thinking is accused of heresy and blasphemy and (is considered) bad. This is how they force political dissidents into silence and strip away the courage of the ordinary people. After all, it is known that people are happier to oppose secular systems and earthly ones rather than religious systems that are given to them by their ancestors.

Against this group is a new group of progressive Muslim thinkers and intellectuals who form a united front, which is borderless and belongs to all Islamic countries. The establishment of a united front of Muslim progressive thinkers, regardless of nationality but sharing in the belief of upholding human dignity for all Muslims, heralds a new era for Islam. This united front does not have a name, does not have a leader, nor a central office nor branches. Rather, it resides in the hearts and minds of every individual who seeks to uphold the sanctity of their ancient religion but at the same time uphold true religious values and democratic ones and not accept any wrongful interpretation of religion. In fact, Islam is a religion of equality. The Prophet Muhammad always said that there really is no difference between a black person and a white person or an Arab and a non-Arab. After taking over Mecca, the Prophet Muhammad set up to establish an Islamic government he himself led, as well as the affairs of the society. And he called for *bay'ah* from all the people, including Muslims and non-Muslims, and *bay'ah* in modern terms means to give a vote. History shows that there were individuals who chose not to give the *bay'ah* but nevertheless enjoyed the right to live freely in those lands.

The Prophet Muhammad respected women tremendously and even sought their *bay'ah* at the beginning of the establishment of an Islamic government. In other words, he granted women the right to vote. This all at a time when women had no rights, including the right to live, and at a time when all individuals had no political rights whatsoever. So it's strange and interesting that, in the twenty-first century, some Muslim countries belittle women and strip them of their rights. Fourteen centuries ago, Prophet Muhammad sought the vote of everyone, so how could we possibly claim today that Islam is incompatible with democracy? Do we want to set ourselves back even further from fourteen centuries ago? Do Islamic governments want to claim that they understand Islam even better than the Prophet Muhammad? In fact, the problem does not lie with Islam as a religion. Rather, for different reasons, some Islamic countries are unwilling to offer an interpretation of Islam that shows that Islam and democracy are in fact compatible. These undemocratic governments are in fact hiding behind Islam as a shield and taking advantage of Islam as a means of justifying their own goals. For this reason, the culture besetting Islamic countries, including their political culture, requires an evolution, so that, with open eyes, they can identify the needs of their society, and, while resorting to the spirit of Islam, bring back laws that show that Islam is compatible with democratic goals and ideals. The best and most important step that can occur in this cultural evolution is to teach Islam, in its correct sense, to people. Dynamic Islam must be taught to people, and people must learn that it is possible to be Muslim and live better at the same time. Muslims should become aware that the key to heaven does not lie in the hands of Islamic governments, that any act by an Islamic government, even in the name of Islam, is not necessarily Islamic. This is only how genuine Islamic movements can rise and replace terrorism.

It is interesting that, in addition to reactionary fundamentalist forces and undemocratic Islamic states, there's another group that resists progressive interpretations of Islam. These are people who seek to identify the wrongful acts of certain individuals and groups as Islam itself and to show that Islam is equivalent to terrorism. By doing that, they can better endorse the theory of the clash of civilizations and justify the wars in the Middle East. In fact, dynamic Islam and Islam that accepts democracy, and Islam that respects cultural pluralism, and Islam that believes in human rights and democracy, is under attack from two fronts—on one front by fundamentalist reactionary religious groups that try to say that, whatever they do, their acts are Islamic, and on a second front by individuals who are in fact enemies of Islam and seek to show a darker image of Islam in order to justify their wars. And this is the commonality between the enemies of Islam, both its ignorant enemies as well as those who are not ignorant. It is therefore incumbent upon every progressive Islamic thinker, at this critical historical juncture, to reveal the true image of Islam, a religion filled with love and forgiveness, and a religion that is against violence and terrorism. Muslims have for centuries lived and worked peacefully and closely with followers of other faiths and religions—Buddhists, Confucianists, Christians, and Jews. Truly, it is possible to live peacefully together, regardless of any creed or belief that we belong to, by respecting those beliefs. Followers of different cultures, while retaining their specific characteristics, can seek their commonalities and accordingly make laws that will be uniform for everyone and will help improve everyone's life simultaneously. Democracy and human rights are the common requirement of all human societies. Every culture and religion respects everyone who respects the life opportunity and the human dignity of others. Every creed and belief believes that it is unacceptable to resort to terrorism, violence, torture, and to demean human dignity. Those who resort to arguments such as cultural relativism to disregard democratic and human rights values are in fact tyrannical reactionaries, who seek to cover their dictatorial faces by resorting to acts of violence and aggression against their own people in the name of national or religious culture.

Regretfully, today the world has another reason to fight human rights, and that is in the name of the fight against terrorism. There's of course no doubt that terror and violence are unacceptable in any society, and fighting terrorism and violence therefore thus constitute a legitimate act. However, fighting terrorism should not turn into a tool for silencing people and dissident voices. Unfortunately, doing so and fighting human rights in the name of fighting terrorism but disregarding human rights values has reached an extent to which the United Nations has been forced to pass a number of resolutions on the subject. There're many examples across the world when we look, but I'd like to refer to a few. In the war against terrorism, people's telephone conversations are listened to and eavesdropped on, an act that is illegal and against the Constitution, to an extent where even the American Bar Association has spoken against it. Or, for example, in the United States, if you're searching for research material and books, even in a small local library, your information can

be connected via computer to Homeland Security, who can then follow and persecute you for the kind of books that you choose to read. If you recall, in the beginning, I did say that undemocratic Islamic states do not have the right to use the name of Islam to oppress their people. Radical Islamic groups do not have the right to touch on the religious sentiments of the people to take advantage of it and convince their followers to resort to acts of violence. By the same token, Western countries, including and especially the United States, do not have the right to take advantage of the name of democracy and human rights and use it as a justification to militarily attack other countries. It is only through democracy that one can materialize human rights, and therefore, no country has the right to attack another state or country in the name of human rights and democracy. Human rights and democracy cannot be granted to a nation through cluster bombs. This is exactly how some groups choose to take advantage of democracy and human rights.

Now that we speak of democracy, I'd like to tell you of my definition of "democracy." We all know that democracy means the majority rule. But a majority that comes to power through free elections still does not have the right to rule in whatever manner it chooses. They cannot disallow a minority to speak their voices, resorting to ideological beliefs that they have. For example, in socialist countries like China, this is what happens. For a majority that reaches power does not have the right to take advantage of the name of Islam, under the pretext of Islam, to oppress half of society; that is to say, women, an act that happens in many Islamic countries today. These examples show that a majority that comes to power does not have the right to carry out its will in whatever manner it chooses. Democracy has a framework that must be respected. Even when a majority-elected government goes beyond this framework, its acts are no longer legitimate, because in fact it has moved away from democracy. Let's not forget that many governments, including many dictators, gained power in the beginning through a majority vote, such as Hitler himself. But since they walk beyond the framework for democracy, they were no longer democratic governments.

But what is this framework of democracy that I refer to? This framework is human-rights laws and principles. That is to say, a majority that gains power through votes has the right to govern only by observing human-rights values and principles. It is only when democracy and human rights are combined together to govern that society can move toward peace. When we speak of human rights, we know that it has many different dimensions. One of the dimensions of human rights, which is unfortunately most often neglected, is the provision of welfare to the people of society, in accordance with the wealth of society. Therefore, the widening gap between the rich and the poor is one example of a violation of human rights. There are many countries in which the gap between rich and poor is enormous. The poor are patient and bear the brunt; nevertheless, this is a violation of human rights. I can refer to India as one example or to Iran. The big gap between the rich and poor is one example of a human-rights violation. National resources should be used for public benefits. Therefore, countries that have enormous military budgets are violating human rights. There are few countries that either don't have an army or have a very low military budget. Regretfully, most countries in the world have very heavy military budgets. Their military budget exceeds the combined budget that they choose to allocate to health and education in their countries. That means that the money that has to be spent to improve the health and education of people is spent on arms, arms that will be used to destroy the lives of people. It seems, unfortunately, that there is a deadly arms race among countries, a fact that has endangered world peace today.

To justify warfare, politicians take advantage of the religious culture and sentiments of their people. It is therefore the duty of people and every individual to shed light on the commonalities of religions and belief systems and therefore take away the excuse from governments to resort to warfare in order to advance their own interests and violate human rights. One place that can be very helpful in this respect is the universities. Having religious studies and especially comparative religions programs and studies, can help raise such awareness among people. I'd like to therefore extend my gratitude once again and to congratulate the organizers and sponsors of this congress, including McGill University, for the initiative they have taken. I pray for lasting peace for your beautiful city and for the entire world. Thank you for your patience, and I am happy to answer any questions you may have. Thank you again.

QUESTIONS AND ANSWERS FOR THE AUTHOR

Question: Speaking about the role of human-rights charters and legislation as the framework for democracy, for many people who have strong religious convictions, human rights charters and legislation seem to be usurping the role of religious doctrines and traditions, in terms of acting as the framework for the state in a democracy. Can you help us understand the relationship between religious beliefs and democracy, and human rights legislation and religious beliefs and traditions? What should prevail? (Which of them enjoys) your confidence? What has ultimate authority in the framework for democracy—human rights legislation or religious doctrines? Thank you.

Answer: There's no doubt that the priority is with human-rights principles. Because if we base things on traditions, the sentiments, and especially religious and belief sentiments of people, it can be taken advantage of. Governments will choose to interpret such traditions in a manner that serves their interests and purposes. But if we accept and choose human rights, it tells us what the principles are with full clarity. At the same time, one should realize the fact that human rights are compatible with any religion and belief system and creed. When the Universal Declaration of Human Rights was drafted, the followers of all major belief systems and faiths were invited to give their input. Human rights is in fact the essence of different belief systems and religions. Do you know of any religion that would endorse killings, murders, belittlement of human dignity, and terror and violence? Do you know of any religion that would take away the rights of a group of people only because of their color or because of their beliefs? Therefore, human rights is the essence of religions and world civilizations. It is not at all incompatible with religious traditions. It is only undemocratic governments that make such a claim so that they can interpret religious traditions in a way that serves their own goals.

Question: To be consistent with what you just said, human rights should prevail on any religion, or, another way to say it would be that, every religion should respect human rights. And to be consistent with that, do you think that we should, or the United Nations should, ask every religious leader to have their own religious writings be censored to make sure that any sentence that promotes violence against women or homosexuals, or violence against any other people from any other religion, should be removed from the religious books?

Answer: It is in practice impossible for the United Nations to force religious leaders to censor their religious texts and teachings. But what would work is that (organizations of) human rights address governments. When human rights are violated, it is governments that are held accountable. If a country legislates a new law, for example, that endorses discrimination against a certain ethnic or religious group, then that is an act of a violation of human rights. And then the government can be condemned. If the government happens to be a member of the International Criminal Court, politicians from that state can also be held accountable by the ICC. Therefore, the relationship of the United Nations is with governments who must legislate and change bad laws, not with religious leaders.

Question: Thank you, Dr. Ebadi, for your book *Iran Awakening,* and for your amazing courage. In many countries, human rights are not extended to gay and lesbian people. My question is, What's the role for international movements like the gay movement, who want to try to impact a country's

laws where, for instance, gays and lesbians are regularly executed. How can the national democracy of a country be respected, while at the same time international organizations try to pressure a country to stop the executions? Boycotts usually hurt the poor or others most. But is there a place for boycotts or other movements to try to change national laws?

Answer: The punishment or the execution of gays and lesbians is an act of human rights violation. So if, by law, a government endorses that, and in some countries this is law, including in some Islamic countries, then the governments have violated human rights. And therefore one has the opportunity to report such acts of violation of human rights, these punishments and executions, to human rights commissions and the international fora that see to these acts. Therefore, gay and lesbian movements should collect the exact figures for the number of individuals who have been persecuted for being gay and lesbian, and, with name and the date of the act of persecution, give a report to international organizations.

Question: Dr. Shirin Ebadi, I congratulate you on your wonderfully inspiring and frank talk, and nations around the world must listen to it. There is, however, a small element that you mentioned in your speech and I would like you to clarify on that point. You mentioned something regarding the enemies of Islam. I'm just wondering, are there such people and how do you conceptualize them, and what is their real intent?

Answer: I believe the enemies of Islam belong to two groups. Their first group is Muslim reactionaries who misinterpret Islam, who hide behind the shield of Islam and justify their oppression in the name of Islam. On the surface, they're Muslims, but in reality, they're the enemy of genuine Islam and dynamic Islam. And the other are groups that, for political interests, choose to, again, take advantage of the name of Islam and represent Islam as a religion that endorses violence and terrorism. They try to say the wrongful deeds and actions of a group of individuals or small group of Muslims is Islam itself. If a group, for example, like al Qaeda, resorts to terror and violence, they'll say, "You see, this is what Islam is about." By representing a darker image of Islam, they try to justify the wars in the Middle East. I want to add here that, like any other religion, Islam can have different interpretations. You can see, in the West itself, one church endorses the marriage of homosexuals whereas the other one refutes it, whereas both are Christians. Even political ideologies have different interpretations. China was not being run the same way the former Soviet Union was. Was there no difference, for example, between Cuba and Albania? It's the same with Islam. The fact that women and humans rights have different status in different Islamic countries shows that Islam can have different interpretations. You can see, in a countries like Saudi Arabia, women can't even drive, let alone have social and political rights. But in other countries, such as Indonesia or Pakistan or Bangladesh, they've had women prime ministers and presidents from many years back. Or, the punishment of stoning or execution is accepted by law in country like Iran and Saudi Arabia, but in other Islamic countries they've been banned. So what Islamic intellectuals are calling for is a correct interpretation of Islam which is compatible with the needs of our time and age.

What Gives a Person Worth?

A Zoroastrian View

Nikan H. Khatibi

What gives a person worth? Many use their religious viewpoints to determine their answer to this question. My belief is that each person has equal worth because each person was created equally by God. If my religious principles do not express this belief adequately or if there is some other framework others use in their determination of a person's worth, be it a national or personal viewpoint, then people in this world are in danger of being seen as less than human or as good-doers (or bad-doers) who must earn their worth in the world. This good to be achieved is often national or religious, and so creating religious and national borders to distance people comes from a wrong view of people to begin with.

From a Zoroastrian perspective, our responsibility as a community is to put the individual's value first and foremost and then proceed with dialogue across borders in the hopes of sustaining peace within the human brotherhood.

The similarities and differences between individual and societal preferences are based on our subjective judgments. In many societies, for example, many would judge men as more capable in many areas of work than women. This is because of the fact that a society places more value on certain kinds of products and services that men traditionally have been placed in charge of providing. These extrinsic, social viewpoints tend to foster social judgments about the intrinsic values of individual human beings. So if such judgments of worth can be made in such ways within one's own religion or society, and the more dissimilar those outside our religion or society are to ourselves, the more likely we are to make black-and-white judgments about the outsiders' intrinsic value as human beings.

This can be seen practically applied in many religions today. Many use extrinsic differences they see in other religions as a barometer for that religion's spiritual worth. As a result, one religion may believe or even declare itself superior to another group. This can also be seen in everyday life. A homeless person on the street may be judged by some to be less religious than a wealthy banker simply because of external attributes. In such an example, we would be judging a person's spirituality by his or her apparent success or appearance, and by so doing, we would be acting as superior judges, a position reserved for God alone.

Furthermore, throughout the world, people of all different religions believe that the only way to reach God is through their religion and thus often see the nonbelievers as subhuman. Institutionalized religions have consistently succumbed to believing that their ordained path is the only true path, as founded on their exclusive belief system. This can be seen in certain strands of Christianity and Islam. Christians believe that the only way to heaven is through Jesus Christ; Muslims believe Muhammad is their path. People from both sides use this as a way of putting themselves "higher" than others, when in fact, differences in religious viewpoints should be respected, celebrated, and allowed to coexist harmoniously.

So what can we do to stop the belief in religious superiority? The Zoroastrian religion, with its unique history, illustrates the fundamental connectedness of the world's religious traditions to support the view that religions are different paths to the same reality. Prophet Zoroaster was the first to propound the freedom of choice for human beings and to affirm that human beings are entitled to the beliefs of their choice so long as they pursue the path of peaceful existence.

Let us use Zoroaster's example of promoting freedom of choice to formulate a solution for a peaceful society. Let us go to our respective communities and share with one another the importance of respecting, and more importantly, celebrating each other's diversity and equality. Let us learn to coexist harmoniously. Only once we accept each other's equality, each other's value in life, can we say we are at peace with one another. Only then can we say, "Yes, we are all of equal worth."

RELIGION, VIOLENCE, AND HUMAN RIGHTS

A Hindu Perspective

Arvind Sharma

HUMAN RIGHTS AND HUMAN DIGNITY

Throughout this essay, I shall assume that it is analytically advantageous to carry out our discussion in terms of the twin concepts of human rights and human dignity. Sometimes these two terms are used almost synonymously; when a distinction is drawn between the two, there is a tendency to view human dignity as the more comprehensive of the two. I shall use both the terms and in both ways—sometimes as interchangeable and sometimes as distinct, sometimes as dual but undivided and yet at other times as two separate concepts, but united, even in tension.

The second introductory remark is not unrelated to the first. In the main body of the chapter, I shall approach my topic through a series of successively broadening circles of orientation. I shall thus begin by examining the question of the dignity of the dead or those about to be killed; that is to say, human dignity in the face of violence, or in the case of a violent end. The next concentric circle will examine the possibility of defending human dignity not against but through violence. A third circle shall encompass the question of maintaining the dignity of combatants and noncombatants in the course of

war—that often secularly ritualized enactment of violence. Finally, I shall draw the largest circle around some concepts of Hindu and Indic civilization that seem to dignify violence itself and examine their implications.

In brief, then, dignity *in* violence, dignity *through* violence, dignity while *engaged* in violence, and finally, *dignifying* violence are the four themes I shall be touching upon.

Before I embark on this exercise, however, I would like to offer a few comments on the timeliness of the topic of the chapter as it was brought home to me even as I was writing it. I use the word *timeliness* advisedly. It is one of the virtues whose cultivation is recommended in Confucianism through the term *chung-yung*. The word is often translated as "the middle way" but possesses a strong connotation of "timeliness," as in being neither too early nor too late, in a Confucian setting. I would like to share two indications of this, one in terms of human rights and the other in terms of human dignity. An op-ed piece by Michael Ignatieff appeared in the *New York Times* on February 5, 2002, under the title "Is the Human Rights Era Ending?" It proposed that the time had come to challenge the regnant mood in the wake of the events of

September 11, 2001, that "national security trumps human rights."[1] On the other hand, when the Śaṅkarācārya of Kanchi, a leading pontiff of India, was asked, with tension building up in Ayodhyā for commencing work on the construction of the Rāma Temple on March 15, 2002, "What is the real meaning of *ahiṁsā* or non-violence in today's world?" he replied, "We need both pacifism and just wars for the good of the land," when such good presumably included maintaining human dignity at least in the good land of India and perhaps the world.[2]

HUMAN RIGHTS OF THE DEAD

I would now like to proceed by referring to one of the earliest episodes I know involving violence and dignity. It is provided by the Greek playwright Sophocles (496–406 B.C.E.). "Human rights theorists refer to [his] *Antigone,* as the classic example from Greek literature. According to Sophocles, King Creon reproaches Antigone for having given her brother a burial, contrary to the law of the city (because her brother had fought against the Polis). She responded that she is obliged to follow a higher, unwritten law which supersedes positive (man-made) law."[3]

One is tempted to ask, Do the dead have human rights—such as the right to a decent burial even at the hands of the enemy? Should a shared humanity not transcend enmity? One is reminded here of an incident in the Hindu epic *Rāmāyaṇa*, in which the demon Rāvaṇa abducts the wife of Rāma. Rāvaṇa is ultimately killed by Rāma, as Rāma proceeds to rescue his wife, Sītā, from him. With Rāvaṇa lying dead, Rāma is asked what is to be done with his dead body. Thereupon Rāma famously replies to the brother of the dead Rāvaṇa:

> Enmities end at death. Our purpose is served. Perform the proper rites. He is as much [a brother] to me as he is to you.[4]

So much for human rights and human dignity of the dead.

VIOLENCE AS PROTECTOR OF HUMAN RIGHTS

Violence comprises both human rights and human dignity. The matter seems fairly straightforward when stated in this way. But when it is put under an analytical lens, it gets more convoluted. It gets more convoluted in terms of human rights in view of the fact that sometimes it may be necessary to resort to violence in order to protect human rights—as in the face of terrorism. This is considered acceptable from a Hindu or even an Indic perspective, since this presents a case when violence recoils on violence, in the memorable phrase of the *Manusmṛti* (VIII. 349–51), a well-known Hindu text usually assigned in its present form to the second century C.E. Bühler translates the relevant verses as follows:

> 349. In their own defence, in a strife for the fees of officiating priests, and in order to protect women and Brāhmaṇas; he who (under such circumstances) kills in the cause of right, commits no sin.
>
> 350. One may slay without hesitation an assassin who approaches (with murderous intent), whether (he be one's) teacher, a child or an aged man, or a Brāhmaṇa deeply versed in the Vedas.
>
> 351. By killing an assassin the slayer incurs no guilt, whether (he does it) publicly or secretly; in that case fury recoils upon fury.[5]

These verses contain an important Sanskrit word, *ātatāyin,* literally "one who has stretched the bow to the extreme," thereby graphically representing an oppressor. The word is also sometimes used in a technical sense to include the following: (1) an arsonist, (2) a murderer, (3) a terrorist, (4) a rapist, (5) a robber, and (6) a felon.[6]

MAINTAINING HUMAN DIGNITY IN VIOLENCE

We turn next to the question of human rights and human dignity *in* violence, namely in the conduct of violence or, briefly, in war. The *Manusmṛti* just alluded to also provides surprisingly relevant material on this point. The famous scholar of Indic civilization Professor A. L. Basham remarks on the provisions relating to war found therein (VII. 90–93) that the "chivalrous rules of warfare, probably based on a very old tradition, and codified in their present form among the martial peoples of western India in pre-Mauryan times, must have had some effect in mitigating the harshness of war for combatant and non-combatant alike."[7] He goes on to add, "It is doubtful if any other ancient civilization set such humane ideals of warfare."[8] Ideals mind you—which means that they were perhaps not always observed in practice, but Basham was sufficiently impressed with them to write elsewhere in his classic study of Indic civilization, "No other ancient law giver proclaimed such noble ideals of fair play in battle as Manu did."[9]

Before we turn to the consideration of the ideals set for the combatants, let us pause for a moment to consider the fate of the noncombatants, who, according to the general code of war, were to be spared. Striking evidence that such was the case at least during some periods of ancient Indian history is provided by the extant fragments of the work of Megasthenes, the Seleucid ambassador at the court of the Mauryan emperor of India in the fourth century B.C.E.. Megasthenes famously (though erroneously) observed that famine was unknown in India, meaning thereby perhaps that is was unknown in India as he knew it. This observation is remarkable in itself, but one of the explanations he provides for it is perhaps even more remarkable, for he goes on to say,

> But, further, there are usages observed by the Indians which contribute to prevent the occurrence of famine among them; for whereas among other nations it is usual, in the contests of war, to ravage the soil, and thus to reduce it to an uncultivated waste, among the Indians, on the contrary, by whom husbandmen are regarded as a class that is sacred and inviolable, the tillers of the soil, even when battle is raging in their neighbourhood, are undisturbed by any sense of danger, for the combatants on either side in waging the conflict make carnage of each other, but allow those engaged in husbandry to remain quite unmolested. Besides, they neither ravage an enemy's land with fire, nor cut down its trees.[10]

Hartmut Scharfe notes that "Alexander's historians observed with amazement how Indian peasants went about their work in the fields unharmed in full view of two fighting armies." He also notes that the *Mahābhārata* (XII. 104.39) "recommends against the destruction of crops in war, at least under certain conditions, and tribal allies are instructed in the proper conduct of war [as follows]: don't destroy crops or fields."[11]

We turn next to the preservation of the dignity of the combatants themselves, or even of their human rights in some ways, speaking anachronistically of course. I now cite from the *Manusmṛti*:

> 90. When he fights with his foes in battle, let him not strike with weapons concealed (in wood), not with (such as are) barbed, poisoned, or the points of which are blazing with fire.
>
> 91. Let him not strike one who (in flight) has climbed on an eminence, nor a eunuch, nor one who joins the palms of his hands (in supplication), nor one who (flees) with flying hair, nor one who sits down, nor one who says "I am thine";
>
> 92. Nor one who sleeps, nor one who has lost his coat of mail, nor one who is naked, nor one who is disarmed, nor one who looks on without taking part in the fight, nor one who is fighting with another (foe);
>
> 93. Nor one whose weapons are broken, nor one afflicted (with sorrow), nor one who has been grievously wounded, nor one who is in fear, nor one who has turned to flight; (but in all these cases let him) remember the duty (of honourable warriors).[12]

Similar rules are also laid down in the epic *Mahābhārata* and elsewhere that, according to P. V. Kane, bear "comparison with the conventions of the Geneva and Hague Conferences."[13] It should be added, however, that the epic also provides instances of their violation.[14]

Human Dignity and Victorious Conquest

Battles end in either victory or defeat—no matter how they are fought. Sometimes the defeated king dies—but what if he survives? And what of his kingdom?

Hindu political theory provides a broad framework that helps answer such questions. It distinguishes between three types of conquests: "The first is conquest in which the defeated king is forced to render homage and tribute, after which he or a member of the family is reinstated as a vassal. The second is victory in which enormous booty is demanded and large portions of enemy territory annexed. The third involves the political annihilation of the conquered kingdom and its incorporation into that of the victor."[15]

The terms used to designate these three types of conquest are not without interest. The first, the least malevolent type, is called *dharma-vijaya,* or righteous conquest; the second is called *lobha-vijaya,* or larcenous or acquisitive conquest in which booty is demanded; the third, in which the ruler is ousted, is called *asura-vijaya,* or demonic conquest, reminiscent of the ruthlessness of the Assyrians.

The idea of *dharma-vijaya,* or righteous conquest, is interesting. It was developed in certain circles to denote conquest only through righteousness as by the Mauryan Buddhist emperor Aśoka; in other circles it may have led to development of the perspective that came to view war as a ritual, as in the analogy of the sacrifice of animals in Vedic ritual.[16]

Violence and Righteousness

Another term found in the Hindu tradition—analogous to that of *dharma-vijaya,* or righteous conquest—is that of *dharma-yuddha,* or righteous battle. An analysis of the word *dharma-yuddha* might help advance our discussion of violence and human dignity further. The word is a compound in which the first word, *dharma,* means righteousness, along with a host of other meanings. The word *yuddha* means battle or war. As a compound expression, it can be analyzed and made meaningful in more than one way. At the most obvious level, it could mean a righteous war, as well as a war fought righteously. That is to say, violence could be "dignified" either in terms of what it is being engaged in *for,* or in terms of *how* it is being carried out. Thus "fighting may be noble or ignoble according to its purpose or object, so also it can be good or bad according to the manner in which it is carried out."[17] In other words, it could mean a just war or a war fought justly, and ideally both. Such a connotation imparts human dignity to an otherwise violent exercise, because justice rubs off on violence, as it were, in terms of both the means and end of violence, thereby dignifying both.

There is also a more specifically Hindu way of dignifying violence by placing it in the context of the so-called caste system. It is not often realized that one of the things performing one's inherited duty in life generated in Indian society was a sense of dignity. There was also a dignified way of discharging one's duty. In this sense, then, it was an honorable thing to be a warrior in itself. Then, there was an honorable way of fighting. In this particular context, it meant not running away from battle or, as graphically stated in the tradition, "not showing one's back to the enemy." This fact of not running away from the field of battle is specifically mentioned in the *Bhagavadgītā* among the qualities of a *kṣatriya,* and also surfaces in the *Manusmṛti* (VII. 89) in the following verse:

> Those kings who, seeking to slay each other in battle, fight with the utmost exertion and do not *turn back,* go to heaven.[18]

This manner of fighting was also dignified soteriologically, to the extent that *what* one fought for became secondary to *how* one fought; that is, bravely. In the *Mahābhārata,* King Yudhiṣṭhira is one of the Pāṇḍava brothers. These Pāṇḍava brothers are the good guys, who win the war against the Kauravas, the evil cousins, who were the bad guys. When Yudhiṣṭhira died and was led into heaven, he was shocked to find the bad guys in heaven as well, and it was explained to him that this was so because they had performed their duty as *kṣatriyas,* or warriors, fittingly.

One feels a certain uneasiness perhaps with such an extension of the concept of dignity in relation to violence, and with good reason. For such an extension may explain a phenomenon that has puzzled cultural historians of India for a long time; namely, that despite its commitment to *ahiṁsā,* or nonviolence, "positive condemnations of war are rare in Indian literature."[19] The same holds true of the death penalty. It is perhaps worth adding, just to emphasize this point, that this holds true even in the case of Jainism, whose commitment to *ahiṁsā,* or nonviolence, is generally believed to exceed that of both Hinduism and Buddhism. The famous historian V. A. Smith found this point of sufficient consequence to include an explanation of it from a Jaina point of view in his history of India, which will not fail to interest us:

> A true Jaina will do nothing to hurt the feelings of another person, man, woman, or child; nor will he violate the principles of Jainism. Jaina ethics are meant for men of all positions—for kings, warriors, traders, artisans, agriculturists, and indeed for men and women in every walk of life. . . . "Do your duty. Do it as humanely as you can." This, in brief, is the primary principle of Jainism. Non-killing cannot interfere with one's duties. The king, or the judge, has to hang a murderer. The murderer's act is the negation of a right of the murdered. The king's or the judge's, order is the negation of this negation, and is enjoined by Jainism as a duty. Similarly, the soldier's killing on the battle-field.[20]

I would like to propose that one reason why in such cases violence may have lost its moral sting—its capacity to shock—may well be because it had been imbued with dignity in the ways we have discussed.

Conclusion

Normally we think of human rights and human dignity as morally synonymous concepts in human-rights discourse. This graded discussion of violence in Hinduism in the context of such discourse generates the possibility that sometimes tension might arise between the two. A dignitarian approach to violence, for instance, might tend to justify it in contexts in which a rights alone approach might consider it unjustified.

CONFUCIAN CONTRIBUTIONS TO THE UNIVERSAL DECLARATION OF HUMAN RIGHTS

A Historical and Philosophical Perspective

Sumner B. Twiss

It is often claimed that the Universal Declaration of Human Rights (UDHR) is a preeminently Western document that promulgates a distinctively Western moral and political ideology of individual human rights incompatible with many of the world's cultural-moral traditions. Given the fact, however, that the UDHR was formulated through a year-and-a-half-long process of drafting and negotiation among representatives of no fewer than fifty-eight nations and cultural traditions, the claim seems prima facie suspect. Since the traditions of East Asia are often regarded (wrongly, I believe) as most in tension with the aspirations and content of the UDHR, it may be especially instructive to trace the Chinese contribution to its formulation: doing so may help correct those myopic perceptions that (1) the UDHR is predominantly or exclusively Western and (2) individual human rights are necessarily irreconcilable with East Asian traditions.[1]

After researching the official United Nations records of 1947–48, as well as consulting the recently published diaries of John Humphrey, the principal coordinator of the drafting process, I have determined that the Chinese delegate P. C. Chang introduced a number of Confucian ideas, strategies, and arguments into the deliberative process leading up to the final formulation of the UDHR, adopted December 10, 1948, by the U.N. General Assembly. This Confucian contribution is considerably more extensive and influential than has ever been reported previously. Chang was described by Humphrey as the towering intellect of the Third Committee (which debated and approved the final UDHR draft sent to the General Assembly) who more than anyone else was responsible for imparting a universal rather than a purely Western character to the UDHR.

Humphrey noted in his diary entry for December 4, 1948, that "in intellectual stature he [Chang] towers over any other member of the committee. I also like his philosophy." And for October 7, 1948, he noted: "The debate in the Third Committee was passionately interesting this morning. P. C. Chang made a particularly brilliant speech in which he pleaded for two-man mindedness. As only he can he drew the attention of those countries that are trying to impose special philosophical concepts such as the law of nature, to the fact that the declaration is meant for all men everywhere." In a footnote to the entry for October 11, 1948, the editor John Hobbins reports that at a four-person meeting of the officers of the Commission on Human Rights held in February 1947, "[Charles] Malik

[Lebanese philosopher and diplomat] believed that the question of rights should be approached through Christian precepts, especially the teachings of St. Thomas Aquinas. Chang argued the necessity of a more universal approach. Humphrey was asked to prepare a draft and Chang suggested, tongue in cheek, that Humphrey go to China for six months to study Confucius before attempting the task."[2]

BIOGRAPHICAL BACKGROUND

The P. C. Chang of the United Nations official records was Chang Peng-chun (1882–1957), who was born and raised in Tientsin, China.[3] He graduated from Nankai Middle School (founded by his older brother, Poling) in 1906, and from Bao-Ding Deng School (high school) in 1910. Supported by the U.S. Boxer Rebellion Indemnity Fund, Chang attended Clark University (Worcester, MA), 1910–13, graduating with a BA in 1913. He then pursued graduate studies at Columbia University, 1913–15, taking two master's degrees in 1915, one from the graduate school and the other from the college of education (Teachers College). In 1919, after working for a few years in China, Chang returned to Columbia and completed Ph.D. requirements in 1922, although the doctorial degree was not formally awarded until 1924, after publication of his dissertation in 1923.

During 1916–19, prior to his doctoral studies, Chang taught at Nankai Middle School, serving as acting president in 1917–19, and helped his brother organize and establish Nankai University in 1919. After completing his doctoral work, Chang returned to China and upgraded Tsingshua School (Beijing) to a college in 1923, serving as its dean, 1923–26. In 1926 he returned to Nankai, becoming the principal of Nankai Middle School, while also serving as professor of philosophy at Nankai University, 1926–37. In 1928–29 Chang was acting president of Nankai University. While on the faculty of Nankai University, Chang also held visiting appointments at the University of Chicago (Chinese philosophy and art) and the Chicago Art Institute in 1931; University of Hawaii (Chinese art and literature) in 1933 and 1934; and Cambridge University (as Ministry of Education Exchange Professor) in 1936. For a brief period at the conclusion of World War II in 1945, Chang also held a visiting appointment at Columbia University.

During his career, Chang authored three books, one on Chinese education (his published dissertation, *Education for Modernization in China* [1923]) and two on Chinese history and culture (*China: Whence and Whither?* [1934]; *China at the Crossroads* [1936]), and edited yet another (*There Is Another China* [1948]). He also wrote a number of original plays, two of which were staged in New York City (including at the Cort Theatre, Broadway), with the others staged in China. Throughout his career, Chang translated many Western plays into Chinese, directed numerous play productions in China, and directed Chinese Classical Theatre tours in the United States (1930) and Soviet Russia (1935). In 1938, he received a doctor of humane letters from his alma mater, Clark University.

Chang's governmental and diplomatic career developed as his academic career was concluding. In 1937, possibly because of the anti-Japanese influence of his plays, Chang was appointed by the Chinese government to pursue anti-Japanese propaganda activities in Europe and America, which included giving public lectures in a number of European cities, including London, as well as lobbying the U.S. Congress for passage of an economic sanctions bill against Japan (1939). Chang was a member of the People's Political Council, 1938–40, and served successively as minister plenipotentiary and envoy extraordinary to Turkey (a neutral country), 1940–42, and ambassador to Chile (another neutral country), 1942–45. In 1942, he negotiated and signed a treaty of amity between China and Iraq. At the conclusion of World War II, Chang served as China's chief delegate (ambassador rank) at the initial organization meetings of the United Nations in London and New York, assuming the role of resident chief delegate to the United Nations Social and Economic Council, 1946–52. In 1947–48, he was a member and vice chairman of the U.N. Commission on Human

Rights (including membership on the drafting committee for the UDHR), and in 1948 he headed the Chinese delegation to the Geneva Conference on Freedom of Information.

Chang was well placed to make a significant contribution to the UDHR, but before examining the specifics of that contribution, we need also to be aware of certain intellectual influences on Chang, as well as the tenor of his thinking immediately preceding the formulation of the UDHR.

INTELLECTUAL INFLUENCES

There were two broad intellectual influences on Chang—John Dewey's philosophy of education and classical Chinese culture—both of which are well represented in his published work. Neither of these influences should be particularly surprising, given Chang's dual passions for education and Chinese culture and given the social context in China at the time he was teaching. Let us, just for the record, begin with the social context before considering Chang's writings.

Dewey's Influence

It is well known that Dewey's philosophy of pragmatism—particularly in its methodological approach of combining critical reflection (logic, scientific method) with a practical emphasis (social problem solving)—influenced Chinese thought in the 1920s.[4] In particular, it provided the New Culture movement with a method of critique, evaluation, and adaptation of new Western ideas to the Chinese social situation. That movement was very critical of traditional Chinese cultural values and emphasized supplanting them with Western cultural values (e.g., science and technology; political ideas and structures). Although Dewey himself proposed the critical evaluation of both Chinese traditional culture and Western culture, with the aim of developing a new culture with the best elements of both, the New Culture movement was less cautious in its rejection of traditional Chinese culture in favor of Western adaptations.[5] As we shall see shortly, Chang's approach

was more similar to Dewey's than that of the New Culture movement.

It is also well known that Dewey's philosophy of education in particular had an extraordinary impact on Chinese educational institutions and programming during the same period, and even lasting to the foundation of the People's Republic in 1949. Many of China's educational leaders at the time had trained at Columbia under Dewey and William Heard Kilpatrick (an educator who put many of Dewey's ideas into practice in the United States). Indeed, Chang's own brother (president of Nankai University) had studied with Dewey and strongly advocated the implementation of his educational theory. Nankai University was known for its Deweyian orientation and influence, along with Peking National University, Peking Teachers College, and Nanking Teachers College. Through the influence of these educational leaders and institutions, Dewey's ideas on experience-centered learning, adapting education to the needs of social evolution, cultivating the individual, and developing democratic spirit in cooperative learning projects were applied to schools and curricula throughout China.

Chang himself in his dissertation and first published book, *Education for Modernization in China*, manifests clear indebtedness to Dewey's educational philosophy. At the outset of this work, Chang argues forcefully for the importance of educating a leadership able to cope with economic problems so as to transform China into a modern industrialized nation with a "wide-awake outlook," "enlightened individuality," and "democratic processes." He does so in a Deweyian way by emphasizing the attainment of an equilibrium between the best of the old (traditional Chinese culture) and the best of the new (Western culture) through a process of critical readjustment from old to new (as contrasted with blind appropriation of Western culture):

> In order to be effective in the present-day world, even as conservatives, each one needs to be equipped with the wide-awake outlook and the strong enlightened individuality

which only the modernized social and moral institutions can produce. . . .

China must change and change very rapidly until a state of more or less adjusted equilibrium is reached. But by modernization we do not imply that China must, even if she could, go through all the stages of change that the modern nations have gone through. For China the process is readjustment and not mere appropriation or reproduction. The products of modernism already formed can serve very well as hypotheses, but should not be too blindly or too closely followed as infallible models. . . .

Modernization is a process. It will call for certain indispensable modern products in the development of the process. But it does not commit itself to uphold any crystallized formulations of the modern West to the entire detriment of the norms and formulations of the old culture. It emphasizes the process rather than the products. The old culture furnishes the basic experiences to be modernized.[6]

Chang goes on to use Dewey's thought in proposing that the immediate aim of education is modernization in the sense of developing in students an appreciation for the scientific method, the rights and liberties of individuals, and democratic decision-making and problem-solving processes. In order to achieve this result, Chang argues that there must be educational analogues for those circumstances that historically produced such characteristics of modernization. In particular, he focuses on the circumstances of expansion, exploration, and frontier community in the U.S. West and then cites Dewey on providing the educational analogues of these circumstances—an expanding and challenging social environment that "encourages the wholesome unification of thinking and doing" in individual exertion and development, conceiving the ideal school as a frontierlike household and community in which are developed discipline, character, order and industry, and responsibility for solving problems that meet communal needs:

At the end of the nineteenth century when industrial transformations were taking place in American life, Professor Dewey saw that the essential powers in men and women who could succeed in adapting themselves to the new environment were the natural products of the mode of living which we may characterize as frontier community-building that had been going on for three hundred years previously in America. He also saw that the most efficient means to adapt the younger generation successfully to cope with the vast problems around them would be the provision in the schools of the substitutes for the environmental forces which in previous generations of frontier life shaped and made possible the characteristics of initiative, keen thinking ability and cooperative endeavor.[7]

As the centerpiece of his argument, Chang then goes on to propose, develop, and apply five "criteria for curriculum construction." Although it is not possible here to report his argument in any detail, the five criteria are clearly Deweyian, ranging across (1) encouraging hypothesis formulation and verification; (2) adapting methods to needs-oriented goals; (3) developing executive, organizing, and vocational capacities; (4) promoting, on the basis of equal opportunity, democratic social conduct and qualities of independent judgment; and (5) humanizing the aims and processes of modern life. The fifth criterion in particular seems to develop Dewey's social vision of creating a new culture with the best elements of both traditional Chinese culture and Western culture, for Chang explicitly adumbrates it as follows: "Does the school activity preserve and readapt the ideals and habits of humanism in the old culture? Does the school activity allow and encourage the searching for 'human' values in the products and processes of modern culture?"[8]

I think it would be fair to infer from Chang's discussion of these criteria that he gained from Dewey a set of social, moral, and political values that are recognizably Western in their orientations.[9] At the same time, however, reflecting on the fifth criterion, Chang also clearly gained from Dewey an affirmation of the value of his own traditional culture, aspects of which might have to be preserved, even if readapted, in order to achieve the goal of a competent leadership for an equilibrated culture that is truly human or humanized. Indeed, one might plausibly discern in Chang's emphasis on "human" and "humanized" a Confucian-influenced concern that the traits of modernization developed in China and its future leadership be humane in a traditional sense, to which we now turn.

Chinese Culture, Especially Confucianism

Although the influence of Dewey's thought on Chang seems obvious and profound, one should not overlook Chang's deep knowledge and appreciation of Chinese culture and its contribution to world history and culture. In his second and third books, *China: Whence and Whither?* and *China at the Crossroads,* Chang displays extraordinary erudition about China's cultural achievements (both material and nonmaterial) prior to the nineteenth century and their impact on the rest of the world.[10] Particularly important for our purposes are Chang's discussions of Confucian and neo-Confucian philosophical and political thought as well as his views on Chinese education. Also important are his views of how traditional Chinese philosophy and related cultural forms were received by and influenced Western thinkers. Let us begin with the latter.

Chang is utterly clear in his belief that Chinese philosophical thought and culture, as transmitted by returning Jesuit missionaries in the sixteenth and seventeenth centuries, positively impressed eighteenth-century European thinkers such as Diderot and Voltaire. For example, he quotes extensively from *The Works of Voltaire* that, in the latter's view, "the life, honour, and fortune of the subject [citizen] was under the protection of the laws . . . [in] China," its "people were not burdened with taxes," "the fundamental law in China being to consider the empire as one family is the reason why the welfare of the community is attended to as the first

principal duty," and Confucius was a philosopher par excellence ("I have read his books with attention; I have made extracts from them; I have found in them nothing but the purest morality, without the slightest tinge of charlatanism"). Although Chang himself is not overly credulous about the historical accuracy of such claims—"It was . . . the glamour of a better organized . . . controlled, and more cultured civilization, attracting the attention of eighteenth century thinkers . . . dissatisfied with the order of things in Europe"—his point is that "descriptions of China and Chinese philosophical thought" were known to eighteenth-century Europe in "a period of rather free speculation concerning political and religious ideas" and "caught the imagination of some thinkers of the period."[11]

Chang goes on to display a rather wide acquaintance with classical Chinese thinkers such as Confucius, Mencius, and Chuang-Tzu, and later neo-Confucian figures such as Ku Yen-wu, Yen Yuan, Huang Chung-his, and Tai Chen. With regard to the classical period, particularly important to Chang are Confucius's ideas on *jen* and its extension to others, the inclusiveness of human responsibility for improving life, an ideal government founded on "ideals of personal conduct" (rather than on formally enacted laws), and the "cultivation of the completely humanized man," as well as Mencius's notions of "the essential goodness of the nature of man," the "fundamental respect for what is 'human' in all men," and the priority of the people in humane governance, emphasizing "the rights of the people as well as the obligation of the ruler to provide for the good of the people."[12] With respect to the neo-Confucians, Chang is particularly taken with Huang Chung-hsi ("a radical political thinker"), from whose treatise, *Waiting for the Dawn,* he quotes the famous opening paragraph criticizing the selfishness of (later) rulers to the detriment of the people being able to consider their own interests, and Yen Yuan, whom he characterizes as "an original educational thinker" and "early formulator of some principles of education . . . familiar to modern educational thinking," for example, "the fact that real learning and doing must go together."[13]

Beyond these discussions of particular Confucian philosophers, Chang also identifies a number of what he regards as general or systematic Confucian contributions to political thought in world history. He cites in particular the competitive civil service examination system (which he regards as "democratizing government structure to a certain extent," well before the time of European and American democracies), the right of the people to rebellion against an unworthy ruler ("early formulated in China"), and the emphasis given to education by the state (about which he quotes Quesnay from the eighteenth century—"with the exception of China, the necessity of this institution, which is the foundation of government, has been ignored by all kingdoms"—and then cites Adolf Reichwein's claim that "national systems of education . . . in the European world . . . owed much to the system of education in China").[14]

All of this extensive and pointed discussion by Chang of Chinese (Confucian) cultural contributions culminates in his concluding claim that "China must strive to achieve a new culture that is creatively modern—yes, but it is also to be hoped that it will contain elements distinctively Chinese."[15] And some pages earlier he had written,

> A more liberal attitude has happily superseded the somewhat superstitious belief in the conflict of East and West. Culturally, there are many "Easts" and many "Wests"; and they are by no means all necessarily irreconcilable. To take just one instance, it is generally agreed that the humanistic attitude and emphasis in the Chinese tradition appear more "modern" than the outlook toward life that prevailed in medieval Europe. . . . Valuable suggestions for the modern world will naturally be sought after, but they can also be found in the earlier Western experiences and in Chinese history as well.[16]

My point in citing these claims, and Chang's discussions of Confucian thought, can be simply put. While it is certainly the case that Dewey's thought—as methodological approach—lies behind Chang's thinking, it is also the case that he is clearly influenced by, and appreciative of, Chinese philosophy and political thought (independent of Dewey), so much so that he hopes to find a reconciliation or bridge between East and West precisely in commonalities that they share at various points in their intersecting histories—for example, Chinese influence on eighteenth-century European thought; articulation of the right of the people to rebellion against injustice; democratization based on universal education; and open opportunity based on merit. In this manner, Chang appears positioned to do comparative philosophy, East and West, steeped as he was in both Chinese and Western intellectual traditions.

Propensity to Use Confucian Thought

Chang delivered a number of lectures and addresses in the years immediately preceding his work with the Commission on Human Rights. Two sets of talks are particularly revealing of the way that he interlaces Chinese thought and Western sources. The first set of addresses was delivered in Baghdad, March 6 and 11, 1942, at King Faisal II Hall, while he was minister to Turkey. The second are pointed statements made at the initial meetings of the first session of the U.N. Economic and Social Council, January 23 and February 7, 1946 (London), and June 4, 1946 (New York).[17] Both sets of speeches indicate Chang's propensity for using Chinese sources (in addition to Western ideas) to argue his case for modernization and humanization in the world. In addition, we can see certain precursors to the content of his contributions to the UDHR.

The lectures in Baghdad were untitled addresses that appear to have been designed to characterize Chinese history and culture for a Muslim audience unacquainted with China and to lay the groundwork for comprehending how to go about the process of cultural change, combining elements of tradition with the realities of the modern world in a self-critical manner that advances the human good (presumably a process faced by both Chinese and Muslims in their respective contexts). Without going into the detailed substance of these lectures, it is sufficient to say that Chang argues strenuously for the importance of the "sound basis" of knowing the contemporary "concrete needs" of the community and then engaging in a process of "comparative study" of other societies and cultures in their environments (their ways of solving problems and meeting needs), followed by making "daring hypotheses" (about what to do) and "verification in application" (of a given hypothesis)—all as a continuous process of refinement, adjustment, and adaptation of both old and new cultural forms, social structures, institutions, and policies.[18] Here we can discern Dewey's influence.

Intriguingly, in these lectures, Chang makes constant use of the thought of Confucius (quoting from the *Analects*) in reiterating the importance of maintaining humanism and humane values in cultural change. He repeats more forcefully (without qualification) than in his earlier book that "Chinese thought influenced the so-called Philosophy of the Enlightenment in 18th century Europe" in its battle against authoritarianism.[19] He also asserts (again, without qualification) that "the civil service system . . . [with] open competitive examination . . . was the foundation of democratic development in China."[20] He has an extended discussion of Confucius's ideas regarding resistance to "class distinction in education" and "emphasis on Humanism . . . mutual understanding and respect."[21] In the latter regard, Chang explicitly discusses Confucius's attitude toward spiritual things and, "concerning the attitude to worship," cites *Analects* 6:22 ("Respect the Spirit as if the Spirit were there"), which Chang interprets as follows: "In other words it is again that humanistic attitude. It is to respect the Spirit as if it were there—emphasizing the influence of that respect on humanity, and not so much the nature of the Spirit itself which we human beings should be humble enough to acknowledge we do not know."[22] And concluding the lectures, Chang returns to "the possible influence of Chinese humanism on modern thinkers," boldly citing the following passage from *The Great Learning* as "a formula . . . to relate ethics and politics and politics to education," as the "way of creative reorientation . . . for all peoples in the present day world":

In order to bring peace to the world, there must be order in the different countries. In order to bring order in the different countries, the family (social relations) must be regulated. In order to regulate the family (social relations) individuals must be cultivated. In order to cultivate individuals, their hearts must be rectified. In order to rectify their hearts, their thoughts must be made sincere. In order to make their thoughts sincere, they must extend their knowledge. In order to extend their knowledge, they must go to things as they are.[23]

Clearly, for Chang, Dewey's thought and Confucian thought are deeply interpenetrated.

In his three 1946 addresses to the U.N. Economic and Social Council, Chang is equally bold (and arguably Confucian) in his conception of the council's role and practical work. In his first address, Chang contends that the council is "designed for human welfare" and that "cooperative effort in the solution of common problems" requires "a new loyalty on the part of the peoples of the world" to the work of the council. In discussing how to cultivate this new loyalty, Chang cites (first in Chinese, then in English) a passage from *Mencius* IV.B.16—"Subdue people with goodness, people can never be subdued. Nourish people with goodness, the whole world will be subdued." In other words, the important thing is to nourish and stimulate the people, not to try to subdue them (even by the force of virtue). Chang adds: "Nourish people with goodness—that is the function of this Council and the whole world is waiting to be thus subdued."[24]

In his second address, Chang proposes a resolution for calling an international health conference under the auspices of the council. He frames this call in the language of declaring war against microbes "causing and conditioning disease and pestilence in the world." Although he does not here cite any Confucian sources or texts, Chang does call for a "spirit of cooperation" that does not give "too much attention to national differentiation" or "indulge over much in national pride and prejudice," since, after all, microbes "go from place to place without passports, visas, and custom barriers" and "have no sense of national pride or distinction." Suggests Chang, let us learn from these microbial enemies something that is "not undesirable but may even be considered supremely beneficial"—namely, that we are united in our humanity and that the "spirit of cooperation" contributes to "the true blessing of man."[25] No Confucian language here obviously, but certainly a concept of brotherhood and cooperation that is compatible with the Confucian idea of an ever-expanding sympathy or benevolence for the welfare of all humankind.

In his third and longest address, Chang argues vigorously for the Economic and Social Council's giving much-needed assistance to "the economically 'low pressure' areas of the world," citing specifically the less-developed areas in the Middle East, Latin America, and the Far East. In making his case, Chang argues that economic assistance for the industrialization of comparatively under-industrialized countries and peoples will enhance their self-determination and self-reliance; that such industrial development will "spur onward the progress in all [countries]"; that it would be desirable to promulgate "a suggested code of international investments, setting down conditions in lending and borrowing countries . . . conducive to such investments"; and that the council needs to give special attention to the way that the economic changes result in "political, social, and intellectual" changes as well.[26] None of these betray any specifically Confucian ideas—other than the general Confucian concern for the material and social welfare of the people—but it seems significant that Chang concludes his address with an extensive passage attributed to Confucius (from *Li Chi*, Book VII, Li Yun), which he [Chang] characterizes as a "statement of the ideal of economic and social adjustment in the world" and which he interpolates for his audience:

When the Ta Tao or Grand Way prevails, the world is for the welfare of all. Officers are selected because of their virtue and competence. Mutual confidence is promoted and peaceful relations are maintained. People regard not only their own parents as parents, nor only their own children as children. Provisions are made for the aged, employment is provided for the able-bodied, and education is afforded to the young. Widows and widowers, orphans and the childless, the deformed and the diseased, are all cared for. Men have their occupations and women have their homes. Surplus goods are not to be wasted: they need not be kept as one's own. Labor is not to be idle: work is not necessarily for self only. [Please allow me to repeat these phrases— they seem so modern. "Surplus goods are not to be wasted: they need not to be kept as one's own. Labor is not to be idle: work is not necessarily for self only."] Scheming and intrigues are repressed and banditry and rebellion do not arise. As a result, there is no need of shutting the house-gate at night. Such is the Age of Grand Harmony.[27]

In retrospect, and in light of this passage, I suggest that Chang's development proposals are very much a modern articulation of a central Confucian ideal for a harmonious world that serves the welfare of people everywhere.

Considering all of the above, I believe that we can find the following traits in Chang, the last three of which are particularly carried into his work on the UDHR:

1. An abiding commitment to modernization in Chinese education, society, and culture, construed along the lines of Dewey's thought, self-critically combining aspects of old and new.
2. A passionate commitment to the humanistic elements and vision of Confucian thought.
3. A deep interest in constructive comparative thought that attempts to reconcile the humanistic values of the Confucian tradition with those of Western traditions.
4. A propensity to use Confucian ideas to advance his case for self-critical and humanized modernization in the world.

UNIVERSAL DECLARATION OF HUMAN RIGHTS

Strategic Contributions

The historical record shows that Chang argued vigorously and successfully for the position that the UDHR should (1) be conceived as the basis and program for the humanization of mankind (here Chang appealed to the Confucian idea of man's moral nature or capacity to become truly human in the sense of moral growth and achievement); (2) incorporate a large measure of pragmatic agreement on norms of conduct despite persisting differences of philosophy and ideology among peoples of the world (here Chang appealed to the Confucian emphasis on the art of living—as contrasted with metaphysics—together with making the argument that no representatives should insist on including controverted metaphysical or theological concepts in the declaration); and (3) be written in a manner readily comprehensible to all people (here Chang implicitly used the Confucian emphasis on the priority of the people to support his view that the UDHR was to be a people's document, not a scholar's or a lawyer's).

Before examining these three points in a bit more detail, it should be remarked that, unlike many of the other more politically motivated representatives to the Third Committee, Chang's contributions to its deliberations on the UDHR were almost uniformly philosophical and ethical in character. Indeed, the historical record reports at one point that "the Chinese representative felt that ethical considerations should play a greater part in the discussion. The question was not purely political."[28] That is to say, Chang attempted to argue for positions based on his understanding of Confucian philosophy and ethics and what they could contribute to constructive debate about, and resolution of, philosophical differences between representatives.

With regard to the humanistic aims of the UDHR, Chang had earlier expressed his view before the U.N. Economic and Social Council (February 1947) that any declaration developed should be based on "the aspiration for a new humanism."[29]

In September 1948, during the Third Committee deliberations, he elaborated on this view considerably by claiming, first, that "in the eighteenth century . . . in Europe, translations of Chinese philosophers had been known to and had inspired such thinkers as Voltaire, Quesnay and Diderot in their humanistic revolt against feudalistic conceptions," to such an extent that "Chinese ideas had been intermingled with European thought and sentiment on human rights at the time when that subject had been first speculated upon in modern Europe." This claim was immediately followed by another, that "stress should be laid upon the human aspect of human rights. A human being had to be constantly conscious of other men, in whose society he lived," resulting in Chang's concluding and ringing statement that "the declaration should be approved as soon as possible, to serve as a basis and a programme for the humanization of man."[30] The point here is not to raise for scrutiny the accuracy or inaccuracy of Chang's first historical claim but rather to show that he quite self-consciously tried to link the Confucian idea of man's moral capacity to the notion of human rights as a development of that very capacity, both in the past and for the future.[31] This linkage of human rights and humanization was an important theme in many of Chang's subsequent interventions, and it went unchallenged.

On the matter of pragmatic agreement on norms despite differences in philosophy and ideology, Chang, again, had introduced this idea earlier before the Economic and Social Council in 1947: "The fact that rights of man were included in thirty-five or forty of the world's constitutions indicated that a large measure of agreement was possible in spite of differences of philosophy or ideology."[32] He also effectively developed this idea further in the Third Committee by stoutly resisting the incorporation of any language that would raise "metaphysical problems" in "a declaration designed to be universally applicable."[33] Here Chang argued that "in the field of human rights popular majority should not be forgotten," adumbrating as follows: "The Chinese representative recalled that the population of his country comprised a large segment of humanity . . . [with] . . . ideals and traditions different from those of the Christian West . . . [e.g.] good manners, decorum, propriety, and consideration for others."[34] Yet, despite the importance of the latter to the Chinese, he "would refrain from proposing that mention of them should be made in the declaration," with the hope "that his colleagues would show equal consideration and withdraw some of the amendments . . . raising metaphysical problems."[35] A subsequent intervention against those wishing to import a theological foundation to the UDHR put the point eloquently and subtly: "without these words [e.g., "God," "natural law," "by nature"] . . . those who believed in God could still find the idea of God [if they wished to so interpret], and at the same time others with different concepts would be able to accept the text [since theology was not its basis]."[36] Chang's point was clearly that pragmatic agreement was possible despite persisting differences of philosophy, theology, and metaphysics.[37] His point and argument carried through the remainder of the Third Committee's deliberations.

Finally, it should be observed that Chang was a great and consistent advocate of having a brief declaration readily understandable by all, which he reported was the rationale for the Chinese delegation's original submission of a ten-article declaration for consideration by the Commission on Human Rights. Although the final draft declaration before the Third Committee was more than twice this length, Chang was nonetheless able to claim that the Chinese "document had aided in making the present draft declaration clear and relatively brief."[38] Time and time again, during the deliberations of the Third Committee, Chang returned to this point of comprehensibility to all people; for example, "It should be a document for all men everywhere, not merely for lawyers and scholars"; "as the declaration was destined for the vast mass of the world's population, it should never be criticized for being too explicit"; not to mention his innumerable interventions stressing the need for "concrete" language, paragraphing of articles that avoided "expressing two sets of ideas in a single paragraph," and "careful consideration

of amendments" in the spirit of the Chinese proverb, "Matters allowed to mature slowly are free from sharp corners."[39] All of these interventions, I interpolate, expressed Chang's great respect for the Confucian emphasis on the importance of the people, whom the UDHR was being designed to serve.

Specific Articles

The historical record also shows that Chang used specifically Confucian ideas to support, and indeed reformulate, various articles of the UDHR.[40] For example, he appealed to Confucian concepts of human moral capacity and *jen* (two-men-mindedness, benevolence) to forward and formulate the claims of Article 1 about the dignity of human beings and acting in the spirit of brotherhood. He used the Confucian orientation toward moral pragmatism to support what he called "pluralistic tolerance" of thought, conscience, and religious belief protected by Article 18. He implicitly used the Confucian emphasis on the importance of the people and explicitly appealed to the tradition's experience with competitive civil service to support, respectively, governance based on the will of the people and equal access to public service forwarded by Article 21. And, for a final example, he appealed to the Confucian emphasis on duties to community to support the balancing of rights with duties in Article 29. Let us now consider Chang's contributions to these illustrative articles in greater detail.

With regard to Article 1, it is reported in some secondary literature that, within the drafting committee's deliberations, which preceded those of the full Third Committee, Chang had argued for the inclusion of *jen* (humaneness) in addition to the ideas of human dignity, rights, and reason.[41] In the fuller, more public, and more completely reported deliberations of the Third Committee, the reasoning behind Chang's earlier contributions was much more developed. First, it became clear that for Chang the idea of *jen* was encapsulated in the phrase "the spirit of brotherhood," which, he claimed, "was perfectly consistent with the Chinese attitude towards manners [*li*] and the importance of kindly and considerate treatment of others [*jen*], wherein both *li* and *jen* were related by him to man's capacity to become truly human—"It was only when man's social behavior rose to that level that he was truly human."[42]

Second, it also became clear that for Chang the language of "the spirit of brotherhood" counterbalanced the statement of rights in this article. Chang explicitly claimed, "A happy balance was struck by the broad statement of rights in the first sentence and the implication of duties in the second," accomplishing the article's important function that "the various rights [of the full declaration] would appear more selfish if they were not preceded by the reference to 'a spirit of brotherhood.'"[43] That is to say, for Chang, "spirit of brotherhood" connoted duties to others in such a manner that human rights and duties were importantly and appropriately interdependent.

Finally, in the Third Committee's debate about whether Article 1 should incorporate metaphysical or theological concepts, Chang made the crucial mediating intervention that it would be acceptable to understand the article on the basis of eighteenth-century European philosophy's claim about man's innate goodness, implying that "although man was largely animal, there was a part of him which distinguished him from the animals. That part was the real man and was good, and that part should therefore be given greater importance" (compare *Mencius* VI.A.14).[44] Why would this be acceptable to Chang? Because this idea was consistent also with the Confucian idea that "human beings" refers to the "non-animal part of man," wherein man has the capacity to "increase his moral stature," "reach a high moral standard," and rise to "that level where he was truly human."[45] By proposing this link between European and Chinese philosophy, Chang effectively quelled further effort to build into the declaration any stronger metaphysical or theological concepts. Collectively considered, the foregoing three points appear to present a genuine Confucian contribution to the formulation and adoption of Article 1.

With respect to Article 18, Chang made another distinctive Confucian contribution to the Third Committee's deliberations, one that

may be somewhat surprising, given the often-cited, though myopic, view that Confucianism is hostile to religious tolerance.[46] Amid the heated debate over protecting the freedom of religious belief, most pointedly the freedom to change one's religious adherence—a point of grave contention between the Saudi and Pakistani delegates representing conflicting Islamic views on the question—Chang introduced his view of another important link between East and West. First, he affirmed that this article dealt with "one of the most important principles in the declaration," stemming "from the eighteenth century, when the idea of human rights was born in Western Europe."[47] Second, in the interest of "studying the problem of religious expression in its true perspective," he wished to explain "how the Chinese approached the religious problem."[48]

What followed was a Confucian-informed argument in five steps:[49] (1) "Chinese philosophy was based essentially on a firm belief in a unitarian cause" [a reference to intra-worldly, organic cosmology]. (2) "That philosophy considered man's actions [also called by Chang "the art of living"] to be more important than metaphysics" [also called by him "knowledge of the causes of life"]. (3) "The best way to testify to the greatness of the Divinity [used by Chang in an all-encompassing way to refer to both theistic and non-theistic beliefs] was to give proof of an exemplary attitude in this world." (4) "In the eyes of Chinese philosophers, it was pluralistic tolerance in every sphere of thought, conscience, and religion, which should inspire men if they wished to base their relations on benevolence and justice" (the exemplary attitude or art of living). (5) QED: against "the objection of the representative from Saudi Arabia," freedom of religious belief was to be protected. To which Chang added the pragmatically compelling point: not "to ensure the inviolability of that profound part of thought and conscience . . . was apt to lead mankind into unreasoned conflict." Shortly after this intervention, Article 18 was adopted by the Third Committee.

Chang's Confucian background also played a large role in his support for Article 21, sometimes explicitly, but often implicitly.[50] It was certainly the case that on numerous occasions at the Economic and Social Council Chang invoked the Chinese experience with "the institution of public civil service," which he claimed had "not yet been realized in the Western world," to support "the right of free and equal access to public service" in one's country.[51] I take the Confucian-inspired influence here to be reasonably uncontroversial.

By the same token, although he strongly supported the principle that "the will of the people shall be the basis of the authority of government," to the extent of proposing that "the will of the people" should be "the subject of the first clause" of subparagraph 3, Chang did not explicitly mention or discuss the Confucian idea of the priority of the people over the ruler or government (as so strongly asserted in Confucian and neo-Confucian texts).[52] Perhaps the closest he came to invoking this idea was when, in his 1947 contribution to the Economic and Social Council, he tied together the ideas of public civil service, representative government, and freedom and equality forming "the basis of social democracy," when referring to the then new 1946 Chinese constitution.[53] This, of course, is hardly convincing evidence, if indeed it is evidence at all, of a Confucian influence. However, I must say that throughout all of his interventions in the Third Committee, including those discussed above, Chang made it utterly clear that the people were his priority. This principle may have been so deeply formative in his thinking—and acceptable to so many other representatives—that he did not feel the need to invoke its Confucian background.

Finally, with respect to Article 29, we return to one of Chang's contributions to Article 1—the notion of balancing rights and duties in the UDHR.[54] In supporting that "happy balance" of explicit human rights and implicit duties (in "the spirit of brotherhood") in Article 1, Chang claimed that "similar reasoning applied to Article [29], which contained a statement of duties."[55] Inasmuch as the "duties to community" mentioned in Article 29 were thereby related to Chang's fuller claim that "the aims of the U.N. were not to ensure the selfish gains of the individual but to try and increase man's

moral stature," for "consciousness of duties enable man to reach a high moral standard," I believe that we have here reasonably clear evidence of a Confucian idea in support of this article. [56]

Comparative Philosophy

Beyond this discussion of Chang's interventions in the Third Committee's deliberations, there are certain philosophical points that may be of particular interest to comparative philosophers. For example, although he referred time and again to the concept of *li* (rites, customs, manners) as central to Confucian ethics, Chang nevertheless clearly accepted the conceptuality of individual rights, so long as these were balanced with duties to the community in a way that would function to increase man's moral stature. For a second example, reiterating a point discussed earlier, although at one time in the deliberations tempted to take no position on the nature of man ("for the purposes of the declaration it was better to start with a clean state"), Chang finally supported the text of Article 1 (referring to human dignity, brotherhood, and rights) understood on the basis of eighteenth-century European philosophy incorporating the idea of man's innate goodness, which he regarded as similar to the Confucian idea that the part of man distinguishing him from the animals is his moral nature, his innate capacity for moral achievement.[57] This similarity was apparently regarded by Chang as an important normative link between Western and Eastern philosophy that could be safely affirmed by both, so long as it was kept clear of any other metaphysical and theological ideas.

What is particularly interesting and important about Chang's Confucian contributions to the debates of the Third Committee is the fact that he often appeared to be engaging in constructive comparative ethics. That is to say, he self-consciously tried to find normative and conceptual bridges between Confucian moral thought and Western European philosophy in a way that forged new angles of vision on both traditions and how they might learn from each other.[58] Cases in point included, for example, (1) linking human rights to humanization (thus producing an understanding of human rights as contributory to mankind's moral growth and maturation, an advance over some Western conceptions of rights as no more than protective fences around individuals); (2) emphasizing the interdependence of rights and duties (thus opening the Confucian tradition to a new, moral-conceptual category [rights] while also reminding Western traditions that rights alone were not conducive to genuine community); (3) highlighting the significance of "the spirit of brotherhood" as a moral concept shared by both East and West (prompting both to take the concept more seriously); (4) identifying mankind's moral capacity as another philosophical bridge or similarity between East and West (which both could profitably explore further in the common project of human rights' humanization of the world); (5) demonstrating how freedom of religion could be soundly protected by both Eastern and Western traditions (in a manner that did not require adopting any specific set of religious premises or beliefs—a model for future cooperation and interaction); and (6) demonstrating how Eastern and Western traditions could agree on certain fundamentals of humane governance (e.g., priority of the will of the people, equal access to public service, implying that neither tradition had a special premium on how to understand humane governance).

Equally important, perhaps, as these constructive achievements were those lines of argument that Chang did not pursue—whether by choice or inadvertence is difficult to determine. He did not, for example, attempt to substitute *li* (rites, customs) for the category of rights or to argue for *li*'s moral superiority, as I believe some Western scholars of Confucianism have attempted to do. He did not argue for the priority of socioeconomic human rights over civil-political rights, as, again, some Western scholars of Confucianism are tempted to do. He did not claim that, as a communitarian tradition, Confucianism was somehow conceptually incompatible with human-rights thinking and advocacy, as, once again, some Western scholars are tempted to claim.[59] Why did Chang not pursue such lines of argument when they seem so obvious to others familiar with the tradition? Was he, for example, so steeped in his Western education that he was blinded to these moves? I personally doubt that this is the right sort of answer, given the extent and subtlety of Chang's Confucian interventions.

A better answer perhaps is this: Chang saw both Confucianism and the West as evolving traditions, originally formed by different historical, political, and social circumstances and yet sharing the same world, equally vulnerable to cruelty, bestiality, inhumanity of man to man, and linked in that bond of vulnerability. Furthermore, in confronting the issues before the Third Committee, Chang came increasingly to appreciate certain similarities of moral thought and action, East and West, which together formed a bridge for intercultural exchange and pragmatic agreement on the really important issues of the postwar world. And he wagered that strengthening and widening that bridge—or at least keeping it open—would allow both traditions to learn from each other, to change and evolve at least to the extent that they could actively cooperate in the grand project of the world's humanization. If Chang so wagered, and I believe he did, then his position is one I share, and one we all can at least appreciate.

A Bahá'í Perspective on the Universal Declaration of Human Rights by the World's Religions

Brian D. Lepard

I would like to comment on the various insightful points raised by Arvind Sharma and to do so from a Bahá'í perspective. These represent my own personal reflections as a Bahá'í and as a scholar of international human-rights law. First, I wish to thank Arvind Sharma and all those religion scholars and believers who have contributed to crafting such a thoughtful and important document—a document that seeks to achieve the type of integration of the best that international law and religion can mutually offer to the critical problem of making human rights a reality for all human beings.

Turning to the first of the three reasons that Sharma has advanced for producing the Universal Declaration of Human Rights by the World's Religions (see Appendix), he emphasizes that "it would be in the interest of everyone if the various religions of the world acted in concert instead of working against each other." The Bahá'í teachings similarly endorse religious amity. Bahá'u'lláh, the prophet-founder of the Bahá'í Faith, counseled: "Consort with the followers of all religions in a spirit of friendliness and fellowship."[1]

Bahá'ís believe that interreligious fellowship is not only a prudent means of ensuring peaceful coexistence among members of different faiths,

but a divine command. This command originates from the fact that, in the Bahá'í view, all the world's great religions represent guidance from one divine source. All their founders have been inspired educators sent by that source, often referred to as God, to provide unerring moral guidance to humanity. In the words of 'Abdu'l-Bahá, the son of Bahá'u'lláh and the authorized interpreter of his teachings, "Blessed souls—whether Moses, Jesus, Zoroaster, Krishna, Buddha, Confucius, or Muhammad—were the cause of the illumination of the world of humanity. . . . All of them have sacrificed life, endured ordeals and tribulations in order that They might educate us."[2] And he further stated: "All the holy Manifestations of God have proclaimed and promulgated the same reality. They have summoned mankind to reality itself, and reality is one."[3] For these reasons, Bahá'ís have vigorously supported interfaith activities aimed at promoting the discovery and reaffirmation of this common reality proclaimed by all the world religions. Indeed, the basis for this interfaith discourse must be a common conviction that "God is one and that, beyond all diversity of cultural expression and human interpretation, religion is likewise one." These are words from a recent statement by the international governing body of the Bahá'í faith, the Universal House of Justice, to the world's religious leaders, issued in April 2002.[4]

Nevertheless, there are clearly also reasons of expediency for promoting interreligious cooperation, particularly on a common affirmation of human rights. Not the least of these is that religious prejudice, sometimes taking the form of fanaticism but more often the form of a claim to exclusive access to truth, is on the ascension. And it is one of the last forms of prejudice still to enjoy general credibility. This fact is highlighted by the April 2002 statement of the Universal House of Justice, which notes that for a brief period of time after the first Parliament of Religions held in 1893 at the Columbian Exposition in Chicago, which the statement praises, it seemed that the world would be emancipated from religious bigotry. But in recent years, those hopes have dimmed. The statement affirms: "The greater part of organized religion stands paralyzed at the threshold of the future, gripped in those very dogmas and claims of privileged access to truth that have been responsible for creating some of the most bitter conflicts dividing the earth's inhabitants."[5]

For all these reasons, it might be fruitful, as Sharma has recognized, to encourage further interreligious collaboration on the Universal Declaration of Human Rights by the World's Religions. In particular, it might be helpful for representatives of different faiths to identify scriptural passages that support the principles elaborated in each article and to work together to prepare an anthology of these passages. Such an endeavor would provide an opportunity for members of various faiths better to perceive the common moral principles in their sacred texts.

The second reason Sharma proposes for supporting the religious Universal Declaration is that the "two main sources of value formation in the world today" are the moral values "embedded in the various religious traditions of the world" and the "liberal humanistic secular traditions" prevalent in the West. He views the UN's Universal Declaration of Human Rights as primarily a product of the latter secular tradition and astutely asks: "Why not also harness the moral resources of the

religious traditions of humanity when they also share many elements of the vision articulated in" the UN's Universal Declaration? This would provide, he argues, another source of inspiration to realize the Universal Declaration's ideals of human dignity and even to broaden these ideals.

Bahá'ís would emphatically agree with Sharma's arguments and might even extend his argument. For Bahá'ís believe that religiously inspired values must support any beneficial concept of human rights. Further, as a matter of history, the so-called secular views of human rights that evolved out of the Enlightenment can be traced to moral principles articulated by the world religions, including Judaism, Christianity, and Islam, as many scholars have demonstrated. And every major world religion has taught, explicitly or implicitly, the concept of human rights, as I have pointed out in my book *Rethinking Humanitarian Intervention*.[6] The promulgation of the teachings of every world religion has led to great advances in respect for human rights in those cultures in which their seeds were planted, even if followers have also perverted those teachings for their own petty and sometimes malicious ends. To take one example, the teachings of Islam spread abroad the principle of religious tolerance, and for well over a millennium granted women far more rights than they enjoyed in the Western Christian world.

For these reasons, it is imperative that the world religions lend their voice and their unique moral perspective to efforts to implement the UN's Universal Declaration. Indeed, the world's leaders must turn to religious inspiration if human-rights ideals are to be made reality. Regarding the role of religion in society, Bahá'u'lláh affirmed: "Religion is verily the chief instrument for the establishment of order in the world and of tranquility amongst its peoples."[7] The Universal House of Justice stated in its letter to the world's religious leaders that religion "reaches to the roots of motivation. When it has been faithful to the spirit and example of the transcendent Figures who gave the world its great belief systems, it has awakened in whole populations capacities to love, to forgive, to create, to dare greatly, to overcome prejudice, to sacrifice for the common good and to discipline the impulses of animal instinct."[8] Bahá'ís are convinced it is inconceivable that we can fashion a world free of human rights violations in a spiritual vacuum and through ideologies of human invention, including a purely secular theory of human rights.

As Sharma has suggested, a religious perspective on human rights can offer important and very unique contributions to the principles already laid down in contemporary international human-rights law. It can do so in a number of ways. First, the scriptures of the world religions articulate as a cardinal moral principle the unity of the human family, as I explore at greater length in *Rethinking Humanitarian Intervention*.[9] This principle of unity provides a secure foundation not only for the recognition of the inherent rights of every human being but also for the existence of *individual duties* to promote and protect the human rights of others. In the words of the Universal House of Justice, the "scriptures of all religions have always taught the believer to see in service to others not only a moral duty, but an avenue for the soul's own approach to God."[10] By contrast, international legal documents, such as the UN's Universal Declaration, primarily stress (and recognize) only the duties of governments to promote human rights. In this connection, an innovative and commendable feature of the religious Universal Declaration is that it places great emphasis on the duties of each individual to take concrete steps to implement the rights it asserts.

The third justification offered by Sharma for promulgating a Universal Declaration of Human Rights by the World's Religions is that religious extremism is on the rise, as horrifyingly demonstrated by the attacks of September 11, 2001, in the United States as well as the attacks of March 11, 2004, in Spain, and that the adoption of the religious Universal Declaration might help stem the tide of religious fanaticism. This is also a laudable objective from a Bahá'í perspective. The Bahá'í writings unequivocally condemn religious hatred and zealotry. The Universal House of Justice has referred to "the horrors being visited upon hapless populations today by outbursts of fanaticism that shame the name of religion."[11] It is essential for the leaders of the world's religions to step forward, roundly condemn acts of extremism committed in the names of their religions, and foster among their followers a spirit of camaraderie with members of other faiths, in keeping with the unadulterated verities and teachings of their own scriptures. Otherwise, as the Universal House of Justice warned in 2002, "With every day that passes, danger grows that the rising fires of religious prejudice will ignite a worldwide conflagration the consequences of which are unthinkable."[12]

In keeping with these broad principles, it might be possible to refine certain specific draft articles of the religious Universal Declaration. For example, in view of the essential role of religiously inspired moral principles in bringing about respect for human rights, the third preambular paragraph might be reworded to convey a more positive emphasis, such as, "Whereas the world religions are positive resources for human rights and ought to be turned to as sources of guidance and inspiration in the conceptualization and implementation of human rights." Second, it might be possible to add a preambular paragraph affirming the unity of the human family as a basis for recognizing fundamental human rights. Third, with respect to Article 26, it might be helpful to include a paragraph promoting interreligious understanding through education, and in particular education in the common moral values shared by the world religions. Last, with respect to Article 29, dealing with duties, it might be possible to add a new paragraph clearly stating that everyone has a duty to promote and help protect the human rights of others. As I have emphasized, this is a unique aspect of a religiously based moral approach to human rights.

In closing, let me underscore the tremendous value of the process of formulating and disseminating the Universal Declaration of Human Rights by the World's Religions, especially after the events of September 11, and I wholeheartedly congratulate all those who have participated in its drafting, including Arvind Sharma.[13]

WORLD'S RELIGIONS, HUMAN RIGHTS, AND SAME-SEX MARRIAGE

Brent Hawkes
Janet Epp Buckingham
Douglas Elliott
Margaret Somerville

BRENT HAWKES

I'm here partly because of my thirty years of involvement in gay and lesbian human-rights movements here in Canada, and as pastor of a church in Toronto that has a special ministry to the gay and lesbian community, and that has also been at the forefront for rights for gays and lesbians. We see a trend throughout the world in many of the world's religions: gay and lesbian participants no longer being satisfied with being pushed out of those religions but wanting to reclaim their opportunity to be part of those faith traditions, to celebrate their spirituality while celebrating their sexuality. The difficulty has been that, for many of our traditional religions, our viewpoints are based on ancient scriptures, ancient texts, when very little was known about homosexuality. And some of the biases and the ignorance of that era have been brought into modern times and the religions of today.

More specifically, I'm here because of the work that our church has done around the issue of equal marriage. We were the first church to have legally recognized the weddings of same-sex male and female couples, on January 14, 2001. A very short history: Through the publication of bannas,

the Ontario Marriage Act says that any two persons can be married, and so on January 14, we had those ceremonies. The government refused to recognize them and refused to register them, so we took them to court. We won the original court case, then we won the appeal, and then the federal government decided not to appeal that to the Supreme Court, and ultimately our Parliament affirmed those decisions.

Since then, the Netherlands, Belgium, Spain, and Massachusetts, and soon, South Africa will have put in law the recognition of same-sex marriage. And here in Canada, we're supported by the largest Protestant denomination, the United Church of Canada, by the Unitarian congregations, and by Hebrew rabbis among others.

When one religion tries to take its perspective and restrict the rights of other religions, then we get into great difficulty. And as an example of that difficulty, there is a bulletproof vest that I had to wear by order of the police when I performed those marriages in 2001. I happen to own it because I've had to wear it on a number of occasions. This is what we do to each other. Seventeen of our churches have been burned to the ground.

The movement for the rights of gays and lesbians in Canada has seen two groups opposed consistently. The public-opinion polls tell us that one group is made up of people who say they don't know anyone who is gay or lesbian. And as that group has declined over the years, as gay people have come out, then support for our causes has risen. What has remained constant is the opposition based on religious reasons. One of the leading legalistic Protestants, Brian Stiller, said in an article that the law in society has two purposes. One is to confine behavior—don't steal. The second is to be instructive in society—stealing is bad. And fundamentalists want the law to say homosexuality is bad. And they have wanted that at every level. The idea that our civil laws should reflect a specific religious viewpoint is scary, and this idea leads to state-sanctioned tyranny of beliefs. We should, all of us, be scared, because it means the majority religious view in any one country could dictate public policy against all other minorities. In the movement toward equal marriage in Canada, we've not been asking any faith tradition, any denomination, to make any changes. Indeed, we have sought to protect the right of denominations and clergy who do not wish to perform equal marriage to have the protection that they not be forced to do so. So while we are trying to expand equal rights to include our religious perspectives, at the same time, we're trying to protect the rights of others who disagree with us.

Homosexuality has been viewed by Dr. Boivert and others as the last acceptable hatred by religions. We have recently seen one rare example of religious leaders in the city of Jerusalem come together and make a joint statement. Very rarely does that happen. But recently they did so to condemn a pride celebration in the city of Jerusalem. And a reward was offered—not by the religious leaders—for the killing of a gay person who came to that parade. Fortunately, no killings occurred. Two thousand gay and lesbian people have been executed in Iran since 1979 purely for religious reasons. And there have been killings and bashings here in North America, spurred on by the religious Right. The Declaration for Human Rights that has been drafted for the world religions is a wonderful, wonderful step in the right direction. And I would hope that we would be able to find a way to disagree theologically on issues, to disagree on public positions, but that we might find a way to do that which doesn't lead to bulletproof vests, that doesn't lead to the denial of human rights, that we could be secure enough in our own religious perspectives that we can allow others who differ from us to be able to have their place as well, and that the civil laws of our land would not reflect one religious perspective to the exclusion of others. Thank you.

Janet Epp Buckingham

Marriage is one of those complex institutions that is both deeply religious and yet is often recognized by the state. In Canada, as in a lot of other countries, not all, but in many countries, it's a shared responsibility between the church or other religious institutions and the state. Seventy-five percent of marriages in Canada are solemnized by clergy, so clearly it is considered a deeply religious institution. It wasn't very many years ago when the church was actually the institution that solemnized all marriages. And if you wanted to go back and track your ancestry and find birth and death certificates, it could only be done through churches. Now, the state has taken on more responsibility on the issue of marriage, which makes us realize how complex this issue is, when we're saying, "What's the state's responsibility for marriage, and what is religion's responsibility for marriage?"

The issue of the definition of marriage, and therefore the nature of marriage, has been debated in Canada for over a decade. It has been an extremely divisive debate, and I can tell you that there are wounded souls on both sides of the issue. In essence, the debate really narrowed down to two possible definitions of marriage, and only one could ultimately predominate. The first definition is the one recognized around the world. Until recently, when someone said to you they were married, it was a given that it was a person of the opposite sex, whether you were Hindu or Muslim or Christian or atheist or any other of the world's religions. If you were married, it was to someone of the opposite sex. This definition of marriage has deep roots in religion and culture. Underlying this understanding of marriage is the recognition that marriage has the expectation of children. Indeed, until about the 1960s, there was little one could do to prevent children resulting from marriage. This is not to denigrate childless marriages but simply to recognize that we make public policy on norms, not on the exceptions. The understanding of marriage as being at the root of families and the raising of children has important implications for how marriage is nurtured and sustained in a culture. Now marriage is understood to involve sacrifice, both sacrifice for one's spouse and sacrifice for the benefit of one's children. Marriage, as historically understood, does not necessarily involve romantic love. Indeed, in many cultures until even now, marriages are still arranged by parents for their children. Marriage is an alliance for the future of the children, and the future of that family.

Much of this has changed in the West. You must understand that to redefine marriage to include same-sex couples requires that one first redefine the understanding of marriage. Marriage is about the two people involved. It does not necessarily involve the bearing and raising of children. In fact, when this issue came before the courts in Canada, the judges ruled that it was abhorrent to say that marriage involved procreation or that it was an important incident of marriage. In this understanding of marriage, it is about affirming the loving, committed relationship between two adults. This means that to exclude any loving, committed couple from marriage is discriminatory and offensive. This understanding of marriage has important implications for how marriage is nurtured and sustained in the culture. If it is about recognizing and affirming romantic love, does this mean the state has a responsibility to encourage ongoing romance? Does it necessitate easy divorce laws so that couple who no longer have romantic feelings for one another can separate and divorce? It raises issues about the state's interest in marriage.

During the debate and discussion on the definition of marriage, I was asked over and over again, "How would this change your marriage to include same-sex couples in the definition of marriage? How could making marriage more inclusive

harm the institution?" The answer is that redefining marriage has huge implications for how it is nurtured and sustained in the culture. If it is nurtured in its traditional or historic form, it is sustained as the foundation for the raising of children. It is family-centered. But if it is nurtured in its new form, it is about the couple, and that is very different. In Canada, we have seen the implications very clearly of the impact on those who hold to the historic definition of marriage once marriage is redefined. Because some of us continue—and I speak for many in the evangelical Christian community—because we continue to recognize marriage as an institution between a man and a woman in a family-centered way and refuse to recognize the new definition in our communities, we are marginalized. This is very serious, and I consider it the biggest threat to religious freedom in Canada.

Recently, the Becket Fund for Religious Liberty, a U.S.-based religious liberty organization, held a symposium on the impact on religious freedom of changing the definition of marriage. They included academics from both sides of the debate. Interestingly, it was academics who supported same-sex marriage who anticipated the most serious impact on religious freedom. These academics view those of us who hold to a traditional view as being the same as racists. Therefore, they would support restrictions on our views of marriage and on our ability to communicate these views in public. Some of the restrictions they foresee include refusal of government funding, tax benefits, and even building permits for religious institutions that refuse to recognize same-sex marriage if it is legalized.

Let me share with you briefly some of the legal issues that have arisen in Canada in the aftermath of the redefinition of marriage. A Catholic men's club faced a legal challenge after refusing to rent their hall to a lesbian couple for a wedding reception. A Catholic bishop faced a legal challenge—in Canada it is called a human-rights complaint—for what he said in a pastoral letter on issues related to homosexual practice and same-sex marriage. A Christian teacher and a Christian university professor have both been disciplined for comments made and published outside the classroom on related issues. Civil officials who solemnize nonreligious marriages have been required to solemnize same-sex marriage or they lose their jobs. School curricula are being revised to reflect the new definition of marriage. Teachers have been told they may not opt out of this material. Parents and students have similarly been told that they may not opt out of classes where this material is being taught. Dr. Somerville—I don't believe she's going to mention this, so I will—Dr. Somerville personally experienced, when she was awarded an honorary doctorate at Ryerson University, a campaign to marginalize her for her views on same-sex marriage. She was protested against, and some of the professors turned their backs on her when she was given an honorary doctoral award. These examples are not all directly related to the definition of marriage, but it's been a factor in the marginalization of the voices of people of faith.

When this issue was being debated in Canada, those from the religious communities who raised alarm bells about this and the potential infringement of our rights were assured that these kinds of issues will not arise. We were told that this was not about enforcing one view of marriage. We were told there would be room in our society for more than one view of marriage. But as we expected, this has not been the case. When the definition of marriage is changed, it follows that the state will enforce and reinforce the new definition of marriage. This seems to necessitate restricting and restraining those who hold to the previous and near-universal definition of marriage.

I think it's clear to everyone that there's a wide variety of religious expression. Some hold to a fairly strict interpretation of their sacred texts. Some are more free and liberal with their interpretation. I do not believe this body, this conference, would argue—and I hope that no one in this room would argue—that those who hold to a more strict interpretation are wrong and should face sanctions in society for holding their views. Evangelical Christians, for example, who number approximately 420 million worldwide, hold to the Bible as the authority in life for faith and religious practice. We derive our understanding of marriage from the creation narratives, from references in the Old Testament, from the words of Jesus Christ, and subsequent instruction from the apostles. These point us to marriage as a monogamous, lifelong union between one man and one woman. All would point to this as our common understanding of marriage. This being a given, we cannot and will not deviate from this definition of marriage, and we cannot adopt a different definition of marriage. We will not accept polygamy, we do not accept those who live together in common-law unions, and we will not accept same-sex marriage. We do not accept our children being indoctrinated into this new view of marriage, and society will try to enforce it on our children. We do not accept being marginalized and being called homophobic and bigots because we espouse certain views about marriage. We will not allow our facilities to be used to celebrate marriage that we do not recognize. Should we, then, face discrimination? The same reasoning that I have just explained for evangelical Christians also applies to Roman Catholics, most Muslims, and many other religious traditions. The implication of changing the definition of marriage is to exclude and marginalize those religious groups who hold to traditional views on marriage. This includes not only my religious tradition but many, many others. One cannot endorse changing the definition of marriage without recognizing the serious implications for the marginalization of minority, and sometimes even majority, religious groups. Thank you.

DOUGLAS ELLIOTT

Marriage is a legal institution, and the right to marry is a legal question. That is so withstanding that marriage is a religious institution in many faiths. The issue of same-sex marriage does raise profound questions about the relationship between the law and religion and about the role of the law in regulating marriage. It will be my contention in these brief remarks that the optimal legal regime is one that permits same-sex couples to marry under the same laws that recognize the right of opposite-sex couples to marry. The historical record makes

121

it clear that the law has been used in the past to improperly restrict access to marriage based on the enforcement of the majority's religious values, at times allied with pseudoscientific notions of the public good. Laws restricting same-sex marriage arose out of traditional religious rules that should not be used to justify restrictions on the liberty of adults to choose their marriage partners in the civil-law system in the twenty-first century. There are no compelling reasons other than religious ones to justify such restrictions.

Religion and law operate in overlapping but distinct spheres, as reflected in Jesus Christ's famous injunction to render unto Caesar that which is Caesar's. In the European systems that are the foundation of the laws of Canada and many other countries, the Roman Catholic Church was once the exclusive regulator of marriage. However, beginning with Henry VIII in England and with the French Revolution in France, both the common-law and civil-law systems have either recognized the supremacy of the state in regulating marriage in the one case or its exclusive power to regulate marriage in the other. Accordingly, the exclusion of the pope from control over the legal institution of marriage did not arise recently, nor in the context of same-same marriage. It is in fact a matter of great antiquity. There's a historic pattern of the state, however, granting special rights to the religious majority in matters of marriage. In this province, under French rule, Protestant marriages did not exist legally. Only Catholic marriages were legally recognized. Similarly, in my home province of Ontario, at one time, only Protestant marriages were legally recognized. Catholic marriages were meaningless to the state, let alone Jewish, Muslim, and other non-Christian marriages.

Most people today would agree that this kind of religious discrimination has no place in the marriage laws of any modern democracy. Marriage laws should respect human rights, freedom of religion, and the dignity of allowing every adult to choose whom to marry based on their own religious beliefs, if any. Laws banning interracial marriage were historically similarly grounded on the social majority's religious notions. In a case decided in the 1960s, *Loving v. Virginia,* the Virginia court reflected traditional views about God, marriage, and race when it said the following: "Almighty God created the races white, black, yellow, malay and red, and he placed them on separate continents, and but for the interference with His arrangement there would be no cause for such marriages. The fact that He separated the races shows that he did not intend for the races to mix." In the case of racial discrimination in marriage, science was also enlisted as an ally, genetics in particular. It was argued that interracial marriages would be bad for children and society because these unions would produce so-called mongrel children that would be genetically inferior. Once again, today I doubt many Christians would share those religious beliefs reflected in those judges' remarks, nor would many scientists propound those particular views on genetics.

This concept that the religious values of the majority should control the legal institution of marriage informs the common-law rule that has been used in many countries, and until recently, in Canada, to limit marriage to opposite-sex couples. It was pronounced back in 1866, in the case of *Hyde v. Hyde,* pronounced by a judge, not by a Parliament. The issue before the court in Hyde was Mormon polygamy, not same-sex marriage. The court was effectively trying to determine whether Mormon marriage was Christian marriage and thereby entitled to recognition under the law, or whether it was some type of infidel marriage that did not warrant legal recognition. The decision was made to refuse to recognize Mormon marriage as Christian marriage, and therefore, legal marriage. This is reflected in the language of the key passage in the ruling as follows: "What then is the nature of this institution, marriage, as understood in Christendom? It be of common acceptance in existence. It must need to have some pervading identity and universal basis." I concede that marriage, as understood in Christendom, may for this purpose be defined as the voluntary union for life for one man and one woman, to the exclusion of all others. I note in passing that there was nothing in this definition that required a willingness or ability to procreate. That was never a condition of either Christian marriage or legal marriage.

On Canada's same-sex marriage statute, our Supreme Court made the following observations about this historic legacy and the need for a modern approach to the issue: "The reference to Christendom is telling. Hyde spoke to a society of shared social values where marriage and religion were thought to be inseparable. This is no longer the case. Canada is a pluralistic society. Marriage, from the perspective of the State, is a civil institution."

Both church and state, of course, for centuries condemned homosexual acts. There's a diversity of religious views on the question among and within religions today. However, there's a somewhat greater consensus on how to approach the problem legally, at least with respect to criminal law. Most democratic states do not criminalize homosexual acts, and there's a principle of equal treatment for gays and lesbians that is recognized under international law. However, there is a greater diversity of views on the question of marriage. It's certainly clear from our two religious panelists there's in fact a diversity of views about whether same-sex marriage should be permitted in the religious context.

In modern states that respect human rights, the state should not choose sides in such religious debates. In my view, that result can best be achieved by having laws that permit religious organizations that wish to perform same-sex marriages to do so while ensuring that those who object to such unions can never be compelled to marry same-sex couples within their religious institutions. This is the legal approach that has served many societies well, including our own, in a context of other religious rules regarding marriage, notably, the rule that many faiths have, that they will only marry two persons who are members in good standing of their own faith communities. And I'll note at this point that in the cases that were argued in Ontario, our church was advocating religious freedom, including the protection of the religious freedom of the churches with which Ms. Buckingham is involved, and it was their organization that was asking the court to restrict our religious

freedom to perform same-sex marriages. Rules based simply on the enforcement of one group's religious precepts on another cannot be justified. However, sometimes rules that have their origins in religion can be justified on some other or different grounds today.

So the question arises apart from religious objections. Are there other grounds for supporting the restriction of marriage to opposite-sex couples? I know from her previous pronouncements that an answer will be offered by my old friend Margaret Somerville, that it is in the best interest of children to justify this restriction, and that we must privilege the best interest of children over the choices of adults. Her argument goes that restricting marriage to opposite-sex couples is justified because it promotes the symbolic ideal that the best environment for raising children is generally in the context of biological married opposite-sex parents. In my view, Margo is wrong in fact, in principle and in law.

Factually, the leading study on this point—that is, how do children do in same-sex households, as compared to opposite-sex households—is the comprehensive survey of all such studies done by Stacy and Dillards that was filed in a Canadian marriage litigation. The authors conclude that the children of same-sex parents do just as well as those raised by opposite-sex couples. But you needn't take my word for it. Their views on this point have been accepted by all the Canadian courts and by all major professional organizations working in this field, such as the American Psychiatric Association.

In principle, we must recognize that marriage has legally never been connected to any ability or willingness to procreate, when it comes to heterosexuals. People who are beyond the age of procreation have always been permitted to marry. We have never barred heterosexuals from marrying because they might create a home environment that we perceive to be less than ideal, such as parents who smoke or parents who are poor. Further, there's simply no logical connection between the decision of heterosexuals to marry and procreate and the restriction on same-sex marriage. In my own informal survey, including an associate of mine who recently married a woman, I have yet

123

to meet any straight couple that has asserted that they would not marry, or would not have children, because same-sex couples are now allowed to marry. To suggest otherwise strikes me as a bizarre comment on the behavior of straight couples. Finally, unless unmarried couples, straight or gay, are to be forbidden to procreate and adopt, the people who would really suffer by refusing to recognize same-sex marriage are the children in non-traditional relationships, gay and straight. Those children will be legally and socially stigmatized by the Somerville approach, which seeks to privilege the children of married, opposite-sex couples.

Finally, there's no legal justification for this concern. Our law has never confused the rules relating to marriage and the rules relating to raising children. Our laws recognize that not all parent-child relationships are the product of married, opposite-sex couples. The irony of Margo's position is that it is only same-sex couples that must generally involve the adoption process and, therefore, have to satisfy a court that it is in a child's best interest that they become parents. This is in stark contrast to straight couples who can reproduce no matter how patently unfit they may be to be parents. And we know that the biological tie between parent and child has not prevented some of the worst possible behavior, including sexual assault and murder. Finally, if procreation were to be the touchstone of marriage, then legal equality would logically require opposite-sex couples who are sterile, or unwilling to reproduce, to not be allowed to marry and that contraception would be mandatory for unmarried heterosexual couples. Naturally, divorce would be out.

I believe these examples illustrate how preposterous it is to restrict the liberty of same-sex couples to marry in the interest of promoting some notion of the best interest of children. Laws that permit same-sex marriage but do not require religions that object to perform same-sex marriages respect freedom of religion and individual autonomy. I completely support the right of the churches that Janet represents to refuse to marry same-sex couples and, indeed, to preach that homosexuality is sinful.

History teaches us that when government gets into the business of enforcing religious rules, great harm results. When a state imposes a religious rule, it can only pick one. Even religious faiths that do not support same-sex marriage within their faiths should, in my view, support civil laws that do permit same-sex marriage. Why? Because this underlines the principle of religious diversity that protects all faiths from the imposition by the state of the rules of other faiths. The old restriction on same-sex marriage was clearly based on religious rules, and there's no legitimate other ground for the exclusion. Contrary to what Ms. Buckingham has said, in my view, nothing bad has happened in the countries that have permitted same-sex marriage. She has selected a few instances where challenges have been made to those who have discriminated against gays and lesbians, but in my view, those cases have nothing to do with the recognition of same-sex marriage. And in fact, if you look at our case law, and particularly the case of Trinity Western University that I know Janet is very familiar with, and the same-sex marriage case itself, it's very clear that in Canada our courts have gone to great lengths to try and strike a balance between the rights of evangelical Christians in particular within their own sphere to have some freedom to reflect their religious beliefs while at the same time protecting gays and lesbians from discrimination in the public sphere. In short, the prophecies of doom that we heard about what would happen in Canada if we recognize same-sex marriage have simply not materialized. Heterosexuality remains remarkably popular in this country. The joy of family weddings has simply been extended to everyone. Thank you.

MARGARET SOMERVILLE

My colleague Douglas Elliott has introduced what I'm going to say, so you might save me a few minutes, Douglas. I'm the attorney for the case of children's rights, and particularly children's human rights. Seeing that this is a conference that has as one of its goals to try to articulate how religions and human rights interact and coalesce, I would very much urge you to consider children's human rights. This is the latest edition of the *McGill Law Journal*, which arrived on my desk yesterday. It contains an article called "Children's and Parent's Rights" by Barbara Bennett Woodhouse, in which she proposes, "Children and juveniles are the latest kids on the human rights block." Until I read this article, which I did just this morning, I hadn't realized why it was so hard to get the issue of children's rights into the marriage debate in Canada—it was almost impossible. The breach of children's rights that same-sex marriage involves is my only objection to same-sex marriage.

I don't have a problem with homosexuality—I think it's absolutely wrong to discriminate against gay people. But I do believe that we have a conflict in the same-sex marriage debate between homosexual people's human rights against discrimination and children's human rights with respect to their parents and the family structure in which they're brought up. And so my colleague Douglas Elliott said that marriage laws should respect human rights. I totally agree with him. But that must include what those laws need to be if they are to respect children's human rights. He also said there's no compelling reasons other than religious ones to reject same-sex marriage. Well, the reason that I reject it has got nothing to do with religion. I reject it on a secular, biological-family-rights-of-children, needs-of-children base. So let's go to the position I take on same-sex marriage, because we're going to have to go fairly quickly for me to set out the arguments that I want to make to you.

The first question we need to ask is: What's the purpose of marriage as a societal institution? To answer, we must take into account a crucial point: Under both national and international law, marriage is a compound right. It's not just the right of adults to marry whom they want. It's the right to marry *and to found a family*. And that latter right establishes both parents' rights with respect to their children and children's rights with respect to their parents. So that question means we have to ask ourselves: Should biology continue to matter to marriage? And that translates into yet another question: Should biology continue to matter to parenthood? I believe that the needs and rights of children, in general—of course, we're going to have to deal with individual children where it's not possible for them to be with their biological parents and raised in their biological family—but the needs and rights of children, in general, mean that we should continue to have as our societal norm that norm established by monogamous opposite-sex marriage; namely, that children have a right to know who their biological parents are and, if at all possible, to be brought up within their biological family. And why is that norm important? Because we need general principles—values and norms—that protect the transmission of life to the next generation and nurture that life in the best possible conditions, until the child becomes independent. That's what I believe marriage has always primarily been about. The adults are really secondary beneficiaries of the institution of marriage; its primary beneficiaries are intended to be the children born into the marriage—above all else, marriage is meant to be for the protection of the transmission of human life to ensure that there is a next generation. Now that view is regarded in Canada at present, and I'm regarded, as quaint, old-fashioned, out-of-date, and, as Janet mentioned, a bigot, and hateful. There have been all sorts of suggestions by advocates of same-sex marriage as to what should be done with me, including that I should be sent back to Australia, where I was born.

So let me explain what I'm on about here. I believe there's a biological reality at the core of opposite-sex marriage; namely, the natural procreative relationship between a man and a woman, and opposite-sex marriage recognizes, symbolizes, and institutionalizes that relationship. It sets up an institution that gives children their rights with respect to their parents and family structure based on their links to their biological parents. The problem with same-sex marriage is not that it's between two homosexuals; it's that it eliminates that biological reality from marriage. It directly and overtly contravenes it and wipes it out as the norm and, in doing that, it negates the rights of all children to contact and connection with their biological parents and to being reared by them within their own biological family structure. And it wipes out

125

those rights, not just for individual children, but on a societal level; and not just for children in a same-sex marriage, but for all children. It also wipes out those rights for children who later on become gay adults, as well as for children who later on become heterosexual adults—I believe all children need a mother and a father, preferably their own biological parents, and have a right to know who those parents and, therefore they themselves, are. Douglas raised the question of infertile, opposite-sex couples or ones who don't want children, why that doesn't have the same effect of negating children's rights in these respects. The reason is that those are individual cases, not a norm, and those situations, unlike same-sex marriage, don't overtly contravene the societal level norm, values, and symbolism established by opposite-sex marriage, and that's why they do not create the same problem.

We can also look at parenthood from another angle, and this is actually explicit in our new Canadian Civil Marriage Act. In Canada, we'd always defined parent as the "natural parent." That was the term, used in our federal legislation. The Civil Marriage Act changed the word from "natural" to "legal"—in other words, the parental bond between parents and children is no longer defined by biological links but is now defined by the law and who it declares as the parents—the natural reality of biological parenthood no longer counts. So the fundamental nature of the primary bond has been radically changed. What that change effectuates is to implement genderless parenting. The arguments in favor of that are based on a belief that it doesn't matter to children whether their parents are two men, two women, or a man and a woman. In making that change, we reverse the basic presumption that as a society we work from a basic presumption—a norm—that children's parents are their natural parents, to which exceptions must be justified. Rather we replace it with a basic presumption that a child's parents are simply who the law says they are. Now, apart from anything else, that directly contravenes a provision in the International Convention on the Rights of the Child, which is the most ratified convention in the history of the United Nations, and which Canada has ratified. (Only two countries in the world, the United States and Somalia, have not ratified that convention.) That convention provides that children have a basic right to be raised in their own family and to know who their parents are.

So what we have here is a conflict of two claims. That's what same-sex marriage presents us with, a conflict between the rights of same-sex adults to have their relationship, as they want it to be, recognized legally as marriage, and to have the public recognition that would engender that it's wrong to discriminate against them—creating that message is the power of same-sex marriage to correct past wrongs of discrimination against homosexual people. It gives a very strong message in that regard. But that goal is achieved at the expense of breaching the fundamental human rights of children with respect to their parents. So we have to make a choice. I believe the choice we should make comes closest to having the best of both worlds, that of upholding rights against discrimination on the basis of sexual orientation and that of respecting children's rights with respect to their biological families and family structure. I support gay rights to equal treatment with heterosexual people with respect to their intimate relationships, and I agree completely that the horrible discrimination against gay people in the past must be decried and never occur again. But I propose we can achieve those goals without breaching children's fundamental human rights through legal recognition of civil unions between same-sex couples rather than marriage. Civil unions do not affect children's rights because, unlike marriage, which is a compound right—the right to marry *and found a family*—they carry no such right. Civil unions, however, have been rejected by the gay community in Canada as instituting what they call second-class citizenship.

I want now to touch on some avant-garde issues that same-sex marriage raises with respect to children's human rights with respect to their biological families and family structure. Because same-sex marriage unlinks the biological bonds between parents and children as the basis for defining parenthood and who constitute a family, it brings in the whole area of new reproductive technologies, an area which I study with respect to the ethics and law which should govern it.

If you look at the literature, up until very recently, when we talked about new reproductive technologies—and I've been working in this area for nearly thirty years—we were always concerned with the physical health of the child whom we brought into existence. But that was almost the only matter that we were concerned about. Now we're starting to realize that there are a whole lot of other matters that we also have to be concerned about.

So what should children's rights be, first of all with respect to know who are their parents, which we've been talking about, but also the way in which they are conceived, or what we can call their "coming into being"? I suggest that one way we can approach this is through a concept of "anticipated consent." That means that we must ask ourselves: Is what we're going to do to these children something that we can reasonably anticipate they would consent to when they're old enough to know and understand what we did? I believe that some of the things that we're now able to do to them, they would not consent to. In fact we already know that many people who were brought into being, for example, through gamete donation—donated sperm or donated ova—are now forming groups— they call themselves "donor-conceived adults"— and they adamantly believe that society did a very serious wrong to them in allowing them to come into existence through the technology that was used to conceive them.

So what I propose is that, in light of all these developments, we need to recognize new human rights for children. And I propose that the rights children in general should have include, first, a right to know the identity of their biological parents. They also have a right to both a mother and a father, preferably their own biological parents. Further, they have a right to be raised by those parents, unless an exception can be justified as in the best interests of a particular child, as in many adoptions. And they have the right to be conceived with a natural, biological heritage; that is, from an untampered-with ovum from one identified, adult, living woman and an untampered-with sperm from one, identified, living adult man.

Now, I would like to explain how same-sex marriage, because it carries the right to found a family, would contravene all of those rights of children. In unlinking marriage from biological parenthood, same-sex marriage contravenes the first two rights. And because same-sex marriage carries the right to found a family—indeed, in the Ontario Court of Appeal case that Douglas Elliott referred to, the judges ruled that "if procreation is important to marriage, [they thought it wasn't, as he said] there's no problem for same-sex couples, because they can use new reproductive technologies to make themselves procreative." That means that same-sex marriage could be seen as endorsing certain uses of new reproductive technologies— for instance, surrogate motherhood—that many people see as unethical and in breach of children's human rights.

In giving same-sex couples the right to found a family, same-sex marriage takes away children's right to both a mother and a father. So another central issue it raises is: Does it matter whether a child has a mother and a father? Mr. Elliott referred to research that says it really doesn't matter; children without a parent of each sex are not disadvantaged. That research is highly challengeable. Even two prominent gay researchers, William Mason and Jonathan Roach, recently put out a report that said, at best, the jury is out on that evidence. Also, for anyone who is really interested in this issue, there is a very long and comprehensive new report on it commissioned by the French government, which rejected same-sex marriage for France precisely on the basis that it would be contrary to respecting children's rights and fulfilling their needs to set up same-sex parenting in the way that same-sex marriage would do. In fact, if we want a general, ethical principle that leads to the same conclusion, we can take the precautionary principle that's used in environmental ethics and law. That requirement says that when we're really uncertain about some great social experiment—and same-sex marriage is a great social experiment—we should err on the side of caution, which means keeping the status quo until deviating from it can be shown to be justified.

Now, children's rights to know the identity of their biological parents is increasingly being recognized in the law of all countries. For instance, the United Kingdom has recently passed laws to that effect. The result of prohibiting gamete donor anonymity is that people are not as willing to donate. Sometimes an argument against requiring donor identification is that many children do not know who their biological father is. But that situation arising by chance differs ethically from it's being created through choice. There's a major difference ethically between a woman getting pregnant and not knowing who the father was, so the child doesn't know, and society setting up systems that condone that situation and accommodate it within the societal norm, which is what we're talking about here. There's a very big difference between respecting people's right to reproductive privacy in the former situation and, as in the latter situation, providing people with positive technological assistance to help them to create, what these children sometimes call themselves, "genetic orphans."

I want to go now to perhaps the most startling situation opened up by same-sex marriage with respect to children's human rights—the right to come into being from natural human origins. Amazing new technologies on the horizon raise a question that we've never had to face before: Does a child have a right to a natural, biological heritage; that is, a right to untampered-with biological origins? These technologies include, as well as cloning, which you've probably seen lots of discussion about, making it possible for two men to have their own genetically shared baby or for two women to do so. And the reason is we can now make sperm or ova from adult stem cells. There was a report in *Nature* yesterday, about Japanese scientists creating a mouse embryo from two female mice. What we can do using our science in animals down the line we can usually also do in humans. And that would mean you would be able to have your own shared genetic baby, even if you were two men or two women. It also means, and even more bizarrely

in a way, that you could have your own baby that wasn't your clone. If you were a woman, scientists could take one of your ova, make a sperm from one of your stem cells, and fertilize the ovum with that sperm. There would be recombination of the chromosomes present in that embryo, and so you'd have a new human life which came only from you, but is not your clone, because there would have been rearrangement of all the genetic material.

Such extraordinary new technoscience possibilities mean that we need new legal and ethical protections. And one of those, I propose, is that we must recognize as the most fundamental human right of all; namely, that every human being who comes into existence has a right to do so from natural untampered-with biological origins; that is, from an untampered-with ovum from one identified, living, adult woman and an untampered-with sperm from one, identified, living, adult man.

The word *living* excludes using postmortem gamete donation. To conceive a child knowing that it could never meet its biological parent is ethically wrong, so postmortem donation of sperm or ova should not be allowed.

The parent must also be an adult human. That excludes using sperm or ova from aborted fetuses, creating a child whose parent was never born, who would need to explain that ". . . actually my mother was a fetus." Or cloning a child from a dying child. These are the unprecedented scientific and ethical issues that we are looking at within these areas.

In other words, we must recognize that the right to bear children does not include the right to deny children their natural rights of natural biological integrity, knowing their biological identity and being part of their biological family. Neither does it include denying children at least the chance, when being conceived, of meeting their biological parents. Society should not be complicit in any procedures that involve breaches of the fundamental human rights of children in this context; that is, it should not approve or fund any procedure for the creation of a child, unless the procedure is consistent with a child's right to a natural biological heritage and other rights that flow from that right. And society should recognize that any genetic procedure that would turn out to be harmful to the future child or to a future generation or contrary to their interests is morally unacceptable and should be prohibited.

Now, the challenges that new reproductive technologies in combination with same-sex marriage raise will include legal challenges in the courts to legislation, such as that in Canada, that bans paying surrogate mothers. Married gay men argue that they have a right to found a family, and that, just as it was discrimination against them not to allow them to marry, it is likewise discrimination against them with respect to exercising their right to found a family to ban payment to surrogate mothers, because that is the only way they can have children. In Canada, we also prohibit payment for sperm or ova. The same arguments are being launched there that the ban on payment is unconstitutional because it constitutes discrimination on the basis of sexual orientation. So these two unprecedented new realities of same-sex marriage and new reproductive technologies are coalescing to present unprecedented challenges to children's most fundamental human rights.

In conclusion, knowing who our biological relatives are and relating to them is central to how we form our human identity, relate to others in the world, and find meaning in life, all complex, intimate realities in every human life that we used to address through religion but now must also deal with as secular societies. Children and their descendents who don't know their genetic origins cannot sense themselves as embedded in a web of people, past, present, and to come in the future, through whom they can trace the thread of life's passage down the generations, to them and from them. As far as we know, humans are the only animals where experiencing genetic relationship is integral to their sense of themselves. What we know and are learning now of the effects of eliminating that experience is that doing so is harmful to children, biological parents, families, and society. And we can only imagine how much more damage would be done to a child who was born, not from the union of a natural sperm and a natural ovum, which is the way of passing on life to the next generation that opposite-sex marriage institutionalizes, but born from gametes constructed through biotechnology. Thank you.

QUESTIONS AND ANSWERS FOR THE AUTHORS

Question: Thank you for putting this together. I have two brief questions. One is, when we talk about in Canada moving toward building the new standards of marriage into the curriculum in school, I wanted to ask about . . . I certainly don't think it's the job of schools to teach children their moral rights. I think there are other issues right now such as evolution in schools, which is a major issue as well. Dr. Buckingham, if you could address that, if that's possible? And then also, for all the legal panelists, if there was ever a possibility of leaving marriage to the religious and spiritual realm and leaving a civil union only to the state realm?

Buckingham: We used to have religion taught in schools, Christian religion taught in schools. And over time, as our society became more pluralistic, there was a decision made to exclude that teaching from the schools. I would suggest that that may be a possible answer to the problem. It seems to be difficult for some schools to teach about sex and sexuality without teaching morals along with it, and it may be appropriate that that issue be left, as with religion, to the education of the parents and that be taught at home. At the moment, it's extremely controversial, and this kind of material and the morality is being taught in schools and is expanding. I will speak just briefly to the issue of leaving marriage to religious institutions and having the public recognition as a civil union. That has been discussed in Canada. Many people thought, or some people thought, that would be a very good resolution. Unfortunately, our constitutional scheme provides some boundaries or some barriers to being able to do that. But it may be a possibility that could be considered down the road for other countries. And some European countries, for example, have a separation between civil marriage and religious marriage, which would facilitate that kind of an approach.

129

Elliott: Just to pick up on what Janet was saying, I think that the principal difficulty here was an internal difficulty in Canada that made the option of separating marriage from the civil and religious realm completely impossible, because we can't have national civil unions in this country. But this raised the further problem on an international level that the civil unions that exist, for example, in France and Germany, they don't move across boundaries very easily, so you do effectively have a second-class-relationship problem when you have a civil-union system, because the French civil union is very different even from the German civil-union system or the British civil-union system or the Australian civil-union system. So it's not universally recognized, and there's a great debate always about what rights go into these civil unions. The French one has very few, the British one has very comprehensive, and that's one of the reasons why we argue, apart from the moral issue that gays and lesbians should be treated the same, we argue that marriage was the most convenient way of ensuring that equality because it is an institution, legally, that means the same thing across Canada and around the world, in terms of the bundle of rights that go with that institution.

Hawkes: The Canadian Human Rights Commission has studied the issue of marriage around the debate of same-sex marriage, and at the end of their study, they put out a report that said, in Canada, we need more options for couples. Right now, it's marriage or common law. And if you're a heterosexual common-law couple, after one to three years, then certain rights and obligations are imposed upon you as a heterosexual couple, whether you like it or not. And they said that in society there should be more options for couples to choose along the way, but that all of those options should be open equally to gay and lesbian couples and heterosexual couples, so that, if we have civil unions, both gay couples and heterosexual couples should have access to it as well as marriage. It should be equally accessible, but we should have more options. At a time, in my province of Ontario, only Protestant marriages were recognized. Catholic and Jewish marriages were not. No one would ever have said, "Let's keep marriage for the Protestants, and we'll give civil union to the Catholics and the Jews." No one would have ever thought that kind of separate but equal would have been acceptable. So we're saying the same thing, that it's not acceptable for us either.

Question: First I'd like to say thank you for the variety of perspectives, and I might have addressed a question to any of you, but I'd like to address this question to Dr. Buckingham. I think I wrote down what you said as clearly as I could. If I got it wrong, I apologize, and you can correct me. I think I heard you say something toward the end of your presentation, like: "The purpose of changing the definition of marriage and the laws that follow is to exclude and marginalize those of us who hold traditional views." I don't know if that is correct or not, but if that is what you said, I'm confused, because I would think that the purpose of changing the definition of marriage and the laws that follow is rather to provide equal opportunity for and the legitimation of caring relationships for all the citizens of Canada. So it seems that it turns the question toward the dominant majority of heterosexual persons and away from the marginalized minority of gay persons.

Buckingham: The answer is quite easy, and it's that you heard me wrong. I said the implication, not the purpose, but the outcome, of doing that.

Question: But does it still, then, focus upon the majority who holds the traditional views rather than focusing it upon those who hold the minority view?

Buckingham: Once the definition of marriage is changed to include another group or the definition of marriage is changed for all of society, it has implications on minority religions who cannot accept that view. And so the implications for those minority religions will be marginalization and restrictions on their religious freedoms. I'm talking about the impact on religious groups. I'm not talking about the impact on the couples.

Somerville: Perhaps I can speak from personal experience to that. The reason that there was such protest about my being awarded this honorary doctor of science degree from Ryerson University was that simply the fact that I opposed same-sex marriage meant, in the protesters' eyes, that I was hateful, bigoted, discriminatory, prejudiced. For instance, I was described as a neo-Nazi, told that I should join the Ku Klux Klan, and there were many other examples of that kind of language. The point I want to make here is that it's not only unacceptable to advocates of same-sex marriage to say, as I did, that you've got problems with same-sex marriage or to explain the reasons why you oppose it, but also, you become labeled as a hateful person simply because you oppose same-sex marriage, and that's exactly what happened to me. It was also claimed that I should not be allowed to speak in the university because of those views, whether or not I was speaking on same-sex marriage. And these protests caused a huge outburst right across the country. In fact, most of the newspapers picked it up and treated it as an issue of academic freedom and freedom of speech, and therefore, were opposed to what happened, even the one's, such as the *Globe and Mail*, that supported same-sex marriage.

We're seeing these sorts of fallouts from the activism around same-sex marriage increasing; for instance, teachers have been suspended because they've expressed the view that they believe homosexuality is not morally acceptable under their beliefs which are founded on the Bible. We also have hate-crime legislation in Canada; that is, a prohibition on inciting hatred against an identified group on certain bases. Relatively recently, the hate-crime provision was amended to include homosexuality expressly, as a prohibited base for inciting hatred. In the protests surrounding my case, it was alleged in the newspapers that maybe I could be prosecuted for hate crime for my opposition to same-sex marriage, along the lines of the arguments that I just gave you.

Hawkes: For years in Canada, we've had a definition of marriage that has allowed for divorce, and many religions do not support divorce. My understanding is none of those have been marginalized. None of those have been discriminated against. None of those have been taken to court because they don't support divorce. We have in Canada this amazing ability to protect minority rights and this ability particularly to protect religious minority rights. Also, I happened to be one of those people who led the protest at Ryerson, and certainly within all of our movements, we have our crazies, and with all of our movements, we have people who would cause death threats and problems within all of our movements. We were protesting Ryerson's decision, specifically the timing of that decision, to honor a leading opponent of gay marriage in the midst of the national debate on gay marriage. We thought the timing was inappropriate, and that was the point we were trying to make at Ryerson. We weren't saying that Ms. Somerville didn't have a right to her opinion or a right to state her opinion, and so on. We just said it was wrong for Ryerson, a university in the middle of the gay community, to honor a leading opponent in the midst of the discussions. Wait until the decision is over if they had wanted to honor that opponent.

Question: We claim the title evangelical also, but we're not fundamentalists. And sometimes we resent not being spoken of as evangelicals. Dr. Buckingham, you contrasted two views of marriage: one was the traditional and one was what you claimed to be modern. The traditional being family-centered and the modern being love-centered, romantic-centered. And yet you, evangelicals and others, have recognized marriage that has been only love-centered, and that's the marriage of people in their forties, fifties, sixties, and seventies, who have been widowed, who come into it not for any children or to raise families but for love and security. I'm sure you don't condemn them. I'm sure you recognize their marriage. Why then, did you use the argument in a disparaging way, associating gay marriage with the love-centered notion in order to reject that position? Would you accept it?

Buckingham: I think I made the point in my talk that we make our public policy based on the norms and expectations rather than the exceptions. So I said we have historically made our public policy based on the family-centered model. The state's interest in strong and stable marriages is for the benefit of the children. Does the state really care whether two people stay together or don't stay together in a loving union? No, I would argue that the state doesn't really have a strong interest in that. And so we have made our public policy based on the family-centered model because it was in the interest of the state to have children raised in homes where they're going to have two parents, they're not going to be in poverty, they're going to have two people to care for them who are their biological parents, because this has historically been considered the best situation for children. Certainly we are not opposed to older couples getting married, and they still follow the norm and fit within the definition of the husband-and-wife marriage. And I don't purport to speak on behalf of all evangelical Christians worldwide. But the majority would follow the family-centered model of marriage, as would many other religious traditions.

Question: First, to the woman from Australia, that was a very insightful presentation. My question to you is: What about the right of life itself? Not only the children's rights or the parents' rights, but life itself? And then to Janet, who to me sounded a little bit . . . [speaker didn't finish the last sentence] I'm very sorry for the victimization. My question to you is: Have you or your organization been engaged in discrimination or active lobbyism against same-sex marriages?

Somerville: We are the first generation of humans ever that hold the essence of life itself in the palm of our collective human hand. We can now transform life. There is a new movement called the transhumanists. (In fact, there was a panel at this conference two days ago that discussed that development.) Transhumanists believe that with our new technoscience we are on our way to what they call a posthuman future, that Homo sapiens is an obsolete model and that we'll be replaced by redesigning ourselves. We can't get into that, but placing my presentation on the implications of same-sex

marriage and new reproductive technologies that I have proposed to you within the context of what the transhumanists are proposing, I would argue we must protect the essence of human life; we must hold it in trust for future generations. And that requires restricting some uses of new reproductive technologies, which, as I've explained, is connected with issues raised by same-sex marriage. In legalizing same-sex marriage we say, as a society, that same-sex couples have a right to found a family, and that, in turn, opens up a very strong argument for their claim that "I've got a right to use these technologies to found that family even though they transform the mode of transmission of life." So the new questions we have to ask, which did not exist in the past because the technology didn't exist, include: What does respect for the transmission of life require? What does respect for the human germ cell line—the basic genes we pass on from generation to generation that form the human gene pool—require? Those are all unprecedented, new questions of immense importance. If it's any comfort, we are working on them in ethics.

Buckingham: In response to the comment or question about my own discriminatory behavior, I will tell you, I have not called anyone names. I have been called bigoted and homophobic. I have been threatened. I have received hate mail. I have not sent any hate mail. I have never commented that gays and lesbians should not be treated with dignity. I've never said that their buildings should be razed or burned. I will say I do not believe that equality, and treating people with equal dignity, requires the definition of marriage to be changed. There are other ways of respecting people's relationships.

Question: Once again, compliments on that work. I'm Daniel Helminiak from the University of West Georgia. Many of you may know me from my book *What the Bible Really Says About Homosexuality* and more recently *Sex and the Sacred: Gay Identity and Spiritual Growth.* In other words, I'm well versed in these issues. I'm highly impressed with this argument about the rights of the children. Except for a doubt that comes up when we're going to have some symbolic meaning of marriage, which casts doubt on the whole agenda behind it. But in contrast to that, what was going on with Dr. Buckingham. . . . I distinguished in religion the (1) inessential, e.g., customs, practices; (2) the indeterminate, e.g., the things with God that no one will ever be able to resolve by agreement; and (3) the indispensable, the things that have to do with this life, which we could, in good reason, settle. You made the statement that you hold things in faith and you hope that no one would think you're wrong for that and you should not be marginalized for holding these views. I think you are wrong. The evidence is against it on every front, and to suppose that just because it's religious opinion it has to be expressed is one of the problems in this discussion we're having here. You want to appeal to the scriptures? You should start holding your slaves, you've got to take all your money out of the bank, and you as a woman should not be speaking to us. Please.

Buckingham: Thanks for those marginalizing comments.

Question: You deserve them.

Question [different person]: A simple question to Margaret Somerville. Given your main focus is the welfare, the well-being, of children, I don't quite understand why you would approve of and be fine with civil union and not with marriage.

Somerville: That's a very good question and it's one I'm often asked. The reason is that civil unions— and it's what Mr. Elliott said—don't automatically carry the same rights as marriage. So civil unions don't carry the right to found a family. My problem with same-sex marriage is not the union of the two people and the public recognition of that. I support that. My problem is that it automatically, and in both national and international law, carries an express right to found a family, which then brings in all these other claims about rights to use these technologies, abolition of children's rights to have both a father and a mother, and so on.

There's new genetic research—we haven't got time to go into this—in rats that shows that some of our genes need to be activated by certain

behavior on the part of our parents, and if we don't experience that behavior within a certain critical window period, those genes shut down for life. So my argument is—and research is starting to show—that men parent differently from women, and we need both forms of parenting. I think we will find genes that are activated by a mother's conduct that wouldn't be activated by a father's, and vice versa. So it's paradoxical: At the same time as we're finding out how important, for instance, complementary parenting of men and women is, rather than just intuitively knowing that and acting on that intuition, for instance, in establishing the institution of opposite-sex marriage, we're abolishing the ways in our society in which we fulfilled those needs of children.

Question: My name is Donald Boisvert. I teach here at Concordia in Montreal. Thank you, the four of you, for a very engaging panel. My question is for Dr. Somerville. This is the first time I've heard you speak, so I'm also grateful for that. I think you mentioned in the beginning of your talk that your position is not religiously based, if I'm not mistaken. I was powerfully struck in your presentation at how it reflects traditional Catholic papal teaching on marriage, procreation, new technologies. I was wondering if you have any comments on that sort of strong Catholic flavor to your position.

Somerville: I'm giving the Massey Lectures in Canada next month. I've written a book to go with them: *The Ethical Imagination: Journeys of the Human Spirit.* And the second Massey Lecture is an argument for what I call a presumption in favor of nature, the natural and life. So I am what you would probably call a modern natural ethics, natural-law-based person. And to the extent that that reflects a Thomas Aquinas kind of approach to issues, and to the extent that it is part of Catholic received wisdom, then there's definitely the same kind of basis. But I don't do it because it's religious, and there are issues where you would hear me speak and you would say, "Well, that doesn't coincide with what the Catholic Church believes." I just think that, in these very fundamental issues that concern life itself, the idea of a presumption in favor of the natural is the wisest one to adopt, in particular in light of the enormous technoscience power we now have to change it. It doesn't mean we can't change the natural, it means that we have to show that we're justified in doing so—I also, in another Massey lecture, develop a concept that I call the secular-sacred. I believe that, traditionally, we accessed the sacred through religion. I don't believe we can do that as a society in the world of the future, if only because, for instance, we're all different religions. And so what I'm trying to do is find some ways that this very ancient human wisdom that for a lot of us is encapsulated and very importantly passed on to us through the religions can be encapsulated and passed on to future generations other than through religion. Religion will still be important, but it can no longer be the sole means of achieving this goal. So obviously then I'm into the same areas as those in which religion plays a very important role. We're into the same tasks. But I'm not basing what I'm proposing on religion, although I hope it will be acceptable to people who are religious, and if so, no matter which religion, and as well to people who are not religious. My basic goal is to try to find a "shared ethics" (a concept that needs careful definition) that as many people as possible can buy into.

Question: My name is Gary Sealey. I'm the president of Servas International, which built 15,000 homes in eighty countries around the world. And my question is: Given the theme of this conference, World's Religions After September 11: A Global Congress—a day which marks a day of hate and terror and fear—what can religions do? . . . What must religions do to celebrate diversity and celebrate loving relationships that support children in their development needs? I'm not talking about law. I'm talking about the religions. So if any of the panelists could reply. . . .

Buckingham: I can say within my community the whole debate over same-sex marriage has caused a lot of self-reflection on how we have treated gays and lesbians in our midst. And I think that has been a very positive move. There has been a lot of discussion about ministry and caring for one

another and reconciliation. I am very troubled by what's happening, in terms of marginalizing language and mudslinging between different religious groups and protests being launched and nasty language being flung about. And I'm very troubled by that, and I would hope that religious organizations, in particular, can find way of bringing peace and reconciliation. Our doors have been open to that and we certainly have met with leaders from the gay and lesbian community on those issues. But I am troubled by those who are not of the reconciliation bent.

Elliott: This isn't really my topic, but I'm going to put my oar in here just very quickly, because it's something that Reverend Hawkes and I were talking about over lunch. Over the years, the mantra from the religious Right has been, we hate the sin but we love the sinner. And I can tell you that it's been my experience as a gay man that we hear an awful lot about hating the sin, and very little, if anything, about loving the sinner. And I'd like to put out a challenge to Janet's group and the other conservative religions that condemn homosexuality, because I think there's one thing that we might be able to agree on, and I think it would be a great step forward toward reconciliation. Right now there are still eight countries in the world that still have capital punishment for homosexual acts. Most of the great religions of the world, including the Roman Catholic Church, condemn capital punishment. I think it would be great if those religions would stand up, united with us, and say it's time to stop the imposition of capital punishment on gays and lesbians just because of their sexual acts. I think that would be a great step forward in trying to reconcile the gay and lesbian community to the world religions that have been extremely critical of them.

Hawkes: In line with that, when I was invited to this conference, I called our regional elder, our bishop of sorts, to tell her that I was coming. And she was just in the midst of writing a letter to the United Nations because ten gay people in Iran were about to be executed, and she was trying to intervene on their behalf. And so I echo what Douglas said. If one of the themes of this conference that keeps coming up is that compassion is a central virtue of all of our religions, and that the golden rule is a central value in all of our religions. And I would just like to invite others who hold a different perspective to think about our families too. When Ms. Somerville continues to repeat the phrase "genetic orphans," people in our church shed tears. One mom came to me when she knew I was coming here and said, "Could you please try to make the point to her to stop using that phrase, because she's talking about my son." And I would ask people to treat our families—because we have families too—to treat our families in the way you want your family to be treated, to treat our marriages in the way you want your marriages to be treated. And I think even if we disagree, if the world religions would start practicing compassion and start practicing the golden rule, then the broader society, instead of running away from religion, would view religion as something to be respected even in the midst of our differences.

Somerville: Just to respond to the plea about the term "genetic orphans," which was actually a term that a young adopted woman used to me. She said, "I am a genetic orphan." It's a term that children who don't know who their genetic parents are, are using, and there are Web sites you can go to where they're trying to contact other children who might be their half siblings, because, for instance, they were conceived from the same sperm bank. And these children tell me things like, "I get up every morning and I look in the mirror, and half of me is missing. Society had no right to do this to me." So those stories are not my invention. The reason you see this as an unacceptable term to use, Reverend Hawkes, is because you are looking at the situation and talking—and I agree that you should do so—from the perspective of the rights of the adults who desperately want to have children and want to set up a family which will not be based on biological bonds. I'm speaking from exactly the opposite side, and I'm telling you how those children feel about themselves. Just as the parents you speak about feel wounded that somebody is saying their kid is a "genetic orphan," those children are wounded because they say, my natural right to know my biological heritage is not being respected. So what we're really looking at here is: Should adults' preferences prevail or should children's needs and rights prevail? You, as I understand what you have said, choose the former; I choose the latter. That is where our views differ.

RELIGION AND HUMAN RIGHTS

A Historical and Contemporary Assessment

Krishna Kanth Tigiripalli
Lalitha Kumari Kadarla

The nature of the debate on a topic such as "Religion and Human Rights" is polemical and paradoxical. Both theses concepts are important for society. And both are complementary and contradictory in nature. Religion is very important for the individual and society. Human societies will crumble like castles made of cards without religion. Religion has been a binding force in society, and it helps build up the ethos and values of society. Without religion and religious-based values, societies will lose sight of direction, and ethics and rationality might even cease to exist. It has been proven since time immemorial that religion helps to inculcate values based on ethics and morality, as well as rational thinking and behavior.[1]

Both Plato and Karl Marx spoke about the importance of religion in society. Marx famously described religion as the opium of the masses. By saying so, Marx underscored the importance of religion in the society. But extreme and divergent religious beliefs brought internecine conflict in the world. It is paradoxical that religion, identified as a cohesive and unifying force, was also seen as a divisive and destructive force that divided societies. Religious fanatics and dogmatists have vitiated the atmosphere and are responsible for the present schism and morass in the world.[2]

For a rational thinker, both religious and human rights are intertwined and inseparable. Without religion there would be no civility and rationality, and the religious outlook, enmeshed with ethics, helps us to formulate certain values and makes us more helpful to others and more humane toward the beliefs of others. Rousseau observed a long time ago that man in nature has certain inalienable rights, and these rights cannot be denied to man by anyone. Men and women of faith are asserting human rights, because human rights are not simply a matter of law. The Universal Declaration of Human Rights, which was passed without dissenting vote by the General Assembly of the United Nations in 1948 and which constitutes the foundation of international human-rights law, affirms the faith of the people in fundamental human rights. Human rights cannot simply be derived from legal precedents of the past, nor from empirical evidence or logic, but require a "leap of faith." This is true whether one is "religious" or not.

Although there is widespread acceptance of the importance of human rights in international governance, there is considerable confusion as to their precise nature and role in international law. There are writers who regard the high incidence of noncompliance with human-rights norms as evidence of state practice that argues against the existence of a structure of human-rights principles in international law. The concept of human rights is closely allied with ethics and morality. Those rights that reflect the values of a community will be those with the most chance of successful implementation. Of course, there may be no necessary connection in particular instances, for not all community values will be enshrined in law, nor do all legal rights reflect moral concerns, since many operate on a technical level as entitlements under specific conditions.

Rights may be seen as emanating from various sources, whether from religion, the nature of humankind, or the nature of society. The natural-law view, as expressed in the traditional formulations of that approach or by virtue of the natural rights movement, maintains that certain rights exist as a result of a higher law above positive or man-made law. Such a higher law constitutes a universal and absolute set of principles, governing all human beings in time and space. The natural-rights approach of the seventeenth century, associated primarily with John Locke, identified the existence of such inalienable rights as the rights to life, liberty, and property, through a social contract marking the end of the conditions governed by the state of nature. This theory enabled recourse to be had to a superior type of law and was thus able to provide a powerful instrument for restraining arbitrary power.

The United Nations System— Human Rights

There are a number of human-rights provisions in the United Nations Charter. Article 1 covers the organization, promotion, and encouragement of respect for human rights and fundamental freedoms for all without distinction as to race, sex, language, or religion. Article 13 (1) notes that the General Assembly shall initiate studies and make recommendations regarding the realization of human rights for all, while Article 55 provides that the U.N. shall promote universal respect for and observance of human rights. In a significant provision, Article 56 states that

all members pledge themselves to take joint and separate action in cooperation with the organization for the achievement of the purposes set forth in article.[3]

Prohibition of Discrimination

Apart from the overwhelming requirement of protection from physical attack upon their very existence as a group, groups need protection against discriminatory treatment as such. The norm of nondiscrimination thus constitutes a principle relevant both to groups and to individual members of groups.

The International Convention on the Elimination of All Forms of Racial Discrimination was signed in 1965 and entered into force in 1969. It builds on the nondiscrimination provision in the U.N. Charter. Racial discrimination is defined as

any distinction, exclusion, restriction or preference based on race, colour, descent or national or ethnic origin which has the purpose or effect of nullifying or impairing the recognition, enjoyment or exercise, on an equal footing, of human rights and fundamental freedoms in the political, economic, social, cultural or any other field of public life.[4]

Under its jurisdiction, state parties undertake to prohibit racial discrimination and guarantee equality for all in the enjoyment of a series of rights, and to assure to all within their jurisdiction effective protection and remedies regarding such human rights.

The Principle of Self-Determination as a Human Right

The right to self-determination has often been examined insofar as it relates to the context of decolonization.[5] The question arises whether this right, which has been widely proclaimed, has an application beyond the colonial context. The first article of both international covenants on human rights provides that all peoples have the right to self-determination. The Helsinki Final Act of 1975 refers to the principle of equal rights and self-determination. People shall be free to determine their political status and to pursue their economic and social development according to the policy they have chosen. However, the 1970 Declaration on Principles of International Law Concerning Friendly Relations referred to the prior period of colonial rule.

International law was simply the law of nations prior to World War II, and thus the rights of a human person were the rights granted by his or her government. No person, therefore, had any rights in a country other than his or her own, unless the person's own country had secured rights for its citizens in that foreign country through a treaty. Persons might claim "natural rights" in the first half of this century, such as those affirmed in the American Declaration of Independence, but these were only recognized and enforceable by the laws of individual countries. Until the middle of this century, legal rights were "citizen rights" rather than human rights.

This understanding of rights was supported by accepted theories of jurisprudence in the West, which defined laws as the decisions of governments and recognized no source of "higher law." The Nuremberg trials after World War II asserted a higher standard of law than that of the sovereign state, and the United Nations codified this as international human-rights law. Since 1948, these human-rights laws have grown to include numerous covenants (treaties) and international regulatory mechanisms, such as the Commission on Human Rights of the United Nations. At the same time, the number of nations in the U.N. has expanded rapidly, primarily as a result of the liberation of peoples in Africa and Asia from colonial rule. The U.N. has become more prominent, if no less controversial, and assertions of human rights have continued to capture international attention.[6]

In the last fifty years, the understanding of human rights has also expanded conceptually. The Universal Declaration of Human Rights was dominated by notions of civil and political rights familiar to Westerners. But economic and social rights concerning employment, food, shelter, education, and health care have also been affirmed. More recently, accompanying the growing strength of formerly colonized peoples in the U.N., cultural and people's rights have been asserted. We see here a shift (at least in emphasis) from the individual to the group and from protection of the dignity of the individual from state intervention to providing for communities, through state intervention, the elements of life deemed necessary for human dignity.

When we reflect on the historical development of human rights, we see immediately that, for most of human history, religious leaders resisted what we today describe as fundamental human rights. Traditionally, religious leaders were primarily concerned with enforcing their authority and with the welfare of their own community rather than with the rights of their followers, especially if recognizing these rights meant permitting dissent. Religious people who today support human rights need to acknowledge humbly that their traditions and teachings have long been used to deny many contemporary civil and political rights and that, until recently, support for human rights has come more consistently from secular political and cultural movements than from religious constituencies.

This is less true for Protestants than for Catholics, as Protestants are quick to claim their right of conscience in opposition to the religious hierarchy from which they are dissenting. Nonetheless, it is common knowledge that Protestant Reformers often suppressed dissent within their own jurisdictions. Religious freedom, as a fundamental right of all individuals, was not effectively institutionalized among Protestants until Roger Williams established Rhode Island as an independent colony.

The Virginia Bill of Rights of 1776 laid the foundation for modern notions of civil and political rights, and in the United States, the Bill of Rights in the Constitution guaranteed these rights for all those who were permitted to vote. In the latter part of the eighteenth century, many of the individuals who embraced the idea of "natural rights" were members of churches, yet it would be misleading to say that religious organizations were active in lobbying for the protection of rights. The protection of civil and political rights was the result of a successful rebellion and the experience of freedom that inspired and sustained it.[7]

American religious leaders were prominent in the nineteenth century in promoting the rights of black Americans, women, prisoners, and children. And in the middle of the twentieth century, Christian and Jewish leaders from the United States were among the first to urge that the United Nations promulgate a Declaration of Human Rights. The newly formed World Council of Churches provided leadership among Protestant Christian groups, and since Vatican II, members of the Roman Catholic Church have been in the forefront of human-rights struggles all over the world. Jewish participants in the human-rights movement are far more numerous than their small numbers in the world would lead one to expect. And more recently, a number of leading Muslim intellectuals have asserted that the Islamic tradition supports fundamental human rights.

Among Christians, there is considerable debate about whether human rights are adequately supported by the scriptures of the Old Testament or can only be affirmed on the basis of the saving event of Jesus Christ. Christian evangelicals have expressed concern, as have Muslims, that the Universal Declaration of Human Rights does not acknowledge God as the ultimate source of human rights and have accused Christian liberals of making "Freedom" their God rather than Jesus Christ. Since Vatican II, Catholics have embraced human rights as the social conditions for human dignity, and many priests, nuns, and lay leaders have been martyred in human-rights struggles in Africa, Asia, and Latin America.[8]

Religious support for human rights among Jews, Christians, and Muslims tends to take the form of arguing that modern notions of rights are implicit in the duties that we owe to God and our neighbors, which are revealed in the ancient scriptures of each community of faith. If I have, for instance, the duty to love you as my neighbor, then you have the right to expect and hold me to the standard of conduct that is consistent with my duty. Hindus derive rights from social, cultural, and religious duties. Buddhists find rights implied in the obligation to be aware of the interconnectedness of all reality and thus affirm animal as well as human rights.

This is very different from the view of those who drafted the Universal Declaration of Human Rights and promoted the development of human-rights law in the first part of the second half of the twentieth century. From this other point of view, which is at the core of recent Western political thought, rights are inherent in the nature of the individuals who join together to form communities. Thus, rights are brought into society by individuals who, in theory, form a "social contract" with one another in order to live together. In this perspective, the community is like a voluntary association, which the individual can leave or join as he or she chooses.

When Asians or Africans practicing Hindu, Buddhist, Islamic, or indigenous traditions assert their cultural rights today and complain that international human rights law is dominated by Western individualism, they are challenging the universality of the idea that communities are formed by individuals who enter into a social contract. In historical terms, of course, they are correct. Until very recently, all societies were formed more around kinship and ethnic identities than by the voluntary decisions of their individual members. Prior to modern democratic forms of government, individuals had little to say about the laws that governed their societies. Any assertion of the universality of human rights, therefore, must be acknowledged as a contemporary claim that such rights are universally the necessary social conditions for human dignity.[9]

In the case of culture, which is an offshoot of religion and ethnicity, individuals have faced racial discrimination in the West, which has denied or denies equal status and opportunities to individuals who happened to be blacks, Latinos, or Asians in their own societies. In this regard, the *Dalits* (also known as untouchables) of India were the product of religious belief, and the Hindu religion did not permit rights to these unfortunate people. The *Dalit* population in India is as large as the population of the United States and numbers about 250 million. The Durban Conference against Racial Discrimination took note of the plight of the large number of the *Dalits*. Untouchables are denied basic human rights, although India is a signatory to the Universal Declaration of Human Rights. Similar discrimination, however, is very much prevalent in different forms in the West, varying in degrees from place to place and time to time.

The International Convention on the Elimination of All Forms of Racial Discrimination, signed in 1965 and entered into force in 1969, builds on the nondiscrimination provisions in the U.N. Charter.[10] Under its provisions, state parties undertake to prohibit racial discrimination and guarantee equality for all in the enjoyment of a series of rights and to assure to all within their jurisdiction effective protection and remedies regarding such human rights. It is also fair to conclude that in addition to the existence of this convention, the prohibition of discrimination on racial grounds is part of customary international law. This may be understood on the basis inter alia of Articles 55 and 56 of the U.N. Charter and Articles 2 and 7 of the Universal Declaration of Human Rights. Discrimination on other grounds of religion and gender may also be contrary to customary international law.[11]

Freedom of religion or belief is defined in the Universal Declaration of Human Rights and the Covenant on Civil and Political Rights as primarily an individual right. In the words of the Universal Declaration, "freedom of thought, conscience and religion" is protected, and this includes the freedom to change one's religion or belief as well as the freedom to join with others in teaching, practicing, worshiping, and observing the religious disciplines of one's faith community. Religious freedom may be asserted by a group of individuals, but it is fundamentally the right of the individual person.

This understanding of the right to religious freedom implies that religion is a voluntary activity on the part of individuals, who join together to practice what their individual consciences tell them

is right. As this is largely a modern, Western notion of religion, it is not surprising that more traditional religious communities are less than enthusiastic about this emphasis on the rights of the individual believer. In their view, if rights are given by God to the community of the faithful, then individual rights are secondary rather than primary. The rights of the community take precedence.

Here the role of civil society is a predominant one, and the theoretical labors of Antonio Gramsci have informed us that a hegemonized civil society can become a handmaiden of the state in its project of social practices.[12] Civil societies are defined by the practices of their inhabitants. These practices may lead to the sphere becoming a captive of the state; however, it could equally realize its potential for mounting a powerful challenge to state-oriented practices. The presence of civil society is a crucial but not an adequate precondition for ensuring state accountability. Whether the state can be made accountable depends upon the self-consciousness, vibrancy, and political vision of civil society. An inactive civil society leads to unresponsive states; a potential, self-conscious civil society imposes limits upon state power. In this context, a self-conscious and a vigilant civil society will visualize what kind of civil society one wants to build up. Hence, the role of civil society is very important in inculcating the values and ethos for itself and for the future generations.

Gramsci understands civil society as the realm existing not just between the state and the family, but also occupying the space outside the market, state, and family—in other words, as the realm of culture, ideology, and political debate. It was Gramsci who drew the distinction between hegemony, based on consent, and domination, based on coercion. The changing definitions of civil society expressed the different ways in which consent was generated in different periods and the different issues that were important at different times. In a way, the civil society in general terms is defined or construed as a process through which individuals negotiate, argue, struggle against, or agree with each other and with the centers of political and economic authority.

Through voluntary associations, movements, parties, and unions, the individual is able to act publicly. Thus, in the early modern period, the main concern of civil rights was fear. Hence, civil society was a society where laws replaced physical coercion, arbitrary arrest, and the like.

Civil society, armed with values of rights and mutual tolerance, has thus to constantly mediate between social forces seeking to assert themselves in the public space and between them and the state. And constant vigilance has to be its creed and dogma. The battles against chauvinistic movements that attempt to hegemonize civil society have to be fought in civil society itself. There is no alternative, since the state, in which at one time great hopes had been reposed, has shown itself to be vulnerable to these chauvinistic passions. It has simply opted out of engagement with these forces and their pernicious ideologies. Only a civil society, armed with a democratic spirit, can provide an alternative.

In order to do so, civil society has to function as a sphere of pedagogy and communication. The values of freedom, equality, and justice have to be extended through communicative action, debate, and publicity. Civil society has to act as an intermediary filter between the particularistic loyalties of society, the individual, and the state. A civil society that is unable to mediate because it suffers from weak communication is both impotent and vulnerable. It can become strong when its members exhibit a commitment to freedom and equality and to democracy, participation, and the mutual recognition of rights. The need is even greater in those societies where civil society is fragile. Kothari and Sethi, while speaking of modern India, put it this way:

> It is in . . . situations where a well-defined civil society does not exist, where the culture, history and experiences of different communities are not only different but at variance with each other, and where the state does not enjoy an overriding moral authority in many spheres of social life, if not itself being the major perpetrator of violations, that a relevant *politics* of human rights needs to be defined.[13]

But whether the voices of reason and sanity will have an impact on particularistic loyalties or on the state, or whether they will be able to modify these projects, depends on the politics and the political vision of civil society. And this means that the inhabitants of civil society have to be deeply committed to the values of democratic life.

For citizens of the United States, religious freedom means separation of church and state. Religious establishment and religious freedom are seen as contradictory. International law, however, does not require "disestablishment." We need only think of England to see why, because there the Church of England is established by law, and the sovereign is the head of the church. The church of England enjoys a status not afforded to other religious communities and, in the religious education classes required in every public school in England, the Church of England generally has a predominant place in the curriculum. Nonetheless, few would seriously argue that there is religious oppression or a lack of religious freedom in England today. Similarly, in many other Western European societies (Sweden, Germany, Switzerland, Greece, to name a few), state churches exist, and such established churches receive favored treatment in some way. The Universal Declaration of Human Rights would never have been passed in 1948 if it had defined freedom of religion (as the United States does in the first amendment of its Constitution) as requiring the separation of church and state.[14]

We may now turn to Eastern Europe to look at societies under the monopolistic control of a secular worldview. Not all the countries concerned can be examined in any detail, but a comparison could be made between the East and West (Poland and Russia) and it could be, perhaps, the best approach for a number of reasons. The material available on these two societies is much greater in volume and quality than found elsewhere. Furthermore, the two countries offer the maximum opportunity for bringing out important contrasts between a dominating and a dominated society, between the Orthodox and the Catholic Church, between total state power and elements of constitutional opposition, between total disruption of the countryside and limited disruption. Nevertheless, other countries warrant a query or an explanation insofar as special developments have occurred in them from time to time. For example, there is some interest in the current situation with regard to church-state relations in Hungary and Serbia (Yugoslavia).

International human-rights law may well favor a "secular" state, as some religious critics claim, but it does not require it. Instead, international human-rights law requires states to "prevent and eliminate discrimination on the grounds of religion or belief" and to "combat intolerance on the grounds of religion or other beliefs." International law names the evil as "discrimination" and "intolerance" rather than "establishment," allowing that some sort of "fair and tolerant establishment" of religion is possible. Put more precisely, it leaves open the question of special relationships between the state and one or more religious traditions and the evaluation of the effects of such relationships on religious freedom, rather than asserting in principle that any support for religion by a government will necessarily be discriminatory.

Religious communities continue to play a significant role in the enforcement of human rights because of the unique nature of international law in our time. Unlike the laws of a state, international human rights law has no coercive authority to back it up. The United Nations does not have enforcement powers, except as granted by its member nations, and then only for very limited purposes. For many, this fact suggests that human-rights law is merely a legal fiction, a romantic idea, until a world government with enforcement powers is created. Others argue, however, that the enforcement of international human-rights law is an experiment in nonviolent community building. Nonviolent methods for enforcing human-rights laws include encouraging more responsible conduct through interfaith cooperation, exposing human rights violations to public scrutiny and shame, and economic and political sanctions.

Religious ideals and discipline may help keep the human-rights struggle nonviolent, may encourage political leaders to live up to the higher aspirations of their religious and cultural traditions, and may help build trust between minority and majority communities in a society. We see examples of this in the movement led by Gandhi in India, in the role of Christians and Jewish leaders during the civil rights movement in the United States during the 1960s, in the leadership of Christians and Muslims in fighting apartheid in South Africa, and in the martyrdom of religious leaders all around the world in the struggle for human rights.[15]

It is worth noting that the type, source, and volume of material in the different societies are indicative of the conditions therein. In Russia, the clearly stated aim of most research is to bring out the optimal conditions and apply the best techniques for eliminating vestiges of the "idealist" worldview. Support in religious traditions not only provides a foundation for human rights, which may otherwise appear to be merely the consensus of a particular culture or a particular time, but also translates the imperatives of human rights into the moral and spiritual language of different religious and cultural traditions. This allows more people to claim these rights as their own heritage and strengthens the contemporary affirmation that fundamental human rights are universal.

RELIGION AND WOMEN

Respecting Gender

INTRODUCTION

The discussion of women in the context of both religion and human rights is subject to a bedeviling paradox: that the very indivisibility of men and women as human beings sometimes contributes to the invisibility of women in the discussion. Special effort is therefore required to prevent this from happening, hence a separate section for this topic.

One point worth keeping in mind is the implicit ambivalence of religions toward women. While religions' guiding moral norms such as justice and compassion resonate with women's needs, their institutional structures often involve their subordination, thereby creating a lasting tension between the religion's moral norms and the social reality over which it presides. The essay on Hinduism is particularly instructive in this context.

Another point worth recognizing is the fact that, while religions may tend to view the role of women ambiguously and even negatively in the *abstract*, their position often softens and even becomes positive when dealing with women in the *concrete*; that is, as mother, sister, daughter, or wife. It is true that the position of the wife may involve subordination to the husband in some settings, but here again such legal subordination does not necessarily imply inferiority but often reflects current power structures which are subject to modification.

Women in World Religions

Discrimination, Liberation, and Backlash

Rosemary Radford Ruether

In this talk on women in world religions, I will attempt some comparisons of the treatment of women in seven major traditions of world religions: Hinduism, Buddhism, Jainism, Confucianism, Judaism, Christianity, and Islam in their classical periods of development. I will then discuss how women's status was modernized in these world religions and how this process of modernization has generated fundamentalist backlash in several of these traditions. Obviously, in such a forty-minute presentation, it is impossible to mention all the historical nuances that would be necessary for a longer study of these issues. One is forced to make broad generalizations.

All of these seven traditions reflect patrilineal, patriarchal patterns of their societies and enshrine somewhat comparable expressions of discrimination against women. This is in contrast to Shamanist traditions that preexisted these patriarchal religions, where women's autonomy and leadership is more highly valued. Daoism, often listed among the world religions, carries on much of the ancient Chinese Shaman traditions and significantly allows a larger place for female leadership and a positive view of the feminine than the more patriarchal world religions I will discuss in this talk.

Comparative Patterns in World Religions

I will compare these seven world religions in terms of six major themes: (1) male and female in cosmic order, and good and evil; (2) purity and impurity; (3) education, teaching, and religious leadership; (4) asceticism and monasticism; (5) marriage, divorce, and widowhood; (6) dress, body, and segregation.

Male and Female in Cosmic Order; Good and Evil

Among world religions, Christianity developed one of the most severe woman-blaming views for the advent of evil. According to the Augustinian tradition that shaped western Christianity, men and women were created with souls equally capable of spiritual life, but the woman was created subordinate to man in the original order of creation. The woman then revolted against this subordination in the primeval garden, causing the expulsion of humanity from paradise and the advent of evil in the world. In order to redeem herself, the woman must subordinate herself to male authority, even to the point of coercion and abuse. Although women of spiritual merit may be equal in heaven, this redemptive transformation entails acceptance of strict subordination on earth.[1]

Christianity also absorbed a Greek dualistic ontological hierarchy of the spiritual over the material, mind over body, and linked the body with physical passions and sin. Women by nature are seen as linked to the body and more prone to bodily passions. For Augustine, women's "natural" subordination is tied to this hierarchy of mind over body, the male representing the mind and the female the body.

Judaism also carries the story of woman's creation from the side or "rib" of Adam, her primacy in disobedience to God and expulsion from paradise. But because Judaism does not have a doctrine of the Fall, this story does not have the same theological consequences as in Christianity. The Qur'an has only the story of man and woman's creation at the same time, lacking the Adam's-rib story and woman-blaming for sin, although this story comes into Islam through later commentary influenced by Christianity. Islam also lacks the idea of the Fall. Both Judaism and Islam see men and women as created for different roles, men for public service and headship of the family and women for domestic duties, but these are not linked to ontological hierarchy of mind over body, as in classical Christianity.

In Hinduism, women are also linked with the material world of appearances and are seen as less capable of spiritual liberation. This is connected with concepts of karma and *samsara* (the cycle of rebirth). Women's lesser capacity for liberation means they are destined to continue in the cycle of rebirth. Being born a woman is itself seen as caused by previous sin, resulting in being born as a female. These ideas also come into Jainism and Buddhism through the influence of Hinduism, but they are contested in these two traditions.

In Jainism, two religious orders developed, the Digambaras, who practice nudity, and the Shevetambaras, who are white-clad. The Digambaras do not admit women to monastic life, claiming women are impure and sensual, incapable of spiritual renunciation, while the Shevetambaras

admit women and see them as having the same capacities as men. In Buddhism, there are traditions that claim that women cannot become a Buddha because of her sensual female body, seen as threatening to the celibate life of male monks, while other traditions insist that male or female bodiliness is an illusory difference, and a woman can equally attain spiritual liberation.[2]

In Confucianism, the cosmos is seen as grounded in a cosmic energy, Ch'i, which works through an interplay of vital forces, yin and yang, linked to male and female. Yin and yang are not dualistic in the same way as mind and body in Western philosophical thought. Rather, they are seen as complementary and interpenetrating, each vitally necessary to the other. In Daoism, the yin, or female force, is even seen as more primary, grounding the male yang. However in Confucianism, the yin-yang complementary forces became linked with a hierarchical concept of society, the outer public world and the inner domestic world. Since woman is strictly confined to the domestic world and is the underside of all of the social relations of authority and obedience, this also shaped the yin-yang interaction as hierarchical. Yin-yang as passive to active is linked to subordination and dominance in social relations.[3]

PURITY AND IMPURITY

The notion of woman's ontological inferiority is related to the idea of woman's impurity or ritual pollution in several traditions. This is particularly true in Hinduism, where the hierarchy of caste is linked to the hierarchy of purity and pollution. The lowest caste, the Sudras, and the outcastes or untouchables, are assigned the dirty work that is ritually polluting. Women, through their bodily activities of menstruation and childbirth and their work in food preparation and cleanup, are linked to ritual impurity and thus equated to the Sudras, the ritually impure caste.

Judaism also has a strong tradition of woman's ritual impurity through her bodily functions of menstruation and childbirth. This deeply affects daily life. A woman must segregate herself from her husband and male relatives for part of each month. The dichotomy of purity and impurity is correlated with the sacred and the profane. In temple Judaism, this meant that women were forbidden to approach the holy of holies and confined to the outer court. Women's impurity is compared to the impurity of the profane Gentile world. In the separations of the pure and the impure, woman falls on the impure side of the separations, by which men keep themselves pure and holy to come into the presence of God. They are, as Jewish feminist Judith Plaskow has said, the "gentile within."[4]

In New Testament Christianity, this tradition of purity and impurity, correlated with the separations of Jew-gentile and male-female, pure and impure foods, is explicit rejected. In the Qur'an, the notion of women's impurity is ignored. But in both Christianity and Islam, ideas of woman's impurity come back in through popular culture, particularly affecting women's public religious participation. Women are told to exclude themselves from church or mosque when menstruating. Christianity developed a rite of purification for women after childbirth.

Even in modern Protestantism, such ideas sometime reenter through popular culture. Thus, when I taught at Gurukul Lutheran Theological Seminary in Madras a few years ago, I was surprised to be told by a woman seminarian that her pastor told her women may not enter the church while menstruating. Both the notions of women's ritual impurity in Hindu-influenced culture, plus the presence of such ideas in Hebrew Scripture, apparently caused this pastor to appropriate these traditions into Christian practice in India.

EDUCATION AND RELIGIOUS LEADERSHIP

Many world religions traditionally excluded women from religious education or at least the higher level of education. This also excluded women from the religious leadership that depended on such education. In Judaism, women were excluded from study of religious texts and directed to take care of the material side of life in order to free the male to study. This also excluded

women from the rabbinate, which depended on a high level of achievement in such study. Islam did not exclude women from private study, but women were not admitted to the role of public teacher or imam.

Christianity also did not exclude women from private study, but women were forbidden to engage in public teaching. This also meant that women's writings were less likely to be preserved, since the fruits of women's intellectual life were not seen as part of the public teaching tradition. The exclusion of women from ordination in Christianity is also linked with the idea that the sacramental priesthood represents Christ. Classical Christianity taught that women's lack of full humanity meant that she could not represent Christ and that Christ had to be a male to represent the fullness of humanity.[5]

In Hinduism, it is the Brahman caste that studies the sacred texts and performs the rituals dependent on such knowledge. Women of Brahman caste are excluded from this study and are linked with ignorance and lack of capacity for knowledge. In Confucianism also, women are excluded from the study that leads to public service as a Confucian scholar. The Jain tradition limited the right of nuns to study, forbidding them access to certain texts.[6] Buddhism does not restrict study by nuns but has put many impediments in the way of women achieving authority as a teacher. Thus, although traditions exist of women's learning, there are few existing texts identified as authored by women.[7]

ASCETICISM AND WOMEN RELIGIOUS

Asceticism created a new layer of spiritual practice, based on rejecting marriage and family for renunciate life. In the ascetic dimension of religion, there arises a debate whether women are capable of renunciate life and are to be admitted to monastic life. Neither Judaism, Islam, nor Confucianism values sexual renunciation, focusing religion on family life, so this issue does not arise, although Judaism apparently had a brief development of celibate religious communities in the first century. Hinduism generally excludes women from renunciate life and the study that is necessary for it, although female Bhakta who renounce marriage for devotion to a particular god do develop.

Buddhism and Jainism admit women to monastic life but put severe constrains on them, insisting that even the oldest and most learned nun must subordinate herself to the youngest monk. Thus, female monastics are marginalized, denied authority, and often lack the same economic resources as monks. Offerings to nuns by the laity are seen as garnering less merit than offerings to monks.

Christianity valued celibate life and promoted female monastic communities, although attempting to put them under male church authority, affording them less mobility and education than males. In medieval Christianity, learned women's monastic communities developed, often playing the key role of education for women in the society. With libraries and scriptoria, women's religious communities have been key to the preservation of women's mystical and religious writings. In modern times, the struggle to improve nuns' education and to afford them wider public ministries has been an area of conflict between Christian women's communities and the male ecclesiastical hierarchy.

Marriage, Divorce, and Widowhood

In all world religions, regulating marriage, divorce, and widowhood have been key functions of religion, linked to supporting the patriarchal family. Hebrew religion in patriarchal times allowed polygamy, but this died out as Judaism developed. Men have the priority in initiating divorce, and this continues to cause great difficulty to Orthodox Jews when the husband is absent but not certified as dead or refuses to give a wife a divorce. This leaves many Orthodox Jewish women in a limbo, unable to remarry.

Christianity preferred celibacy to marriage and rejected polygamy. Remarriage of widows or widowers was discouraged. Marriage was banned between cousins to the seventh degree of kinship, and divorce was not allowed.[8] Islam allowed a man four wives, if he could treat them all equally,

a Qur'anic teaching which has been used to insist that a male should have only one wife, since no man could treat multiple wives equally. Traditionally, Islam also allowed a man to divorce his wife simply by announcing three times that he divorced her.

Hinduism and Confucianism prefer the one legal wife, although concubines and secondary wives maintained by a husband were not criticized. Moreover, both of these traditions developed practices of child marriage in order to assure that the bride would be a virgin. Males have the prerogative in divorce. Both Hinduism and Confucianism discourage remarriage of widows. This most severely affected the Hindu widow, who was faced with the choice of burning herself on the funeral pyre of her husband or becoming an impoverished beggar on the margins of family life. How well women were able to live as widows or divorced women depended on women's rights to inherit and maintain control of property from their families and husbands, rights which most patriarchal religions have restricted.

Separation, Veiling, and the Female Body

Much of the discourse about women and religion in recent decades has centered on the insistence of modern Islamists on women's complete body covering, including in some cases covering of the face. This is seen as evidence of the extreme subordination of women in Islam, in contrast to greater freedom of Western Christian and Jewish women. But this Islam-blaming for women's subordination, focused on veiling, is ahistorical. The issue of women's veiling needs to be put in the context of practices in many cultures of restricting women to the household, insistence on full body covering, and accompaniment when women leave the protected domestic space. Such separation of women has applied mostly to upper-class women, with peasant women much freer to move around in the outside world, although also seen as disreputable because of this greater freedom.

Hinduism sought to restrict female activities, particularly of upper-caste women, to the domestic sphere. This separation is believed to have become more severe under the influence of Islam in India after 1200 C.E. Confucianism also sought to restrict the upper-class women to the domestic space and forbid women presence in the public world. The practice of foot-binding in Chinese culture had the obvious effect of severely restricting female mobility, confining them to a sedentary life within the home. Although it began for elite women, it came to be identified with respectable and valued women of affluent men who could afford such restrictions of their wife's work. Peasant women, who worked in the fields, could not afford such a luxury, but this also meant that women with "natural" feet were seen as crude and low class.

Veiling of women was not unknown in Christianity and Judaism. In the New Testament, uncovered hair is connected with women's sensuality and sinfulness, which causes temptation in men and angels. Thus, women are particularly enjoined to wear a veil in church. This idea continued into modern times in practices of women wearing a veil or hat in church. In Judaism, uncovered hair was seen as seductive, an indication of a "loose" woman. The respectable women should wear a veil and full body covering without jewelry or attractive clothing in public. Orthodox Judaism developed the custom of demanding that the wife shave her head and wear a wig, since uncovered hair was seen as dangerously sensual. This continues among ultra-Orthodox women today, while mainline Orthodox women generally wear some kind of hat or scarf to cover her hair in public.

Islam was influenced by these customs in Judaism and Christianity. It developed an insistence on women remaining primarily in the domestic space and wearing a veil in public, although again this was primarily a custom for upper-class women, with peasant women who had to work in the fields less likely to wear a head covering. The contemporary Islamist insistence on complete body and head covering, including the face, and restriction of any contact with males outside the family, has primarily developed in the context of a modern Islamist fundamentalism that is shaped by reaction to what is perceived as Western colonialism and corruption of family morals.

MODERNIZATION AND BACKLASH

To explain this fixation on female veiling and separation in contemporary Islamism, one needs to turn to the issue of modernization of women's status from the mid-nineteenth century to the present and the way in which certain processes of modernizing women's status in the context of secularism and colonialism have lent themselves to antifeminism backlash in several world religions.

Women in the United States and England began to agitate for women's rights from the mid-nineteenth century. They sought higher education; access to valued male professions, such as medicine and law; and legal civil status, including the vote, property rights, and the possibility of political office. From the 1880s to 1930s, there was some success in winning more equal legal status with men in these societies.

Rights for women were argued on two different grounds. For Christian feminists in the United States, depatriarchalization of American society reflected their views of true Christianity. Women were said to have been created equal by God and affirmed in this equality by Christ. Patriarchy was seen as a sinful deviation from God's true intentions. This view in original equality was particularly cultivated by Quaker feminists such as Angelina Grimké Lucretia Mott and Susan B. Anthony, important in the nineteenth-century feminist movement.[9] But most of the changed status of women in America and Britain coincided with secularization and the loss of influence of the churches over society, with the clerical class mostly resisting rights for women. The hierarchy of the Catholic Church in the United States and Europe generally rejected women's suffrage in the 1920s.

This period of amelioration of women's status corresponded with the high point of British imperialism. Britain forged an empire on which the "sun never set," from Egypt to India and Burma. The British colonial leaders established a discourse about the favorable treatment of women in Western societies as evidence for the superiority of Western civilization. This colonial discourse about women was used both to establish the inferiority of

Asian cultures and religions, especially Hinduism and Islam, and to justify British right to rule, based on its "uplift" to women in the Middle Eastern and Asian world. Missionary men and women also adopted versions of this discourse on women, positioning indigenous women as oppressed by Islam, Hinduism, and other Asian religions. Christian conversion was promoted as uplifting women.[10]

This kind of discourse about Western civilization as liberating women has returned today as a tool against the Islamic world. For example, when President Bush invaded Afghanistan in 2002, one of his arguments to justify the invasion was the oppression of Afghani women by the Taliban, even though the American government had shown no concern about the oppression of Afghani women earlier, when they were allies whom the Americans helped put into power. The superiority of American culture was touted as democratic and liberating by presenting the Americans as liberating women, promoting their education and political rights.

This colonial discourse about women created two kinds of reactions on the part of men of the colonized societies. Indigenous women were seldom consulted by either side and only with difficulty began to articulate their own voice in this conflict. These two responses I will call "militant secular nationalism" and "militant anti-Western religious fundamentalism."

The first response predominated in the late nineteenth century to the 1980s. The second response has grown in the last thirty-five years as secular nationalist governments, established by anticolonial liberation movements, have failed to establish just societies freed from western neocolonialism.

Some national liberation movements linked themselves with Marxism, such as in the China and Vietnam. Religions, whether Confucian, Buddhist, or Christian, were discredited as reactionary and superstitious vestiges of a backward era, to be overcome by a socialist society that would bring both freedom from Western colonialism and an equalitarian and just society for all. The equality of women was seen as an integral part of this just society. Such male socialist feminism discouraged independent feminist movements, seen as "bourgeois Western" feminism, since socialism would take care of assuring women's equality in society.

India and the Islamic world also sought liberation from Western colonialism, promoting secular democratic societies, rather than a socialism which aroused Western anticommunist interventions. Modernization of women's status, the vote, equal education, inclusion in professions, removal of oppressive restrictions and practices, such as foot-binding in China, widow burning and child marriage in India, or purdah and the veil in Islamic countries, were seen as part of this secular modernization.

The failure of many of these secular liberal or socialist societies to establish real justice for the majority and to free the society from Western economic neocolonialism sparked a second anticolonial movement that has focused on religious renewal. Islamism, sometimes called Islamic fundamentalism, has become the strongest version of this second movement, which attacks the corrupt leadership of their own society and continued Western dominance. Religious fundamentalist movements are also found in Hinduism and Confucianism, and right-wing or fundamentalist Judaism and Christianity are also on the rise. U.S. right-wing Christianity particularly has been a key ally of the neoconservatives of the Bush administration.

The Islamic revolution in Iran in 1979 became the key turning point in the advent of this second response to colonialism. Iran had been penetrated by Britain from the late nineteenth century, who early saw the value of its oil resources. When a newly independent Iran sought to nationalize its oil resources under nationalist leader Mohammed Mossadegh, he was overthrown by a combination of British and American power in 1953, reestablishing the Shah of Iran as a Western puppet, who severely repressed internal dissent. The Shah also supported the modernization of women's status.

When the Shah's oppressive rule was overthrown by an Islamic regime in 1979, this took the form of a militant anti-Western policy and insistence on reestablishing traditional Islamic restrictions on women. The modernization of women's status, symbolized by the adoption of Western dress, came to be the concrete expression of the corruption of Muslim societies and values by western neocolonialism. The vindication of Muslim masculinity against Western power thus came to be expressed by a combination of antiwestern militancy and reestablishment of strict control over women.

The psychological connections between control over women in family and society and overthrowing western control over the resources of the society have deep emotional links. The humiliation of Muslim men by the West, which claims to prove its superiority through its liberation of their women, is rebuffed by insisting that such liberation of women is in fact their corruption and the corruption of the whole society, while the purity and divine favor of the society is vindicated by reestablishing traditional gender relations.

Although the historical context is different for a Western society such as the United States, the psychological and cultural dynamics are somewhat similar. In the 1880s, conservative Christians rejected historical-critical methods of biblical interpretation, writing a series of books called *The Fundamentals*, from which comes the name fundamentalism. In the 1920s–50s, conservative Christians lost out politically and culturally to liberal Christians in the seminaries and National Council of Churches and to secularism and pluralism in the larger culture. Such liberal and secular leaders made conservatives feel humiliated and culturally backward on issues such as teaching evolution in the schools.

Since the late 1970s with the Reagan presidency and now that of George W. Bush, right-wing Christianity has made a spectacular political comeback and has sought to assert its cultural agenda in the society, ideally seeking to reestablish their definition of an American Christian state. Attacks on abortion and on homosexual marriage have become their key issues. Feminism in general is seen as corrupting society and destroying "family values." Conservative Christians seek to claim to be the true Christian believers, over against secular godlessness. To quote Christian fundamentalist

leader Pat Robertson, "Feminism makes women leave their husbands, kill their children, practice witchcraft, destroy capitalism and become lesbians."

Progressive Christians are currently busy trying to reestablish a progressive alternative to religious fundamentalism, but progressive Christian men often fail to see how basic sexual and gender politics is to the right-wing Christian agenda. Thus, they abandon issues such as women reproductive rights as too controversial while trying to establish their credentials as authentic Christians through issues of war, poverty, and environmental sustainability.

I suggest that it is religious or theological feminism that is the key alternative to this false dualism between antifeminist religious fundamentalism and liberal secularism. In each of the world religions, most notably Buddhism, Judaism, Christianity, and Islam, significant movements of religious feminism have developed that seek to vindicate the full equality of women as equal partners with men, not by repudiating the religious tradition altogether but by drawing out its deeper ethical and spiritual values. Thus for Jewish feminist Ellen Umansky, Jewish feminism reaffirms the deeper values of Judaism of women and men's equal dignity, equality, and worth.[11] Christian feminists search the New Testament for an affirmation of the essentially liberating message of Jesus.[12] Islamic feminists such as Riffat Hassan seek to establish the egalitarian message of Muhammad in his social context. She cites the lack of traditions, such as women as created second from Adam's rib, within the Qur'anic teaching.[13]

Thus, religious feminists in the various world religions seek a renewal of the ethical and spiritual traditions, not the repudiation of religion by secular materialism. It is this renewal of religious and ethical values based on the equal sacred worth of all humans, women as much as men, which is the only answer to the false dichotomy of antiwomen religious fundamentalism, on the one hand, and a secular materialism unconcerned with values of the common good, on the other.

Women and Human Rights

The Status of Women in the *Smṛti* Texts of Hinduism

Abha Singh

Literally, the word *smṛti* means "recollection." It signifies "a record of tradition that was based on Vedas" (*śruti*). As a compilation of approved rules and customs, promulgated at different times by or under the sanction of eminent sages, these texts enjoy the status of authority among the Hindus. In a way, these texts serve as a guide to the Hindu society with regard to religious and mundane matters. Hindu society was basically hierarchical. As a result, the thrust of *smṛti* texts appears to help one fulfill the goal of one's birth.[1] So these texts provide a comprehensive code of conduct for each and every person in society. This chapter is an attempt to examine the status of Hindu women against the backdrop of the *smṛti* texts.[2]

Smṛti texts were compiled, broadly, in the period ranging between the Vedic era and Buddhist era. Scores of the texts are available. However, three of these—Manusmṛti, Yājñavalkyasmṛti, and Parāśarasmṛti—were quite prominent. Among the three, Manusmṛti in particular has held a position of preeminence since its dicta have influenced the lives and ideals of Hindus down the ages. Manusmṛti has been compared in its extent and thoroughness to that of Confucius in China. The paramount position of Manusmṛti among Indian literature is based on the fact that this ethical work deals more with civil matters than any other work. Since Manusmṛti has had the utmost influence on the social order of Hindus, we shall concentrate on it.

Context

The main context of description of any *smṛti* text is social morality. In congruence with *śruti* (Vedas), *smṛtis* present their picture of social morality blended with ritualism. Although ritualism pervades the entire outlook of Hindu religious texts, the basic thrust appears to be the stability of the social organization and the advocacy of a social morality that would be conducive to it. To be clearer, Hindu seers presupposed the world as meaningful. Therefore, by the performance of rituals and through the fulfillment of social obligations one can achieve one's ultimate goal. It would not be out of place to mention here that morality comprises the legitimacy of the pursuit of one's self-interest, as it concedes that there is no conflict between the good of the individual and that of the society. Nevertheless, Hindu seers did not discuss morality as a separate discipline. Still, their concern for the sociomoral life of the individual and of society undeniably put them on the high pedestal of lawgivers (*smṛtikāras*).

The basic precept of morality is that it is relative to time and space. Hindu social morality is also relative, but in a wider spectrum. In addition to time (*yuga*) and space (*deśa*), the Hindu concept of morality is also relative to one's *varṇa* (class), stage of life (*āśrama*), and sex (*liṅga*). This is for the reason that women of all the four *varṇas* of Hinduism (*brāhmaṇa, kṣatriya, vaiśya,* and *śudra*) are treated as a class apart. Hence, their duties and virtues have been depicted quite differently from those of men. Since *smṛtis* aim at presenting guidelines for the entire life of human beings, including religion, morality, culture, and sociolegal aspects, it would not be an exaggeration to state that the morality rendered by *smṛti* (*dharmaśāstra*) is essentially social in character.

One should remember the fact that the status of morality in a society can be determined by dissecting the treatment it imparts to its weaker class and sex. In this case, as mentioned earlier, the weaker sex (i.e., women) is under the scanner. Against this backdrop, an attempt has been made to document, in detail, the account of the status of women in *smṛti* texts in a society that was on the threshold of Vedic and Buddhist India. It seems extremely difficult to construct a picture of women in the age of *smṛtis* because initially these texts were passed over verbally, and they were documented much later. Lest we forget, no tall claims can be made, and in this regard, one needs to be cautious and careful. However, the influence of *smṛti* texts on Hindu society makes one depend on that influence to a large extent, and it gives a fairly authentic picture of women in that age. Still, one of the more important features of the Vedic texts—of which *smṛtis* constitute a synthesis—is the large number of female deities, such as Uṣā, Rātri, Prithvī, Sarasvatī, Kuhu, Rākā, Sinīvāli, and many others. The religion of people reflects their mental framework. If so, then a religion that respects and worships so many female deities provides a clear image of people who respect and honor women. But at the same time, we find that *smṛtis* have an ambivalent attitude toward women. As regards worldly pleasures, women are seen as obstacles in the path of spiritual quest. But in the view of dharma (comprehending both religion and morality), women are seen as wives and mothers, and are well respected.

Negative Attitude toward Women

The entire gamut of the existence of women in *smṛti* texts is based on the theory of *bīja-kṣetra-nyāya*.[3] Man-woman relationships have been explained through this analogy. Indian literature takes recourse to various analogies in order to explain complex concepts. This literary model, which was used for the purpose of easing the day-to-day functioning of life, was in due course believed to be a scientific truth. Thereupon, the metaphor became a tool to justify the supremacy of men over women. The dichotomy of man and woman where the two were presumed to be unequal was manifested through the *bīja-kṣetra-nyāya*. Nevertheless, it was used by *smṛtikāras* to underline the significance of woman's contribution to biological reproduction. In a way, these *smṛtikāras* helped proclaim a morality based on hierarchy. For women, there is a code of conduct in terms of *strī dharma* (i.e., duty of women) that gave women a subordinate status in personal and social life. Hence, all activity, be it concerning literature, art, lawmaking, rituals, or the practice of medicine or politics, echoes the basic prejudice that women are lesser beings. *Smṛtikāras* adopted various ways of glorifying the prescribed and condemning the unwanted and unexpected. These glorifications and condemnations were, in fact, subtle ways of control and exploitation.

In *bīja-kṣetra-nyāya*, the word *bīja* means "seeds" or "semen," whereas *kṣetra* means "field" or "land." In the said metaphor, *kṣetra* depicts woman. It is held that woman acts as a nourishing agent for the growth of a seed. On the other hand, man is called a seed that has the power to reproduce its own kind.[4] Analyzing the concept of *bīja-kṣetra-nyāya*, Manu, the author of Manusmṛti, comprehends three possibilities. First, one may give importance to *bīja*, some others may regard *kṣetra* as prominent, and still others may hold both *bīja* and *kṣetra* to be equally important.[5] Manu holds that normally a seed sown in a defective field gets destroyed without giving any result. A field without the seed being sown into it is simply barren land. Still, the seed is given greater importance because it is only because of the influence of good seed that even a person born in *tiryagyoni* (i.e., animal species) could also become a seer simply by being an offspring of a worthy seed.[6]

The above view, which projects man at the helm of affairs, implies that in Manusmṛti the relation between man and woman is never taken to be a relation between two equals. A woman has no identity, and she also is not supposed to have one. The identity she is supposed to have is conferred on her by the males with whom she is associated. This particular articulation of *bīja-kṣetra-nyāya* influenced the social life of Hindus in such a way that, even after hundreds of years, it is projected in the treatment meted out to the women even in contemporary India. *Bīja-kṣetra-nyāya* trivialized the status of women to such an extent that women were forced to spend their lives giving birth to children. A woman was expected to take care of her children until they were grown up. She was sandwiched between training children for their roles and doing household work. Like barren land, a woman who was unable to bear children was thought to be useless. It was thought natural for the husband of such a woman to go to another woman. Consequently, a sharp boundary line and division of labor between domestic and public life was drawn. Obviously, domestic life (held as secondary in importance) was part and parcel of woman's world.

Disparities arose right at birth: a son was seen as a rescuing boat and a daughter as a sorrow. Almost all rituals, especially the funeral rites, were essentially supposed to be performed by the son. Rites and rituals, to a large extent, contributed to the devaluation of woman in Hindu society. "The importance of the sons grew with the importance of obsequial rites which were supposedly essential to ensure man's eschatological destiny, and which could be performed only by sons."[7] Shakuntala Rao Shastry observes that the growing importance of sons in funeral rites resulted in a proportional devaluation of women in Vedic and post-Vedic society:

The imperative necessity of a son who could offer oblations dominated the whole sphere of thought. . . . Women who hitherto had a share in the intellectual and religious field, came to be considered as having no purpose in life except that of being the mothers of sons.[8]

Manu contends that men of three upper classes—*brāhmaṇas, kṣatriyas, and vaiśyas*—are twice born.[9] Their second birth is attributed to the initiation ceremony. The detailed exposition of the said ceremony enlightens the reader regarding the importance of these ceremonies for the male child.[10] But there is no such provision for the girl child. As so, the female child is called "once born." Manu, showing his magnanimity toward women, permits a few ceremonies for them.[11] Still, he contends that these ceremonies should be performed without the recitation of Vedic mantras.[12] Manu strongly holds that, since women cannot recite Vedic mantras, they are essentially impure and sinful. It seems that the idea of ritualistic impurity, from which women were supposed to suffer *for certain periods* of their lives, was used to emphasize the impurity and inferior status of women. Hence, women were degraded to the status of the once born, or *śudras* (fourth and the lowest class of the society).

The lumping together of women and *śudras* implicitly presupposes the prejudice that a woman has no mind and hence no capacity to think. She is like a slave, and a male is like a master. Just as a slave does not have an independent wish, a woman also cannot act according to her wish. Apropos of the master-slave relationship, the man-woman relationship was shaped so thoroughly that it was natural for man to rule his wife—exactly the way a despot ruled or dominated his subjects. It appears that to enslave others and to become a slave was the way of life in those early years. The following expression is a classic example of such morality: "It is not the horse, not the elephant, not the tiger that should be sacrificed but the goat because even fate does not favour those that are weak."[13] A woman has to follow the duties that are prescribed by the man. The moral code of conduct, which is supposed to be followed religiously apropos of the ancient Indian law, looks upon a woman as the property of a man. Manusmṛti, as well as other *smṛtis,* state that it is the woman's duty to give sexual satisfaction to the male and to procreate. Laziness, fickleness, and lying are described as the natural, inborn characteristics of women in the Manusmṛti.[14] Speaking further, of course derogatively, Manu describes women as naturally lustful and ever ready to seduce men. For him, women have an insatiable passion for men, so much so that they are not even bothered by who their partner is. Women are frivolous, heartless, and full of untruth and malice.[15] Hence, Manu contends that a husband must carefully guard his wife. Various lawmakers and authors of epics and *Purāṇas,* toeing the line with Manu's views, unanimously hold that a woman must never be left independent. It is emphasized that she always has to be under the control and protective guardianship of her father, husband, or son.[16] All this suggests a thoroughly dependent and slavelike existence for women.

The plight of woman continued in marriage. Early Aryans were apparently not very particular about sexual mores. Later on, in the Vedic period itself, Aryans seemingly became unyielding regarding the virginity of women, which led to the establishment of the marriage institution. Thenceforth, marriage received the status of a religious sacrament. The primal male-female relationship was transformed into a social tie and emotional bond. In this way, Vedic seers thus saved women from being reduced to nothing more than sex machines. The Vedas offered respect and honor to women through marriage. Women reciprocated by becoming extra careful in performing various roles assigned to them. As a result, the puritanical Hindu society in the period of *dharmaśāstra* became more rigid toward the said institution. In the *smṛti* texts, we find descriptions of eight kinds of marriages.[17] Several kinds of progenies also are discussed, albeit many of them are offspring of extramarital unions.

The importance of marriage is further emphasized by the fact that the concerned parties must scrutinize the lineage (*kula*), conduct, and additional qualities of each other. In other words, ancestry, health, and family history must be thoroughly examined. Mating should be made only between those parties who have no physical defects, no trace of heritable disease, and no health problems. It was also emphasized that the bride must be younger than the groom. For Manu, a bride belonging to even a wealthy family must be rejected if the family is one in which religious rites have been neglected, and the Veda is not recited. If in a marriage a male child is not born, the husband can remarry. Since the object of marriage is to carry on the male line, Manu recommends the rejection of a girl who has no brother; for Manu, there is a risk of her being made a *putrikā* or of her son being taken by her father (the son's grandfather) as his son, or whose father is not known.[18]

Apparently *smṛtikāras* legitimized such issues through these classifications.[19] There is a serious discussion as to whom such children belong: to the biological father or the husband of the mother?[20] It appears that, in the *smṛti* period, Hindu society was not very rigid or particular about sexual mores, and a considerable amount of promiscuity in sex relations was tolerated in the society. *Niyoga* (levirate, or compulsory marriage) was allowed not only in the case of childless widows, but women also practiced it with an impotent husband as well.[21] Although, on the one hand, almost all *smṛtikāras* had accepted such relations, at the same time most of them disapproved of them, which appears to be a mockery of rational thinking. While clearly admitting the custom of *niyoga,* Manu goes to the extent of condemning it as immoral and against the duty (dharma) of the wife to remain loyal to her husband throughout her life and even in death.[22]

The Hindu ideal of extreme loyalty to one's husband (*pativrata dharma*) is probably the most important factor responsible for the total suppression and subjugation of women. *Smṛtikāras* never tired of listing the duties of wives toward their husbands. Hindu thinkers of that age unanimously declared that service to husband is the only duty of a wife. To emphasize the importance of such service, they vehemently asserted that only by scrupulously performing that "supreme duty" would she be able to achieve heaven.[23] A woman's life is insignificant;

she should sacrifice her life for the good of her husband.[24] While remaining totally obedient and loyal to her husband, she should worship him as a god, even if he is full of blemishes.[25] Even after widowhood she was to remain loyal to him, as there was no question of widow remarriage or the marriage of a deserted wife. In the absence or after the death of the husband, a woman was forced to live in total deprivation and strictest self-discipline.[26]

As stated in the beginning, the act of procreation was heralded as a sacrifice. Since procreation was not possible without women, Hindu thinkers were forced to view them as partners in life. But the so-called mature brains condemned pleasure-seeking since it appreciated the value of the idea of detachment, which entailed the condemnation of women as well. Women were perceived as the source of all temptations and as an obstruction in men's quest for liberation. Men, seeking to overcome the sufferings of worldly life, preferred to control their women instead of controlling their minds. It was the shortcut and the easiest way to exonerate oneself of one's pitfalls and shortcomings. Hence, the upper hand of man was manifested in the condemnation and despisement of woman.[27] As a result, emphasis was placed on the chastity of women, which implied more restraint on their freedom and other rights. The marriage age of girls was constantly lowered to such an extent that a rather ridiculous norm came to prevail: that a girl should be married while she was still an infant (nagnikā). In addition, participation of women in social functions was prohibited, and they were, on the whole, reduced to the level of second-class citizens.

The fact of the matter is that the condition of women deteriorated considerably over time; that is, between the śruti and smṛti period and on. A bird's-eye view of śruti texts reveals that, in the early days, Hindu women enjoyed considerable freedom and a respectable position in society. It appears that in the beginning women could perform at least some Vedic sacrifices and recite Vedic mantras. Gradually, these rights were denied to them, including the initiation ceremony. Additionally, the widespread practice of polygamy also seems to be responsible,

to a considerable extent, for the devaluation of the position of women in society. We also find indications of the deplorable practice of giving several maids as gifts to an honored guest, or as dowry to a bridegroom.[28] On the basis of above discussion, one may infer that in the smṛti texts, by denying women's independence, women were denied the basic value as a human being. They were deprived of personhood itself. This is a glaring example of transgression of social justice.

POSITIVE ATTITUDE TOWARD WOMEN

The above discussion, which posits a grim picture of the status of women in smṛti texts, is only one side of the coin. We come across several verses in these texts exhibiting the brighter side of women's treatment. In other words, a positive approach toward women is found in almost all the texts from the Vedas to the dharmaśāstras. Of course, in all these texts, the main field of work for woman was recognized to be the home and hearth, and in those affairs, she undoubtedly enjoyed maximum freedom and power. While blessing the bride, for example, one Vedic hymn says that she may rule over her husband's household, including the parents-in-law and servants.[29]

As the central Hindu ethos, to a great extent, has continued to be Vedic, such positive sentiments are found in almost all later religious texts. Smṛti texts, in general, declared women (of all the four classes) as worthy of protection. Manu regards the murder of woman on par with the murder of a brāhmaṇa or that of a child. It has been declared to be the greatest crime, from which no redemption is possible.[30]

Another positive note is that the male partner was held responsible for any adulterous relation, whereas the guilt of the female was minimized. Therefore, smṛti texts prescribe very harsh punishment for men in the case of adultery. All men, except brāhmaṇas, were liable for capital punishment in cases of adultery with an unwilling partner.[31]

It was the duty of the king to protect the victim and return her to her family after she had performed the prescribed, so-called mild penance.[32] Thereupon, even an adulterous woman was declared fit to be accepted by her family and society.[33] The fallen woman must be given food and shelter.[34] Manu and Yājñavalkya, the author of *Yājñavalkyasmṛti*, appear to be more generous on this point since they clearly declare that a woman does not need any purificatory rite. She is always pure.[35] Again, all the *smṛtis* unanimously recognize the rights of women over their personal property.[36] In this regard, the concept of *strī-dhana* (personal property of women) is already recognized.

Of course, for *smṛtikāras*, the two sexes are complementary to each other, and their attraction is deeply rooted in their respective natures. Manu never intended to look down on *kāma* (the domain of desire). He was only eager to voice safeguards against improper yearning for its urges. For him, unchecked sexual unions might lead to the lowering of a human being, and an unrestrained person might become a slave of desires. It is for this simple reason that celibacy was prescribed for a male student. Both men and women are expected to be united in wedlock without premarital sexual experience. In fact, the passages in the Manusmṛti, which seem to condemn the nature of women, are in reality warnings against improper sex.[37] *Smṛtikāras* never hesitated in admitting that it is a man's world. Therefore, woman must live under the protection of men. Still, we come across passages of repeated admonitions for husbands, fathers, and sons to look after their female relations properly and keep them well satisfied.[38]

In a way, the emphasis on the duties of woman has been counterbalanced by the emphasis on the duties of man. *Smṛtikāras* point out that women are like the goddess Lakshmi, for they bring prosperity to the household. Manu says that women are essential for the welfare of the family. They give birth to children, bring them up, serve the elders of the family, and look after the entire household, as well as all the socioreligious customs. Moreover, a wife is a must for the proper fulfillment of a man's religious duties.[39]

Polygamy was permitted and practiced by ancient Hindus, but it was always under compulsion.

Certain conditions were stipulated under which a man was permitted to remarry. Hence, *smṛti* texts were conscientious enough to safeguard the interests of the wife. Deserting a wife was declared a serious crime.[40] The tears of dependent women blight a family. The grateful smiles of women make the fortune of the family blossom, while their curse withers the home.

Moreover, the concept of mother symbolizes unselfish love, tender care, and willingness to sacrifice to the utmost. Hence, mothers are the most respected and loved persons in Hindu homes. A mother deserved greatest respect and was raised to the rank of divinity along with the teacher and the father. But the latter were placed immeasurably below her in the right to be loved and venerated.[41] A mother was served properly, even if she had become a fallen woman.[42]

Regarding the denial of the initiation ceremony (*upanayana*, which symbolized the beginning of student life), these thinkers hold that the denial of it does not mean denial of a right to education for women. Women were supposed to obtain education without undergoing the rite.[43] For Manu, marriage is the rite of initiation for women, and the contingent duties of living with the teacher and of tending the household fire, which a *Brahmacārī* does, are fulfilled by the woman while serving her husband and attending to the domestic duties.[44]

Even some positive trend is evidenced in regard to the widows. *Smṛitikaras* have never denied the existence of widows in the society. While discussing the ideal mode of conduct for a widow, rules were also formulated for a widow's inheritance of family property in the absence of any male issue. Widows were even allowed to have a son through *niyoga* with a man appointed by the elders for the purpose. In a nutshell, there is no evidence of the ghastly custom of self-immolation of the widow (*satī*) in *smṛti* texts.

Apropos of the above explanation of the recognition of the worth of a woman in the family and, thereupon, in society, Hindu women developed immense moral strength and self-respect. History speaks of various legendary ladies who showed ready intelligence and a strong moral character in the hour of crises. Their character was an amalgamation of the conventional ideal of loyalty to one's husband and a progressive outlook on life. They asserted themselves in all fields of society, be it a matter of right or duty, and above all in free choice in marriage.

OBSERVATIONS

The attempt to understand the status of women requires the understanding of the social structure of that time that was pyramidal in nature, wherein women and *śudras* formed the base; that is, they were on the lowest level. The inequality and injustice in the society were inherent in the basic social structure itself. Women were considered lower among the lowest, as they were not supposed to have any specific *varṇa*. The woman's *varṇa*, or class, used to be determined either by that of her father or her husband (a practice which is still prevalent). She was not considered to be able to pursue *mokṣa* (liberation) since she was not eligible for *sannyāsāśrama*. Besides, she was not allotted any share in the wealth of her father or that of her husband.

Smṛtis enslaved the brains of women in such a way that they presumed that their nature is and should be according to such descriptions. Because of such hammering and brainwashing, either by the social structure or through literature, women became unaware and ignorant of their true selves. *Smṛtis* have described the behavior of ideal woman with ample illustrations drawn from various sources. Pārvatī and Sāvitrī symbolize total devotion to the husband, a virtue essential for an ideal woman. Framing woman as a weak creature and then advocating protection for her is showing her nothing but disrespect.

The image of woman, in terms of an ideal housewife, brings out the enormous difficulties in concretizing the entirety of womanhood as such. It appears to be the greatest hindrance to the free development of women as human beings. A woman doesn't find herself capable of anything except being a daughter, wife, or mother. In other words, her whole existence is for the man.

This belief in her supposed unstable and irrational nature is prevalent in Hindu society to this day. Women with a refined self-awareness and stable state of mind have been and are still being oppressed by the institutions of family and society to such an extent that they even are compelled to destroy themselves.

The psychology of man and woman has all along been dominated by the firm belief that the man is superior and, therefore, he must rule over the woman. As a mother, a woman was respected and is still respected, but as a wife, she is bashed even today. Various rituals and customs express this attitude. Even now, giving away one's own daughter (*kanyādāna*) is considered to be a holy act that achieves great virtue (*puṇya*) for her father. On the other hand, in certain tribal societies, the father actually sells his daughter, and the bridegroom has to pay the price for the girl. Both the options are based on the same proposition that woman has an instrumental value, be it the case of glorification or as a clear-cut exchange, such as in a barter system.

Apropos of *smṛti* texts, the son remains with his parents throughout life, while a girl is treated as an outsider since she is supposed to leave the house after the marriage. Such is the way life is lived in Hindu society. Such practice is clearly based upon the belief that a male child is the giver of seed, *bīja-dātā*, and a creator of culture, while a girl is looked at as the field and a carrier of culture.

Today, even after the passage of thousands of years, Hindu society is not free from the prejudice in which it became engulfed through the *smṛti* texts that man is superior to woman. Although the democratic legal system puts every human being on the same platform and makes them equal irrespective of sex, religion, or race, in actual practice this is rarely followed. Society is still male dominated, and people are afraid of losing their patriarchal status and modifying rights that are based on the superiority of the male. On the other hand, vast, illiterate populations of women are not ready to lose their so-called secure life and face the world. Neither of the two parties is ready to overcome the myth, realize reality, and evolve a new system that would transcend the ghost of *śruti* and *smṛti* culture.

Hindu seers tried to overcome the prejudices regarding woman in the post-*smṛti* era. They have suggested that, even within the male-dominated discourse, there is a possibility of progress in terms of a better attitude toward woman. In this regard, the temperament of two independent substances, *Puruṣa* and *Prakṛti,* in the *Sāṅkhya* system is suggestive. These two substances exhibit a form of man-woman relationship. Both *Puruṣa* (man) and *Prakṛti* (woman) have their own identities with distinctive qualities. *Puruṣa* has consciousness and therefore knowledge, but *Prakṛti* is devoid of it. Capacity to act is the distinctive quality of *Prakṛti.* These two come together with the purpose of compensating the imperfections of each other. *Puruṣa* is pure and free and thereby does not undertake any activity. But because of his contact with *Prakṛti,* he is dragged into the cycle of the phenomenal world. *Puruṣa* does not act in spite of being conscious. Similarly, a man, by nature, is supposed to be superior. A woman is not supposed to possess intelligence. She is on par with unconscious inanimate objects, and her existence itself is of a lower level. The concept of *Prakṛti* expresses the view that a woman lures and hypnotizes. Yet their coming together is governed by pragmatic considerations. Still, the recognition of *Prakṛti* as an embodiment of existence shows the utility of considering the *Sāṅkhya* system. The relationship between *Puruṣa* and *Prakṛti* appears to be like that of the relationship between two equal beings. However, the qualities attributed to woman show that she has no identity of her own and lacks the power of decision making. Hence, in the *Sāṅkhya* philosophy, the independent status of women has not been fully asserted.

The status of women achieved its pinnacle in the *Śākta* philosophy. According to the *Śākta* philosophy, the reality on which the existence of the world depends is both the formal and efficient cause of the world. The belief that there is a feminine element at the root of every creation is central to the *Śākta* philosophy. Lord *Śiva* is also considered as the form of *Śakti.* His mother is considered to be the mother of everything. By way of contrast with earlier Hindu thinking, in the *Śākta* philosophy, woman is neither inert nor like an animal but is a living and intelligent agent. She is not the object of enjoyment, but, like man, she is an enjoyer. She helps in liberating the self and does not act as an obstruction to liberation. In fact, for the *Śākta* philosophers, realization of self is the result of the awakening of a power (*Śakti*), which is called *Kundalinī.* Therefore, in the *Śākta* philosophy, man and woman are on par with one another. Neither of them (although each has distinctive qualities) is either superior or inferior. This theory, which realizes the coexistence of man and woman, ultimately presents an epitome of human relationship. It explicitly expresses equality and therefore advocates peace. It is suggestive of a new way of life wherein women are granted equal footing with men and are therefore respected.

Conclusion

In the background of this detailed account of the positive and negative aspects of the status of women apropos of *smṛti* texts, one can safely say that throughout the texts, women have been viewed as lesser beings. Hindu seers promulgated their code of conduct for woman with the basic presumption that man, by nature, is better informed, can counter violence, can provide a shield safety, and can ensure security. Woman acquiesced in this, thinking that the difference in nature based on sex has ordained them for only the secondary, subservient roles, which are based on the expectations of men. Since secondary roles do not have a direct economic value, those who perform these roles are not counted as productive members of society. Hence, a woman's value in her own eyes is much less than that of man. We can, therefore, understand why the life of woman was never valued highly in Hindu religion. Its worth depended on the convenience or contribution she could make to the man in the form of helping him realize his roles and satisfy his desires. Ever since the *smṛti* age, women have always been deprived of power. Possession of power by a person implies that the person has the authority to discriminate. Not being vested with any power directly, women then do not possess the means of changing the situation and emancipating themselves physically, mentally, and emotionally since they never had access to resources that could support their efforts. Through a system of rewards and punishments, this power structure has been perpetuated down the ages.

The second half of the last century witnessed great liberation movements on all fronts. The women's liberation movement is one of them. But when seen from the point of view of Hindu women, it is clear they were offered certain concessions and privileges within the age-old, traditional structure that is itself on the verge of stagnation. Discussion of the rights and roles of women is often misconstrued as a threat to man's position in society. Similarly, concern for the plight of woman and repulsion against injustices done to them are sometimes mistaken as Westernization. Even after independence, the Constitution provided special considerations to the *śudras* (lower-caste people) because of past injustices to them, but no such consideration was shown to women. Although the lifestyle of women has gone through many reforms and phases, economically and academically women today are more independent than their predecessors. Women are more and more emerging as working women. In spite of all this, however, there is little change in women's social status.

One could claim that in order to understand the specific nature of the problem of Hindu women, men as well as women have to be freed from the hold of traditional values and ideas. But I totally disagree with this type of solution of the problem. To my thinking, the strength of Hindu women lies in the Hindu tradition itself. As stated in the beginning, morality is relative to time and space. Since the *smṛti* and post-*smṛti* eras, lots of changes are in evidence in the outlook of people. Accordingly, their attitudes toward women also have seen several changes. Therefore, the solution to the problem lies in the thorough and unbiased study of traditional Hindu philosophy. I have discussed earlier that women received their due in the *Śākta* philosophy, in which women are granted equal footing with men and therefore respected as persons.

Hence, the proper perception of Hindu texts would bring woman closer to her proper place in society. As a chain reaction, people would be ready to accept women as individuals and recognize their worth as rational and moral agents.

WOMEN'S INTERFAITH INITIATIVES IN THE UNITED STATES AFTER 9/11

Kathryn Lohre

In the years since 9/11, women's interfaith initiatives have gained ground in many parts of the United States, providing a new model for inter-religious engagement. These initiatives, although each unique to its own context, have several things in common: they are inspired by a deep-seated commitment to community-building in the aftermath of a crisis; they are often formed at the behest of a personal invitation from one individual to another individual or group; they tend toward common action in the form of group or social projects; and they honor the centrality of storytelling and relationship building for their own sake.

In this post-9/11 era, women's interfaith initiatives offer an exciting alternative to the standard model for interfaith engagement, which often presumes male (clergy) leadership. For one thing, academic and professional authorities on inter-faith relations are replaced with real-life experts: women who live and breathe the challenges of reli-gious coexistence in times of crisis. Second, formal dialogue is replaced with storytelling. Personal tes-timonies, reflections, and engagement in difficult dialogues are not limited to theological arenas of overlap and divergence but instead focus on the day-to-day experiences where conflicts of identity, more often than ideology, are commonplace.

What follows is a sketch of the multireligious women's networks of the Pluralism Project at Har-vard University as well as a snapshot of women's initiatives that have developed in various parts of the United States over the past five years. The intention is to explore this new model of women's interfaith initiatives, with the idea that it is comple-mentary to traditional models and as such will be critical to multireligious societies in the years to come. In the spirit of honoring these efforts, let me begin with a story.

BEGINNING TO TELL THE STORY: THE PLURALISM PROJECT WOMEN'S NETWORKS

In the days after 9/11, a Christian radio station in Ohio put out a call to the community to come and form a human ring of solidarity around the Islamic Center of Greater Toledo. The dome of the mosque had been damaged by rifle fire, as one of many acts of backlash against Muslims in the United States. Many of us who keep our fingers on the pulse of religious issues expected this kind of backlash. What we didn't anticipate, however, was the out-pouring of acts of solidarity that were used to overpower acts of hatred. In Toledo, the organizers

161

expected three hundred—maybe five hundred at the most—but over 1,000 people turned out for the event.

Cherrefe Kadri, the first woman president of the Islamic Center of Greater Toledo, told this story to a group of women around a table at the Harvard Club in New York City. It was November 2, and smoke still billowed from ground zero some blocks away. The Pluralism Project at Harvard University, a research organization dedicated to the study and documentation of the changing religious landscape in the United States, had convened its Women's Networks in Multi-Religious America at short notice. The one-day consultation was an attempt to learn about the backlash that Americans of minority religious traditions, primarily Muslims and Sikhs, were experiencing in cities throughout the United States, with a focus on the experiences of women within those communities.[1]

In the days after 9/11, a number of interfaith initiatives were immediately brought to task. Many of them were dominated by male clergy. Women's voices—in particular the voices of women from minority religious communities—were difficult to hear. In contrast, the Pluralism Project's consultation included representatives from Women of Reform Judaism, the Jewish Orthodox Feminist Alliance, United Methodist Women, the North American Council for Muslim Women, the Muslim Women's League, Manavi, the Sikh Mediawatch and Resource Task Force (now the Sikh American Legal Defense and Education Fund), and others.

What was different about the Pluralism Project's consultation was precisely that it sought to give voice to the critical perspectives of Muslim, Sikh, and other South Asian American women. Participants from these communities articulated their sense of feeling "under siege." Many of the women spoke to the hate crimes that had marred their communities, the misdirected acts of vengeance that seemed to have become socially acceptable in a climate of xenophobia and a culture of war. Stories of detentions, hate crimes, and discriminations—perpetrated by the U.S. government and fellow U.S. citizens—set off new alarms for other participants, namely those from the mainstream Christian denominations. Sikh men and women had been attacked for wearing their turbans; South Asians were attacked for the color of their skin; Muslim women were harassed for covering their heads; and guilt by association, or at least perceived association, was the order of the days that followed the terrorist attacks.

Like many of the women's interfaith initiatives that have been formed since 9/11, stories were central to the women's networks meeting that day. The stories that were told of personal anxieties, fears, and hopes had been lost to the sensational media coverage of the unfolding "war on terror." As far as the women were concerned, however, the stories they shared with each other were a life raft in a sea of suspicions, assumptions, and ignorance. Of course, their stories did not solve the complex religio-political problems of the day, but they did open up doors to unexpected connections and understandings.

The tensions present in the room begged the question: Would the events of September 11 pose an irreversible setback to dialogue and common action? Each woman at the meeting carried her own set of tensions and constraints, as an individual, and as a representative of an organization. In fact, the representative of one of the Jewish women's organizations had been constrained by her board from attending because of voiced concerns about a representative of one of the Muslim women's organizations. Thus the ability to sit at the same table was not taken for granted; nor was the women's courage to tell their stories in a context with its own fears and suspicions.

We have had three other formal consultations, including an event at the National Press Club in Washington, D.C., in 2004 to discuss issues of common concern for women of faith leading up to the presidential election. Today, members of our women's networks continue to build relationships with one another and to take measures of common action and advocacy. Local and regional groupings have also met to address issues of concern and to share resources and strategies.

As an extension of our women's networks consultations, we released the film *Acting on Faith:*

Women's New Religious Activism in America in April of 2005. This documentary chronicles the lives of three of our women's networks members—a Buddhist, a Hindu, and a Muslim—for whom faith, activism, and identity are deeply intertwined. Filmed in 2003, their stories capture some of the challenges of women living in a post-9/11 era. In combination with our online study guide, this resource has been used by educators, corporate diversity trainers, and local congregations to widen the public conversation. Looking ahead, our focus will remain on local, grassroots expressions of women's networks. Thus, the research to which I will now turn forms the basis of our ongoing work in this area.

ACTING ON OUR STORIES: TOWARD A PARADIGM OF SHARED ACTION AND ACTIVISM

The Pluralism Project has long been documenting the interfaith movement in the United States. Over the past five years, we have also been tracking those initiatives that were created or bolstered in response to 9/11. Many of these initiatives were formed by women or developed women's components in order to serve particular needs. These women's interfaith initiatives range from small to large, dialogue groups to action groups, social groups to social transformation groups, and day-long conferences to lifelong relationships. The personal invitations that formed the basis for many of these initiatives were extended because an individual or group was moved by current events—September 11, the earthquake in Pakistan, the London bombings, or the recent unrest in Israel and Lebanon—to take personal action toward engagement with the religious "other." I will turn now to an exploration of these initiatives.

INTERFAITH INITIATIVES WITH A WOMEN'S COMPONENT

Several women's interfaith initiatives have grown out of broader, co-ed initiatives. In some cases, there was a deliberate attempt to address the particular concerns of women. In other cases, the women felt a compelling bond with one another and formed a subgroup to explore this bond.

JAM Women's Group[2]

In southern Florida, for example, JAM and All (Jews, Muslims, Christians and All Peoples), an interfaith group founded by a Jew and a Muslim, was formed in response to September 11. The group's mission statement is presented on its Web site: "JAM and ALL is a nonprofit organization of Jews, Muslims, and Christians, and all peoples dedicated to fostering understanding, social harmony, and peace through dialogue, multicultural interaction and educational projects."[3] As this organization was getting off the ground, the temple's women's spirituality group invited some Muslim women to one of its meetings.

Subsequently, a women's offshoot group was formed in early 2002, with a core group of thirty women ranging in age from eighteen to eighty who attend regularly.

JAM Women's Group seeks to "delve deeply into each others' cultures and beliefs for a greater understanding, to create strong friendships and to treat all the world's children with compassion."[4] The group has no formal staff structure, unlike the umbrella organization, but instead relies on volunteerism and the hospitality of its members who open their homes for meetings. The meetings are centered on storytelling and sharing of personal experiences in order to overcome stereotypes and to build strong, resilient relationships. Naheed Khan, JAM member and owner of a local restaurant where the Women's Group often meets, remarked, "The end products of our meetings are beautiful relationships. We are all about unity and uniting for peace."[5]

Spiritual and Religious Alliance for Hope[6]

On the other side of the country, in Orange County, California, the Human Relations Commission hosted an interfaith dialogue series among Jews, Christians, and Muslims shortly after 9/11. As the experience was very productive, members decided that they wanted to continue their work with a trip to Mexico to build a house for a low-income family. Sande Hart, one of the Jewish participants, noticed a particular bond among the women. She invited them to her home, and the Spiritual and Religious Alliance for Hope (SARAH) was formed.[7]

Today, ten to twenty women gather at the monthly meetings. Discussion topics include faith, empowerment, and peace. As with JAM Women's Group, participants are encouraged to share their stories, and they have also discussed various life-cycle events and rituals particular to their traditions. Other activities have included site visits to local religious centers, celebration of religious holidays, creation of "peace tapestries," and leadership development for service work in the community.

In recent months, unrest in the Middle East has strained the efforts of SARAH. In the past, the group had prided itself on the relationship between a Jewish woman and a Lebanese woman who worked hard to build common ground. However, in a recent article in *The Jewish Journal of Greater Los Angeles,* Hart lamented that the Jewish and Muslim members of the group had both decided not to interact for the time being, saying they needed "space."[8]

Woman to Woman Project of the Interfaith Association of Snohomish County

A bit further north, in Washington State, Therese Quinn and a few acquaintances decided that they wanted to get to know the Iraqis in their community as the war in Iraq raged in the aftermath of 9/11. Under the auspices of the Interfaith Association of Snohomish County, they put up fliers around town. Soon there were forty Jewish, Christian, and Muslim women gathered at the local YMCA for the first of the group's weekly meetings. Through various activities, such as baking baklava and storytelling, the women gathered get to know one another.

The initial impulse to "get to know their neighbors" has proved fruitful in challenging stereotypes. The formation of friendships has helped many of

the women to see the religious "other" as a person like herself. Participant Phyllis Rainey remarked, quoted in a *Seattle Times* article, that "you can't judge one person by the foolish way their government is acting. It's things like this, meeting people and seeing them as individuals, that makes us all realize we're more alike than we are different."[9]

WOMEN'S INTERFAITH INITIATIVES

Other women's interfaith initiatives have simply been formed by and for women. Some have evolved from historically ecumenical women's groups into interfaith groups. New technologies are also providing a venue for dialogue and common action.

Women Transcending Boundaries[10]

Women Transcending Boundaries (WTB) is a women's interfaith group in Syracuse, New York. After an adult forum at her church following September 11, cofounder Betsy Wiggins struggled with the desire to reach out to the Muslim women in her community. Through various connections, she was introduced to Danya Wellmon. The two met for coffee, and after hours of conversation about their beliefs and experiences, they decided to extend the invitation to other women they thought would be interested. Within a month of 9/11, the first meeting of the group took place in Wiggins's home. Twenty-two women attended, including eleven Muslim women and eleven others from the Buddhist, Jewish, and Christian faiths.

The group continues to meet monthly on Sunday afternoons in a local private school, with between forty and sixty participants at each meeting. The organization's three core commitments are storytelling, service, and socializing. Storytelling has played a prominent role since the early days of the organization when women gathered to share their experiences of 9/11. Later on, a "life-cycle" series helped women to share the various rites of passage that shape their faith lives. Service projects have ranged from local to international, such as assisting with a literacy project and raising funds for a girls' school in rural Pakistan. Finally, with an intention to foster lifelong relationships, WTB places a premium on informal socializing. These three commitments are managed by a large leadership council, an advisory board, and six committees.

Sacred Circles Conferences at the Washington National Cathedral[11]

Other women's organizations have expanded their initial ecumenical vision to one that is now interfaith. Since 1996, the Washington National Cathedral in D.C. has hosted a biannual conference called Sacred Circles. Attended by more than one thousand women, these events were historically ecumenical, drawing women from various Christian denominations and diverse spiritual practices. After 9/11, Grace Ogden, Sacred Circles founder, felt the need to explicitly expand the conference into an interfaith initiative. Jewish, Muslim, Hindu, and Buddhist women were invited to join the planning committee, and the November 2002 meeting was called "Four Faces of Faith."

Silent meditation, labyrinth walking, workshops on numerous topics, keynote speakers, dancing, and singing are all part of the conference. The thematic focus for 2007 will be an exploration of love and fear in women's lives. The mission of the conference says, "In these times, we must choose love over fear. Deep, wise love is the spiritual ground from which we draw strength, vision and courage."[12]

Women of Spirit Conference

Another similar type of conference called Women of Spirit has occurred for the last twenty-one years in Omaha, Nebraska. Since 9/11, participation has evolved from predominately Christian to multifaith. This year, Jewish, Christian, and Muslim storytellers will share their faith journeys. Following the first interfaith conference of Women of Spirit, monthly breakfasts were organized to keep the dialogue going. Prayers from the various faith traditions are offered, and different topics are chosen for discussion.

Gather the Women

As e-mail and other communications technologies have become more accessible, relationship building across national and international boundaries has become easier and more affordable. As Kathlyn Schaaf watched violent images on her television in California on 9/11 and the days that followed, she felt a clear impetus to do something to connect women. With the help of eleven others, she created Gather the Women, an interactive website and communications hub that is utilized by thousands of women all over the world. The purpose of the website is to provide a space for women to chronicle local events that support world peace. The women who contribute come from a variety of religious traditions, and the site seems to be indicative of a new form of "political activism that's guided and sustained by spirituality."[13]

Picking Up the Phone and Taking Simple Risks

The events of 9/11 continue to affect the way in which interfaith initiatives unfold in the United States, but newer global events continue to threaten progress. Perhaps a hopeful example to conclude with is an initiative that is still in its early, informal stages. In July, Ellen Bloomfield, a resident of Blue Ash, Ohio, read a news account of local Muslims' concerns regarding violence in the Middle East. She picked up the phone and called Zenab Schwen, one of the women quoted in the article. She invited her to her home, as Ellen put it, to "sort through issues that threatened to divide the region, the world, and Jewish and Muslim women like themselves."[14]

Schwen immediately accepted the invitation, and the two have continued to meet informally, with no set expectations. Schwen said, "The success of our meeting was that it was just that somebody reached out and wasn't afraid to do it, and somebody accepted willingly. It was the personal connection."[15] It is this connection that they hope to eventually extend to others.

CONCLUSION

Storytelling and relationship building through a wide variety of activities are the bedrock for many of these women's interfaith initiatives—with the understanding that new insights into who we are, and who we are to each other, are the foundation for building stronger, more connected communities. Yet precisely because of this fact, women's interfaith efforts are rarely covered in the mainstream media or endorsed by interfaith professionals.

After 9/11, women have made critical innovations in interfaith action: with a focus on one-to-one relationships, experiential dialogue, and an embrace of social activities as a necessary part of their agenda, this new model is complementary to more traditional interfaith initiatives and is constructive in finding a new way forward when dialogue is stalled by escalating world events. In many ways, laughing and singing, playing and praying together as humans are precisely the activities that make it possible to return to a common table in times of crisis.

These women's initiatives are a model for linking ourselves in this way. Since 9/11, women in cities across the United States have taught us a powerful lesson about the possibilities for a hopeful future. Through their example, we can see that our courage to connect with one another must overwhelm our fears, in very personal and political terms. Then, and only then, does our shared story begin to emerge.

TURNING WAR INSIDE OUT

New Perspectives for the Nuclear Age

Marcia Sichol

To understand or change the war system, we need to understand the constituent elements at lower levels of analysis in a sophisticated way. The cook knows salt, the composer strings, and the gardener soil; the war scholar should know gender.[1]

During these post-9/11 days, we are witnessing something greater and of longer duration than armed conflicts. As a member of a congregation of women religious who believe that God lives and acts in our world, and as an ethicist who also believes in the power of human reason, I have felt the need to address not only the regional armed conflicts that have ensued but also what I believe is the growing global conflict between religion and reason. Both religion and reason have a role to play during the current violence. Certainly religion should help people of all faiths to purify intention and to rid the mind and heart of hatred and prejudice. Whereas people's religious beliefs emerge from a variety of religious sects and cultures, reason appeals to universal ethical principles. Religion can help one to live by such principles; it ought not to be abused by appealing to sectarian beliefs that contradict them. No side in a conflict can use revelation to prove it is on God's side; rather, I maintain

that God works through human beings who do their best to reason rightly.

In this essay, I assume that the role of theology and religion is and ought to be different from the role of philosophy and reason in making the case for war or for pacifism. Theology and philosophy have long been close partners in the Christian just-war tradition, with each appealing to human reason in making its arguments for and against war. In our century, the presence of nuclear weapons has given rise to new theories about war. These theories are but the latest within a tradition in the West dating back to the Greeks four thousand years ago. In my book, *The Making of a Nuclear Peace,* I analyzed three contemporary just-war theorists, each of a different academic discipline and religious faith, but each male, and found that none of them succeeds in giving an ethical justification for the use of nuclear weapons. The fact that both religion and reason—theology and philosophy—have been dominated by men for centuries prompted me to ask, What if I change one piece of the matrix and examine female thinkers? Does gender make a significant difference in making judgments about war? Will taking a "feminine turn" in moral reasoning offer clues to the uncovering of the underlying principle governing centuries of the just-war tradition? Will I find a new paradigm for a more adequate just-war theory for the twenty-first century? What I discovered was not what I expected and yet turned out to be more than I expected.

DOES GENDER MAKE A DIFFERENCE? YES . . . AND NO!

The first step toward answering my questions followed from the realization that nuclear war is a bioethical issue on a global scale, affecting the lives of the human race as well as the planet's entire ecosystem. Bioethics has brought casuistry back to respectability in moral philosophy, and its widespread practice signals a change in perspective, what I have called a "feminine turn." Women customarily pull out moral principles from cases at hand, much as lawyers, physicians, and business-people function. Today many men, too, are finding that this "feminine turn" in moral thought holds great promise of providing a more adequate approach to resolving today's moral dilemmas than the deductive approaches of the past.

Not Gender, but Perspective

In my research, I discovered that Hannah Arendt, a woman who did not actually write much about just war per se, has nevertheless developed concepts that illumine the moral ground on which the just-war tradition stands. A Jewish American philosopher who escaped from Nazi Germany, Hannah Arendt is a woman many feminists have abandoned as not "feminist" enough. Nevertheless, her work has invigorated feminist thought.

What captured my attention was Arendt's explication of Immanuel Kant in relation to aesthetics and the perspectives of "actors" and "spectators"—whom I call "insiders" and "outsiders." The "best people," Kant says, come to a situation not as actors but as spectators, for only the spectator gets to see the whole while the actor focuses on the part he or she plays. More important, it is the spectator who serves as judge—he or she determines what is and is not acceptable. When it comes to war, this

analysis aptly pertains to the role of the majority of women in the world.

THREE TWENTIETH-CENTURY WOMEN

The claim that most women are outsiders, as along with many men who are excluded from war-fighting or policymaking for whatever reason, is supported by the fascinating stories and statistics in the writings of three twentieth-century women: Vera Brittain (1893–1970), Jean Bethke Elshtain (1940–), and Joanna Bourke (1963–).[2] Of the three, Vera Brittain's published letters reveal a woman who is closest to being an insider in that she served as a nurse on the front in World War I. After losing the four most significant men in her life and then seeing her own British soldiers treating injured Germans with dignity and respect, she moved from being an avid war supporter to becoming an active pacifist. In her book *Women and War*, the American historian Jean Bethke Elshtain analyzes women's behaviors in wartime and finds that there are no simplistic divisions between "violent men and pacific women."[3] She cites statistics to show that only 15 percent of the men engaged in combat in World War II, for example, actually fired their weapons in battle. Wartime analyses show that men are strongly opposed to killing even when society gives them permission to do so. Joanna Bourke, now professor of history at Birkbeck College, University of London, in what has been called "a masterpiece of revisionist history," *An Intimate History of Killing: Face-to-Face Killing in Twentieth Century Warfare*, shows how women are an integral part of the slaughter of war and the myths surrounding it.[4] Her position, which the writings of the two other women support, is that society is the chief determinant in deciding what aspects of gender should dominate in men and women. As women become insiders, such as, war-fighters and policymakers, society encourages them to shed their more "feminine" qualities. In the nuclear age, it is easy to see that the barriers against women in the military are fast disappearing. Little physical strength is needed to push a button. As a former Marine Vietnam veteran has said:

All you do is move that finger so impercepti-bly, just a wish flashing across your mind like a shadow, not even a full brain synapse, and poof! in a blast of sound and energy and light a truck or a house or even people disappear, everything flying and settling back into dust.[5]

THE *DIS*-COVERING OF THE DEEP VALUE IN THE JUST-WAR TRADITION

Relating Arendt's analysis to war, the three authors show that *most* men and women are not actors, not insiders, but spectators. As outsiders, they are the majority affected by war. As judges who determine what is acceptable, they also have tre-mendous power—the power that, I believe, gave rise to the just-war tradition. The outsiders were the ones who needed a safe space to make homes, to care for families, to attain human flourishing. In prehistoric days, defense of one's borders fell to the physically strong male. In our time, defense of one's borders has expanded beyond individ-ual nations to regions and alliances. But what underlies this concern for defense of borders is the desire to preserve that kinship or bondedness that now reveals itself as global in scope. In the eighteenth century, Kant spoke of the bondedness of peoples in his *Perpetual Peace* (1795) when he referred to the kinship "steadily increasing between the nations of the earth [that] has now extended so enormously that a violation of right in one part of the world is felt all over it."[6] In the twenty-first century, we have actually reached the point where war threatens the entire global fam-ily. This situation demands human action to save ourselves from ourselves.

A NEW PARADIGM

One can find instances of individuals' acts to resolve conflicts without resort to war-fighting in the twentieth century in Gandhi, King, Mandela, and others. Thinkers from the East are among those "previously excluded," to whom I have referred. If the twenty-first century does turn out to be, as some have suggested, the century of India

or China, the West would do well to enter into con-versation with these thinkers in what Arendt calls the "public space." Respect for such a public space offers the best chance to resolve conflict because discussion can focus on the boundaries beyond which policymakers may not go. Such public dia-logue is called for by the bondedness of peoples, which provides justification for self-defense or defense of one's neighbors against unjust aggres-sion.[7] The presence of nuclear weapons makes it impossible to conduct a just war because these weapons threaten the very value just wars are meant to preserve.

In her analysis of the human condition, Arendt finds that the greatest surprises in history come about through one human being's act. And it is through the human act that religion can assist rea-son. Ironically, Arendt turns to a religious figure—to Jesus of Nazareth, who, she says, links the power to forgive with the power of performing miracles. In fact, she, a scholar from a Jewish background, calls the incarnation the "most succinct expression of hope for the world."[8] The incarnation is God's way of seeing humanity from the perspective of the lowly, a child born into a people among the most despised by the powerful elite in Rome. This is the very perspective we have been considering as the perspective of the outsider—the perspective of the most vulnerable of the world. Paradoxically, it is at the same time the perspective of power, for if the marginalized act in concert against policies and actions that are harmful to them, their com-bined power can force changes made by global insiders. In the United States, women's movements led by such women as Sojourner Truth, a former slave; Elizabeth Cady Stanton; and others show the changes such combined power can effect. The civil rights movements in the United States and South Africa and Gandhi's independence move-ment in India are but three examples of this use of power from the twentieth century. This perspec-tive of power is available to each woman and each man, regardless of where they stand in society. Peace will only be possible if both genders make this "feminine turn"—perhaps it should be called a "more fully human turn"—and stand with the most marginalized to examine social and political realities from the perspective of those underneath. Such is the human act that is "the miracle in the making"—a peace that is more than a truce, but a peace that is forged through sustained work: not the work of war, but the struggle to enter into conversation with those from many perspectives, especially the perspective of the most vulnerable, still overwhelmingly a woman's perspective.

PART 4

RELIGION AND THE ENVIRONMENT

Science and Ethics

Human-rights discourse segues into a discussion of religion and the environment in an illuminating way. Scholars now recognize three phases in the evolution of human-rights discourse. In the first phase, it was mainly concerned with civil and political rights. In the second, the focus shifted to economic and social rights. In its third stage it now focuses on the rights of women and the environment.

Modern secular perspective in this respect offers an interesting contrast with religious worldviews. The religious perspective often starts with the cosmos and moves toward the individual through the intervening layer of the community. Such an ecological vision contrasts with the modern secular one, which takes the individual as the starting point and then moves on through the community to the cosmos. Although concern with ecology is a modern development, most religions seem to contain, no doubt in their own idiom statements of what we would regard as ecological concerns today. The Christian apostle Paul can see the cosmos in travail, human beings are designated God's vice-gerents on the earth in Islam, and in Hindu myths the oppressed earth assumes the form of a cow as it approaches the gods for relief.

These ancient motifs can now be enlivened by modern ecological concerns. All three papers in this section break remarkably fresh ground, as ecological considerations increasingly impinge on our collective imagination.

Religion and Science

Huston Smith

I want to begin by saluting Professor Arvind Sharma for having brought this important conference into being. Of all the people I know, I think of Arvind as the man who gets things done. I've seen that over the years, and this is only the last evidence of it. I want to mention one other thing. I have not attended any session, not at all because of disinterest, but because I have had a cochlear implant last month, and I can only hear by lip reading now, and that does one no good at sessions like this. It can work one-on-one, but within two months I should be able to hear. This new development in hearing is not quite as good as spectacles for seeing, but still a great breakthrough. And by the end of the year, my hearing will be 95 percent normal without hearing aid. So I want to spread the word, because there is a lot of deafness out there, and it's worth looking into.

Now, as we all know, the title, the subject, of this conference is World's Religions after September 11. However, there's something that was assumed but not stated, and the explicit full title would read World's Religions and Politics after September 11. Because I go through this final schedule and I was going to see how many had politics mixed up in the title and included in the title, and then I gave up counting because almost all of them had

something about justice and equity and rights of various kinds. And that leads me to another kind of introductory thing. This, you may know, is the sixtieth anniversary of the founding of the United Nations. I suspect that I am the only survivor of those who were in that majestic hall that day. How did I make it? Well, as a gesture toward democracy, all the heads of state of the various countries filled this immense and stately auditorium, but up in the balcony, they reserved three rows for first come first get in, and I was a student at the University of California. I got up and took the first bus from Berkeley to San Francisco 5 a.m., and I got in. And it was a thrilling event. I mean the hope that rang through that building. Finally, we are going to put war behind us, and we will settle our differences through Parliament or congresses. Now, fifty years later, I am a citizen of the United States, and I am ashamed of the way that my administration and my country plainly brushed the United Nations aside and launched a unilateral war in Iraq, and I just feel I want to apologize for my country in doing that.

Now, to settle into the topic, my announced topic is religion and science. Now, logically, it's very interesting and very convenient, easy, to diagram it—two concentric circles, the smaller one labelled as science and the larger one as religion. That's the way it has always been up until modern times. The greatest historical divide in all of history is modernity and the premodern. Let me explain that. In the sixteenth and seventeenth century, eastern Europe stumbled on a new way of knowing. We call it the scientific method, and it introduced proof. Before that there could be speculations and arguments. But as the story has it—I'm not sure this is quite right—(if it pertains to) Galileo, (but)—it used to be thought the larger objects fell faster than smaller objects. So, he took—if it was Galileo, I'm not sure but—took a large canon ball and a small canon ball to the top of the Leaning Tower of Pisa and with a piece of wood pushed them over the edge at the same time and, what do you know, they both hit the ground at the same time. So much for the notion that larger objects fall faster than smaller. Now, this new way of knowing—proof—which retired false hypotheses and put in place their alternative—ones that were confirmed—and went on into laboratory experiment. This new way of knowing very quickly began to produce three great benefits. First, materials could be multiplied very quickly. The spinning mills of Birmingham practically ruined the economy of India, where weaving was an important industry. Second, drudgery could be reduced—washing machines, microwaves, vacuum cleaners. Third, life expectancy could be extended. In all the countries that have been caught up in the scientific revolution, the age of life expectancy has risen very dramatically.

Now, these are not inconsiderable benefits—multiplication of goods, reduction of drudgery, extension of life. So we wrote science a blank check. If it had been a blank check for knowledge of the physical world, that would have been correct. We just were swept up in these benefits and fell for science hook, line, and sinker, and therein lay a very serious mistake, because science spins off of our physical senses. Very important, but they are not the only senses we have. No one has ever seen a thought. No one has ever seen a feeling. And yet the world of our thoughts and feeling is the world that we are primarily involved with. Now, the upshot of this mistake was that those two circles that I began by saying the way

to relate science and religion is science, a small circle, inside religion, a big circle. That has been reversed, and now we have religion as the small circle within science, the big circle. "Now, what's wrong with that?" you might say. It's that science can deal with only the ground floor of existence, our physical world, whereas religion can deal with other worlds. *World* is a very elastic word. I mean, we can say, "Oh, he lives in a small village. It's a very small world." But it can be expanded to be the whole of everything that is. And because we have turned the field over to science as the reliable way of knowing, it has put religion in the shadow. And that is a disaster. Everyone of us at this conference is involved with religion. I wondered if in any of these innumerable papers, the question was raised, "Why is religion important?" I suspect that it was not explicitly relayed and raised because we just take it for granted that religion is important. But that is not the way our secular scientist society sees it. And so, religion is in the eclipse today, and it's worth raising the question.

Let's just think about this subject that has brought us together. *Religio* is Latin for rebinding. And religion involves belonging and, when that belonging has been sundered, then work toward rebinding it. And that rebinding occurs in three levels, one with the whole of the thing. Rebinding. If you want to use the word *God* in whatsoever name, whatsoever idiom, it's reconciliation with the whole and with God. But it's also a reconciliation with people to one another. I just got word on my way over here of the tragic shooting that occurred today. The opposite of bonding is sundering. It's the splintering, and every society works toward the best possible rebinding of the people in that society through greater equality, greater justice. And then, there are face-to-face relationships. And religion—all of them—instructs that we should rejoice with those who rejoice and weep with those who mourn.

Now I'm going to move, Mr. Chairman, into a conclusion that will take a little while, but it's a very clear indication of the way science has thrown religion into eclipse. I have a lifelong friend. He is a scientist at Penn State University and a world-class scientist. He founded and monitors the premier materials science laboratory in the world, and for the last year, the topic that has raged through the papers of the United States—I can't speak to the others—is the controversy between evolution and intelligent design. Did we come here by the survival of the fittest? Is that what brought us here? Or was there a mind behind it? And we tracked this practically everyday for about nine months. There was something on that in one op-ed or other. And the balance fell on evolution, not intelligent design. And then one morning, the telephone rang. And Rustrum—he was Indian, not American Indian, but Indian Indian—and Rustrum said, "Huston, we got to get in on this." And I said, "You're right. We do have to." So we batted out a statement and kept it short, just about one page, because that would increase the likelihood of it getting printed. And I can almost remember. This is how it went: "In this yearlong controversy between evolution and intelligent design, there is one authority who we have not seen mentioned: Julius Caesar." Now, in journalism, that's known as a hook. You hook the reader because it's so absurd that he has to go on and find out what kind of justification. So, then, we quote, "Julius said that people tend to believe what they want to believe." And that's true. And then we went on to say, "This short piece on this subject is being co-written by a scientist and a historian of religion." By the way, in the end, we give our credentials. They're massive. I'll speak only to his, but I have a few too. Then we go on to say, "We believe in science. The fossil record shows that it took 3.5 billion years to evolve from the smallest micro-organisms on this planet all the way up to Homo sapiens, human beings. And that being true, we want to believe it. However, we also want to believe in religion, because no amount of survival of the fittest, natural selection, will produce—the Latin word is the *imago Dei*—the image of God within us. Or we could cut through the jargon and say the spirit of God, which is the fundamental component of our being. And so, wanting to believe in both science and religion—we do believe in both science and religion—and believe that a little clear thinking will show this yearlong controversy as a tempest in a teapot." Now, I'm not through. We kept it short,

sent it to the *New York Times* op-ed. No response. *Wall Street Journal,* no response. *Washington Post,* no response. *Los Angeles Times,* no response. And then we moved now into the news magazine that had also been covering it. Ten submissions. Zero response. And then Rustrum and I said, "We could spent our year just spinning our wheels trying to get some substantial journal to publish this." So we gave up.

But let me remind you, the only submission by true people, a scientist and religionist, was the only one they wouldn't touch. What does that tell us about our society? It's clear that the media or the intelligentsia don't want to hear a good word for religion. Of course, religion is all over the map, but what kind? George W. Bush's kind. And the fundamentalists, yes. That's all over the map. But for the intelligentsia and their paper and their television program, no. That is the situation we are in. I do not want to end on a totally despondent note. The good thing about mistakes, is when they are discovered, they can be corrected. And I think we are seeing some glimmering in those who are on the frontier of the intelligentsia's media that this mistake is being discovered and that would open the way to its being corrected.

Questions and Answers for the Author

Question: I would like to ask you about your recent reaction to this so-called ID—intelligent design. Do you think that this is a way that is open for the future of the relationship between science and religion?

Answer: Oh yes! I do. Needless to say, we thought we had it just right and everybody else for a whole year had missed it. But it's going to take a little time for the mistake—the mistake, however, mind you, is making science, the big circle, and religion, the smaller one—it's going to take some time for that to seep down, especially into the masses. I think the best thinkers at the frontier are acknowledging this a little bit cautiously, but they are raising that possibility.

Question: Do you think this question of intelligent design is really something that brings us forward in the relation between science and religion, and the notion of God, for instance?

Answer: Well, if I heard correctly, intelligent implies an intelligent being, and one that could orchestrate all these things is another word for a divine being.

Question: What is the best scientific hope for intelligent design? DNA, consciousness, or. . . .

Answer: Well, DNA I do not know very much about. And I'm not sure that anyone really sees the full implication of that. Consciousness, I don't think . . . Oh, it is, and this is important. It opens another subject, because science deals only with matter. It has assumed and led us to believe that matter is the fundamental reality in the universe. Now, I don't have time here, but if I did, I think I could prove to you that that's just an assumption and it is not true. Consciousness is the fundamental reality. But we can take a leap from the notebook of the scientist on this point, because they say matter—and remember, in their opinion, the fundamental reality—cannot be destroyed. It can be changed from corporeality to energy, and then back from energy to corporeality. But you can't destroy it. Now, if you can't destroy the most fundamental reality when it is matter, the same holds for consciousness, and it cannot be destroyed. And to my mind, this is a knockdown proof that life, when it drops the body, as the Indians say, that is not the end. The light on the television screen stays on. Of course, nobody has any idea what image it will be on the television screen, but the light will still be on.

Question: In this age, the polarity of science and religion seems to be moving instead when absorption of sorts of religion by science. That is, science is now being called a religion in and of itself. Is science, as a religion, any less valuable than traditional religion, in your opinion?

Answer: I think my answer is going to be yes, but . . . Well, that's playing pretty fast and loose with the word *religion*. You can be very elastic and say your religion is what you really believe in. And if

so, why, sure, for dyed-in-the-wool scientists, it is their religion. But I think that's playing fast and loose with words.

Question: Your model of concentric circles suggests that science should be a subset of religion. But do they really overlap in the questions they seek to answer? In other words, doesn't science answer "what," "where," "when," and "how," while religion seeks to answer "why"?

Answer: Well, I didn't absorb the first part, but the last part sounds right, science answering "what," "where," "when," and "how"—space, time, and matter—the three rubrics of science. Yes, but why? The author of this is exactly right. It cannot give any reason why.

Question: As a historian of religion, can you please comment briefly on the way different religions of the world, or major spokespersons of these religions, relate to science?

Answer: It's mostly historical, because in premodern and some parts of the world are still in that state. They don't brush up against religion. But where they have. . . . Well, there are opinions all over the map, but I think when they move beyond opinions to thought—calculated and carefully thought-through thought—they come out in the same place.

Question: If you have to summarize your thesis about why religion matters, what would you say?

Answer: Okay, that's good. It matters because after the physical needs of the body are met—food, shelter—it is the most important component in life, for giving us orientation, for giving us hope, for giving us compassion.

Question: A question regarding your joint submission to the media you talked about—Could the lack of response from the media to your submission be a reflection of how you approached the media and not the media's agenda to steer clear of religion?

Answer: Well, it's always possible. But I'm at a loss. How should we have approached the media? It seems to me that we were courteous, we stated our opinion which was our job to submit to them, and so, well, that's my answer. I cannot understand that they could have been offset by how. . . .

Question: I was asked to answer a question that I have no answer to, because I find it evident and clear for myself. Why do we need to believe?

Answer: Interesting. What is the alternative to believing? Skepticism. But you cannot live a totally skeptical life. You have to believe. When every time we take a step, we believe that the floor or the platform will support us. Every time we wake up in the morning, we believe that the basic fixtures of the world will not have changed overnight. So, that's my answer. Unbelief, disbelief, skepticism is an unlivable philosophy.

Question: Do you believe God is supreme intelligence?

Answer: Yes and yes. Yes, my definition of God is: List all the virtues you can think of—creativity, kindness, compassion, truth, beauty, goodness, such as another. List them all and then draw a line from each of those up to a point at the top, and the ascent of the lines means that each virtue is gaining in degree as it ascends. And if I want to play this analogy one point further, that final point in which all these virtues to the maximum that we can conceive and, even beyond that, converge—it's like a mathematical point. It has no space at all. And that puts it outside the space-time world, which is where God is.

Incarnation and the Environment

Mary Ann Buckley

When I say "we" are facing a crisis, I mean all of earth's creatures—humankind, plant and animal life, water, air, and land—the whole of our living planet. Many say that this crisis is the major sign and call of our time, because if we don't respond to this one, it won't matter what response we make in other situations. Furthermore, the violence that has been unleashed in the post-9/11 world exacerbates the crisis and accentuates the truth that nothing happens in isolation from anything else. We're an interdependent, earth community—for good and for ill—whether we're from a part of the world that marks time by the September 11 event or not.

So, within the time frame of the years since September 11, I'd like first to tell you a story of one small yet bold agricultural project that is, in its own modest way, beginning to make a positive difference to the earth community. Then I'll explore briefly how this project is nourished and sustained by an incarnational vision.

The story begins in 2003. That's when a few of my Nigerian sisters and their colleagues opened what is now called the Holy Child Integrated Agricultural Center. It's in the village of Owowo Lala in southwestern Nigeria—West Africa—in the homeland of one of Africa's largest ethnic groups, the Yoruba people.

This agricultural center is one sign of hope in the much larger context of the vast, marvelously diverse continent of Africa—a continent with an enormous wealth of peoples and natural resources, and a heavy weight of human suffering and the degradation of life-supporting habitats. Owowo Lala village is situated in a rural area in the region around the big urban center of Abeokuta, a city important, among other things, for its University of Agriculture. Our sisters went to this locale to be at the service of a new and burgeoning diocese of the Roman Catholic Church. They wanted to meet the people at the point of their most pressing needs. And they found that what the people needed first of all was food and better-balanced diets, and then they needed to be taught how to produce affordable, nutritious food for themselves in an ongoing, sustainable way. As they responded to these immediate needs, our sisters and their co-workers also dreamed of creating jobs and training future farmers in innovative methods that would enable them to be independent and self-reliant. This was the vision that fired the launching of the project.

And the story has continued its hopeful trajectory through the past three years. Five Holy Child sisters have worked hard with a staff of local people to translate that vision into practical reality. They have purchased, cleared, and cultivated forty-eight acres of land (the size of about forty-eight soccer fields); they've installed an infrastructure for water and electrical power, and have constructed housing; they've begun to raise pigs, chickens, turkeys, and rabbits; they built and stocked ten fish ponds; and they've started biogas energy production. In effect, they've incarnated their vision. The farm is up and running now. But that's just the first chapter of the story. The plan for the next six years is to raise funds to expand all of this over 197 acres and eventually construct classrooms for workshops and courses on organic farming. And it's really happening, day by day.

This dedicated team of Holy Child sisters and local people has created an organic farm. That means they're committed to not using any chemical fertilizers, but what they do use very creatively is an "integrated" method of agriculture. Therefore, every process on the farm is designed to be incorporated into every other process: waste from latrines is filtered to irrigate crops; when a chicken is slaughtered, its waste is fed to the catfish, then water from the catfish pond is used for the crops, and so on. Everything is recycled, nothing is lost, and thus the whole becomes greater than the sum of all the parts. This is the underlying philosophy—the soul, really—of integrated agriculture. It's a very ecologically friendly approach. I see it as a mirror that reflects back to us the basic principles of the universe: that life in all its myriad forms is essentially one, and that all living things are interconnected, interdependent. This approach is like a model, not just for organic farming, but for every dimension of living. Our sisters say, in their mission statement for this center, that "we [Holy Child sisters] are passionate that our dream of organic agriculture will bring food, hope and a better life to the people of Nigeria."

How then do they sustain that passion? What belief system and spirituality ground and nourish a project like this, day in and day out? I'd like to answer those questions in two ways—by saying what I think sustains the people involved, and by sharing with you what they say gives them energy and will from day to day.

I believe that if you were to put those questions to any member of my international community, sooner or later she would start talking about the mystery of the incarnation. And that's where I would start.

Tobie Tondi writes that incarnation is "the creative and nurturing activity of the Transcendent One." Those who designed and now run the agricultural center continue this creative, nurturing activity through the very earthy ordinariness of raising animals, planting crops, grinding grain, and teaching others to do likewise, so that everyone may share the table of earth's bounty and live more fully human lives and so that earth itself will flourish and not be depleted. Their farming activities give expression to the love of the transcendent one. Their lives repeat the pattern of the incarnation and continue it in a new time, place, and situation. That idea of continuing the incarnation happens to be expressed in the very first line of my community's constitution—that God needs men and women in every age to make known the reality of the incarnation. This belief is the deep source of our life and energy.

And that fundamental belief has even further theological depths. The lives of those who run the center repeat the pattern of the incarnation, and in so doing, they also express the pattern of the inner life of God, the transcendent one. The incarnation is the outward manifestation of this inward life of God. And in my Catholic Christian tradition, we say that the inner life of God is communitarian; it's trinitarian—Father, Son, and Holy Spirit—is how we say it in classical language. The Trinity is simply a way of talking about the inner life of God, and incarnation is simply the outward expression of that rich interior life of love—love made accessible as something we can touch, taste, and see with our own eyes in our distinctive human way.

The philosopher/theologian Beatrice Bruteau says this in more contemporary language, in an article titled "Eucharistic Ecology and Ecological Spirituality." For her, the symbol of the Trinity means that the inner life of God is a "mutually feeding, mutually indwelling, community, in which all the persons give themselves to one another as food, for the sake of life, abundant life."[1] So, quite literally, the agricultural center staff is committed to becoming that mutually feeding, interdependent community of love that is a sure sign of God's sustaining presence among us. And their integrated approach to organic farming, in which everything gives itself to be redirected to some further need, is an expression of this communitarian life. This dynamic of interdependent love is at the very heart of the cosmos too—for creation bears the stamp of the Creator.

But these are lofty ideas, and I doubt that the staff of the Holy Child Integrated Agricultural Center has time to think such thoughts when the chickens are cackling to be fed in the cool of the early morning—or when the bore hole fails and they have to haul water in drums from the village to keep the crops from withering in the heat of the midday sun.

Maybe, in the press of daily life, those at the farm are more in touch with the simple fact that the incarnation is essentially a movement toward earth and its needs rather than away from it in retreat—a movement toward the world out of love, because they've fallen so deeply in love with it that they're part of it, inseparable from it. They and the pigs and the cassava plants are all one, so to roll up their sleeves and do what needs to be done is the way they love.

When there is some leisure to ponder the meaning of all that's entailed in running a small organic farm, I think the staff would be encouraged by a revelation of an eleventh-century German woman. She's Hildegard of Bingen, a mystic who saw deeply into the mystery of the incarnation in relation to earth. This is what she had to say:

> The earth . . . is the mother of all,
> for contained in her are the seeds of all.
> The earth . . . is in so many ways fruitful.
> All creation comes from it.
> Yet it forms not only the basic raw material for
>   humankind,
> but also the substance of the incarnation of
>   God's Son.[2]

Earth itself is the substance of the incarnation of God's Son. If you take time to think about this, you can see that it must be very nourishing indeed to touch into the truth that the soil that collects under one's fingernails in the course of a day's work is the same substance from which the body of Christ was formed. It all erupted from the same, original flaring forth of creation 15 billion years ago. Whether these truths are at the level of consciousness or not, I think they are the deep truths that must nourish and sustain the passionate commitment of my sisters on their wonderful farm in Yorubaland.

When I asked them to speak for themselves about what sustains their passion, my sisters spoke excitedly about the nourishment they receive from the enthusiasm and joy of the villagers. The people of the area are very poor, and the farm has become for them a place where they really can buy good food at an affordable price, find employment, and learn methods for producing their own food. In the process, they grow personally in a sense of their own power and dignity. One of the added side effects of this growth has been an increased respect for the capabilities of women. Farming is men's work in this part of Nigeria, and little by little, the men are growing in admiration for what our sisters have achieved on the land with the help of other women.

So the realization of the dream that launched the farm just a few years ago is like daily bread, on many levels, for staff and villagers. And my sisters continue to be fed by even more dreams. As I listened to their reflections on what sustains their passion, I heard them say that new dreams keep on exploding in their minds and hearts. In fact, they dream that one day the farm will even become a village—Holy Child Village is what they'll call it! They dream there will be a school, a conference center, and a library there; a restaurant too, and a pastoral center, and perhaps even a clinic. Women and men will farm side by side in this village. University students will continue to come to study methods of integrated agriculture. It will be a place of refreshment and renewal—tourists from far and wide will travel there to enjoy an eco-holiday.

Others will come in search of spiritual nourishment and a time of prayer and retreat.

In other words, the Holy Child Integrated Agricultural Center, and the village it could someday become, is essentially a place of unbounded hope for life, a metaphor for a worldview, a very real sign of the reign of God. That's the "fire in the belly" that burns in my sisters and their friends from day to day.

ECO-JUSTICE ETHICS

A Brief Overview

Dieter T. Hessel

Ecological responsibility linked to social justice is what the world needs now. A healthy earth community requires advocacy and action on urgent environmental issues in ways that connect with struggles for social and economic justice. "Eco-justice" envisions and values ecology and justice together, since there will be little environmental health without socioeconomic justice, and vice versa. Some discussions of "sustainability," a prominent concept in environmental studies and political discourse, have parallel ethical meaning, to the extent that they also encompass social justice principles.[1]

Today, there is growing appreciation for a "construction of what is often called an 'eco-justice' ethic . . . that holds together concerns for the natural world and for human life, that recognizes that devastation of the environment and economic injustice go hand in hand, and that affirms that environmental and human rights are indivisible."[2] The vision and values of eco-justice ethics express a spiritually grounded moral posture of respect and fairness toward all creation, human and nonhuman. Eco-justice ethics are shaped by religious insights and scientific knowledge, interwoven with social, economic, and political experience.

HOW THE TERM EMERGED

After the first Earth Day, "eco-justice" became the theme of a group of North American, ecumenically engaged Christian ethicists (including this author). In a seminal article, "Ecological Responsibility and Economic Justice," Episcopal priest Norman Faramelli of the Boston Industrial Mission emphasized that "choosing [to work for] ecology instead of [against] poverty, or vice versa, is to make a bad choice"; the way ahead is to choose both.[3] That posture was not characteristic of the emerging environmental movement, which even today too often lacks passion for, or adequate principles of, social justice. Conversely, many social justice and peace activists have viewed environmentalism as a distraction (and even today can remain rather disinterested in ecological aspects or environmental dimensions of their concerns). To foster converging commitments to ecology and justice, American Baptist leaders Richard Jones and Owen Owens introduced the term *eco-justice*.

By 1973, a strategy to advance integrative ethics of ecology and justice became the focus of an ecumenical campus ministry initiative at Cornell University called the Eco-Justice Project and Network (EJPN), initiated and then coordinated for two decades by Presbyterian social ethicist William E. Gibson. He defined eco-justice as

> the well-being of humankind on a thriving earth . . . an earth productive of sufficient food, with water fit for all to drink, air fit to breathe, forests kept replenished, renewable resources continuously renewed, nonrenewable resources used as sparingly as possible so that they will be available [to future generations] for their most important uses. . . . On a thriving earth, providing sustainable sufficiency for all, human well-being is nurtured not only by the provision of these material necessities but also by a way of living within the natural order that is fitting: respectful of the integrity of natural systems and of the worth of nonhuman creatures, appreciative of the beauty and mystery of the world of nature.[4]

In addition to authoring several substantive essays on the subject, Gibson solicited short articles by engaged scholars on a range of eco-justice topics and published them in a quarterly journal he edited called *The Egg*, selections from which were recently republished under one cover.[5] Within two decades, a significant body of writings emerged that emphasize respect for everykind and show intersecting concern for ecology, justice, and faith.[6]

Norms of Eco-Justice Ethics

The basic norms of eco-justice ethics can be summarized as follows:

1. *solidarity* with other people and creatures—companions, victims, and allies—in earth community, reflecting deep respect for diverse creation;
2. ecological *sustainability*—environmentally fitting habits of living and working that enable life to flourish, and utilize ecologically and socially appropriate technology;
3. *sufficiency* as a standard of organized sharing, which requires basic floors and definite ceilings for equitable or "fair" consumption;

4. socially just *participation* in decisions about how to obtain sustenance and to manage community life for the good in common and the good of the commons.

The solidarity norm comprehends the full dimensions of earth community and of inter-human obligation. Sustainability gives high visibility to ecological integrity and wise, conserving behavior throughout the resource-use cycle. The norms of sufficiency and participation highlight the distributive and participatory dimensions of basic social justice. These norms illumine an overarching imperative: to pursue right relations in reinforcing ways that are both ecologically fitting and socially just.[7]

Each norm is ends-oriented and means-clarifying, illumining both where we want to go and how to get there. The observance of each ethical norm reinforces and qualifies the others in contextual decision-making oriented to just and sustainable community. All four are core values or criteria to guide personal and institutional practice, issue analysis, and government policy. An ethic of eco-justice applies comprehensively to ominous environmental threats intersecting with major societal problems.

Breadth of Concern

Authentic expressions of eco-justice ethics seek ecological justice in tandem with socio-economic justice. That makes the ethical focus of the eco-justice movement wider than most "environmentalism." Conferences, forums, networks, and publications of the movement have ranged from presenting big-picture analyses of the eco-*injustice* crisis to explorations of specific environmental problems and related issues of hunger action, sustainable agriculture, energy production and use, lifestyle integrity, economic development, debt relief, fair trade, good work, peacemaking, and environmental justice for poor people, racial minorities, and women. In that list of concerns, one can see the breadth of our subject that now also includes grappling with global warming by reducing carbon emissions while attending to impacts on poor communities, lowlands, oceans, deteriorating places, and threatened species.

The basic objective of earth ethics that seek eco-justice is to shape just and sustainable community. This purpose connects well with some emphases expressed in related discourse about achieving "sustainability," "ecological justice," "earth justice," or "environmental justice."

For example, "environmental justice" is an important facet of eco-justice, but the latter has wider concerns. Some recent programs of eco-justice education and action fostered by religious denominations have confused matters by calling all that they do "environmental justice" work. This posture does underline the importance of meeting the justice claims of vulnerable human communities and individuals. Obviously, there is much to be done to secure human environmental rights for affected communities (often racial minorities, and predominantly women and children) that are oppressed by indifferent or corrupt governments, privileged classes, and powerful polluting corporations.[8]

Nevertheless, environmental justice is essential but only part of the larger agenda of seeking the common good for humans in harmony with the sustaining matrix of life. Therefore,

> Eco-justice [also] recognizes in other creatures and natural systems the claim to be respected and valued and taken into account in societal arrangements. . . . The concern for ecological soundness and sustainability includes but transcends the concern of humans for themselves.[9]

The converse is also true. Those who equate eco-justice with "ecological justice" inadvertently tend to play down or to lose sight of major social justice requirements in a world of predatory economic exploitation driven by market fundamentalism that widens the rich-poor gap while intensifying pollution and waste. Some recent publications such as the substantive four-volume Earth Bible series, initiated by an ecumenical team of Australian scholars, use the term "ecojustice"—without a hyphen—to name their ecologically focused principles of Earth Justice, namely, "ecological interdependence, intrinsic worth, human custodianship, and resistance."[10] The Earth Bible project offers a fresh approach to and new interpretations of scriptural passages, but it does not quite address social and economic justice requirements for achieving sustainable earth community.

ECUMENICAL AND SECULAR DEVELOPMENT

The ecumenical movement worldwide, through deliberations and programs spanning more than three decades, has fostered eco-justice ethics, beginning with a thematic focus on "just, participatory, and sustainable society," initiated at the 1975 Nairobi Assembly of the World Council of Churches (WCC). That theme was influenced by insights of the 1972 United Nations Stockholm Conference on Environment and Development, but ecumenical openness to being instructed by emergent global discourse about sustainability was also shaped by biblical-theological reflection on the eco-injustice crisis. Eco-justice ethics have deep biblical roots in the Bible's opening vision of creation's Sabbath, the story of God's rainbow covenant with "all flesh on earth" after the flood (Gen 9), and key summaries of covenant obligations to respond to the poor, to give animals Sabbath rest, to let the land lie fallow, and to cancel debts periodically, if not to redistribute land (see Exod 23, Lev 19 and 25, and Deut 15). The same spiritually grounded ethical posture permeates Jesus' teachings (for example, in the Gospel of Luke) about living into the kingdom of God (today we might call it "kindom"). Abrahamic monotheists informed by this fresh view of the human-earth relationship can now comprehend that all beings on earth are one household (*oikos*) requiring an economy (*oikonomia*) that takes ecological and social stewardship (*oikonomos*) seriously.

As Australian biologist Charles Birch, addressing the 1975 WCC gathering, explained,

> A prior requirement of any global society is that it be so organized that human life and other

living creatures on which human life depends can be sustained indefinitely within the limits of the Earth. A second requirement is that it be sustained at a quality that makes possible fulfillment of human life for all people. A society so organized to achieve both these ends we can call a sustainable global society . . . with a new sort of science and technology governed by a new sort of economics and politics.[11]

A follow-up ecumenical conference at MIT in 1979 on "Faith, Science, and the Future" pursued the subject in more detail, and the next WCC Assembly (Vancouver, 1983) focused on "Justice, Peace, and Integrity of Creation." In response, member communions of the WCC began to develop earth ministries. In the United States, initiatives of that kind were led by the Eco-Justice Working Group of the National Council of Churches.[12]

A Roman Catholic response began to unfold with the pope's 1979 trip to the Americas (first Puebla, Mexico, and then Des Moines, Iowa), where John Paul II emphasized land stewardship. Pastoral letters on the same subject issued by Catholic Bishops in Appalachia and the Great Plains preceded the pope's visit.[13] A decade later, the Vatican issued the 1990 message, "The Ecological Crisis: A Common Responsibility." Then on Pentecost 1992 in Brazil, parallel to the 1992 United Nations Conference on Environment and Development (the "Earth Summit" in Rio de Janeiro), an inclusive gathering of Protestant, Orthodox, Roman Catholic, and Anglican leaders facilitated by the WCC issued its *Letter to the Churches*, which concluded its confession of complicity and expression of commitment with these words:

The Spirit teaches us to go first to those places where community and creation are most obviously languishing, those melancholy places where the cry of the people and the cry of the earth are intermingled. [There] we meet Jesus, who goes before, in solidarity and healing.[14]

Thought and action for just and sustainable community, post-Rio, have animated a religiously and ethnically pluralistic network of engaged persons on six continents. (In this brief essay I will not discuss parallel expressions of eco-justice ethics in other world religions, such as Judaism and Confucianism. See the Forum on Religion and Ecology volumes on Judaism and Ecology and on Confucianism and Ecology.)

Even as ecumenical earth ethics developed, a parallel secular focus on sustainability—seeking to protect the environment while combating poverty—gained momentum in a series of United Nations–sponsored events, beginning with the 1972 Stockholm Conference on Environment and Development, followed by the 1987 Bruntland Commission Report, the Rio Declaration of the 1992 Earth Summit, and the 2002 World Summit on Sustainable Development in Johannesburg. Cumulatively, these global deliberations exposed the inseparable link between environmental issues and socioeconomic problems and the geopolitical proportions of the struggle to integrate them.

The Stockholm Conference underlined the significance of sustainability as a standard of authentic, healthy development, and the need for both inter generational and intra generational equity among humans to move toward achieving it. The Stockholm Declaration called on the nations to improve the environment "for present and future generations . . . a goal to be pursued together with, and in harmony with, the established and fundamental goals of peace and worldwide economic and social development."

This set the stage for two important shifts of emphasis in global ethics discourse: seeing holistic connections between humanity's social, ecological, and economic obligations and asserting responsibility for future as well as present generations. The two shifts in ethical sensibility show up quite clearly in the 1987 Brundtland Commission's definition of sustainable development; that is, it "meets the needs of the present without compromising the ability of future generations to meet their own needs." The ethical thrust, however, was still toward meeting the needs of humankind without direct attention to the well-being of otherkind, beyond their instrumental value to humans. The 1992 Earth

Summit had a similarly anthropocentric emphasis on the use value of the environment, though there were some leads toward more environmentally promising ethics. . . . For example, Principle 1 of the Rio Declaration asserts that "human beings are at the center of concerns for sustainable development" and that "they are entitled to a healthy and productive life in harmony with nature." Principle 7 asserts that "states shall cooperate in a spirit of global partnership to conserve, protect, and restore the health and integrity of Earth's ecosystem." And Principle 25 declares that "peace, development, and environmental protection are independent and indivisible."

A decade later, the United Nations Report of the World Summit on Sustainable Development (2002) emphasized that "sound environmental, social, and economic policies, democratic institutions responsive to the needs of the people, the rule of law, anti-corruption measures, gender equality, and an enabling environment for investment are the basis for sustainable development." Note the ambiguity of its call for an "enabling" investment environment.

Meanwhile, anthropocentric thinking, shallow views of "sustainable development," along with unrealistic cornucopian optimism about the results of deregulated economic growth and innovative technology have remained dominant in most government and business circles. Increasingly, these ethically barren approaches are being challenged by a more substantial, holistic paradigm of sustainable community,[15] or "Earth Democracy."[16] Vandana Shiva favors Earth Democracy as an alternate name for an ethic of justice, sustainability, and peace that "allows us to reclaim our common humanity and our unity with all life" over against development schemes that enclose or privatize the commons and deny poor communities sustainable livelihoods.

> Earth Democracy relocates the sanctity of life in all beings and all people irrespective of class, gender, religion, or caste. And it redefines 'upholding family values' as respecting the limits on greed and violence set by belonging to the earth family.[17]

Twenty-First-Century Earth Ethics

The global reach and intercultural salience of deepening eco-justice ethics show up most cogently in sixteen "interdependent principles for a sustainable way of life" that the Earth Charter (2000) articulates. The charter is an international "peoples treaty" endorsed by a growing number of NGOs and government representatives in the International Union for the Conservation of Nature (IUCN or World Conservation Union). Its ethical imperatives (presented as sets of four principles in Parts 1–4 of the charter) actually unpack and broaden the meaning of the four basic eco-justice norms—solidarity, sustainability, sufficiency, and participation—in that order. As Earth Charter drafting committee member J. Ronald Engel, Professor of Social Ethics emeritus at Meadville-Lombard Theological School in Chicago, points out:

> The Charter repeatedly drives home the message that . . . only through the elimination of poverty and other human deprivation, and the establishment of just and nonviolent social and economic relationships, will the citizens of the world be in a position to protect and restore the integrity of Earth's ecological systems. . . . The Earth Charter thus embraces what has come to be called an 'eco-justice' ethic—a comprehensive and holistic moral approach in which ecological and social (including economic and cultural) well-being are considered both dependent and independent variables. It is not possible to adequately address one without also addressing the other; yet each also needs to be addressed on its own terms.[18]

Mature eco-justice ethics contribute to shaping just and sustainable community in a socially conflicted and ecologically stressed world by resisting two popular false assumptions. The first is that the natural environment should be a focus of responsibility apart from considerations of human well-being. Eco-justice ethics assert to the contrary that interhuman justice is part of environmental wholeness. Not only is nature's health inseparable from human well-being; environmental health will never get the priority attention it deserves in religion, ethics, business, or politics if nature is viewed as external to human society or we to it. The second false assumption being challenged is that societies can wait to become ecologically sustainable until they "develop" economically. Neoliberals and Marxists alike have assumed the priority of economic development, to be followed eventually by environmental protection measures. But that is an impossible scenario for today's crowded, technologically toxic world facing severe biophysical limits and increasing socioeconomic inequity. Healthy society depends upon ecological security and vice versa. Eco-justice ethics emphasize that ecology and justice are nonsequential, simultaneous requirements, all the more so when economic problems become dire.

Eco-justice ethics will be all the more pertinent as the world community seeks to meet the challenges of global warming and severe social inequality. Wealthy countries that account for two-thirds of the atmospheric buildup of carbon dioxide over recent decades must recognize their ecological debt to poor countries that experienced little social benefit from natural-resource exploitation by corporate investors allied with corrupt governments and that are experiencing disproportionate negative effects of climate change.

In retrospect, a posture that first emerged to reconcile post–Earth Day competition between social justice and environmental action groups turns out to offer much more than tradeoffs. Eco-justice vision and values provide a dynamic framework for philosophical and ethical reflection that animates religious communities, environmental and economic organizations, government entities, educational institutions, and the media to meet the real needs of distressed Earth community. That is the urgent moral assignment of our time.

5 RELIGION AND DIVERSITY

Embracing Pluralism

INTRODUCTION

The crucial but unacknowledged role of diversity in our lives becomes apparent the moment we try to answer the question: Do two people who follow the same religion understand it in exactly the same way? And if they don't, then it is obvious that there are really as many Christianities as there are Christians, or as many Buddhisms as there are Buddhists, and so on. This recognition is in addition to the diversity which already characterizes the various religions of the world in the form of major subdivisions within them, such as Catholic, Protestant and Orthodox Christianity, or Sunni and Shii (or, Shia) Islam, and so on; as well as the many further subdivisions within them, in the form of, say, the various denominations of Protestantism in Christianity, the various schools of law within Islam, the various schools of philosophy within Hinduism, and so on. Then, apart from this internal diversity within the various religious traditions, we must reckon with the fact of the variety of the religious traditions themselves, as represented by Judaism, Christianity, Islam, Hinduism, Buddhism, Confucianism, Taoism, and others. Our familiarity with this diversity serves to conceal its immensity from us, but once we become conscious of it, we realize the significance of the theme which is addressed in this section.

Pluralism as a Way of Dealing with Religious Diversity

Caitlin Crowley

Interactions between religions take place along a continuum. At one end of the spectrum is pluralism. At the other end is intolerance. Intolerant relationships consist of hatred and prejudice. One group may believe that another group should be exterminated. Intolerance can also be nonviolent, but lead a group to believe that the rights and privileges of the other should be less than one's own.

At the pluralistic end of the spectrum, interactions are marked by the effort to create peaceful coexistence based on acknowledgement and respect for religious, cultural, and ideological differences. It is not to be confused with diversity. Diversity is already a social reality in North America. On account of diversity, there are many ideas and opinions that are forced into coexistence. Sometimes coexistence works and sometimes it causes friction. The uneven response to diversity begs the question: What is the best way to deal with diversity? The answers to this question span this long, varied continuum from intolerance to pluralism.

There is an area on the tolerance continuum that could be called nonaccepting tolerance. In this case, a person maintains that their religious truth is greater or more true than others. Although all those not participating in that person's tradition are excluded from salvation, those in the darkness

are allowed to be in darkness. This is because "it is preferable to allow others the freedom of error than for believers to lose their integrity."[1] There is no effort to forcibly convert or eliminate those of another faith; their existence is tolerated. However, their beliefs are not acceptable for salvation. That is why it is called nonaccepting tolerance.

A little farther along the continuum is acceptance of those who are similar to you and rejection of those who are too different. Vaishnavites and Shaivites are not the same, but they are close. Jews and Christians share a similar history. Ideas and beliefs that are shared make it easier to understand and accept someone of another faith tradition. People may identify those close to them as being on somewhat of the right path.

There are people in another place on the spectrum who believe that, although their religion has the ultimate truth, those who live good lives will be rewarded in the next life or the afterlife, despite their rejection or ignorance of the truth. This seems like tolerance because those of other faiths will be given some reward for good behavior. However, these people still consider other faith traditions to be in some way inferior in their religious beliefs.

Universalism is a concept that spans the spectrum. It is the idea that all human beings are able to access the religious truths of particular traditions and achieve salvation through that religion. However, the concept of universalism does not guarantee that those who practice other traditions will achieve salvation. Some people who are universalists believe that humans can achieve salvation no matter what their traditions. There are also universalists who believe that anyone can join their religious tradition but that joining their tradition is essential for salvation.

At the far end of the spectrum is pluralism. Diana Eck, Harvard professor of comparative religions and Indian studies, defines pluralism in her book *A New Religious America:* "Pluralism is not an ideology, not a leftist scheme, and not a free-form relativism. Rather, pluralism is the dynamic process through which we engage with one another in and through our very deepest differences."[2] Professor Robert Wuthnow agrees that this engagement is both broad and deep. He writes, "Religious differences are instantiated in dress, food, holidays, and family rituals; they also reflect historic teachings and deeply held patterns of belief and practice. These beliefs and practices may be personal and private, but they cannot easily be divorced from questions about truth and morality."[3] In active pluralism, these beliefs, practices, and commitments cannot be checked at the door. They are a necessary part of debate and dialogue.

The first thing required for active pluralism is the renunciation of the supremacy of one's own religion. Pastor Scott Gustafson explains that "religion might be understood in such a way that the variety of religious expressions are assumed to be diverse expressions of a more ultimate reality. In this case religious toleration seems logically to follow. However, the toleration of any particular expression that claims ultimate status for itself is quite problematic because such claims undermine the assumption that individual religious expressions are indicative of some other, more fundamental reality."[4] Pluralism also requires some level of relativism. There are elements common between different religions and among all religions. However, there are also incompatible differences—for instance, reincarnation and the belief that a soul

gets one life to live are theologically irreconcilable. There is more than one way to approach these differences. A religious person could view the difference as unimportant—as a culturally specific detail that is important for the practice of that religion but exists outside of the realm of truths that are common to all religions. A person could also refuse to decide which belief is more true—only their higher power really knows. They do not know whether what they do or what someone else does is more right, and they agree not to choose. This person would recognize a difference but move on to focus on the common truths between religions.

Pluralism, then, requires interest in and sincere study of other religions—how they began, their history, their theology, their rituals, and so forth. It is important to realize that although there is a huge difference in the outer aspects of religions from the names, history, rituals, and organizations, the essence of religions is almost identical as to guide humanity in their physical life observing love, the unintentional love, and justice, and in the ultimate goal of unification with the supreme being. It is important to realize that studying a text or ritual by itself does not approximate the lived experience of that text or ritual. The process of encountering both a text and the lived experience of a text can be challenging in many ways. As Professor Louis Hammann of Gettysburg College puts it, "Practicing [religious tolerance] may strain one's own commitments, unless tolerance is itself required by the logic of those commitments."[5] Interest and study may be seen as a part of one's own religious experience. This can be highly successful and fulfilling personally and can facilitate achieving real pluralism.

In the beginning of the twentieth century, CaoDai faith was founded in Vietnam, stating that all religions are of one same divine origin (which is God called by different names), have the same teachings based on love and justice, and are just diverse manifestations of the same truth. With its universal teaching, CaoDai paves a way for more tolerance in pluralism.

One way to focus pluralism is around concern for our common interests—peace and the well-being of humanity. Sister Joan Kirby writes in an essay: "We will meet outside the walls; we will meet on our way up the mountain; we will meet in the search for our deepest roots in God. This does not imply a religious consensus as a negotiation of our faith convictions. Rather, it acknowledges that we all draw from the deepest and most life-giving sources and that we share everyone's concern for the future of humanity."[6]

Professor Diana Eck illustrates this complicated process best: "Pluralism is not simply relativism. It does not replace or eliminate deep religious commitments or secular commitments for that matter. It is, rather, the encounter of commitments. While the encounter with other faiths in a pluralist society may lead one to a less myopic view of one's own faith, pluralism is premised not on a reductive relativism but on the significance of and engagement with real differences."[7] Pluralism is a feasible paradox. And even if it was found that particular faiths tended more toward exclusivism, the fact that there are scholars in every tradition who believe that real pluralism is possible demonstrates the potential in all religions for activating pluralism. Respecting deep religious differences while maintaining one's own commitments is intense but possible. Argument and dissension will happen. The key will be to create truly pluralistic environments, make them the norm, and prepare the next generations to inherit and preserve it.

CaoDai, recognizing the merit of all religions, propounding that all religions have one same origin and teach the same principles, always encourages people to open their heart to have interest and study of other religions as part of their own religious practice in order to fulfill pluralism and thus create harmony for humanity.

ORIENTALIST FEMINISM AND ISLAMOPHOBIA/IRANOPHOBIA

Roksana Bahramitash

In the aftermath of September 11, two countries have been attacked as part of a global war on terror. The United States of America, under its current administration run under a neoconservative political ideology, sees a global threat of terrorism as harbored by Islamic fundamentalism. In order to mobilize support, a wide range of strategies has been used by Washington. One of them is to insist upon Muslim women's rights. The irony is that this administration relies for its support on the religious Right of evangelicalism and is itself conservative in its approach toward women's rights. For instance, it supports pro-life politics and has sought to curb women's access to abortion on demand. The United States has not signed CEDAW, the Convention for the Elimination of Discrimination against Women. It continues to refuse to sign because of articles such as equal pay for men and women. Yet, it forced Iraq to sign, and remains critical of Muslim countries with regard to their treatment of women. Prior to invading Afghanistan, President Bush expressed deep concern about the status of women in the country and intimated that the war was going to free them. This sudden support for women's rights came as a shock to many advocates of women's rights who had been campaigning against the Taliban—a campaign that had fallen on deaf ears

prior to September 11. In fact, the United States had supported the Taliban in the aftermath of the Cold War. But suddenly, the situation of Afghan women became extremely important to the United States, and a war was the answer.

To an objective mind, the position of this current administration may appear to be very surprising; but surprising as it is, it is nonetheless not new. There has been a long history of legitimizing foreign policy under the pretext of defending women's rights. Dating back to colonial times in many parts of the colonial world—namely, Egypt, India, and Algeria—the presence of Western powers was part of an effort to civilize these nations. Western domination and military action against the colonized has been legitimized thanks to the assumption that the colonized world is inferior to the Western world. In the case of the Middle East and North Africa, Edward Said's groundbreaking work on Orientalism articulates the way the West has viewed the Orient.[1] As Said points out, the Orient has been regarded as the place of corrupt despotism, mystical religiosity, irrationality, backwardness, and the Other. As for evidence of this Other's inferiority, one element is the treatment of women.

In Algeria, the colonization of Arabs was legitimized under the so-called civilizing mission of the French. As Frantz Fanon argues, the French attempt to "civilize" Algerians was focused on "liberating women" from so-called retrograde Islamic traditions by methods such as forced deveiling.[2] Forced deveiling and Gallicization constituted the road to women's liberation and ultimately to the country's civilization. Interestingly enough, while Algerian women were being "rescued" from their men by the French, many women in France were fighting for their rights against those very men who fantasized about liberating Muslim women. The official position of the French colonial powers was that until Algerian men became civilized (and treated women appropriately) they should not have the right to vote.

Civilizing the Muslims was not an entirely male enterprise. White middle-class women adapted the Orientalist discourse and in fact used their position as women to enter Muslim female space to collect evidence of victimhood of Muslim women. For instance, the nineteenth-century painter Henrietta Brown became famous for her paintings of the Ottoman court—a sight hidden from European men. But the depiction of Muslim women in Brown's Orientalist painting became popular, giving access to what European men could not portray. According to Yegenoglu, "It is with the assistance of the Western woman (for she is the only 'foreigner' allowed to enter into the 'forbidden zone') that the mysteries of this inaccessible 'inner space' and the 'essence' of the Orient secluded in it could be unconcealed; it is she who can remedy the long-lasting lack of the Western subject."[3] Her paintings illustrated Muslim women's victimization through the cruel Islamic practices of polygamy and the sexual segregation of harems.

Although polygamy and other misogynistic practices did exist and still do, the context under which such depictions are brought into light is the problem. Just as there is no doubt that the Taliban is oppressive toward women, the way Afghan women's position has been contextualized to justify the mobilizing of forces for war is at the heart of the dilemma. Women like Brown are numerous, and in fact a certain type of feminism lends itself to this sort of Orientalist thought and analysis. This type of feminism has been defined as Orientalist feminism. Parvin Paydar identifies such feminism as that which assumes a dichotomy between the West and the Orient.[4] In this paradigm, the Orient is seen as a place of backwardness, irrationality, and religious dogma, and the proof of that is the treatment of women. Orientalist feminism paints a monolithic picture of victimized women of the Orient who need to be rescued.

Similar to colonial times when white middle-class women from the West joined colonial civilizing missions, in the postcolonial era there is a growing body of literature on the oppression of women in the Muslim world—literature written by women, many of them feminists. These feminists, Orientalist feminists, are not limited to the West; in the postcolonial context, women of Muslim origin have also joined the mission. This chapter focuses on an Iranian woman, Azar Nafisi, whose book *Reading Lolita in Tehran* claims to defend women's rights. The book is full of evidence of the oppression of women and is reminiscent of another book written in the 1980s, *Not Without My Daughter*, by Betty Mahmoody, an American woman. In her book, Mahmoody writes about the horrors of Iran. The book became a bestseller and was later made into a Hollywood movie. The consequence of the book's publication and the film's release was a wave of attacks motivated by racial hatred against Iranians throughout Europe and North America.

Nafisi's book remained the number-one bestseller for several months on the *New York Times Book Review* list. What is interesting is that, unlike Betty Mahmoody's book, Nafisi's work is formally endorsed by Washington. The book is highly recommended and promoted by the neoconservatives of the current administration. Nafisi says that her neoconservative mentor Fouad Ajami, her superior at the School of Advanced International Studies in Washington, has been among her best supporters. In the book, in a list of people who endorsed it, Bernard Lewis, a neoconservative guru, describes the book as "a memoir about teaching Western literature in revolutionary Iran with profound and fascinating insights into both."[5]

Nafisi's book is a personal account of the lives of women in Iran from an insider's point of view. Nafisi places her depiction of her own life and the lives of eight women within a context of supposed total horror in Iran—the Iran of President Bush's Axis of Evil. Nafisi claims to have been dismissed from university and forced to resort to teaching eight women English literature in her home. Her book and her experience have come to be representative of Iranian women's experience as an indication of Muslim/Iranian men's misogyny. Again, there is no question that women suffer from oppression in Iran, yet there is a major problem with a depiction that feeds negative stereotypes about Muslim/Iranian men.

As Hamid Dabbashi has argued,

So far as its unfailing hatred of everything Iranian—from its literary masterpieces to its ordinary people—is concerned, not since Betty Mahmoody's notorious book *Not Without My Daughter* (1984) has a text exuded so systematic a visceral hatred of everything Iranian. Meanwhile, by seeking to recycle a kaffeeklatsch version of English literature as the ideological foregrounding of American empire, *Reading Lolita in Tehran* is reminiscent of the most pestiferous colonial projects of the British in India, when, for example, in 1835 a colonial officer like Thomas Macaulay decreed: "We must do our best to form a class who may be interpreters between us and the millions whom we govern, a class of persons Indian in blood and colour, but English in taste, in opinions, words and intellect." Azar Nafisi is the personification of that native informer and colonial agent, polishing her services for an American version of the very same project.[6]

Nafisi's work is not only a celebration of U.S. foreign policy; it is equally a major contribution to the Islamophobia that exists in North America. "It is a truth universally acknowledged that a Muslim man, regardless of his fortune, must be in want of a nine-year-old virgin wife."[7] Nafisi repeats this idea again and again. In addition, even secular Iranian men come into the picture; Nafisi makes them seem not very different from those who are religious and portrays them as fanatical, hypocritical, and generally oppressive behind their liberated appearance. Nafisi mentions the changing of the legal marriage age to nine years old in accordance with Islamic jurisprudence as an act that reinforced the misogyny of Islamic religion. However, although it is true that the legal age of marriage was lowered after the regime change, in reality, as Moslem points out, the average age of marriage has risen from 18.7 in 1956 to 21 in 1991, and any deviation from this pattern is statistically marginal. In other words, although there is no doubt that such a legal age is unacceptable, the law hardly reflects a social reality.[8]

The same applies to polygamy. Since I mention Nafisi's negative account of Iranian men and their desire to have many wives, it should also be taken into account that in reality polygamy is a very uncommon practice. Only 1 percent of all marriages are polygamous, according to recent research conducted at the University of Tehran.[9] These are just two examples of how facts and fiction intertwine to create a book that pretends to give a true story of Iran and of the oppression of Iranian women. Moreover, millions of Iranian women have entered university education in the period following the revolution.[10]

Such denunciation of Iran as a backward, barbaric place for women because of Islam takes place within a context where millions of Muslim men throughout North America are being profiled as potential terrorists. There has been rising anti-Muslim/Iranian/Arab sentiment in North America. Altaf Ali, executive director for the Florida chapter of the Council on American-Islamic Relations, said his organization released a report in July indicating that anti-Muslim incidents in the state had increased by ninety-five percent during 2002.[11] Hate crimes against Muslims are also linked to the war in Iraq.[12] The situation of women in the Muslim world in general and in Iran in particular leaves a great deal to be desired, and feminists in Iran and other parts of the Muslim world, as well as many other countries, have a huge battle to fight.

What is unclear is how neoconservatives and their current foreign policy are going to help the situation. It is very likely that further destabilization of the region will make the situation worse for men as well as women.

The tragedy of the situation is that, to justify a war in the region, support has been mobilized under the pretext of liberating women and at the expense of Muslim and Iranian people in North America. Rising Islamophobia is a major concern for antiracist groups and anti-war activists. If the defense of women's rights is tackled separately from antiracist and antiwar endeavors, that defense can not only work against antiracist and antiwar activism but in the long run it will make the situation worse for the women it purports to defend. Neither Afghanistan nor Iraq are markedly better than they were prior to the United States' invasion. An attack on Iran, which the current administration is contemplating, will produce the same result as it has in the other two cases—increased instability and increased hardship for women. (In Afghanistan, this is thanks to the regrouping of the Taliban; in Iraq, the situation is approaching civil war thanks to the failure of Western-style democracy.) It is important therefore to emphasize the link between women's rights advocacy and that of antiracist and antiwar activism; otherwise, all three battles will be lost together.

Along a Path Less Traveled

A Plurality of Religious Ultimates?

Arvind Sharma

It would be well to begin by recalling the task one has set out for oneself. The task is to persuade the reader to think in terms of the possibility of a plurality of religious ultimates. I have no illusions regarding the magnitude of my venture. Indeed, the very consideration of this possibility might have occasioned a measure of surprise that I hope to mitigate as we proceed. In fact, if the eyebrows raised in disbelief at the beginning of this chapter are reduced at its end to furrowed eyebrows contemplating, howsoever reluctantly, the possibility indicated in the title, I would consider myself adequately recompensed for my labors.

And a labor it has been. For although religious plurality is a dominant feature of the religious life of our century both inside and outside academia, there is, in the technical sense of the word, a "rational" reluctance to concede it in the context of religious ultimacy. We are familiar with a plurality of religious traditions as well as a plurality of methods of studying them—both when such methods are sympathetic to religion, or neutral or antagonistic toward it. There is even a plurality of paths admitted within a religious tradition. There is also a growing if somewhat problematic realization that there could be plurality of revelations of or from the same reality, compared to which the acceptance of a plurality

of expressions of the experience of the same reality is perhaps considered somewhat less of a problem. Such magnanimity of disposition, however, seems to desert us when the question of the plurality of religious ultimates is raised. This is perhaps in part because the idea appears like a philosophical version of a religious position that is not even a rejected option in the Abrahamic religions of Judaism, Christianity, and Islam, namely, polytheism. The word tends to sink out of sight under the weight of its own negative associations. Perhaps the rejection is too quick, as the Sikh scholar noted at an ecumenical conference. After hearing a Jewish, a Christian, and a Muslim scholar vehemently assert by turns that they believed in "one God," he is said to have exclaimed: "Will someone tell me how many one Gods there are?" But surely there is more to it. Even an apparently polytheistic religion such as Hinduism, for instance, upon investigation, it turns out, believes in one God. Klaus K. Klostermaier writes:

> Many Hindu homes are lavishly decorated with color prints of a great many Hindu gods and goddesses, often joined by the gods and goddesses of other religions and the pictures of contemporary heroes. Thus, side by side with Śiva, Viṣṇu, and Devī one can see Jesus and

Zoroaster, Gautama Buddha and Jina Mahāvīra, Mahātmā Gāndhī and Jawaharlal Nehru, and many others. But, if questioned about the many gods, even illiterate villages will answer: *bhagvān ek hai,* the Lord is One. They may not be able to figure out in theological terms how the many gods and the One God hang together and they may not be sure about the hierarchy among the many manifestations, but they know that ultimately there is only One and that the many somehow merge into the one.[1]

The Problem of Monolatry

How deeply entrenched this monolatrous tendency is in religion and philosophy becomes evident even from a cursory inspection of the philosophies and religions of East and West. Contrary to the Kiplingesque formulation, the East and the West do meet at least in this respect. Both mind and matter are equally given in common experience. I see a table. The perception is mental; the object perceived is material. Yet Western idealism in one way or another, from Plato to Hegel, manages to either explain it or explain it away in terms of mind or spirit or some such entity. Western materialism—from its most ancient forms to its modern incarnation as scientific materialism and Marxism—manages to perform the diametrically opposite feat of accounting for mind in terms of matter. In either case, the many have been reduced to two and two to one.

Indian philosophy does not like being left behind. Various forms of Indian idealism and Indian materialism perform similar maneuvers to achieve similar results. It is perhaps a matter of further interest, however, that sometimes, although one is reduced to the other, the reduction is not to one but several material or spiritual principles. And now the plot begins to thicken.

Religious Ultimates in Nyāya-Vaiśeṣika and Sāṅkhya

One Hindu system of thought is known as Nyāya-Vaiśeṣika. According to it an entity, in order to

be ultimate, must be eternal. It argues that as only composite objects can dissolve, only a partless entity can be eternal and therefore ultimate. In order to be devoid of parts, an entity must be either infinitesimal or all-pervasive. This principle allows it to posit nine fundamental substances: earth, water, fire, and air (all atoms); ether; space; and time, souls, and mind. Thus, the system is plural but it is not pluralistic; that is, all of them do not enjoy the same status. The soul enjoys a higher status, and among the souls is the supreme soul—God.[2] Another Hindu system, the Sāṅkhya, subsumes all matter under a single entity and is also atheistic so that in the end one is left with a plurality of souls. However, in their state of salvation, they are all qualitatively (though not numerically) the same: spiritual clones, as it were.[3] It would be tedious to multiply the examples, all of which point in the same direction—that even the apparently pluralistic systems possess a monistic bias if probed far enough or deep enough.

Religious Ultimates and Soteriology

Thus are we led to the crux of the matter. Religious or philosophical systems can be pluralistic, but such pluralism tends to become attenuated and even vanish when it comes to soteriology. In the guise of oneness masquerading as sameness, or as the one goal to which all paths lead, or the one emptiness that characterizes everything including itself as empty, or as the one Buddha or the one Buddha-nature in all—in one way or another—monistically or henotheistically—somehow salvation comes to hinge on the one. In this deck of cards even drawing an ace will not help—salvation is the joker.

But why must this be so? In the Hibbert Lectures that he delivered at Manchester College and published under the title *A Pluralistic Universe,* William James raised a similar issue. It would be convenient to pursue our investigation further in the light of what he has to say. In the present context, the manner in which he contrasts monism and pluralism is particularly helpful. According to him, monism "insists that when you come down to reality as such, to the reality of realities, everything is present to everything else in one vast instantaneous co-implicated completeness," whereas for "pluralism, all that we are required to admit as the constitution of reality is what we ourselves find empirically realized in every minimum of finite life."[4] Elsewhere, he distinguishes between them as follows: "Pluralism lets things really exist in the each-form or distributively. Monism thinks that the all-form or collective-unit form is the only form that is rational."[5] The way William James contrasts rationalism and empiricism helps turn the key further in the lock: "Empiricism means the habit of explaining wholes by parts, and rationalism means the habit of explaining parts by wholes."[6] It is apparent now why empiricism would invite the charge of incoherence,[7] for it is open-ended. Toward the end of his lectures, William James offers some concluding remarks with great economy and courtesy. He says:

> Whatever I may say, each of you will be sure to take pluralism or leave it, just as your own sense of rationality moves and inclines. The only thing I emphatically insist upon is that it is a fully co-ordinate hypothesis with monism. This world *may,* in the last resort, be a block-universe; but on the other hand it *may* be a universe only strung-along, not rounded in and closed. Reality *may* exist distributively just as it sensibly seems to, after all. On that possibility I do insist.[8]

It seems that James's views have suffered from benign neglect because the possibility he insisted on has not been fully explored. One may explore it further with the famous Indian metaphor of the elephant and the blind men. Thereby hangs a tale.

THE PARABLE OF THE BLIND MEN AND THE ELEPHANT

Buddha, the Blessed One, gives the parable of the blind men and the elephant to illustrate that partial knowledge always breeds bigotry and fanaticism. Once a group of disciples entered the city of Śrāvasti to beg alms. They found there a number of sectarians holding disputations with one another and maintaining "This is the truth, that is not the truth. That is not the truth, this is the truth." After listening to these conflicting views, the brethren came back to the Exalted One and described to him what they had seen and heard at Śrāvasti.

Then said the Exalted One:

"These sectarians, brethren, are blind and unseeing. They know not the real, they know not the unreal; they know not the truth, they know not the untruth. In such a state of ignorance do they dispute and quarrel as ye describe. Now in former times, brethren, there was a Rājā (king) in this same Śrāvasti. Then, brethren, the Rājā called to a certain man, saying: "Come thou, good fellow! Go, gather together all the blind men that are in Śrāvasti!"

"'Very good, Your Majesty,' replied that man, and in obedience to the Rājā, gathered together all the blind men, took them with him to the Rājā, and said: 'Your Majesty, all the blind men of Śrāvasti are now assembled.'

"'Then, my good man, show the blind men an elephant.'

"'Very good, Your Majesty,' said the man and did as he was told, saying: 'O ye blind men, such as this is an elephant.'

"And to one he presented the head of the elephant, to another, the ear, to another a tusk, the trunk, the foot, back, tail and tuft of the tail, saying to each one that that was the elephant.

"Now, brethren, that man, having presented the elephant to the blind men, came to the Rājā and said: 'Your Majesty, the elephant has been presented to the blind men. Do what is your will.'

"Thereupon, brethren, the Rājā went up to the blind men and said to each: 'Have you studied the elephant?'

"'Yes, Your Majesty.'

"'Then tell me your conclusions about him.'

"Thereupon those who had been presented with the head answered 'Your Majesty, an elephant is just like a pot.' And those who had only observed the ear replied: 'An elephant is just like a winnowing basket.' Those who had been presented with the tusk said it was a ploughshare. Those who knew only the trunk said it was a plough. 'The body,' said they, 'is a granary; the foot, a pillar; the back, a mortar; the tail, a pestle; the tuft of the tail, just a besom.'

"Then they began to quarrel, shouting, 'Yes, it is!' 'No, it isn't!' 'An elephant is not that!' 'Yes it is like that!' and so on, till they came to fisticuffs about the matter.

"Then, brethren, that Rājā was delighted with the scene."[9]

The moral the Buddha draws from the tale is "those who think truth is in their exclusive keeping and their religion is the only approach to reality 'see only one side of a thing,' like the blind men in the parable."[10]

Such an interpretation of the parable is helpful if one is contrasting religious exclusivism with religious pluralism.[11] However, it does pose a problem. The person who is not blind knows the elephant as the whole, as an object that possesses the various parts grabbed hold of by the blind men. Hence this situation corresponds to that of rationalism (and not empiricism) as defined by William James: the habit of explaining the parts by the whole.

Let us, however, take another look at the situation. Even a person who is not blind never sees the elephant simultaneously as a whole. He can see only one part or side of the elephant. Moreover, one cannot quite say that the blind men did not know the elephant as such according to their mode of knowing. They utilized the sense of touch; the person with vision uses sight. Is a wooden bat the same object in the hands of a player who can see it and a blind person who can only feel it? Moreover, does the person with eyes really see the object called "elephant" as it is? If the person possessed x-ray vision, would the person still see the same elephant? Moreover, in a less dramatic vein, let us only imagine that we as human beings possessed a sixth sense—as different from all our senses as sound is from sight. What creature would we "see" then?

The point then is this: all knowledge is partial in its own way. How are we to know that in another way of knowing the elephant would not appear in a very different way—even as two distinct objects? We are out-Jamesing William James in our pursuit of radical empiricism to be sure, but the implications of empiricism in this light are truly radical. And this is when we haven't even introduced the notion of a universe that is changing all the time!

PLURALISM AND POLYTHEISM

We must plunge now into the forest a little deeper. In the parable, the blind men are groping for the elephant; is it possible that at some level of experience they may construct one by their groping for it in some psychedelic way? Let us discard this possibility as rather far-fetched but consider another. In the parable, the elephant represented reality; the blind men grasped one part of it. The reality of the elephant itself, however, was taken for granted, as known or knowable. But our situation in life is different. We are holding onto different parts and do not know whether they are all connected. They may be or they may not be. Are all the religions connected? Is the ultimate of all the religions the same? It is rationalism that leads us to this assumption, and this becomes clear in the discussions of the point in Indian and Western philosophy where Occam's razor is deliberately invoked to establish the case for one God or reality.[12] But are we then not begging the question? It is rationalism itself that is being called into question. Indian discussions of the issue are helpful here. The Nyāya-Vaśeṣika school was referred to earlier. In this pair, it is the Nyāya school that emphasizes rationalism and sure enough argues for monotheism on the basis that "wherever there is scope for the consideration whether we should admit a single principle or a multiplicity of principles, all logicians are unanimous that the former course should be followed."[13] It should be added, however, that critics of the highest caliber such as Appayya Dīkṣita, the seventeenth-century South Indian polymath, "are of the view that the argument does not prove that there is only one maker of the world, and they do not admit 'parsimony' as a consideration which can clinch the issue. To this [a logician] replies: 'Is parsimony to be rejected here only, or everywhere?' Surely, in view of the fact that almost all modern developments in scientific theory are based on a recognition of 'parsimony', it is hard to reject parsimony in this case. But (as Appayya Dīkṣita says) since we are proceeding on the basis of observed facts, it is not simpler to suppose that the world is the co-operative endeavour of many intelligent beings?"[14]

William James's statement that "a philosophy of pure experience must tend to pluralism in its ontology"[15] sounds like a grand and radical restatement of the point just made.

Conclusion

One might conclude by trying to push this point of view a little further with some passion, aroused not by my partiality to it but by indignation at its neglect. One may advert to the parable of the elephant for this purpose. Let us suppose that not one but two elephants were placed in the midst of the blind men. Now their descriptions might still be the same, but they could apply to either of the two elephants. If the metaphor is thus extended, two similar statements need not necessarily relate to one reality; two realities could be involved. Or to press a different metaphor into service to make the same point: identical symptoms, such as a headache, can be generated by different diseases. In the study of religious pluralism, much attention has been devoted to the point that the self-same identical reality is perhaps experienced differently. One may conclude this chapter with the plea that at least more attention, if not the same measure of attention, be accorded to the possibility that it is possible to experience different ultimate realities identically.

RELIGION IS ABOUT HOW YOU BEHAVE

The Essential Virtue Is Compassion

Karen Armstrong

On this day, which commemorates that terrible atrocity in which religion became associated with horror, violence, and hatred, I was reminded of an event in the fifth century B.C.E. in Athens. Every year, on the festival of Dionysus, god of transformation, as part of a religious celebration, all Athenian citizens were required to attend the tragedies, tragic dramas put on each year which usually reflected in a mythical form some of the dilemmas of the city at that time. Five years after the battle of Salamis, when the Greeks had eventually defeated the very mighty Persian army, Aeschylus put on his play *The Persians*, and there was no hint of gloating, no triumphalism. Five years earlier, the Persians had rampaged through Athens, had vandalized the city, and had destroyed the beautiful new buildings, the new temples built on the Acropolis. But Aeschylus presents the Persians as a people in mourning, a people like the Greeks themselves, a sister people to the Greeks. And the defeated hero of Persia, Xerxes, is led, with great honor and respect, into his house. And I think we have to ask ourselves whether it would be possible for such a play to be put on today.

We don't usually think of the Greeks contributing to the Axial Age (c. 900–200 B.C.E.), that extraordinary transformative period in religious consciousness, when the great world traditions that have continued to nourish humanity either came into being or had their roots. But in their tragic drama, they came close to the essential core spirit that lies at the heart of all our traditions, that religion is not about what you believe or what you think. It's about how you behave, and the essential virtue is compassion.

One of the very first people, as far as we know, to make it absolutely crystal clear that religion was essentially altruism was Confucius. And it was he who, again, as far as we know, was first to promulgate the golden rule: do not do to others what you would not like them to do to you. And most of the world traditions have come in their own way to formulate this rule. Confucius was asked, "What was the essential thread that bound all your teaching together, Master?" And he said, " *Shu*, likening to the self." Look into your own heart. Discover what it is that gives *you* pain, and then refrain, under any circumstances whatsoever, from inflicting that pain upon anybody else. "Do not do to others, as you would not have done to you." "Master," said one of his disciples, "which one of your teachings can we put into practice all day and everyday?" And, again, Confucius said, "Do not do to others, what you would not have done to you." The practice of the golden rule teaches us to dethrone ourselves from the center of our world and put another there. It is this which would introduce people to the Dao, the ultimate reality. The Buddha came to the same conclusion, when he said it was by compassion that we reach *ceto-vimutti*, the release of the mind, which, in the early Buddhist scriptures, is a synonym for the ultimate enlightenment of nirvana. But all these sages insisted that it was not enough simply to confine your compassion and benevolence to your own group. You must have what one Chinese sage called *jian ai*, concern for everybody, because love for your own group or people with whom you agree becomes simply a form of group egotism, and it is egotism that imprisons us in ourselves and holds us back from the divine.

In Jewish law, we're told to love the stranger. "If a stranger lives with you in your land," says Leviticus, "do not molest him. You must treat him as one of your own people and love him as yourself, for you were strangers in Egypt." And it's the same principle of empathy. Look into your own heart, your own past. Remember what it was that gave you pain when you were strangers in Egypt and then apply that understanding of your own pain to the understanding of the other. The word love here needs a little decoding. Leviticus is a legal text, and we were not required to emote or to feel filled with warm tender affection for the stranger. The word *love*, was used in international treaties; and it implied that kings and allies would look out for each other's interests, give them practical support and help, and that is something to which we can all aspire. "Love your enemies," said Jesus. Give your love, concern, and benevolence where there is no hope of any return. And that is the task of religion in our day. The great Rabbi Hillel, the older contemporary of Jesus, was one day approached by a pagan who promised to convert to Judaism on condition that the rabbi recited the whole of Jewish teaching while he stood on one leg. Hillel stood on one leg and replied: "That which is hateful to you do not do to your neighbour. That is the Torah. The rest is commentary. Go and study it." And that's an extraordinary statement—no mention of God or the creation of the world in six days or the

613 compartments of the Torah or the promised land. "Do not do unto others, as you would not have done to you." And in the endless performance of that duty to compassion, you will encounter the divine.

While researching my last book, I was astonished to learn that during the Axial Age, every single one of the major world traditions that developed during this time began its reform with a principled revulsion from the violence of their time. These were very violent societies, violence that seems pitiful compared with what we're facing today, and yet it shocked the people of the Axial Age. And in searching for a cure for violence in the human psyche, the sages began to discover the inner world and a whole range of inner peace, but compassion lay always at the core.

Today the challenge is to apply the golden rule globally. In the Axial Age, the individual was coming to the fore. People were beginning to discover themselves as autonomous individuals, and one of the Axial Age's concerns was to prevent the clash of warring egos in a newly urbanized society. And now we're living in one world, and what happens today in Afghanistan or Iraq or Palestine will have repercussions tomorrow in London, New York, or Washington. We all share the same predicament, and that means that it is a religious duty not to treat others as we would not wish to be treated ourselves, to realize that other nations are as important as our own. This is the only way we're going to bring peace to our world, and this is the religious challenge.

I'd like to conclude with two stories. When the Prophet Muhammad finally conquered Mecca, he eventually abandoned violence and adopted a course of nonviolence that was worthy of Gandhi. Mecca opened its gates to him voluntarily, and he went and stood beside the Kaaba, and he invited his tribe, the Quraysh, to enter Islam. No one was forced or coerced, but Muhammad invited them. "Oh Quraysh," he said, "God is calling you from the chauvinism of paganism, with its pride in ancestors. But remember: All men come from Adam and Adam came from dust." And then he recited these words from the Qur'an, where God says to humanity, "Oh people, we have created you from a male and a female and have formed you into tribes and nations, so that you may know one another." Not so that you may terrorize or convert or exploit or colonize or dominate, but so that you may know one another, because when we live together in community, we inevitably come up against uncongenial people, and that experience enables us to deal with the more challenging Other that we meet in other tribes or nations.

My second story comes from the Hebrew Bible, a story of Abraham, regarded as the father of believers by Jews, Christians, and Muslims alike. It's said that one day, Abraham was sitting outside his tent in Mamre, near Hebron, and saw three strangers on the horizon. Strangers are frightening people at any time. Very few of us today would take three total strangers off the streets and bring them into our own home. But Abraham ran out, in the heat of the Middle Eastern afternoon, and prostrated himself before these three strangers, as though they were gods or kings. And then he brought them back into his encampment and gave them, not just a sandwich or a glass of water, but poured out for them an elaborate meal, giving these three total strangers all the love and refreshment that he could for their journey. And I think it is of the utmost importance that these people were strangers. The word in Hebrew, *qadosh*, "holy," as used in the "holiness of God," means "separate," "other." And sometimes, the initial revulsion or fear that we may feel, when we encounter the stranger can give us intimations of that holiness that is God. Thus, the effort to understand and reach out to the other, to reach out to enemies, should become not just a political but a spiritual process. We don't need any new prophets, any new revelations. We all simply need to uncover the call of compassion that lies at the heart of all our great religious traditions.

RELIGIOUS TOLERANCE AND PEACE-BUILDING IN A WORLD OF DIVERSITY

Issa Kirarira

Throughout history, religious differences have divided men and women from their neighbors and have served as justification for some of humankind's bloodiest conflicts. In the modern world, it has become clear that people of all religions must bridge these differences and work together to ensure our survival and realize the vision of peace that all faiths share.

Presently, the "clash of religions" is resonating so powerfully and worryingly around the world that finding answers to the old questions of how best to manage and mitigate conflicts over religions has taken on renewed importance.

The earliest recorded evidence of religious activity dates from only about 60,000 B.C.E. However, anthropologists and historians of religion believe that some form of religion has been practiced since people first appeared on earth about 2.5 million years ago.

Religion (Latin *religare,* "to bind," perhaps human beings to God) is a code of belief or philosophy that often involves worship of a God or gods. Belief in a supernatural power is not essential (absent in, for example, Buddhism and Confucianism), but faithful adherence is usually considered to be rewarded, for example, by escape from human existence (Buddhism), by future existence (Christianity, Islam), or by worldly benefit (Soka Gakkai, Buddhism).

Among the chief religions are

- Ancient and pantheist religions: Babylonia, Assyria, Egypt, Greece, and Rome;
- Oriental: Hinduism, Buddhism, Jainism, Parseeism, Confucianism, Taoism, and Shinto;
- Religions of a book: Judaism, Christianity (the principal divisions are Roman Catholic, Eastern Orthodox, and Protestant), and Islam (the principle divisions are Sunni and Shi'ite);
- Combined derivation such as Bahá'í Faith, the Unification Church, and Mormonism.

On the other hand, theology is the study of religion. The word itself refers to the interpretation of the doctrines of God. But modern theology includes the study of various religions and such topics as church history, sacred writings, and the relationship between religion and human needs.

Theology teaches the importance of rejecting violence and adapting to peaceful and civilized means of resolving conflicts and disagreements. It is a vital instrument in enhancing societal transition without recourse to volatile methods. This is through revelation as in the scriptures of Christianity, Islam, or other religions that religious communities are formed by people coming and staying together. Each religion therefore serves as an example for the other.

If we are to live peacefully in our diversity, we must first successfully confront the challenge of how to build all-inclusive, tolerant societies and look at religion as a better way of fostering peace than of fueling war. People of different religions must be allowed to express and practice their beliefs, and at the same time, they should respect the beliefs of others. There can be no coherent social life unless there are social relationships that bind people together to at least some degree of order. As the dictum goes, when Christ enters, sectarianism has to leave. To maintain an orderly system, every individual should be left to exercise the religion of his or her choice.

The Holy Qur'an says, "I worship not which you worship nor will you worship that which I worship. And I shall not worship that which you are worshipping nor will you worship that which I worship. To you be your religion and to me my religion."[1] People of one religion must be allowed to not only to criticize the practices and beliefs of other religions but to respect them.

RELIGIOUS TOLERANCE IN PEACE-BUILDING

We both commemorate the sad events of September 11 and celebrate the heroes whose spirit of oneness soared above the grief and pain of that time. I wish to categorically state that we are in every way opposed to the acts of September 11. The perpetrators of those acts were evil and have absolutely no connection with the truth of Islam or any other religion.

The true spirit of heroism that ensued in the wake of the events of September 11 should be emulated by future generations without the need for more tragedies to convince them of the fact that we are really one people of different tongues, races, educational backgrounds, cultures, and religious orientation, and yet of very like needs.

We may pray differently, but our destiny is the same.

What brings us together is the universal cry for peace, peace that leaves us the freedom to bring up our families in an atmosphere of love and conviviality with our neighbors. Our cry is for a future of prosperity that can spread around our nations that there may be no more frustration in our communities and that there may be less disagreement and more of a spirit of working together in the very ultimate of tolerance to differences in beliefs and in choices of nonantagonistic behaviors.

Religious communities are, without question, the largest and best-organized civil institutions in the world today. They claim the allegiance of billions of believers and bridge the divides of race, class, and nationality. They are uniquely equipped to meet the challenges of our time: resolving conflicts, caring for the sick and needy, promoting peaceful coexistence among all people, and allowing some degree of tolerance.

Islamic civilization has in the past proved capable of, for the times, extraordinary feats of toleration. Under the Muslims, medieval Spain became a haven for diverse religions and sects. Following the Christian reconquest, the Inquisition eliminated all dissent. The notion that Islamic civilization is inherently less capable of tolerance and compassion than any other religion is hard to square with facts.

When Meccan pagans severely persecuted the early Muslims, Prophet Muhammad himself instructed a group of his followers to migrate to neighboring Abyssinia, now Ethiopia, which was ruled by a Christian king. He was known as a just ruler, and so the prophet trusted that his followers would be safe under this king's rule. The king not only provided them safe refuge but also refused to deport them back to Mecca when a Meccan delegation requested him to do so. It should be noted that the Muslims sought protection under a Christian king, which goes against the generalization that a Muslim cannot take a Christian as his protector. There are numerous examples of good relations, tolerance, and neighborliness shown by non-Muslims in authority or otherwise to Muslims the world over.

It is a relief that the mainstream theologians have came out so unanimously against the terrorists. What we must now ask them is to campaign more strongly against the aberrant doctrines that underpin them. It is the responsibility of the Islamic world to defeat the terrorist aberration theologically. In what sense were the World Trade Center bombers members of Islam? This question has been sidelined by many Western analysts impatient with the niceties of theology, but it may be the key to understanding the attack, and to assessing the long-term prospects for peace in the Muslim world.

Without a theological position justifying the rejection of the mainstream position, the frustration would have led to a frustration with religion and then to a search for secular responses. It should be noted that religious studies involves instruction in the beliefs of a particular religion. This type of education is the work of organized religions, through their school and religious organizations. Religious education therefore may be defined as general education that follows religious instructions and ideals. It is the clergy and various religious orders that offer the best opportunities for religious study and education.

At the heart of the global crisis currently afflicting humanity exists a pervasive lack of moral leadership in all sectors of human society. The lack of moral leadership is demonstrated in the continuous uncovering of unethical behavior at all levels of society in all parts of the world. Religions traditionally offer guiding wisdom, yet the disparity of belief systems results in fragmentation and often works against the common good. Are religions responsible for caring for the soul of humanity? If so, how can we encourage religious leaders to move beyond concern for their specific faith communities to caring for the whole of humanity?

It is true that because of the politicization of religions and cultures, political elites and religious leaders fail to consolidate unity in their countries or communities. In turn, the international community (the U.N., Amnesty International, Human Rights Watch, etc.) comes in with solutions that it deems reasonable for cushioning or ending a crisis. However, these solutions ignore the real and fundamental issues at the back and front of the crisis. In turn, they produce short-lived solutions and answers to complex and complicated problems.

Rarely is religion the principal cause of international conflict, even though some adversaries may argue differently. Religious adherence continues to play a significant role in legitimizing the social order as well as reducing conflicts. This becomes an effective mechanism for power sharing between diverse religious groups. Power-sharing arrangements between different groups prevent conflicts and violence. This conception of democracy emerges when the "study of politics" is linked to the "study of religion" by the concept of power.

For instance, high government officials are sworn into office while holding Bibles and Qur'ans, and they make public demonstrations of church attendance and prayers in mosques. Legislative sessions are opened with public prayers, and court proceedings involve taking oaths involving the name of God. Such arrangements are important in legitimizing social order while at the same time reducing conflicts in countries without social order. There is no serious attempt to achieve world peace that can ignore religion.

Many religions suffer from various forms of exclusion, sometimes resulting from explicit suppression of religious freedom or discrimination against that group—a problem particularly common in nonsecular countries where the state upholds an established religion.

But in other cases, the exclusion may be less direct and often unintended, as when the public calendar does not recognize a minority's religious holidays. India officially celebrates five Hindu holidays but also four Muslim, two Christian, one Buddhist, one Jain, and one Sikh holiday in recognition of the diverse population. France celebrates eleven national holidays: five are nondenominational, but the six religious holidays all celebrate events in the Christian calendar even though 7 percent of the population is Muslim and 1 percent is Jewish. Similarly, the dress codes in public institutions may conflict with a minority's religious dress, or state rules about marriage and inheritance may differ from those of religious codes.

These sorts of conflicts can arise even in secular states with strong democratic institutions that protect civil and political rights. Given the profound importance of religion to people's identities, it is not surprising that religious minorities often mobilize to contest these exclusions. Some religious practices are not difficult to accommodate, but often they present difficult choices and trade-offs.

France is grappling with whether the wearing of headscarves in state schools violates state principles of secularism and democratic values of gender equality that state education aims to impart. Although a law was passed in 2004 banning headscarves in state schools, the debate continues today. Nigeria is struggling with whether to uphold the ruling of Sharia courts in the case of adultery. A high-profile case involved a woman, Safiya Husaini, being convicted of adultery in 2001 for having a child out of wedlock and sentenced to death by stoning. She has since mounted a successful appeal of the conviction.

What is important is to expand human freedoms and human rights and to recognize equality. Secular and democratic states are most likely to achieve these goals when the state provides reasonable accommodations for religious practices, where all religions have the same relation to the state and where the state protects human rights.

In order to live peacefully in the world, one must first successfully meet the challenge of building religiously tolerant societies that allow people religious freedom. Such a world would be more stable, more peaceful, and free from much disturbance and confusion.

Religion can have a strong role of guiding wisdom and enabling individuals to weigh their cultures and decide on those aspects that might be of benefit or of detriment to themselves and to society. The Holy Qur'an says, "Piety doesn't lie in turning your face to the East or West. Piety lies in believing in God."[2] This through the influence of faith has encouraged the followers to move beyond concern for their specific faith communities into caring for the whole of humanity.

Having noted these relationships, we should become particularly interested in how best to enable students and academics to become agents of social change imbued with spiritual, technical, moral, and spiritual capacities. The maintenance of a liberal society depends largely on respecting the rule of law, listening to political claims, protecting fundamental human rights, and securing the rights of diverse cultural groups and minorities. The need to find ways of forging unity amid this diversity is the responsibility of the states; it is also their responsibility to protect rights and secure freedoms for all their members, and not discriminate on the grounds of race, religion, or culture. Religious adherence plays a significant role in legitimizing the social order as well as reducing conflict.

Islam as a religion is an organized system of beliefs, ceremonies, practices, and worship that center on one supreme God (Allah). Islam developed a form of religious life during the eighth century C.E. through the Sufi movement. The members met regularly to recite the Qur'an and worship together. The Islamic system has preserved and even maintained prior cultural expressions, including the Egyptian sphinx and the Persian persepolis, all signs of religious tolerance.

The Qur'anic command of tolerance explains why Greece, in spite of five hundred years of Ottoman rule, emerged as a Greek Orthodox nation; why en route to the Cairo airport, one sees more Coptic churches than mosques; why the Bible is available in Moroccan bookshops; and why church steeples in Damascus bear neon-lit crosses at night. All these are examples of the willingness to live together in tolerance.

The principal aim and object of every religion is service to humanity, and both prayers and fasting have been the basic teachings of every religion the world over. To Muslims, fasting during the month of Ramadan inculcates within them tolerance, sacrifice, purity, and total submission, and helps strengthen them to live by their faith within the realities of life. The impact of fasting is immense. It teaches us in a practical way to live up to the human standards that Allah has ordained for humankind.

Islam places great emphasis on the unity, both of thought and action, of the Muslim *Ummah* ("community"). The objective is to establish peace on earth and eradicate oppression and mischief from society; failing that, crisis, turmoil, and catastrophes will prevail in the world.

Muslims have uniformity in their religious practices. Allah created different groups of people, and they were expected to get to know one another. Allah says, "O mankind, we created you from a single male and female, and made you into nations and tribes that you may know one another (not that you may despise each other)."[3]

Dividing people into sects, denominations, and group is a sinful act. In this regard, Allah says, "As for those who divide their religion and break up into sects, you have no part in them in the least their affair is with Allah; He will in the end tell them the truth of all they did."[4] Allah commands believers to "hold fast together to Allah's code (the way prescribed by Allah) and let nothing divide you."[5]

Muslims must strive to create this unity not only among themselves but also with other religious faiths. If we unite, then Allah will send his mercy and grace upon us. He will also guide each of us on the straight path and grant us peace and honor.

We do agree that some Muslims, as men themselves, have not been followers of the truth of their religion. There are cases of discrimination, and even humiliation, of Jews, Christians, and even of their own Muslim brethren living under some Muslim rulers. That is why it comes out as particularly painful to the entire Muslim world whenever, in sharp contrast to the Qur'anic teachings, a few extremists attack and hurt non-Muslims as happened in Pakistan when some innocent Christian worshipers were killed. The Afghanistan war, Osama Bin Laden, Saddam Hussein's attacks of Kuwait, and the July 7, 2005, bombing in Britain are some additional examples.

On behalf of the peace-loving peoples of the Islamic world, we do advocate that perpetrators of these heinous crimes be exposed to real Islam. We ask both Muslims and the non-Muslims in the rest of the world to do their utmost to protect the security and welfare of the minority communities living under their protection.

Although it is understandable that the expression of anger and loss of tolerance is not too infrequent a phenomenon during times of warfare or political crisis, it is just as important to balance out this understanding with a deep contemplation of the possibility of what could happen if threats and other proclamations are acted upon. The bottom line is that the resulting effect on our planet earth on the next years and next centuries has to be thoroughly analyzed before conflict should be permitted.

There are misled Muslims who may cherish disrespect or even hatred for Westerners or non-Muslims. That can, however, be found among people of other faiths as well. Numbers of such people are not many. I believe we, the majority, Muslim, Christian, Hindu, Buddhist, Bahá'í, and all other world religions, can overcome the power they have amassed. History has replayed this scenario over and over. Let us emulate the example of our more balanced forbearers and stamp out these social evils by developing a culture of forgiveness, mercy, peace, love, and tolerance.

WAY FORWARD

Dr. Hassan Hathout, a scholar of Islam, says, "In my late sixties, and after life-long study, reflection and insight into my Islamic faith, I feel my heart bursting with love. It is non-specific love that has no address attached to it. I feel love towards my fellow humans, animals, birds, trees, things, and the earth and universe in which we live and deep in my heart I wish it were contagious."[6]

Such is the result of his true understanding of his faith and its reflection in him. Hopefully many of us and our own children will be able to walk in his footsteps. It is our heartfelt belief that our planet earth can adapt his culture of thinking and action. The question should be, Why not? What has gone wrong, and can the situation be salvaged and how? The answer to these questions is quite simple.

It is important to realize that our fellowship is with God alone and not with the belief system that we have. In many cases, even though we proclaim our loyalty to God, in our actions, we really adhere to the teachings of the school of thought with which we associate ourselves. Loyalty to God, in contrast, means evaluating our actions with this question: Is this want God wants?

Related to the above is that the shape and substance of the value of teaching religious studies needs to provide a better understanding of the common values of all religions and assist in the formulation of nonsectarian curricula. The curricula considered should meet the needs of quality, access, and lifestyle; they should be all inclusive and flexible, and should be undertaken after a comparative analysis of different values. Also, a program in moral leadership should be considered for school teachers to understand relationships of domination and contribute to their transformation into relationships based on interconnectedness, reciprocity, and service.

We have seen the effect of media, both positive and negative, on the masses. We can harness this same power and bestow this one good above all upon our own future.

The religious opinion concerning the acts of terrorism provides for deterrent punishment against persons who carry out bombing attacks against installations and housing complexes, or hijack airplanes, trains, and other means of transportation with the intent to intimidate or terrify innocent people—the so-called refugees. Islam urges the protection of human life and honors property, religion, and intellect—Allah says: "If any do transgress the limits ordained by God, such persons wrong themselves as well as others."[7] Peace-loving nations, people, and organizations should endeavor to protect humankind from all forms of evil and contribute to any effort that aims at realizing security and peace for humankind.

By studying Islam rationally rather than emotionally, one would be able to see the equity of Islam and its compatibility with humankind's natural disposition on one hand and scientific realities on the other. Islam is not only a religion of peace and nonaggression; but it also contains solutions to humankind's problems as well as its favorable view of justice, tolerance, dialogue, and human interaction.

Identifying the facts, both causative and resultant, nurtures a culture of tolerance that creates an atmosphere for peace to thrive and enables people of diverse religious and cultural backgrounds to live together in harmony. Hence, due rights are returned to their rightful owners, and wrongdoing is stopped.

The media, the government systems, the donor community, and all sympathetic to the cry for peace need to agree on an immediate plan of action and work with communities the world over to bring about realization of this dream.

CONCLUSION

Overall, the world must address the challenge of how to build inclusive, religiously diverse societies in order to achieve the goals of reducing tensions in the world and solving the problems facing humanity. When we talk about tolerance, we don't necessarily mean that we should agree with or love one another, but we mean that we should respect the rights of others, especially the right to be different. At times, intolerance should be promoted. By this I mean let's not tolerate acts such as those of September 11, Bali, Nairobi, July 7 in Britain, and Pakistan, to name just a few, because they only make us insecure and cause untold suffering to us all. Freedom of self-expression is not without restrictions, however. Transgressing the sanctity of others' honor and spreading rumors lead to confusion and disorder, and upset the atmosphere of stability and the feeling of security among citizens. None of these can be condoned in the name of religious freedom.

RELIGION AND TRANSFORMATION

Interreligious Dialogue

INTRODUCTION

Dialogue is a word which has almost suffered semantic abasement on account of its frequent invocation, but two aspects of it continue to remain potentially revolutionary. The first is that genuine dialogue always implies a willingness to change in encounter with the other, although the exact nature of this change remains nobly unpredictable. The second is that, contrary to our notions of possessing the "truth," dialogue seems to imply that it may lie not with us but inbetween us.

According to a well-known typology, the parties which come to the table may be characterized as subscribing to exclusivism, inclusivism, or pluralism; and it needs to be recognized that the dialogue must occur not merely among those who share the rubric "pluralism" but also with and among those who espouse "exclusivism" and "inclusivism" as well.

It would be useful to examine the readings in the light of the presuppositions of dialogue. One must also not overlook the possibility of fruitful dialogue not just among the religions but also between the religious and secular dimensions of life—an area in which Gregory Baum's piece is particularly instructive.

PROMOTION OF INTERRELIGIOUS DIALOGUE

Mihai Valentin Vladimirescu

I cannot persuade myself that without love to others, and without, as far as rests with me, peaceableness towards all, I can be called a worthy servant of Jesus Christ.
—St. Basil the Great (329–79 C.E.),
Letter 203, 2

It is obvious that dialogue between cultures and religions has become one of the main pillars of modern cultures, and one of the ways we judge the maturity of today's religious traditions. Having recourse to dialogue only as an emergency measure, when conflicts and dramatic events have made both cohabitation and understanding much more tense, only adds to the difficulties inherent in already very complex situations. For this reason, more and more of these types of meetings are held every day, giving people an opportunity to share thoughts and exchange ideas, opening up new channels of understanding and collaboration.

The organization of the conference on the world's religions after September 11 is a display of confidence in the power of communicative reason. It aims to bring together different lines of thought and action and sit experts and stakeholders down at the same table, with a full awareness of the magnitude of the work to be carried out.

One of the basic aims of this meeting should be to raise awareness among as much of the population as possible regarding the challenges that need to be faced in order to create, strengthen, and maintain a culture of peace, with positive contribution of peaceful religions creatively committed to peace-seeking initiatives. Our meeting is targeted at all those who have dedicated, or are willing to dedicate, their lives to intellectual, social, political, and religious commitment, aimed at exploring human cohabitation in all its complexity. It is also aimed at those who want to be stimulated by programs of action that will enable them to overcome the obstacles that have long deadlocked collective situations paralyzed by ancestral prejudices, banal interests, and sterile attitudes.

Underlining the importance of promoting understanding, tolerance, and friendship among human beings in all their diversity of religion, belief, culture, and language, and affirming that interreligious dialogue is an integral part of efforts to translate shared values into actions, in particular efforts to promote a culture of peace and dialogue among civilizations, we should acknowledge that respect for the diversity of religions and cultures, tolerance, dialogue, and cooperation can contribute to combating ideologies and practices based on discrimination, intolerance, and hatred and help reinforce world peace, social justice, and friendship among peoples.

Based on these considerations, the leaders of religions should encourage and urge governments and states to take a number of measures aimed at, inter alia, promoting, including through education, understanding, tolerance, and friendship among human beings in their diversity of religion, belief, culture, and language; protecting religious sites and preventing acts or threats of damage to and destruction of these sites; preventing and eliminating discrimination on the grounds of religion or belief, in the recognition, exercise, and enjoyment of human rights and fundamental freedoms in all fields of civil, economic, political, social, and cultural life; and ensuring that, in the course of their official duties, members of law enforcement bodies and the military, civil servants, educators, and other public officials respect different religions and beliefs and do not discriminate against persons professing them.

We are living in a very exciting moment in history. Something profound and wonderful is happening, which can be seen only if we stand back and observe the spectrum of cultures and religions that have been evolving over the centuries. If we can do this and enter into alternative religious and cultural worlds, something amazing begins to show itself, a deep pattern that has been centuries in the making. It appears that the different religions and cultural consciousnesses shaped a new humanity. We see as we look across religious worlds that they are all deeply concerned with a stage of being human that needs to be overcome.

The Bible does not directly address interreligious dialogue as it is understood and practiced today. The Greek word *dialegomai,* which appears in such verses as Acts 17:17 and Jude 9, means to "discuss, conduct a discussion."[1] The New Testament writers were thus using *dialegomai* to describe a period of questions and answers following the proclamation of the gospel. Nonetheless, the Bible gives several examples of sustained interreligious conversation. Jesus spent several days in the temple as a young man, discussing religious

issues with the teachers. Jesus questioned the teachers on various points, amazing them in turn with his responses to their questions. Although an example of interfaith rather than interreligious dialogue, this discussion almost certainly involved insights from Jesus that would have been understood by the teachers as transcending the common boundaries of contemporary Judaism.

The method of education through questioning was common among both Jews and Greeks: the rabbinical method of teaching involved mutual questioning and discussion, and even earlier the Greek philosopher Socrates utilized this method in what is now called Socratic dialogue. Such mutual discussion is at the heart of interreligious dialogue. Paul's discourse on the hill in Athens exhibits a similar willingness to engage in interreligious dialogue. Rather than avoiding any contact with the idolatrous practices of the Athenians, Paul closely observed them and then used these practices as the springboard for presenting his beliefs. Note that Paul did not initially engage in evangelism or debate: he debated with the Jews and the "devout" (i.e., God-fearing Gentiles), but he merely "beheld" the practices of the people outside his religious community. Paul was fulfilling the first purpose listed in the first section of this chapter: Paul examined the religions of the Athenians to determine their spiritual state and to present the gospel in a way that would be most comprehensible to them. The knowledge used by Paul could be obtained only through direct interaction with the practitioners of the Athenian philosophies and religions. Paul also shows that Christians can acknowledge truth in other religions without accepting the entirety of the religion as true. His affirmative quotation from the Cretan poet Epimenides (whom he again quotes in Titus 1:12) is an example of approvingly noting a truth in the beliefs of the Athenians. The fact that he was nonetheless presenting the gospel, however, also shows that acknowledging the limited truth to which the Athenians held does not mean one should compromise advocating the supremacy of God's full revelation in Christ. The episode on the hill is an example of Paul's becoming all things to all people in order to win some. Through the clarified understanding of other religions that results from interreligious dialogue, evangelists are able to express their beliefs so that they will be correctly understood by people in other religions and cultures. This can only result from, to use the old cliché, walking in the shoes of others. Dialogue is a way for understanding how non-Christians perceive Christianity.

Interest in a Christian approach to people of other faiths can already be seen in the New Testament. In the book of Acts, Peter, responding to the realities of a multifaith context, says to the gentile Cornelius, "I truly understand that God shows no partiality, but in every nation anyone who fears him and does what is right is acceptable to him."[2]

This basic understanding of God's direct access to all people echoes what is asserted in the Hebrew scriptures by the prophet Malachi when he says, "For from the rising of the sun to its setting my name is great among the nations, and in every place incense is offered to my name, and a pure offering for my name is great among the nations says the Lord of hosts."[3]

In Jesus's words and action, in his proclamation, in his ministry of healing and service, God was establishing his reign on earth, a sovereign rule whose presence and power cannot be limited to any one community or culture. The attitudes of Jesus as he reached out to those beyond the house of Israel testify to this universal reign. He spoke with the woman of Samaria, affirming all who would worship God in Spirit and truth.[4] He marveled at the faith of a centurion, acknowledging that he had not found such faith in all Israel.[5] For the sake of a Syro-Phoenician woman, and in response to her faith, he performed a miracle of healing.[6]

But while it appears that the saving power of the reign of God made present in Jesus during his earthly ministry was in some sense limited, through the event of his death and resurrection, the paschal mystery itself, these limits were transcended.[7] The cross and the resurrection disclose for us the universal dimension of the saving mystery of God.

This saving mystery is mediated and expressed in many and various ways as God's plan unfolds toward its fulfillment. It may be available to those outside the fold of Christ in ways we cannot understand, as they live faithful and truthful lives in their concrete circumstances and in the framework of the religious traditions that guide and inspire them.[8] The Christ event is for us the clearest expression of the salvific will of God in all human history.[9]

It is our Christian faith in God that challenges us to take seriously the whole realm of religious plurality. We see this not so much as an obstacle to be overcome but rather as an opportunity for deepening our encounter with God and with our neighbors as we await the fulfillment when "God will be all in all."[10]

If we look at the teachings of Jesus, the deepest concern and command to love one another, to awaken spiritually, and to go through a profound rebirth calls for a renovation of our being and the move to a dialogical consciousness. Thus, in the Judeo-Christian roots, we find this call for the awakening of a new awareness that centers upon God and the presence of God as the primary concern for human beings, which in turn calls for the deepest change in our lives.

A model of interdependence of individuals within the family and larger communities is much more realistic and healthy for both the person and the community. If autonomy implies anonymity in the city or neighborhood and absence of intimate bonds that are rooted in mutual commitments, then the person is fleeing from the association of life and love with duty and responsibility. If a large number of people are motivated solely or in the majority of cases by self-interest alone, society at large will suffer. All decisions that involve collaboration with others must be based on a prudent trust that the people will be true to their word. In time of peace, societies in the ancient Middle East defined their relations on the international level in terms of treaties and the responsibilities that flowed from such commitments. Such an agreement was usually imposed by an emperor upon the petty states that came under his control. His self-description at the beginning of a treaty portrayed him as a benefactor whose gracious attitude would continue, but the treaty itself obliged only the vassal. Transgression of the stipulations laid upon the subordinate party was the reason for war or for a court case and corrective punishment.

In every modern society, people should have a perspective or viewpoint whereby the intricacies of daily life can be evaluated from the outside. This can be achieved in the context of dialogue, because each partner is listening to the other express a vision of life and community. It can be discovered also when we enter the literature of an ancient civilization, stepping back into a world quite different from our own. Both Jews and Christians share the Hebrew Bible and accept it as God's word; even though methods of interpretation differ, we can continue to learn from the way the other community experiences and lives this word.

The dialogical human somehow awakens to the realization that to be human is a profoundly interrelational, interconnected, interactive way of living and being. This means that everything in human life requires the living through of this interactive principle of reality itself. At this deepest level, we see a contrast and tension playing out through history between the ego-centered culture and the dialogical way of life. This brings us to the question of the importance of interreligious dialogue. Religions are deeply established patterns of life that have been distilled over centuries and millennia of ongoing cultural evolution and experimentation. Religious worldviews attempt to get to what is most fundamental in human culture and human reality. They are alternative, narrative, corporate expressions of what is profoundly first, the vital core of our cultural life. As we look across the spectrum of religions, we find profoundly alternative ways of recognizing something primordial that is the common source of our diverse worldviews.

We need to respect their religious convictions, different as these may be from our own, and to admire the things that God has accomplished and continues to accomplish in them through the Holy Spirit. Interreligious dialogue is therefore a "two-way street." Christians must enter into it in a spirit of openness, prepared to receive from others, while on their part, they give witness to their own faith. Authentic dialogue opens both partners to a deeper conversion to the God who speaks to each through the other. Through the witness of others, we Christians can truly discover facets of the divine mystery that we have not yet seen or responded to. The practice of dialogue will then result in the deepening of our own life of faith. We believe that walking together with people of other living faiths will bring us to a fuller understanding and experience of truth.

The different religious teachings agree that the egocentric life is the source of diverse human problems. The great world teachers through the ages have attempted to show that the essence of being human is in overcoming the ego-centered way. This can be seen, for example, deep in the Judaic tradition with the ultimate command to love God with all our heart and all our being.

This primal reality is so profound and deep that there is no one name that can approach it or exhaust it, and no name has emerged in the evolution of global cultures to presume to name it. And yet it is important to have a word that may function to help us focus our thoughts and attention on this deep common ground that emerges out of interreligious dialogue.

A religion is a way of life that shapes a culture, so if we understand the interactions and interplay between and among religions, we see that there is a profound common reality emerging from this creative encounter, found right at the core of the diverse religions. One of the greatest lessons of the centuries of interreligious dialogue and interaction is that logos is so deep in its unity that multiplicity and plurality and diversity are of its essence. Here we see the deepest roots of the origin of dialogue and the evolution of dialogical consciousness. In this historic drama of logos we see that human evolution inexorably moves beyond the egocentric culture to the awakening of global consciousness through dialogue. This deeper story of human evolution could not be seen clearly until we advanced to the global perspective that comes from creative dialogue between worlds. Perhaps the deepest lesson that we might learn from the evolution of cultures is that human beings are essentially beings in dialogue. We do not stand alone. The vision of human as an ego-centered, independently existing entity has simply been shown to be unacceptable and disastrous in the evolution of cultures.

This brings us to the condition in which we are living, an exciting moment in this evolution over centuries. The birthing of this dialogical consciousness is accelerating and peaking in contemporary times. The religions can encounter one another only by delving more deeply into the truth, not by giving up. What is required, however, is reverence for others' belief, along with the willingness to seek truth in what I find alien, a truth that concerns me and that can correct me and lead me further. What is required is the willingness to look behind what may appear strange in order to find the deeper reality it conceals.

The promotion of dialogue among different communities and civilizations is, at present, a priority for the international community. It is only in dialogue that communities can truly meet and understand one another. Choosing the route of dialogue however, involves facing a number of difficulties and challenges. First of all, throughout history there have been clashes between groups of people bearing different truths or worldviews. This difficulty is ingrained in the centuries-long history of every group and its own self-understanding and, therefore, can be eliminated neither quickly nor through pure will.

Interreligious dialogue also helps Christians to better understand their own faith. Because the focus of interreligious dialogue is on the differences between religions, Christians are forced to examine their own beliefs in order to support these positions. This examination will increase the self-understanding of Christians, helping them to differentiate between the pure gospel and the cultural lenses through which people too frequently interpret the gospel. Interreligious dialogue enhances apologetics and discernment. By better understanding the beliefs and practices of other religions, Christians are able to understand how true Christianity is different. This enables Christians to both identify and contextualize the teachings of other religions and to present a reason why Christians believe differently. Finally, interreligious dialogue

increases the ability of Christians to love their neighbors. Dialogue will enhance our ability to see that each person is their moral equal—the only difference is that Christians are sinners who have been saved through God's grace. The knowledge that Christians had nothing to do with their salvation should inspire them to reach out and share the undeserved love of God with their neighbors. Relational evangelism will improve as clarified understanding of the faith and lives of neighbors erases misconceptions about other religions.

Interreligious dialogue is a very elastic concept. Sharing experiences and sharing lives, working on common projects for a better world, wrestling together with questions of religious truth—these are some of the approaches to interreligious dialogue. Interreligious dialogue changes our normative understanding of religious meaning. It represents a shift from self-sufficiency in religious understandings of identity and truth to an appreciation of potentially multiple sources of identity and truth. And the shift is not simply a matter of observation in the face of the facts—there just happens to be many religions. It is a shift toward appreciating that one cannot now think theologically or intellectually about one's own faith outside of the relationship of this dialogue. In this sense, dialogue changes our perception of reality itself. Dialogue is a transaction between people and not systems. This point is often made but seldom taken fully to heart. Through friendship, we learn to value the religious experience of the other in ways that overcome stereotypes and move beyond textbook definitions. But friendships also thrive on the cut and thrust of human inquiry. Not everything that a friend says need be taken at face value. There is a critical edge to our conversations, and this is what keeps friendship alive. Once we take one another for granted, the relationship declines. Friendship reaches across differences between people, and critical friendship commits the integrity of friends to both honesty and shared life.

Religions are deep wells of social value; that is, they provide ethical frameworks, binding beliefs, and a sense of human solidarity in community. They harbor values such as justice, peace, compassion for the suffering, friendship with the stranger, and connectedness to the earth. Historically, these values have been mostly directed toward shaping self-sufficient communities, in spite of the universalist thrust at the heart of the postaxial religious consciousness. In a plural world, this is no longer tenable. The question arises how to transcend self-sufficiency and thereby crosspollinate the spiritual and ethical resourcefulness of each.

In his Homily on the Beatitudes, the holy Hierarch Gregory of Nyssa extols peace and concord among people:

> Of everything that people seek to enjoy in life, is there anything sweeter than a peaceful life? Everything that you would call pleasant in life, is pleasant only when it is united with peace. Let there be everything that is valued in life: wealth, health, a wife, children, a home, relatives, friends; let there be beautiful gardens, places for merry banquets and all contrivances for amusement . . . let all this be, but if there not be peace, what use is it? . . . And so, peace is not only pleasant in itself for those who enjoy peace, but it makes all the good things of life enjoyable. If there should occur with us, as often happens with people, some kind of misfortune in a time of peace, it too becomes more tolerable, because in such a case evil is pacified by good. . . . Judge for thyself: What sort of life do those who are at enmity with each other and are suspicious of one another have? They meet sullenly and one abhors everything in the other; their lips are mute, their glance is averted and the hearing of one is closed to the words of the other.
>
> Everything that is pleasing to one of them is hateful to the other; and, on the contrary, that which is hateful and hostile to one, is pleasing to the other. Therefore, the Lord wants that thou wouldst multiply in thyself the grace of peace with such abundance, so that not only wouldst thou enjoy it, but that thy life would serve as a medicine against the illness of others . . . Whoever turns others away from this shameful vice, such a one renders the greatest benefit and may justly be called blessed; such a one performs a work of God's power, by destroying evil in human nature, and by introducing in place of it fellowship with good things. That is why the Lord also calls the peacemaker a son of God, because he who procures such tranquility for human society becomes an imitator of the true God. The Bestower and Lord of good things completely exterminates and destroys all that is unnatural and alien to good. A similar activity does He command also of thee; and thou must extinguish hatred, cut off enmity and vengeance, destroy quarrels, expel hypocrisy, extinguish the remembrance of wrongs which corrupts the heart, and in place of it introduce everything contrary . . . love, joy, peace, goodness, magnanimity, in a word the whole assemblage of good things. And so, is not he blessed who distributes the divine gifts, who imitates God in his gifts, whose benefactions are similar to God's great gifts?[11]

We feel called to allow the practice of interreligious dialogue to transform the way in which we do theology. We need to move toward a dialogical theology in which the praxis of dialogue, together with that of human liberation, will constitute a true *locus theologicus;* that is, both a source of and basis for theological work. The challenge of religious plurality and the praxis of dialogue are part of the context in which we must search for fresh understandings, new questions, and better expressions of our Christian faith and commitment.

In their encounters with neighbors of other religious traditions, many Christians have come to experience the meaning of a "common humanity" before God. This experience is rooted in the biblical affirmation that God is the Creator and sustainer of all creation. "The earth is the Lord's and all that is in it, the world, and those who live in it."[12] God called the people of Israel to be witnesses among the nations while, at the same time, affirming that God is the God of all nations.[13] The eschatological visions in the Bible anticipate all nations coming together and the creation being restored to the fullness that God intends for all. This conviction is reflected in the affirmation that God is not without witness among any people or at any time.[14]

A particularly important dimension of the dialogue among civilizations is interreligious dialogue, which implies dialogue both among religions and within a single religion. Indeed, the key issue raised by the dialogue among civilizations is the place of ethics in the relationship between societies, peoples, and individuals. Hence, interreligious dialogue constitutes an essential dimension of the dialogue among civilizations. Many interreligious conflicts are fuelled largely by a search for identity expressed by a retreat into a particular religion or spiritual tradition to the exclusion of all others. Beyond the political factors at work, these antagonistic manifestations or retreats are rooted in ignorance of the intrinsic ideals and objectives shared by all faiths. Interreligious dialogue could be an important factor in highlighting the dynamic interplay between spiritual traditions and their specific cultures, by focusing on their mutual contributions and exchanges. It is therefore even more imperative in this age of globalization for all faiths to work together through joint action to reinvent forms of coexistence for the peoples of the world whose experience of conflict or coexistence constitutes the building blocks of the collective memory of humanity.

INTERRELIGIOUS DIALOGUE ATTENTIVE TO WESTERN ENLIGHTENMENT

Gregory Baum

We are grateful that the world religions have learned to respect one another, engage in dialogue, and act jointly in the service of peace. We are grateful for the World Conference of Religions for Peace, the Parliament of the World Religions, and other interreligious world organizations that foster mutual understanding and cooperative action. I am personally grateful for the development in my own church at the Second Vatican Council that acknowledged God's universal mercy, respected religious pluralism, and recommended interreligious dialogue.

At the same time, the September 11 attacks and the preemptive strike against Iraq have made us keenly aware of the dark side of religion; that is to say, the power of religion to encourage arrogance, generate contempt, produce hatred, create conflicts, encourage aggression, and even legitimate violence. How do we explain this dark side of religion?

This is a question that greatly troubles me. I cannot forget that the history of my own Christian tradition includes acts of arrogance, aggression, and violence. I am unable to forget the crusades, the Inquisition, the use of torture to defend the truth, the religious wars between Catholics and Protestants, and the blessing of empire and colonialism by the Christian churches. At the same time, I believe that Christianity and the other world religions are luminous traditions, bringing light to the world, illuminating the path that leads to love, justice, and peace. How then do we account for the dark side?

Here is how the Kyoto Declaration of 1970 answers this question: "As men and women of religion, we confess in humility and penitence that we have very often betrayed our religious ideals and our commitment to peace. It is not religion that has failed the cause of peace, but religious people."[1] The religions are here seen as flawless: to be blamed are the acts of religious people. But is this an adequate answer? Are the religions really flawless?

We often hear the argument that people who in the name of their religion foster hatred or commit acts of violence use their religion as an instrument to enhance their power. Here again the religions are seen as flawless; responsibility for the evil deeds rests upon the actors who have instrumentalized their religion. But is this analysis sufficient? Is the harm done by religious actors simply their personal choice? Or may it not also be structural; that is, the result of flaws in the religious tradition itself?

This is a troubling question. Let me give an example from the Christian tradition. For centuries, the churches promoted contempt for Jews and Jewish religion, resulting in destructive consequences for the Jewish communities in Europe. Who is responsible for this contempt? Should we simply blame individual Christians who violated the divine commandment of neighborly love? Or did the anti-Jewish bias have a structural cause? Was the flaw in the tradition itself? Today, we have answered this question. We recognize that the church's official liturgy condemned the Jews for their unbelief and depicted them as deserted by God. Contempt for the Jews was thus structurally mediated: it was produced by a flaw in the tradition—a flaw introduced by actors in the past who sinned against the love of neighbor. It was only after the Holocaust that the churches recognized their flawed inheritance and reread the Holy Scriptures and found in them resources for changing their teaching. Today the Catholic Church and the major Protestant churches honor Judaism and respect the world religions in the name of Jesus.

Religious traditions are complex historical movements, constituted by diverse currents and engaged in a never-ending debate about the meaning and power of their sacred inheritance in the ever-changing cultural contexts. The preceding reflections force us to admit that religious traditions have a dark side, even as we greatly admire these traditions for their capacity to renew themselves and respond creatively to new historical challenges. Most of the presentations at the congress on world religions deal with the luminous side of religion, promoting love, justice, and peace and rendering an indispensable service to the well-being of humanity. What I wish to do is quite different: with a heavy heart, I wish to explore the dark side of religion. The examples I use shall all be taken from my own tradition. I leave it to members of other religious tradition to test whether my analysis sheds light on their own history.

To gain a better understanding of the dark side of religion, I wish to engage in dialogue with an intellectual current of the Western Enlightenment. I realize of course that the Enlightenment was an ambiguous intellectual movement. On the one hand, the movement, boasting that its values were universal, generated contempt for traditional societies and in particular for non-Western cultures. This was the imperialist dimension of the Enlightenment. At the same time, the movement also advocated the rescue of people from oppressive institutions. This was the emancipatory dimension of the Enlightenment. The desire for emancipation or rescue from oppressive structures is, in my opinion, truly universal. All colonized peoples want to be free; all hungry people want to live in conditions that allow them to eat and feed their families; all despised people want to live in a culture that honors them.

Dialogue with this emancipatory current of the Enlightenment promises to be helpful in my inquiry into the dark side of religion. I shall pay attention in particular to the sociology of knowledge that analyzes the capacity of ideas and symbols to affect cultural development and influence people's behavior.

THE DESTRUCTIVE POTENTIAL OF RELIGION

Prior to my turn to the sociology of knowledge, I wish to make two more general remarks on the destructive potential of religions.

First, the venerated sacred texts of religion contain certain harsh passages that, if applied literally, cause damage to innocent people. Some passages in our sacred literature praise conquest by the sword, foster contempt for outsiders, and even legitimate violence in the name of God. We have to wrestle with these harsh texts, show their location in a particular historical situation, and demonstrate that they have been transcended and therefore invalidated by subsequent currents in the same tradition.

Christians are troubled by passages in the early parts of the Old Testament that depict God as a heavenly warrior, describe the conquest of Palestine as a genocidal military campaign, and present the tribes surrounding the people of Israel as steeped in evil. These passages are transcended and invalidated in parts of the Old Testament written in a later period, telling us that God is merciful, that God has made a covenant with the whole of humanity, and that God's mercy and justice are operative in all the nations. Here God is revealed, not in the loud clap of the thunder but in the still, small voice.

Christians are also troubled by the passages in the New Testament according to which all who do not believe in Jesus Christ will be condemned—a verdict that excludes the majority of humankind from God's mercy and creates a division in humanity that can never be healed. These passages are transcended and invalidated by texts in the New Testament according to which people will be saved by their love of God and neighbor and their solidarity with the poor and the needy. In a parable of Matthew's Gospel, Jesus addresses a group of persons who had never heard of him yet selflessly offered help to people in trouble. To them he said, "What you have done to the least of them, you have done to me."[2]

Not all believers are willing to transcend and invalidate the harsh texts of their tradition. They prefer to apply the harsh texts literally, even if in doing so they do harm to innocent people. In my opinion, the harsh texts of the sacred literature contribute to the ambiguity of the religious traditions.

Second, the sacred literature we have inherited is to a large extent written in a poetic style, using images, similes, and hyperboles. It is thus not surprising that the commandments and counsels we read in them are not always rationally consistent and may even be contradictory. They may reflect different contexts or represent different forms of speech.

Thus, in one place in the New Testament, we read that all worldly authority comes from God and to disobey this authority is disobedience to God, yet in another context we read that disobedience to authority may be justified because "it is better to obey God than man."[3] Here is another conundrum: at one point, Jesus says, "Any one who is not with me is against me," whereas at another point he tells his disciples, "Anyone who is not against you is with you."[4] A simplistic reading of the scriptures, relying on a single text, without qualifying it with reference to other texts, may well inspire extreme and unbalanced behavior harmful to society.

A Definition of Ideology

Let me now turn to the sociology of knowledge, in particular to the concept of ideology, which is here defined as the distortion of truth for the sake of collective self-interest. Societies tend to generate ideologies in a largely unconscious process to secure their identity, enhance their power, and legitimate or disguise their oppressive structures. Not only do societies want to look good; they want to hide their unjust practices and look better than they are. The dominant culture of any society is thus affected by an ideological bias; as a result, its members tend to assimilate this distortion as the truth and defend it with passion. By contrast, the carefully disguised institutional injustices are clearly recognized by the victims of the society and by persons in solidarity with them.

In the early 1960s, the American author John Howard Griffin decided to color his skin and travel through the United States as a black man in order to see the world through the eyes of the disadvantaged and despised. In his book *Black Like Me,* he told us that moving through the streets as a black man, he was unable to recognize the cities with which he had been familiar. The same experience is recounted by Dorothee Sölle, a German Protestant theologian who was radicalized in the 1950s when she, a young woman of a comfortable class, accompanied a group of women refugees searching the city for employment and a place to live. As she walked with these women through her own city, she no longer recognized it. These women, she wrote, helped her to discover the truth. She became aware that the dominant culture makes the sinister aspects of society invisible.

Ideological Bias: Us versus Them

Can we admit that religious traditions are also affected by ideologies? Every religion has the sacred duty of defining its identity and articulating the faith and practice that distinguish it from other religions and from the surrounding culture. The legitimate discourse distinguishing between "us" and "them" is a mechanism that easily generates ideology. We hold the truth, they are in error; we are enlightened, they live in blindness; we live holy lives, they practice vices. The us-and-them discourse tends to produce an elevated self-understanding and a false sense of superiority of our own community, accompanied by a denigrating perception of other communities seen as inferior. Because in their history most religions have defined themselves against a competing religion or against a culture that resisted them, their sacred literature tends to refer to outsiders in a manner that demeans them and generates conflicts.

Distinguishing between us and them does not have to produce ideological distortions. In every religion, the truth is received in humility as a gift for which one is grateful. We embrace the truth that has been granted to us, yet without boasting about it as if we had achieved it ourselves. To have contempt for religious traditions other than our own sins against humility reveals false pride and misappropriates the truth entrusted to us. Feeling superior is not the work of faith but of arrogance. Looking down upon other religions is therefore a self-damaging process. The ideological self-elevation that leads to the contempt of outsiders actually distorts one's own religious inheritance.

In a Christian context, this point was strongly made by St. Paul. He told Christians to remember that despising the Jews for refusing to believe in Jesus was a sign that they—the Christians—looked upon their faith as a personal achievement, not as a free gift, thus endangering their justification before God.[5] One wishes that the church had listened to St. Paul.

It was only in the twentieth century, largely as a response to the horrors of World War II and the Holocaust, that the Christian church began a critical examination of its inherited discourse about outsiders—about Jews, members of the world religions, native peoples, unbelievers, Christians deemed heretical, and homosexuals. Rereading the Scriptures with a new openness, the churches discovered theological foundation for addressing outsiders with respect and engaging in interreligious dialogue. A similar process of self-correction is taking place in other religious traditions.

Respect for outsiders and, more especially, for other religious traditions does not make us into sentimental observers of human history, refusing to recognize the conflictive world in which we live. We are not naïve: we do distinguish between good and evil in the world. Yet the distinction between good and evil is quite different from the distinction between us and them. Good and evil are dimensions present in all communities: they pervade us, that is, our own community, as well as them, that is, the communities of the others. Standing against injustice, oppression, and exploitation is an ethical struggle that focuses first on the faults in our own community before we turn to what is wrong and damaging in others.

I conclude from the preceding remarks that the discourse used by a tradition to distinguish between believers and nonbelievers easily generates ideologies that damage the purity of the tradition, produce conflict in society, and allow themselves to be instrumentalized for the enhancement of political power.

IDEOLOGICAL BIAS: TRUTH AS AN INSTRUMENT OF DOMINATION

Another principle of the sociology of knowledge is that the meaning of a sentence changes as the speaker moves to a different social location. An example I often refer to is the anthem "Germany, Germany Above All," which was the song of the failed liberal revolution of 1848 calling for a united Germany over all the divisions produced by the feudal order. Yet, after the creation of the German Empire in 1870, the same song acquired a totally different meaning: "Germany, Germany Above All" now became an expression of political arrogance. The meaning of a message changes dramatically if it is uttered by a powerful actor.

It is a recognized principle of hermeneutics that to understand the literal meaning of a scriptural passage one must situate it in its historical context. The sociology of knowledge draws attention to the fact that when this passage is recited in a new historical context, its meaning may change significantly. In particular, the rhetoric of resistance employed by individuals or small communities threatened by an aggressive enemy will acquire a different meaning when repeated by persons or communities in possession of power. When the prophet or the sage faces strong opposition or suffers persecution, he expresses his resistance by predicting the ultimate victory of truth and pronouncing God's judgment on his enemies. Yet if the identical sentences are used by persons or institutions possessing great power, they become a discourse of domination, asserting the victory of truth over all dissidents and God's judgment on all who challenge the establishment. The truth uttered by the weak becomes ideology when repeated by the powerful.

To illustrate this point, I remind my students of the song, "We Shall Overcome," sung by powerless people in the civil rights struggle to express their trust that in the long run truth and justice will prevail. Yet, if the police department had adopted "We Shall Overcome" as their theme song, its meaning would have been quite different: it would have meant that they shall use their guns and their armored cars to quell dissent and establish order.

Let me apply this principle to the Christian discourse about truth. Jesus, we read in Scripture, came to reveal the hidden truth of God. Jesus said to those who believed in him, "If you make my word your home you will indeed be my disciples; you will come to know the truth, and the truth will set you free."[6] The truth he proclaimed would free people—it would "give sight to the blind, set the captives free and liberate the oppressed."[7] Jesus and the first Christian community preached the truth with great courage against the imperial culture of Rome, the worship of the emperor, and the Jewish aristocracy complicit with the empire. The early witnesses were willing to die for the liberating truth.

Yet, in subsequent centuries, when the Christian communities had become powerful churches, commitment to the truth became the source of endless quarrels, the justification for persecuting dissidents, and the legitimation of violent conflicts. The truth uttered in resistance to empire now became an instrument to promote the power of the churches. Truth came to be looked upon increasingly in conceptual terms, separated from the practice of love: it came to be used as an instrument to promote the establishment and suppress alternative interpretations. Today, we remember with embarrassment the Inquisition and the use of torture in the name of God's truth and are unable to forget the religious wars between Catholics and Protestants in the sixteenth and seventeenth centuries. The atheism of many Enlightenment thinkers, we now recognize, had been a reaction to the endless religious violence. The religious compromise achieved by the Peace of Westphalia in 1648 initiated long centuries of noncommunication between Catholics and Protestants, each side using the truth as an instrument to triumph over the other. We are grateful to God that the ecumenical movement of the twentieth century has radically changed the religious situation: we have learned to respect ecclesiastical pluralism and hope to move closer to one another.

IDEOLOGICAL BIAS: RELIGION AS SACRED LEGITIMATION OF AN UNJUST SOCIETY

We now turn to the infamous critique of religion proposed in the nineteenth century by Karl Marx. He argued that religion was an ideology designed to protect the existing social order, to utter blessings on the prince and the royal court, to demand obedience from the people, and to console them in their misery with promises of a higher life in the spirit, as a reward for their virtue. We reject the Marxist critique of religion. As counterevidence, we turn to the message and the actions of the founders of religions and to the lives of the sages, prophets, and saints. At the beginning and, later, at its best, religion has always been at odds with political domination. At the same time, the grain of truth in the Marxist critique deserves attention.

When religion is welcomed in society, encouraged by government, and supported by public funds, it tends to understand itself as the spiritual guardian of society and a defender of the established order. Religion here becomes the sacred canopy of the secular realm. In this situation, religion may call for social reforms to create a more just society, yet religion may also become a reactionary force, defending the power of the dominant elite and offering ideological support for the status quo.

Taking my examples from the Christian tradition, I recall that the colonial conquest of the European empires was blessed by the Christian churches. They interpreted the colonial expansion of the European powers as a providential event opening the door to the worldwide Christian mission. With few exceptions, the churches were so deeply identified with European culture and European arrogance that their religious mission acquired a political meaning: they preached obedience to the king and promoted what they regarded as a superior civilization. Here religion clearly assumed the ideological character denounced by the Marxist critique.

There are many other examples in which the ecclesiastical establishment wedded itself to the political order or the economic elite. I am thinking, for instance, of the unbelievable spectacle during the First World War when the European churches prayed against one another, each for the victory of its own nation—an experience that contributed to the subsequent secularization of European society.

This leads me to the topic of war, which deserves careful attention, but which I cannot treat in detail at this occasion. The Christian tradition has, in the past, accepted the so-called just-war theory, specifying the conditions under which a defensive war was ethically permissible. Most religions have developed such a theory, even as all of them had—and still have—ardent believers committed to nonviolence. Because the American war against Iraq was a preemptive strike against a nation that had not been a threat to the United States, the leaders of the major American churches refused to recognize the ethical legitimacy of this war, even if the organized Christian Right in America strongly supported the war.

To illustrate the ideological distortions of religion, I draw upon examples from my own tradition. I am fully aware that similar examples can be drawn from other religious traditions, but I leave this task to their own followers. All over the world, religion has repeatedly legitimated conquest.

In some historical situations, religion has also motivated resistance to domination. In the Christian tradition, the just-war theory has been applied to justify revolutionary violence. Most of the American churches approved of the American revolution against the British crown in the 1770s, arguing that in the struggle against domination the rational and disciplined use of violence was ethically acceptable. Yet Christian teachers—and teachers in all religious traditions—have always repudiated the irrational and arbitrary use of violence, even when practiced in defense of a just cause. Violence is irrational and arbitrary when it is an expression of rage, directed at innocent people, and devoid of a rational plan for improving the unjust situation. In the face of oppression and exploitation, religion may well produce anger, but if it blesses the practice of random violence, it becomes ideologically distorted.

We are grateful to God for people of faith in all the world religions who recognize the ideological taint in their tradition and summon their fellow believers to reembrace the authentic message and the deepest values of their faith. The religions are sent to offer light to the world.

IDEOLOGICAL BIAS: RELIGION SUPPORTING AN EXCLUSIVELY MALE PERSPECTIVE

I must make a brief remark about another ideological bias. According to the sociology of knowledge, the perception of reality depends in part on the social location of the observer. Implied in this principle is that men and women, located as they are on different levels of social power, will have different perceptions of reality. To understand who we are as human beings and what our inherited religion means for human life, we will have to listen to both men and women. Limiting ourselves to the male perspective produces an ideological distortion of the truth. In my opinion, the stubborn commitment to the male perspective in the world religions is a mental disease.

BLIND IDEALISM

I have offered a brief description of four ideology-producing processes operative in religious traditions: (1) the unreflective us-and-them discourse, (2) the language of the powerless adopted by the powerful, (3) the uncritical support of religion for the political or economic elites, and (4) the exclusion of the feminine perspective. I have also briefly mentioned the danger of religion legitimating rage.

As I am exploring the dark side of religion, I will now turn to another problematic dimension of the role of religion has played in human society. Let me return to an idea of Karl Marx, with whom we are in disagreement, but whose proposals demand reflection. In his book *The German Ideology*, Marx made fun of the German intellectuals of his day who, influenced by the philosopher Hegel, would spend all day debating the problems of society. In their discussions, Marx claimed, they analyzed the irrationalities of society and tried to resolve them in theory, and then, when the day was over, they would leave their meeting satisfied, believing that they had changed the world. Marx called this German intellectual approach "idealism"; that is, the belief that changing the ideas in the head is sufficient for changing the world. He conceded that new ideas are necessary for restructuring society, yet they are never sufficient: changing the world also demands action.

The question I ask myself is whether the religious believers are sometimes inclined to practice this problematic idealism. Responding to the violation of peace and justice, religious leaders often propose that what is needed is a change of mind and heart and a renewed commitment to the love of neighbor. Implied in this proposal is the idea that, if people become more loving, more forgiving, and more generous, then oppressive practices and violent conflicts will disappear. There is an element of truth in this proposal: a conversion of mind and heart is indeed necessary for the reconstruction of a defective social order. But a change of consciousness is not sufficient; we must also wrestle with the concrete conditions of society.

Let me be more specific: if a religious group wants to promote peace in society, it is not sufficient to call for the spiritual conversion of people; it is also necessary to join the public debate dealing with the causes of the conflict, the policies of the government, and the interests of the weapons industries. Canada is an arms-producing country, and its industries make millions of dollars selling them all over the world. Dedication to peace demands more than a change of heart; it calls for a critique of the arms industries and the participation in political debates. Should we who stand for peace demand that laborers in the arms industries give up their jobs? But then, where will they then find new jobs at a time when unemployment is on the rise? The point I am making is that advocating peace demands more than a conversion of the heart; it includes a wresting with the concrete problems of society.

Confronted by issues of grave injustice, religious people of good will often think that all we need is love, forgiveness, and generosity. This is the message of many religious leaders. The recent encyclical of Benedict XVI *Deus caritas est* is an expression of this kind of idealism. A different counsel was given many decades ago by Pope Pius XI when he said that justice demands "the correction of morals and the reform of institutions."[8] We who are prompted by our faith to promote justice must not only purge our hearts of selfishness and deal justly with our neighbors; we must also challenge the structures of injustice that exploit and oppress innocent people. Under the apartheid regime in South Africa, many courageous people resisted the government at great risk, including Christians, Jews, Muslims, Hindus, and secular men and women. The Kairos Circle, a group of courageous Christians, criticized the churches in their county: they denounced the Afrikaans-speaking church for legitimating apartheid with arguments drawn from the Bible and then accused the English-speaking churches of asking their members to reject apartheid in their heart and not demanding that they stand against apartheid in the public sphere. The English-speaking church practiced what we have called "idealism."

I greatly admire the World Conference of Religions for Peace because it urges religious leaders and religious communities to purify their hearts and seek the peace of soul, and at the same time join the public debate, reveal the causes of conflicts and wars, and cooperate with nonreligious actors who share their commitment to justice and peace.

GRATITUDE

We are now participating in a spiritual movement for which there is no precedent prior to the twentieth century. We now have access to a new spiritual energy. In this chapter, I have concentrated on the ideologies that have marred religious traditions because I believe we must face the dark inheritance of our own tradition to open ourselves to spiritual renewal. All our traditions have a hidden potential enabling us to become partners in a movement that offers light to the world, illuminating the path that leads to justice and peace.

Movement and Institution

Necessary Elements of Sustaining the Interfaith Vision

David A. Leslie

Movements are born out of deeply held convictions that the status quo needs to change. The movements of the day are many: environmental, gay rights, women's rights, nuclear freeze, Jubilee, disability rights, farmworkers' rights, and many others. At times, broad societal movements emerge out of the religious community. Other times, religious community support gives these movements new adherents, strength, and direction. In each case, people and collectives of people are called, sometimes driven, to improve the world as they and others experience it. Out of the mantra "something needs to change," movements are born.

The goal of such movements is to change *both* perspectives on specific issues and worldviews *and* individual and corporate practices. This is especially so for those movements that have strong interfaith characteristics. During the last decade, for example, Jubilee committees were formed to educate faith communities about the debilitating consequences of immense debt in developing nations and to raise the collective voice for debt retirement for developing nations.

Likewise, environmental concerns, in particular global warming, have been the impetus for faith communities revisiting Holy Scriptures and developing faith and environmental sustainability study

and action initiatives. The mission of these efforts is to change religious thinking about the environment and to change individual and corporate practices such as how electric power is purchased and how buildings are built and to enhance religious communities' voices in support of policies such as the Kyoto Protocol.

In the Pacific Northwest, where environmental consciousness is quite strong, the Catholic bishops in the dioceses along the Columbia River released the pastoral letter "The Columbia River Watershed: Caring for Creation and the Common Good." This letter added an important faith-based perspective to the environmental movement in our region of the United States and Canada. Coalitions of denominational and interreligious organizations regularly convene forums on a wide range of environmental issues including dam breeching on the lower Snake River as proposed by tribal governments in an effort to restore salmon runs, as promised in treaties with the U.S. government signed in the 1850s. Dialogue on land usage, water rights, and small-farm sustainability are also interfaith action priorities. In addition, interreligious advocacy efforts to support the Endangered Species Act and to oppose drilling in the Arctic National Wildlife Refuge are also part of the faith community's active participation in the broader environmental movement.

There are numerous other issues on which people of differing faiths converge. There are interfaith groups that study scriptural texts, and interreligious marriages are increasingly the order of the day. Pastoral care in hospitals and chaplaincy programs in correctional institutions have clearly identifiable interfaith dimensions. There is probably no issue today—either inside or outside of one's faith community—that does not have some aspect of interreligiousness. We live in an increasingly pluralistic society, and even our most sacred and parochial convictions, such as the concept of salvation, are often processed through an interfaith lens.

As such, being engaged in and knowledgeable of interfaith relations and affairs is not optional. As I have found in my vocational endeavors and suggested earlier, there is hardly an issue or societal concern that does not have (or should not have) interfaith dimensions. If part of our collective mission is to work for the improvement of the world, to positively change the status quo for all of God's people, then the building of respectful, constructive, and issue-oriented interfaith relationships is a must. Peacemaking, human rights, and environmental sustainability are best done cooperatively, and pose the opportunity for the faith community to collectively model a different type of temporal behavior; namely, suspending partisan parochialism and engaging cooperatively in a mutually agreed-upon action-oriented manner.

Today's interfaith movement—and the movements within the movement—have many reflections, and its proponents have many goals and objectives. If there is any doubt, just review closely this congress's program. Although seeming at times quite diffuse and disjointed, there is an important keystone or hinge point that brings in focus a central purpose for all interfaith work. This purpose, I believe, is found in the answer to the question that is posed poignantly in the subtheme of the Congress, "Can religion be a force for good?" Clearly, this question can be answered both in the affirmative and the negative. Religion can be a force for good, and religion can be a force for evil. Yet most of us, I would suspect, are driven to see most fully the force of religion as a force for good and to work ethically and morally to mitigate the not-so-good aspects of religion.

As the world continues to have its share of sectarian violence, some of which is clearly religion-inspired, the need for religion as a force for the good becomes more critical. And, as more and more people of faith and others outside of the religious community develop this conviction, there is a growing sense of the urgency for new reflections and commitment to interfaith relations, dialogue, and action. Central to this growing awareness is the corresponding awareness that together we can make more positive differences, and conversely, apart, the potential for destruction is enhanced.

To further this point, Can religion be a force for good? is answered most fully when numerous people of faith from numerous religious traditions and convictions come together in joint efforts. Interfaith efforts within South Africa played a critical role in sustaining the movement that eventually ended the apartheid regime and brought about a new political reality. Likewise, interfaith efforts in the United States helped end our own apartheid, Jim Crow, segregationist practices. The picture of the Reverend Dr. Martin Luther King Jr., Greek Orthodox Archbishop Iakovos, and Rabbi Abraham Heschel walking together in Selma, Alabama, during the civil rights struggles in the United States visually confirms this point. In Iraq, there are efforts to build an interfaith alliance developed through the Iraqi Institute of Peace, which helped develop the Baghdad Religious Accord that states publicly the need for interfaith cooperation and the end of bloodshed. In urban and rural communities throughout much of the world, interfaith cooperation is seen as a necessary aspect of creating respectful and healthy communities spawning courageous efforts to address the needs of the poor and disenfranchised through health and human services.

Yet, in spite of all this positive energy and movement, there are detractors. Several millennia ago, King Solomon of ancient Israel developed the political and religious alliances that allowed the kingdom to experience peace, prosperity, and power as never before. However, as biblical writers warned, "If you turn aside from following me . . . serve other gods and worship them, then I will cut Israel off from the land that I have given them; and the house that I have consecrated for my name I will cast out of my sight."[1] According to these observers, Solomon's tolerance and interest in the "other" opened the way to apostasy—a type of religious treason—and the ultimate downfall of the kingdom.

More recently, this story has repeated itself in different forms. Remember, one person's openness is another person's apostasy. When Pastor David Benke, president of the Atlantic District of the Lutheran Church Missouri Synod, joined in a community commemoration for the victims of September 11 at Yankee Stadium, he was suspended from the clergy roster for promoting religious "syncretism (mixing religions), defending false doctrines and unionism (worshipping with non-LCMS clergy)."[2] In other places in the world, interfaith interest and cooperation—even *intra*religious cooperation—can result in ostracism and, sadly, even death.

Like most movements, those engaged in interfaith efforts are confronted daily with critics, people who are apathetic, and those who would deny the value of and the opportunity to engage in interfaith work. Yet the interfaith movement is critical to the well-being of the world and must be nurtured, sustained, and grown. So how is this to happen? How is the movement to keep its focus and develop its passion and the new leadership necessary to keep the interfaith movement creatively alive? It is in these questions that we find the convergence of movement and institution.

For twenty years, I have worked within interfaith organizations and for Christian-based organizations like my current employer, Ecumenical Ministries of Oregon, that have a strong commitment to engaging with other faith traditions. From my experience, I know firsthand the wonderful opportunities and the soul-numbing challenges in these efforts. I have learned that healthy interfaith organizations are *movement*-infused and committed to working on tangible issues of our time

and developing the consciousness and leadership important to today's and tomorrow's societal crises and transformational opportunities. They are not stagnating and diffuse but focused and flexible, able to change with the times.

So how then do healthy interfaith organizations develop and grow in depth of purpose and program? Let me share with you several things I have learned and work on daily to ensure that our part in the interfaith movement is alive, relevant, rich in passion, and sustainable:

1. Interfaith work is holy and sacred. Clearly, this for many is the root of the passion that allows the interfaith movement to flourish; yet it is also at the root of much of the resistance to the movement. What personally is sacred and from God may be seen as anathema to the faith of another. Ultimately, interfaith organizing is an enterprise that should not be taken for granted or lightly, and the religious principles that undergird the interfaith institution and the movement as a whole should be clearly developed.

2. Interfaith work must therefore be based on the respect of faith traditions. It is important to create a learning environment where those participating can share not only their own faith commitments but learn about others. A healthy interfaith institution is grounded in intellectual and spiritual curiosity and openness where learning and seeking are honored and individual faith traditions, commitments, and beliefs are acknowledged and respected.

3. With that said, however, vibrant interfaith organizations seek to find the "we"—that is, the point of convergence of common or shared goals, dreams, aspirations, and inspirations. Creative interfaith work cannot be a forum for unilateral dominance of one faith tradition—a series of monologues—rather, it is a dialogical, mutual, and reciprocal process.

4. The organization that flourishes is one that has clarity of purpose and a mission that is

developed by all stakeholders. Additionally, it is one where the mission is regularly revisited and adjusted as needed over time. Taking time in retreats and planning sessions to deliberate and discuss how the mission is being carried out, who is "at the table" as well as who is not, and issues that need to be addressed and those that may no longer need attention is critical to health and sustainability.

5. Creative interfaith organizations are characterized by a public aspect of the work of the organization; they offer opportunities for the public—religious and secular—to engage one another. Publicly available prayer and worship events, lectures, dialogue circles, social service programs, and social-action initiatives offer the opportunity for people to put their faith into action and discover others previously unknown who share common interests, beliefs, and commitments from differing faith traditions. This is a powerful witness that is much needed in our broken, fractured world.

6. Movement-filled institutions have the ability to risk and stretch in developing programs but also know their limits. In other words, it is important to be driven by big visions (for example, the end of war) yet understand that the single institution cannot do everything alone and accomplish everything immediately. There has to be a sense of "urgent patience" and a congruence of initiatives with resources available, including financial, human, spiritual, and in-kind. Too many movements and corresponding organizations burn out or do not reach their full potential because of taking on too much with little planning and inadequate resources. There is also a tendency to be unwilling to share the opportunities of service with other organizations in common cause. It is important to avoid institutional arrogance that excludes rather than includes potential allies and friends.

7. Sustainability is related to the rhythms and ebbs and flows of the people in a community and the historical circumstances of life. The interfaith movement is very relational-oriented, and organizational sustainability can often rest on the passions of a few committed individuals. As people come and go, organizations may fluctuate depending on movement leadership (or lack thereof). Likewise, historical circumstances can radically influence interfaith relationships. The situation in the Middle East, for example, is both the impetus for critical and extraordinary interfaith relationships and, at the same time, creates great stress for the interfaith movement. Understanding this means that there is an unending commitment to develop new leaders and practitioners, as well as to not despair when all is not perfect.

8. Finally, as we all know, the interfaith movement is not always an easy place to put one's energies and commitments. The interfaith movement is about change, about new ways to think about one's faith and to practice and live in community. At its root, the interfaith movement challenges extreme parochialism and a religious orthodoxy that holds all others outside of a particular faith as doomed to hell. Those engaged must realize that the road traveled will not be easy. Fortunately, however, the movement's strength is found in those through the millennia as well as those here today and those yet to be discovered whose interfaith commitments sustain the joint efforts to build healthy and respectful societies and address society's inequities and self-destructive tendencies. Knowing that we are not alone ensures the future of the movement.

As I have discovered, the interfaith movement in its many reflections is critical to the well-being of the world in which we live. My hope is that you will find your place within this sacred and mighty endeavor and build bridges and empower hope in the days to come.

BUDDHISM MEETS HINDUISM

Interaction and Influence in India

Arvind Sharma

Although as academics we are supposed to put our subjectivity on hold and pontificate with magisterial, and even Olympian, detachment, it might not be out of place to start with a personal reminiscence. In the spirit in which a picture can be worth a thousand words, sometimes an ounce of emotion is worth a ton of facts. I must have been nineteen, straining at the leash to get out of my teens, when I looked at a morning paper one day in 1959 that announced with banner headlines: "The Dalai Lama Crosses Over into India." This was electrifying. After all, a news report is the first draft of history. But what I want to share with the reader is not the banner headlines but the fine print, which stated that when the then Prime Minister of India, Jawahar Lal Nehru, announced in the Indian Parliament that the Dalai Lama had set foot on Indian soil, the Indian Parliament, I can still remember the expression, "burst into spontaneous applause."

Presumably, most of the members of the Indian Parliament were Hindus. And presumably they knew that the Dalai Lama was a Buddhist monk. Then what made them erupt in spontaneous applause? I have put this question to myself often, and this chapter will be yet another attempt on my part to answer it.

Had the members of the Parliament by an act of intuition—or emotional intelligence—grasped something in the situation that eludes us as scholars? One raises this question because when I became a student of comparative religion I was told that Hinduism and Buddhism are two different religions. This was news to me. I had known that they were distinct, but that they were different was news to me. Once I had barely accustomed myself to looking at the Indian religious reality in this way, I was next told that Hinduism was responsible for the disappearance of Buddhism in India. I was led to wonder whether Buddhism had disappeared from India, or whether it had disappeared into India. And if one were to think on these lines, I also wondered whether anyone had asked the question, Was Hinduism responsible for the emergence of Buddhism in India? As one whose formative years of life were spent in India, I was now confronted with what is now fashionably referred to as cognitive dissonance on a massive scale in a foreign land, where I was studying comparative religion, a field of study virtually unknown in India.

It gradually became clear, as one tried to come to terms with this cognitive dissonance, that the appearance or disappearance of Buddhism in

India, in relation to Hinduism, was viewed in the literature on the subject from three perspectives. From one perspective, Buddhism arose as a protest against Hinduism in both its metaphysical and sociopolitical orientation and seemed set to displace it, when somehow the tide gradually turned, and Hinduism regained lost ground and ultimately succeeded in absorbing Buddhism. The following passage from Pandit Nehru's well-known book *The Discovery of India* grants surprising vivacity to this perspective. He writes:

> Eight or nine years ago, when I was in Paris, André Malraux put me a strange question at the very beginning of our conversation. What was it, he asked me, that enabled Hinduism to push away organized Buddhism from India, without major conflict, over a thousand years ago? How did Hinduism succeed in absorbing, as it were, a great and widespread popular religion, without the usual wars of religion which disfigure the history of so many countries? What inner vitality or strength did Hinduism possess then which enabled it to perform this remarkable feat? And does India possess this inner vitality and strength today? If so, her freedom and greatness were assured.[1]

These lines were written in 1946. In 1947, India became free. One rarely sees a prediction fulfilled so quickly!

Note, however, the way the argument is framed. Hinduism and Buddhism are "opposed" to each other, and ultimately Hinduism overcomes or overpowers Buddhism, or more diplomatically, absorbs it. There is also a hint of Hindu triumphalism when the matter is put that way. A second perspective retains the oppositional framework but attributes the disappearance of Buddhism in India less to Hindu success and more to Buddhist failure.

Many permutations and combinations of these two positions are possible, which claim to explain the decline of Buddhism in India as prefigured in Xuanzang's well-known dismal dream in the seventh century recorded in his biography by

Hwui-Li: "Yuan Chwang dreamt one night while residing at Nālandā that, soon after the death of Śilāditya Harṣavardhana, the doctrine of Buddha would be visited by a terrible calamity and the great hall of Nālandā would be deserted, its glorious chambers turned into dwellings of the water-buffaloes and that a devastating fire would reduce to ashes all its structures and towns around it."[2]

HINDU-BUDDHIST INTERACTION IN ANCIENT INDIA

One could, however, also view the interaction between Hinduism and Buddhism in India in a slightly different light, visualizing these traditions not so much in opposition to each other as in apposition with each other, interacting in creative tension rather than in destructive conflict. One outstanding scholar of the Buddhist presence in India sums up the history of Buddhism in India in this one line: "The rich stream of cultural life inspired by the Buddha progressed during the centuries following his Parinirvāṇa, gradually acquiring a varied and individual aspect but ever remaining a tributary to that larger stream of Indian culture into which it ultimately merged."[3]

Teasing this suggestion out a little further, one could view the interaction between Hinduism and Buddhism as an interaction between two strands of what we might call the Indic religious tradition as a whole and to demonstrate how our perception of the same data are altered if we adopt such an attitude. The possibilities generated by this approach may be illustrated with two concrete examples in the following sections.

It is well-known that the Buddha was accepted as an incarnation of Viṣṇu by the sixth or seventh century.[4] When this point is adduced as indicating the hospitality of the two traditions to each other, scholars are quick to point out it really constitutes proof of hostility between them, because, according to the Viṣṇu Purāṇa, the Buddha appeared in the world to lead people away from the Vedic path, because the world was becoming overburdened by an excess of virtue. Klaus K. Klostermaier summarizes this view as follows:

Some authors seem to think that the reception of Buddha among the *avatāras* of Viṣṇu would express a spirit of tolerance. But the way in which this Buddha-*avatāra* is described in the *Viṣṇupurāṇa*, and the general Hindu attitude of considering both good and evil as coming from the same Supreme being, would suggest that we have here an early and unmistakably hostile Hindu text dealing with Buddhism.

Buddha is introduced as one of many forms of the *māyā-moha* (delusive power) of Viṣṇu: he engages in what may be termed psychological warfare against the *daityas* on behalf of the *devas*, who have come to take refuge with him. He is sent to destroy the enemies of the Vaiṣṇavas from within. He is characterized as *raktāṃbara*, dressed in a red garment, as *mṛdvalpamadhurākṣara*, speaking gently, calmly, and sweetly. The teachings, which he communicates for the self-destruction of the *daityas*, considered as pernicious and heretical by the Hindus, are

1. The killing of animals for sacrifices should be discontinued.
2. The whole world is a product of the mind.
3. The world is without support.
4. The world is engaged in pursuit of error, which it mistakes for knowledge.

As a result of this teaching the *daityas* abandoned the dharma of the Vedas and the *smṛtis*, and they induced others to do the same. The same *māyā-moha* of Viṣṇu had appeared before Buddha as "a naked mendicant with shaven head and a bunch of peacock feathers in his hands," and he would appear again as the preacher of the Cārvāka doctrines.

The *Viṣṇupurāṇa* calls the Ṛk, Yajus, and Sāmaveda the "garments" of a man: a man is naked if he goes without them. The *daityas*, seduced by Buddha are in such a position. Whereas the *devas* were unable to dislodge the *daityas* before, they now defeat them: "The armor of dharma, which had formerly protected the *daityas* had been discarded by them

and upon its abandonment followed their destruction."[5]

This is fairly damning evidence of Hindu hostility to Buddhism in the face of the thesis of enriching interaction of the two traditions one intends to propose, so let us see how this challenge may be faced. A point to keep in mind here is that the Purāṇas tend to carry their sectarian loyalties to the point of vilifying other gods and that this holds true not just of the Buddha and Viṣṇu but also of so-called Hindu gods as well, such as Viṣṇu and Śiva themselves. For the sake of consistency, one should therefore also present a similar example, to which attention is drawn by Professor Klostermaier himself. While commenting on the sectarian rivalries of the Hindu gods, he writes:

> A telling story is that of Vikra, who, after practicing severe *tapas* for many years, called on Śiva, asking him to grant the boon, that whosoever's head he would touch, that man should die instantly. Śiva laughingly granted the boon, realizing his folly only when Vikra chased his wife and him, to try out the new art. Śiva in his despair sought refuge with Viṣṇu, asking for advice. Viṣṇu, cunningly, induced doubt in Vikra. Śiva, he told Vikra, cannot always be taken seriously. He might have been joking or lying—so better try it first on yourself. Vikra did so, and thus killed himself with the boon he had received. The story has as its main theme the superiority of Viṣṇu over Śiva, who has to appeal to Viṣṇu to save his life.[6]

The point then is that Buddha is not singled out for vilification in the Purāṇas; other gods are also shown up.

Moreover, there are other ways of viewing this question. Even if the Buddha leads demons astray, it might be worth recalling the mystic utterance here, that "the light which leads astray is also light from heaven." But the issue is also capable of resolution at a less lofty level. It is true that the Viṣṇu Purāṇa presents the Buddha even as an incarnation of Viṣṇu in a negative light. We need to ask if the Hindu tradition ascribes other motives to his incarnation elsewhere. A. L. Basham offers the following helpful observation on this point:

> According to most theologians the god became Buddha in order to delude the wicked, lead them to deny the Vedas, and thus ensure their damnation. Jayadeva's *Gīta Govinda*, however, which contains one of the earliest lists of incarnations, states that Viṣṇu became Buddha out of compassion for animals, in order to put an end to bloody sacrifice. This probably gives a clue to the true background of the Buddha avatāra. He was included in the list, as other deities were included, in order to assimilate heterodox elements into the Vaiṣṇavite fold.[7]

HINDUISM AND BUDDHISM: SOME PHILOSOPHICAL CONSIDERATIONS

It might, however, be argued that it is the Vedas and not the Purāṇas that are the foundational texts of Hinduism, and the Buddhists are known to explicitly reject Vedic authority. This then fixes a gulf between the two that no amount of goodwill can bridge. This argument possesses considerable force, but once again it seems that the spectacle of two Indic religious traditions grappling with ultimate concerns seems to generate a new perspective much more consistent with the evidence on hand. For instance, the Hindu revealed texts are known as śruti. Is it a mere accident that Buddhist texts often commence with the following line or a variant of it: evaṁ me śrutam.[8] It could be argued that the Buddhist texts are claiming to set themselves up as rivals to the Hindu śruti, and this could be the case. It could however also be argued that the word *Veda* had come to signify the accumulated wisdom of both the brāhmaṇas and the śramaṇas, which we may accept for our purposes here as referring to the Buddhists. So the point shifts from competition to convergence.

Of far greater significance, however, is the recognition that both the traditions are trying to grasp the ultimate truth. The foundational insights of Buddhism are the four noble truths (ariya saccāni) and the quintessential Hindu pronouncement—*Om tat sat*—also openly appeals to truth. What is crucial then is to recognize how these two traditions grapple with this angel, maybe the same angel: how they position themselves in relation to truth—engagement with which alone contains their ultimate justification.

A section from a sermon of the Buddha from the Majjhima Nikāya, which deals with the nature of consciousness and the chain of causation, becomes relevant at this point. This chain of causation itself, however, is not the focus of our interest at the moment but another simple and curious point, which is suggested by the reading of the following short passage from the sermon in which the Buddha puts questions to the monks and they respond.

> "Do you agree, monks, that any given organism is a living being?" "Yes, sir."
>
> "Do you agree that it is produced by food?" "Yes, sir."
>
> "And that when the food is cut off the living being is cut off and dies?" "Yes, sir."
>
> "And that doubt on any of these points will lead to perplexity?" "Yes, sir."
>
> "And that Right Recognition is knowledge of the true facts as they really are?" "Yes, sir."
>
> "Now if you cling to this pure and unvitiated view, if you cherish it, treasure it, and make it your own, will you be able to develop a state of consciousness with which you can cross the stream of transmigration as on a raft, which you use but do not keep?" "No, sir."
>
> "But only if you maintain this pure view, but don't cling to it or cherish it . . . only if you use it but are ready to give it up?" "Yes, sir."[9]

Please make a special note of the fact that when the Buddha asks the monks, "Do you hold these views?" they say "yes," but when he asks them, "Do you cling to these views?" they say "no."

Professor A. L. Basham explains the significance of the difference in these reactions as follows:

> Buddhism is a practical system, with the single aim of freeing living beings from suffering. This passage apparently implies that even the most fundamental doctrines of Buddhism are only means to that end and must not be maintained dogmatically for their own sake. It suggests also that there may be higher truths, which can only be realized as Nirvāṇa is approached.[10]

In other words, the sayings of the Buddha themselves must not be allowed to become dogma. They are not identical with the truth; they lead to the truth. Now what is the attitude of the Hindu school of thought often discussed in the context of Buddhism, namely, Advaita Vedānta, in this respect? We have seen how Buddhists are supposed to relate to Buddhist scriptures, let us now hear M. Hiriyanna explain how Advaita Vedāntins need to view the Vedas. He explains the "exact function of revelation" as follows:

> The aim here, as in the case of other Indian doctrines, is not merely to grasp the ultimate truth intellectually but to realize it in one's own experience. The scripture as such, being a form of verbal testimony, can however convey only mediate knowledge. To attain the ideal therefore means to advance farther than merely comprehending the scriptural truth. Scriptural knowledge, accordingly, is not sufficient, though necessary; and like reason, it also therefore becomes only a subsidiary aid to the attainment of the goal. The Upanishads themselves declare that when a person has seen this truth for himself, he outgrows the need for the scriptures. "There a father becomes no father; a mother, no mother; the world, no world; the gods, no gods; the Vedas, no Vedas." Thus we finally get beyond both reason and revelation, and rest on direct experience (*anubhava*). Hence if Advaita is dogmatic the dogma is there only to be transcended. Further, we should not forget that revelation itself, as

stated in an earlier chapter, goes back to the intuitive experience of the great seers of the past. It is that experience which is to be personally corroborated by the disciple.[11]

The similarity of the two traditions in their attitudes toward scriptural authority is hard to miss. It is easy to suggest that one has been influenced by the other. But to do so would be to miss the real point—that both are reflecting an attitude of the Indic religious tradition in common, rather than a case of mutual influence. In this common search for truth, however, it is possible to come up with different conclusions. And again it is a part of the spirit of the Indic religious tradition to honor the various conclusions, even if they differ, on account of the sublimely ambiguous nature of the enterprise one is engaged in.

Consider the following two statements pertaining to the ultimate reality. The first is found in the Upaniṣads and is translated as follows by the Buddhist scholar who has drawn attention to it:

> The sun shines not there, nor the moon and stars,
>
> These lightings shine not, much less this (earthly) fire!
>
> After Him, as He shines, doth everything shine,
>
> This whole world is illuminated with His light.[12]

He goes on to refer then to a Buddhist parallel and says:

> In the *Udāna* we find a similar passage, which reads as follows:
>
> Where earth, water, fire and air do not penetrate;
>
> There the stars do not glitter, nor the sun shed its light;
>
> The moon too shines not but there is no darkness there.

Here there is no theistic interpretation of the experience and we earlier explained why such an interpretation would be erroneous. Besides, many of the metaphysical ideas about soul (ātman) which are rejected in Buddhism are to be found in the Upaniṣads, so that it would be quite misleading to identify the two.[13]

True, the two should not be identified, but does one exclude the other? What is being suggested is that once one begins to look upon Hinduism and Buddhism as two subsystems within a more encompassing Indic religious tradition, these differences take on a different hue—they take on not the color of violence but that color that any description of ultimate reality must take on, once it is refracted by the mind. To cite an example from physics, it is no longer a question of whether the wave theory of light is correct or the particle theory of light is correct. It is rather the case that certain aspects of the behavior of light are better understood on the assumption that light behaves like a wave, while certain other aspects of its behavior are better understood on the assumption that light behaves like a particle. But there is no doubting of the fact of light, just as there is no need to ab initio doubt the claim that according to both Advaita Vedānta and Buddhism enlightenment is possible in this very life. Thus, when it comes to the crunch, it could be plausibly argued that Hinduism and Buddhism cover the same ground, although one might wish to add that, while traveling over the same ground, Hinduism tends to take the more scenic route.

Some may be inclined to consider the lens being proposed for viewing the interaction between Hinduism and Buddhism in the past and in the present, and in the future as well, as too academic or esoteric, perhaps even idiosyncratic. One would therefore like to say something by way of self-extenuation regarding the suspicion that the approach adopted here may be an armchair one and not one drawn from the field. However, it finds support in the field as well, provided one is willing to step over from India into Nepal.

In the year 2004, Princeton University Press published an English translation of a book on Hinduism written in German by Professor Axel Michaels, under the title *Hinduism: Past and Present*. Therein Axel Michaels reports:

A Nepali, asked if he was a Hindu or a Buddhist, answered: "Yes." All these answers may be imagined with a typical Indian gesture: the head slightly bent and softly tilted, the eyelids shut, the mouth smiling.[14]

Apparently, this experience made quite an impression on the German scholar, because he alludes to it again later on at the end of the following passage:

Therefore, the views of "there is only one god" and "all gods are one" are not so far from one another in the Hindu religions as has often been held. "Thou shalt not make unto thee any graven image" (Exodus 20:4) can also lead to the conclusion: Thou shalt not make only a single graven image. Hence, there is not *one* single word for god in Sanskrit, but many: *īśa/ īśvara* ("ruler"), *bhagavat* ("elevated"), *prabhu* ("mighty"), *deva* ("god"), among others; the poet-saint Kabīr uses eighty-six terms for "god." . . .

The consequences of this notion of god are tangible in popular religiosity all over. To use an example I have already cited (chapter 1), if a Newar in Nepal is asked if he is a Hindu or a Buddhist, he might simply answer "yes." To restrict oneself to one position, one god, would be a stingy perspective of divinity for him: He can worship both Buddha and Śiva without getting into a conflict of belief.[15]

Conclusion

The time has now come to conclude. One hopes enough evidence has been presented to render the third option of viewing Hinduism and Buddhism credible. If the first option would put the primary focus on Hinduism and the second one on Buddhism, a hyphenated Hindu-Buddhist approach, which views them as dual but undivided, has its own insights to offer in the context of the history of Buddhism in India. One might even add that such a view might find favor with his Holiness, the Dalai Lama. As he was mentioned at the very outset of the chapter, concluding it with his remark might lend the presentation a certain symmetry and even help conceal such lack of coherence as it might have possessed.

During the course of an interview conducted on November 22, 1992, the Dalai Lama made the following statement, which one might wish to cite as one concludes:

> When I say that Buddhism is a part of Hinduism, certain people criticize me. But if I were to say that Hinduism and Buddhism are totally different, it would not be in conformity with truth.[16]

Fundamentalism and Interfaith Dialogue

Harvey Cox Jr.

It was the best of times; it was the worst of times." These are the opening words of Charles Dickens's famous novel *A Tale of Two Cities*. The phrase might, however, very well describe the situation of interreligious relations in the world since that terrible day five years ago. It's a time of paradox in the relations of the religious traditions to each other. On the one hand, interreligious dialogue seems to be, and indeed is, flourishing. There are more organizations and conferences and seminars and centers and programs devoted to this topic and these themes than in any previous time in history. They're flowering. However, we also live in a world of dangerous animosity, between and among religious traditions. My colleague Professor Samuel Huntington warns that we may be heading for a bloody clash of civilizations between what he designates as Islamic on one side and Judeo-Christian civilizations on the other. Sometimes he calls it the West against the rest. I think he is wrong for a number of reasons, one of which is the "welcome marbling" of religious expressions around the world. We're all mixed in with each other, and we're not really any longer centered in any particular civilizational blocs, a very healthy development. Between these two contradictory trends—all these positive things that are going on and this dangerous animosity—we have an explanation for what is going on. It has to do with the fact that, due to immigration, travel, Internet, diaspora of all religions around the world, we are now in each other's faces; we are now each other's neighbors.

So I want to direct my remarks here to three angles that we need to address in a triangle of challenges and that present themselves to us as we take a step into the future, away from the five years that have passed since September 11. These all have to do with some tendencies that should not go unnoticed as we proceed with these conversations. The first is the appearance, in the last century, in each of the traditions, of what some refer to as a fundamentalist movement; that is, a strong reaction against interfaith dialogue, which is viewed as a lethal danger to the integrity of the faith. The second is a certain lack of candor in interfaith dialogue, a kind of politeness, a kind of a reticence, that sometimes inadvertently hampers interfaith communication. And the third is a reluctance to speak about or exchange views on the inevitable political dimension of interfaith conversation, the context in which these dialogues go on. Let me speak a little bit about each of these.

I'm concerned about the term *fundamentalist* in particular. It is a word that was coined in the early part of the twentieth century in the United States by those conservative Protestants who believed that biblical scholarship, the theory of evolution, and social gospel were threatening what they took to be the very core of Christianity—the "fundamentals." They issued a number of pamphlets called *The Fundamentals* and began calling themselves "fundamentalists" who would defend these fundamentals—all of them theological fundamentals—the virgin birth; the divine inspiration, and indeed the inerrancy, of scriptures; physical resurrection—all theological terms. One of the great mysteries of fundamentalism, in the United States at least, in the last hundred years, has been its transmutation from an explicitly theological religious movement to an almost entirely political movement with strong political influence.

The term *fundamentalism*, however, very quickly began to be applied elsewhere, to some Muslims and some Jews, all of whom do not like the term to be applied to them. It doesn't help very much in describing radical movements in Hinduism or Buddhism or Shinto. Nevertheless, it is still used to designate those allegedly conservative wings appearing in each of the traditions. I use the word "allegedly" here because I don't believe these are really conservative movements. They are modern movements. They are modern movements that seek to retrieve, very selectively, elements from the past of a tradition, from a text, from a ritual, from a particular period, and then deploy that on certain fronts in the religious and political modern world. They're modern movements that call themselves "conservative."

The two fronts on which fundamentalists in all traditions fight their battles are what might be called the outside front and the inside front. The outside front is against certain tendencies in the modern world, especially in the equality of women and other such things. Yet, at the same time, they embrace eagerly and uncritically certain aspects of modernity, such as advertising, the latest management techniques, communications technologies. I've noticed, though, in studying these movements, that they often reserve their most vitriolic comments, their most vigorous opposition, not for

the outsider, but what they consider to be the fifth column within their own traditions, those who are abandoning or betraying their tradition. So nobody is blamed more vociferously by right-wing Jews than other Jews, or Hindus by other Hindus, or Christians by fundamentalist Christians.

The Muslim Brotherhood, for example, which was founded in Egypt—one of its earliest leaders was Sayyid Qutb, one of the intellectual founders of Muslim renewal—opposed, at the time, most of the movements of the modern world—communism, capitalism, nationalism—in the interest of establishing what they wanted to call an original Islamic *ummah,* informed by Qur'anic justice and equality. The attacks, however, the criticisms, were focused almost entirely on what they called "pseudo-Muslims," not primarily on the West, but only secondarily, because what they consider to be "pseudo-Muslims" were the ones who were playing into the hands of ruling elites and of colonial powers and were taking their societies back to what they call *jahiliya;* that is, the period of impiety and chaos and injustice preceding the coming of the Qur'an. The leaders of al Qaeda have said time and time again that their major enemies are the allegedly Muslim regimes, the West—and only secondarily, the United States in particular—for supporting those regimes which they believe are tyrannizing their own people. This is why they're especially opposed to Saudi Arabia, which rules explicitly in the name of Islam, protecting the sacred sites.

Something similar is happening in Israel. Sometimes the internal confrontation there is depicted as one between secular and religious Israelis, but it really is between two different forms of religion, even though the early founders of Zionism called themselves secular, even agnostic, like Ben-Gurion and others. Still, the language of Zionism is redolent with biblical and religious references. The word *Zion* itself, for example, is derived from the biblical name for Jerusalem. On the other side is the newly arisen movement of what some people call messianic Zionism; that is, a mixture of Orthodox Judaism and Zionism, the inspiration for which was Rabbi Abraham Kook, sparked especially by the Israeli victory in the 1967 war and inspiring the settler movement, which claims to want to conquer and settle the whole of the Eretz Yisrael. Some people call this the land of fundamentalism.

In the United States we see the same thing. The American religious Right condemns Hollywood and activist judges, but they reserve their most potent fusillades for other Christians who disagree with them on all kinds of issues. Notice, however, again, that the main agenda for the religious Right in America today is not one of theological content. It is not about biblical inerrancy or the atonement but what they call traditional values, much of which has only a very peripheral connection with historic Christianity. Remember also that Gandhi was not assassinated by a Muslim but by a fellow Hindu, and Prime Minister Rabin was not assassinated by a Palestinian Muslim but by a devoted Zionist Jew, enacting what he believes the Torah instructed him to do. In tradition after tradition, everywhere in the world, we can observe this burgeoning of a fundamentalist wing, which fights both within its own tradition and outside, sometimes with a special venom toward those on the inside.

So where does this leave interfaith dialogue? We have three difficulties to overcome, and I want to call them the difficulty of achieving religious candor in interfaith conversation, in stimulating intrafaith, as well as interfaith, communication, and in being willing to include a discussion of the political dimension within which all of this goes on. I've noticed, in many interfaith meetings, that there's a certain reluctance to bring up questions that might seem to be disruptive, irrelevant, or a threat to the atmosphere of congeniality and collegiality. This often happens. We avoid, either consciously or unconsciously, bringing up things that might offend the other party. We don't want to rock the boat. So, we as Christians, for example, just love to talk about how Jewish Jesus was, what a prominent place he has in the Qur'an, and to be so grateful for that. We should be. Or we muse about how much we need to learn from the lovely Buddhist tolerance or from the generous Hindu inclusivism, as indeed we do have to learn. But at the

same time, all of our traditions are enmeshed in political and cultural turmoil. This pattern of tactical avoidance, though it may preserve a certain atmosphere, eventually leads to evading hard questions. It leads to obscuring the involvement, the inconvenient factor, that throughout history, conflicts within and between religious traditions have been suffused with political element, and such detextualized conversations—and I repeat, not all of the meetings are like this—can therefore lead to a false sense of optimism about the interfaith relationships and the inevitable disillusionment that sets in when they don't seem to work out as we had hoped. For this reason, I warmly commend the planners of this conference for being bold enough to schedule discussions of the Middle East conflict while we are here in Montreal, and of same-sex marriage. This was courageous and a step certainly in the right direction, which I hope sets an example for other conferences in the future, where we need to do more of that, in a delicate, diplomatic, and frank way.

It's also becoming clear that religious peacemaking, which is a better term than interreligious dialogue—we have an objective in these dialogues, not just to talk to each other, but to make peace among the religions and therefore contribute to peace among the nations and civilizations. We need to do three things. We need to deepen our conversation with other traditions, but also with the other wing of our own traditions, and with the political world in which these two inevitably take place. So I'd like to suggest a couple of changes here, in how we proceed with interreligious conversations. The first is, we need to recognize this other wing and to recognize the candor which is needed if we're going to talk with each other, both within and without our traditions, moving away from an exclusive emphasis on cultivating harmony—good feelings—into a phase of honest questioning, especially questioning the toxic ingredients in both our own tradition and in other traditions. And we all have them. They leap out of the pages of the scriptures. They blemish the historical records of each of our faiths. Any reader of the Hebrew scriptures or the book of Revelation in the New Testament knows about slaying all the Canaanites in order to take back the land, or casting the unbelievers into the sea of fire. The Qur'an, unfortunately, has certain such passages as well. Some people call them the "texts of terror." Now unfortunately a lot of people seem adept at uncovering these texts in other people's scripture but are less aware of the ones in their own. We all have them. And we have them in our histories as well. Think about the Crusades, the rivers of blood (unleashed) in Jerusalem by the fourth Crusade, the sacking of Constantinople, in my own tradition. There it is. And to deny it is a kind of false innocence, a kind of disingenuousness, if you will, which in the long run really doesn't contribute to religious peacemaking. We're embarrassed by these elements in our own tradition. We're embarrassed by these texts of terror. But we simply have to uncover them, cope with them, and ask the question of why they often remain moribund for centuries and then suddenly they spark into flames in order to incite violence in other times. How does that happen? It's a hermeneutical question: How are texts interpreted? But it's also a political question: How are texts used, resurrected, deployed for strategic, tactical, political purposes?

I want to suggest that this is an issue that, although we need to struggle with it within our own traditions, we need to help each other. Perhaps a Muslim or a Hindu reading the Christian scriptures can help uncover these texts and gently force us to confront them, and we might even be able to help Muslims or Hindus to confront those elements and ask those questions about their own. It's a risky enterprise. It exposes vulnerabilities on both sides. But I think it's a necessary step to take. If we can move beyond, for example, constantly quoting those lovely exhortations to peacemaking in the Hebrew scriptures—how many times have we heard those during conferences such as this? Or Jesus' recommendation that we love our neighbors? And rarely Jesus' statement that "I come to bring a sword." That isn't often quoted. What do we do with that? But there it is. And to candidly face these, discuss them with each other and recognize we have a common problem, and not just a singular problem in each of the traditions, is something we need to do.

I want to also stress the need for what I call *intra*faith conversation. We must move with more energy to meet, to understand, to appreciate, to argue with those who have circled the wagons within each of our traditions. We don't do enough of that. And unless we do, we face the grim prospect of a future in which open-minded members of each faith devote increasing amounts of time to dialogue and colloquies with other open-minded members of other traditions, and the fundamentalist wings of all of our traditions are left behind. But they're not left behind to wane. They're growing and getting stronger, in many instances, because they are isolated and even more truculent. So we'll end up, paradoxically, with more and deeper divisions than we once had, only running along internal instead of external fault lines. In this case, the interfaith movement would then be defeated by its own apparent success, and no one wants to see that.

I recognize the objection to these suggestions I'm making: "You simply can't talk to these people!" I've heard this a number of times. "You can't talk to fundamentalists. They won't listen. They already have the answer, so why talk?" Well, I want to report here from a personal perspective. In the last ten years, I've been trying very hard to make sure we include intrafaith conversations in our program at Harvard at the Center for the Study of World Religions. We have invited delegations, first from Liberty University, founded by Jerry Falwell. Faculty and students came, visited us. We visited them. Later we had a similar delegation from Regent University, founded by Pat Robertson, and we found that the people who came thought nobody wanted to hear them, nobody wanted to meet them. They considered themselves to be treated dismissively, as hicks or rednecks, or out of step with the world. And to be invited to have a conversation, even though the conversation might not have produced very much, was a very important step for them, and, I think, also for us. Of course it would be difficult. But this signals, perhaps even more emphatically, the need to do so. It can be done. The discussion we had with the faculty from Regent University was on how to present and advocate religious values in the public realm. We took one of the most controversial subjects. We had a private gathering of five or six faculty members from our faculty, and five or six from theirs. Congenial. Then we had a whole evening of discussion, open to the public, which filled one of the largest halls at the university. It just isn't true that you just can't talk with these people. It's hard. It's difficult. But it isn't impossible, and I'm here to testify to that.

Most Christians I know of who are interested in interfaith dialogue would far prefer to spend an afternoon talking with the Dalai Lama than with Jerry Falwell, and I can well understand how, because I've talked with both of them. I can understand that. But you should not avoid dialogue because it's difficult. It is a reason to try to enter into it. Of course these conversations will be difficult. They're difficult because these are folks in our own tradition who share many of the core beliefs that we share, and therefore it grates on us more when we disagree on what we think is so essential. But this means that both sides try, understandably, to avoid it. We have to make special efforts to include these fellow Muslims, these fellow Christians, these fellow Jews in our conversations. Otherwise, what we're going to see is the deepening of the confrontation, the calumny, the condemnation, and the constant threat of poisonous schism, which will get us nowhere. Sibling rivalry, that say, is one of the nastiest kinds, and here I think we have an illustration of how difficult it is. I remember the first murder recorded in the Bible was a brother who killed his own brother, strikingly over the proper way to sacrifice to the God they both worshiped.

Now the possibility of such *intra*faith dialogue is not as foreboding. And after years of effort, the Divinity School at Harvard has just appointed its first fully tenured and permanent professor of evangelical theology. It'll be a permanent position on our faculty. This is a recognition that the evangelical tradition is not simply something transient. It's there. It's changing. It has its own history. It is an important part of the conversation—the ecumenical conversation and the interfaith conversation. We are hoping, and already finding, that more evangelical and Pentecostal students are enrolling, and I think this is all for the good.

[It is interesting] reaching back into history and finding that, back in the nineteenth century, with evangelicals in the United States, who were the sponsors and champions of abolitionism and the peace movement. William Jennings Bryan, in the early twentieth century, was a great champion of peacemaking in the world. So there is that tradition to be reclaimed. The president of the National Association of Evangelicals gave a blistering speech in which he condemned the religious Right, including the Christian Right, in the United States, as an aberration, and a regrettable one at that. Interesting statement. An aberration and a regrettable one. I can't think what an unregrettable aberration would be. He put it pretty strongly. Now if somebody who was the director secretary of the National Council of Churches, or of the World Council of Churches, had said that, no one would have taken notice. But this was a high official in the National Association of Evangelicals. Something was happening. The *Boston Globe* reporting his speech, carrying the headline: "Official Chides Christian Right." The following year, Rick Warren, pastor of the huge church in Saddleback, California, led efforts by evangelicals and other Christians to organize a movement called Creation Caretakers against Global Warming and later that same year organized evangelicals to join with Jewish leaders, Catholics, and mainline Protestants to sign a courageous statement opposing torture and publishing the statement in the *New York Times*, just as the administration was dodging the issue and even advocating certain forms of what it euphemistically calls "harsh interrogation" of detainees. So there're a lot of possibilities. We had a wonderful discussion last year with some members of the Gordon-Conwell Faculty, an evangelical seminary in Boston, in which we talked about the impact of the so-called Left Behind novels, which they all deplored as much as we did. These were not universally accepted by evangelicals in the United States. Not at all. It's also true that, in other parts of the world, in Latin America in particular, the growth of evangelical Christianity is not replicating the American religious Right. If anything, it tends to be a little bit toward the democratic left in its voting records according to surveys of evangelicals in Latin America. And evangelicals there are looking for something equivalent to the social gospel they once condemned. They want it to come from their tradition and not to be borrowed from somebody else's.

So, maybe at the next session of our World Parliament of Religions, we could have some attention, maybe quite a bit of attention, to intrafaith as well as interfaith dialogue, and we could be more candid and open about the political contours in which these conversations go on.

So here we are, in a paradoxical age, the best of times and the worst of times. We need to face these three directions: toward other faiths, toward those in our own tradition, and to the larger political context. Let's make it the best of times instead of the worst of times. I think we're making a good start in Montreal this week. Thank you.

QUESTIONS AND ANSWERS FOR THE AUTHOR

Question: When one is thinking about an example of what might be the best of times, or a good time at least, in interfaith dialogue, a period that comes to mind is the ninth to the twelfth centuries in Andalusia. There we have an instance, it seems to me, of a very rich conversation that begins to develop initially between Jewish peripatetics and Islamic peripatetics. The religions in some sense can talk to one another in that time precisely because there's a dialogue between religion and philosophy. And the Christians are introduced into this with the translation of the texts of Aristotle from Arabic into Latin, and Thomas Aquinas becomes part of the project invoking Maimonides' *Moreh* in his *Summa Theologica*. And it seems to me that—charging into the Enlightenment—the Protestant tradition, the Anglo-American liberal Protestant tradition, has a lot to answer for for undoing the rich dialogue of religion and philosophy. Places like Oxford and Cambridge and Harvard have

contributed mightily to preventing this rich dialogue between religion and philosophy. I think it is one of the great scandals, from my perspective, of what the Enlightenment has accomplished. It may be that the difficulty of interfaith dialogue may owe a great deal to the lack of a dialogue between religion and philosophy. I guess my question is: Do you think the revival of dialogue between religion and philosophy might be the necessary condition for a dialogue among the religions?

Answer: That's a very provocative question. [One thinks of the] period in Andalus, in which southern Spain and northern Morocco were part of a Muslim-ruled province for four hundred years or more, in which Jews, Christians, and Muslims lived together in relative harmony. There was some tension here and there, but it was a remarkable period. Last year, I was part of a travel-study seminar of Harvard alumni and others, studying that period of Andalus. I was very impressed with that, and sorry that it is not given as much attention as it should be. Christian artisans were helping to build the mosques. St. John of the Cross was reading Arabic texts as he composed his *Dark Night of the Soul*. We know there was an awful lot of interaction. One astonishing thing was the sultan of one of the great cities there—the Muslim sultan—appointed the head of the Jewish community as his foreign minister and in fact sent him over to Constantinople to try to forge an alliance between Andalus and the Byzantine Empire against the other wing of the Muslims in and around Baghdad. But as a matter of fact enlisting the rabbi of the Jewish community seems to be a sign of interfaith vitality.

Now, to the issue of science, I think you're entirely right about that, and I plead guilty. I think what a lot of the big secular research universities have done in the last hundred years is abandon the historical, philosophical task of trying to understand the big picture, which necessarily includes religious dimensions. This wasn't the case with William James and Whitehead—the giants that strode the earth at our faculty in those days. It has, however, happened, and it is to the expense of philosophy as well as religion. I think it has impoverished both sides. I attribute some of it, indeed, not so much perhaps to Protestant liberalism as to the influence of neo-orthodoxy—Protestant neo-orthodoxy—which didn't think you need philosophy. You had the word of God and that was it. Fortunately, the conversation between religion and philosophy is coming back, and it's coming back, interestingly, through two avenues. One is what you might call the philosophy of public life, public ethics. What do you base public values on? Michael Sandel of the Government Department is a philosopher who's inviting that kind of conversation. The other way it's coming back is, of course, the vexing issues raised by science and technology, which philosophers are beginning to deal with and which they now believe that some of the ways of thinking about these issues, especially end-of-life issues, have been part of the long tradition of Christian ethical theological discourse. So it is really beginning to happen again, and I think it will make an important contribution, because I do think that the three traditions you mentioned, that were there in Andalus—the Muslim, Christian, and Jewish—profiting precisely from having some of the same philosophical texts. They were sitting around the table having each other translate them. They were working together, and that may happen again.

Question: [You spoke about] our own ability to put our own houses in order, especially relations between moderates and extremists. Since you have some expertise on the rights concerning cows, may I ask how one can manage this when it would appear that both groups, the moderates and the extremists, have it as a sacred cow that they are not to dialogue with each other?

Answer: [Let's say], for the moment, the fundamentalist wing has as at least part of their credo, "You don't talk to those guys." And those of us on the other side have as part of our credo, "There's no point talking to them." Now, there's a kind of fatalism in this. Somebody has to break the fatalistic chain. Now believe me, it took a lot of time for me to convince my colleagues to invite people from Liberty University or from Regent to come to

Harvard. I was criticized for that. "Why give these people a platform? Why do that?" Well, it is important if you are not going to allow the division, the chasm, to deepen and become even more poisonous. Somebody has to break the ice. And I think it's probably more our responsibility to break the ice. At least try. We were surprised by how quickly they responded. I think being invited to a major university probably helped, giving them a chance to be there and talk to other people. I think there are a hundred other universities and church groups that would do the same thing. We have an annual meeting, sponsored by the Massachusetts Council of Churches, which they call an "evangelical-liberal dialogue." We meet once a year, spend the whole day talking about this. The progress can be very slow, but what I want to say here. . . . Let me repeat a sentence or two from what I just said. These groups . . . neither of these groups is monolithic. There're changes within the evangelical community. It's growing, it's dispersing, it's changing, it's fragmenting. The old leadership of Robertson, Dobson, and Falwell is being displaced now by a new generation of young leaders. When President Bush went to Calvin College in Michigan last spring, his aides told him this was a good, safe place to go. It was a conservative, Calvinist college, and he would be welcome there. He was welcomed all right. He was welcomed by a huge student demonstration bearing banners saying the war in Iraq doesn't qualify, according to Christian standards, as just war. He was welcomed by a faculty petition, signed by a third of the faculty, that said the same thing. I was told that he was as nice as he could be, but he really blistered his aides when he got back to Washington for not warning him in advance about what to expect. Let us not think of this whole group now as a singular bloc, with an unmovable creed that they're not going to talk to anybody else. I think we simply have to keep trying.

Question: Just one last thing if I may. Dialogue is fine and is important. But what does one do about violence and terror and apathy, which seem to be equally if not more important than long-term dialogue?

Answer: You have to start by conversing with people. I'm a strong believer in the power of dialogue. I'm still influenced by Martin Buber, whom I read as a college student. I think we just have to keep trying. It's people who don't understand each other, with faulty information about each other, have stereotypes, images, who are willing to engage in violence against each other, and that can be, to some extent, mitigated by face-to-face meeting, even if the meetings are argumentative, even if the meetings are heated. At least you are meeting and you're talking and trying to listen to each other. I think that's better than nothing.

Question: I want to share with you some of my own experience and insight into this thing to see if you could give me another perspective on it. Coming from rural Georgia, where attempting such a thing with people in the community, I have found them dishonest, duplicitous, demeaning of other people, publicly defaming other people's character. I stopped talking with them. That's just a personal thing. The theological perspective, the notion of intrafaith dialogue. . . . I begin to wonder if we're still within the same faith. And the reason I say that is because when I look at the central claim of the fundamentalist tradition, they do not consider history central to the tradition. To me, they have branched off from Judaism and Christianity as much as Islam did, or Buddhism did out of Hinduism. The core of that position seems to be not Judeo-Christian in the least. And the point is, I'm not looking at ethics and I'm not even looking at this personal stuff, but it's the theological issue that Judaism and Christianity were always historical religions, and when you disregard that, you have vitiated the essence of that tradition.

Answer: That's true, and that's a very serious observation. It is also true, however, that even fundamentalists, if they eschew history, live in history. They live in history. History is changing around them. Regions they live in are changing. There are lots and lots of people in the world who are ex-fundamentalists. I could introduce you to a number of them, who once were but no longer are. And one of the reasons is, in order to keep up that kind of a bastion of nonrecognition of your own history or others' history, it takes a lot of energy. It takes a lot of energy to do that and to keep it going, especially if you meet more and more people who don't share exactly your perspective. Notice that the Southern Baptist Convention a couple of months ago wanted to pass a resolution suggesting that all Southern Baptists should withdraw from any kind of participation in the public school system. And it didn't pass at the meeting. However, the very idea that that could be thought of and then rejected by the hundreds and hundreds of Southern Baptists who teach in public schools or are principles or administrators suggests that it's not going to be possible for them to withdraw from certain elements of American religious pluralism. The girlfriend, the boyfriend, the pal down the street, the brother-in-law are not going to be people who agree with this, and the historical and personal interactions are going to go on. So maybe I'm really entirely too optimistic or innocent about this, but I don't think it hurts to try to have a conversation. I'm sorry that you've been impugned and insulted that way. I've had a little of that myself, and it's hard to take. It's very hard to take, but it shouldn't turn us around. I can remember the time when—not too many years ago, twenty-five years ago—someone donated some money to the Harvard Divinity School to add a Chair of Roman Catholic theological studies, and some of my friends and colleagues on the faculty said, "We can't do that! Catholics can't engage in free and open academic research and teaching. They have to do what the pope tell them. How can we have a Catholic on this faculty?" Well, that group was voted down, mainly because it was a 2.5-million-dollar grant, and we've had some of the finest and most cooperative kinds of Catholic scholars who are now not only teaching Catholic theology but teaching Bible and church history. So we can't allow the stereotype to continue to inform our perception of other groups when what we really need, and they need, is the experience of mutual exchange.

Question: I have a very quick question. Would Harvard be prepared to go to Liberty or Regent? Or is it just the other way around?

Answer: We did both. We had an exchange, and I actually gave a lecture at Regent. I was not introduced by President Robertson. But I spoke openly to a large group of students and faculty and had a wonderful evening talking to them. We plan to do some more of it.

Question: Thanks for inviting other religions to review the scriptures of major religions, at least the Christian traditions and the Jewish traditions. I'm talking for the Hindu traditions. How would you help Hindu traditional scholars or pundits to take a look at the major religious works and make their own observations? If you look back, seventeenth century onward, the Asian traditions, especially the Indic traditions, boiling down to the Vedic traditions, have been abused, misused, misinterpreted, or whatever you want to call it. And this team, they will have an opportunity to voice themselves in the West here. How would you help the traditional scholars of Hinduism to make their views known on the current world religions?

Answer: Fine question. One of my favorite examples of how a text can be read is, of course, the *Bhagavadgītā,* which is about war and about the encouragement by Krishna of Arjuna to engage in war. On one level, this can read as a very militaristic and violent text. However, it was the favorite text of Gandhi, because Gandhi read it as a metaphor of the struggle we all have against the violence within us. He read it as a spiritually informative text. So a lot of the question, I think, is what is technically called a hermeneutical question: How do we read such texts, not just on a scholarly level, but in what kind of historical setting and circumstance are they read? One method for this that we found rather useful and productive is to have scholars from, say, two traditions, say, Hindu and Christian, to come together and read a Jewish text. Or have a Hindu and Jewish scholar come together and read a text which is not theirs, like something from the New Testament. While we do this, we have the people for whom that is a primary text listening in but not necessarily contributing. And they learn something. I think we are now entering an era in which we cannot simply ponder our own texts. We have

to ponder each other's texts and do it together with each other, and we'll discover things that we hadn't seen before.

Question: Probably I did not clarify my issue. It is not about hermeneutics. It is about the foundational economics and trends in the publication industry in the academia. That's what I want you to make your observations please.

Answer: Well, you may be right. Maybe we should get another question because we're running out of time.

Question: Dr. Cox, I was fascinated with the idea that Harvard Divinity School has named its first evangelical professor of theology. And you mentioned that right in the context of inviting Regent and Liberty. Should we try to invite someone who has a diametrically opposed theological perspective to be a permanent part of our faculty or a permanent part of our group to have that opposing perspective? Or just from time to time to bring someone in and to maintain a particular perspective as a faculty that believes in this direction or that direction? You see the question?

Answer: I see exactly the question, and I think that would vary from one school to another. Our underlying perspective is, we want these major voices in at least the American religious landscape represented by those who are both scholars of that tradition and also, to some extent, practitioners of that tradition. We make no apology for that. That's the most valuable kind of voice we can have, and we want them to be a permanent part of our faculty conversation among ourselves and with our students. There may be schools in which that would not be relevant, but there are Jesuits schools now that have Muslims on their faculty. There are Jewish schools that have Christian members of the faculty. This is becoming more common, and I think it is a good thing. I think somehow maintaining the underlying thematic of a particular school is good, but that underlying thematic can even be strengthened and sharpened with the presence within the school of people with other perspectives.

Question: We have seen right now that, though the world is going toward secularism, but, at the time, theocratic stresses are increasing. But in the whole conference today, I've not seen much of an example of how the advancement or more growth of the theocratic states actually hampers the well-being of all secular nations all over the world. And I have seen quite a fraction of different lectures by different speakers in today's session, and I have found that they're trying to say that United States is the ultimate enemy of Islam, and this kind of talk is going around. There may be something in this, but one thing is not examined at all in any way, that in theocratic countries like Bangladesh and Pakistan, how the minorities are treated. [Their proportion] has come down in Bangladesh from 30 percent to 9 percent, in Pakistan from 24 percent to 1 percent. [These facts are never explained.] And also, if everyone thinks that my religion is to spread my religion, whether Islam or Christianity, how can that be at all possible when my outward motto is to Christianize the world or Islamize the world?

Answer: That's a very dangerous trend you point to, and I think the diminishing of religious minorities in any country, especially ones where their presence has been there for a long time, is a disastrous development and ought to be opposed at every turn. One of the great pleasures I have is the pleasure of teaching. And almost every class I give, teaching young men and women from Islamic countries, they all seem to be intensely interested in comparative religion, other religions, Christianity, Judaism, as well as their own. And they're living in a country in which there is religious pluralism and tolerance, and they will eventually be going back to leadership positions in their own countries. But I think it's a particularly foreboding development that countries that have had minorities that have been part of the weft and woof of their culture, sometimes for centuries, are making it harder for those minorities to stay there. I think it's a matter that needs all our attention.

Question: Good afternoon, Professor Cox. Thank you for hearing me. My husband and I run the New Seminary in New York, which ordained interfaith ministers, and something has come to our attention in the last couple of months that is particularly disturbing. We have heard that the religious Right, if you want to call it that, has called interfaith the next antichrist. I was wondering if you have heard that and if you could talk about that for a second.

Answer: I have not heard that, but I'm not, alas, entirely surprised by it. I think one has to be careful of how we say "the religious Right," as it's called. The religious Right is also not as monolithic as you might think, and there are different voices within it. But they're very suspicious. That's what I said in my talk. They're very, very suspicious of interfaith dialogue, many of them, and calling it antichrist, I guess, is just raising it to the highest caliber. So I wish we could have stopped on a better note than that, but thank you. It shows us we still have a lot of work to do.

Question: If I may . . . just a minute. . . . One thing I want to add. . . . The only words that we've been missing are—and I want to remind us of it in our teaching—and I'm going to say it in an old Latin expression that I learned when I was four years old. Shall I say it for you?

Answer: Yes.

Question: Ego amo tua. Shall I translate it?

Answer: Yes.

Questioner: I love you.

Toward a Culture of Peace

Fabrice Blée

In today's world, we are desperately in need of a culture of peace. Interreligious dialogue is seen as a key element in such a development. Although many initiatives have been taken in this area since the first Parliament of Religions was held in Chicago in 1893, we are reaching a point when we must consider what to do to foster more realistic and less idealistic relations. This concern was raised by the World Council of Churches in a congress titled Critical Moment in Interreligious Dialogue, held in Geneva in June 2005.[1] Being sensitive to this need, I am skeptical regarding the tendency to focus only on common points, an attitude that consists in avoiding all situations that might lead to conflict. Is it fair to ask religious leaders to support peace at all costs? Does this serve peace? If yes, what kind of peace? Or does it serve a specific world order? How then can a culture of peace be developed?

A culture of peace cannot be reduced to simply the effort of reaching a peace accord. Rather, it must be based on a pluralistic attitude that holds together an awareness of the interdependency of people, cultures, nations, and religions, and the respect for what makes us truly different and unique. Unity, peace, and harmony cannot gloss over or ignore the difficulties in dealing with the differences, in particular hopes and concerns, either doctrinal or

political. Such a confrontation is a necessary step on the path of interreligious dialogue. That is why I find the role of a spirituality of dialogue so important.

The central idea of my presentation is this: there is no culture of peace possible without the emergence of a spirituality of dialogue. Only such a spirituality can promote respect for religious otherness while accepting that there is no real separation between religion, politics, and spirituality. Here are three elements that must be considered as interactive if our intention is to promote mutual respect and understanding.

I propose to develop this idea briefly in four points. First, I would like to say something about what I mean by spirituality of dialogue. Second, I want to point out the relevance in not separating religion and political concern too quickly. Third, it is vital to reconnect religion and spirituality. Fourth, examining the last two points will allow me to show the importance of considering the link between spirituality and political concern. Finally, all these points will be followed by some concluding thoughts.

What Do I Mean by Spirituality of Dialogue?

My intention is neither to describe the historical development of a spirituality of dialogue nor to point out its theological implications. Instead, I refer you to my book *Le désert de l'altérité,* published in 2004. Here, let us just ask this question: What is at stake in a spirituality of dialogue? As soon as a dialogue is more than a mere conversation, as soon as our partner is received in our heart, as soon as we accept that we are received in our partner's milieu (that is, in another religious context), as soon as we are touched by another universal truth and worldview, dialogue becomes existential and begins to transform us deeply.

The relationship that comes out of such an encounter is certainly enriching and promising, but it also becomes a question for oneself, a source of tension, a challenging space wherein we face ourselves with our strengths as well as our weaknesses, a space wherein God talks to us in unknown ways. The inner dialogue resulting from this relationship is not easy. Our faith and beliefs are put at risk. Then the meeting, which is going on within oneself between two religious universes, two ways of feeling and praying, requires spiritual qualities and virtues. That is the reason why dialogue is seen as a spiritual act in itself.

A spirituality of dialogue comes out of a hospitality process through which we can accept being deeply touched by another religious experience while witnessing our own faith. It refers to a new religious consciousness stemming from a dialogue of religious experience, one of the four types of dialogue identified by the Pontifical Council for Interreligious Dialogue; that is, a sharing focused on each other's connection to the living God, the divine mystery.

In a spirituality of dialogue, religious otherness, that is, other believers as received in their religious differences and uniqueness, is not seen as a threat to our own religious identity but as the space where our identity is fully expressed, where I apply concretely what it means to be a Christian. Therefore, a spirituality of dialogue is not universal; it is always specific and has to be developed by each religious assembly in accordance with its own worldviews and doctrinal characteristics. However, in every case, a spirituality of dialogue will promote deep respect for religious otherness, true

listening to those who are different from us, and sincere mutual understanding. But this cannot be done unless we accept the impossibility of separating religion, political concern, and spirituality.

RELIGION AND POLITICAL CONCERN

The events of 9/11 have changed the perception of religion and its role regarding society and world development. Since then, it has become common to talk about religion on TV, in the news, and in political debates, a situation which would have appeared odd and unusual ten or fifteen years ago. Religions have become an issue. More and more people want to explore religions in order to understand more deeply the world they live in as well as many local and international tensions and conflicts. Peace has no future on this planet unless we pay attention to the various religious claims and hopes, unless we promote dialogue and mutual understanding among them.

One thing, however, must be remembered: for the majority of believers, religion is not a private activity; rather, it plays a great part in determining their behavior and decisions on social and political levels. In other words, religious identity "has direct repercussions for ethnic, political, and national identity."[2] Religions are not something added to cultures that would otherwise be naturally secular in themselves. On the contrary, culture and religion are often so intertwined that it would be impossible to extract what is properly cultural or religious. Each culture promotes a specific order and social organization, and the religious dimension is never neutral in such representations.

The ideal that promotes the separation between religion and politics certainly serves valuable and pragmatic goals, but it does not neutralize the will of many believers to act for a better world and society in accordance with their own religious values. In our global context, however, such an ideal cannot be imposed, even by force, as the only one to be applied in all contexts and cultures.

We are, therefore, led to ask this question: Within religion, how can we determine the correct course of action? In most religions, at least in the way they have been applied for centuries, a right action is determined not primarily by the welfare of the individual but in accordance with a specific cosmotheandric order that has to be preserved and promoted. From a religious point of view, peace cannot be reduced to individual security and the absence of conflicts, two elements that are overestimated in our Western world.[3] Considering this point, is it realistic and fair to invite all religious leaders, especially Muslim leaders, to promote a specific vision of peace at all costs?

If a culture of peace is vital, it should not be based on such a request. The shock between religious worldviews will be dramatic in today's world unless we facilitate dialogue. However, dialogue cannot succeed unless we pay serious attention to the interconnection between religion and political concern—between one's relationship to the sacred and the momentum to be involved in the structure of the city (polis). This momentum is inherent in all relationships involving the sacred.

If religions are not political institutions, they are at least circles wherein political actions are made. It is possible to ignore the social and political concerns of Hindus, Muslims, Jews, or Christians in various contexts, but this will not serve dialogue and peace; we will only play the game of a dominating political worldview, nourishing by the same token fundamentalism and violence. Here Raimundo Panikkar's question is relevant: "Is pluralism the stratagem to induce people to give up their own identities in order to create a new world order in which all cats are gray, all differences abolished under the pretext of tolerance and peace?"[4] It is precisely because the link between religion and political concern must not be neglected that it is necessary to recognize the interconnection between religion and spirituality.

Religion and Spirituality

A spirituality of dialogue can be seen as part of today's spiritual renewal, especially in the West. However, it does not yield to the current tendency to see spirituality as exclusive of religion. Such an opposition is inappropriate and damaging in many respects. Three remarks will help in understanding the present situation: First, religions have not become irrelevant, as was predicted decades ago; they have not been replaced by a disincarnated and multiform spirituality. Second, religions have no future except in the revitalization of their spiritual dimension. Third, in our pluralistic context, such a revitalization will be accomplished by taking an interreligious approach. Keeping these points in mind, it is clear why a spirituality of dialogue is so relevant: it actually prevents two dangers threatening interreligious dialogue and peace.

First of all, there is the danger that interreligious dialogue will be reduced to a mere diplomatic activity. This risk is all the more real because current political conflicts often have a religious dimension, and because the word dialogue itself, so often mentioned in the news regarding the geopolitical scene, refers to negotiation and aims at compromises.

The danger here is to see this approach becoming the main one: the opportunity to talk about peace and at the same time the pretext to stop the development of a spirituality of dialogue that would engage the church in new and challenging ways. Are we actually ready as Christians to make this step? Are we ready to lose in some ways to gain in others? The question is important, because if we refuse to make the step, dialogue could become simply a new strategy to meet particular and provincial interests; then it would become a tool at the service of political powers, and if so, peace has no chance.

Generally speaking, we see religions only as sociopolitical structures that have a strong influence on people. However, when we come to talk about faith and the spiritual dimension, we often focus on pathological, irrational, or other extreme behaviors. In my opinion, this means that, even though religions have a space in our society, they are not yet taken seriously. This will be the case as long as their deepest hopes, linked to salvation or liberation, of the spiritual encounter with the divine, or inner awakening, are not heard and respected. Only a spirituality of dialogue can preserve the "prophetic" voice of an interreligious encounter, in the sense that such a spirituality is rooted in a more profound dialogue with the divine presence, in the silence of love and humility.

What is at stake, then, in interreligious dialogue is not peace at all costs, for the simple reason that peace cannot be forced, just as the rules of dialogue cannot be imposed. We cannot control the other in dialogue; the little control we have, however, is over ourselves. What is at stake in dialogue is our openness to religious otherness, our effort to understand and respect the religious system and experience of the Hindu or Muslim partner, in the full affirmation of our own faith and identity. Here, compromises do not exist.

A second danger related to the opposition between spirituality and religion is to believe in a universal spirituality beyond all religious belonging to which everybody would join sooner or later. This would be the pretext to call every religious leader to promote peace without paying attention to local and contextual problems and concerns. A spirituality of dialogue rejects such an opposition between spirituality and religion. It does not yield to the temptation that consists of believing that religion is an obstacle to dialogue and spirituality its solution. On the contrary, religious structure can offer an important support in helping dialogue last and progress, whereas circles known as the most spiritual sometimes sustain rivalries and unhealthy tensions.

A spirituality of dialogue does not aim at the fusion of interacting religious systems or at the creation of a universal spirituality beyond all religious structure. It does not promote a unique and abstract truth that every believer should adopt, whatever his or her religion. If a dialogue lived at the spiritual level is considered promising, it is neither because it requires ignoring religious doctrines and structures of one's partner nor because one minimizes the fact that they are different from ours. It is because these religious doctrines and structures are considered seriously and rooted in the effort to reconnect with the divine mystery in which they find their raison d'être.

A spirituality of dialogue takes seriously religious systems while opening them to the unlimited and uncontrolled presence of God. This prevents all risk of absolutism. Hence, religious systems are kept incomplete, therefore always open to dialogue, and to mutual understanding and enrichment.

SPIRITUALITY AND POLITICAL CONCERN

It is perilous to think that spirituality has nothing to do with political concern or that it leads necessarily to peace and harmony. True, spirituality is the driving force allowing religion to accomplish its goal of peace—peace understood, however, not as an absence of war but as liberation or salvation, a fullness transcending both the visible and invisible worlds.

Now, this liberation has an individual aspect as well as a collective aspect, and implies, to some extent, a fight. There is the fight within, the battle of Jacob against the angel, and there is also the fight without, a fight for social justice and liberation. Both of these battles go together. Even though the call for liberation is universal, it is always rooted in a specific community facing specific problems requiring specific battles for justice and freedom.

Liberation, justice, and freedom are based on the search for respect, dignity, and integrity. No one can contribute to peace without first receiving respect and dignity. When there is no respect, there is humiliation, and humiliation nourishes hatred and violence. Respect is the key condition to peace, and respect is sustained by love and humility. In many ways, respect is beyond our own capability; that is why it can be seen as a divine gift, sustained by the Holy Spirit. The divine power helps us to pay respect as well as to receive respect and dignity. This is true at the individual and collective levels.

It is not surprising, therefore, to see spiritual people, or mystics, involved in political debates, in battles and conflicts in order to fight for what they think is right, for justice and dignity. History teaches that interiority has a great impact on the organization of the city. Saint Benedict, Saint Bernard, Saint Joan of Arc, and Martin Luther are among those who have initiated great changes in social consciousness and behaviors. The more the fight for change is rooted in faith and transcending reality, the deeper the changes.

Each religion has its own understanding and vision about liberation and its process. Certainly there are similar ethics among religions, but I doubt these ethics are applied with the same logic and priorities. The idea of global peace including and involving all particular religious communities and cultural contexts is a new idea. I do not say that such an idea is impossible to concretize; I say only it is not an automatic process.

It is a demanding process that requires the participation of everyone, every partner of dialogue. In this process, one cannot avoid the step that consists of understanding with respect the doctrinal and political coherence of our partner's religious experience. We need to elaborate a new approach of religious otherness, an approach in which religious otherness is not an obstacle to the process of liberation but part of it.

Conclusion

I like Panikkar's idea: there is no "pluralistic religion" but only a "pluralistic attitude" toward religion.[5] This means that Christians, Muslims, and Hindus have their own conceptions of the ultimate reality, the absolute, the universal, and from their conception comes their approach to other religions. A Christian will never be fully at home among Muslims or Hindus; the Muslim never fully at home among Christians and Hindus; and so on. However, each of them can choose to practice hospitality, to welcome the religious otherness, and to develop this approach within their own tradition and from their own categories.

As far as Christians are concerned, they are called to apply Jesus's commandment in a new way: to love their enemies. In Christian history, enemies par excellence have been members of other religious traditions and heretics, those who prayed and believed in a different way. Christians are called to receive others in their hearts with what is important to them: their faith, beliefs, hopes, and deepest aspirations. This can be done only if we accept the connection between religion, politics, and spirituality.

It is much easier to deal with political concerns in interreligious dialogue when this dialogue is rooted in a spiritual perspective, supported with a spirituality of dialogue, and based on values such as faith, love, humility, and detachment. Peace does not depend on security, on building a fortress around us. Rather, it depends on faith and confidence: confidence that friendship can grow out of tensions and conflicts; confidence in the divine presence who, in her glory, transforms us and the world toward harmony; confidence that this divine presence expresses herself through unknown ways; and confidence that love awakens love, respect awakens respect, whereas too much security kills it.

However, a "pluralistic attitude" toward religions cannot be improvised. A spirituality of dialogue must be elaborated, developed, and taught. Spirituality does not lead necessarily to this attitude, and it can promote sectarian views. That is why interreligious education is so important in our societies. It is urgent that a new spiritual and religious consciousness prevail, a new consciousness based on respect and dignity. But the question still remains: are we ready to go in this direction, and to face the difficulties attached to it?

RELIGION AND THE TWENTY-FIRST CENTURY

Toward a Global Spirituality

INTRODUCTION

Many observers have noticed a trend away from "religion" and toward "spirituality," with spirituality coming more and more to be seen as antithetical to religion when religion is identified with institutional religion. And thus, almost by definition, spirituality is something which is not structured like religion. Yet spirituality too has its own myriad structures, not so much institutional as ideational. This section is devoted to an examination of the varieties of spiritual experience.

The word *spiritual* is an ambiguous one but could perhaps be given a clearer provenance by relating it to states of consciousness. We are all aware of our body; let us call this physical consciousness. But it is sometimes transcended when we become engaged in, say, reading an absorbing book. At that time, we are in a state of mental rather than physical consciousness. Spirituality consists of the claim that there is a deeper state of consciousness, absorption which results in the loss of both physical and mental consciousness, just as the absorption in mental consciousness can result in loss of physical consciousness.

This global trend toward spirituality acts as a counterweight to the global trend toward fundamentalism, and the reader might feel inclined to welcome it on that account even as one feasts on its enormous variety.

Religion Is Central to Human Affairs

Part of the Problem, Part of the Solution

Didiji

My Divine Brothers and Sisters, Namaskar! Today I stand here to represent Revered Pandurang Shastri Athavale—Dadaji, my father, and Swadhyaya, the grassroots initiative he founded in India in the early forties of the last century. His life was an expression of his love for God and humankind. He inspired Swadhyayees to love and work selflessly in the society and live as one divine family. I bring with me love and greetings of this family of millions of Swadhyayees from across the world.

We have gathered here to discuss and understand issues that are of immense importance for the existence and well-being of humankind. I take it that, behind the invitation extended to me, the conveners of this congress too have recognized the contribution and the potential of Swadhyaya. I deeply and sincerely thank them.

Quest for development and improvement of quality of life on this planet has been a constant driving force of humankind. Many initiatives have been taken in that direction by various concerned agencies. Science and technology is one such agency that has succeeded in lowering the barriers of geographical distance and has made the world a global village. It has eased the way for globalizing any idea or concept. Industry, trade, commerce, and services have taken the lead in this drive toward globalization. Different cultures from different parts of the world too have found their way to distant hearts and minds.

However, in the last few decades or so, we have witnessed widespread resistance to changes taking place in the name of development, modernization, nation-building, and world order in different global settings. The resistance has taken many shapes. Convulsions resulting from the rise of fundamentalism in almost all the major religions of the world seem to be one of them. Religion, in one form or the other, is as old as humanity and is an inseparable part of human life. It has a profound impact on individual life as well as social arrangements. Any idea of development that does not consider this aspect of human life tends to generate resistance. Even today, the role of religion has not diminished in human affairs. Indeed, it is not only involved and concerned with human problems but has also deeply affected contemporary developments.

At one level, September 11 could be seen as a metaphor of this resistance that has also triggered an accelerated search for some kind of lightning rod to cope with certain hurt religious feelings. At another level, it has served to emphasize the centrality of religions in human affairs. It has forced us to accept or rather concede that religions do play

259

a significant role in human life—an integrative role as society's essential enzyme and, at the same time, a disintegrative role leading to contemporary dilemmas and unrest.

If, then, religions have so many facets, the question is: What is religion? Despite the serious threat of being undermined by science and technology, why has it survived? We need to better our understanding of it. Instead of getting into any typology, I will limit my search for definitions of religion within my own tradition, that is, the "Indic" tradition. Our commonly used word for religion is *dharma*, though it is an unsatisfactory synonym of the word *religion* as understood today. Be that as it may, for us dharma is a meta-idea that includes philosophy, spirituality, and practices.

Yato Abhyudaya Nisreyasa Siddhi Sa Dharma. It is that which leads to success in material as well as spiritual life.

Dharanat Dharma Ityahu, Dharmo Dharayate Praja. It is that which sustains the individual and the society; that is, self-development and social good.

Na Manushyat Paro Dharmah. There is no greater religion than human religion.

These facets of dharma are not unique or exclusive to Indic faith traditions. Such a list only illustrates a significant overlap between ideas inherent in dharma with the ideas of, say, justice and prosperity inherent in Judaic tradition, all-embracing and self-effacing love of "agape," solidarity and compassion in the Qur'an, noninjury in holy books of Jains, the idea of service in Sikhism, and compassion in Buddhism.

Indeed, at least at the level of shared values, it is not difficult to find and cite similarities between various faith traditions. It only serves to emphasize that at one level the meaning of religion is anchored in relatively similar humanistic/spiritual/ethical values such as love, justice, sharing, equity, and peace—a feeling of oneness with entire reality. The integrative aspects of these values have helped

people to live in harmony with "the other" on the basis of inspirations derived from different sources of spiritual insights located in different cultural, historical, or psychosocial backgrounds.

However, today, religion is popularly understood in an almost sectarian sense. This leads to arrangements sanctified by legal systems or conventions that seek to keep away religions from the public arena. What is sought is to treat religion as a matter of private conscience, to avoid violent contestations and encourage tolerance, if not respect, of the other. This is seen as the most feasible way of coexisting in an increasingly multicultural, globalized world. However, it is apparent now that the separation of the private and the public has been most difficult to achieve.

Reverend Dadaji believed that religion is the necessity of human life. According to him:

Religion is that which upholds human dignity;
it is that which inculcates love for life;
it is that which kindles righteousness;
it is that which teaches to live in adversity;
it is that which imparts moral and ethical education.

His view of religion is, and I quote:

Even as mankind is achieving greater heights in material sphere, human bonding is cracking at every level. Religion that instills self-esteem evokes emotion and sublimates ego will strengthen this bonding and bring man closer to man . . . without which the social structure will continue to collapse bit by bit, men and women will continue to be pitched in conflict with themselves, with community and with the Creator.

Religion is meant to give an intellectual introduction to God and reveal the relationship of the Self with the Divine and with the fellow human beings.

In his opinion, the religions also go through various phases in human society. Whenever the philosophical and rational base of the religion is eroded, the intellectuals distance themselves from the religion. Such a religion becomes ritualistic, and it drives away the youth as well. Whenever religion becomes otherworldly and filled with superstitions, it looses its relevance in the contemporary context.

It is our experience that exclusion of any religion from public arena is extremely difficult to achieve. Therefore, it would be more relevant to examine, given the basic harmony and unity of experiences of human beings, how we can achieve a participatory understanding of the humanistic values of the world's religions and relate the individual with the other in the larger order of the cosmos.

Since we have not been able to achieve that, we have problems of sustainable peace; we have issues related to justice; we have to demand equality; and we have to fight against discrimination. Every nation on this earth faces these challenges. And there is a dominant feeling of the political and financial establishment the world over that globalization is the solution to these challenges. Economy, trade, and industry have taken the lead in spreading their wings across the globe. It promises to eventually eradicate poverty and ensure justice and equity for all. These promises are not believed by those who have suffered displacement, including cultural displacement, and they have turned into opponents of the concept of globalization. The people promoting globalization tend to blame religion as one of the main sources of such resistance. And those who want religion to be the mainstay of humanity blame economic globalization for many of today's dilemmas.

These challenges have evoked half-hearted and uneven responses from the world's religions. As of now, these religions seem haunted by two fixations—preoccupation with established religious frameworks, rituals, and procedures and how to prevent attraction of its followers for any new thought or new forms of spirituality. Grown out of alienation, mainly from mainline sectarian and denominational constraints, these new forms of spirituality seek spiritual wisdom of other faiths and from other sources of knowledge without

formally giving up the faith of their birth. They also seek creative interpretations from tenets of their own faith traditions. Such creative syntheses by these forms of spirituality become meaningful because of their deep commitment to various social action programs. The faith establishments either ignore or oppose such forms of spirituality, but they are often unable to prevent them from attracting mass following. As a result, usually, serious efforts are made to woo them and to co-opt these forms of spiritualities as part of the larger mainline faith.

The initiative that I represent, Swadhyaya, too, is one such phenomenon that is based on *Vedantic* ideals of universal divinity and universal humanity which, in active and dynamic interaction, promote both spirituality and sociality. We owe it to one person—Rev. Pandurang Shastri Athavale—Dadaji.

We have our own views on globalization, eradication of poverty, peace, justice, and equality. We believe that the essential aspect of globalization is acceptance of the other. Mere acceptance of existence of the other is not sufficient. One has to learn to view the other as oneself; one has to learn to relate with the other. This presupposes an internal change in the mindset of people, and unless it is brought about, we will neither have peace nor justice. Tolerance of the other is a quality born mainly out of helplessness and is devoid of warmth, love, and care. This leads to neutrality in relations, which is not a desirable situation. The point is how to bring man closer to man in a loving and unselfish relationship.

For us, peace is maintenance of equilibrium within and without, and the way to peace is through harmony and justice. For Dadaji, peace is neither mere absence of violence nor mere nonviolent resolution of conflicts. For him, peace is building of loving and cohesive relationships in and across societies.

It is apparent that Dadaji has put great emphasis on selfless relationship, equality, and unity. For a Swadhyayee, the other is a divine brother, and one is encouraged to relate the divine in the other with the divine within oneself. It makes one trust the positive in everyone. Out of such feelings more than sixty years ago, Dadaji started his journey. For him, this inner journey was not to be a lonely and meditative pursuit. He instilled this understanding and feeling in everyone that came in touch with him.

Different people have different ideas of the divine and the sacred. Dadaji derived his understanding of indwelling presence of God from the Indic wisdom. Through inculcating this understanding, Dadaji could instill self-esteem, sense of dignity, and self-worth in the common man. He also took care that this sense of self-esteem does not inflate into problematic ego. He fully recognized the possibilities and pitfalls of ego. Therefore, he stressed the need and awareness of *swa,* or self, not based on cultural isolationism but on an expansion of the idea of self. He sought to reorient ego by relating it to a "self" that is divine. Through an activist orientation of "bhakti"—devotion. He sought to make bhakti the vehicle of non-egocentric, collective, constructive activities. Indeed, bhakti is the foundational term in Swadhyaya. He gave new meaning to the idea of bhakti. His idea of bhakti is not that of a passive agency that promotes retreat or reduces it to observance of rituals. For him, bhakti is a loving expression of gratefulness to God, and such expression finds its way through meditative worship and action-oriented devotion that is radically different from ritualistic worship.

Bhaktipheri, or devotional outreach, is Swadhyaya's main activation agency. Swadhyaya places very high value on face-to-face personal contacts in contrast to impersonal, formal contacts, as bonds of mutual trust are most vital for development of sustainable community initiatives. Swadhyayee activists (*krutsheels*) travel repeatedly on their own initiative and own resources to villages, towns, and cities to link with others in the divine family. This family, ever expanding, is inclusive and admits of no economic or social barrier and has embraced nearly twenty million people in twenty-two countries across the globe with more than 600,000 activist *krutisheels.* It has empowered millions of people and has successfully developed communities that cut across caste rigidities. Dadaji

notably focused on the marginal communities and the dispossessed. He never insisted upon them to change their lifestyles. While meeting economic and social problems of various microcommunities head on, he never sought external financial or material assistance. Though by now, spread over nearly 100,000 villages and among Indian expatriate communities in all continents, Swadhyaya has maintained a low profile, notably in the "development community." That is the way Dadaji wanted it.

Action-oriented devotion finds its expression in various socioeconomic programs. One may not have riches to offer to God, but everyone has one's efficiency to offer in the form of devotion to God. Farmers devote their efficiency—farming skill—to God and generate impersonal wealth for distribution to the needy as Prasad—benefaction of God (in contrast to charity or loans) through the experiment of Yogeshwar Krushi (Farms of God). There are nearly 10,000 such farms in India today. Likewise, fishermen, artisans, skilled and semiskilled workers give their efficiency in various other experiments connected with their respective fields of skills. Doctors, chartered accountants, engineers, and other professionals too give their excellence as devotional offering to the Creator. All experiments under the aegis of Swadhyaya are devotion based on and involving offering in the form of time and efficiency. The *krutisheels* derive satisfaction of performing worship of God; at the same time, the experiments generate impersonal wealth. The undercurrent is that of doing God's work and not social service. Work for God would continue forever and that is why we know that through Swadhyaya, the work for humanity would continue for a long time to come.

The understanding of indwelling presence of the divine creates self-worth, and the understanding of divine pervasiveness magnifies such self-worth. It changes the outlook toward the other and nature. Science told us that there is life in plants and vegetation; Dadaji inspired us to see God in them. Out of this understanding, Vruksha mandirs (tree temples), Shree Darshanam (divine communes), and Madhav Vrund (tree plantations) have come into existence so far. These experiments bring people from twenty surrounding villages into forming a kind of divine commune. Here the trees and plants are nurtured and worshiped as manifestations of God. Millions of trees have been planted in the past decade by Swadhyayees, with almost 100 percent survival rate. These experiments also address the complex problem of ecology. At world level, these experiments can be viewed as a nursery, but in terms of validation of a principle, it has a great significance.

There are nearly twenty such experiments inspired by Dadaji covering such wide areas as augmenting community water resources, vocational training, dairy farming, potable water supply, drainage, sanitation, informal education, and so on, that are changing the socioeconomic face of society. Dadaji's insights are effective through these experiments to increase self-esteem and counteract conventional social ills like alcoholism, domestic violence, gambling, petty crime, ethnic violence, and so forth. Swadhyaya reveals that devotion can influence all spheres of human life and can lead to holistic reconstruction and development of the society.

Swadhyaya embraces everyone: children, the youth, women, marginal sections of the society, people from different faith establishments, villagers, and city-dwellers, in short, the cross section of society. It brings man closer to man in a selfless loving relationship of a divine family.

There are about 25,000 cultural centers of children the world over, in which about 850,000 children, on an average, become culturally enriched.

Alienation of youth from the culture is the concern of thinkers the world over, and everyone finds it difficult if not impossible to address this concern. At such a time, nearly 2.5 million youth participating in about 27,000 youth cultural centers and related activities can be considered an achievement of Swadhyaya and blessing of God.

Active participation of women in a major way is a strength of Swadhyaya. Today more than 250,000 young and elderly women involve their time and talents in Swadhyaya.

Aadivaasis and Vanvaasis (forest dwellers) have been rerooted to their culture through Swadhyaya, and together with other marginal communities, they have been made a part of mainstream society.

And all of the above has become possible only because Dadaji created a family different from an institution or social organization. Relationship based on devotion is the foundation of the Swadhyaya family. What he has done in essence is to inspire us to view the sacred not only in idols or holy books but in the entire universe. By instilling the understanding of relation with the other through the indwelling presence of common divine in all, he could create a vast family of millions, and community living assumed a radically different meaning. The understanding of divine relationship is a revolutionary thought, wherein there is no discrimination; no generation gap; no barriers of caste, creed, class, color, education; and all live as children of one God. This is the emotional revolution. Dadaji brought the devotion out from the narrow confines of ritualistic observance and made it a powerful and all-encompassing aspect of human life.

He has proved that bhakti is a social force. This is what Dadaji proclaimed at the World's Religions Congress in Japan in 1954, and we Swadhyayees experience this in all our endeavors. It is our endeavor to create a nursery of the alternate society that Dadaji worked for. Since it is an uncharted course, we expect hurdles and opposition. But understanding of God's nearness and selfless love for humanity as Dadaji taught us is our enduring strength.

It is practically impossible for anyone even to imagine one world-religion. Different regions, societies, communities would continue to have different religions. Religions would continue to give moral orders and regulate conduct of the individual, and the society and would continue to strive to create good human beings. Every religion and faith-establishment should not only accept the existence of other religions and faith-establishments but should also have catholicity to accept the profound insights of the world's great spirits. If we can do that, we can certainly hope for a much better world with harmony, peace, justice, and equity.

From our own experience, we believe that inculcation of the understanding of bhakti or devotion in every person would be indispensable toward achieving such a goal. We are, in our own way, incessantly striving to give shape to the vision of Dadaji and create such an alternate society.

On behalf of the Swadhyaya pariwar, I take this opportunity to invite you to join us, whenever the spirit moves you, to witness and experience the transformation that is taking place wherever Swadhyaya has struck roots.

REDEFINING HUMANITY AND CIVILIZATION

Nadine Sultana d'Osman Han

Human beings are like parts of a body, created from the same essence, When one part is hurt and in pain, the others cannot remain in peace and be quiet.

—Sa'adi[1]

Humanity can be defined by looking into another's eyes and seeing one's own reflection. Civilization is a living orchestra in which humankind's diversity must be harmonized like a symphony of various instruments.

Søren Aakye Kierkegaard said that "life can only be understood backwards; but it must be lived forwards."[2]

What does this mean? It means that we must look to the past for guidance, because the past is our stable point of reference, and thus avoid repeating past errors.

Humanity is spirituality with a form. It bridges the outer and inner life. From divine origin, spirituality is the essence of compassion, unbiased justice, tolerance, morality, honesty, integrity, and humility. Without spirituality, there can be no humanity or civilization. Spirituality is the direct communication between our conscience and the divine. There can be no compromise or shield of justification for our bad deeds.

It is assumable that originally all humans were not aware of this divine revelation and that it had to be taught to us in a framework that could be understood. Thus, holy prophets were chosen among us to enlighten us. These teachings gave rise to religion. For Muslims, the *Ummah* is made comprehensible by the teachings transmitted by the Prophet Muhammad.

With the passing of time, religion split into various branches to accommodate various cultures in the same manner as languages. Thus, it is ridiculous to declare that only one religion represents the only truth, in the same context that only one language cannot be accepted as the sole means of communication. Only spirituality is indivisible. Religion itself must be diversified to meet the needs of a multicultural humanity and geographical differences.

WHAT IS THE BASIC DIFFERENCE BETWEEN ISLAM AND CHRISTIANITY?

Islam is oriented toward the heart and follows the emotional process reflected in the Sufi music, with its flight into the ecstasy of the imaginary, an aspect of spiritualism. Christianity is oriented toward the intellectual process of its followers and is rigidly controlled, much like Western classical music. Thus, wisdom would require that instead of fighting one another, we harmonize both for a balance between the head and the heart.

Both language and religion are modified over time by human interpretation. In the first instance, on the positive side, it accommodates new discoveries or understanding. On the negative side, ambiguous wordings mislead the unwary. In the second case, it is more complex. The interpretation or misinterpretation of religion gives rise to the temptation of manipulation in order to justify and legitimize objectionable actions or behavior, including cruelty and all sorts of abuses. It is a sad fact that humans are handicapped by genes inherited from nature's law of survival, which is the fate of animals on this planet.

In fact, due to the very faulty and aggressive nature of humankind, several prophets had to periodically redirect us to the right path away from barbarism. Humans were blessed at some point in time by the revelation of spirituality, enabling them to escape the cruel law of the jungle affecting the animal kingdom. But most of us could not or would not relinquish the thrill of power over the weak.

Civilization for most people translated into the gratification of insatiable greed. It is a defect that has survived in spite of the example set by prophets and that shall ultimately destroy humanity.

Although religion proclaims to mirror spirituality, in practice it is a tool of control for the power and ambitions of a few. Today more than ever, religions are exploited to justify the injustices and imbalance carried out in their name in all areas of our lives: political, racial, between genders, between the poor and rich, economic, health, environment, and so forth. The list goes on and on.

Spirituality that is the internal journey of one's soul cannot be confused with religion, nor with so-called righteous humane secular democracies that are the imperfect laws of men in which self-interests are the ultimate goal. Spirituality cannot be applied to the self-appointed judges of conscience and behavior, governed by the law of the strongest over the voiceless and defenseless multitude who cannot challenge them.

Spirituality is the uncorrupted word from the divine found in the consciences of those untainted by sins of cruelty, oppression, injustice, and self-serving motives in contempt of others' rights. No one can interfere between an individual conscience and the divine. The divine (Allah or God) is the only judge of the soul and the dispenser of punishment. No one has the right to anticipate what the divine's punishment shall be for an individual.

The only person one may be allowed to judge is oneself, in order to improve oneself. In the same way, a true democracy cannot be a banner of justification in the oppression and exploitation of the weak in the name of so-called humanitarian goodness without substance.

In the same context, the ideology of democracy has become a slogan without meaning. It has become a propaganda of deceits and inequalities that are carried out with impunity. Unless we urgently attend to justice for all in a global framework, with respect to individual rights, to dignity and well-being, to tolerance—indulgent with our human brothers and sisters worldwide and severe with our own shortcomings—we shall drive ourselves to extinction.

Although we are still hoping for a miracle to save ourselves from our destructive selves, it is my humble opinion that the long-awaited final prophet shall not save us this time from our follies, but shall come as a stern judge. This time, humans shall have to account for their evils. Humankind has taken too much for granted for its rescue by exceptional prophets. We have disregarded too often the warnings to amend our ways.

From the beginning of time, we have indulged in wars to appropriate what belongs to others, to justify falsely our oppression of the weak, and generally to live by the dictate of the law of the jungle. This century shall see the accountability that we deserve. Perhaps we should prepare for it, for there is no more escape. In this, we shall be all equals, just as death does not spare any human.

The past is the compass of time. It guides our steps in the present toward the future. Without a past we are lost, blindly seeking our reason for being.

It may be that life on earth is a glitch in an otherwise perfect cosmos. However, it is a point I shall not debate because its knowledge is outside the scope of human intelligence.

On the other hand, we know that life on earth is one of cruelty, in which both animals and humans killed (and kill) each other for basic survival. At some point in time, only humans were blessed with the potential to distance themselves from this vicious circle and to progress toward what we call humanity and civilization. Yet, as of this century, we have been unable to achieve either. We have only achieved degrees of humanity and civilization, but at the same time, we have also achieved greater ability to inflict greater destruction and barbarism upon ourselves, the animal kingdom, and the planet itself.

Primitive man's aggressiveness was limited in scope and without a clear understanding of consequences, which were relatively minor. Today, aggressiveness cannot be discounted in the same light manner, for the very survival of the planet as a whole is at stake.

A civilized humanity and wars are incompatible, and unless we can resolve disputes without violence, there can be no civilization and in fact we may be considered more barbaric than animals: a form of destructive virus.

Why wars? We have heard countless justifications for it over the centuries and particularly today, in which the aggressors are trying to convince their victims that the sufferings inflicted upon them are for their own good and thus not only morally acceptable but something to celebrate! We are back to the gladiator mentality.

Do not be deceived by slogans of self-justification in the name of righteous humanity.

Wars are nothing less than legalized organized crimes. Regardless of the many shields to justify such aggressive behavior, the truth of the matter remains that wars are being waged to appropriate what belongs to others.

In theory, it is all very well to assume that prosperity comes from steady hard work and honesty, but realities show otherwise. The most expedient means to acquire wealth is by the exploitation of others. Most drug dealers clearly understand this reality; most governments use the same tactics to appropriate the coveted commodities such as petroleum from the Middle East, diamonds from Africa, gold from Latin America, and a cheap labor force from poverty-stricken countries and immigrants. The list goes on and on. Wars are thus to control the right to exploit with impunity another country, for self-interest. The slogan of "human rights" seems overused and quite irrelevant in regard to wars when one analyzes the laissez-faire martyrdom of children worldwide or the plight of the Palestinians who were ruthlessly uprooted from their country and way of life to make room for the Israelites, victims of World War II, a conflict that had nothing to do with the Palestinians. Today, millions are persecuted, tortured, displaced, and made homeless by government policies and wars, and although some murmurs of disapproval may be heard, no actions are taken; for these unfortunate people are deemed expendable by our uncivilized mentality in which the law of the jungle prevails—for it has never left us.

It is obvious that humans do not learn from past lessons of barbarism. History repeats itself, only with different victims.

The twentieth century should have been a century of peace and growth as the logical outcome of technological advances. We should have expected a better quality of life—physically, emotionally, and intellectually—as progress eliminated arduous manual work. Yet, this has clearly not happened. On the contrary, the twentieth century claims, to its shame, two world wars, and the new century is heading toward a bloodier third one, not by necessity but by choice. We would do well to urgently examine our motives.

A superpower does not look kindly on self-reliant nations. Any nation that does not need charity or protection is viewed as a threat. Yet, this attitude is self-defeating.

Warfare is big business. No other business could claim such exchange of billions of dollars, yet ironically, it benefits no one. The consumer's needs are just a speck in the economic scale in comparison to military needs. Thus, as such, warfare has

267

to be promoted and expanded, to permit military trade. Such a giant investment must produce dividends to avoid the bankruptcy of its nation, hence the wars.

The uncontrollable addiction to greed of big businesses could only lead to the present innovation of "preventive wars." We are deceiving ourselves if we believe that peace can be achieved by warfare. History has shown time after time that wars can only lead to retaliation and thus more bloodshed and misery for humankind.

It is also nonsense to declare that nuclear weapons should be the privilege of a few nations, under the belief that they will use "mature restraint" in the use of such weapons. The use of the atomic bomb by the United States in Japan belies such an assumption, as do repeated threats to use nuclear weapons to intimidate nations that are not viewed favorably. Again, any stockpile of weapons has to be eventually used, for the titanic investment made to its production cannot be left to rust. Hence, propaganda justifies "preventive wars."

Only banishment of all nuclear weapons worldwide could be a step toward peace.

Double-standard policies have never worked. It is undeniable that quality of life cannot be achieved by warfare and injustice.

The new world order was presented as a gift of happy promises for the future of mankind in the twenty-first century. But as soon as the door opened, it transformed itself into a new world labeled "ethnic cleansing" and "profiling as potential criminals" mostly the followers of Islam. Yesterday, other groups were the victims, and tomorrow we may see a totally different group victimized.

If we look at the state of affairs in our society, we would recognize the truths of our behavior reflected in our contempt of human lives resulting in child neglect, abuse, birth defects, famine, homelessness, discarded elders for whom the golden years have turned into the pauper years, and the addiction to drugs, sex, and violence so prized as entertainment. But our greatest modern crime today is war—mass murder of civilians and the random imprisonment and torture of prisoners, most of them held without charges, but based on a system of discrimination

toward the least favored ethnicity of the moment. The second most unspeakable evil is committed by enlisting children-soldiers. Even animals protect their young!

Where are the promises of our scientists and politicians? Their discoveries have not resulted in the betterment of humankind, but its destruction. Farmers were removed to be replaced by scientists that thought they were better qualified than nature itself. The result is the pollution of the food chain, both vegetal and animal, leading to numerous new viruses and the destruction of the human immune system. As to the new abundance of genetically modified food, besides being of doubtful nutritional value, it has brought its own problem of an overfed, dependent society, and along with it sickness and obesity in one corner of the planet and famine in another. In addition, drug discoveries do not fare better, and most experiments bring untold catastrophes that we are only perceiving now in our environment, health, and so forth. We have even gone as far as to deny the basic right to die with dignity. Science without wisdom is very dangerous indeed. Even the computers have become powerful devices to spy on and control individuals and groups, curtailing the precious right to privacy and political ethics.

It is time that the public demand maturity and decency toward human lives from their leaders.

THE TWENTY-FIRST CENTURY IS THE BLOOMING OF OUR PAST EXCESSES

Most politicians and futurists like to remind us that the burden of our bad deeds shall not mature before the next generations, but I tend to disagree, for our ancestors made the same reasoning—thus, in the twenty-first century, we are that next generation. We are their future, and the burden is ours to solve.

The twenty-first century shall see either our salvation or our extinction. The choice is ours, and it can no longer be delayed and hidden under veils of illusions.

It is my humble opinion that unless we come to realize that wars must be banned worldwide, along with weapons, we cannot save this planet nor achieve true civilization.

Globalization must be defined not in terms of imposing one culture over another but to safeguard the security, economy, well-being, and justice for all nations without discrimination. Corporations must be regulated on the same standards worldwide. In addition, profits and salaries for both employers and employees must provide a fair maximum for employers and fair minimum for employees. A global currency should be introduced so as to end currency inequality.

When an employer receives several millions in salary, and his employee at the bottom of the ladder receives an estimated ten dollars an hour, it is not a fair division of profits, but the impunity of organized corporate Mafia-style organization. Societies cannot function along this kind of inequity and thievery. Corporate profits must determine the fair equity of salary for both employer and employee. We cannot return to a slavery mentality in a civilized world. It would be useful if an international language were taught to small children along with a native language. All humans should be bilingual.

Religions are the threads that unify a community or nations, thus they interweave deeply with governmental affairs. As such, religions have been used time and again by political leaders to divide rather than unify human beings. This must change without delay. Religious conflicts deny the purpose of religion as an expression of spirituality and humane decency. It becomes like today's democracies, just a superficial platform of talk without substance.

It is imperative that religions be unified in a commitment for the betterment of humankind without any discrimination against diversity of creed, belief, or culture. Religions must speak with one voice against governmental abuses of power. Religion must be a forceful preemptive tool against the evil of declaration of war.

Religions are powerful entities, and if they have the goodwill to do so, they have the power to strengthen the United Nations by implementing the following:

1. An independent truly international court (much expanded and more effective than the model of today), in which all nations are represented fairly, must enforce that any declaration of war be considered a crime against humanity, and the court must have the authority to demand the immediate resignation of the government in violation, and a new one voted in office, regardless of the size or power of the nation.

2. An independent international court must oversee the protection of children and bring to justice without delay any perpetrator of child abuse (individual or organized). Trafficking and exploitation of children must never be tolerated, and officials who do not enforce protection of children within their borders must be made accountable. Any act of violence should be severely punished, and torture of any kind should never be tolerated under any circumstance. We must look at the planet's resources in global terms for a fair distribution to all mankind. We must all contribute to the healing of the earth and rediscover a healthier lifestyle.

3. Laws must be reviewed to protect the well-being of the family, the vulnerable, and the sick (both physical and mental). Leisure time and proper education in morality (without oppression) must be reintroduced for a happy earthly journey. Entertainment must be joyful, without vices or violence. It must be a tool of civilized relaxation, a model of inspiration of the finer qualities possible within human abilities.

Suffering must never be inflicted upon others in reality or in imaginary entertainment. The young look upon their elders for their future adulthood, thus it is important to show excellence in all our behavior if we can hope to attain the goal of civilization as intended by the divine. Other laws governing marriage, sickness, death, and so forth must be for the happiness of humankind. Marriage and motherhood are not for children. Marriage under the age of eighteen (and possibly twenty-one) years old should be banned world-wide. Maturity is essential for a healthy society. Children must not be rushed into adult responsibilities that overwhelm them.

SOCIETIES ARE ALWAYS REFLECTED IN THE TREATMENT AND THE EDUCATION RECEIVED BY CHILDREN

The children are always the adults of tomorrow; thus, they must be our priority.

There is no doubt that criminals shall always exist, even under the best of circumstances. So how to deal with this problem? Prisons are not the answer in most cases. Petty crimes such as theft or disorderly conduct should be fined to compensate victims, or community services performed.

For heinous murders, if not due to mental disorder or uncontrollable emotional disturbance, perhaps the death penalty could be considered, but never in a physically painful manner. For other crimes, all efforts toward rehabilitation should be considered. Children should never be judged as adults.

These recommendations may seem too idealistic, yet if profound reforms are not implemented urgently, this century shall see the extinction of humankind in the worst kind of nightmare. Possibly, it is already too late, for the earth itself has its rhythm as well as its own immune system defense. Although most futurist politicians believe that the answer lies by preparing remote survival quarters while annihilating most of humankind, that is an unrealistic vision.

Their agony may be even more painful than the ones that they intend to inflict on the masses.

Do not believe for a moment that our present induced hysteria toward so-called national security, the Patriot Act against terrorist threats, terror from Islam, and all similar propaganda slogans are sprouting from a sudden momentum of aggression by so-called fundamentalist crazy states or nations. First, let me say that the present turmoil has nothing to do with religious spirituality. The basic message of all religions, as taught by every prophet, was one of compassion, tolerance, and justice. Islam is

a peace-oriented religion. This is supported by the facts that warriors of Islam have shown time and again mercy in time of wars, respecting Islamic teachings that conquered populations should be spared. The generosity of hospitality to strangers is also a direct influence from Islam. At no time did the Muslims commit atrocities as was done in Europe at the time of the Inquisition or the Crusaders or such cruelty as to nail a prophet on a cross. Islam has always promoted tolerance and justice, as amply demonstrated by the Ottoman Sultans during their very long reign, for nearly seven hundred years.

This said, to this century, humankind has not reached the goal of idyllic societies, and the future looks gloomier. Not because this is inevitable but because the leaders of today, controlled by the all-powerful corporate world of our times, have no intention whatsoever to work toward the betterment of human beings but rather toward their alienation in order that a chosen few can capitalize and benefit from the diminishing resources of the planet. In addition, we have reached that level in our development where the people who decide our fate have progressed toward the fantasy that they can match their creator and create themselves a humanity that suits their needs and desire for total control of life surrounding them. In the role model that they have been taught, this small group wants to be the ultimate master, with engineered slaves or servants who would worship them.

Hence, the creation after World War II (and before that under different names) of such future global planners as the think tank RAND and so forth. The present turmoil has nothing to do with the sudden appearance of so-called terrorists but is a well-thought-out plan to rid the planet of those "they" consider undesirable and the realization that their previous encouragement for a population explosion to meet the expansion of a consumerist market has served its purpose both in term of profits and resources, and is no longer needed. It may have even become a liability to the survival of these manipulators who created dependent artificial societies.

We should not be so surprised, for from the beginning of time, the fate of mankind has always been shaped by an "elite" class. Perhaps what has changed is the commitment or goals toward the betterment of humankind. Kings were committed to safeguard the well-being of their subjects, and those who erred were promptly removed by an intolerant public. Kings had their privileges, but they knew their limits. Also, they were very conscious of their obedience to a divine force.

This is not so today. Although numerous so-called religious sects of all sorts have sprung up to mislead and capitalize on a naive people who have lost touch with true spirituality and search desperately for the right path to their inner being, the masterminds of today, futurists, consider themselves the new creator, or in other words, the equal of the divine.

The divine is not a presence that we can categorize or understand easily with our limited human intelligence. Yet some have the mere breeziest of intuition that we may have been created as perhaps a sort of experiment. If we prove ourselves to be a defective experiment, we might be destroyed, very much like humans do in their own laboratories with both animals and bacteria, once they are through with their own "live" experiment. We are well aware that the animals we use as "guinea pigs" feel the pain of their suffering but are not conscious of the source of their pain and are powerless against the scientists who decide their fate.

Our fate may have been already decided. However, it is our moral duty to help ease the suffering of our fellow-beings as long as the divine allows us a breath. Evil might triumph over truth, but we must stand strong at the side of justice and tolerance and not falter in our determination to remain true to spirituality within our inner self. We must not waste in vain the precious gift of life, in the here and thereafter, that the divine has bestowed on us. The incomprehensible shall be made comprehensible in due course to the deserving souls.

Futurists are nothing new, only the wording has changed. In addition, all futurists do not have the same agendas.

The greatest futurist of his time was Nostradamus. Nostradamus was not some sort of magician nor a medium with the meaning that we usually associate with those who perceive what is obscure to the majority. Nostradamus was an exceptionally perceptive psychologist of human nature and very much conscious of the interrelation between the cosmos, the earth, and life itself. He could read the map of humankind's journey on earth as revealed to him by his exceptional awareness of the world around him and the presence of the divine in all things.

Nostradamus tried to transmit his knowledge to us, and his message is not as nebulous as it may first appear. However, Nostradamus did not conform to the knowledge and mentality of his own time, thus he had to take care to reveal truths in layers of veils so as not to antagonize the authorities of his time. Thanks to his wisdom, his words were not lost to those who would eventually comprehend his message. In the same way, the "experts" during his time did not accept the concept of earth as a sphere. This kind of mentality is still with us today, for the "experts" in each era do not look kindly on those whose insight or intuition look further into the future than the accepted scientists of the time. Thus, the visionary of this world must always take care not to make too-obvious waves in a sea of ignorance, or they may risk becoming the victim of persecution or slander.

Conclusion

The twenty-first century is going to be the century of truth, in which we shall all be accountable for our actions to a higher court than the corrupt courts of humankind.

The twenty-first century is not going to bring back to us a messiah to redeem us from our sins. Humans were unable or unwilling to recognize messiahs when they came in the past. The Prophet Jesus Christ (peace and blessings be upon him) was crucified, and later his teachings were distorted to the extreme extent as applied by the Christians' Inquisition.

Another Prophet, Muhammad (peace and blessings be upon him), was sent to us to bring us back to the path of compassionate justice and behavior.

The passing of time brought its forgetfulness, and with it brought forth struggles for power with the consequences of division within Islam.

Allah the Merciful sent again a messenger as revealed by the Prophet (peace and blessings be upon him) for preparing his recognition by the faithful. This messenger was the Ottoman Sultan Fatih Mehmet, who reestablished the spiritual path leading to the Ottoman Caliphate for the preservation of Allah's will. Under its protective umbrella, Islam flourished in peace, justice, and prosperity, benefiting the Christians as well.

Again, with the passing of time, corruption led to self-serving disloyalties and misinterpretations of his teachings. This brought forth in the twentieth century the vengeful sword of evil—leading to unprecedented mass deportation or massacre called justified "ethnic cleansing" for the good of humanity and democratic ideals, just as the Taliban (and other oppressive regimes) believed that prayers would absolve them from their daily crime of cruelty and injustice.

Needless to say, these politicians and religious leaders do not abide by the rules and teachings that they impose on others by force.

As the twentieth century of sorrows was approaching its end, a last merciful reprieve was granted to us, so as not to carry forth the destructive path of doom to the new millennium. But again, promises of instant material and power gratification clouded our judgment.

Thus, divine signs went unrecognized by many and were ignored or exploited by a few. Henceforth, this modest messenger came to us with the softness of the mist, and left us with the quietness of humility. Alas! This is so.

Our mentality of presumptuousness to unlimited forgiveness for our sins looks toward a glorified messiah to absolve us of wrongdoing. This is not going to happen. The time has come for the accountability of our actions toward others.

Unless the spiritual truth can triumph over the evils of the law of the jungle, it is my observation that we are reaching the end of our journey on earth. For we have reached the future. We are the children upon which the sins of the fathers have been visited.

The planet Earth is a circular sphere,
Every point of departure is every point of
    arrival.
Life has a circular rhythm,
Everything returns to its starting point.
The seeds of nature grow from the Earth,
Give their leaves and fruits,
Then return to the Earth.
The animal's earthly envelope
Composed of nutrients of the Earth,
Returns to the latter, to nourish the Earth
    itself.
The spiritual soul comes from the realm of
    purity of Allah,
And must return pure to the realm of Allah.
The Qur'an is the book of Heavens,
The first chapter,
Opens with the first Prophet, Adam.
The last chapter,
Will end with the return of Adam's posterity.
The circle of Khalifat is reaching its end.
Its last mission:
The unity of mankind
In universal beneficence.
The 21st century will be the point of arrival of
    the Universal Soul,
At its point of departure from the realm of
    Allah.
The Earth itself must return to its cosmic
    origin.
A new voyage is being drafted in the infinity
    of time.[3]

Religion in an Age of Anxiety

Seyyed Hossein Nasr

I don't know if he is here or not because I'm in the dark as far as you're concerned. I see nothing and you see me. That's the way God looks at the world. So you're put in a "divine position"; you're very much responsible.

I made this trip to the wonderful city of Montreal after almost two decades of absence. I first lectured here over forty-five years ago—how life passes—at McGill University when Wilfred Cantwell Smith was director of the Islamic Center here. I accepted this invitation for two reasons. One is the theme itself, which is of very, very great pertinence to the world today. So much misunderstanding has come about concerning the role of religion and human life, especially after the seminal and tragic events of September 11. And second, because I feel that the group of people who deal with this issue here, assembled by Professor Sharma and his colleagues at McGill University, are aptly suited to deal with these issues, a bit farther away from the center of political contention than one finds often in these debates in the United States, of course, not everywhere, but in many places.

I titled my talk Religion in the Age of Anxiety. This might seem a strange title, but I want to begin—since I was asked to speak about disagreements of religion after September 11— with a truth that anxiety itself is not against religious attachment. To speak a bit more philosophically or mystically, our denial of heaven precludes our having our feet firmly on the earth. When the earth begins to shake under our feet, for many people, their eyes look upward toward the heavens. And in every period of human history, periods of uncertitude and anxiety have turned a large number of people toward religion in general and spiritual life in particular, the best example in the history of Asia being perhaps the Mongol invasion, by the descendents of Genghis Khan, which devastated both eastern Asia and western Asia. And Persia, Iran, where I come from, lost practically half its population and some twenty to thirty million people were killed in this invasion. But the result of it was not only devastation but rejuvenation of the spiritual life in many, many ways. And the same occurred in China, mutatis mutandis, under another condition.

Now what has happened since September 11, therefore, has presented both an advantage and a disadvantage for the teaching and understanding of religion. And I will say at the outset that I do not believe that the September 11 events have had a deep effect upon Hinduism and Buddhism and

Sikhism and Neo-Confucianism and Taoism and Shintoism and the other great religions of Asia, nor the primal religions of Australian aborigines or Africans or the Native Americans. So I shall limit my comments to Christianity, to some extent Judaism, and to Islam, in a sense, Islam in the West. It's paradoxical that this event has essentially affected the children of Abraham, not religion globally, although we have the bad habit today of looking out of our window and whatever we see out there we say, "That's the whole world. It's global." That is not true. The globe is much larger than globalists think, thank God for that. Anyway, I shall limit my comments to the West, and to Christianity primarily, and then turn to Islam, because I suppose you expect me to say something about that.

I believe there are four major effects of September 11 on religion in America. America and Europe are very different in this sense. It was only three days ago that the pope in Munich bewailed the loss of Christianity in Europe and that Europeans have become deaf to the call of God—just three days ago, and at a center, a very, very important center, of traditional Catholic Christianity for 1,500 years, in Europe since the Christianization of the Germanic people. And this has not changed very much with September 11. So I shall leave Europe aside for the most part. That is, September 11 did not make Europe more Christian, but it did make them more hateful of Islam, something which earlier European history had already manifested, going back to the tenth and eleventh centuries. So let me concentrate my attention on America.

Now, first of all, the group of people who are secularists, or against religion as a whole, and believe that religion has been the source of confrontation and contention and conflict and death over the centuries in human history are forgetting the First World War and the Second World War, but that's beside the point. A sizeable group of people in the West, who have a rather deep historical, intellectual background, people who, after the Hundred Years' War between Protestants and Catholics, in which so many people were killed, have since turned away from all religious discourse

in disgust at the conflicts that had been created, and who blame—these are the grandfathers of the present-day secularists—and have blamed religion as the source of violence. September 11 gave an important impetus to this group. And it is only this group that joins most Europeans, where Christian practice is in the minority—nominal Christianity is there but practice is for a minority—this group, which is a minority in the United States in reverse, is very similar in the further alienation from religion, and attacks religion, as a result of seeing a dastardly act, a great tragedy carried out in the name of a religion.

Of course, here, there are remarkable incongruities and lack of a just and harmonious way of looking at the two sides of the story. Just two days ago, the tragic death of 3,000 people during September 11 was being commemorated in the United States, almost everywhere. But I didn't hear anyone speak of the over 100,000 Muslims who were killed as a result of that. This statement of mine is based on what the *Manchester Guardian* and other Western newspapers have written, not on some conjecture by some Muslim extremist. Over 100,000 people have perished as a result of that act. So one evil act has resulted in another evil act, but the second evil act is hardly ever spoken about, because it is not seen as an evil act. And this also brings up, therefore, very, very important Christian and also Jewish theological issues, which some very honest Christian and Jewish theologians have had to tackle. But in the mass media, in the general ambiance of discourse, such a thing is absent. At least I have not seen it, or have very rarely seen it.

The second reaction that came from September 11 is what is associated with Christian fundamentalism. And this needs a lot of clarification. I do not have time to go into it in depth. Very briefly, fundamentalism began in the early twentieth century by a number of Protestant American southerners. All those three characteristics (are important). There were no fundamentalists in Maine and New Hampshire. Nor were there Catholics. They were Protestants, Americans, and southerners, who, being attacked left and right, by Darwinists and evolutionists from Ivy League colleges in the north, and from the northern intelligentsia, which was much more secularized, thought that the only defense of the Bible would come through a literal interpretation of it. And they said we should stick to a literal interpretation of the Bible and became known as fundamentalists. Unfortunately, this term was used very rapidly in 1979 by the media for the Iranian Revolution, the Islamic Revolution of 1979. So after that, the term *fundamentalism* became very prevalent politically, predominantly for the Islamic world, but also elsewhere. So now, if I used the words *Christian fundamentalist*, we have to remind ourselves that it is within the context of the political discourse about this term, which was brought into being after 1979.

Now, this group, called the Christian fundamentalists, comprises sixty to seventy million people perhap—some people say fifty million—evangelicals, most of whom belong to the southern parts of the United States, and it excludes Catholicism, American Catholicism, and the mainstream Protestant Churches, like Episcopalianism and Methodism and so forth. This group became more strengthened after 9/11. It became strengthened for many, many reasons, but one of them was a greater definition of the enemy as being an anti-Christian and an antireligious force. Now the enemy was no longer Charles Darwin; it was Osama bin Laden. There's of course a very, very big difference. And because this was seen as a living threat—whether all of the threat is true or not is for others to debate, but certainly a threat of some dimension—this movement grew and, because of the events of September 11, gained a great deal of political power, which it had never exercised in the United States since perhaps the foundation of the Republic, and that was in any case another kind of Christian fundamentalism. And as you know, today it's a very powerful force, and it is in close relationship with what one could call Jewish fundamentalism, in the same way that the nonfundamentalistic elements of Christianity are in close dialogue with nonfundamentalist elements of both Islam and Judaism.

The flowering of what is called fundamentalism is to be seen, of course, in all of the three monotheistic religions, and they were all strengthened during the period after September 11. But it is not unique to them. There's such a thing as Hindu fundamentalism, which resulted in the destruction of the Babri Mosque or the killing of 3,000 Gujaratis in one day a couple of years ago and many other phenomena such as Tamil Tigers and what they're doing in Sri Lanka. There are all kinds of things that are going on. This phenomenon, fundamentalism, extremism, is all over the place, and it is augmented everywhere across the world, but especially in the Abrahamic world, by the political events that are carried out by the West against the Islamic world or those parts of the Islamic world which are considered to have abetted the activities of these terrorists who do terrible acts in the name of Islam.

Anyway, one of the important characteristics of Christian fundamentalism, until about two or three years ago—now one detects a little bit of a change—is bringing Islamophobia back to life. What do I mean by bringing back to life? For almost a thousand years, from the rise of Islam in the seventh century to, when Islam occupied the Iberian Peninsula up to southern France, there were Christian political writings against Islam, trying to refute Islam. And since Christ was a central figure of Christianity, they thought the Prophet of Islam, Muhammad, was also the central figure of Islam. So they thought by defaming him, by attacking him, they would attack Islam. And therefore horrendous biographies appeared against the Prophet. Every accusation you can think of in the dictionary was made against him, from being, God forbid, a thief to doing promiscuous sexual acts and all kinds of things that I, as a Muslim, don't feel comfortable to repeat. This came out in Latin very, very early and determined, for a very long time, the general Western attitude toward him and toward Islam.

But things began to change, especially since the Second World War. It really goes back to Pope Pius XII, before the Second World War, who, sending one of his emissaries to Libya as ambassador, as nuncio of Libya, said to him: "Do not think that you're going to a country of a people who are faithless, infidels, or pagans, or heathens. You're going to a country where people believe in God as we do." This was a most remarkable statement made by a pope since the foundation of Christianity concerning relation between Islam and Christianity. But because of the political situation of Pope Pius XII through the Second World War, this very important statement is usually covered over. Everything is, unfortunately, determined so much by politics rather than reality. Anyway, after the Second World War, long ecumenical meetings between Catholics and Muslims as well as Protestants and Muslims began in Europe and later on in America. One of the foremost figures in that movement came from your country; that is, the late Wilfred Cantwell Smith, my very close friend, who first invited me to Montreal here. I remember that this year is the forty-ninth year since I first participated in an ecumenical meeting in Morocco between leading Catholic theologians and Muslims and also Catholic scholars.

What this rise of Islamophobia has done is practically to have destroyed this fifty years of effort that has been made by well-intentioned Christians and Muslims. Never in the twentieth century, after the debacle, of course, of fascism and those very bitter and demonic political moments in Europe in the thirties and forties, has a religious leader attacked the founder of another religion in terms that people like Jerry Falwell and Robertson and Marshal Graham have attacked the Prophet of Islam. Never. We keep talking about political correctness. Political correctness is correct as long as it does not involve Islam. With Islam, you have a heyday. You can attack anyone you want in any way that you want. I mean, no American station would accept some Christian minister coming and saying that blacks are less intelligent than whites, or the Jews did this and that. There would be fires in the streets the next day. But calling the Prophet of Islam a thief is all right. It doesn't really matter. And this rise of Islamophobia, caused by many Christian fundamentalists who are completely exclusivist in every way, is not being confronted by the mainstream of Christian Churches. I've had a lot of debate with Catholics and Protestants

over the last few years, and I'm very angry at this, because their silence, in a sense, helps the destruction of mutual understanding built over such a long time, silence in attacking these people, not silence while continuing to debate and to dialogue with Muslims. This has been, I think, one of the very unfortunate consequences of religious reaction after September 11, because it makes more difficult the very much needed discourse between Christianity and Islam. There're many, many people to blame on both sides. On the Islamic side, however, the most extreme accusation of the most strident terrorist-oriented preachers is to call the Christians "the Crusaders." I do not recall a single pronouncement, by anyone, even the most bigoted Saudi preacher, calling Christ a name. I've never heard that. So we do not have parity here by any means, and this has created a problem which is going to cost everybody very dearly.

But parallel with these two reactions, first, further secularization and opposition to religion, second, greater rise of the power of Christian fundamentalism, we have something on the other side, and that is the search for greater inclusivism. September 11 has caused many people in the West, and in America especially, to learn and read more about Islam. Now, of all the great religions of the world, no religion has more difficulty accepting the truth of other religions than does Christianity. For Islam and Hinduism, two of the major religions of the world, it is much easier to accommodate the presence of other revelations. But Christianity is so Christocentric that to accept the idea that God spoke elsewhere is not accepted by most people. And there are some Christian theologian—Hans Küng, John Hick—who have been moving gradually toward this direction during the last half century, but they are not the orthodox theologians of their denominations anyway. And now you see, since September 11, a greater interest in becoming more inclusivist, including Islam. Interest in learning more about Islam has suddenly arisen immensely in the United States. The number of Qur'ans that were sold between 2001 and 2002 was several hundred percent more than the number sold before.

The great problem in this, of course, was that the very fact that there was interest in Islam brought pseudoexperts to the market. And I've said, jokingly, there are so many people who are supposed to be experts on Islam and they do not know whether Islam is spelled with an "s" or a "z." They don't even know how to pronounce the (name of the) country of Iraq, whose Islamic heritage has been half demolished and destroyed. This has made the interest in Islam not a very positive matter in certain circles and has also caused the writing of a large number of books about Islam by people who purport to be scholars. It's like having Goebbels write a book about American democracy. Exactly like that. But they're all in markets, and there's an invisible hand unfortunately whereby these things are made to be widespread. The serious books about Islam are somewhere on the back shelf. If you ask for it, they'll get it for you. So this need for inclusivism, which is a very positive thing, and you see it in the rise of interest in teaching of Islam in various American universities, and Canada is very similar, in the sense all of this also has this backlash, as I said, of a major campaign to preserve present-day ignorance, increasing misinformation, and, worst of all, propagating disinformation. Whenever I listen to television—unfortunately I have to do it once in a while to keep up with what's going on—but some 80 percent of every statement made about Islam is factually false. But it goes on and is repeated and repeated and repeated. That is the condition we're in.

Finally, one of the consequences of September 11 has been the rise of messianism in Christianity. Now Christianity, of course, has always had a messianic element. There were medieval saints who expected the coming of Christ and the age of the Holy Ghost. In the very first century of Christianity, Christians expected the second coming of Christ, but he decided not to come, and here we are, two thousand years later. But every time there is crisis in the world, messianism becomes more powerful among not only Christianity but all religions, including Hinduism, including the expectation of the Cakravarti [Universal Monarch] and the Kalki Avatar, and the Mahdi in Islam, who we're

expecting is coming, and Christians believe in the second coming of Christ. Of course, Muslims also believe there's a second coming of Christ, but coming after that of the Mahdi. Anyway, this movement, of course, was strengthened, and it made millions of dollars for those who wrote of this very exclusivist eschatology, in which you would have a number of these nice Southern Baptists be lifted up in rapture to heaven, without even experiencing death, and the rest of us would have to go through the pain of death and go to hell. This, what I call an exclusivist eschatology, has a devastating effect upon the relationship between Christianity and other religions of the world and has caused a major crisis within Christian thought itself.

Now all I've said about Christianity is also true, to a large extent, in Judaism, of course, mutatis mutandis. There're Jews who are messianists. There're Jews who are fundamentalists. There're Jews who've gone in the other direction to try to open themselves up like Christians, who pay attention to a more traditional understanding of religion and participate even in peace movements with Muslims. Dialogue going on right now, as we stand here, with major Jewish figures is much more prevalent than it was twenty years ago, which is one of the very good signs upon the horizons.

Now let me turn to the Islamic world, to which I want to pay most of my attention. In the Islamic world, September 11 did not have an effect of turning people against religion. First of all, there're very few secularists in the Islamic world. This has been debated to a large extent: Why is it that there're so many secularists in the West, where the major religion is Christianity, and so few secularists in the Islamic world, where the major religion is Islam? And, for a long time, the answer was, "Well, of course, the Europeans are much more intelligent than Muslims and Hindus and everybody else. Their intelligence allows them to see that religion is false, and they were one of the first people to really have a postreligious phase, that is, a post-Christian history." Now, of course, nobody buys that nonsense anymore, and one has to reach for deeper causes, which is not the subject of my discussion here today. But there's no doubt that there are very few people who are secularists in the Islamic world. The only ones I can remember are a few Iranians in exile in California, who talk nonsense from morning to night, and that's about it. I know hardly anyone within the Islamic world who's secularist. And so that first reaction that came in this country, of already convinced secularists becoming firmer in their opposition to religion because of the events of September 11, did not take place. And the idea of the forced secularization of society by certain governments in fact began to take a back seat, in such countries as Tunisia, Turkey, and Egypt, where the governments are supposed to be secularist, where the people are devoutly Muslim, and the governments are all supported by the West, precisely because they espouse the cause of secularism. In these countries, the pressure to secularize society has become confronted more and more with sterner opposition.

Perhaps the most important effect of September 11 on the Islamic world is the weakening of the Salafi/Wahhabi heritage and influence. For many of you in the audience who are probably not from the Islamic world, the word *Salafi* in Arabic means ancestors, *Salaf* being the person who has come before. It's somewhat like Confucianism. It's a name given to a movement that began in the eighteenth century and became strong in the nineteenth century by trying to go back to a simple Islam at the origin of Islam, opposition to all of the complexities of city life, of urban life, to Islamic theology and philosophy and art, and especially to the mystical dimension of Islam, which is Sufism, and which is the most universalist and inclusive view within Islam, parallels to what we find in Christianity and Judaism. The Salafi movement has spread through Iraq, and most of the Muslim East, that is, the Arab East. It did not have any influence on Iran, less so on the western part of the Arab world; that is, North Africa, some influence in Pakistan and India, and some influence in Indonesia, but little. After the First World War, the Wahhabis, of course—that was a special branch of Salafism which was much more militaristic and politically inclined, and which opposed both Sufism and Shi'ism very strongly—have been ruling Saudi Arabia and gained greater

power with petrodollars, which became plenty in the 1970s. They came to have the means of projecting their ideology elsewhere. And with the coming of the Iranian Revolution and the fear of the United States and the rest of the West that the revolution of Ayatollah Khomeini would take over surrounding countries, a green light was given, you might say, for the Saudis to spend millions and millions of dollars in schools in Afghanistan, Pakistan, India, and later on central Asia when the Soviet government fell, all across the Asian landmass, and of course within the Arab world itself. And all of this talk you hear about the Taliban being trained in madrasas—*madrasa* simply means college—being attacked in newspapers, comes back to a decision that somebody made probably a few blocks from where my office is on 22nd Street and H in Washington—I don't know which side, but a decision was made there.

Now, the Salafi movement controlled until recently about 80 percent of the mosques in the United States because of the money that was paid by Saudi Arabia to bring imams and other people who were bound to follow the Wahhabi line. Now all of that has weakened. It is amazing how much it has weakened. Because, of course, the people who participated in September 11 all came from an ideological background that was related to this extremist interpretation of Islam, besides the fact that most of them were Saudis, besides that, of course, Bin Laden is a Saudi, and other leaders of the terrorist movement are related to this ideology. And what is called international global Jihadism and so forth comes out of this background. Now, this movement began to be opposed in the United States, once authorities found out what its consequences were. And the Saudis are not sending imams to American mosques any more now. Within Saudi Arabia itself, what is most interesting is that the royal family, after 150 years, is now opening the door to Sufism, even in Mecca and Medina. And although they don't come out openly and say it, a number of very eminent Saudi functionaries now belong to Sufi orders which were underground during all this time because they were not officially accepted. And also, for the first time in the history of Saudi Arabia, recently the Shi'ites of Saudi Arabia are allowed to appear on television—to appear on television as Muslims. So there's a great change coming about. But within the rest of the Islamic world, this change depends on the condition—political condition—of the day. As soon as you bomb Lebanese children and people see those sights, interest in this kind of activist, sometimes militaristic, violent interpretation of Islam increases. And when there is more peace and harmony, it decreases. But I would say that, intellectually, no matter what the newspapers say in this country and in the United States, the Salafi Wahhabi movement is on the wane—intellectually, purely intellectually. It is not on the rise. It is weakening, especially in the last three or four years. You get articles written by people in Turkey, in Egypt, and other places who were once supporters of the Salafi movement, who now try to distance themselves from them.

This current has been complemented by the greater interest in Sufism throughout the Islamic world. Now, this does not mean that this movement itself directly helps Sufism. It means that, by removing the dike of Wahhabism, it allowed the water of Sufism to pour down into the valley of Islamic civilization. In Morocco, already, the year before last—I was there—the Sultan of Morocco reestablished a very important ceremony which had gone back for centuries, bringing authorities of Sufism from North Africa together in a place named Marrakesh, which the French shut down when they were colonizing North Africa for fear of people from different places meeting each other. In Turkey, there are now much less strict restrictions placed on Sufi orders and in many other places. You have local conditions, like in certain parts of Pakistan, sometimes among certain groups in Iran—although right now, Sufism is flowering, especially intellectually in Iran—who oppose this or that Sufi order, but that's an epiphenomenon. The major phenomenon is much greater interest in Sufism, which means also inclusivism, religiously speaking. Long before the modern world, Persian poets like Jalal al-Din Rumi and Hafiz wrote about the universality of religion, that God speaks to all

people. They took the message of the Qur'an seriously, that revelation is universal. I don't have the time today to quote some poems by these men.

But parallel with that, there's no doubt that, as the struggle with the West continues, as the major problems, such as that of the Palestinians and Israelis, such as Kashmir, such as the massacres of Chechnya and other places continue unabated, and as the tragic wars of Afghanistan and Iraq result in very large number of deaths of Muslims, who are hardly mentioned in Western papers—only if one soldier dies it's in the paper and nobody even mentions how many civilians die—as these things continue, the other wave of a religious exclusivism of the Other also continues, and this is going to be very dangerous for small Christian and Jewish minorities who are still living in the Islamic world, where they've lived together for a long, long time in peace. This includes Iran, where we have Armenians and Assyrians, and includes Syria, which has a large Christian population. It even includes Lebanon, where the recent war in a sense created a crack in the unity of Lebanese society, by the West continuing to call the war a war between Islam and Hezbollah, while the rest of Lebanon was being bombed to smithereens.

Moreover, in Islam, we have something very similar to the messianic movement in Christianity, and it is called Mahdiism. Just three to four days ago it was the birthday of the Mahdi, the fifteenth of Shahban, the month before Ramadan, the fasting month which starts in less than ten days from now. I was giving a talk in Washington at the time. This very issue came up, and I mentioned its politicization. It was at Georgetown. And I said then that the politicization of Mahdiism by the present government of Iran, and, to some extent Iraq, is just a mirror image of the politicization of messianism in Christianity, in what can be called right or extreme Christianity. But it's a phenomenon that's definitely a consequence of September 11. Before September 11, there was already a wave of messianism, going back to Ayatollah Khomeini. People saw his picture in the moon. Some even thought he was the twelfth imam, or the Mahdi, and so forth. And yet this movement was not that strong. But in the last few years, it's become more and more strong, and as we know, all these messianic movements are revolutionary movements, whether it's in Christianity or the Jewish Messiah or Mahdi—whatever it is in any religion.

And finally, [there is ferment in] the Islamic world because of the lack of seriousness of modernism or fundamentalism as an alternative, toward the revival of interest in traditional Islam. I've said for many years, even before all these events took place, that we do not have in the Islamic world only this division between modern and traditional. That's false. What we have is distinction between modern, fundamentalist, and traditional. And much of what the West calls fundamentalist is traditional, while fundamentalism is the other side of the coin of modernism. You cannot say, in the context of Christianity, that St. Bernard of Clairvaux is a Christian fundamentalist because he was such a devout Christian, because there was no modernism at that time. Fundamentalism cannot exist without modernism, and much of its attitude is the same as modernism. But there's the third way, which is that of the majority of Muslims as they have always lived historically, and that is called traditional Islam, in which there has been a much greater interest because of these events. I can tell you that personally. My life has been devoted to it for the last fifty years; I've been writing on this subject, this subject of bringing back to life traditionalist Islam, with its dimension of inclusivism, openness, and vast intellectual and spiritual heritage, which is refuted by both the Salafis and the modernists—by both the Islamic fundamentalists and the modernists—to make use of this intellectual and spiritual heritage to find a modus vivendi with Christianity and Judaism and to present a version of Islam to the world that can live with the contemporary world without submitting itself to the follies of the world in which we live.

QUESTIONS AND ANSWERS
FOR THE AUTHOR

Question: Professor Nasr, thank you very much for your talk. You made a little remark about Islam and Hinduism, and you spoke about other revelations of God. I want to just draw your attention to the fact that Hinduism is not a religion of revelation. Judaism, Christianity, Islam, and perhaps Bahá'í, are religions of revelation. But the question that I wanted to ask you is: After having revealed, making a revelation that brought into existence Judaism and Christianity, are you in a position to tell me, in one or two sentences, why exactly the revelation that brought into existence Islam was necessary? Thank you.

Answer: From the human point of view, Christianity had not been able to hold its very birthplace together. You had these eastern churches that would fight against each other, and the Byzantines, whenever they could get their hands on these people, would massacre them. Just a century before the rise of Islam, the Byzantine army captured the city of Edessa and put over five thousand Christian priests to death. And so obviously, this was not going to work out, in contrast to the West, where Christianity became a unified force to create Western civilization. As for Judaism, Judaism was not a religion for the whole world. The Jews never claimed that. They were considered the chosen people. And what about guidance for the rest of the people? And, obviously, each religion has a certain dynamic. It only spreads to a certain amount of area, in light of its own inner structure and the energy which God has given to it. How come that Islam spread so easily over the Christian East, but never to the Christian West? Why is it that Islam didn't sweep over France and Germany and finish Christianity off? God had not willed it. And so the idea that a new religion begins is not one that can be determined by us. But one can also see the need—like today, many people feel the need. Those people who are not devoted to traditional religions say, "Oh, we are in need of a new religion." I've heard that a thousand times. Those who are followers of religions, whichever one it is, they believe that there will not be a new religion, but a return—heaven, once again, manifesting itself in the world in the context the great religions already created. It's remarkable how universal this idea is. As I said, we have the Kalki Avatar, and Mahdi, and the second coming of Christ, and Lao-tzu coming back from the west, and so on and so on. And the North American Indians have very elaborate teachings about this. As for Hinduism not being a revelation, it depends on how you define the word *revelation*. If the Srutis are inspired texts, like the Upanishads and the Vedas, received by the rishis in India, should one not call it a revelation? It's not simply something human. If it were, it would not have lasted for so many thousands of years. Nothing human endures like that.

Question: I'm a Roman Catholic who has struggled over the political influence of the Vatican in the war against global feminism and its seeking of allies within conservative Islamic movements, as also now, with the government of George Bush with the Christian Right in the United States. Now, the Vatican opposes the entry of Turkey into the European Union—or elements of the Vatican do—because they are now concerned with reestablishing Christendom as a basis of European identity. And this has been opposed by the European Parliament, but the entry of Turkey into the European Union was opposed by the Vatican. So there's that kind of division there. However, in the last decade, if you look at the United Nations and the conferences on women—I was there in New York, and I saw the alliance that builds between conservative Christian movements and conservative Islam over the rise of global feminism. And I wondered if you would comment on that as an element. I know it's outside the purview of specifically September 11, but I think there's an interesting element that is now there in the modern world about the alliance between these conservative elements in these three religions.

Answer: Think of the global air industry, (which) comes from the West, captures the world, and it's called "global." You must remember that, therefore, resistance to it in non-Western society, which did not inaugurate this movement, is somewhat different from what one sees in societies which did. Having said that, when you have an international situation, you have major organizations with religious or political clout. They make alliances on the basis of convenience, on certain issues. For example, right now, the United States might be in perfect accord with Russia on some matters but differ completely on other issues. The church has found an ally in Islam, which emphasizes the importance of the family, composed of male, female, and children. And all the experimentations with new kinds of families and so forth have until now been opposed in Islam and also by the Catholic Church. It is a diplomatic move by the church to try to join forces with Islam on this particular issue. On another issue, it will join forces with Western secularists or the Russian Orthodox Church or something else. But you're right. It's not a theological black-and-white declaration of doctrine. It's a kind of diplomacy to further the agenda of each of these churches or organizations.

Question: With your permission, I'd like to first of all thank you for the broad scope of phenomena you pointed to, but I want to ask your permission also to take exception with two words, and those two words were *mutatis mutandis*. In your presentation, you argued, or suggested, that the situation vis-à-vis Judaism in relationship to Islam is more or less a copy or a clone or close enough to simply be dismissed within two sentences as similar to what's taking place within Christianity. And I'd like to take exception to that. First, the nature of Jewish fundamentalism is very, very different. As a religion, it is based on oral tradition together with a written tradition. It is simply impossible to have a similar return to scripture. Jewish fundamentalists are much more like Bernard of Clairvaux. Of course, there is this aspect of a flip side of modernity that you pointed to applies also, within certain segments. But I think the key element concerning Jewish fundamentalism as applies to Islam is that Jewish-Muslim relations are almost completely overshadowed by the situation of Israel and the Arab states, primarily the Palestinians. And as a consequence of that, the image of Muslims that occupy the Jewish consciousness has much more to do with what's going on in Israel than what they have to do in what's going on with September 11. As an organizer of a meeting of a hundred imams and rabbis in Brussels last year, I can testify to the fact that what was uppermost on the minds of Jews and Muslims had to do with what's happening with mutual images, the perception and the loss of centuries of common understanding, common living, that have been, in the same way that you described the erosion of Muslim-Christian relations over the past fifty years, similar movements happening in Muslim-Jewish relations but having very, very little to do with the events of September 11. And consequently, I would ask for your permission to exclude Judaism from your presentation and to recognize the different dynamics, both as far as how the religion is constituted but, even more so, vis-à-vis how the recent events and their politicization play into contemporary Muslim-Jewish relations.

Answer: First of all, Jewish fundamentalism is like Christian fundamentalism in one way, in that it takes the text of the Old Testament literally and therefore claims the land of Israel for the Jews. It's not just a symbolic understanding. It's a literal understanding. It's the foundation for Zionism. And the Christian fundamentalist also takes the Bible literally. But of course, as far as other matters are concerned, Jewish fundamentalism is most of all involved with land. Christian fundamentalism is not involved with its own land, although there're now Christian Zionists, of course, who are as defensive that the land belongs to Jews in the Holy Land as the Jews are. I'm not saying the two are the same. But I was not even talking about Jewish fundamentalism in relation to Islam. I was talking of Jewish fundamentalism as religious attitude within the Jewish community in the West. You have the same things you have in Christianity—further secularism, inclusivism, and exclusivism. All these three currents you also have within Judaism. That's what I really wanted to say. Obviously, vis-à-vis Islam, the situation is based on many different parameters that don't exist within Islam in relation to Western Christianity.

Question: Can we just agree that not every reference to the meaning of a text is necessarily fundamentalist? Otherwise, we run into the impossible situation that only figurative and allegorical readings have meaning. So not every reference to text is necessarily fundamentalist. The rest has to be explored beyond this conversation.

Answer: You're pushing the situation, but since I'm a philosopher and theologian, I have to answer you. It's those very texts of the Bible that have been considered to be contentious from the point of view of modern ideologies that are not accepted literally. That's the answer to it. Alright, next.

Question: I refer to your remark about secularists in the Muslim world. There are very few of them because none are permitted to live. I give you a few examples of Indonesia. In 1965, half a million of them were massacred by the military over there. Your own Iran had fifty thousand people from the Left, ranging from Islamic Marxists to the Communists, who were completely eradicated. I come from Pakistan, where if one was a secularist, one would be determined to be an apostate and a blasphemer and, therefore, liable to be killed or persecuted or set aside. I've lived in Saudi Arabia for ten years. I can assure you that the sheer presence, or sheer uttering of the words "separation of religion and state" would get me deported, arrested, or sent out. So, to suggest that there are very few secularists in the Islamic world is a consequence of an open choice is not correct. I would suggest to you that Mosaddeq was a secularist, was eliminated by the CIA, but his large support base came from the secular Left. And to justify their demands and not explain why they have disappeared from Morocco or Tunisia, or that they were the core elements in the anticolonial movement is, in my opinion, a bit simplistic.

Answer: Mosaddeq was a very close friend of our family. Mosaddeq was not a secularist in a modern sense. He was a modernized Iranian. And the effects of the colonization of the Islamic world throughout was to turn a number of people to modernism, and, therefore, they could be called, in a sense, secularist, but not philosophically. There were people in whose lives religion no longer played such an important role. Let it be noted that the effect of centuries of colonialism of the West on the Islamic world, or, in fact, the rest of Asia, was not to convert the rest of Asia to Christianity—a very small number of people did—but to try to cut them off from their own religion; that is, to create secularized Hindus, secularized Buddhists, secularized Muslims. And I did not deny that. The 500,000 people killed in Indonesia were Communists. And there are a number of people in the Islamic world who turn to the Left and become out-and-out secularists who are Communists, including in Iran. But it's interesting that in both Indonesia and Iran, they lost. It's not enough to say that President Roosevelt spent sixty thousand dollars to carry out a coup to bring the Shah back to power and Mosaddeq found that it was physically impossible (to resist). He was totally upset. There had not been the political and religious background ready for it. The fact is that the result has been what we see before us today. Even if you have two million, three million, five million, ten million secularists in the Islamic world—and I do not think there is more than that number—even if they're left alone, compared to a population of 1.3 billion people, that is not very much.

Question: For me personally, I view science as being in a continual or perpetual state of revelation, and I'd like to hear your views about science and our understanding of physical realities. In the introduction, you made it clear that you had spent some time studying science. I would like to hear you either speak to the reasons you divorced your studies from it or how they could be tied in to the studies you currently pursue.

Answer: I would like to refer to the series of books in the Library of Living Philosophers, those big thousand-page volumes. The first volume for the twenty-first century is about yours truly. And there're two long articles about this very issue that you ask. It is impossible for me in two minutes to really satisfy your need in a way as to be honest and to do justice to this very important subject. But as for science being revelation, the word *revelation*

of course can be used in many ways. You can be playing on the piano and say, "Suddenly a revelation came to me and I composed this melody for a Broadway show." That's also possible. We, however, use the word *revelation* technically and theologically, on the basis of a worldview which, first of all, believes that the physical or psychophysical world is not the only reality. There is a spiritual reality, and above that, a pure, absolute Reality which is even above the spiritual. And revelation is the coming down, the descent, of something from that upper world to the psychophysical world. That's what revelation is. Now, modern science, as a way of knowing, is not based on that. I'm the last person in the world to say that there's such a thing as scientific method. I think that is absurd for a person who knows the history of science. The major scientists, let's say Einstein's 1905 paper—that is not based upon the scientific method. The theory of special relativity was not based on carrying out experiments in a laboratory and all these things that we learn to test a theory. His work was based on intuition and not ordinary scientific method. If you want to call that intuition a revelation, we have no qualms. And there have been remarkable "revelations" of this kind, especially in the early twentieth century, with Heisenberg, Schrödinger, Einstein, Max Planck, and so on. These four especially should be noted in this context. There's no doubt about that. Now that's not the same thing as the revelation of the Upanishads or the Qur'an or the Torah. Such revelation assumes another structure of reality. Schrödinger who, in fact, followed the Vedantic philosophy as he said, never said that: "I wrote the Schrödinger equation as a result of hearing it from on high, from a divine power." And that's where the difference comes. It's a question of clarifying your vocabulary. But I do believe that much of modern science is intuitive. Most of it is cranking things out from day to day, but for those people who are at the forefront of modern science, they are creative thinkers, and science should not be reduced to what you learn in first-year college as the scientific method. That's all. Good luck to you.

Religion and Media

Satguru Bodhinatha Veylanswami

As a publisher of *Hinduism Today* magazine, I've been asked to speak on the topic of religion and the media. The media obviously has played the central role in disseminating information on September 11, subsequent terrorist attacks, and the military actions in Afghanistan, Iraq, and the Middle East, all of which have a religious component. By *media*, we specifically mean journalistic reporting, be it newspapers, magazines, television, or the Internet, and not including fictional presentations, such as art, movies, music, and the stage, though these too have significant impact on how religion is viewed. The question arises naturally as to the media's ability to deal with this religious component, given its limitations of expertise, time, and known institutional peculiarities. We're going to talk about these limitations over the next hour, as well as the opportunities which religious people and groups have to educate and favorably impact the media, locally and globally. The organizer of the congress, Professor Arvind Sharma, mentioned in his letter inviting us to give this presentation that he hoped we would be able to show how the media might use its persuasive power to promote harmony among religions and bridge the secular-religious divide. In our opinion, this is a challenging possibility. But the media will not be able to accomplish this by itself,

for the media to promote harmony among religions requires religious groups to work with the media in specific ways, which we shall detail in this presentation. The same effort to promote harmony among religions should also enable the nonreligious, secular members of society to gain greater understanding, and perhaps even appreciation, of the religions within society.

Our experience with the media comes from *Hinduism Today* magazine, which was founded in 1979 and has since evolved into a full-color magazine, published quarterly, supplemented by our daily Hindu Press International e-mail news summary service. We publish *Hinduism Today* as a nonprofit service to our faith to record the modern history of a billion-strong religion in renaissance. We have no political agenda and report on all the various sects and lineages of our religion. Mostly, we promote everyone's good works, though when necessary, we investigate controversies, especially those covered poorly in the mainstream media. Our goals are to foster Hindu solidarity, inform and inspire Hindus, and dispel misinformation about Hinduism. The following slides show our covers and articles from several of our issues over the last few years. This talk is first setting some basic definitions, then discussing the realities of journalism, in order to offer some strategies for better relationships between religionists and the media.

The media is a business. It's an obvious but crucial point that media such as newspapers, magazines, and television are a business. With the exception of public broadcasting and government-controlled outlets, they're expected to turn a profit. This business sells as news both information and entertainment. Media have criteria for determining what is news. Everyday, journalists around the world ponder whether some event or issue is news according to established criteria. So then, what is this news the media wants to provide us? Here's one typical set of criteria, illustrated with photos from the major wire services. First, effect: How many people were, are, or will be affected, and by how much? For example, the 2004 tsunami pictured here, the war in Iraq or Lebanon have affected tens of millions of people. In terms of religion, a split in the Anglican Church or a change in Catholic doctrine would affect a large number of people and hence is news. In general, war, crime, violence of any sort, accidents, and natural disasters are all news because they have such a dramatic impact on those affected. Second, timeliness. Did the event occur very recently? As information becomes older, it becomes less newsworthy. A major accident snarling traffic downtown is news the day it happens but not the next morning. Annual reporting of religious holidays is also an example. They are news when they happen but not at other times of the year. This Zuma press photo [I am showing now] is of the festival commemorating the culmination of the annual pilgrimage to Mecca as celebrated in West Palm Beach, Florida. Third, revelation. Is there significant new information previously unknown, for example, a new cure for a disease, an archeological discovery, uncovered criminal activity or, for a religious example, the discovery of the *Gospel of Judas*, pictured here in its original bundle, before conservation work began. Fourth, proximity. Was the event nearby geographically? Perhaps the most common example being the local weather, which is always news. For example, your July heat wave, for which the wires posted this photo from Zuma press

on electrical demand. Fifth, oddity. Was the event highly unusual? In the journalism books, they say dog bites man is not news, but man bites dog is. Two months ago, in Ottawa, a fleeing suspect did actually bite a police dog named Pago, generating news stories as far away as South Africa and Malaysia. Unfortunately, religion often ends up in this category. Be it Shi'ite Muslims flaying themselves to mark the martyrdom of Imam Hussein or Christian ministers handling poisonous snakes, both acts of testament to their faith. And you'll likely find in articles using these photos that nothing is made of the Shi'ite man's ability to withstand pain or the fact that the minister does not get bit by the snake. Sixth, entertainment. Does it make for a fun or engaging story? Good stories about children and animals fall in this category, as does the entire realm of sports. A number of religious activities can come in this category, such as a traditional wedding, a festival, or a coming-of-age event that are colorful and interesting to people of other faiths. For example, this wire photo of a 2005 Sikh wedding here in Toronto qualifies on three counts. The groom is part of a colorful wedding, but also the child and the horse add diverting or amusing elements. Seventh, celebrity. Was anyone famous involved? Entire publications operate within this single category. They deem it news to take a photo of a movie star walking down the street. So if a celebrity does something religious, it becomes news. For example, pop singer Britney Spears visiting a Hindu temple in Los Angeles to have her baby blessed. She generated many stories, most of them unexplainably critical of her. The celebrity effect is also cumulative, so if you have the Dalai Lama paired with celebrity actor Richard Gere, it becomes even more important news. These categories are often applied collectively. For example, this photo combined a culturally significant Toronto Film Festival with the appealing children and a celebrity. That would be the movie-star dog, Lassie.

You'll note that this method of categorizing news doesn't necessarily identify truly important issues or events. And they may actually marginalize them. In practice, the media tends to focus on open conflict and not necessarily on truly critical issues. Professor Beverly Keever of the School of Communications at the University of Hawaii told us there is an inverse relationship to what is considered news and what is important. She gives the example of the breakdown of the foster care system in Hawaii, which will ultimately have a disastrous societal impact, that never appears in the news. Global warming tends to get some press these days, much more than it did twenty years ago, but still not much, considering the consequences. It got more when Al Gore, a celebrity, made a documentary on it, adding to its news value. Important religious issues may not qualify as news. How often does one see a story on the declining religiosity among youth or the decline in the number of youth entering the clergy, both issues in all religions? What, in the long run, is the human consequence of an unreligious generation compared to, say, the results of a province's next elections, which could be but a minor blip in political history?

Are conferences news? People who want to change the world such as our organizer, Professor Arvind Sharma, arrange conferences to bring together the best and the brightest to tackle important issues. The media will likely ignore these conference proceedings. Why? Because a conference by itself doesn't fit into the news criteria. To be news, something has to be present other than the fact of a conference. You've just seen here in Toronto the fairly good coverage of the AIDS conference, but what did it focus on? Bill Gates, Bill Clinton, and Richard Gere, the celebrities. The AIDS conference cochair, Dr. Helene Gale, fairly acknowledged, "It's been wonderful to have people come to the conference, who, by definition of their visibility, create more visibility for the conference." The boycotting of the conference by Uganda AIDS activist Marvin Simpa created additional news, as did the debate at the conference over the dominance of the celebrities. Street protests also bring out the media, and had Dr. Sharma assigned several dozen graduate students to picket this venue on any pretense, media coverage would have increased.

We have asked several prominent Hindus to contribute comments for this presentation, which we will share as we proceed through the talk. The first is from Dr. Karan Singh. He is a son of the last Maharaja of Kashmir and a prominent Indian politician and scholar of religion. He has been elected to India's Parliament, held cabinet post, and served as India's ambassador to the United States. He has represented Hinduism at several international conferences and is a major figure in the interfaith movement. He specifically addressed the issue of how the media selects its news. He said, "It is the big responsibility of the media to report factually and accurately on what has happened. At the same time, the media should throw its weight in favor of communal harmony. Presently, the media hardly takes note of the interfaith movement. For example, there was a huge gathering for the Parliament of the World's Religions in Cape Town, South Africa in 1999. There was not a word in the press about it. Twenty years ago, the environmental movement was similarly ignored or on the periphery of media coverage. Now, it has moved to the center. The same needs to happen with the interfaith movement." He also remarked: "Prior to the England August arrests for the plane plot using liquid explosives, a million Muslims have lived peacefully in England for thirty or forty years. Now the whole community is under suspicion. This is a tragedy, but brought on by the way these jihadists have acted, which has demonized Islam. The press should report on the softer aspects of Islam. The teachings of Sufism, for example, should be brought to the fore, whereas now, Wahhabi Islam has more exposure. In general, religions need to project more universal principles. Hinduism has a strong tradition of pluralism."

Now, we will talk about the world of the journalist. Experienced reporters are excellent writers well trained in information gathering. They are a quick study of complex issues and expert at sniffing out deception and trickery. Reporters are almost always working under time deadlines. They are not researchers with weeks or months to investigate their topic. A report on an event today often needs to be filed tonight for publishing in the morning or even for today's evening news. So reporters can only include in their report the information they can gather in the short time they have to gather it. The job of the reporter often reveals to him the underbelly of life—crime, drugs, fraud in conflict. After a number of years of seeing the worst humankind has to offer, reporters can become jaded, even cynical. They've run into too many people willing to say anything to get into the news, been lied to by too many politicians or crafty businessmen with a hidden agenda, and seen too often in firsthand man's inhumanity to man. It's not a profession that attracts religious people. We encountered one reporter, a prominent member of the profession in the United States, who said, "We don't talk about religion in the newsroom. We consider religion just another special interest group." Another reporter confided, "We'll report on your activity, but we don't care about your core beliefs." To be sure, other reporters we consulted did not endorse these cynical attitudes, yet acknowledged they were not uncommon. It is unlikely this institutional attitude will change any time soon.

Just because reporters are in a hurry doesn't mean they're not prepared to observe minute details in their reports. Associated Press is the largest news-gathering organization in the world. It publishes a style book which is a mini-encyclopedia, containing entries ranging from the correct spelling of certain words to the proper use of acronyms to short descriptions of major religious denominations. There is one on every English-speaking reporter's desk in the world. We suggest you buy one and study it. Understand the minutiae a reporter can manage. For example, what is this? Right on page 38 of the AP style manual: Canada goose, not Canadian goose. Similarly, any reporter can tell you that Jeep should be capitalized, as should Jacuzzi and Rollerblades, because they're all trademarks, as the stylebook explains. Reporters are instructed to use letter carriers instead of mailman, because women hold the job, and that there is no apostrophe in Pikes Peak. The stylebook contains a number of entries on religion. The stylebook is fairly comprehensive for Christian sects, with multiple entries covering several pages. Here's the entry on Islam, all of Islam, which amounts to just a single page. Hinduism at left and Buddhism at right each get only one

column. Neither Sikhs nor Jains are even mentioned. The information on Hinduism is simplistic and contains the astoundingly inaccurate statement that, in Hinduism, there is no formal clergy, when there are thousands of formal priestly and monastic lineages. It also says there are one million Hindus in the United States, when there are 2.2 million. Reporters obviously are resourceful enough to find other sources of information than the stylebook. However, the stylebook is considered authoritative. The lesson to be learned from the stylebook is that reporters are quite capable of dealing with minute details of a subject. We're not asking too much that they learn and understand the history, the theology, and the current manifestation of any religion or religious movement which enters their sphere of reporting.

To summarize our first section, the media is a business, with all that means in terms of selling a product. News is what the media say it is and not necessarily what is important. What we, as religious people, consider significant about our faith or what's vitally important to the future of humankind may be dismissed as not newsworthy. The criteria for news are effect, timeliness, revelation, proximity, oddity, entertainment, and celebrity. There are cynical people in the media business who do not regard religion kindly. The media is quite capable of dealing with complex issues and subtle distinctions. It is up to religious groups to educate them as to how to do so with regard to a particular religion.

Moving on to our second part. There are two general circumstances under which religion comes into the media: proactive interaction and reactive interaction. Proactive interaction is when religious groups or persons seek out the press with the intent of creating a news item. Proactive interaction is the topic of this section, section two of our talk. The second manner in which religion comes into the press is through reactive interaction, when something has happened, like terrorist attacks by members of our faiths, for example, and suddenly the press comes looking for us. Or we approach them because something published provoked and outraged us. This will be the subject of our third section.

It's our thesis that religious groups should take the time and make the effort to create proactive interactions with the media, as a means of educating the community about their faith. In this section of our talk, we're going to explore the various means of getting religion in the media in benign circumstances; that is, when not faced with some crisis. Environmentalists have a saying that, to save the planet, we must think globally and act locally. We recommend applying the same concept to media relations. It means that we evaluate the global situation about religion and determine those things which we can do at a local level to bring about some improvement. The first step in proactive interaction is getting to know your local media. The goal with the local press is not to hit the front page or the prime-time TV report. It is rather to establish a constant low-key presence through news items, photo opportunities, educational features, opinion pieces, and letters to the editor. In North America, most newspapers and magazines have an editor responsible for religious reporting. TV stations may have a reporter assigned part-time to religion. Religious leaders should meet the local religion editors and get to know them personally. The leaders should make themselves easily available. Religious leaders can facilitate the flow of news about their community to the media. Religion editors want to reflect their community's religious diversity in the publication. The religion editor at the *Honolulu Advertiser* newspaper told us that most of the material she receives is from Christian evangelicals. She, like other religion editors, has to seek out other religious groups and develop stories. And media conglomerate Gannett Corporation, of which the *Advertiser* is a part, actually grades its publications on the number of ethnic religious voices which appear. One fruitful area of news, she explains, is the intersecting circles between religious communities; that is, areas of concern, activity, or ceremony, which are pretty much the same across religions. For example, one religious community's concern for passing on their religious heritage to the next generation makes a good story to a religion editor, as all other communities will be interested in it. Celebrations common to all religions, such as marriage or coming of age, likewise make interesting stories and serve to educate the entire community in particular traditions. Color ceremonies, such as the Sikh wedding we saw earlier, can serve, for example, as a means to explain the Sikh view of marriage and family.

Next, for both local and wider coverage, religious groups need to have a clear Internet presence, a Web site which explains the basics of the faith in simple terms. Religious groups should also have a section on their Web site for the media. One critical aspect to this section is well-written press releases on recent events complete with high resolution photos and contact information for any reporter wanting more specifics. A group with the resources can hire a public relations firm to manage a Web site, issue press releases, and respond to the media. Here, for example, is a nicely organized main page of the immense Vatican Web site. By clicking on the information button, one quickly goes to a page which includes press contacts. This, on the other hand, is the first web page listed for a Google search on Islam. While it is a vast Web site, it is not clearly organized and provides no links for the media to use.

There are many opportunities in a community to generate favorable news coverage. One that works well for us is our open house, which we hold once every two years, inviting friends on that island, local clergy, politicians, and the media. There is a tour, entertainment, and small talk, all of which allow those of other religions to understand what we are doing. Weddings are also of general interest, especially for one that is colorful. The local press will be delighted to cover it, either as part of the religion page or the society page. A church, mosque, or temple can work out coverage of a festival or holy days with the local press. Most communities have interfaith organizations. Participation is not likely to generate media coverage but is a valuable opportunity to educate other ministers on one's faith. All ministers of religion in one area should be considered as one's natural allies regardless of sect, and an effort made to personally know each. Not to be overlooked is the simple but expensive method of buying paid advertising space in newspapers, magazines, television, or, in this case, on a billboard calling for the ordination of women as priests in the Catholic Church. Ads can be used noncontroversially to explain a particular religious holiday or be a carefully crafted statement in response to a tragic event.

One can gain favorable media coverage and community appreciation through social service activities, such as feeding the poor, holding medical camps, and disaster relief. The Sikh religion has a tradition of free feeding, the langar, which they put into action during disasters in the United States. The langar, or community kitchen, was established by Sikh Gurus five hundred years ago to provide food to everyone. Those in India are familiar with the tradition and expect the appearance of langar during relief work, such as this one after the tsunami struck South India. But this is something new in the West, a colorful and charitable tradition which made for news in the context of the Katrina relief efforts. Here, Christian charity presents a check for twenty thousand dollars to the Red Cross for Katrina relief. One U.S. Hindu temple had no such programs and told me they were regarded as a cult by the local community. Other Hindu temples, on the other hand, are major supporters of the food bank and local charities and are well regarded by their community. A religious group helping with a disaster that is not nearby should definitely contact their local press to inform them of their efforts.

Swami Pragyanand, the spokesperson for one of India's largest monastic orders, the Avahan Akhara, was interviewed by *Hinduism Today* for this event and spoke to the role of media in India. He said: "At the moment in India, the media role is not satisfactory. They publish exclusively negative news, giving full coverage to every explosion, and nothing positive. If they give news of crime, why not also religion? The readers need positive news, too, and the media should be helpful to religion and can play a prominent role in the character-building of our youth. In India now, they will report negative information on religion but not the positive work that is being done."

Religious groups need to be prepared to take advantage of opportunities, for example, by having well-trained speakers available on short notice. Speaking opportunities range from public forums organized by politicians to TV programs to elementary school presentations. A recent program on the Public Broadcasting System assembled a group of moderate Muslims, including one woman, to discuss issues about Islam. Speakers should be people educated in the faith who speak from their heart. Community interfaith groups can organize speakers of the religions of the community. For example, the Milwaukee Wisconsin Interfaith Group has a speaker's bureau. The Catholic Church there took the lead to manage this Web site for the speakers who represent the Buddhist, Christian, Christian Science, Hindu, Jewish, and Muslim communities. In Honolulu, following September 11, the Muslim community formed a speaker's bureau that was available for just about any occasion or venue, from TV interviews to elementary school presentations. The Southern Poverty Law Center in the United States has a program called Teaching Tolerance. One part of it is to have children meet children of other religions. Instituting such programs is an effective way of becoming known in your community. Some religions have succeeded in creating national and international groups which monitor and respond to the press, such as B'nai Brith, Council on American Islamic Relations, and the Hindu American Foundation. Those groups respond both to events that have involved their faith as well as the way their religion is treated in the media itself. Advocacy groups necessarily work to influence the political process, which is why we ourselves don't engage in this kind of activity.

A religious group can also be its own press, as we have done with *Hinduism Today* and our daily e-mail news summary service, Hindu Press International. But being your own press is different from being a watchdog or advocacy group, as just discussed. To be effective, it needs to be done in a thoroughly professional manner, on a par with *Newsweek* or *Time* magazines. Its reporting needs to be accurate and unbiased, something that can be trusted by the media. While not begun by a religious group, a useful illustration is Al Jazeera, the Qatar-based news channel and Web site. Prior to September 11, hardly anyone in the West had heard of it, and when they did, they thought it perhaps a radical Muslim operation. But its factual reporting quickly dispelled that impression, at least among those who explored the organization. Al Jazeera has a skilled team of reporters on the scene of major events and from this basis generates accurate news. In doing so, it follows standard journalism practices. What Al Jazeera has accomplished is to bring an Arab viewpoint to events which would otherwise be seen only through the eyes of Western journalists.

In summary then, the elements of proactive interaction with the media are as follows: be a part of your local community by bringing your lives into theirs—the reports on holidays, religious rights, and so on—and by making your religion's voice heard on important issues; personally get to know the local journalists and television reporters; make it easy for them to collect a story on your community; understand how the media thinks and what it considers news; run regular programs of social service, such as medical camps or food distribution; be prepared to respond to local and national disasters, either by direct efforts or by donating money; create or join a speaker's bureau; form a local or national activist organization; become your own media with a newspaper, magazine, or television or radio station; develop a comprehensive, media-friendly Web site; invite the media to an open house, regular services, special events and holidays; let them meet the congregation; participate in local interfaith activities; and—if all else fails—buy an ad.

Dr. A Vaithilingam is the president of the Malaysia Hindu Sangam. We interviewed him for this presentation here as a representative of a country where the media is watched quite closely. His perspective is one of someone living in a potentially volatile country, where sections of the media have in the past instigated disruptive activities. We are not in any way endorsing suppression of a free press as is done in Malaysia but include his testimony to show the underlying motivation and mechanics of such suppression. He said,

Let me first give some background about Malaysia and freedom of the press. There are three groups in Malaysia: the Malays, who are the majority; the Chinese, who control the economy; and the Indians, who are about seven percent. In 1959, there were racial riots, especially in Kuala Lumpur. Following these racial riots, restrictions were imposed on the press in the 1960s and 70s. Then things got a little bit more liberal until, in the 80s, the issue of religion conversion of Muslims by certain Christian groups happened. Dr. Mahathir Mohamad became Prime Minister in 1981 and he imposed a lot of restrictions on the press. Personally, I feel that because of the seriousness of either race or religion, sometimes there is a need for a bit of restrictions. Recently we faced the claim that Moorthy, a Hindu, an ex-army man who was part of Malaysia's Everest climbing team, had converted to Islam shortly before he died. He was already unconscious when the conversion claim was announced. And after he died, he was given a Muslim burial. Attempts by his Hindu wife to claim his body for cremation were rejected by the courts on the basis that they could not overrule the Muslim Shari'ah court, which had already decided that Moorthy had converted. This became a very emotional issue for both Muslims and non-Muslims. Now, there is the case of Lena Joy, a Malay Muslim girl who converted to Christianity and now demands that this conversion be officially recognized on her ID card. Shari'ah court will not recognize the conversion and the High Court has declined to intervene. Now the case has gone to the Supreme Court and it is yet to be decided. We, the non-Muslims, have campaigned that Article 11 of the Constitution assuring the freedom of choice and worship be upheld. Muslims want Article 12-11A to prevail. This article was added in Mahathir's time and states that all matters pertaining to Islam should be decided by the Shari'ah court. The issue is highly sensitive and soon will be decided by the Supreme Court.

Moving on to our part three. In this third part of our presentation, we're going to talk about reactive interaction with the press. That is, how should religious people and groups deal with a breaking news event that reflects upon them as a religion? The day a religion or religious group is badly portrayed in the press is not the best day to start developing a working relationship with the media. An existing, well-developed relationship is a better starting point. Events that attract global attention require a response on both the global and local levels. Unfortunately, only the Catholic Church is really organized so as to respond in a unified manner. The lack of centralized authority in most religions can make it difficult for the majority feelings to be heard.

An immediate response is important. As an example of responding to a major event, we'll take the July 28 shooting at a Seattle synagogue, which left one dead and five wounded. The attack occurred in the afternoon of July 28 and is reported in the *Seattle Times*. The Council on American Islamic Relations issued a press release shortly after midnight of the following day, just hours after the shooting occurred. It includes names and contact information for seven Islamic organizations in the Seattle area. Excerpts from the Council on American Islamic Relations' statement are included at the end of the *Seattle Times'* report which appeared the day after the shooting. On the following day, the 30th, a conciliatory article appears in the *Seattle Times* containing statements from Jews and Muslims, including community organizations mentioned in the Council on American Islamic Relations' press release and Aziz Junejo, a columnist for the *Seattle Times'* Faith and Values page, that is, their religion page. This is an example of a good response to a crisis, which involved both the issuing of a timely statement by the Council on American Islamic Relations and the use of a long-standing relationship with the *Seattle Times'* religion page columnist Aziz Junejo.

Anuttama Dasa is the North American director of communications for the International Society for Krishna Consciousness. As such, he is responsible for dealing with the national press and for educating local chapters on public relations. He's had many years of experience. Asked by us for his suggestions to religions for dealing with the media, he responded:

> The media is the gatekeeper to the minds and hearts of most of the world's population. As people of faith, we need to understand that media and work with media people to promote the important truths we have to offer the world. The media is composed of people like you and I that have feelings, limitations, and a job to do under tremendous pressure. They're paid to get out the story, whether it is positive or not. Sadly, sensational news sells. Don't take it personally. Instead, be proactive. For example, promote significant, positive events to the media. Know your facts and present them in an easily understandable way. Be ready to provide photo opportunities and interviews with a variety of interesting people in your community, not just the institutional head. Do not be defensive if the media takes a negative perspective. Help them see a balanced and fair perspective. If you don't know the answer to something, say so, and get back with the correct information as soon as possible. Don't be evasive. Do not assume the media hates you. They don't. They're only trying to fill their paper, magazine, or TV news with something of interest.

Next, we'll look at an October 4, 2003, report in the *Toronto Star* which upset the Hindu community in Canada. It's an example of media coverage which is biased, unfair, or demeaning to a community and how to deal with it. The *Star* published a photo of a Durga statue being prepared for the annual Durga festival in India, a multiday celebration involving hundreds of millions of Hindus. In the photo, the statue is nearly finished but is yet undressed. The naked lady was a provocative depiction of a sacred festival. Hindus found the publishing of this one photo to represent one of Hinduism's largest festivals to be insulting, presenting Hinduism in a bizarre manner. We would say

291

this incident was an exception to the *Toronto Star*'s exemplary record of inclusiveness and respect in its reporting on minority religions.

Hindus were offended by the photo and informed the *Star*, leading to this sequence of events, which is, to our experience, typical of such protests against the media. Initial complaints were ignored, including a thousand e-mail letters to the editor. Demonstrations in front of their office, coupled with contact from concerned Hindu community leaders got their attention. Community leaders met with the editors and explained the photo by itself simply showed part of a normal process of festival preparation. But the selection of this particular photo as the only picture to publish in *Toronto* about the festival was obviously done to highlight the bizarre and to present something that the non-Hindus would laugh or snicker at. The paper's response was to issue a half-hearted apology on October 11, which ended with a statement that, "when asked, several Hindus said the photo didn't offend them." It didn't identify these several Hindus as qualified people, such as community leaders, temple priests, scholars of Hindu iconography, or even devout Hindus, but still used their opinion to justify their photo. Hindus rejected the apology and continued to protest. Editors ultimately concluded Hindus were genuinely offended by the photo and issued a proper apology. In the course of doing so, they also acknowledged to community leaders that the *Star* already had a policy in place to present religious images in a dignified manner. They admitted they had failed to abide by their own policy. Here's the photo the *Star* published. Available at the same time to them from Reuters and other wire services were the following photos, which they could have chosen from. Clearly, the *Toronto Star* had many fine photos to choose from but chose the most bizarre, vulgar, and salacious. In summary, the elements of this successful protest to a publication are—they clearly stated their objectives; gathered community support, including from politicians, academics, and other religions; did not settle for anything less than a full change of heart; insisted the *Star* enforced its existing policies with regard to how it treats religion.

Madhu Kishwar of Delhi, India, is the editor of *Manushi* magazine. She is one of India's leading activists for women's rights and social justice for disadvantaged communities. She was interviewed for this presentation by Rajiv Malik, our Delhi correspondent. She focused on the larger problems of bias in the academic arena which trains reporters, one result of which is bias in the media. Among her comments, she said:

> India is the one country in the world where the majority community, the Hindus, complain that they are not given a sympathetic coverage by the press as against the minority communities of Islam and Christianity, which get a better treatment by the press. Our mainstream national press is greatly influenced by the Leftists, who in turn are influenced by the colonial critique of Hinduism. As well, they are influenced by Karl Marx, who portrayed Hinduism as a stagnant civilization, which is a cesspool of dehumanizing practices. So that is the Marxist description and that of British missionaries through which most of the scholars and media see Hinduism in India. Our educated elite is poorly informed about our own religion and culture. Experts on Hinduism are in short supply. The best that exists have inadequate knowledge and are biased as well. The whole information structure is of a shoddy quality. Now if certain people of a religion do demonic things in the name of Islam, what can others do? It is the actions of a community that determines a popular perception and image about it. I must say, that so far as Indian mainstream media is concerned, they have acted very responsibly and have not done anything to demonize Islam. The role of Indian mainstream media, which I keep track of, has been very fair and balanced. I can only speak about the relationship with my religion, that is, Hinduism, with the media. If I can understand my own religion and represent it in the best way possible, that is enough. Some kind of a concrete initiative has to come from India-based groups of scholars and institu-

tions to create world-class institutions and scholars here in India.

There are various ways to protest to the media. Call a newspaper or magazine and complain about an article, and they'll tell you to write a letter to the editor. It's simple and quick for them. Letters to the editor are useful in responding to other letters to the editor, some editorial pieces, and factual errors in reports. But they don't do anything to change bad attitudes or newspaper policy. There's a great tendency on the part of religious groups to call for a public campaign by their members, deluging the local press and politicians with all sorts of mail. This approach will backfire if people get hostile. Most campaigns we've seen launched online by Hindus degenerate into ugly name-calling, even threats, and do more harm than good. Such public campaigns will only be effective when organized and moderated by a well-known group. A thoughtful and polite approach is much more productive than condemning, accusatory diatribes. For example, the Muslim community in Phoenix, Arizona, arranged a face-to-face meeting with the editors of the local newspaper. They said, "We don't see our community in your newspaper." This polite objection resulted in a permanent shift, and one reporter was assigned part-time to cover news and events in the Muslim community, which numbers over seventy thousand.

The recent case of the cartoons insulting the Prophet Muhammad is instructive as a public campaign that got out of hand. What was notable to us was the hypocrisy of the Western press defending the cartoons as an expression of free speech. Muslims rightly pointed out that in several countries in Europe it is actually against the law to publish anti-Semitic cartoons. It is as well against the policy of every major Western publication to publish anti-Semitic or racist cartoons. Now the Western media understands it must extend this policy to Muslims. Whether this was best accomplished by deadly riots and death threats against the cartoonists is another question. Making enemies of the press is never a good strategy. Community leaders in Denmark could have tried to solve the issue locally before others became involved who saw an opportunity to create civil unrest. A group from any religion could have taken the lead had the papers and cartoonists been convinced to apologize early, and it would have been much more difficult for the matter to become an international disaster complete with loss of life.

Let's summarize the elements of reactive response to negative or incorrect media coverage. Be prepared in advance, both in terms of establishing working relationships with both local and national media and in terms of forming advocacy groups to respond. Have press releases prepared for various eventualities. Timing is important. Be able to respond immediately with an authoritative voice. Reach out to the local community in each area that is impacted by the event, including through interfaith connections. And media is not the enemy just because they're accurately reporting on something that reflects badly on your religion and neglecting all the good you do. Don't be overly defensive. Protest improper reporting politely and firmly. Don't make threats. Persist until a proper resolution is reached. We do not have to accept brush-offs or half-hearted apologies when the religious community is involved. Many in the media are cynical and inherently skeptical about religion. This is not likely to change. Bias in the media can also have deep roots in the nation's academic structure and tradition, as is the case in India. The religious leaders in your community and secular leaders should meet the editors of your local press. Quick action in response to negative reports may prevent further trouble from radical elements.

So, we're going to summarize now. Doctor Sharma originally asked how the media might use its persuasive power to promote harmony among religions and bridge the religious and secular divide. In our opinion, the responsibility to make this happen belongs with religious groups. Each group needs to work to improve its relationship with the media. They should understand how the media thinks and works. It has its institutional peculiarities, some of which work against religion. They need to be proactive and open more channels to those who report the news, understand their world in both its opportunities and restrictions,

293

and make it easy for the media to accurately and sympathetically report on religious events. They need to be organized to quickly respond reactively when crisis situations occur. One way to bridge the secular-religious divide is to share our lives with each other, which can be done in part by stories in the media. People can then learn that we all have many experiences, concerns, and challenges in common. We all seek to live life for a higher purpose, even if we don't conceive of that purpose in terms of God. Through programs such as Teaching Tolerance, our children can meet children of different races and religions and learn from an early age of their commonalities. In this way, we can develop an honest respect for each other and for the religious or nonreligious path we each follow in life. Thank you very much.

QUESTIONS AND ANSWERS
FOR THE AUTHOR

Question: I wonder if you could throw some light on the comprehensive role of the media. Differentiate the media, print media versus the image media, and that kind of thing, and how one might relate to them in a nuanced fashion.

Answer: Image media means, like, television?

Question: Television on the one hand, print on the other.

Answer: It's easier to appeal to the print media. For example, when I travel to various places, quite often, someone from the local newspaper would interview me. But very seldom do I get a television interview. So it shows that television is looking for something that is graphically appealing, that will do well on the screen. So it needs to be better choreographed, better thought out. It has to be in the sense of an attractive event. We talked about events such as a wedding, for example, or some ceremony of a child. It could be done in an interesting way, kind of a minidocumentary for the media. In general, it has to be more interesting, more thought out, more choreographed in order to get into the visual media.

Question: Could you very briefly focus on the success that *Hinduism Today* has achieved in the last twenty or thirty years that it has been in existence?

Answer: What makes it different is that it talks about all of Hinduism. In Hinduism, we have so many different denominations, so many different teachers. And quite often, the publications within Hinduism just talk about one denomination or one teacher. How ours is different is we talk about them all, and that's a specific goal of our publication. And, in fact, we limit the amount we can talk about ourselves to a very small amount. And because of that, we're well respected by Hindu leaders around the world and Hindu educators, and it serves a unique function in that it is more educational. It is able to present the overview of the Hindu religion more than any other publications because of what I've just described.

Question: Do you have anything to say about investigative journalism pieces or reportage over a longer time frame, and how religions can address that?

Answer: Could you ask your question again? I didn't quite grasp it.

Question: Sure. A lot of what you spoke about related to how reporters face time pressure in beat reporting. But there's also a lot of investigative journalism pieces that take a much longer period of time but still obviously have bias involved. I was wondering if you can speak to how religion should deal with that.

Answer: Well, I think one of the key points we talked about is knowing the editors at the local newspapers. And if you know they are doing a story, then hopefully they would allow you to contribute in some way. Of course, they won't let you edit it—they have the last word—but they may let you look at it, or at least solicit your input on important points. So I would say, try and participate in that way. Try and get your input accepted as part of the story. And, of course, that is based on knowing them in the first place, which is one of the important keys we've brought out.

Question: Is it foreseeable that a magazine like *Hinduism Today* could influence media studies in terms of students coming out as reporters and journalists with a religious perspective or some sort of religious training background? There seems to be a huge divide between coverage of political issues or world affairs and religious studies or religion issues.

Answer: Yes. To influence journalist students, *Hinduism Today* and other religious magazines would need to be studied as part of the curriculum; that is, make sure journalist curriculum devoted some time to this area.

Question: What about new forms, for example, through the Internet, to communicate with their members?

Answer: Well, yes. That's a very good point. What has our experience been? Well, we rely heavily on the Internet for our communications. We have a number of Web sites. One of them has daily news, for example. It changes everyday. Part of it follows me around the world. I just went to Malaysia and Singapore, and now I'm here. So you can see photographs—photographs of all the people we met—and summaries of the talk right on it, so that our members and supporters can see what we're doing on a daily basis. What we find particularly effective is a Web site that changes everyday. There's nothing worse on the web than a site that changes once a year. So we use that, plus we send out various e-mail publications to different categories of members and supporters. That's why we have our Hindu Press International, which we send out to thousands of people everyday, just general Hindu news. Because our magazine is only quarterly, we send this out everyday so people can know about current events in a timely way. Plus we have other newsletters we send out on e-mail to select groups. So we think it's very important for religion to also be a part of the Internet and utilize both web and e-mail in terms of influencing its members of supporters.

Question: As a person who spent some years working as a reporter at a local newspaper here in Montreal, I would like to congratulate you on your presentation. You seem to know what you're talking about, and I would endorse much of what you said. I think there's lots of good stuff that religious people could well pay attention to. Would you not agree that there can sometimes be a problem with hypersensitivity and worse? From some of my reading—and I have followed the matter—in the case of the Scandinavian cartoon controversy, the impression I get is that the original cartoons were published by a publication which set out to be controversial. There was some discussion with the local Muslim community in that case locally and that there was a certain time lag, and then riots and so on broke out in some of the Islamic world. If I'm not mistaken, they were fueled more than anything by collections of pictures which were circulated, presumably by Muslims, which were far more offensive to Islam than what appeared in the original publication. And that was one element in fueling the controversy.

Answer: Our simple point was that an apology somewhere along the line early on would have been appropriate. Because such sensitivities were fueled, it's good to quell the situation before it gets out of hand. If the media starts an international incident unknowingly, it can also stop it knowingly. Our sense was that not enough was done early on to respond in some kind of sensitive way to the concerns. Thank you very much again.

Lessons from Hinduism for the World after 9/11

Ashok Vohra

Nothing is so hostile to religion as other religions. . . . The world would be a much more religious place if all religions were removed from it.
—Radhakrishnan,
An Idealist View of Life[1]

Each religion and its subsect; every civilization and every nation for one reason or the other considers itself "to be better than the others. The Greeks looked down upon all non-Greeks as barbarians, while the Jews' contempt for the uncircumcised and the Muslims' hatred for the Kafirs is [sic] well-known. The Chinese always thought of themselves as a superior race. . . . Europeans fancied themselves—many still do—to be civilizers and saviours of the Asians and Africans and considered themselves to be superior. . . . All this shows that there never were a people who considered themselves to be just as good as the others only."[2] This feeling of superiority gives rise to conflict psychology among the members of communities, which in turn is responsible for the state of perennial discord, dispute, and conflict situations in society. In such a society, there is no peace and harmony. It is dominated by xenophobia and constant fear, tension, and threat of the flaring of the clash, skirmish, battle, or even war with the other.

Sanatana Dharma or Hinduism was the earliest religion in the world to face opposition to the doctrines it held dearly. The challenge was not just against the corrupt and degraded brahmanical (priestly) traditions and practices that had for various reasons come into vogue but questioned its very foundational doctrine; namely, that the Vedas are the source of all knowledge. The challenge was faced from the Shramanic traditions. Buddhism and Jainism formed the core of the Shramanic tradition. The founders of the Shramanic religions, with all the force at their command, rejected the authority of the Hindu scriptures (Vedas) and deities, denied the efficacy of sacrifice, and displayed unequivocal hostility to the practices of brahmanical supremacy. The laity or the followers of these religions, in all their faith and rituals, abandoned the brahmanical practices. The exponents and commentators on the doctrines of the founders of the Shramanic religions, with all their logical equipment, demolished the theoretical foundations of the brahmanical religion and demonstrated the futility of its practices. These traditions criticized Hinduism quite severely. For example, talking about the Brāhmaṇas and Brahmā, Buddha said in the *Tevijja Sutta,* "the teachers who talk about Brahmā have not seen him face to face.

They are like a man in love who cannot say who the lady is, or like one who builds a staircase without knowing where the place is to be, or like one wishing to cross a river who should call the other side to come to him."[3] Criticizing the authority of the shruti tradition, he said in *Mahātaṇhāsaṅkhaya Sutta,* "Accept not what you hear by report, accept not tradition. . . . Do not accept a statement on the ground that it is found in our books."[4] He criticized the priestly class, who claimed to be in possession of some secret knowledge in most disparaging terms thus: "O disciples, there are three to whom secrecy belongs and not openness: secrecy belongs to women, not openness; secrecy belongs to priestly wisdom, not openness; secrecy belongs to false doctrine, not openness."[5] According to Radhakrishnan, "As a matter of fact, the Buddha was more definitely opposed to Vedic orthodoxy and ceremonialism than was Socrates to the State religion of Athens, or Jesus to Judaism."[6] History tells us that there was a "war" for establishing the supremacy between Hinduism and Shramana religions, though this conflict, as is the case with all other conflicts, was more on the ideological plane. The two continuously tried to find fault with the other's doctrine, logic, and arguments. As a result, Buddha, in the words of Gandhi, "carried the war into the enemy's camp and brought down on its knees an arrogant priesthood."[7]

In the course of time, Hinduism faced the ideological challenge, many a time culminating in violent conflict resulting in loss of lives and property and in all-around destruction, not only from its own factions such as Shaivites, Shaktas, and Vaishnavites, but also from Christianity, Islam, and Judaism—religions born on alien soil. These religions are generally exclusive and believe in the doctrine of the day of judgment, God, and divine creation; the religions of Indian origin generally subscribe to the doctrine of rebirth and transmigration of the soul and are inclusive of all other beliefs. So Hinduism had to confront religious doctrines that were diametrically opposed to their own belief systems. This glaring doctrinal conflict was compounded by the fact that these alien doctrines and belief systems had the patronage of the rulers who had brought the other religions to Indian soil.

Hinduism realized long before others that those who are opposed to us, and are keen to harm us both materially and spiritually, are our own brothers, who for one reason or the other are estranged from us. We need not be angry at them or be depressed by the fact that they are alienated from us. It does not recommend that we should even feel rightful indignation at their separation from us and their acts of commission and omission to hurt us. It has always advocated that they can be won over by love and understanding. It has never supported revengeful destructive action against those who oppose our ideology, philosophy, and form of life. This is primarily because it upholds the view that retribution and revenge can never annihilate violence. Retribution and revenge only perpetuate violence. In this respect, violence can be compared with desire for material goods. "Desires are never satiated by the enjoyment of desires; thereby they only flame forth ever more like fire with butter," and however much wealth and material goods man may possess, he "is never satisfied by wealth alone."[8] But it is through voluntary renunciation that a man enjoys the real bliss— *tena tyaktena bhunījthāh.*[9]

The same applies to violence. Violence can never come to an end with violence. Violence only breeds more ferocious, brutal, unruly, and inhumane violence. Buddha condemned violence and hate thus: "Not by hate is hate destroyed: by love alone is hate destroyed."[10] He commands his followers not to retaliate to the violence they are subjected to by violence. He says, "Ye monks, if robbers and murderers should sever your joints and ribs with a saw, he who fell into anger and threat would not be fulfilling my commands."[11] If violence is met with violence, the whole of humanity would surely come to an end. Mahatma Gandhi put it thus: "To answer brutality with brutality is to admit one's moral and intellectual bankruptcy and it can only start a vicious circle."[12] That is why he went on, to the extent of saying, "If untruth and violence are necessary for furthering the interest of my country, let my country go under."[13] In saying this, Gandhi

297

has shown that he is far superior a religious man than the self-proclaimed religious leaders who uphold the view that it is their and their followers' duty to kill all those who differ from them in their views, or belong to other religions and do not agree to covert to their religion or their ideology or their stream of thought.

"In this imperfect world," as Radhakrishnan says, "it may be an urgent political duty to make our defences as secure as possible against attack, but under no circumstances can it be one's religious duty to slaughter one's fellow-men."[14] Nor can it be one's political duty. The principle that nonviolence, rather than violence, is an effective tool in bringing about the change of mind of our adversary, and changing his mindset ever after, is not a theoretical or abstract construct. It is based on the experience of our *rishis*—sages.

Mahatma Gandhi in his essay "The Doctrine of the Sword" says,

> The rishis who discovered the law of nonviolence in the midst of violence, were greater geniuses than Newton. They were themselves greater warriors than Wellington. Having themselves known the use of arms, they realized their uselessness and taught a weary world that its salvation lay not through violence but through non-violence. Non-violence in its dynamic condition means conscious suffering. It does not mean meek submission to the will of the evil-doer, but putting of one's whole self against the will of the tyrant.[15]

Explaining it further, he says that nonviolence "never implies that a non-violent man should bend before the violence of an aggressor."[16] All he is expected to do is not to return "the latter's violence by violence," but "refuse to submit to the latter's illegitimate demand even to the point of death. . . . He is not to return violence by violence but neutralize it by withholding one's hand and, at the same time, refusing to submit to the demand."[17]

This according to him is "the only civilized way of going on in the world."[18] This assures a permanent peaceful world order. "All other courses can only lead to a race for armaments interspersed by periods of peace which is by necessity and brought about by exhaustion, when preparations would be going on for violence of a superior order."[19] Our recent experience of dealing with terrorists corroborates this hypothesis of Gandhi. The terrorists lie low after a misadventure, and during this period of hibernation, they prepare for a bigger and more heinous misadventure. The world in the meantime waits with bated breath for a new mishap and lives in a constant and continuous state of fear. It invests all its precious and limited resources just to find out and combat the next move of the terrorists.

A permanent peaceful world order cannot be established till the time we are able to strike at the root of the problem that gives rise to terrorism and violence. It cannot be established merely by creating a sense of fear of punishment in the minds of the misadventurers. "If I cease stealing for fear of punishment, I would recommence the operation as soon as the fear is withdrawn from me."[20] According to Gandhi,

> A cause suffers exactly to the extent that it is supported by violence. If I kill a man who obstructs me, I may experience a sense of false security. But this security will be short lived. For I shall not have dealt with the root cause. In due course, other men will surely rise to obstruct me. My business, therefore, is not to kill the man or men who obstruct me, but to discover the cause that impels them to obstruct me, and deal with them.[21]

That is why he always preached the maxim, "Hate the sin and not the sinner."[22]

Gandhi, with the help of a hypothetical example of an armed robber who has robbed you of your property, illustrates how to deal with the root cause of violence and terrorism in the chapter titled "Brute Force" in his *Hind Swaraj*. I discuss the example in detail, for it bears close similarities to our post-9/11 world scenario. He argues thus:

> That well-armed man has stolen your property; you have harbored the thought of his act; you

are filled with anger; you argue that you want to punish that rogue, not for your own sake, but for the good of your neighbors; you have collected a number of armed men, you want to take his house by assault; he is duly informed of it, he runs away; he too is incensed. He collects his brother robbers, and sends you a defiant message that he will commit robbery in broad day light. You are strong, you do not fear him, you are prepared to receive him. Meanwhile the robber pesters your neighbors. They complain before you. You reply that you are doing all for their sake, you do not mind that your own goods have been stolen. Your neighbors reply that the robber never pestered them before, and that he commenced his depredations only after you declared hostilities against him. You are between Scylla and Charybdis. You are full of pity for the poor men. What they say is true. What are you to do? You will be disgraced if you now leave the robber alone. You, therefore, tell the poor men: "Never mind. Come, my wealth is yours, I will give you arms, I will teach you how to use them; you should belabor the rogue; don't you leave him alone." And so the battle grows; the robbers increase in numbers; your neighbors have deliberately put themselves to inconvenience. Thus the result of wanting to take revenge upon the robber is that you have disturbed your own peace; you are in perpetual fear of being robbed and assaulted; your courage has given place to cowardice.[23]

Gandhi goes on to compare this way of treating the errant robber, which results in the disturbance of one's own as well as one's neighbors' peace of mind, with another way of dealing with him that is based not on revenge and retribution but on compassion and pity. He describes this new way thus:

You set this armed robber down as an ignorant brother; you intend to reason with him at a suitable opportunity; you argue that he is, after all, a fellow-man; you do not know what prompted him to steal. You, therefore, decide that, when you can, you will destroy the man's motive for stealing. Whilst you are thus reasoning with yourself, the man comes again to steal. Instead of being angry with him you take pity on him. You think that this stealing habit must be a disease with him. Henceforth, you, therefore, keep your doors and windows open, you change your sleeping-place, and you keep your things in a manner most accessible to him. The robber comes again and is confused as all this is new to him; nevertheless, he takes away your things. But his mind is agitated. He inquires about you in the village, he comes to learn about your broad and loving heart, he repents, he begs your pardon, returns you your things, and leaves off the stealing habit. He becomes your servant, and you find for him honorable employment.[24]

Gandhi being a realist does not deduce from the above example "that robbers will act in the above manner or that all will have the same pity like you."[25] The purpose of taking this example is to show that "at least in the majority of cases, if not indeed in all, the force of love and pity is infinitely greater than the force of arms. There is harm in the exercise of brute force, never in that of pity."[26] During all this process of solving the issues through nonviolent technique, one has to remember that "he is expected not to be angry with one who has injured him. He will not wish him harm; he will wish him well; he will not swear at him; he will not cause him any physical hurt. He will put up with all the injury to which he is subjected by the wrong-doer."[27] It is with an open mind that one will enter into a dialogue and debate with an enemy. One will restrain from saying or doing anything that is likely to hurt the opponent in thought, word, or deed.

The Hindus practiced this method in dealing with their opponents. Hindus believed in one God, though called by an infinite variety of names, including *Paramātmā, Ishwara,* Shiva, Vishnu, Rama, *Allāh, Khuda,* Dada Hormuzada, Jehova, and God. They uphold that "He is the one and yet many; He is smaller than an atom, and bigger than the Himalayas. He is contained even in a drop of the ocean, and yet not even the seven seas can encompass Him."[28] But that does not mean that the Hindu sages and seers swept under the carpet the fact of plurality of religions and a possible conflict among them, their teachings, and their scriptures. According to Hindus, these diverse forms of worship and texts are created by God to suit different men, in accordance with their respective stages of knowledge.

Saint Nammalvar in Tiruviruttam admits, "The Lord has created diverse ways of worship. He has created faiths that differ among themselves, according to the differences in the understanding of their followers. He has created various gods of these faiths. He has filled the gods with His form."[29] Since the gods of all faiths are but different forms of the same supreme being, in Tiruvaymoli 1.1.5 he says, "The followers of different faiths attain to the feet of the gods they worship, according to their lights. The gods they worship are not deficient. The Supreme Lord pervading everyone has ordained that everyone should follow his destined course."[30]

This conclusion, according to Ramakrishna Paramahamsa, is not the outcome of a theory but is based on experience. According to him,

> I have practised all religions, Hinduism, Islam, Christianity, and I have also followed the paths of the different Hindu sects. . . . I have found that the same God towards whom all are directing their steps, though along different paths. . . . You must try all beliefs, and traverse all the different ways once. . . . The tank has several ghats. At one, Hindus draw water in pitchers, and call it *jal;* at another, Musalmaans draw water in leather bottles, and call it *pani;* at a third, Christians and call it water. Can we imagine that the water is not *jal,* but only *pani* or water? How ridiculous! The substance is one under different names and everyone is seeking the same substance; nothing but climate, temperament and name varies.[31]

Keeping this essential unity behind the diversity of appearance, he recommends, "Let each man follow his own path. If he sincerely and ardently wishes to know God, peace be unto him. He will surely realize Him."[32]

Whenever there is a conflict between two religions and religious texts, the Hindu saints suggest a method of resolving them. According to Arulnandi Shivacharya, a thirteenth-century Shaivite saint, accepting the fact that "religions and religious texts are many; they conflict and are at variance with one another" suggests that "if the question is which is *the* religion and which is *the* text among these, the answer is that is *the* religion and that *the* text which, without rancour and without rejecting one of them and accepting another, find a place for all of them in a spirit of fairness."[33]

This method of judgment rejects completely the attitude of condescension and superciliousness as it admits ab initio that all religions and all texts are valuable in their own right. It is based on the fact that the theology of a land is the product of its environment and the specific modes of cognitive, intellectual, aesthetic, moral, and religious experience. One can choose any one of them on the basis of one's preference, or on what one considers to be more harmonious and more inclusive than the others. If one chooses the religion or culture from among different and at times conflicting ones on the above basis, then one is likely to derive the maximum possible benefits from them.

This method has the singular advantage of arousing in an individual not a dogmatic thought about God or the authority of a particular scripture but to awaken in him the quest for ultimate reality and truth. It takes him away from theology and leads him to spiritualism. What prevents one from seeing this is one's own ideas, prejudices, inclinations, virtues, and defects. These factors are responsible for wrong knowledge (*viparyaya*). The wrong or false knowledge (*mithyājñāna*) is the fountainhead of *rāga* and *dveśa* (attachment and jealousy). These in turn are the root cause of our delusion and our erratic conduct. Men who are vitiated by *rāga* and *dveśa* utter falsehoods and commit thefts, debaucheries, and murder. They entertain wicked thoughts and perpetuate falsehoods and make unfounded claims. The only way to win over the opponent who has wrong knowledge is through discussion and rational persuasion. He has to be convinced by our argument that so far he has been subscribing to wrong knowledge and therefore has been behaving in the manner he has been behaving so far. For a meaningful and scrupulously exact and fruitful discussion with our opponents, we need certain rules that are acceptable to both parties to the dispute before we enter into the debate. The Upaniṣads consider discussion (*vāda*) with set rules to be a valid method of arriving at truth. *Chandogya Upaniṣad* calls it *vākovakya*—the science of connecting sentence with sentence or the science of argument or logic. *Kaṭha Upaniṣad* refers to the art of *vāda* as *tarka*-logic—and *Aitreya Brahmana* refers to it as *yukti*—plausible reasoning. The importance given to discussion (*vāda*) in the Indian tradition is summed up in the aphorism *vāde vāde jāyate tattvabodhaḥ* ("true knowledge of reality grows out of discussion"). Aristotle too supported discussion as a valid method of grasping the true nature of reality when he said, "Some see one side of a matter and others another, but all together can see all sides."[34]

To regulate debates and with a view to provide criteria for judging the validity or invalidity of arguments, the Indian thinkers, especially those belonging to the Nyāya school of Indian philosophy, laid down standards for distinguishing the true from the false, discussed the nature and number of *pramāṇas* and *prameyas* (means and objects of knowledge), classified arguments into various kinds, developed rules of valid reasoning, pointed out the fallacies that one can commit in reasoning, and laid down the techniques for avoiding them. Naiyāyikas, therefore, present us with an explicit and elaborate formulation of the principles of inquiry to enable us "to initiate and promote right discussion on things that matter—the saving truths."[35]

The Naiyāyikas not only discuss in detail the techniques for arriving at right knowledge; but they also make an in-depth study of the techniques for rooting out false knowledge. Among the first category come the source of the cognition of a thing (*pramāṇa*), object of right knowledge, doubt,

motive, example, theory, members of a syllogism, *tarka,* and certain conclusion. Discussion, wrangling, cavil, apparent reasoning, quibbling, futile rejoinder, and clinchers constitute the latter.

The prerequisite and precondition for a meaningful discussion (*vāda*) is an entirely friendly spirit. It can be between a teacher and a pupil or between two opponents, each keen to find out the truth or the true nature of reality. When entering into a debate, one should remember that its sole aim is to arrive at truth. In a discussion, the premises and conclusion as well as the means and criteria of knowledge are clearly stated. There is no ambiguity about its purpose. Its aim is not to show off one's debating skill or somehow or other to attempt to cloud the issue so as to make the other person yield to one's own view at any cost. The purpose of *vāda* is not to be victorious but to bring the truth to light. In a debate proper, one arrives at new insights regarding the grounds and consequences of the principles held and in their light either becomes more convinced about their truth or revises or even abandons them. One has at all costs to avoid wrangling (*jalpa*); that is, the tendency to ignore the quest for truth and resort to quibbling with the sole aim of scoring a victory over the opponent. One should also avoid entering into an argument in which each party is merely interested in refuting and discrediting the other's position rather than establishing its own (*vitaṇḍā*). One has also to refrain from offering something as valid reasoning that in fact is not so (*hetvābhāsa*). Each of the parties in the debate has also to desist from dodging the issue in question by resorting to the distortion of the intended meaning of the opponent even though his meaning is clear and distinct in the given context (*chala*). In other words, one should not make undue use of the ambiguity and inexactness that is an integral part of our ordinary language to confuse the issue. One should only take the words in the sense in which they are used. Finally, one should strictly avoid using inappropriate similes and false analogies to defend one's position and refute that of the others (*jāti*). Having followed all these dos and don'ts, one should finally present a clincher (*nigrahasthāna*) on the basis of which he should demand the opponent to concede or give up his stand on the principle which he had set out to defend. A clincher establishes beyond doubt that the latter has either grossly misunderstood his own position or is unaware of the implications of his own thesis.

The lesson that one has to learn from Hinduism, which has survived a large number of turbulences and attacks from various quarters—from insiders as well as outsiders—is to avoid violence and overcome the tendency of retaliation and develop techniques of debate suitable to our times. With a stable, open, unprejudiced, and friendly mind, and with the help of these techniques, one has to dialogue with the opponents and win them over. They have to be treated as our misguided brothers who have for one reason or the other gone astray. One has to remember that egoism, desire, greed, hatred, and fear are the root cause of the degradation of our nature and our miserable state, which is far from our ideal of perfection. Radhakrishnan had drawn our attention to the fact that "perfection can be achieved only through self-conquest, through courage and austerity, through unity and brotherhood in life."[36]

Without actual trial of this method of rule-governed discussion, it would be wrong to say that terrorists will not accept our invitation as they "are considered to be advocates of brute force."[37] Murty seems to support this: "When one believes one's cause to be just and when one fails to assert one's own right through discussion and rational persuasion, the moral and manly thing seems to be to fight for one's cause."[38] This, according to Gandhi, is our prejudice, because if it were true, then "why do they (terrorists), talk about obeying laws?"[39] For Murty, Gandhi's advice is, "Those who believe in the justice of their cause have need to possess boundless patience."[40] Arguing about nonviolence being the very nature of man, he says, "If mankind was not habitually non-violent, it would have been self-destroyed ages ago. But in the duel between forces of violence and non-violence, the latter have always come out victorious at the end."[41]

THE FUTURE OF MANKIND

The Bhagavadgītā Doctrine

T. N. Achuta Rao

Humanity is at the crossroads. The horrible incident of September 11, 2001, that reduced the World Trade Center to rubble stirred the conscience of people all over the world. It calls for a new approach to our religions, our religious faiths and beliefs, our scientific and technological achievements, and our goals. Suddenly we feel lost in wilderness and need a proper guide—the Bhagavadgītā. The world is divided into power blocs, including groups of developing and developed nations, and nations based on various religious faiths. There is mutual distrust, ill will, strife, terrorism, and war among nations, particularly in the Middle East. The world is divided on the basis of religious faith and economic disparity; there is competition among nations to possess nuclear arsenals, and one of the main concerns today is to find ways and means of preventing nuclear war.

This essay addresses what underlies these crucial problems facing us all and tries to find an appropriate solution. The underlying problem of division is so crucial that the very existence of humankind depends on it. In addition, human beings are the most delicate animals on earth and are constantly faced with the dilemmas of good and bad, right and wrong, happiness and misery—and no one is sure what it all means. Man faces the imminent threat of total extinction any time at the press of a button. Even without that threat, humanity's very existence has become problematic because of hunger, malnutrition, scarcity of water, scarcity of food, and disease. The very structure of the human body is always susceptible to infectious diseases such as AIDS and viral fevers (the dengue, Asian flu, etc.) of unknown origin—in addition to the ever-present problems of diabetes, cancer, and diseases of the heart and kidney. These are very real problems that need urgent remedies and solutions of a different type than the ones science and technology can provide. The more the science and technology advance, the more day-to-day life becomes expensive and complicated.

The three major components to man are the body, mind, and soul. Science and technology can provide answers to the questions pertaining to the human body to some extent, but only in an incomplete way. The two other major aspects relate to the functions of mind and senses, and to the spirit or the soul. Many problems remain to be addressed in these more abstract fields.

The answer to the question of human survival lies in spirituality, which is not an easy approach to follow in a materialistic world. However, it is essential to make an earnest effort in this direction.

303

The Bhagavadgītā could be considered the most appropriate guide for humankind at this time, and its relevance is discussed below.

THE BHAGAVADGĪTĀ

The Bhagavadgītā, popularly known as the Gītā, is well known all over the world because its translation is available in various languages. It contains the *udhgīta*: the utterances of Śrī Kṛṣṇa. According to the ancient Hindu scriptures, the people who migrated from the Nordic regions south to the valley of the Indus River, known as the River Sindhu, followed this tradition, and the text dates back to ancient times. In fact, it is stated in these ancient writings that the Lord delivered sermons and commandments to human beings about the secrets of his creation and the ways to help human beings survive on this planet, living along with other creatures. The secret of success, peace, and happiness was first revealed to Manu, the first man to appear on earth. Again, this secret was revealed to Arjuna on the battlefield of Kurukṣetra (near Delhi, India) and again was repeated to him after the war, at the end of Dvāpara Yuga; it was again told in brief to Uddhava, an ardent devotee of Śrī Kṛṣṇa. Thus, time and again, the secret of happiness has been revealed to us by no less a person than the Lord. It is not surprising that such a revelation should have occurred since even today an enlightened person may receive revelations of this kind if he or she lives a life of austerity; is of absolute purity in mind, thoughts, and deeds; and is devoted to transcendental meditation.

Whatever the Lord has said has been heard by man—the ancient seer, the Ṛṣi or the sage—and he has preserved the Lord's words intact, strictly adhering to the rules and regulations of the Vedic grammar and phonetics in all its perfection; these words have been transmitted with devotion, knowledge, and firm faith to future generations. These sermons or commandments are known as *śruti* (what is heard) and *smṛti* (what is remembered), and they hold good even to this day. The preaching of the Lord is still practiced in India by a sect called the Bhāgavatas, the ardent devotees of Bhagavān

Śrī Kṛṣṇa. They are a small proportion of the world population known as the Vaiṣṇavaites. They follow the ancient scriptures such as the Vedas, the Upaniṣads, the Brahmasūtras, and the Purāṇas including the Bhāgavata, Mahābhārata, Rāmāyaṇa, and the Bhagavadgītā. The Bhagavadgītā is the best among these since it is the sum and substance of all the scriptures, and it is also the most respected word of the Lord.

Among the ancient scriptures, three scriptures stand out as the prominent foundation trinity of scriptures—the *prasthānathrayī*—on which Hindu philosophy is based. These are the *Upaniṣads*, the *Brahmasūtras*, and the Bhagavadgītā. But the basis for all these is the ṚgVeda. The ṚgVeda is also the words of the creator Lord Brahmā; those uttered to his first son, Atharvan, came to be known as the Atharva Veda. These were later subdivided into four distinct parts: the ṚgVeda, the Sāma Veda, the Yajur Veda, and the Atharva Veda. However, the ṚgVeda Saṃhitā (totality of knowledge), also called *apauruṣeya* (unwritten by man) is a beautiful record of supreme knowledge. These scriptures contain the knowledge of the entire universe in brief, and they stand as eternal truth (*sat*). Such knowledge (*jñāna*) brings bliss. Brahman, or the ultimate reality, is therefore called *saccidānada* for short.

The Bhagavadgītā deals with most pertinent question of war fought to establish righteousness, not war fought to obtain peace, as present-day advocates of war describe it. Today, wars are being fought against unknown enemies in unfamiliar countries, involving the madness of killing innocent people. But in the Bhagavadgītā, Śrī Kṛṣṇa advocates war to fight injustice and even goes to the extent of adopting unfair means to establish righteousness (dharma). He asks the unwilling warrior Arjuna to take up arms against injustice and asks him not to think of kith and kin when it comes to establishing righteousness. He fears or favors no one when it comes to establishing truth and justice. "Truth only will reign supreme" (*Satyam eva jayate*) is the Upaniṣadic doctrine. Truth is Brahman/Brahm/Supreme Consciousness.

Here, it is pertinent to ask whether war that involves killing, bloodshed, and loss of property, and that brings misery and poverty, is worthwhile when people are already suffering from hunger, disease, misery, and poverty. The answer to this question is as follows: who dies in war or who wins it is not the issue. The issue is the eradication of injustice (adharma) and the removal of people who adopt unfair means to achieve their goals. War is considered a necessary evil. All these utterances, however, pertain to the physical aspects that are of no concern to a spiritual seeker, one who wants to establish supreme order everywhere and to bring peace and prosperity, as well as emancipation or liberation (*mukti*) to the entire population of the world. Although the latter brings an everlasting solution to mankind, the former will only bring about an immediate and temporary solution. As Śrī Kṛṣṇa said at the end of the Dvāpara Yuga before departing from the earth, it is not possible to eradicate evil, since good and evil exist in the mind as the product of ignorance; duality is the quality of the universe, and that exists in the minds of the people too. But a person of true knowledge and enlightenment can usher in equity and justice wherever he goes, by his mere presence, provided he adheres to the principles enunciated in the Bhagavadgītā. As Confucius has said, even if one person is transformed, there will be one less scoundrel in this world. Thus, our aim is to transform the entire population and make this earth a better place in which to live. It is the quality of the people that ultimately matters in civilization.

Bhagavadgītā teaches the secret of attaining to enlightenment through adherence to truth (*satyam*), self-less service (*niḥsvārtha sevā*), love (*prema*), and sacrifice (*tyāga*). The ancient Hindu way of life was one of austerity that followed the principles of universal brotherhood (*vasudhaiva kuṭumbakam*). This is confirmed by the *śānti* mantra from Upaniṣad texts. The proper approach to the problems of the world is through the practice of transcendental meditation and purification of the soul through pure thoughts, good words, and good deeds; thus, cleansing body, mind, and soul is the most important thing. This aspect is considered again at the end of this chapter. Bhagavadgītā is the guide to sensible living. It teaches Yoga to achieve purity in life through selfless action (*niṣ kāma karma*); it is action without the motive of profit for the self but rather action for common good. This is exactly the opposite of the principles of modern business practices, where profit is the sole motive.

THE FUTURE OF MANKIND

The entire problem concerning world peace, security, and the welfare of mankind should be addressed in totality (*saṁhitā*) in a way that brings together the body, mind, and soul to work harmoniously and in unison. Hence, a holistic approach is required. Any other attempt to find a social, cultural, or a political solution to human problems will not yield the desired results. This holistic approach is discussed below.

There is already a loose political organization called the United Nations, with its associated cultural organization, UNESCO. There is a U.N. Security Council to watch over global security aspects. The extent to which these organizations have addressed the human problems and the results they have attained so far are inconclusive, and terrible problems remain. How long will the innocent continue to suffer? Can we not find a solution to these problems now? The solution lies in the principle of live and let live. Let there be peace everywhere; let each country enjoy its sovereign power without any foreign interference, so that vested interests are kept away from trouble spots. The principles of natural law and dharma (righteousness) should prevail.

THE DOCTRINES OF THE BHAGAVADGĪTĀ

The doctrines enunciated in the Bhagavadgītā are very clear. First, it implores everyone to work in a selfless manner for the welfare of society, for the common good. The principle involved here is that of sacrifice on the basis of the Vedic ritual of fire sacrifice *yajña* (Yajur Veda). The Lord offers himself as the *āhuti* sacrifice in the form of a horse (*aśva*), as in Śvetāśvatara Upaniṣad. The sun offers itself as the sacrificial offering (*āhuti*): it burns to

305

provide light, heat, and life to the world. The moon is the food to sun; the plants offer themselves as food to man and beasts, and so on. Every object in this material world is for enjoyment and consumption, and each one sacrifices itself for the benefit of the other and thereby attains liberation (*mukti*). According to this principle of sacrifice (*yajña*), the correct path is to sacrifice individual interest for family interest, sacrifice family interest for community interest, and in the same way, sacrifice community interest for the sake of the state or the national interest. It is clear that universal peace depends on the sacrifice on the part of nations even when their vested interests are concerned. Hence, we have the principle of *vasudhaiva kuṭumabakam*, which means that the world is one large family (*vishva-kuṭumba*), and that all men, women, and children are children of God, living with a common interest in sacrifice and survival.

The ancient wisdom implores us that we should respect nature. All living creatures, including plants and birds, are included in this one large, extended family. The mantra is: *prithvivye namaḥ, vanaspataye namaḥ.* The principle of *vasudhaiva kuṭumbakam* is the noblest principle to usher in world peace. There is no room for any selfish interest here, be it religious or economic in nature. The supreme goal is the common good of all.

It should be clarified here when it comes to religious faith, one should not mistake religious faith for spirituality. Religious faith is sheer ignorance, and spirituality is the knowledge of the soul (ātman). Everybody should be concerned more about salvation through knowledge of the soul, ātma jñāna, and not about God, who is everywhere but is nowhere to be found. Clear knowledge about all these abstract subjects comes from purity of mind, thoughts, words, and deeds. There is no place for dogmatism or fundamentalism or groupism here. Religious faith is a purely personal affair. It is a personal communication between the Almighty and the person's soul, in the privacy of one's inner heart. Any outward display of religious faith is based on ignorance about God and is an insult to God. To realize God needs an inner eye. It is the inward-focused senses and mind that receive

revelations. Absence of all external activities is the basic rule in religious faith and liberation. In view of this, Lord Śrī Kṛṣṇa advocates *bhakti mārga* and *jñāna mārga*. The proper way to emancipation is through total dedication to public service without any selfish or family interest. The fundamental principle may be formulated as follows: service to mankind is service to God.

The second important doctrine enunciated in the Gītā is that everyone should fight injustice wherever and whenever it occurs. When Śrī Kṛṣṇa says that he will descend to earth whenever unrighteousness (adharma) gains the upper hand, what he means is that everyone (since God resides in the cavity of everyone's heart) should realize the presence of the supreme spirit and fight injustice. This sends a clear signal to all concerned not to indulge in violence or adopt unfair means to promote one's own selfish interest even in the name of God and religious faith. Everyone should find his own God in his or her heart and not search for it in any public places such as the temples, churches, mosques, or pagodas.

The ṚgVeda says that the Lord resides in the cavity of the heart (hṛdaya). The Upaniṣads reiterate this, and the Bhagavadgītā makes it very clear that the Lord exists in the myriad eyes and limbs of living creatures. It says that the Lord sees through the eyes of the beholder, and there is only the Lord everywhere in different names, forms, and functions—and none else. This point is further elaborated in Ishavaysa Upaniṣad as *iṣāvāsyam idam sarvam*. So, before one makes a decision in matters of war, adopts revolutionary methods, takes extreme steps toward destruction, or adopts terrorist ways to achieve goals, one should think about the real meaning and purpose of salvation. Nothing else other than salvation should be the goal. This view deserves to be endorsed unanimously. Let there be peace everywhere on earth.

It has been made very clear that this concept of God, religion, and religious faith should be clearly understood not only in a rational way but in a spiritual way as well. The latter is very important. God is nothing but one's own pure consciousness; God needs no external support for his existence through priests and prophets or preachers. Everyone should mind his or her own business, the business (busyness) of his soul, without disturbing the faith of others in this regard. If one turns inward and finds God in the cavity of his or her own heart, one has found salvation; if one finds God in every eye one beholds, one has attained perfection; and if one attains the knowledge of the soul (ātmā), namely that it is eternal, unborn, and immortal, and if one also knows that the Lord created man in his own image, that everything is an illusion (māyā), and that we are all a mirror reflection (pratibimba) of the supreme being and nothing else, then one becomes a jñānī. Whoever has realized this truth has attained complete knowledge. He has attained universal consciousness (vishva prajñā). This level of consciousness helps one see things as they are, in their true nature. It gives complete knowledge (pūrṇa prajñā), which redeems us from the cycle of rebirths whether one believes in it or not. It is this level of consciousness that is required in our rulers. It is, however, not forthcoming unless these national leaders become spiritually awakened and tap their hidden resources. Rather, they operate at the mūlādhāra level of lower self, which is full of lust, attachment, greed, and selfishness.

The simplest way to develop spirituality is to think of a supreme power that rules the destiny of this world. Just as the sun gets its power from this one single source, the power of Parabrahman rests nowhere else but within the heart of every organic and inorganic substance as miniscule energy, consciousness, or prajñā. By constantly chanting of the name of the Lord, dhyānam, japam, and attaining to the state of transcendental ecstasy (samādhi), anybody can raise oneself to this level. It is difficult but not impossible. A little time reserved for contemplation (dhāraṇā) every day will help achieve this transcendental state easily and quickly. At this stage of consciousness, the world looks beautiful; one forgets about one's own selfish interests and strives for the welfare of the society at large. This is the secret. Here, in the Bhagavadgītā, Śrī Kṛṣṇa and Arjuna stand respectively for the spiritually attained person as the supreme consciousness and for the individual mind confused by dualities. The

very battlefield of Kurukṣetra is the human body and mind, riddled with dualities, doubts, ego, hunger for power, and selfishness. The battle is between the good and the bad, likes and dislikes, love and hate, the beautiful and the ugly—all positive and negative forces personified. Man is torn between these two opposites. At times, many people lose their balance, torn by this conflict, and find it difficult to cope with the world. Some even take such extreme steps, such as committing suicide or engaging in terrorist activities, either under wrong influence or through sheer ignorance. The right solution given in the Gītā is to rise above all these dualities, see things as they are, and realize oneness (ekatvam), thereby attaining unity consciousness.

How to Attain Unity Consciousness?

Normally, people in all walks of life function in a routine manner at the level of their lower selves, which exhibits attachment, greed, selfishness, anger, fear, jealousy, hatred, likes, and dislikes, and do not hesitate to practice unfair means to achieve their selfish ends. They are full of ego, and they fail to understand and cooperate with their fellow beings unless it is pleasurable and profitable to them. This attitude is responsible for all the maladies of the present-day world, where each person vies with others in trying to maximize profits and corner the resources of the world.

On the other hand, there are a few divine souls who operate at higher levels of consciousness. They are full of love and respect for their fellow beings, and exhibit divine qualities such as compassion, sympathy, and consideration. They strive relentlessly for the welfare of the society at large and serve others with devotion selflessly without fear, favor, or profit.

These levels of consciousness, broadly speaking, may be identified as follows:

1. The lower self. It starts from mūlādhāra at the end of the spinal cord and rises above, up to maṇipūraka near the navel via svādhiṣṭhāna, which comes in between. These plexuses are the seats of qualities displaying a

307

mixture of *tamas* and *rajas*, which explains the behavior mentioned above.

2. The higher self. It starts from the plexus *anāhata*, near the heart, and goes up to the *sahasrāra* plexus over the head via *viśuddha* (near the throat) and the *ājñā* plexus (at the point between the eyebrows). It also consists of the third eye that looks inward. These are the levels of divine qualities that ultimately bring knowledge of Brahman (Brahma-Prajñā) and supreme bliss (Brhamānanda).

3. The highest self. A spiritual seeker should be able to reach the *sahasrār* plexus level of consciousness from the *mūlādhāra* by *sādhanā* following Haṭha Yoga or Kundalīṇī Yoga. But it is important to synthesize the *sapta vyāhṛtis*, such as *the bhū, bhuvaḥ, svaḥ, mahaḥ, janaḥ, tapaḥ,* and *satyam*, along with the seven levels of awareness, along with the Gāyatrī japam and Prāṇāyāma. Progress here is gradual progress, depending on the purity of the person in all aspects of his physical, mental, and spiritual life.

Only such persons who can achieve this level of consciousness can lead the world.

There are well-laid paths of Yoga to attain these higher levels of consciousness, and one cannot attain higher levels without spiritual practices (*sādhanā*). Bhagavadgītā is a textbook of Yoga, where Lord Śrī Kṛṣṇa teaches Yoga to Arjuna, as, for instance, in the chapter on Yogavidyā.

There is no need to go into further details here. Suffice it to say that it is essential for man to think and act at higher levels of consciousness. All the corrupt practices can be attributed to a man's thoughts and actions at a lower level of consciousness. Thinking and acting at a lower level of consciousness also breeds corruption. Slums and dirty surroundings are to be found wherever people operate at lower levels of consciousness. People may occupy any position in society in the economic, social, political, or even religious fields, but their actions will result in total destruction of society if they do not raise their levels of consciousness. Doing so also helps people obtain divine intuitional knowledge at higher levels of consciousness.

Thus, Bhagavadgītā is the storehouse of knowledge and wisdom, and it is useful for persons of any age; it also serves for all ages to come. It is the only hope for mankind to survive all natural and cultural tragedies.

It is heartening to note that India leads the world in this aspect, and more than 10 million persons have become realized souls, giving the world their spiritual knowledge and experience, and another 10 million persons are on their way to spiritual attainment. However, it must be cautioned here that not all people who pose as spiritualists are really realized souls, and many pose as gurus while lacking spiritual attainment. It is not hard to find such black sheep in the spiritual congregations.

Conclusion

Philosophically speaking, the future of mankind rests in the hands of the Lord Almighty, since only his will prevails. There is no escape for the mortals but to surrender their individual will to the supreme will of the Lord (Śrī Hari Icchā). Śrī Kṛṣṇa implores everyone to surrender to him and to his will unconditionally, and he promises to deliver *mukti* (emancipation) to whoever approaches him with wisdom (*viveka*), knowledge (*vicāra*) and renunciation of worldly pleasures (*vairāgya*). It may not be possible for everyone to reach these heights at one stretch, or in one or two lives. However, there is ample scope for everybody to reach higher and higher levels of consciousness and attain supreme bliss. This objective world of dualities does not simply exist, for all practical purposes, to such realized souls (*jñānīs*). There are numerous instances where such yogis live happily despite all the commotion in the world, contributing their mite to the betterment of the world. They can use their spiritual powers to change the hearts of people who matter. They can create a new world where people have no ill will or strife, war or misery, hunger or disease; otherwise, how can the present Kali Yuga usher in the Satya Yug, that is, the Kṛta Yuga?

Now, the task before us is to accelerate the rate of spiritual process, raise the tempo of practices, increase the number of spiritual seekers to the maximum possible, and thereby make this world a better place. Spiritual seekers are those who seek nothing in this world of objects but supreme bliss of solitude, selfless service, and total surrender to the will of the supreme force. The world will change with a change of heart in people. It is the natural law. Everyone should strive to attain the higher level of consciousness from that of the animal level to that of man, and the human and the divine within the lifespan of a hundred years, if one is lucky to live to that mark.

But the problem remains. When the lower creatures are elevated to higher forms of life, such as through the process advocated by Darwin in his theory of evolution, the creatures of lower levels of consciousness also continue to exist. But this problem can be solved by governing the lower creatures and making even the people of lower levels of consciousness obey dharma (righteousness).

There are the teachings of great saints—Shri Ramana Maharshi, Shri Aurobindo, Shri Ramakrishna, Shri Swami Rama, Shri Yogananada, Mahesh Yogi, Maata Amrita, and Aanandamayi—whose thoughts and work lead us now in this critical period. There are many spiritually attained persons who are not even seen in public but who remain incognito and transmit their spiritual vibrations for the welfare of people all over the world. These are the eternal sources of wisdom, the light of Asia. Their teachings are to be imbibed, and their principles are to be practiced.

The Bhagavadgītā, as a unifying force, will play a significant role in shaping the future. It is already evident that such a change is possible with the practice of the principles of the Bhagavadgītā. It can transform people and help them raise their level of perception and consciousness. But it requires total dedication, steadfastness, and sincere effort to attain perfection and enlightenment. Only an enlightened soul can reform others. It is not so with the present-day preachers who use their mystic experiences to enrich themselves and forget about the main goal. Such people cannot transform other people. Only a few great souls, such as the Mahavīra, the Buddha, and Jesus Christ, have been able to bring some solace to disturbed souls. All others have either disappeared or divided people on the basis of faith and religion instead of unifying people.

The doctrines of Bhagavadgītā are nothing but the doctrines enunciated in the Upaniṣads. The Vedas are the basis of all divine knowledge, and the Brahmasūtras help one to understand Brahmajñāna and bring about unity consciousness. But the Bhagavadgītā contains all these and much more, including the Yogasūtras (formulas) and the secret path of liberation.

THIS MAGDALENE MOMENT

Joanna Manning

Justice and equality for women and the marginalized, the earth, and all its religions, plus the fire of an integration of the feminine and the erotic into Christian spirituality and a new respect for religious pluralism: that's what the current "Magdalene moment" in history is about, and it is very relevant to a discussion of the role of religion in a post-9/11 world.

One of the earliest symbols associated with Mary Magdalene in art is the egg. Many religious icons portray her holding an egg. The egg is the Easter symbol of resurrection, fertility, new life. But I think there is also another meaning. Once the growing chick inside the shell has used up all the nourishment of the egg, it has to break out of the shell. The old shells of religious structures, of religious institutions that came into being in contexts of hyperpatriarchy, no longer nourish the human spirit. The shell is now suffocating and will be death-dealing if the new spirituality does not break out. The current Magdalene moment is about breaking out of these old shells and taking a risk to venture out into the new, the unknown. As Jesus himself indicated, you can't put the new wine into old wineskins.

Jane Schaberg is the author of a book published in 2002 called *The Resurrection of Mary Magdalene.*[1] Schaberg contends that there have been two models of Christianity in the West, and they're now both in deep trouble. The Petrine model of Christianity is the Roman Catholic Church—now wracked by revelations of clergy sexual abuse and experiencing a steep decline in membership among the young. The Pauline model is the reformed Protestant tradition—now splintering over issues such as homosexuality and contending with the rise of the so-called religious Right in the United States. Schaberg calls for a new "Magdalene Christianity," which would reestablish the prophetic leadership of women that was suppressed early in Christian history and recognize that Mary Magdalene, at least as much as Peter or Paul, played a crucial role in transmitting the message of Jesus. Schaberg calls Mary Magdalene "the creator of the Church's Easter faith." The time is right for Mary to be resurrected.

And she is being resurrected in popular culture, as we've seen from the phenomenal success of Dan Brown's *The Da Vinci Code.* Of course, it's a novel. It's a fast-paced story. But I think the reason for its popularity is because it has touched a nerve in the zeitgeist of our age—it has opened a quest for a new meaning, a longing for the sacred. At the end of the book, the main character, Robert

Langdon, comes to a realization that the Holy Grail represents not literally the offspring of Jesus and Mary Magdalene, but the whole of the lost sacred feminine that has been suppressed by the church for almost two thousand years. The loss of the feminine is also linked to the loss of the earth as a place where we are at home. Too often, religion has led to a distancing from the earth—the "vale of sorrows," as it is named in several traditional Catholic prayers—to the view that our true home lies after death; the siren call to the suicide bomber that heaven awaits him in the hereafter, replete with willing virgins available to assuage his every desire, is an example. The body and the earth have been desacralized by Christianity for so long. The recovery of the sacred feminine within the world's religions (and the most ancient have never lost it) and the return to honoring the sacred power of women—somehow intuitively we know that this is what is necessary to heal the troubles of our age.

The study of ancient Christian texts, such as the *Gospel of Mary* that first came to light in 1896, the scrolls discovered at Nag Hammadi in 1945, and others, is revolutionizing our understanding of early Christianity. The texts of these early Christian writings other than the Gospels show that the companionship of women was highly valued by Jesus. These texts also show that Mary Magdalene played a key role as the close companion of Jesus and as a leader, visionary, and healer within the mixed group of men and women who were his closest associates.

The synchronicity of the time here is extraordinary: the discovery of these texts has coincided with the beginnings of the feminine scholarship of theology and scripture, and this has been exhilarating. Women themselves are now able to reappraise the importance of female leadership within the early church. This has allowed many to hope that this combination of the human experience of women in the twenty-first century and the rediscovery of the ancient practices of women's leadership in the Christian community will support their efforts to open up the structures of Christian communities in our own day to mutual partnerships

between men and women at every level. These texts also demonstrate the pluralism that existed in the first two centuries of Christianity and the diversity of interpretations regarding the meaning of Jesus's life and teaching.

After the conversion of the emperor Constantine to Christianity in the early fourth century and the adoption of the Roman imperial government within the church, and as a Roman imperial structure and mentality gradually encroached on the church, Mary Magdalene was first edited out of the Christian tradition and then labeled as a repentant prostitute. And as the early Christian communities spread within the Roman Empire, the mutual leadership of women and men declined under the impact of Roman familial structure, which emphasized the role of the man as paterfamilias, head of household. The church's internal structure took on the same pattern.

But the impact of the 1945 discovery of the suppressed texts has exposed the fact that the deliberate exclusion of women from church leadership represented a departure from the earliest tradition. The initial impetus of the Jesus movement, stemming from Jesus himself, was to value female leadership. The theological position outlined in these early texts lost out in the battle for orthodoxy, which saw the Roman church emerge as the triumphant seat of Western orthodoxy. As a result, the Roman imperial view of the early church won out in the struggle for orthodoxy.

The rediscovery of the early texts has given us an insight into the Christian world of the first few centuries. The rediscovery of the early texts that the Roman group had ruled out of the canon has stirred up subversive memories. Contemporary human experience is bringing these texts alive again. The Magdalene moment in Christianity can enable us to rethink what it means to be a Christian in a pluralistic world: not a world circumscribed by the boundaries of the Roman Empire of old but one that now spans the whole globe. The models of Christianity that we have now came into existence as a result of being shaped by a context where hierarchical and authoritarian structures were the modus operandi of society. These structures no longer serve the modern world at all well. This egg needs cracking open.

I believe that it is no mere coincidence that this conjunction of modern human experience, especially the experience of women, with the newly discovered ancient texts is taking place at this particular time in history. It is part of the work of the ever-creative Spirit of God to empower men and women of goodwill inside and outside of religious traditions to wake up and save the planet.

Sometimes I fear that we may have entered into a very dark and hopeless period of history indeed. Religious fundamentalism in both Islam and Christianity threatens to plunge the world into a new age of war. The world is divided not only along religious fault lines but also between the haves and the have-nots within each nation. The earth itself is at risk from continuing excessive greed and consumption. The AIDS epidemic threatens to wipe out millions in Africa—the list goes on. Christian fundamentalism has both a Catholic and a Protestant section. Catholic papal fundamentalists believe in a rigidly hierarchical structure of the church and unquestioning obedience to the pope, and Protestant biblical fundamentalists extrapolate certain passages from the Bible and interpret them literally without any consideration of their context. Protestant and Catholic fundamentalists in the United States have forged a new alliance because they have discovered much common ground around issues such as gay rights, abstinence-only sex education, women's equality, Christian exclusivism, individual family values, free market capitalism, and contempt for creation-centered environmental values. Many in the Protestant religious Right hold to the theory of the rapture: war in the Middle East is part of a series of events that will lead to the rapture of the God-fearing and Armageddon for the rest.

But all that this religious Right stands for is diametrically opposed to the initial thrust of Christianity, which respected pluralism, diversity, and the leadership of women. I believe that in a multiplicity of diverse churches and movements focused on the service of the poor and marginalized, humanity, and the earth, there is now a new

energy rising that cuts across denominational and religious boundaries. The leadership role of women is a key factor in this new dynamic.

In many communities inside and outside the churches, the human race is moving into a new awareness of our interconnectedness with the rest of creation. The realization of human kinship with the natural world and the dangers that humanity's depredations of the earth pose for the survival of the natural world is growing. Human consciousness is changing as we become more aware of global warming, species extinction, inequities between rich and poor, and the ravages of runaway consumption in the one-third of the world that is called "rich." An emerging planetary awareness that celebrates unity and searches for the common ground on which we can base the survival of future generations is increasingly compelling.

A new creation story is emerging from the discoveries of the origins of the universe. Beginning with the original burst of energy—some call it the big bang—approximately 13 billion years ago, the first stars that exploded and then died out released the material constituents of life that were to evolve into the myriad forms of living organisms in the universe. We now know that everything in this universe hears the imprint of that original flaring forth: that all life is connected by the stardust that floated and scattered from the primal flaring forth of light.

Through eons of evolution, the forces of mutual attraction within the universe resulted in the solar system and planets within their orbits. The origin and survival of life rests on relationality. This new understanding of cosmology calls for an evolution in the human understanding of God and of the relationship of God with humanity and with the earth. I like to call this the greening of spirituality. Medieval history was my first academic interest, and I can remember the glow of excitement I felt when I discovered the writings of the mystics of that period. One of the greatest, Hildegard of Bingen, speaks of the greening of the soul:

> We need a greening of the soul of humanity and of religion.

In the account of the resurrection in the Gospel of John, Jesus and Mary Magdalene meet and embrace in the garden on that first Easter morning. They are the new Adam and the new Eve in the restored Garden of Eden. Within their embrace lies the hope and promise of a new creation, a new mutuality of men and women in the Christian community. The light of that first Easter morning lit up the world with an inner radiance that is present within all of creation, renewing all life. It could do the same today. The recovery of the inner radiance, the fire of love at the heart of creation, is the great work of our age. The reinstatement of women within the heart of Christianity would represent the possibility of a greening of spirituality, a new and dynamic consciousness of the rich life of the universe.

But the greening of the earth and of religion, the preservation of the delicate ecological balance of the earth, is not just a poetic dream. It also demands a deep and difficult conversion of our lives. It means that people like us in more affluent countries, most of which have had significant exposure to Christian tradition, embrace a more frugal, altruistic lifestyle. Such a conversion also would remove one of the most potent contributors to terrorism and war: the poverty of the majority of the world's population and the overweening control of corporate values and interests.

Here again the women around Jesus, led by Mary Magdalene, provide a role model for a recovery of Magdalene economics in Christian households. It was the women disciples who placed their wealth at the service of the common table. They supported Jesus out of their funds and thus organized the new economy of the reign of God preached by Jesus and practiced by his community. In the Acts of the Apostles, the sharing and redistribution of wealth, modeled on the example of the women, became a condition of entry into the Christian community.

The apostolic role of the women followers of Jesus, who placed their economic resources at the disposal of the community, also became a key component in early Christian tradition. The most ancient Christian tradition around wealth was not about charity: it involved real redistribution of resources. The church was not a place of brokerage between rich and poor, a place where the rich came to give checks or dump used clothing, and the poor came to get stuff. It was an organic community where rich and poor broke bread at the same table. As I read in one book recently, "If we really rediscovered the communal love of the early church then capitalism would not be possible and communism would not be necessary."[2]

The current Magdalene moment calls us to a difficult conversion: to come home to our roots of simple living inherent in the origins of our tradition. This simplicity of life will also call us home to the earth. The earth, the Garden of Eden, the green grove of the resurrection, is calling us to come home after a period of long exile. We have been exiled from our roots in the earth and cut off from the sacredness of its waters and forests. Patriarchal religion in the West has suppressed the sacred feminine and dishonored the healing power of sex. But now, more and more women and men are waking up from a deep sleep, and we are seeing the world around us again with new eyes. We are cracking the shell of the egg of patriarchal thinking and systems in readiness for a new resurrection. We are realizing the connections between the fate of the earth and our ecological environment with the way we live out our economic, political, sexual, and religious lives.

So what would a Magdalene leadership mean for the world today? The novelist Virginia Woolf once wrote, "As a woman I have no country. As a woman I want no country. As a woman my country is the whole world."[3] Substitute the word *spirituality* or *religion* for "country," and what do you get? So if my spirituality is the whole world, who then is my God? Is my God only for some and against others? It's time to let go of the petty God of patriarchy. How can God's activity be confined to any one continent, culture, or church? The supreme mystery who is God can no longer be held within the shell of any one religious boundary. "There will be no peace in the world until there is peace among the world's religions" says Hans Küng.[4] Religious pluralism is not just one of the foundations for peace:

it is about rediscovering the true nature of God: a God who is for all, not just a God of a privileged few.

There is now a common context of human and ecological suffering that overlaps religious boundaries. The Magdalene moment demands that all religions take as the starting point for their dialogue a solidarity with the suffering earth and its peoples. It was Mary of Magdala and Mary the Mother of Jesus who stood by the cross to accompany the crucified one on his great journey through the gates of death. It was they who showed the way toward a praxis of solidarity with the suffering. I was reminded of this just last month during the AIDS conference in Toronto, where Stephen Lewis spearheaded the formation of a new international group: grandmothers to grandmothers. With the loss of the middle generation of parents to AIDS, it is the grandmothers of Africa who are standing by the children. It is the brave stand of these women who are sheltering the generation that has lost parents to AIDS that will carry Africa to a new resurrection.

Solidarity with the suffering earth and its peoples opens the door to dialogue among the world's religions: dialogue that is based on solidarity of service, not on gabfests about dogmatic teachings and unanchored truths that float around in a transcendent soup of abstractions.

This shared process directed toward compassion will open up a third space for dialogue—a new threshold, a liminal third space—that is beyond the enclosed areas occupied by competing traditions that have contributed to competition and war, and one which, from a Christian perspective, is a lot like the original ideals of Christianity: "To find an ecumene of peace and solidarity with the suffering and the victims of war and violence."[5] This is the great call of all contemporary religions. The task of the present moment calls for a willingness among all religions to stop competing and proselytizing and to find common ground in a spirituality of service to the poor and the earth.

God's spirit at work is forcing us to rethink our place in this vast universe, to honor the wonder of creation's diversity, and to embrace it with awe and graciousness instead of exploiting it. There is only one earth. There is just one flesh—the human flesh—that we can wound in war. God's Spirit is at work on the margins inside and outside the churches, empowering women to announce the good news that God has chosen them as witnesses to justice and love in all creation.

This new Magdalene movement has awakened a subversive memory buried within Christian tradition. Another future is possible. The subversive memory of Mary Magdalene could light a fire in many hearts—and this is the year of fire. It will give us the courage to crack open the shell of old ways of thinking. A new eruption of women into spirituality and religion is already happening. But it is fragile. The egg that the Magdalene holds is only just breaking open, and the new life that is emerging, like the newborn chick, is small fragile and undernourished. We need courage like Mary Magdalene's so that we too can go out to renew the earth.

CaoDai

A Way to Harmony

Hum D. Bui

Along with materialism, differences in religions have brought conflicts to people resulting in many wars all over the world. The Inland Empire Interfaith group in California has been working to bring religions together in harmony, cooperation, and understanding. In this effort, we would like to introduce CaoDai, a new faith founded in Vietnam in 1926 by the supreme being via spiritism, based on the principle that all religions are of one same origin (which is God, although called by various names or no name), having the same teachings based on love and justice, and are just diverse manifestations of the same truth.[1]

CaoDai, literally meaning "High Tower" or "Roofless Tower," is used as the name of God. It embraces all religions ranging from what is termed the way of humanity (Confucianism) to the way of genies (geniism or Shintoism or the veneration of ancestors), the way of saints (Judaism, Christianity, Islam), the way of immortals (Taoism), and the way of Buddhas (Hinduism, Buddhism). Although they have different physical manifestations, all religions have the same ethical teachings based on love and justice—love being unconditional and without desire, and Justice being equated with the golden rule: "Do not do to others what you do not want done to you."[2]

In addition to these teachings, there are other similarities among religions; the conception of God is one example.

CaoDai believes that the supreme being is from the Hu Vo (the nothingness or cosmic ether). In the cosmic ether appeared a great source of divine light called Thai Cuc (monad), or the supreme being. The monad then created yin and yang energies, the two opposite logos, the interaction of which led to the formation of the universe.[3] The supreme being, in giving the following message, confirmed that God's energy had manifested through different prophets in the world:

Nhien Dang (Dipankara) is Me,
Sakya Muni the Gautama (Buddha) is Me,
Thai Thuong Nguon Thi (Lao Tse) is Me,
Who is CaoDai.

and

Buddha, God; God, Buddha are Me,
Although different, all branches belong to one same trunk (family).
Buddhism, Taoism, Christianity are in my hands;

Because of love, I come to save humanity for the third time.[4]

With the same conception that the nothingness is the origin of everything, in the Tao Te Ching, Lao Tse says:

There was something nebulous,
Existing before heaven and earth,
Silent, empty, standing alone, altering not,
Moving cyclically without being exhausted,
Which may be called the mother of all under heaven.
I do not know its name; therefore, call it the Tao.[5]

A similar conception that God is the nothingness is found in Buddhism: "There is an unborn, not become, not made, unmanifest, which is called Brahmakaya or Sunyata, the Void, or the Nothingness."[6]

Sadly, it was because of this conception that Buddhism was misunderstood as not believing in the existence of God.

In the same light, Confucius says that God has done nothing but created everything:

Does Heaven ever speak?
The four seasons come and go,
And all creatures thrive and grow.
Does Heaven ever speak?[7]

Judaism believes that God, or Elohim, is a state of consciousness that pertains neither to perception nor to nonperception; or, in other words, the state of consciousness perceiving nothingness, which comes from the chaos.[8]

Christianity believes that God is the Word: "In the beginning was the Word and the Word was with God, and the Word was God. All things are made by Him, and without Him was not anything made that was made."[9]

Not only religions but science theorizes that the universe came from the nothingness: "The Big Bang took place about 13 billion years ago. From nothing, a tiny speck of brilliant light appeared.

It was infinitely hot. Inside this fireball was all of space. With the creation of space, came the birth of time. The infant universe was searingly hot, brimming with the energy of intense radiation."[10]

Modern science has also conceptualized the void, which, according to field theory, is far from empty but, on the contrary, contains an unlimited number of particles that come into being and vanish without end.[11]

This scientific conception so far has brought science closer to the contradictory Eastern idea of nothingness, the void, or cosmic ether, which is considered as "the suchness," as stated in the following phrase from the Buddhist Prajñ-Pāramitā-Hṛdaya Sūtra: "Form is emptiness, and emptiness is indeed form. Emptiness is not different from form; form is not different from emptiness. What is form that is emptiness; what is emptiness that is form."[12]

Isn't it wondrous how much religions and even science have in common? If one takes time to study others' religions, one would realize that religions are but one unified truth that has been expressed in different ways. At this moment, in this current world situation, CaoDai's purpose is to remind humanity and all religions that all religions are of the same origin and principle, and are just different manifestations of the same truth.

A thorough study of all religions leads to the conclusion that all religions are one, not in their historical accuracy or separate customs, but in their essential messages:

All religions come from one common divine source.
All ethics are essentially contained in the Golden Rule and Love.
All humanity is one common family.
Divinity can be experienced and realized in the individual through prayer/mediation.
Good deeds are rewarded, and evil deeds are punished.

The noble effort of CaoDai is to unite all of humanity through a common vision of the supreme being, whatever our minor differences, in order to promote peace and understanding throughout the world. CaoDai does not seek to create a gray world, where all religions are exactly the same, but only to create a more tolerant world, where we can all see each other as sisters and brothers coming from a common divine source, reaching out to a common divine destiny.

If people are open to independently read from and study each other's religions or to contact other religious communities in their areas—to simply build an ongoing dialogue of understanding between them—this likely would be the most powerful weapon against hatred and intolerance and the most powerful force toward friendship and peaceful coexistence.

In addition, various faith groups could organize meetings where different religions could be discussed, speakers could be invited, videos and music of different traditions could be presented, and understanding between people could be enhanced.

Also, charity projects could be established for communities in which everyone could participate, regardless of their different religious and ethnic origins, so that through love and compassion for the needy, humans would become closer to each other, love would develop between them as a solid bond, and peace would subsequently come to prevail, between individuals at first, and then progressively in local communities and finally, throughout the world.

The Glory
of the Divine Feminine

Her Holiness Sai Maa Lakshmi Devi

The Global Congress on the World's Religions gives us all a golden opportunity to transform our consciousness so we can all live on a common ground, transcending the boundaries of religions and thereby creating a violence-free society, a resentment-free society, with a commitment to serve each other. Thus it provides the basis for forming a nonjudgmental community, based on education and knowledge, allowing for the revival of ancient wisdom and creating an empowerment to be shared. It can be a place where we could care for each other, and move from an individual, family-minded consciousness to a global consciousness to become citizens of this world, for which we have great respect.

Such an individual peace could create a peaceful world, in which we promote love, celebrate life, and divinize our minds. The result is the creation of a one-world family, where identification with a limited religion resulting from our limited minds is dissolved, and where we could discipline our minds, discipline our emotions, dare to look inside, face our challenges, and take ownership of our actions—all of which naturally creates peace, which is an attribute of Spirit, of God, of natural law. Religious, pious people have always wished to serve others. During the present shift in planetary consciousness, as people are being challenged in their own religions, they are redefining meaning and purpose as true service to humanity. It is high time for us to realize the meaning of the word *freedom*: What does it really mean to be free?

The conflict we see in the world first starts from individual conflict. It is a war going on within that is then projected outside. We are not honoring our higher selves, the grandeur within us; we worship the material world. The shift demands that we stop being so selfish toward others, serve others, become full human beings, be of service, feel others' pain and suffering, discover the dignity of human life, and build a strong foundation within in order to serve and protect all life. We should act with maturity, take responsibility, and live with grace and humility.

Lack of knowledge and lack of education, meaning ignorance, create contractions in the mind, whereas knowledge uplifts and liberates us. We have a choice today in the twenty-first century between contraction and liberation. Most religions, in their own ways, speak of "self," the indwelling power of God, of life, the presence, where we contemplate and practice introspection. A change in mind leads to a change in behavior and attitude and leads to a life of righteousness containing the beginning of knowledge, of the light of wisdom. With the realization that we are all children of the same source, we can treat the other as one's self, also acknowledging the self in the other. The shift in one's awareness is felt as a vibration by others; a feeling of sisterhood and brotherhood, a feeling of knowing one's self, emerges. Are we not all brothers, sisters, beloveds of the divine? When we transform ourselves, we are transforming the world. Our transformation, a shift of our own consciousness, a transformation of it, is now an imperative.

What is our dharma? When are we going to be awakened? When will we dare to open our hearts to love our brothers and sisters, to accept each other? An awakening happens with education and knowledge of the higher self. The awareness of nonviolence lifts our identity to a self level, a divinity level. There is only one spirit, one light, one God, one source.

If we remember that we are all from one and the same source, we will naturally create a safer place on this planet, realizing we are all human beings. Then we will honor all human values; we will honor life within each of us and a life of wisdom as a wise one. Technology can be used to serve the world, promote a better life, eradicate poverty, stop domestic violence, and revive the law. It is the Shakti that binds us all as pearls on one thread. Technology can be used with wisdom to reinterpret religion in the twenty-first century and to breathe new life into religion and revive it. Technology can help our government bring wisdom to our schools, so that our students will become wiser. Each child should know that there are many different religions. We should put before them the global ideal of general knowledge of religion, which is an inseparable part of human life. These young children have a different consciousness and are so awake. Our role is to take the step toward globalized wisdom and if needed reinterpret, revise, or modify philosophical concepts.

Spiritualizing our everyday life will serve as the greatest example. We can be models of compassion, of nobility, an expression of divine love, apply the golden rule in our daily lives as we grow.

Religious texts, although they have been translated so many, many times, do not often address the feminine aspect of God. Esoteric teachings are very beautiful and respectful of both man and woman, and they seem to understand that both male and female energies go together. They offer a higher level of religious life. There are many references in different traditions of the feminine aspect of God, of life, of Source. The feminine principle was created with the Shakti of life itself. Jesus used to speak of the mother, the Cosmic Mother, Father Creator. The roles of Jesus's grandmother, Anna, and mother, Mary, remind us of the law of forgiveness, that which we carry within each of us. Sophia, principle of feminine wisdom, is one aspect of Shakti. In the creation, there is no evolution without the feminine aspect.

In India, the word *Shakti,* the divine feminine principle, encompasses all the feminine aspects of the cosmos. This has not changed since the beginning of the human race. Shakti is the embodiment of the omnipresent, omnipotent, and omniscient that is worshiped, even though adorned in different forms. Shakti is a recognized form of women in Hinduism, even though in some areas of India, women are still badly treated. Meditation, stillness, is important to be a better vehicle of that divine feminine principle. As meditation liberates one from inner conflict, it dissolves the "stuff," clears the sense of separation, and brings forgiveness, thereby leading to a better life, better behavior, better relationships, an uplifting of consciousness, and higher frequencies of our energies in the *chakras* of our subtle bodies. The power of meditation also brings unity, love, peace, sacredness, and mindfulness to all. It is urgent that we allow our divine feminine to reveal herself so that spiritual growth occurs, allowing spiritual integration in everyday life. There is a lot that can be derived from the feminine principle.

What has happened to the feminine in religion? Our role is to cultivate that love and teach others how to respect, understand, and accept other faiths and how to be awakened to a higher vibration and to the virtue in each human heart. Cultivating the feminine principle in religion leads to a deeper understanding of who we really are, enabling us to articulate the wisdom of responsibility. It contributes to maturity, healthy relationships, caring behavior, commitment, and oneness in our diversity in all aspects of our daily life experience. Peace will prevail when individuals are at peace. The foundation of religion is to be relevant and coherent. Another aspect of religious evolution is to collaborate with different faiths and traditions, interact in interreligious activities, share one's knowledge, and promote discussion and dialogue.

If God possesses both feminine and masculine energy, how could God, as Creator, diminish the dignity of its own creation? Religion is here to sustain society, teach sharing and caring, and share the feeling of oneness, respect, and love of the Creator.

When we consider the fact of birth, what would life be without the feminine? Could there be life? Impossible! If a child does not receive the love of the mother, the brain does not grow. A loved heart has such potential for growth. We need to ask such questions as these: What are we passing to the next generation? How are we educating our children, the custodians of planet Earth? What are our moral values? How can we find a common ground, a togetherness, to uplift human consciousness? How do we kindle the heart of the human race? In most religions, we have golden rules, vows that have embodied respect and justice since the beginning of the human family. Such is the dignity and nobility of being human.

Love, compassion, respect, and communication can really create and establish harmony. These are ways to bring out the best in human beings. The power of forgiveness provides us with the path of healing.

Now for the feminine to be empowered, the masculine has to be reeducated. Man must reevaluate women in his eyes, even the way he sees women. Women are so precious, so important for both peace and spiritual advancement. Both the masculine and feminine aspects must become enlightened and balanced so we can all understand each other. It is possible to achieve this balance since we are all part of the cosmos. The Creator does not discriminate between the two. A mindful person, man or woman, honors and empowers the other. It's all about education, education with awareness, education with heart, education with wisdom, education with love, education with kindness. An inner peace that reveres life is innate in women, because women carry life within their wombs. We women in harmony with men can bring global spiritual wisdom in this world with our love. Peace will prevail when our compassionate transformation of consciousness occurs, as our heart *chakras* open more and more, and our consciousness expands. Such is the potential glory of divine feminine right here now.

RELIGION, FUNDAMENTAL QUESTIONS, AND HUMAN SOCIETY

Vinesh Saxena

Our universe began 13.7 billion years ago, and the earth was formed 4.5 billion years ago. Invertebrate life started to appear 600 million years ago. Fish evolved 150 million years ago. Dinosaurs started roaming the earth about 80 million years ago. Evolution continued—humans as we know them appeared 70,000 years ago. They started to use words about 30,000 years ago, to farm about 11,000 years ago, and to write about 5,000 years ago.

The first organized religion was Judaism, which started in 2085 B.C.E. Then came Hinduism in approximately 1500 B.C.E., then Buddhism about 560 B.C.E. Jainism and Taoism originated at about the same time as Buddhism. Christianity goes back to 30 C.E., and Islam originated about 610 C.E. Sikhism originated about 1500 C.E. Thereafter, only subreligions seem to spring up: Protestantism in 1515 C.E., Mormonism in 1830 C.E., Baháʼí faith in 1844, Jehovah's Witness in 1870, and so on. More recently, Scientology originated in 1955, and the Hare Krishna movement began in 1968. There are many more that I have not mentioned here.

We have briefly reviewed the evolution of human society on the one hand and of religions on the other. It seems that religions originated at different places and at different times, in response to human needs in a specific part of the society at a specific time. When we gaze at the universe and ponder over its mystery, many questions come to mind, including these: Where do we come from? Why are we here on the earth? Where do we go after death? Are we just this mortal body or something more?

To me, the principal fundamental unanswered questions are

1. Does the soul exist?
2. Is there life after death?
3. Does God exist?

The first two questions are interconnected. If we are more than this mortal body—that is, if there is a kind of life force in our body—then it is likely that this life force, which we can call soul, does not die with the mortal body. Hence, it is quite likely that this soul can continue, and the notion of life after death becomes a likelihood.

The third question is very basic. When we look at a house, there is an owner and creator of that house. Similarly, for this immense universe, there must be a creator or owner. Thus we can arrive at the existence of the God. This is simple deductive logic; however, to provide a universally acceptable rational answer is another matter.

I find it very strange and kind of sad that we as humans have existed for 40,000–70,000 years, but there are no universally acceptable and proven answers to these basic questions. Maybe it is not easy to answer them, but society owes itself answers to these questions. Let us look at the religions and see what they say.

DOES SOUL EXIST?

- Judaism: Yes. It is only through the granting of a soul that man becomes animate flesh.
- Hinduism: Yes. Ātman is eternal, invisible, imperishable, and unchanging.
- Buddhism denies the existence of an eternal soul but believes in the notion of constant change.
- Christianity: Yes. Each soul is judged upon death.
- Islam: Yes. The soul has distinct parts: non-rational and rational.

IS THERE LIFE AFTER DEATH?

- Judaism: Jewish ideas are relatively fluid. A Jew might believe that the souls of Jewish people go to heaven, reincarnate into new beings, or get resurrected at the coming of the Messiah.
- Hinduism: Yes. After death, the soul goes to heaven or hell to be rewarded or punished, and then is placed in a new body depending upon deeds performed in this life. This cycle continues till one attains the state of nirvana.
- Buddhism: Yes. People are reborn until they are free from the cycle of birth and decay.
- Christianity: All who have died are immediately judged, and their souls are sent to heaven, hell, or in some belief systems, purgatory. At the time of the second coming of Jesus, the bodies of the righteous will be resurrected and united with their souls.
- Islam: On the day of resurrection, all people will be held accountable for their actions.

DOES GOD EXIST?

- Judaism: Yes. There are two words for it: Yahweh, or Lord, and Elohim, or God
- Hinduism: Yes. God is eternal. Millions of deities are but manifestations to help us visualize the unknowable Godhead.
- Buddhism does not believe in God but believes that there are beings that inhabit the various celestial realms.
- Christianity: Yes. God is both one and triune as the Father, the Son, and the Holy Spirit.
- Islam: Yes. Allah is absolute, eternal, incorporeal, and unknowable.

While examining different religions regarding the three fundamental questions, I see contradictions and marked differences in the answers. For example, Hindus say that there is reincarnation; according to Islam, there is no reincarnation; and Christians believe in resurrection. What does this mean? Then there are atheists, communists, the followers of Jedi, and so on. If religions are true as their followers strongly feel, then there would have to be pigeonholes in God's administrative kingdom that pertain to adherents of different established religions and diverse nonreligious people; in other words, each faction will go to a different distinctive quarter after death. Does this make sense? To me it does not. I believe that all religions are manmade and do not provide logical, rational, or universal answers to the fundamental unanswered questions mentioned earlier. Furthermore, humans have been on the earth for seventy thousand years, while organized religions have been here for fewer than three thousand years, so what was happening when humans were dying earlier than three thousand years ago?

Furthermore, we have been witnessing horrific events. Certainly, 9/11 was one of them. Fundamentalists are even killing people of other religions in the name of religion. Hindus and Muslims fight each other, Catholics and Protestants do the same, and Jews and Muslims are killing each other in the Middle East. The situation is so horrific and baseless. Communists were and are even today suppressing all religions. Christians and Muslims (as well as followers of other religions) convert people of other religions to their religion to "save the souls." I am sad. To me, religions may be acceptable so long as they teach some morality and as long as they respect each other. That is it, but no more.

I am baffled and concerned that society has existed for so long without making any concerted effort to answer the unanswered questions listed earlier. Society has spent more than 10 million dollars to develop an artificial heart, trillions of dollars on space programs, and so on. Then why has society not even established an institute to examine and research the answers to the above questions?

One may explain why it is important to have answers to the fundamental questions listed earlier.

- If soul exists, and if there is life after death in the form of reincarnation based on deeds performed in this life, then the implications would be very different. There will be fewer criminals and less criminal activity; monsters such as Hitler, Idi Amin, and so on would not evolve. People will not be killing each other. Episodes such as 9/11 and the bombings in England, Madrid, and Bom-

bay will not occur. People will be concerned about the moral implications of their deeds. They will become busy preparing for the next life.

- On the other hand, if the answers to the above questions are negative, then we, as well as all events, are random and statistical. Under this scenario, people will want to own and enjoy all material goods and comforts in this one lifetime—imagine how ultramaterialistic such a society would be. Further, what would prevent human beings from carrying out immoral acts and turning into monsters if they can do so with impunity? We would need more laws and more expenditure on law enforcement, otherwise society would in all likelihood just disintegrate.

To conclude, we should encourage society to establish an institute and spend funds to carry out impartial research into answering the questions mentioned above. For my small part, I have established a registered charitable foundation.[1] This foundation has two objectives: the first is to help the needy, and the other is to fund research to provide logical and universally acceptable answers to the three fundamental questions mentioned above.

Beyond Religion

A Holistic Spirituality

Mabel Aranha

What does "holistic" mean in reference to "spirituality"?

- A desire for integration and wholeness, an awareness of equality and reciprocity
- An understanding of the connections between various aspects of our reality as we know it
- A harmonious relationship for the ultimate welfare and productivity of a person and those that inhabit our universe
- A dynamic process that includes every dimension of one's life—including every object and every person that constitutes our world and connecting us with every aspect of human development
- A religious maturity accepting human life and our earth as a gift

A holistic spirituality means an outlook that will integrate our lives sufficiently to give us a sense of increasing wholeness in order to heal the dichotomy between the human and the holy, the secular and the sacred.

A holistic spirituality starts from the premise that there are many ways to achieve peace: through prayer, social action, singing, chanting, writing good literature, painting beautiful pictures, and creating beautiful artifacts and sculptures. The greatest way is the training of the mind in love, kindness, contentment, compassion, and wisdom.

In *By Way of the Heart*, Wilkie Au, a Jesuit, says, "By way of the heart is to take a path to holiness or spirituality that is both graceful and human. It is a spirituality wherein our cold hearts of stone are replaced with warm hearts of flesh capable of loving—a transformation that calls for personal responsibility and effort. It is human because it requires the whole self—body, mind and feeling, as spiritual growth is a multifaceted process."[1] So is human growth.

Many factors contribute to violence in society. We are born with the legacy of greed, hatred, and ignorance passed down through generations and the social and cultural consciousness of a nation or groups of people. Children imitate adults around them because children are still in the process of forming their identities and their sense of right and wrong. Often, they are confused by the behavior of adults—exploitation and competition at the expense of the other. If we want our children to be happy, we have to present alternatives for a happy and peaceful life.

Our understanding of the world comes to us through our senses. Our perceptions and reactions are colored or sieved through individual, family, and social legacies of the past. Conditioned patterns of living and beliefs must be constantly replaced with patterns of understanding, tolerance, and friendliness by leading the people to a place of peace within themselves, when the stress of life and their emotions overwhelm them. We use the feeling of love they are familiar with and widen the circle of that love in boundless ripples touching most aspects of their life with the meditation of loving-kindness.

Loving-kindness is like radiating the rays of the sun in all directions; it is like the rain falling on every person and creature irrespective of who or what they are. A loving-kindness meditation helps us put loving-kindness into practice. When we are constantly sending love, a transformation of the consciousness is initiated. We will not fight or say harsh words. We will not harm or plan to harm others. Loving-kindness understands one's own suffering and through that experience understands the suffering of others. It is a mental attitude that does not want us or others to suffer. Loving-kindness is the beginning stage of compassion. A person of compassion wants all beings to have everything they wish for. The main idea is that all beings must have happiness and the causes for happiness.

Based on a scheme from Donald Goergen, used by Wilkie Au to explain "A Holistic Christian Spirituality," I have attempted to create a framework for the practice of loving-kindness within a holistic spirituality. According to it, the practice of loving-kindness, known as *metta* in Pali and *maitrī* in Sanskrit, can be divided into

1. Self sphere
2. Family sphere
3. Friend/Foe sphere
4. Community and the mediator sphere

Within this holistic framework, self-love must be looked at first. Self-esteem is primary because all other healthy love springs from it. This love is different from the egoistic or narcissistic love of oneself; it is a love that accepts the humanity within us, whenever or wherever we come across it. Embracing the totality of who we are gradually helps us accept the totality of others and the worth of us all. By understanding our pain, our success, our joys, and our need to be happy, we understand the pain and needs of all beings.

Self-denial and self-hatred block us from loving others, and such self-rejection often leads to rejection of the sacred in us and other people. Self-denial is not a negation but an understanding that we are more than what we think we are and recognition of the inherent goodness, which is our true self. Wishing for our own well-being is the root of the wish for the well-being of all beings.

The family, which is the cornerstone of society, is the cradle of love, for here it is that we see the pure love, the unconditional love of a mother and a father for a child, for whom they are willing to give up everything to nurture and keep safe from harm. Love that makes us whole usually begins with our family.

Leisure for all, including parents, must be a component of family life to avoid conflicts, resentments, and the feeling of helplessness. It is necessary to give each member a certain amount of space, time, and opportunity for responsibility, interests, and creativity to flourish and be fulfilled.

Healthy family life must strike a balance between fostering intimacy within the home and developing life-enhancing ties outside domestic walls. We all have known the value of friends and the attachment we have for them. Good friends are like the summer roses, whose fragrance makes the garden smell sweeter. We love our friends but have to use a certain amount of discernment in our friendships. Discernment and discretion distinguish between right and wrong associations and lead to wisdom.

Our reaction to those who are not our friends—a picky boss or spiteful colleagues—is a story we are familiar with. They are also part of our lives, and we need to use the same discernment not to bring on suffering for ourselves and others. If there is a problem, send loving-kindness to a hostile person. Try to persist or leave it aside for the moment and come back to it later. When there is no distinction, we truly radiate kindness.

Our community today is far beyond the little village or town in which we were born. It includes all those who inhabit the planet. Mindless actions in one part of the country or the world have tremendous consequences thousands of miles away. Too much in one place means too little in another. Misuse of mother earth and her exploitation bring about tremendous loss of life in the remotest parts of the globe. We have to understand our needs are the same as the needs of those living in other parts of the world.

All of us deserve to live with sufficient means and achieve happiness. Yet it takes just a few thoughts to convey our empathy and feel the unity in our innermost being. We are able to make this connection through loving-kindness meditation. Sending vibrations of love and friendliness can heal the world and ourselves. Practicing it often will work at the innermost cellular structure of the body, making us truly happy.

LOVING-KINDNESS MEDITATION

We will do a simple loving-kindness meditation. Because of lack of space, we will not follow the pattern in the book, which gives readers a greater understanding of the practice.

The meditation is divided into four parts. When we first introduce the meditation, we do some reflection on the part we are going to meditate.

1. Myself, my parents, my children, relatives, and teachers
2. Friendly persons, indifferent persons, and unfriendly persons
3. Beings in our country, the world, and the universe
4. All living creatures

Sit quietly with your spine straight, eyes closed gently, and hands in your lap. Try to be as relaxed as possible. Send all your tensions through the windows at least for the next twenty minutes. Concentrate on good thoughts. Take three deep inhalations and exhalations.

THE FIRST GROUP

1a: Reflections on Myself

I suffer from discomfort, pain, and sickness. I am hard on myself because I want everything to be perfect according to my wishes. I suffer when I cannot get the things I want. I also suffer when I get what I do not want or have to give up what I have. I have faults, but only if I love myself, I can accept myself as I am, and that will make me happy. That will help me to accept others and to come to love others. So, I send loving-kindness to myself.

Now I send loving-kindness to myself, accepting fully all that I am. Let the feeling of warmth and radiance start from my heart and flow through my whole body.

1b: Meditation of Loving-kindness for Myself

May I be well, happy, and peaceful
May I be free from every harm
May I be free from difficulties
May I have patience and courage
To overcome anger and suffering
And have success in all that I do

2a: Reflections on My Family

My parents worked hard to make a home, give me the things I needed, and good values. I think they did the best they could for me, but sometimes I do not agree with them. My parents suffer too. My brothers and sisters have the same needs, desires, and ambition that I have. This brings conflict in the family. If I try to understand that in some ways they are different and unique, like myself, and send love and kindness to them, I can find a way of making myself peaceful and making them happy, too. If I understand that we all suffer, it will make it easier for me to make allowances for the members of my family and my relatives.

Now send loving-kindness to family members, accepting all that they are. Let the feeling of warmth and radiance start from the heart and flow toward each of them.

2b: Meditation of Loving-kindness for My Family

> May my family be happy and peaceful
> May they be free from every harm
> May they be free from difficulties
> May they have patience and courage
> To overcome anger and suffering
> And have success in all that they do

At this point, we can extend our love to our children, relatives, and teachers, with the appropriate reflection on their lives and their suffering, and be grateful to them for what we have received.

The Second Group

3a: Reflections on Friendly Persons at School or Work

> We know we suffer, and sometimes we know why we suffer. Our friends suffer too. Start with good thoughts about a friend and send him/her loving-kindness, then include all those with whom you have had good times or who have helped you when you were sad or were in difficulties. However, we should not do things that are not right just because we love them. If anyone is sick, send extra love.

Being thankful, we send loving-kindness to them. True love is wishing for their ultimate happiness.

3b: Meditation of Loving-kindness for Friendly Persons

> May friendly persons be happy and peaceful
> May they be free from every harm
> May they be free from difficulties
> May they have patience and courage

> To overcome anger and suffering
> And have success in all that they do

4a: Reflections on Indifferent Persons

> There are many people who pass us by on the streets, in trains and buses, in buildings, and on the highways. Although we do not know them, they suffer because they have the same legacy we have. They also have the same potential for goodness. Until our craving and ill will toward others is eliminated, we will be ignorant of our true self and we will suffer.

With increasing compassion in our hearts, let us send loving-kindness to indifferent people we meet. You can send loving-kindness to people who are neutral but help you in your life, such as the letter carrier, store attendant, newspaper carrier, grocery attendants, garbage collectors, bank officials, and others.

4b: Meditation of Loving-kindness for Indifferent Persons

> May indifferent persons be happy and peaceful
> May they be free from every harm
> May they be free from difficulties
> May they have patience and courage
> To overcome anger and suffering
> And have success in all that they do

5a: Reflections on Unfriendly Persons at School or Work

> We would like everyone in our life to love us. If we do not do that, how can we expect everyone to be friendly to us? People have different ways of behaving with people. Sometimes our friends turn against us, or people who do not seem to like us are not friendly to us. Perhaps we have given them cause at some time without knowing it, or they are doing it out of ignorance without paying attention to the hurt they cause. We should calm ourselves, and think of the

harm and suffering they bring on themselves. If we change this bad result into a good cause by sending kind feelings, we get more credit and ensure our greater happiness in the future.

With the constant practice of sending loving-kindness to those who hurt us, we will not have any enemies. Even if they try to harm us, it will not offend us so much the next time we feel hurt.

5b: Meditation of Loving-kindness for Unfriendly Persons

May unfriendly persons be happy and peaceful
May they be free from every harm
May they be free from difficulties
May they have patience and courage
To overcome anger and suffering
And have success in all that they do

THE THIRD GROUP

6a: Reflections on Beings in My Country

We have people of different states and nationalities living in our country. They follow different religions and come from various cultures. We all want enough food, drink, clothing, and shelter, and good air to breathe. Some are hungry and unemployed; others have no shelter or clothing. Some are addicted to drugs and alcohol and cannot think of the consequences of their actions. Some suffer because of floods, earthquakes, natural disasters, or terrorist actions. Every human being wants caring and loving.

Let us send loving-kindness to all the infants and all the people in our country that they may be loved, that their wishes may be met, and that they may be able to live without hurting each other.

6b: Meditation of Loving-kindness for All Beings in My Country

May all beings in my country be happy and peaceful

May they be free from every harm
May they be free from difficulties
May they have patience and courage
To overcome anger and suffering
And have success in all that they do

7a: Reflections on Beings in Our World

In our world, there are people of many cultures we know nothing about. Some people live on hills and mountains and in dense forests. Whatever they are—rich or poor; white, brown, yellow or black; advanced, underdeveloped, or primitive; with resources or trying hard to make a living—all go through wanting, sickness, aging, and death. The desire to want more and more than we need is a sickness. We suffer because we cannot get the things we want. If we do get them, we are satisfied for brief intervals, but our lack of satisfaction is a permanent state in our life.

Let us think of the suffering of the people in the world, make a wish that everyone will have what they need, including ourselves, and send loving-kindness.

7b: Meditation of Loving-kindness for All Beings in the World

May all beings in the world be happy and peaceful
May they be free from every harm
May they be free from difficulties
May they have patience and courage
To overcome anger and suffering
And have success in all that they do

THE FOURTH GROUP

Let us visualize the creatures of the universe, and then follow it with a loving-kindness meditation.

8a: Reflection on Creatures

Imagine you are transformed into a snow-white dove with beautiful, silver-tipped wings and a heart of gold. Golden rays of loving-kindness are streaming from your heart. You gently lift yourself and are now flying through the air. As you fly over the lakes, seas, and oceans, you see the most beautiful creatures in the waters. Their life appears peaceful, but it is full of danger. Now we fly over the meadows, woods, and forests. There are all kinds of creatures, small as the ant and big as the elephant. Some have to hide from other animals, which may eat them; others are hungry and thirsty and have to travel long distances to get food and water; many are cold, sick, aging, and dying. We see that creatures of the air have the same difficulties. We return back to the city. Dogs and cats are homeless and are scrounging for food. We see some animals ill treated by their masters and horses and oxen that are overworked.

Send loving-kindness to all creatures of the world, including our pets, that they may have good lives.

8b: Meditation of Loving-kindness for All Creatures in the World

May all creatures in the world be happy and peaceful

In the sea and in the air
On the land and everywhere
May they have patience and courage
To overcome danger and suffering
And live in harmony all the time.

The benefits of a wishing prayer cannot be seen. The results of purely mental activities are not visible immediately, yet the extent of their power is very great. The conditioned walls of our own prison gradually break down, and we experience a freedom of mind and spirit.

A loving-kindness meditation can be done during the day in parts or when we face a particular situation before we react to it. We will become calm and do our work with more energy. Our perceptions of others will gradually change. It does not have to be in a structured order. It can be done while standing, walking, playing, or driving, and it is recommended to be done when we start our day or before going to sleep. By teaching children a loving-kindness meditation, teachers, parents, and significant others can replace disintegration with integration, hatred with love, brokenness with wholeness, and division with unity in their lives.

APPENDICES

Primary Documents

APPENDIX 1

United Nations Universal Declaration of Human Rights
December 10, 1948

PREAMBLE

Whereas recognition of the inherent dignity and of the equal and inalienable rights of all members of the human family is the foundation of freedom, justice and peace in the world,

Whereas disregard and contempt for human rights have resulted in barbarous acts which have outraged the conscience of mankind, and the advent of a world in which human beings shall enjoy freedom of speech and belief and freedom from fear and want has been proclaimed as the highest aspiration of the common people,

Whereas it is essential, if man is not to be compelled to have recourse, as a last resort, to rebellion against tyranny and oppression, that human rights should be protected by the rule of law,

Whereas it is essential to promote the development of friendly relations between nations,

Whereas the peoples of the United Nations have in the Charter reaffirmed their faith in fundamental human rights, in the dignity and worth of the human person and in the equal rights of men and women and have determined to promote social progress and better standards of life in larger freedom,

Whereas Member States have pledged themselves to achieve, in co-operation with the United Nations, the promotion of universal respect for and observance of human rights and fundamental freedoms,

Whereas a common understanding of these rights and freedoms is of the greatest importance for the full realization of this pledge,

Now, Therefore THE GENERAL ASSEMBLY proclaims THIS UNIVERSAL DECLARATION OF HUMAN RIGHTS as a common standard of achievement for all peoples and all nations, to the end that every individual and every organ of society, keeping this Declaration constantly in mind, shall strive by teaching and education to promote respect for these rights and freedoms and by progressive measures, national and international, to secure their universal and effective recognition and observance, both among the peoples of Member States themselves and among the peoples of territories under their jurisdiction.

ARTICLE 1

All human beings are born free and equal in dignity and rights. They are endowed with reason and conscience and should act towards one another in a spirit of brotherhood.

ARTICLE 2

Everyone is entitled to all the rights and freedoms set forth in this Declaration, without distinction of any kind, such as race, colour, sex, language, religion, political or other opinion, national or social origin, property, birth or other status. Furthermore, no distinction shall be made on the basis of the political, jurisdictional or international status of the country or territory to which a person belongs, whether it be independent, trust, non-self-governing or under any other limitation of sovereignty.

ARTICLE 3

Everyone has the right to life, liberty and security of person.

ARTICLE 4

No one shall be held in slavery or servitude; slavery and the slave trade shall be prohibited in all their forms.

ARTICLE 5

No one shall be subjected to torture or to cruel, inhuman or degrading treatment or punishment.

ARTICLE 6

Everyone has the right to recognition everywhere as a person before the law.

ARTICLE 7

All are equal before the law and are entitled without any discrimination to equal protection of the law. All are entitled to equal protection against any discrimination in violation of this Declaration and against any incitement to such discrimination.

ARTICLE 8

Everyone has the right to an effective remedy by the competent national tribunals for acts violating the fundamental rights granted him by the constitution or by law.

ARTICLE 9

No one shall be subjected to arbitrary arrest, detention or exile.

ARTICLE 10

Everyone is entitled in full equality to a fair and public hearing by an independent and impartial tribunal, in the determination of his rights and obligations and of any criminal charge against him.

ARTICLE 11

(1) Everyone charged with a penal offence has the right to be presumed innocent until proved guilty according to law in a public trial at which he has had all the guarantees necessary for his defence.

(2) No one shall be held guilty of any penal offence on account of any act or omission which did not constitute a penal offence, under national or international law, at the time when it was committed. Nor shall a heavier penalty be imposed than the one that was applicable at the time the penal offence was committed.

ARTICLE 12

No one shall be subjected to arbitrary interference with his privacy, family, home or correspondence, nor to attacks upon his honour and reputation. Everyone has the right to the protection of the law against such interference or attacks.

ARTICLE 13

(1) Everyone has the right to freedom of movement and residence within the borders of each state.

(2) Everyone has the right to leave any country, including his own, and to return to his country.

ARTICLE 14

(1) Everyone has the right to seek and to enjoy in other countries asylum from persecution.

(2) This right may not be invoked in the case of prosecutions genuinely arising from non-political crimes or from acts contrary to the purposes and principles of the United Nations.

ARTICLE 15

(1) Everyone has the right to a nationality.

(2) No one shall be arbitrarily deprived of his nationality nor denied the right to change his nationality.

ARTICLE 16

(1) Men and women of full age, without any limitation due to race, nationality or religion, have the right to marry and to found a family. They are entitled to equal rights as to marriage, during marriage and at its dissolution.

(2) Marriage shall be entered into only with the free and full consent of the intending spouses.

(3) The family is the natural and fundamental group unit of society and is entitled to protection by society and the State.

ARTICLE 17

(1) Everyone has the right to own property alone as well as in association with others.

(2) No one shall be arbitrarily deprived of his property.

ARTICLE 18

Everyone has the right to freedom of thought, conscience and religion; this right includes freedom to change his religion or belief, and freedom, either alone or in community with others and in public or private, to manifest his religion or belief in teaching, practice, worship and observance.

ARTICLE 19

Everyone has the right to freedom of opinion and expression; this right includes freedom to hold opinions without interference and to seek, receive and impart information and ideas through any media and regardless of frontiers.

ARTICLE 20

(1) Everyone has the right to freedom of peaceful assembly and association.

(2) No one may be compelled to belong to an association.

ARTICLE 21

(1) Everyone has the right to take part in the government of his country, directly or through freely chosen representatives.

(2) Everyone has the right of equal access to public service in his country.

(3) The will of the people shall be the basis of the authority of government; this will shall be expressed in periodic and genuine elections which shall be by universal and equal suffrage and shall be held by secret vote or by equivalent free voting procedures.

ARTICLE 22

Everyone, as a member of society, has the right to social security and is entitled to realization, through national effort and international co-operation and in accordance with the organization and resources of each State, of the economic, social and cultural rights indispensable for his dignity and the free development of his personality.

ARTICLE 23

(1) Everyone has the right to work, to free choice of employment, to just and favourable conditions of work and to protection against unemployment.

(2) Everyone, without any discrimination, has the right to equal pay for equal work.

(3) Everyone who works has the right to just and favourable remuneration ensuring for himself and his family an existence worthy of human dignity, and supplemented, if necessary, by other means of social protection.

(4) Everyone has the right to form and to join trade unions for the protection of his interests.

ARTICLE 24

Everyone has the right to rest and leisure, including reasonable limitation of working hours and periodic holidays with pay.

ARTICLE 25

(1) Everyone has the right to a standard of living adequate for the health and well-being of himself and of his family, including food, clothing, housing and medical care and necessary social services, and the right to security in the event of unemployment, sickness, disability, widowhood, old age or other lack of livelihood in circumstances beyond his control.

(2) Motherhood and childhood are entitled to special care and assistance. All children, whether born in or out of wedlock, shall enjoy the same social protection.

ARTICLE 26

(1) Everyone has the right to education. Education shall be free, at least in the elementary and fundamental stages. Elementary education shall be compulsory. Technical and professional education shall be made generally available and higher education shall be equally accessible to all on the basis of merit.

(2) Education shall be directed to the full development of the human personality and to the strengthening of respect for human rights and fundamental freedoms. It shall promote understanding, tolerance and friendship among all nations, racial or religious groups, and shall further the activities of the United Nations for the maintenance of peace.

(3) Parents have a prior right to choose the kind of education that shall be given to their children.

ARTICLE 27

(1) Everyone has the right freely to participate in the cultural life of the community, to enjoy the arts and to share in scientific advancement and its benefits.

(2) Everyone has the right to the protection of the moral and material interests resulting from any scientific, literary or artistic production of which he is the author.

ARTICLE 28

Everyone is entitled to a social and international order in which the rights and freedoms set forth in this Declaration can be fully realized.

ARTICLE 29

(1) Everyone has duties to the community in which alone the free and full development of his personality is possible.

(2) In the exercise of his rights and freedoms, everyone shall be subject only to such limitations as are determined by law solely for the purpose of securing due recognition and respect for the rights and freedoms of others and of meeting the just requirements of morality, public order and the general welfare in a democratic society.

(3) These rights and freedoms may in no case be exercised contrary to the purposes and principles of the United Nations.

ARTICLE 30

Nothing in this Declaration may be interpreted as implying for any State, group or person any right to engage in any activity or to perform any act aimed at the destruction of any of the rights and freedoms set forth herein.

Appendix 2

Universal Declaration of Human Rights by the World's Religions
December 10, 1998

Whereas human beings are led to affirm that there is more to life than life itself by inspiration human and divine;

Whereas the Universal Declaration of Human Rights, as adopted by the General Assembly of the United Nations on December 10, 1948, bases itself on the former;

Whereas any exclusion of the world's religions as positive resources for human rights is obnoxious to the evidence of daily life;

Whereas the various communities constituting the peoples of the world must exchange not only ideas but also ideals;

Whereas religions ideally urge human beings to live in a just society and not just in any society;

Whereas one must not idealize the actual but strive to realize the ideal;

Whereas not to compensate victims of imperialism, racism, casteism, and sexism is itself imperialist, racist, casteist, and sexist;

Whereas rights are independent of duties in their protection but integrally related to them in conception and execution;

Whereas human rights are intended to secure peace, freedom, equality, and justice—and to mitigate departures therefrom—when these come in conflict or the rights themselves;

Now, therefore, on the fiftieth anniversary of the Universal Declaration of Human Rights and the fiftieth anniversary of the founding of the Faculty of Religious Studies at McGill University, Montreal, Quebec, Canada.

The signatories to this *Universal Declaration of Human Rights by the World's Religions,* as legatees of the religious heritage of humanity do hereby propose the following as the common standard of achievement for the followers of all religions or none, on the 10th day of December, 1998, as all people are brothers and sisters on the face of the earth.

ARTICLE 1

All human beings have the right to be treated as human beings and have the duty to treat everyone as a human being.

ARTICLE 2

Everyone has the right to freedom from violence, in any of its forms, individual or collective; whether based on race, religion, gender, caste or class, or arising from any other cause.

ARTICLE 3

(1) Everyone has the right to food.

(2) Everyone has the right to life, longevity, and liveability and the right to food, clothing, and shelter to sustain them.

(3) Everyone has the duty to support and sustain life, longevity, and liveability of all.

ARTICLE 4

(1) No one shall be subjected to slavery or servitude, forced labor, bonded labor, or child labor. Slavery and the slave trade shall be prohibited in all its forms.

(2) No one shall subject anyone to slavery or servitude in any of its forms.

ARTICLE 5

(1) No one shall be subjected to torture or to cruel, inhuman, or degrading treatment or punishment, inflicted either physically or mentally, whether on secular or religious grounds, inside the home or outside it.

(2) No one shall subject anybody to such treatment.

ARTICLE 6

(1) Everyone has a right to recognition everywhere as a person before law; and by everyone everywhere as a human being deserving humane treatment, even when law and order has broken down.

(2) Everyone has the duty to treat everyone else as a human being both in the eyes of law and one's own.

ARTICLE 7

All are equal before law and entitled to equal protection before law without any discrimination on grounds of race, religion, caste, class, sex, or sexual orientation. It is the right of everyone to be so treated and the duty of everyone to so treat others.

ARTICLE 8

Everybody has the duty to prevent the perpetuation of historical, social, economic, cultural and other wrongs.

ARTICLE 9

(1) No one shall be subjected to arbitrary arrest, detention, or exile by the state or by anyone else. The attempt to proselytize against the will of the person shall amount to arbitrary detention, so also the detention, against their will, of teenage children by the parents, and among spouses.

(2) It is the duty of everyone to secure everyone's liberty.

ARTICLE 10

Everybody has the right to public trial in the face of criminal charges, and it is the duty of the state to ensure it. Everyone who cannot afford a lawyer must be provided one by the state.

ARTICLE 11

Everyone charged with a penal offence has the right to be considered innocent until proven guilty.

ARTICLE 12

(1) Everyone has the right to privacy. This right includes the right not to be subjected to arbitrary interference with one's privacy; of one's own; or of one's family, home or correspondence.

(2) Everyone has the right to one's good name.

(3) It is the duty of everyone to protect the privacy and reputation of everyone else.

(4) Everyone has the right not to have one's religion denigrated in the media or academia.

(5) It is the duty of the follower of every religion to ensure that no religion is denigrated in the media or academia.

ARTICLE 13

(1) Everyone has the right to freedom of movement and residence anywhere in the world.

(2) Everyone has the duty to abide by the laws and regulations applicable in that part of the world.

ARTICLE 14

Everyone has the right to seek and secure asylum in any country from any form of persecution, religious or otherwise, and the right not to be deported. It is the duty of every country to provide such asylum.

ARTICLE 15

(1) Everyone has the right to a nationality;

(2) No one shall be arbitrarily deprived of one's nationality nor denied the right to change one's nationality.

(3) Everyone has the duty to promote the emergence of a global constitutional order.

ARTICLE 16

(1) Everyone has the right to marriage.

(2) Members of a family have the right to retain and practice their own religion or beliefs.

(3) Everyone has the right to raise a family.

(4) Everybody has the right to renounce the world and join a monastery, provided that one shall do so after making adequate arrangement for one's dependents.

(5) Marriage and monasticism are two of the most successful institutional innovations of humanity and are entitled to protection by the society and the state.

(6) Motherhood and childhood are entitled to special care and assistance. It is the duty of everyone to extend special consideration to mothers and children.

(7) Everyone shall promote the outlook that the entire world constitutes an extended family.

ARTICLE 17

(1) Everybody has the right to own property, alone as well as in association with others. An association also has a similar right to own property.

(2) Everyone has a right not to be deprived of property arbitrarily. It is the duty of everyone not to deprive others of their property arbitrarily. Property shall be understood to mean material as well as intellectual, aesthetic, and spiritual property.

(3) Everyone has the duty not to deprive anyone of their property or appropriate it in an unauthorized manner.

ARTICLE 18

(1) There shall be no compulsion in religion. It is a matter of choice.

(2) Everyone has the right to retain one's religion and to change one's religion.

(3) Everyone has the duty to promote peace and tolerance among different religions and ideologies.

ARTICLE 19

(1) Everyone has the right to freedom of opinion and expression, where the term *expression* includes the language one speaks; the food one eats; the clothes one wears; and the religion one practices and professes, provided that one conforms generally to the accustomed rules of decorum recognized in the neighborhood.

(2) It is the duty of everyone to ensure that everyone enjoys such freedom.

(3) Children have the right to express themselves freely in all matters affecting the child, to which it is the duty of their caretakers to give due weight in accordance with the age and maturity of the child.

ARTICLE 20

(1) Everyone has the right to freedom of assembly and association and the duty to do so peacefully.

(2) No one may be compelled to belong to an association, or to leave one without due process.

ARTICLE 21

(1) Everybody over the age of eighteen has the right to vote, to elect or be elected, and thus to take

part in the government or governance of the country, directly or indirectly.

(2) Everyone has the right of equal access to public service in one's country and the duty to provide such access.

(3) It is the duty of everyone to participate in the political process.

ARTICLE 22

Everyone, as a member of society, has a right to social security and a duty to contribute to it.

ARTICLE 23

(1) Everyone has the right to same pay for same work and a duty to offer same pay for same work.

(2) Everyone has the right for just remuneration for one's work and the duty to justly recompense for work done.

(3) Everyone has the right to form and to join trade unions for the protection of one's interests.

(4) Everyone has the right not to join a trade union.

ARTICLE 24

(1) Everyone has the right to work and to rest, including the right to support while seeking work and the right to periodic holidays with pay.

(2) The right to rest extends to the earth.

ARTICLE 25

(1) Everyone has the right to health and to universal medical insurance. It is the duty of the state or society to provide it.

(2) Every child has the right to a childhood free from violence, and it is the duty of the parents to provide it.

ARTICLE 26

Everyone has the right to free education and the right to equality of opportunity for any form of education involving restricted enrollment.

ARTICLE 27

(1) Everyone has the right to freely participate in the cultural life of the community and the right to freely contribute to it.

(2) Everyone has the right to share scientific advances and its benefits and the duty to disseminate them, and wherever possible to contribute to such advances.

(3) Everyone has the right to the protection of their cultural heritage. It is the duty of everyone to protect and enrich everyone's heritage, including one's own.

ARTICLE 28

Everyone has the right to socioeconomic and political order at a global, national, regional, and local level which enables the realization of social, political, economic, racial, and gender justice and the duty to give precedence to universal, national, regional, and local interests in that order.

ARTICLE 29

(1) One is duty-bound, when asserting one's rights, to take the rights of other human beings; of past, present, and future generations; the rights of humanity; and the rights of nature and the earth into account.

(2) One is duty-bound, when asserting one's rights, to prefer nonviolence over violence.

ARTICLE 30

(1) Everyone has the right to require the formation of a supervisory committee within one's community, defined religiously or otherwise, to monitor the implementation of the articles of this declaration and to serve on it and present one's case before such a committee.

(2) It is everyone's duty to ensure that such a committee satisfactorily supervises the implementation of these articles.

NOTES

PART 1

Stephen Healey—Religion and Terror

1. Cited by Harry Emerson Fosdick in *The Manhood of the Master* (New York: Association Press, 1917), p. 167. The original reference is Horace Bushnell's *The Character of Jesus* (1860).

2. For two shrill denunciations that obscure historical Islam, see R. L. Hymers and John S. Waldrip, *Demons in the Smoke of the World Trade Center: The Invasion of Evil Spirits and the Blight of Islam* (Oklahoma City: Hearthstone, 2002) and Robert Spencer, *Islam Unveiled: Disturbing Questions about the World's Fastest Growing Faith* (San Francisco: Encounter, 2003). For a defense of Islam, see Feisal Abdul Rauf, *What's Right with Islam: A New Vision for Muslims and the West* (San Francisco: HarperSanFrancisco, 2004). In addition, see Tariq Ramadan, *Western Muslims and the Future of Islam* (Oxford: Oxford University Press, 2005); Omid Safi, *Progressive Muslims: On Justice, Gender, and Pluralism* (Oxford: Oneworld, 2003); Khaled Abou El Fadl, *The Place of Tolerance in Islam* (Boston: Beacon, 2002). Sam Harris, treated below (see note 5 and *passim*), holds the view that Islam is more reprobate than other religions.

3. For some of the historical reasons behind this, see the articles by Abdou Filali-Ansary in Larry Diamond, Marc Plattner, and Phillip Costopoulos, *World Religions and Democracy* (Baltimore: Johns Hopkins University Press, 2005).

4. Sam Harris, *The End of Faith: Religion, Terror, and the Future of Reason* (New York: Norton, 2004); Diamond, Plattner, and Costopoulos.

5. Harris makes many claims about this. A representative one is that "while religious people are not generally mad, their core beliefs absolutely are" (p. 72).

6. Harris, pp. 16–23, *passim.*

7. In chapter 1, which sets the framework for those that follow, Alfred Stepan criticizes the "assumption of univocality" and suggests that religions are multivocal. See "Religion, Democracy, and 'Twin Tolerations,'" in Diamond, Plattner, and Costopoulos, pp. 9–10. I use the concept of valence (multivalent) to render Stepan's concept of "vocality" (multivocal, univocal).

8. Harris, pp. 192–97.

9. "A belief is a lever that, once pulled, moves almost everything else in a person's life" (Harris, p. 12). See also, Harris, pp. 44–46, 50–79.

10. Ibid., pp. 14–15, *passim.*

11. Ibid., p. 46.

12. Ibid., p. 47.

13. Ibid., pp. 48–49.

14. Ibid., ch. 4–6.

15. Ibid., p. 16.

16. Philip Costopoulos, "Introduction," in Diamond, Plattner, and Costopoulos, p. xi.

17. Stepan, p. 5.

18. Stepan, p. 9.

19. See Costopoulos, "Introduction," and Abdou Filali-Ansary, ch. 12, 15–16, in Diamond, Plattner, and Costopoulos. For the reference to enduring significance of Al-Afghani, see pp. 154–56.

20. "We are at war with Islam" (Harris, p. 109). See Harris, ch. 4.

21. Harris, p. 283, emphasis added.

22. Harris's view that "Buddhism is not a religion at all" squares with the historical and nonessentialist way of thinking about "religion" that derives from the work of comparativist Wilfred Cantwell Smith. See Wilfred Cantwell Smith, *The Meaning and End of Religion* (Minneapolis: Augsburg Fortress Publishers, 1991). However, Harris does not benefit from this theoretical perspective, because he treats meditation as the essence of Buddhism. Harris also does not apply the insight to other religions. Abdou Filali-Ansary shows the importance of this insight for interpreting Islam (see Abdou Filali-Ansary, "Muslims and Democracy," in Diamond, Plattner, and Costopoulos, pp. 153–67; Bernard Lewis, "A Historical Overview," in Diamond, Plattner, and Costopoulos, pp. 168–79).

23. Readers who share Harris's general approval of Buddhism will benefit from reading the *Mahāvaṃsa* of Sri Lankan Buddhism, Stanley Tambiah, *Buddhism Betrayed? Religion, Politics, and Violence in Sri Lanka* (Chicago: University of Chicago Press, 1992), and Tessa J. Bartholomeusz, *In Defense of Dharma: Just-War Ideology in Buddhist Sri Lanka* (London: Routledge Curzon, 2002).

24. Peter Berger, "Christianity: The Global Picture," in Diamond, Plattner, and Costopoulos, pp. 146–50.

25. Hahm Chaibong, "The Ironies of Confucianism," in Diamond, Plattner, and Costopoulos, p. 34.

26. Harris, p. 172.

27. A classic source for this with respect to Christianity is Ernst Troeltsch, *The Social Teachings of the Christian Churches and Sects* (Louisville, KY: Westminster John Knox, 1992 [reprint]).

28. This notion of "ethics of compromise" comes from Ernst Troeltsch, *Christian Thought: Its History and Application*, ed. Baron von Hugel (London: University of London Press, 1923).

29. Harris, pp. 199–203.

30. See Harris, p. 81, for a description of this outrageous device; Harris, p. 193.

31. This is a key task of religious ethics. Readers interested in pursuing this can start with the works of Max Stackhouse, David Hollenbach, Mark Heim, Lisa Cahill, Robert Benne, Ronald Thiemann, and James Gustafson. Readers will find in these authors a type of theological analysis (publicly inclined, fair-minded conversation, argument, and debate) that Harris believes impossible.

32. Harris focuses on extremes (burning heretics, for example). It is true that some such extremes will not be overcome through conversation and will require physical resistance. The cause of civilization in the post-9/11 era, however, is not furthered by imputing religious extremism to entire communities. See Max Stackhouse's discussion of religious-ethical judgment in *Creeds, Society, and Human Rights: A Study in Three Cultures* (Grand Rapids: Eerdmans, 1984), ch. 10, for an example of how judgments can be made in a more ecumenical tone. Also see Reinhold Niebuhr, *Human Destiny*, vol. 2 of *The Nature and Destiny of Man* (New York: Charles Scribner's Sons, 1946).

33. In the post-9/11 era, the ideas of religious communitarians and antiapologists, such as Stanley Hauerwas and John Milbank will increase this sort of ignorance of the other, should these ideas prevail. Hauerwas and Milbank both publish voluminously, and readers would do well to critically digest their views. But in spite of the erudition of Hauerwas and Milbank, Harris's criticism of the unintelligibility of faith applies to them. Milbank, for example, goes to great lengths to show that Christian doctrines are "baseless" and thus not open to intellectual defense or apologia. See Milbank's *Theology and Social Theory* (Oxford: Blackwell, 1990) and "On Baseless Suspicion: Christianity and the Crisis of Socialism," *New Blackfriars* 69 (Jan. 1988).

34. Harris, pp. 45–46.

35. Harris holds, for example, that the "spirit of mutual inquiry is the very antithesis of religious faith" (p. 48).

36. "Buddhism, Asian Values, and Democracy," in Diamond, Plattner, and Costopoulos, pp. 70–74.

37. Samuel Huntington's *The Clash of Civilizations and the Remaking of the World Order* (New York: Simon and Schuster, 1998) presents the valuable insight that the post–Cold War era is not a dyadic contest but a multi-civilizational one.

38. Harris believes that Jainism might be exempt from this claim. On the whole, that is correct. However, the Jain tradition differentiates between monastics and lay believers and recognizes that the latter may need to use violence in self-defense. Consult the Jaina Shrāvakāchār Code. Harris also sanctions violence in such

cases; chapter 4 in Harris is titled "The Problem with Islam."

39. Bernard Lewis's controversial book *What Went Wrong? The Clash between Islam and Modernity in the Middle East* (San Francisco: Harper Perennial, 2003) discusses reasons behind current Islamic anger toward the West. A very different analysis is presented by Mahmood Mamdani, *Good Muslim, Bad Muslim: America, the Cold War, and the Roots of Terror* (New York: Doubleday, 2004).

40. For a more convincing analysis, see Bruce Lincoln's *Holy Terrors: Thinking about Religion after September 11* (Chicago: University of Chicago Press, 2003).

41. Criticism of the penchant of Islamic states to adopt secular socialism goes back to Qutb, Mawdudi, and Khomeini. None of these figures were able to see the nonsecular dimensions of democracy. Reasons for that blindness are explored in Abdou Filali-Ansary, "Muslims and Democracy." Also see Lewis for a very different interpretation.

42. See chapters 12–20 in Diamond, Plattner, and Costopoulos.

43. This provision applies to all actors, not only Muslims. It is true, however, that Islam's place in the newly emerging world is especially problematic, especially given the wager the Islamic world made on the socialistic aspects of modernity, which seem to have been refuted.

44. Most Muslims live outside of the Arab world, but Muslim terrorism is largely the product of Arab Muslims or their non-Arab Muslim converts; it goes without saying that this analysis does not suggest that terrorism is caused by these factors. The issue is considerably more complex.

45. Among theologians working on this, in my view the most important are those who champion so-called public theology. (See the authors listed in note 31.)

46. This portrait of liberalism is, of course, drawn from John Locke's *Letter Concerning Toleration*. Few contemporary liberals engage in the kind of religious disputation supported by Locke. He encouraged vigorous (but nonpolitical) interreligious argument. The primary contribution of *World Religions and Democracy* is the questions it raises about this view.

47. Harris, p. 44.

48. For a thoughtful treatment of this issue, see David Held, Anthony McGrew, et al., *Global Transformations: Politics, Economics and Culture* (Stanford, Calif.: Stanford University Press, 1999).

49. The acts of 9/11 were not by Islam but by certain fanatical Muslims. Harris profoundly errs when he suggests the West and Islam are at war. "The West" and "Islam" are categories, not actors. It is also important to focus on how global forces allow individuals to have dramatic results. An important treatment of this issue is Thomas Friedman's *The World Is Flat: A Brief History of the Twenty-first Century* (New York: Farrar, Straus, and Giroux, 2005); this point is made by Bruce Lincoln in *Holy Terrors* (see note 40).

50. Jürgen Habermas, *The Philosophical Discourse of Modernity: Twelve Lectures* (Cambridge, Mass.: MIT Press, 1990).

51. For the question of democracy, a good resource is Reinhold Niebuhr's *The Children of Light and the Child of Darkness* (New York: Charles Scribner's Sons, 1960).

ARVIND SHARMA—THE BHAGAVADGĪTĀ AND WAR

1. This statement, though substantially true, is not entirely accurate, as later chapters do contain references to fighting (e.g., IX.34). However "in thirteen out of eighteen chapters of the Gītā (viz. Chap. IV–X and Chap. XII–XVIII) we do not meet with a single reference to the scene of the battlefield of Kurukṣetra, nor to the Epic story or incidents of any kind, which might remind us of the fact that Kṛṣṇa and Arjuna had anything to do with the Bhārata war or that the object of the teaching of the Gītā was to induce Arjuna to fight, so preoccupied and deeply absorbed are both the speakers of the dialogue in topics relating to modes of spiritual culture, the ethical ideal and subtle metaphysical concepts" (S. C. Roy, *The Bhagavad-gītā and Modern Scholarship* [London: Luzac & Co., 1941], pp. 146–47).

2. M. K. Gandhi, *Hindu Dharma* (Ahmedabad: Navajivan Press, 1958), pp. 178–79.

3. Gandhi, p. 159.

4. Gandhi, p. 140.

5. T. S. Rukmani, *A Critical Study of the Bhāgavata Purāṇa* (Varanasi: Chowkhamba Sanskrit Series, 1970), p. 6.

6. Rukmani, p. 6; *Bhāgavata Purāṇa* 1.5.15.

7. Mahatma Gandhi, *Anasakti Yoga* (Ahmedabad: Navajivan Prakasana, 1970).

8. Mahadev Desai, *The Gītā According to Gandhi* (Ahmedabad: Navajivan, 1946), p. 135.

9. Desai, *The Gītā According to Gandhi*, p. 135.

10. See Benjamin Walker, *Hindu World* (London: George Allen & Unwin Ltd., 1968), p. 2:221; Kanti Chandra Pandey, *Abhinavagupta: An Historical and Philosophical Study* (Varanasi: Chowkhamba Sanskrit Series Office, 1935), p. 9.

Notes

11. See A. L. Basham, *The Wonder That Was India* (London: Sidgwick and Jackson, 1956), p. 335.

12. Pandey, p. 8; Basham, p. 335.

13. See Pandey, pp. 52–55.

14. K. S. Ramaswamy Sastrigal seems to attribute this view to Abhinavagupta himself when he remarks: "Abhinava Guptacarya says that kṣetra means the body and that the war referred to is between the righteous and the unrighteous tendencies in man" (*The Bhagavadgītā* with translation and notes [Srirangam: Sri Vani Vilas Press, 1927], p. 1:47). But Abhinavagupta introduces this discussion with the remark: "In this respect some offer the following alternative explanation," and hence seems to be citing an alternative interpretation rather than developing his own (see Wasudev Laksman Shastri Pansikar, ed., *Śrīmadbhagavadgītā* [Bombay: Niranayasagar Press, 1912], p. 8).

15. Translation by the author.

16. The allegorical interpretation of the Gītā became quite current around the turn of the century (see W. Douglas Hill, *The Bhagavadgītā* [London: Oxford University Press, 1928], p. 99) and continues to be popular (see A. L. Herman, *The Bhagavad Gītā: A Translation and Critical Commentary* [Springfield, IL: Charles C. Thomas, 1973], pp. 107–8). It is important to realize, however, that Mahatma Gandhi seems to come by the allegorical interpretation on his own, for he says quite clearly that "even in 1888–89, when I first became acquainted with the Gītā, I felt that it was not a historical work, but that, under the guise of physical warfare, it described the duel that perpetually went on in the hearts of mankind and that physical warfare was brought in merely to make the description of the internal duel more alluring" (Mahadev Desai, p. 127). It should be further noted that according to Mahatma Gandhi his "first acquaintance with the Gītā began in 1888–89 with the verse translation by Sir Edwin Arnold known as the Song Celestial" (Mahadev Desai, p. 126). This translation does not project the Gītā as an allegory (see Edwin Arnold, *The Song Celestial or Bhagavad-Gītā* [Boston: Roberts Brothers, 1888], p. 9), unlike the translations or studies by Annie Besant (*The Bhagavad Gītā or The Lord's Song* [London: Theosophical Publishing Society, 1904], preface; *Hints on the Study of the Bhagavad-Gītā* [London: Theosophical Publishing Society, 1906], pp. 6ff). Hence, it is potentially misleading to state, as some have done, that Mahatma Gandhi was first introduced to the Gītā through Annie Besant's translation (see Agehananda Bharati, "The Hindu Renaissance and Its Apologetic Patterns," *The Journal of Asian Studies*, 29, no. 2

[1970]: 274–75). Similarly, Mahatma Gandhi refers to his attempts to read Bal Gangadhar Tilak's commentary on the Gītā (Mahadev Desai, p. 125.), which again does not espouse an allegorical interpretation of the Gītā. It seems that the similarity in the exposition of the Gītā referred to by Abhinavagupta and its exposition by Mahatma Gandhi provides a case of exegetical convergence that spans several centuries.

17. This paper was delivered at the first conference of the Australian Association for the Study of Religions, held at Adelaide in 1976.

WILLIAM R. O'NEILL—THE VIOLENT BEAR IT AWAY

1. Karl von Clausewitz, *On War*, trans. Edward M. Collins, in *War, Politics, and Power* (Chicago: Henry Regnery, 1962), p. 65; cited by Michael Walzer, *Just and Unjust Wars: A Moral Argument with Historical Illustrations*, 3rd ed. (New York: Basic, 1977), p. 23.

2. Walzer, p. 36. Walzer speaks of the "moral reality" of war as "a rule-governed activity."

3. For the ideal of an "overlapping consensus" see John Rawls, *Political Liberalism*, rev. ed. (New York: Columbia University Press, 1996), pp. xlvii ff., 133–72; "The Idea of Public Reason Revisited," in *The Law of Peoples* (Cambridge, Mass.: Harvard University Press, 1999), pp. 164–80.

4. Hugo Grotius, *De Jure Belli ac Pacis, Prolegomena*, trans. F. W. Kelsey (*The Classics of International Law*, Publication of the Carnegie Endowment for International Peace, no. 3, 1925), par. 11. For the notion of human rights as a "secular religion," see Elie Wiesel, "A Tribute to Human Rights," in *The Universal Declaration of Human Rights: Fifty Years and Beyond*, ed. Y. Danieli et al. (Amityville, N.Y.: Baywood, 1999), p. 3.

5. See Michael Walzer, *Thick and Thin: Moral Argument at Home and Abroad* (Notre Dame: University of Notre Dame Press, 1994), pp. 7, 10, 16–19.

6. Grotius, *De Jure Belli ac Pacis, Prolegomena*, par. 39.

7. A. P. D'Entrèves, *Natural Law: An Introduction to Legal Philosophy*, 2d ed. (London: Hutchinson, 1970), p. 55.

8. James Turner Johnson, *Morality and Contemporary Warfare* (New Haven, Conn.: Yale University Press, 1999), p. 219.

9. Cf. Theodor W. Adorno, *Negative Dialectics*, trans. E. B. Ashton (London: Routledge & Kegan Paul, 1973).

10. James F. Childress, "Just-War Criteria," in *War in the Twentieth Century: Sources in Theological Ethics*,

ed. Richard B. Miller (Louisville, KY: Westminster John Knox Press, 1992), pp. 352; see U.S. Bishops, "The Challenge of Peace," par. 80 in David J. O'Brien and Thomas A. Shannon, *Catholic Social Thought: The Documentary Heritage* (Maryknoll, N.Y.: Orbis, 1992), pp. 510–11. "The moral theory of the 'just-war' or 'limited-war' doctrine begins with the presumption which binds all Christians: we should do no harm to our neighbors." For commentary, see Todd D. Whitmore, "The Reception of Catholic Approaches to Peace and War in the United States," in *Modern Catholic Social Teaching: Commentaries and Interpretations*, ed. Kenneth Himes (Washington, D.C.: Georgetown University Press, 2004), pp. 493–521.

11. Johnson, pp. 35ff.

12. See Jacques Derrida, "Difference," in *Speech and Phenomena*, trans. David B. Allison (Evanston, Ill.: Northwestern University Press, 1973), pp. 126–60.

13. I am indebted to John Kelsay for this term.

14. Francisco Suárez, *De legibus ac Deo legislatore*, in *Selections from Three Works*, trans. Gwladys L. Williams et al. (Oxford: Clarendon, 1944), p. 2:349. Cf. Quentin Skinner, *The Foundations of Modern Political Thought* (Cambridge: Cambridge University Press, 1978), pp. 2:174–78.

15. Suárez, pp. 348–49.

16. See Immanuel Kant, *Critique of Practical Reason*, trans. Lewis White Beck (Indianapolis: Bobbs-Merrill Educational Publishing, 1956), pp. 68–71. Kant describes the schema of a concept as "a rule for the synthesis of the imagination," i.e., a rule linking concepts (a posteriori or a priori) to perception (*Critique of Pure Reason*, B 180, trans. Stephan Körner, in Kant [New Haven, Conn.: Yale University Press, 1955]), p. 70. The ideal of a well-formed narrative extends the Kantian ideal of a kingdom of ends diachronically (as inscribed in a narrative tradition) and synchronically (as intersubjectively rather than monologically realized). Construed thus, the kingdom of ends is not a type for the abstract, ahistorical subject, but historicized concretely in social narrative. Cf. Wittgenstein, *Philosophical Investigations*, 3rd ed., trans. G. E. M. Anscombe (New York: Macmillan, 1958), pt. 1, par. 497, 664.

17. See Robert Audi, *Religious Commitment and Secular Reason* (Cambridge: Cambridge University Press, 2000), pp. 86–100.

18. *ST.* I–II, Q. 91, art. 1 and 2.

19. Cf. *Epist.* 189, and 209, 2; *De Civitate Dei*, XIX, 12–13, XXII, 6; *Quest. Heat.* VI, 10, *SEL.*, XXVIII, 2, p. 428, IV, 44, CSEL, XXVIII, 2, p. 353; *De Libero Arbitrio*, V, 12, Migne, PL, XXXXII, 1227; *Contra Faustum*, XXIII,

76 and 79; Epist., 138, ii, 14. Cited in Roland Herbert Bainton, *Christian Attitudes Toward War and Peace: A Historical Survey and Critical Evaluation* (New York: Abingdon Press, 1960), pp. 91ff.

20. Luke 10:37.

21. Hans-Georg Gadamer, *Truth and Method*, 2nd revised ed., trans. Joel Weinsheimer and Donald G. Marshall (New York: Crossroad, 1989), p. 270. As Louis Dupré observes, "The Enlightenment's fight against [prejudices] stemmed itself from a prejudice and followed the Cartesian methodical rule that no position ought to be considered intellectually 'justified' before it was proven" (*The Enlightenment and the Intellectual Foundations of Modern Culture* [New Haven, Conn.: Yale University Press, 2004], p. 10).

22. Thomas Hobbes, *Leviathan*, ed. C. B. Macpherson (London: Penguin, 1968), pp. 185–86.

23. Matt 11:12.

24. Johnson, p. 23; following classical rhetorical usage, *loci* comprise the "storehouse of arguments" whereby general warrants are "topically" applied to specific cases. Such "commonplaces," deriving from consensual ("common sense") presumptions, schematize warrants (and backing), in part, by fixing motives. Cf. Cicero *Topics* II, 7; *Partitiones Oratoriae* 5; Chaim Perelman and L. Olbrechts-Tyteca, *The New Rhetoric: A Treatise on Argumentation*, trans. John Wilkinson and Purcell Weaver (Notre Dame: University of Notre Dame Press, 1969), pp. 83–85.

25. Jean Bethke Elshtain, "Reflections on War and Political Discourse: Realism, Just War, and Feminism in a Nuclear Age," in Miller, p. 400.

26. As Michael Walzer observes, "Hobbes argues that only an absolute sovereign can free [citizens] from . . . fearfulness and break the cycle of threats and 'anticipations' (that is, pre-emptive violence)" (Walzer, p. 77).

27. Locke argues that "the not taking God into this hypothesis has been the great reason of Mr Hobbeses [sic] mistake that the laws of nature are not properly laws nor do oblige mankind to their observation when out of a civil state of commonwealth" (John Locke, *Two Treatises of Government*, ed. P. Laslett [Cambridge: Cambridge University Press, 1963], pp. 93–94).

28. Elshtain, p. 407.

29. John Paul II, "Address of His Holiness Pope John Paul II to the Diplomatic Corps" (January 13, 2003) (http://www.vatican.va/holy_father/john_paul_ii/speeches/2003/january/documents/hf_jp-ii_spe_2003 0113_diplomatic-corps_en.html).

30. H. Richard Niebuhr, "War as Crucifixion," in Miler, p. 70.

31. Niebuhr, p. 70.

32. Lisa Sowle Cahill, *Love Your Enemies: Discipleship, Pacifism, and Just War Theory* (Minneapolis: Fortress Press, 1989), pp. 1–14.

33. Karl Rahner, "On the Question of a Formal Existential Ethics," in *Theological Investigations* 2, trans. Karl H. Kruger (Baltimore: Helicon, 1963), pp. 217–34. "Essential ethics" refers to the set of universal, action-guiding moral norms ascertained by natural reason (e.g., respect for persons' basic rights); we need not assume that such norms rest upon a foundationalist or essentialist metaphysics.

34. Such a mediating approach permits a limited rapprochement with Islamic emphasis upon divine obedience as the primary sanction for just war. See John Kelsay, *Islam and War: A Study in Comparative Ethics* (Louisville, KY: Westminster John Knox, 1993); John Kelsay, "Islam, Politics, and War," *Sewanee Theological Review* 47, no. 1 (Christmas 2003): 11–19; John Kelsay, "Islamic Tradition and the Justice of War," in *The Ethics of War in Asian Civilizations*, ed. Torkel Brekke (London: Routledge, 2006), pp. 81–110.

35. Lance Morrow, "The Case for Rage and Retribution," *Time Magazine*, Sept. 11, 2001.

36. Dorothy Day, "Love Is the Measure," *The Catholic Worker*, June 1946, p. 2.

RAMAZAN BICER—THE APPROACH OF MUSLIM TURKS TO RELIGIOUS TERROR

1. *The Oxford English Dictionary*, 2nd ed., s.v. "terrorism"; Michael E. Vlahos, *Terror's Mask: Insurgency within Islam* (Laurel, Md.: Johns Hopkins University Applied Physics Laboratory, 2002), p. 2.

2. *Macma al-luga al-arabiya: Mustalahat al-ilmiya wal-fanniya* (Kahire: Mecmaü'l-Lugati'l-Arabi, 1967), s.v. "fitnah."

3. Thomas P. Hughes, *A Dictionary of Islam* (London: W. H. Allen & Co., 1895), p. 129, s.v. "fitan."

4. M. H. Kamali, "Freedom of Expression in Islam: An Analysis of *Fitnah*," *American Journal of Islamic Social Sciences* 10, no. 2 (1993): 178–201.

5. Y. Tacar Pulat, *Teror ve Demokrasi* (Ankara: Bilgi Yayinevi, 1999), p. 30.

6. Hannah Arendt, *On Violence* (New York: Harcourt Brace & Co., 1970), pp. 46–56; Antony Arblaster, "Terrorism: Myths, Meaning and Morals," *Political Studies* 25, no. 3 (1977): 414–21.

7. M. S. Denker, *Uluslararası Teror ve Turkiye* (Istanbul: Boğaziçi Yayınları, 1997), pp. 9–15.

8. Emile Durkheim, *The Elementary Forms of Religious Life*, ed. Mark S. Cladis (Oxford: Oxford University Press, 2001), p. 308.

9. Orhan Turkdogan, *Sosyal Siddet ve Tirkiye Gerçegi* (Ankara: Mayas Yayinlari, 1985), p. 122; Necati Alkan, *Genclik ve Terorizm* (Ankara: TEMUH Dairesi Baskanligi, 2002), p. 46.

10. Cihat Ozunder, "Terorun Sosyo-Kulturel Yonleri", Dogu Anadolu Guvenlik ve Huzur Sempozyumu, Elazig 1998, p. 292; Abdülkadir Aygan, "Bir Itirafcinin Kaleminden PKK ve Terorun Sosyal Temelleri", Cilginliktan Sagduyuya, Itirafcilar Anlatiyor, Ankara 1987, pp. 101–2.

11. Aydin Yalcin, *Demokrasi, Sosyalizm ve Genclik* (Istanbul: Ak Yayinlari, 1969), pp. 238–42; Denker, pp. 10–12.

12. www.teror.gen.tr (May 23, 2006).

13. Alkan, pp. 50–51.

14. Pulat, p. 49; Olivier Mongin, "Les Engrenages de la Terreur: Une Renonciation Politique," *Esprit*, 1994–1995, p. 48; Lawrence Hamilton, "Ecology of Terrorism: A Historical and Statistical Study" (Ph.D. diss., University of Colorado, 1978), pp. 91–92.

15. Yalcin, pp. 246–48.

16. www.teror.gen.tr (May 12, 2006).

17. Leslie Macfarlane, *Violence and the State* (London: Thomas Nelson & Sons, 1974) p. 46.

18. Nasai, "Qasāma," 48; "Tahrim," 2; Ibn Maca, "Diyat," 2; Ahmad b. Hanbal, al-Musnad, I, 222.

19. Nuriye Akman, "A Real Muslim Cannot Be a Terrorist," http://www.fgulen.org/index.php?id=1727&option=content&task=view (June 11, 2008).

20. David Cook, *Understanding Jihad* (University of California Press, 2005), p. 42

21. Carole Hillenbrand, *The Crusades: Islamic Perspectives* (New York: Routledge, 2000), p. 243.

22. See Halil Inalcik, "The Question of the Emergence of the Ottoman State," *International Journal of Turkish Studies* 2 (1980): 71–79.

23. See Bernard Lewis, "The Significance of Heresy in Islam," in *Islam in History* (Chicago: Open Court, 2001), pp. 293, 351, 361.

24. Hillenbrand, p. 99.

25. Rudolph Peters, *Jihad in Classical and Modern Islam* (Princeton: Markus Wiener Publication, 1996), p. 324.

26. Cook, p. 93.

27. Sukran Vahide, "Jihad in the Modern Age: Bediuzzaman Said Nursi's Interpretation of Jihad," http://www.nur.org/en/nurcenter/nurlibrary/Bediuzzaman_

Said_ Nursi_s_Interpretation_of_Jihad_168 (April 12, 2008).

28. Said Nursi, *Hutbe-i Samiye* (Istanbul: Sinan Matbaasi, 1960), p. 86.

29. M. Hakan Yavuz, "The Sufi Conception of Jihad: The Case of Said Nursi," at International Conference on "Jihad, War and Peace in the Islamic Authoritative Texts," Georgetown University, November 2–4, 2002, http://forum.talktopics.com/2983/sufi-conception-jihad-case-said-nursi (May 16, 2008).

30. Cevdet Said, *İslami Mücadelede Siddet Sorunu*, trans. H. I. Kaçar (Istanbul: Pinar Yayinlari, 1995), p. 98.

31. Bruno Etienne, *L'Islamisme Radical* (Paris: Hachette, 1987), pp. 21–22.

32. Etienne, p. 177.

33. Hillenbrand, p. 243.

34. M. Sami Denker, *Uluslararası Terör ve Türkiye* (İstanbul, 1997), pp. 5–7; P. J. Vatikiotis, "Islamic Resurgence: A Critical View," in *Islam and Power*, ed. A. Cudsi, H. Dessuki, and E. Ali (London: Croom Helm, 1981), p. 169.

35. Ira Marvin Lapius, *Contemporary Islamic Movements in Historical Perspective* (Berkeley: University of California Press, 1983), p. 54.

36. Vatikiotis, p. 170.

37. Ozer Ozankaya, "Türkiye'de Terorun Etkenleri ve Cozum Yollari," SBF Dergisi, XXXIV/I–IV (1979): 51–61; Denker, p. 5; Mustafa Gunduz, *Basin ve Teror* (Izmir: Saray Medikal Yayıncılık, 1996), pp. 54–57; Suat Ilham, *Teror: Neden Turkiye* (Ankara: Nu-Do Yayın Dağıtım, 1998); Doğu Ergil, *Turkiye'de Teror ve Siddet* (Ankara: Turhan Kitabevi, 1980), pp. 26–48; Pulat, pp. 47–48.

38. Mehmet Dalkilic, "Critiques of Dissimulation in Islamic Sects," *Review of the Faculty of Divinity of Istanbul University* 5 (2003): 113–39.

39. J. Lloyd Dumas, "Is Development an Effective Way to Fight Terrorism?" in *War after September 11*, ed. Verna V. Gehring (Lanham, Md.: Rowman & Littlefield, 2003), pp. 74–75.

40. http://www.twocircles.net/2008jun01/indias_islamic_scholars_issue_fatwa_against_terrorism.html (June 2, 2008).

Muhammad Hammad Lakhvi— The Concept of Peace and Security in Islam

1. Al-Qur'an, Yunus 10:25.

2. Al-Qur'an, Al-An'am 6:127.

3. Al-Qur'an, Al-Ahzab 33:44.

4. Al-Qur'an, Ar-Ra'd 13:23–24.

5. Al-Qur'an, Al-Mā'idah 5:32.

6. Al-Qur'an, Al-Mā'idah 5:32.

7. Al-Tabarani, *Jame'-us-Saghir,* 11/10; *Kanz-ul-Ummal,* 44154.

8. *Sahih Al-Bukhari,* I (Kitab ul Iman), 9; *Tirmizi,* Iman, 2627.

9. Al-Qur'an, An-Nisaa 4:58.

10. Al-Qur'an, Al-An'am 6:152.

11. *Sahih Muslim,* Kitab ul Birr, 2577.

12. Al-Qur'an, Al-Hajj 22:39.

13. Al-Qur'an, Al-Baqarah 2:190.

14. Al-Qur'an, An-Nisaa 4:75–76.

15. Al-Qur'an, Al-Anfal 8:61.

Patricia A. Keefe—The Golden Rule and World Peace

1. Jeffrey Wattles, *The Golden Rule* (London: Oxford University Press, 1996), p. 189.

2. Interview of Karen Armstrong by Krista Tippett on National Public Radio, June 17, 2006. Also see Carpenter's piece on Minnesota Public Radio on June 15, 2006.

3. Wattles, pp. 19–22.

4. Ibid., p. 22.

5. Ibid., p. 42.

6. Joan Chittister, Murshid Saadi Shakur Chishti, and Arthur Waskow, *The Tent of Abraham: Stories of Hope and Peace for Jews, Christians, and Muslims* (Boston: Beacon, 2006), p. 65.

7. Wattles, p. 67.

8. Karen Armstrong interview.

9. Mahābhārata, 5.49.57

10. Mahābhārata, 12.252.251

11. Mahābhārata, 12.279.23

12. Mahābhārata, 13.113; also in *The Mahābhārata of Krishna-Dwaipayana Vyasa*, 3rd ed., trans. Pratap Chandra Roy, (New Delhi: Munshiram Manoharlal, 1972), p. 11:240.

13. Wattles, p. 112 and n. 27.

14. Ibid., p. 113.

15. Ibid., p. 112.

16. Ibid., p. 172, adapted from *The Great Learning*, in *A Source Book in Chinese Philosophy*, trans. and comp. Wing-Tsit Chan (Princeton, N.J.: Princeton University Press, 1963), p. 88.

17. Wattles, p. 172

18. Analysis in this section is from Ibid., pp. 171–74.

19. Martin Luther King Jr., *Strength to Love* (Philadelphia: Fortress Press, 1977), pp. 51–53.

20. Ibid., p. 51.

21. Mahatma Gandhi, *All Men Are Brothers, Life and Thoughts of Mahatma Gandhi as Told in His Own Words*, comp. Krishna Kripalani (Ahmedabad: Navajivan, 1960), p. 128.

22. Ibid., p. 128.

23. Thich Nhat Hanh, *Anger, Wisdom for Cooling the Flames* (New York: Riverhead Trade, 2002), pp. 65–70.

24. Chris Richards, "The Challenge to Violence," *New Internationalist* 381 (2005): 9–12.

25. Ibid., pp. 9–12.

Brian D. Lepard—World Religions and World Peace

1. Brian D. Lepard, *Hope for a Global Ethic: Shared Principles in Religious Scriptures* (Wilmette, Ill.: Bahá'í Publishing, 2005).

2. Edward Conze, trans., *Buddhist Scriptures* (London: Penguin, 1959), p. 186.

3. Matt 5:48. All quotations from the New Testament are from *The Holy Bible Containing the Old and New Testaments: New Revised Standard Version* (New York: Oxford University Press, 1977).

4. 49:13. All quotations from the Qur'an are from A. J. Arberry, trans., *The Koran Interpreted* (New York: Simon and Schuster, 1955).

5. Bahá'u'lláh, *Gleanings from the Writings of Bahá'u'lláh*, 2nd rev. ed., trans. Shoghi Effendi (Wilmette, Ill.: Bahá'í Publishing Trust, 1976), p. 196.

6. See, for example, 5:7, 11:7. All quotations from the Bhagavadgītā are from Franklin Edgerton, trans., *The Bhagavad* Gītā (Cambridge, Mass.: Harvard University Press, 1972).

7. Mal 2:10. All quotations from the Hebrew scriptures are from *Tanakh: A New Translation of the Holy Scriptures according to the Traditional Hebrew Text* (Philadelphia: The Jewish Publication Society, 1985).

8. See Conze, p. 186.

9. See *Analects* 12:5, as translated in E. Bruce Brooks and A. Taeko Brooks, trans., *The Original Analects: Sayings of Confucius and His Successors* (New York: Columbia University Press, 1998).

10. 4:1.

11. 'Abdu'l-Bahá, *Paris Talks: Addresses Given by 'Abdu'l-Bahá in Paris in 1911–1912*, 12th ed. (London: Bahá'í Publishing Trust, 1995), no. 42.11.

12. See 30:21.

13. Ps 34:15.

14. Matt 5:9.

15. 5:18.

16. 'Abdu'l-Bahá, no. 6.7.

17. Isa 32:17.

18. See, for example, *Analects* 14:34.

19. 'Abdu'l-Bahá, *The Compilation of Compilations Prepared by the Universal House of Justice, 1963–1990* (Maryborough, Victoria: Bahá'í Publications Australia, 1991), p. 2:165.

20. Matt 5:42.

21. 76:8–9.

22. Bahá'u'lláh, *Epistle to the Son of the Wolf*, rev. ed., trans. Shoghi Effendi (Wilmette, Ill.: Bahá'í Publishing Trust, 1979), p. 93.

23. Deut 1:17.

24. See, for example, 1 Cor 14:26, 14:29–31.

25. 3:153.

26. Bahá'u'lláh, *Tablets of Bahá'u'lláh Revealed after the Kitáb-i-Aqdas*, trans. Habib Taherzadeh (Haifa: Bahá'í World Centre, 1978), p. 168.

27. Paul Carus, comp., *The Gospel of Buddha* (Chicago: Open Court, 1915), p. 148.

28. See, for example, 'Abdu'l-Bahá, *The Secret of Divine Civilization*, 2nd ed., trans. Marzieh Gail (Wilmette, Ill.: Bahá'í Publishing Trust, 1970), pp. 70–71; Bahá'u'lláh, *Tablets of Bahá'u'lláh*, p. 165.

29. See, for example, U.N. Charter articles 2(4), 39–51.

Part 2

James Kellenberger—Religion and an Implicit Fundamental Human Right

1. Alasdair MacIntyre, *After Virtue*, 2nd ed. (Notre Dame: University of Notre Dame Press, 1984), p. 69.

2. *ST* I–II, q. 102, a. 6., in *Basic Writings of Saint Thomas Aquinas*, ed. Anton C. Pegis (New York: Random House, 1944), p. 2:905.

3. Khaled Abou El Fadl, "The Human Rights Commitment in Modern Islam," in *Human Rights and Responsibilities in the World Religions*, ed. Joseph Runzo, Nancy M. Martin, and Arvind Sharma (Oxford: Oneworld, 2003), pp. 338, 335. The jurist is Ibn al-'Arabi.

4. Amir Hussain makes this point in "'This

Tremor of Western Wisdom': A Muslim Response to Human Rights and the Declaration," in *Human Rights and Responsibilities in the World Religions*, pp. 175–76.

5. John Hick, *An Interpretation of Religion* (New Haven, Conn.: Yale University Press, 1989), pp. 313, 316.

6. James Fredericks, "Buddhism and Human Rights: The Recent Buddhist Discussion and Its Implications for Christianity," in *Human Rights and Responsibilities in the World Religions*, p. 259.

7. Damien Keown, "Are There Human Rights in Buddhism?" in *Buddhism and Human Rights*, ed. Damien V. Keown, Charles S. Prebish, and Wayne R. Husted (Surrey: Curzon, 1998), p. 21.

8. John Stuart Mill, *Utilitarianism* (Indianapolis: Hackett, 1979), pp. 48–49.

9. Craig Ihara, "Why There Are No Rights in Buddhism: A Reply to Damien Keown," in *Buddhism and Human Rights*, p. 45. Ihara quotes with approval Feinberg's claim that "duties of charity, for example, require us to contribute to one or another of a large number of eligible recipients, no one of whom can claim our contribution from us as his due." Ihara cites Feinberg's "The Nature and Value of Rights" in *The Philosophy of Human Rights*, ed. Morton E. Winston (Belmont, Calif.: Wadsworth, 1989), pp. 61–74.

10. Or at least our noninterference. I will assume that most if not all the specific human-rights examples I have been citing are "positive-claim" in rem rights, which require the positive assistance of others.

11. Ihara, "Why There are no Rights in Buddhism: A Reply to Damien Keown," p. 44.

12. Ibid., pp. 45–47.

13. Fredericks also makes this observation. See "Buddhism and Human Rights: The Recent Buddhist Discussion and Its Implications for Christianity," p. 259. He cites Ihara as another with this concern. On page 255 Fredericks, drawing upon Sallie King's work on rights in Buddhism, says that "Buddhist human rights, in contrast to rights as understood by Western Liberalism, are non-adversarial." See Sallie B. King, "Human Rights in Contemporary Engaged Buddhism," in *Buddhist Theology: Critical Reflections by Contemporary Buddhist Scholars*, ed. Roger R. Jackson, and John J. Makransky (Surrey: Curzon, 2000), pp. 295–96.

14. Abou El Fadl, "The Human Rights Commitment in Modern Islam," p. 339.

15. Basil Mitchell regarded "morality" and "sin" as being very different in their demands. Although when human beings do what is morally wrong they sin, sin is much more demanding. For him, a lack of sensitivity could be a sin, but it was not an instance of moral wrongdoing. Mitchell does not, however, address the status of human rights. Basil Mitchell, "How Is the Concept of Sin Related to the Concept of Moral Wrongdoing?" *Religious Studies* 29 (1984): pp. 165–73.

ARVIND SHARMA—RELIGION, VIOLENCE, AND HUMAN RIGHTS

1. Michael Ignatieff, "Is the Human Rights Era Ending?" *New York Times,* February 5, 2002, p. A 29.

2. Rajeev Srinivasan, "Sri Jayendra Sarasvati," *India Abroad,* March 8, 2002, p. 20.

3. Alison Dundes Renteln, *International Human Rights: Universalism versus Relativism* (Newbury Park, Calif.: Sage, 1990), p. 17.

4. *Rāmāyaṇa* VI. 109.25 (vulgate); VI. 99.39 (critical text).

5. G. Bühler, trans., *The Laws of Manu* (Delhi: Motilal Banarsidass, 1967 [1886]), p. 315.

6. Vaman Shrivram Apte, *The Practical Sanskrit-English Dictionary* (Delhi: Motilal Banarsidass, 1965), p. 208.

7. A. L. Basham, *The Wonder That Was India* (New Delhi: Rupa & Co. 1999 [1954]), p. 126.

8. Basham, p. 126.

9. Ibid., p. 9.

10. J. W. McCrindle, *Ancient India as Described by Megasthenes and Arrian* (Calcutta: Chuckervertty, Chatterjee & Co., 1960 [1876–77]), pp. 21–32.

11. Hartmut Scharfe, *The State in Indian Tradition* (Leiden: E. J. Brill, 1989), p. 185.

12. Bühler, pp. 230–31.

13. P. V. Kane, *History of Dharmaśāstra*, 2nd ed. (Poona: Bhandarkar Oriental Research Institute, 1973), p. 3:209.

14. Basham, p. 126.

15. Ibid., p. 124.

16. Ibid., p. 54, 126.

17. K. B. Panda, *Sanātan Dharma and Law* (Cuttack: Goswami Press, n.d.), p. 69.

18. Bühler, p. 230 (emphasis added).

19. Basham, p. 123.

20. Percival Spear, ed., *The Oxford History of India by the Late Vincent A. Smith, C. J. E.* (Delhi: Oxford University Press, 1994), p. 79.

SUMNER B. TWISS—CONFUCIAN CONTRIBUTIONS TO THE UNIVERSAL DECLARATION OF HUMAN RIGHTS

1. An earlier and much briefer version of this paper was presented and discussed at the Academic Seminar on Perceptions of Being Human in Confucian Thought, sponsored by the International Confucian Association, Beijing 1998. A much longer version was published in Chinese in *International Confucian Research*, vol. 6 (1999) (journal of the International Confucian Association), and was presented and discussed at the Fairbank Center for East Asian Research, Harvard University, April 1999. Parts of the longer version formed the basis for sections of some other papers that have been published, namely, "Confucian Values and Human Rights," in Joseph Runzo, Nancy M. Martin, and Arvind Sharma, eds., *Human Rights and Responsibilities in the World Religions* (Oxford: Oneworld, 2003), pp. 283–99 (specifically the section on P. C. Chang, pp. 292–96), and "Confucian Ethics, Concept-Clusters, and Human Rights," in *Polishing the Chinese Mirror: Essays in Honor of Henry Rosemont, Jr.*, ed. Marthe Chandler and Ronnie Littlejohn, ACPA Series of Chinese and Comparative Philosophy (New York: Global Scholarly Publications, 2008), pp. 49–66 (again, specifically the section on P. C. Chang, pp. 60–63). I am indebted to Wm. Theodore de Bary (Columbia University) for his critical comments on the longer version, and I also wish to acknowledge the research and secretarial assistance, respectively, of Caroline Johnson and Kathleen Pappas in the preparation of this chapter.

2. A. J. Hobbins, ed., *On the Edge of Greatness: The Diaries of John Humphrey, First Director of the United Nations Division of Human Rights*, vol. 1 (1948–49) and vol. 2 (1950–51) (Montreal: McGill University Libraries, 1994 and 1996, respectively). The quotations in this paragraph are from pp. 1:55–56, 58, and 88.

3. This information on the biography and career of Chang is drawn from the following sources: "Peng Chun Chang, Diplomat, 65, Dies" (obituary), *New York Times* (July 21, 1957); *Yearbook of the United Nations*, 1947–48 (Lake Success, N.Y.: United Nations Department of Public Information, 1948), p. 1055; "Dr. Peng-chun Chang," online biography produced by the National Coordinating Committee for UDHR50, Franklin and Eleanor Roosevelt Institute, revised April 12, 1998, and available at http://www.udhr50.org/history/Biographies/biopcc.htm; and Ruth H. C. Cheng, and Sze-Chuh Cheng, eds., *Peng Chun Chang 1892–1957: Biography and Collected Works* (privately published, 1995), p. 8 (Chang's own resume) and pp. 20–36 ("A Chronological Biography" by the editors, Chang's daughter and her husband). The last-mentioned source is the most comprehensive and useful.

4. The information in this paragraph and the next is drawn from John Dewey, *Lectures in China, 1919–1921*, trans. and ed. Robert W. Clopton, and Tsuin-chen Ou (Honolulu: University of Hawaii Press, 1973), the editors' Introduction, pp. 1–39 (esp. pp. 4–7, 10–26). See also George Dykhuizen, *The Life and Mind of John Dewey* (Carbondale, Ill.: Southern Illinois University Press, 1973), ch. 10 ("The Far East, 1919–1921").

5. See, for example, John Dewey, "New Culture in China" and "Transforming the Mind of China," reprinted in his *Characters and Events: Popular Essays in Social and Political Philosophy*, ed. Joseph Ratner (New York: Henry Holt, 1929), pp. 1:270–95.

6. The quotations are from Chang Peng-chun, *Education for Modernization in China: A Search for Criteria of Curriculum Construction in View of the Transition in National Life, with Special Reference to Secondary Education*, Contributions to Education 137 (New York: Teachers College, Columbia University, 1923), pp. 14–15.

7. The quotations are from Chang, *Education for Modernization in China*, pp. 28–29. The volumes by Dewey cited by Chang in his own book include *Democracy and Education* (New York: Macmillan, 1916), *School and Society* (Chicago: University of Chicago Press, 1899), *My Pedagogic Creed* (New York: Kellogg, 1897), *How We Think* (Boston: Heath, 1910), *Creative Intelligence* (New York: Holt, 1917), *Influence of Darwin on Philosophy* (New York: Holt, 1910), and (with J. H. Tufts), *Ethics* (Holt, 1908). In addition, Chang discusses briefly Dewey's 1921 article, "Old China and New," reprinted under the title, "Young China and Old," in Dewey, *Characters and Events*, pp. 1:255–69.

8. The five criteria are listed and discussed in Chang, *Education for Modernization in China*, pp. 34–55; the quotation is from p. 35.

9. Beyond this general influence of Dewey's thought on Chang, it might be asked whether Dewey's lectures in China 1919–21—and specifically the lectures on political liberalism and the rights of individuals—influenced Chang in any direct way. So far as I can ascertain, they did not. First, it is highly probable that Chang was studying at Columbia University during the entire period that Dewey was in China. This lack of contact may account in part for why Chang acknowledges in the preface to *Education for Modernization in China* his particular debt to Kilpatrick rather than Dewey. Second, in none of his

published writings does Chang ever refer to these lectures or even to Dewey's more focused works on social and political philosophy. Third, when in his third book, *China at the Crossroads,* Chang draws comparisons between Chinese and European thought, he nowhere cites the standard philosophers associated with the development of political liberalism in the eighteenth and nineteenth centuries—for example, Locke, Rousseau, and the English utilitarians—figures with whom Dewey was well acquainted and himself discussed in his China lectures *(Lectures in China,* pp. 141–46).

None of this is to say that Dewey's political philosophy had no influence on Chang's thought, but rather to suggest that such influence was likely mediated only through Dewey's educational writings. It is also not to say that Dewey's approach to individual rights (in his China lectures) and Chang's approach to human rights (in the UDHR context) are vastly different. There is, for example, a broad parallel between Dewey's pragmatic, historicist position on individual rights (as the product of a historical process and struggle by particular societies, with no appeal to philosophical argumentation) and Chang's pragmatic, antimetaphysical stance on human rights (see below). And Dewey did himself invoke Mencius's name in suggesting that China's "traditional concept of the state's obligation to protect its people" could "be readily modified into the concept of the protection of its citizens by a democratic government" *(Lectures in China,* p. 154). These few, rough parallels, however, are not sufficient to demonstrate a direct impact of Dewey's China lectures on Chang. Again, influence mediated by Dewey's educational writings is more plausible and defensible.

10. These two books are related (as preliminary and final versions), with the first being more fully titled *China: Whence and Whither? An Outline of a High School Unit of Study,* A Preliminary Draft for Experimental Use in the Senior High Schools of the Territory of Hawaii (Honolulu: Institute of Pacific Relations, 1934), and the second and more polished version, *China at the Crossroads: The Chinese Situation in Perspective* (London: Evans Brothers, 1936). Although I have read and compared both versions, I quote only from the second one.

11. Chang, *China at the Crossroads,* quotations from pp. 30–32. Chang himself is quoting Voltaire from *The Works of Voltaire,* trans. William F. Fleming (London: Craftsmen of St. Hubert Guild, 1901), vols. 4 and 15.

12. Chang, *China at the Crossroads,* pp. 44–50; quotations from pp. 47, 49, and 50. Chang's discussion includes extensive quotations from the *Analects* and *Mencius.*

13. Chang, *China at the Crossroads,* pp. 94–97; quotations from pp. 95, 96. Although Chang does not note the source for the Huang quotation, it is from the *Ming-i-tai-fang lit,* recently translated and analyzed by Wm. Theodore de Bary, *Waiting for the Dawn: A Plan for the Prince* (New York: Columbia University Press, 1993).

14. Ibid., pp. 64–68, 150–55; quotations from pp. 66, 68, 150–51. The quotation concerning Reichwein's claim are Chang's words, not Reichwein's, reflecting on the latter's book *China and Europe* (New York: Alfred A. Knopf, 1925), pp. 86, 107–8.

15. Chang, *China at the Crossroads,* p. 171.

16. Ibid., pp. 124–25. Interestingly, John Dewey is nowhere named in this book, although Chang does cite Bertrand Russell's book, *The Problem of China* (London: George Allen and Unwin, 1922) from the same period that both Dewey and Russell lectured in China.

17. The texts of both sets of addresses are reproduced (in their original published form as pamphlets) in Cheng, and Cheng, *Peng Chun Chang,* pp. 143–53, but no original publication information is supplied by the editors. The pamphlets, with their own integrally numbered pages, are titled, respectively, "Text of Two Lectures Delivered by H. E. Dr. P. C. Chang, Chinese Minister to Turkey, in King Faisal II Hall, Baghdad, on March 11, 1942, with an Introductory Speech by H. E. General Nuri As-said, Prime Minister of Iraq" (28 pages) and "A New Loyalty, War Against Microbes, and World Significance of Economically 'Low-Pressure' Areas: Three Speeches by Dr. P. C. Chang, Chinese Representative to the Economic and Social Council of the United Nations" (8 pages). I will refer to first set of lectures as "Two Lectures," and I will refer to the second set as "Three Speeches." In referencing quotations from these two sets of lectures, I will cite the pamphlet page number followed in brackets with the pagination of Cheng, and Cheng's *Peng Chun Chang.*

18. Chang, "Two Lectures," pp. 18–25 [147–49]; quotations from pp. 19 [147], 20 [148], 24 [149].

19. Ibid., pp. 8–9 [145].

20. Ibid., p. 10 [145].

21. Ibid., pp. 14–15 [146].

22. Ibid., p. 16 [147]. Chang does not explicitly cite the source from the *Analects* other than to attribute the quotation to Confucius. D. C. Lau in his translation of the *Analects* (London: Penguin, 1979) renders the passage as follows: "To work for the things the common people have a right to and to keep one's distance from the gods and spirits while showing them reverence can be called wisdom" (p. 84).

23. Chang, "Two Lectures," pp. 27–28 [149]. Again, Chang does not explicitly cite the source from *The Great Learning* other than to attribute the quotation to "a certain philosopher in China." For identification purposes, I used the following translation of *The Great Learning*: Wing-tsit Chan, *A Source Book in Chinese Philosophy* (Princeton: Princeton University Press, 1963), pp. 84–94.

24. Chang, "Three Speeches," p. 2 [150]. Although Chang cites "a saying from the Chinese thinker, Mencius," no precise source is provided in the text. D. C. Lau in his translation of *Mencius* (London: Penguin, 1970) renders the passage as follows: "You can never succeed in winning the allegiance of men by trying to dominate them through goodness. You can only succeed by using this goodness for their welfare. You can never gain the Empire without the heart-felt admiration of the people in it" (p. 130). Compare the translation of James Legge from his *The Works of Mencius* (New York: Dover, 1970; originally published, 1885, by Clarendon Press, Oxford): "Never has he who would by his excellence subdue men been able to subdue them. Let a prince seek by his excellence to nourish men, and he will be able to subdue the whole kingdom" (p. 323).

25. Chang, "Three Speeches," p. 3 [151]; all quotations from this page.

26. Ibid., pp. 5–7 [152–53]; quotations from pp. 6–7.

27. Ibid., p. 8 [153]. Chang does not cite the specific source for this quotation, but it is clearly from the *Li Chi*. The edition I used was *Li Chi, Book of Rites,* trans. James Legge (New York: University Books, 1967; originally published, 1885, by Clarendon Press, Oxford), pp. 1:364–66.

28. *Official Records of the Third Session of the General Assembly, Part I, Social, Humanitarian and Cultural Questions, Third Committee, Summary Records of Meetings 21 September-8 December, 1948*, with Annexes, printed in both English and French (Lake Success, N.Y.: United Nations, 1948), p. 87. It should be noted that these records represent a historical summary of proceedings, not necessarily a precise word-for-word transcription of quotations from speakers. Hereinafter I will cite this work as *Third Committee*, followed by page references.

29. *Economic and Social Council Official Records, Second Year: Fourth Session 28 February 1947–29 March 1947*, with Supplements 1–10, printed in both English and French (Lake Success, N.Y.: United Nations, 1947), p. 111. Again, it should be noted that these records represent a historical summary of proceedings, not necessarily a precise word-for-word transcription. Hereinafter I will cite this work as *Economic and Social Council*, followed by page references.

30. Chang's earlier claims about the influence of Chinese (Confucian) philosophy on eighteenth-century European thought are now being extended by him to the foundations of human rights thinking in the West.

31. Although Chang does not here explicitly identify the idea of man's moral capacity, it is implicit in his emphasis on "the human aspect of human rights," which is further developed by him in connection with his support of Article 1 (see below).

32. *Economic and Social Council*, p. 111.

33. *Third Committee*, p. 98.

34. Ibid., p. 98.

35. Ibid., p. 98.

36. Ibid., p. 98.

37. Chang's notion of pragmatic agreement, despite philosophical and ideological differences, parallels Jacques Maritain's claim that "the goal of UNESCO is a practical goal, agreement between minds can be reached spontaneously, not on the basis of common speculative ideas, but on common practical ideas, not on the affirmation of one and the same conception of the world, of man and of knowledge, but upon the affirmation of a single body of beliefs for guidance in action." Neither Chang nor Maritain cited the other, but the parallelism is remarkable. (The French representative to the Third Committee does refer to the position of Maritain as partial support for Chang's position on Article 1; see *Third Committee*, p. 117.) For Maritain's fuller reasoning, see UNESCO's 1948 typescript volume, *Human Rights: Comments and Interpretations, A Symposium edited by UNESCO, With an Introduction by Jacques Maritain* (Paris: UNESCO, July 25, 1948), pp. I–IX; preceding quotation from page II.

38. *Third Committee*, p. 48.

39. Ibid., p. 48, 397, 177.

40. I have changed the numbering of these articles—which was in flux during the Third Committee debate—to conform with the numbering order finally adopted. I used the edition of UDHR published in *The International Bill of Human Rights* (New York: United Nations, 1993), pp. 4–9.

41. Article 1 reads as follows: "All human beings are born free and equal in dignity and rights. They are endowed with reason and conscience and should act towards one another in a spirit of brotherhood." I reported on Chang's earlier contribution to the drafting committee in my "A Constructive Framework for Discussing Confucianism and Human Rights," in *Confucianism and Human Rights*, ed. Wm. Theodore de Bary, and Tu Weiming (New York: Columbia University Press, 1998), pp. 27–53:

Pier Cesare Bori, referring to records of the debates surrounding the drafting of the Universal Declaration of Human Rights, reports that the Confucian tradition, as represented by the Chinese delegate P. Chang, influenced the formulation of Article 1. As reported by Bori, the first version of this article stated: "All men are brothers. As human beings with the gift of reason and members of a single family, they are free and equal in dignity and rights." With respect to this article, Chang argued for the inclusion of "two-men-mindedness" (the basic Confucian idea of *jen*) in addition to the mention of "reason." At the forefront of Chang's mind, suggests Bori, was the idea of a fundamental sympathy, benevolence, or compassion (as represented by Mencius) as constitutive of human beings generally. The wording finally adopted included "conscience" in addition to "reason," with the understanding that "conscience" was not the voice of an internal moral court but rather the emotional and sympathetic basis of morality, "a 'germ' objectively present" in all persons, "which reason must cultivate."

Bori reconstructs Chang's contributions from his reading of A. Verdoodt, *Naissance et signification de le déclaration universelle des droits de l'homme,* preface by Rene Cassin (Louvain-Paris: Naunelaerts, 1964), pp. 47ff. After consulting that volume, I believe that Bori's reconstruction is a fair inference from the text. See Pier Bori, *From Hermeneutics to Ethical Consensus among Cultures* (Atlanta, Ga.: Scholars, 1994), ch. 7.

42. *Third Committee,* p. 99.

43. Ibid., p. 98.

44. Ibid., pp. 113-114. This passage appears to capture the basic thrust of Book VI.A of *The Mencius. Mencius* VI.A.14 reads, in part, "the parts of the person differ in value and importance. Never harm the parts of greater importance for the sake of those of smaller importance, or the more valuable for the sake of the less valuable. He who nurtures the parts of smaller importance is a small man; he who nurtures the parts of greater importance is a great man. . . . A man who cares only about food and drink is despised by others because he takes care of the parts of smaller importance to the detriment of the parts of greater importance."

45. *Third Committee,* pp. 87, 98, 114, respectively.

46. Article 18 reads as follows: "Everyone has the right to freedom of thought, conscience and religion; this right includes freedom to change his religion or belief, and freedom, either alone or in community with others and in public or private, to manifest his religion or belief in teaching, practice, worship and observance."

47. *Third Committee,* p. 397.

48. Ibid., p. 397.

49. Chang's reasoning here appears to reaffirm and build upon his earlier position in "Two Lectures" about humanistic respect for spiritual matters, based on *Analects* 6:22.

50. Article 21 reads as follows: "1. Everyone has the right to take part in the government of his country, directly or through freely chosen representatives. 2. Everyone has the right of equal access to public service in his country. 3. The will of the people shall be the basis of the authority of government; this will shall be expressed in periodic and genuine elections which shall be by universal and equal suffrage and shall be held by secret vote or by equivalent free voting procedures."

51. The first quotation is from *Economic and Social Council,* p. 110, and the other two from *Third Committee,* p. 462. We have seen from his earlier writings that this is a favored theme of Chang.

52. *Third Committee,* p. 462.

53. *Economic and Social Council,* p. 111.

54. Article 29 reads as follows: "1. Everyone has duties to the community in which alone the free and full development of his personality is possible. 2. In the exercise of his rights and freedoms, everyone shall be subject only to such limitations as are determined by law solely for the purpose of securing due recognition and respect for the rights and freedoms of others and of meeting the just requirements of morality, public order and the general welfare in a democratic society. 3. These rights and freedoms may in no case be exercised contrary to the purposes and principles of the United Nations."

55. *Third Committee,* p. 98.

56. Ibid., p. 98.

57. Ibid., p. 98.

58. This is similar to Chang's earlier effort to point to such bridges in *China at the Crossroads.*

59. I have in mind here the work of such scholars as Roger Ames and Henry Rosemont. See, for example, Henry Rosemont, "Why Take Rights Seriously? A Confucian Critique," and Roger T. Ames, "Rites as Rights: The Confucian Alternative," in *Human Rights and the World's Religions,* ed. Leroy Rouner (Notre Dame: University of Notre Dame Press, 1988), pp. 167–82, 199–216, respectively.

BRIAN D. LEPARD—A BAHÁ'Í PERSPECTIVE ON THE UNIVERSAL DECLARATION OF HUMAN RIGHTS

1. Bahá'u'lláh, *Tablets of Bahá'u'lláh Revealed after the Kitáb-i-Aqdas* (Haifa: Bahá'í World Centre, 1978), p. 22.

2. 'Abdu'l-Bahá, *The Promulgation of Universal Peace: Talks Delivered by 'Abdu'l-Bahá during His Visit to the United States and Canada in 1912*, comp. Howard MacNutt, 2nd ed. (Wilmette, Ill.: Bahá'í Publishing Trust, 1982), p. 346.

3. Ibid., p. 96.

4. The Universal House of Justice, "To the World's Religious Leaders," April 2002, p. 6 (available at http://info.bahai.org/pdf/letter_april2002_english.pdf).

5. Ibid., p. 3.

6. See Brian D. Lepard, *Rethinking Humanitarian Intervention: A Fresh Legal Approach Based on Fundamental Ethical Principles in International Law and World Religions* (University Park, Pa.: Pennsylvania State University Press, 2002), pp. 53–75.

7. Bahá'u'lláh, *Tablets of Bahá'u'lláh*, pp. 63–64.

8. The Universal House of Justice, "To the World's Religious Leaders," p. 3.

9. See Lepard, *Rethinking Humanitarian Intervention*, pp. 45–47.

10. The Universal House of Justice, "To the World's Religious Leaders," p. 5.

11. Ibid., p. 3.

12. Ibid., p. 6.

13. For the perspective of religions other than the Bahá'í faith on this document, see Joseph Runzo, Nancy M. Martin, and Arvind Sharma, eds., *Human Rights and Responsibilities in the World Religions* (Oxford: Oneworld, 2003), part 3.

KRISHNA KANTH TIGIRIPALLI AND LALITHA KUMARI KADARLA: RELIGION AND HUMAN RIGHTS

1. John Rawls, *Theory of Justice* (Oxford: Oxford University Press, 1983), pp. 7–15.

2. *World Christian Encyclopedia: A Comparative Study of Churches and Religions in the Modern World*, ed. David B. Barrett, George Thomas Kurian, and Todd M. Johnson (London: Oxford University Press, 1982), p. 65.

3. Carrie Gustafson and Peter H. Juviler, eds., *Religion and Human Rights: Competing Claims* (New York: Macmillan, 2002), pp. 32–45.

4. James Petras, *Culture and the Challenges of Contemporary World* (New York: Macmillan, 2004), p. 15.

5. James Petras, "Globalisation: A Socialist Perspective," *Economic and Political Weekly* (Feb. 20, 2005), pp. 459–69.

6. Adam Hochschild, "Globalisation and Culture," *Economic and Political Weekly* (May 23, 2005), pp. 1235–38.

7. Manouchehr Ganji, *The International Protection of Human Rights* (London: Oxford University Press, 1980), p. 56.

8. J. Humphrey, "The United Nations Charter and the Universal Declaration of Human Rights," in *The International Protection of Human Rights*, ed. Evan Luard (Oxford: Oxford University Press, 1985), pp. 62–69.

9. Natan Lerner, *The UN Convention on the Elimination of All Forms of Racial Discrimination*, 2nd ed. (Alphen aan den Rijn, the Netherlands: Sijthoff & Noordhoff, 1980). See also Theodor Meron, *Human Rights Law-Making in the United Nations* (Oxford: Oxford University Press, 1986), pp. 46–54.

10. Lerner, *The UN Convention.*, passim; also Matthew C. Craven, *The International Covenant on Economic, Social and Cultural Rights* (Oxford: Oxford University Press, 1995), pp. 45–62.

11. Neera Chandoke, *State and Civil Society: Explorations in Political Theory* (New Delhi: Sage Publications, 1995), pp. 15–25.

12. Roger Simon, *Gramsci's Political Thought: An Introduction* (London: Lawrence and Wishart, 1982), pp. 37–42.

13. Smitu Kothari and Harsh Sethi, eds., *Rethinking Human Rights: Challenges For Theory And Action* (New York: New Horizons, 1989), pp. 66–71.

14. Quentin Skinner, "On Justice, the Common Good and the Priority of Liberty," in *Dimensions of Radical Democracy Pluralism, Citizenship Community*, ed. Chantel Mouffe (London: Verso, 1992), pp. 32–42.

15. Leo Strauss, *Natural Rights and History* (Chicago: University of Chicago Press, 1953), pp. 45–52.

PART 3

ROSEMARY RADFORD RUETHER— WOMEN IN WORLD RELIGIONS

1. See Rosemary Ruether, *Women and Redemption: A Theological History* (Minneapolis: Fortress Press, 1998), 71–7.

2. See Nancy S. Barnes, "Buddhism," in *Women in World Religions,* ed. Arvind Sharma (Albany: State University of New York Press, 1987), 119–21.

3. Theresa Kelleher, "Confucianism," in *Women in World Religions,* 140.

4. Judith Plaskow, *Standing Again at Sinai* (San Francisco: Harper and Row, 1990), 94.

5. This is particularly developed by Thomas Aquinas, under the influence of Aristotelian anthropology: see Ruether, *Women and Redemption,* 94–96.

6. See Padmanabh S. Jaini, *Gender and Salvation: Jaina Debates on the Spiritual Liberation of Women* (Berkeley: University of California Press, 1991).

7. Barnes, *Women in World Religions,* 129–31.

8. For a fuller development of Christian teachings on marriage and divorce, see Rosemary Ruether, *Christianity and the Making of the Modern Family* (Boston: Beacon, 2000), 47–59.

9. Ruether, *Women and Redemption,* 160–64.

10. On "colonial feminism," as promoted by colonial leaders and Christian missionaries, see "Women in South and Southeast Asia," in Barbara N. Ramusack, *Women in Asia: Restoring Women to History* (Indianapolis: Indiana University Press, 1999), 41–43.

11. Ellen Umansky, "Feminism in Judaism," in *Feminism and World Religions,* ed. Arvind Sharma and Katherine K. Young (Albany: State University of New York Press, 1999), 180.

12. For example, Elisabeth Schüssler Fiorenza, *In Memory of Her: A Feminist Theological Reconstruction of Christian Origins* (New York: Crossroad, 1983).

13. Riffat Hassan, "Feminism in Islam," in *Feminism and World Religions,* ed. Arvind Sharma and Katherine K. Young (Albany: State University of New York Press, 1999), 248–55.

Abha Singh—Women and Human Rights

1. *Smṛtis* are the products of different and widely separated ages. In consequence, we come across several such texts, some of which are entirely in prose or in mixed prose and verse, while the large majority are in verse. Nevertheless, most of the *smṛtis* are, indeed, obscure and rarely cited even by ancient commentators. To my mind, apart from the epics (Rāmāyaṇa and Mahābhārata), three *smṛtis*, Manusmṛti, Yājñavalkyasmṛti, and Parāśarasmṛti, have had lasting effects on Hindu religion. These *smṛtis* belong to a different class of composition that was not meant for oral exposition in a narrow Vedic school. These texts were written for grownup householders and learned *brāhmaṇas* as well. Since *brāhmaṇas* were supposed to be spiritual guides of the society, they were competent in determining doubtful points of dharma (righteousness). Hence, *smṛti* texts were intended to be studied by themselves and not as part of wider curriculum. As so, the best minds among the Hindus, educated along traditional lines, have made these texts the subject of study since these texts are still supposed to illuminate the lives of future generations. Among these, Manusmṛti held a position of preeminence, and its dicta still govern society.

2. "Status" needs to be distinguished from the concepts of "position" and "role." Position is accorded to a person by the society. It is a passive concept, and one has to receive it, whether one likes it or not. Role, on the other hand, is something that the person actively takes up and plays on his or her own, and is responsible for that. Hence, the position of a person is, or at least should be, directly dependent on and proportional to the role one plays. Whenever there is a perfect balance between position and role, one may infer that the people have a strong sense of social justice.

3. *Manusmṛti*, trans. Ramchandra Verma Shastri (New Delhi: Vidya Vihar, 1982), *Adhyāya* IX, *Ślokas* 32–52; *Adhyāya* X, *Ślokas* 68–70.

4. *Manusmṛti, Adhyāya* IX, *Śloka* 32.

5. *Manusmṛti, Adhyāya* IX, *Ślokas* 33–69.

6. *Manusmṛti, Adhyāya* X, *Ślokas* 69–71.

7. Saral Jhingran, *Aspects of Hindu Morality* (Delhi: Motilal Banarasidass, 1999), p. 92.

8. Shakuntala Rao Shastry, *Women in the Vedic Age,* (Bombay: Bharatiya Vidya Bhavan, 1952), p. 69.

9. *Manusmṛti, Adhyāya* I, *Śloka* 109; *Adhyāya* II, *Ślokas* 36–68.

10. *Manusmṛti, Adhyāya* II, *Ślokas* 36–68.

11. *Manusmṛti, Adhyāya* II, *Śloka* 69.

12. *Manusmṛti, Adhyāya* IX, *Śloka* 18.

13. *Sāṅkhya Kārikā*, ed. and trans. Ramashankar Tripathi (Varanasi: Chawkhamba Vidya Bhawan, 1970), *Śloka* 19.

14. *Manusmṛti, Adhyāya* IX, *Ślokas* 13, 14, 16, 17.

15. *Manusmṛti, Adhyāya* IX, *Ślokas* 13–18.

16. *Manusmṛti, Adhyāya* V, *Ślokas* 147–49; *Adhyāya* IX, *Ślokas* 2–3; *Yājñavalkyasmṛti*, trans. Umesh Chandra Pandey (Varanasi: Chawkhamba Sanskrit Sansthan, 2003), *Adhyāya* I, *Śloka* 85.

17. *Manusmṛti, Adhyāya* III, *Ślokas* 20–33.

18. *Manusmṛti, Adhyāya* III, *Śloka* 5.

19. *Manusmṛti, Adhyāya* III, *Ślokas* 37–40; *Adhyāya* IX, *Ślokas* 120–25, 138 ff.

20. *Manusmṛti, Adhyāya* IX, *Ślokas* 32–44.

21. *Manusmṛti, Adhyāya* IX, *Ślokas* 59–61.

22. *Manusmṛti, Adhyāya* IX, *Ślokas* 64–65.

23. *Manusmṛti, Adhyāya* IV, *Śloka* 155; *Adhyāya* IX, *Śloka* 29; *Mahābhārata*, vol. VI, *Anuśāsana Parva*, trans.

Pandit Ramnarain Shastri Pandey 'Ram,' (Gorakhpur: Geeta Press), XLVI. Also see Saral Jhingran, p. 95.

24. *Rāmāyaṇa*, trans. Makhan Lal Sen (Delhi: Munshiram Manoharlal, 1978). *Uttara Kāṇḍa*, chapter XVI, p. 592.

25. *Manusmṛti, Adhyāya* V, *Ślokas* 153, 166.

26. *Manusmṛti, Adhyāya* IV, *Ślokas* 156–58; *Adhyāya* IX, *Śloka* 75.

27. *Yoga-Vashiṣṭha,* trans. Viharilal Mitra (Delhi: Bharatiya Publishing House, 1976). *Vairāgya Kāṇḍa*, vol. I, ch. XII and XXII, pp. 45ff, 77ff.

28. Mahābhārata, *Śantiparva, Adhāyaya* XXIX, *Ślokas* 58–59.

29. *ṚgVeda, Adhyāya* X, *Śloka* 85, as cited in Saral Jhingran, p. 96.

30. *Manusmṛti, Adhyāya* VIII, *Śloka* 359; *Adhyāya* XI, *Śloka* 191.

31. *Manusmṛti, Adhyāya* VIII, *Ślokas* 359, 364–66.

32. *Āpastamba Dharma Sutra, Adhāyaya* II, 10.21–24, as cited in Saral Jhingran, p. 96.

33. *Āpastamba Dharma Sutra, Adhāyaya* IV, *Śloka* 10.271.1; Yājñavalkyasmṛti, *Śloka* 1.72.

34. *Manusmṛti, Adhyāya* XI, *Śloka* 189.

35. *Manusmṛti, Adhyāya* V, *Śloka* 130;* Yājñavalkyasmṛti, *Śloka*, 71–72.

36. *Manusmṛti, Adhyāya* III, *Śloka* 52; *Adhyāya* IX, *Ślokas* 192–96.

37. *Manusmṛti, Adhyāya* II, *Ślokas* 213–15.

38. *Manusmṛti, Adhyāya* III, *Ślokas* 55–61; *Adhyāya* IX, *Śloka* 95.

39. *Manusmṛti, Adhyāya* IX, *Ślokas* 27–28.

40. *Manusmṛti, Adhyāya* IX, *Ślokas* 72–79; *Apastamba Dharma Sutra, Adhāyaya* I:10.28.19.

41. *Manusmṛti, Adhyāya* II, *Śloka* 145.

42. *Āpastamba Dharma Sutra, Adhāyaya* I:10.28.9.

43. *Manusmṛti, Adhyāya* II, *Śloka* 66.

44. *Manusmṛti, Adhyāya* II, *Śloka* 67.

KATHRYN LOHRE— WOMEN'S INTERFAITH INITIATIVES IN THE UNITED STATES AFTER 9/11

1. More information about this consultation is available on our website, www.pluralism.org, and in Diana Eck's essay, "Dialogue and the Echo Boom of Terror: Religious Women's Voices after 9/11," in *After Terror: Promoting Dialogue among Civilizations*, ed. Akbar Ahmed and Brian Forst (Cambridge: Polity Press, 2005), pp. 21–28.

2. JAM and ALL: JAM Women's Group Profile, http://www.pluralism.org/research/profiles/display.php?profile=74396 (accessed August 24, 2006).

3. JAM & All Website, "Mission Statement," http://jamandall.org/aboutus.html (accessed August 23, 2006).

4. JAM & All Website, http://jamandall.org/activities_post.asp?id=6. (accessed July 20, 2006).

5. Linda Reeves, "Bridging the Gap: Women of All Faiths Erase Mistrust through Friendship and Understanding," *South Florida Sun-Sentinel*, June 27, 2003, Boca Raton edition, http://jamforall.org/archives/event072704.asp (accessed July 19, 2006).

6. Spiritual and Religious Alliance for Hope Profile, http://www.pluralism.org/research/profiles/display.php?profile=74406 (accessed August 23, 2006).

7. SARAH also refers to the wife of Abraham, given that the project was initially begun as an interfaith venture among the "Abrahamic" traditions.

8. Mark Ballon, "Mideast Fighting Strains Fragile Interfaith Ties," *The Jewish Journal of Greater Los Angeles*, August 4, 2006, http://www.jewishjournal.com/home/preview.php?id=16265 (accessed August 23, 2006).

9. Leslie Moriarty, "Women's Group Stirs Culture Together: Participants in an Interfaith Project Discover 'We're More Alike Than We Are Different,'" *The Times of Snohomish County*, December 24, 2003, p. H4.

10. Women Transcending Boundaries Research Report, http://pluralism.org/research/profiles/display.php?profile=74184 (accessed August 23, 2006).

11. Sacred Circles Conferences at the Washington National Cathedral Profile, http://www.pluralism.org/research/profiles/display.php?profile=74416 (accessed August 23, 2006).

12. Sacred Circles Website. Online at http://www.cathedral.org/cathedral/sacredcircles2007/index.shtml (accessed August 24, 2006).

13. Pythia Peay, "Feminism's Spiritual Wave: A New Women's Spiritual Activist Movement That Has Emerged Since September 11 Is Gathering Women across Faiths," *Utne Reader*, June 8, 2006, http://www.feminist.com/resources/artspeech/insp/spiritualwave.html (accessed August 3, 2006).

14. "2 Women, 2 Faiths, 1 Goal: Peace," editorial, *The Enquirer*, August 1, 2006, http://news.enquirer.com/apps/pbcs.dll/article?AID=/20060801/EDIT01/608010370/1090/EDIT (accessed August 23, 2006).

15. *Enquirer,* August 1, 2006.

MARCIA SICHOL—TURNING WAR INSIDE OUT

1. Joshua S. Goldstein, *War and Gender* (Cambridge: Cambridge University Press, 2001), p. 408.

2. Brittain was an English woman studying at Oxford

who left her studies to serve as a nurse in World War I. Her wartime experience would mark her for life. Elshtain, an American, now the Laura Spelman Rockefeller Professor of Ethics at the University of Chicago, co-chairs the recently established Pew Forum on Religion and American Public Life. She was born just as America was entering World War II; the wartime culture seems to have marked her as a woman and an academic. Bourke, born in New Zealand to Christian missionary parents, traveled widely. Bourke is a revisionist historian who is presently professor of history at Birkbeck College, University of London. Her work ranges from social and economic history to the history of the emotions. She says of her work, "Gender has always been a major site of investigation."

3. Jean Bethke Elshtain, *Women and War* (Brighton: Harvester, 1987).

4. Joanna Bourke, *An Intimate History of Killing: Face-to-Face Killing in Twentieth Century Warfare* (London: Granta, 2000).

5. Bourke, p. 14, citing William Broyles, a former Marine and editor of the *Texas Monthly* and *Newsweek*.

6. Immanuel Kant, *Perpetual Peace: A Philosophical Essay,* trans. with introduction and notes by M. Campbell Smith (New York: Garland, 1972), p. 142.

7. Marcia Sichol, *The Making of a Nuclear Peace* (Washington, D.C.: Georgetown University Press, 1990). This is the topic of the final chapter, in which I trace this core value throughout the just-war theories of Walzer, Ramsey, and O'Brien, as well as in the work of the classical just-war theorists.

8. Hannah Arendt, *The Human Condition* (London: University of Chicago Press, 1998), p. 247.

PART 4

MARY ANN BUCKLEY—INCARNATION AND THE ENVIRONMENT

1. Beatrice Bruteau, "Eucharistic Ecology and Ecological Spirituality," http://www.crosscurrents.org/eucharist.htm.

2. Gabriele Uhlein, *Meditations with Hildegard of Bingen* (Santa Fe, NM: Bear & Co., 1983), p. 58.

DIETER HESSEL—ECO-JUSTICE ETHICS

1. John B. Cobb Jr., *Sustainability: Economics, Ecology, and Justice* (Maryknoll, N.Y.: Orbis, 1992).

2. Kusumita Pedersen, "Environmentalism in Interreligious Perspective," in *Explorations in Global Ethics*, ed. Sumner Twiss and Bruce Grelle (Boulder: Westview, 1998), 254.

3. Norman Faramelli, "Ecological Responsibility and Economic Justice," *Andover Newton Quarterly* 11 (November 1970).

4. William E. Gibson, "Eco-Justice: New Perspective for a Time of Turning," in *For Creation's Sake: Preaching, Ecology, and Justice*, ed. D. T. Hessel (Philadelphia: Geneva), 25.

5. William E. Gibson, *Eco-Justice: The Unfinished Journey* (Albany: SUNY Press, 2004).

6. Peter Bakken, Joan Gibb Engel, and J. Ronald Engel, *Ecology, Justice, and Christian Faith: A Critical Guide to the Literature* (Westport: Greenwood, 1995). See the Venn diagram depicting the intersection of these spheres of concern.

7. For a more detailed discussion, see Dieter T. Hessel, "Ecumenical Ethics for Earth Community," in *Theology and Public Policy* 8/1,2 (Summer and Winter 1996): 22.

8. Aaron Sachs, "Upholding Human Rights and Environmental Justice," in *State of the World*, ed. Lester Brown (New York: Norton, 1996), 133-51. Sachs offers a brief international overview. On the relationship between a healthy environment and poverty reduction, see David Reed, *Escaping Poverty's Grasp: The Environmental Foundations of Poverty Reduction* (London: Earthscan Publications, 2006). Jim Schwab, *Deeper Shades of Green: The Rise of Blue-Collar and Minority Environmentalism in America* (San Francisco: Sierra Club Books, 1994) describes the emergence of environmental justice activism in the United States.

9. Gibson, *Eco-Justice*, 34.

10. Norman C. Habel, editor, "Guiding Ecojustice Principles," in *Earth Bible 1: Readings from the Perspectives of the Earth* (Cleveland: Pilgrim Press, 2000), 42–53.

11. Charles Birch, "Creation, Technology, and Human Survival," taped recording, reels 1 and 2 (World Council of Churches Assembly, Nairobi, Kenya, 1975).

12. Dieter T. Hessel, "Becoming a Church for Ecology and Justice," in *The Prophetic Call: Celebrating Community, Earth, Justice, and Peace*, ed. Hugh Sanborn (Saint Louis: Chalice, 2004), 86-90.

13. John Hart, *The Spirit of the Earth: A Theology of the Land* (New York: Paulist, 1984).

14. Wesley Granberg-Michaelson, *Redeeming the Creation* (Geneva: WCC Publications, 1992), 70, 73.

15. Larry Rasmussen, "Sustainable Development and Sustainable Community: Divergent Paths," in *Development Assessed: Ecumenical Reflections and Actions on Development* (Geneva: WCC, 1995), 165-181.

16. Vandana Shiva, *Earth Democracy: Justice, Sustainability, and Peace* (Cambridge: South End, 2005).

17. Ibid., 8.

18. J. Ronald Engel, "The Earth Charter as a New Covenant for Democracy," Religion and Culture Web, 2007.

Part 5

Caitlin Crowley—Pluralism as a Way of Dealing with Religious Diversity

1. Charles Teague, "Freedom of Religion: The Freedom to Draw Circles," in *Religious Traditions and the Limits of Tolerance*, ed. Louis J. Hammann and Harry M. Buck (Chambersburg, Pa.: Anima, 1988), p. 18.

2. Diana L. Eck, *A New Religious America* (San Francisco: HarperCollins, 2001), p. 70.

3. Robert Wuthnow, *America and the Challenges of Religious Diversity* (Princeton: Princeton University Press, 2005), p. 3.

4. Scott W. Gustafson, "The Scandal of Particularity and the Universality of Grace," in Hammann and Buck, pp. 24–25.

5. Louis J. Hammann, "Defining the Boundaries of a Community," in Hammann and Buck, p. 44.

6. Sister Joan Kirby, "Walls, Fences, and Homes for the Homeless," in Hammann and Buck, p. 149.

7. Eck, p. 71.

Roksana Bahramitash—Orientalist Feminism and Islamophobia/Iranophobia

1. Edward Said, *Orientalism* (New York: Vintage, 1978).

2. Frantz Fanon, *Black Skin White Masks* (New York: Grove, 1967), p. 42.

3. Meda Yegenoglu, *Colonial Fantasies: Towards a Feminist Reading of Orientalism* (Cambridge: Cambridge University Press, 1998), p. 47.

4. Parvin Paydar, *Women in the Political Process in Twentieth-Century Iran* (Cambridge: Cambridge University Press, 1995).

5. Bernard Lewis, in Azar Nafisi, *Reading Lolita in Tehran* (New York: Random House, 2003).

6. Hamid Dabbashi, "Native Informers and the Making of the American Empire," *Al-Ahram Weekly*, June 1–7, 2006.

7. Azar Nafisi, *Reading Lolita in Tehran* (New York: Random House, 2003), p. 257.

8. Mehdi Moslem, "The State and Fractional Politics in the Islamic Republic of Iran," in *Twenty Years of Islamic Revolution: Political and Social Transition in Iran since 1979*, ed. Eric Hooglund (New York: Syracuse University Press, 2002), p. 16.

9. Zhaleh Shaditalab, "Women in the Twentieth Century Iran" (paper presented at the Symposium on Women's Struggle for Peace in the Middle East, Concordia University, Montreal, Canada, 2004).

10. Roksana Bahramitash, "Market Fundamentalism versus Religious Fundamentalism," *Critique* 13, no. 1 (Spring 2004): 33–46.

11. Hannah Sampson, "Hate Crimes Rise Here," Council on American-Islamic Relations, Florida chapter (http://www.cair-florida.org/ViewArticle.asp?Code=CM&ArticleID=142).

12. Jeffrey Kaplan, "Islamophobia in America? September 11 and Islamophobic Hate Crime," *Terrorism and Political Violence*, 18:1 (2006): 1–33.

Arvind Sharma—Along a Path Less Traveled

1. Klaus K. Klostermaier, *A Survey of Hinduism* (Albany: State University of New York Press, 1989), p. 144.

2. See M. Hiriyanna, *The Essentials of Indian Philosophy* (London: George Allen and Unwin, 1948), pp. 86, 90.

3. Hiriyanna, pp. 107, 115.

4. William James, *A Pluralistic Universe* (London: Longmans, Green and Co., 1916), p. 322.

5. James, p. 324.

6. Ibid., pp. 7, 8.

7. Ibid., p. 325.

8. Ibid., p. 328.

9. As narrated by T. M. P. Mahadevan, *Outlines of Hinduism* (Bombay: Chetana, 1960), pp. 18–19.

10. Mahadevan, p. 20, the word "God" replaced by "reality."

11. See John Hick, "Religious Pluralism," in *The Encyclopedia of Religion*, ed. Mircea Eliade (New York:

Macmillan Publishing Company, 1987), pp. 12:331–33. However, whereas the pluralism position in these contexts is understood as questioning the "sole possession of reality," this paper questions the assumption that we possess a "sole reality."

12. See Satchidananda Murty, *Revelation and Reason in Advaita Vedānta* (Delhi: Motilal Banarsidass, 1974 reprint), pp. 119–203.

13. Murty, p. 202.

14. Ibid., p. 208, emphasis added.

15. James, p. 361.

ISSA KIRARIRA—RELIGIOUS TOLERANCE AND PEACE-BUILDING IN A WORLD OF DIVERSITY

1. Qur'an 109:2–6.

2. Qur'an 2:17.

3. Qur'an 49:13.

4. Qur'an 6:159.

5. Qur'an 111:103.

6. Hassan Hathout, *Reading the Muslim Mind* (Plainfield, Ind.: American Trust Publications, 1995), p. 141.

7. Qur'an 2:229.

PART 6

MIHAI VALENTIN VLADIMIRESCU—PROMOTION OF INTERRELIGIOUS DIALOGUE

1. William F. Arnt and F. Wilbur Gingrich, eds., *A Greek-English Lexicon of the New Testament and Other Early Christian Literature*, 2nd ed. (Chicago: University of Chicago Press, 1979), p. 185.

2. Acts 10:34–35 (New Revised Standard Version).

3. Mal 1:11.

4. John 4:7–24.

5. Matt 8:5–11.

6. Matt 15:21–28.

7. Cf. Matt 10:23.

8. John 10:16.

9. I Tim 2:4.

10. I Cor 15–18.

11. Stuart Hall, trans., *Gregory of Nyssa: Homilies on the Beatitudes* (Leiden: Brill, 2000), p. 77.

12. Ps 24:1.

13. Exod 19:5–6.

14. Acts 14:17.

GREGORY BAUM—INTERRELIGIOUS DIALOGUE ATTENTIVE TO WESTERN ENLIGHTENMENT

1. Homer A. Jack, ed., *WCRP: A History of the World Conference on Religion and Peace* (New York: Conference on Religion and Peace, 1993), p. 438.

2. Matt 25:40.

3. Rom 13:1–5; Acts 4:19.

4. Luke 11:23; 9:50.

5. Rom 11:17–22.

6. John 8:31–32.

7. Luke 4:18.

8. *Quadragesimo anno*, n. 77.

DAVID A. LESLIE—MOVEMENT AND INSTITUTION

1. 1 Kings 9:6–7a (New Revised Standard Version).

2. Todd Hertz, "Benke Case Closed, but Tensions Remain," *Christianity Today*, Vol. 47, May 21, 2003 (www.christianitytoday.com/ct/2003/mayweb-only/31.0.html).

ARVIND SHARMA—BUDDHISM MEETS HINDUISM

1. Jawaharlal Nehru, *The Discovery of India* (Calcutta: Signet, 1946), p. 178.

2. Lalmani Joshi, *Studies in the Buddhistic Culture of India* (Delhi: Motilal Banarsidass, 1967), p. 386.

3. Ibid., p. 1.

4. Ibid., p. 400.

5. Klaus K. Klostermaier, *A Survey of Hinduism*, 2nd ed. (Albany: State University of New York Press, 1994), p. 58.

6. Ibid., p. 56.

7. Basham, pp. 306–7. He goes on to add: "Until quite recently the temple of Buddha at Gayā was in the hands of Hindus, and the teacher there was worshipped by Hindus as a Hindu god; but in general little attention was paid to the Buddha Avatāra." There is some evidence that more attention was paid to Buddha as an incarnation than might be apparent; see Joshi, pp. 400–401.

8. Joshi, p. 5.

9. Ainslie T. Embree, ed., *Sources of Indian Tradition*, 2nd ed. (New York: Columbia University Press, 1988 [1958]), p. 102.

10. Embree, p. 150.

11. M. Hiriyanna, *The Essentials of Indian Philosophy* (London: George Allen & Unwin, 1949), p. 173.

12. K. N. Jayatilleke, *The Message of the Buddha* (London: George Allen & Unwin, 1975), p. 126.

13. Ibid., pp. 126–27.

14. Axel Michaels, *Hinduism: Past and Present*, trans. Barbara Harshav (Princeton: Princeton University Press, 2004), p. 6.

15. Michaels, p. 211.

16. Dalai Lama, interview in *Organiser*, November 22, 1992, quoted in Koenraad Elst, *Who Is a Hindu?* (Delhi: Voice of India, 2002), p. 233.

FABRICE BLÉE—TOWARD A CULTURE OF PEACE

1. See the World Council of Churches website, http://www.oikoumene.org.

PART 7

NADINE SULTANA D'OSMAN HAN—REDEFINING HUMANITY AND CIVILIZATION

1. This quote is from the motto of the Tehran School of Social Work (1958–79), as quoted in Sattareh Farman Farmaian (with Dona Munken), *Daughter of Persia: A Woman's Journey from Her Father's Harem through the Islamic Revolution* (New York: Crown, 1992). However, the original source for this motto is the "Book of Gulistan," a work of prose, poems, and maxims by Sa'adi, a thirteenth-century Persian poet.

2. Søren Kierkegaard, *The Journals of Soren Kierkegaard*, ed. and trans. Alexander Dru (New York: Oxford University Press, 1938). Søren Aakye Kierkegaard (1813–55) was a Danish philosopher and theologian.

3. This poem appears in Nadine Sultana d'Osman Han, "The Ummah" (unpublished paper, 1993).

ASHOK VOHRA—LESSONS FROM HINDUISM FOR THE WORLD AFTER 9/11

1. London: George Allen and Unwin, 1947, p. 34.

2. K. Satchidananda Murty, *The Indian Spirit* (Waltair: Andhra University Press, 1965), p. 42.

3. *Dighanikayasutt*, i, 235, quoted in S. Radhakrishnan, *The Dhammapada* (London: Oxford University Press, 1966), p. 9.

4. Quoted in *The Dhammapada*, p. 10.

5. *Mahāparinibbana Sutta*, 32, quoted in *The Dhammapada*, p. 11.

6. *The Dhammapada*, p. 15.

7. "Politics and Religion," in *The Writings of Gandhi*, ed. Ronald Duncan (London: Fontana, 1971), p. 125.

8. *Kaṭha Upanishad*, 1.27; *Bhagvata*, IX, xix.

9. *Isha Upanishad*, 1.

10. *Sānyukta Nikāya* (Nalanda: Pali Publication Board, 1.5.6, 1960).

11. *The Anguttara Nikāya* (Nalanda: Pali Publication Board, Vol.13.7.5, 1960).

12. M. K. Gandhi, *From Yarvada Mandir* (Ahmedabad: Navjivan Publishing House, 1945), pp. 15–16.

13. *Harijan*, June 1, 1947.

14. *Radhakrishnan Reader: An Anthology* (Bombay: Bharatiya Vidya Bhavan, 1969), p. 155.

15. *Young India*, August 11, 1920.

16. *Harijan*, March, 30, 1947.

17. Ibid.

18. Ibid.

19. *Harijan*, March 30, 1947.

20. M. K. Gandhi, *Hind Swaraj* (Ahmedabad: Navjivan, 1945), chapter XVI.

21. *Young India*, February 26, 1931.

22. *The Story of My Experiments with Truth* (Ahmedabad: Navjivan Publishing House, 1948), p. 337.

23. Ibid., pp. 165–66.

24. Ibid., p. 166.

25. Ibid., p. 167.

26. Ibid.

27. *Writings of Gandhi*, p. 69.

28. M. K. Gandhi, *Young India*, January 21, 1926.

29. P. B. Annangaracariyar, ed., *Nalayira Tivyapirabantam* (Kanchi: V.N. Tevanathan, 1971).

30. *A Free Translation of Tiruvalmoli of Sathakopa (Ten Parts)*, translated by N. Kurattalvar Aiyengar (Trichinopoly: Vakulabharanam, 1929).

2. Raimundo Panikkar, "Religious Identity and Pluralism," in *A Dome of Many Colors: Studies in Religious Pluralism, Identity, and Unity*, ed. Arvind Sharma and Kathleen M. Dugan (Harrisburg, PA: Trinity Press International, 1999), p. 27.

3. See Douglas Hall, *Bound and Free: A Theologian's Journey* (Minneapolis: Fortress Press, 2005), p. 112.

4. Panikkar, pp. 28–29.

5. Panikkar, p. 26.

31. *The Gospel of Sri Ramakrishna* (Kolkata: Advaita Ashrama, n/d), p. 39.

32. Ibid., p. 40.

33. *Shivajnanacittyar* (Chennai: Shiava Siddhan Kazhkam, 1984).

34. Quoted in Mortimer J. Adler, *Aristotle for Everybody* (New York: Macmillan, 1978), p. 17.

35. Haribhadra, *Shad Darshana Samuccaya*, trans. K. Satchidananda Murty (Delhi: Eastern Book Linkers, 1986), p. 26.

36. S. Radhakrishnan, *A Hindu View of Life* (London: Unwin, 1971), p. 64.

37. *Hind Swaraj*, op. cit., p. 175.

38. *Indian Spirit*, op. cit., p. 231.

39. *Hind Swaraj*, op. cit., p. 175.

40. *Young India*, April 28, 1920.

41. *Young India*, February 1, 1930.

JOANNA MANNING—THIS MAGDALENE MOMENT

1. Jane Schaberg, *The Resurrection of Mary Magdalene: Legends, Apocrypha and the Christian Testament* (New York: Continuum, 2002).

2. Shane Claiborne, *The Irresistible Revolution: Living as an Ordinary Radical* (Grand Rapids: Zondervan, 2006), p. 164.

3. Virginia Woolf, *Three Guineas* (London: Harcourt Brace Jovanovich, 1966), p. 109.

4. Hans Küng, "Address to the Parliament of World Religions at the Signing of the Document *Towards a Global Ethic: An Initial Declaration*" (Chicago, 1993).

5. Ibid.

HUM D. BUI—CAODAI

1. Hum D. Bui, *Cao Dai: Faith of Unity* (Fayetteville, Ark.: Emerald Wave, 2000), pp. 16–18.

2. Ibid., pp. 92–99.

3. Ibid., pp. 32–33.

4. Ibid., p. 39.

5. Gia-Fu Feng and Jane English, *Tao Te Ching* (New York: Vintage, 1997), p. 25.

6. Bhikkhu Bodhi, trans., *The Connected Discourses of the Buddha: A Translation of the Saṃyutta-Nikāya* (Somerville, Mass.: Wisdom Publications, 2000).

7. Bryan W. Van Norden, Confucius: *Analects* 17:19. *Confucius and the Analects: New Essays*, p. 73. (Available at http://books.google.com/books?id=nqb0Fa8Umv4C&pg=PA73&lpg=PA73&dq=Does+Heaven+ever+speak%3F&source=web&ots= 8CUNBvI5np&sig=bt8DBNBIneBy8wKrVBIBMmt3drc&hl=en#PPA73,M1.)

8. Job 26:7. The Holy Bible. New International Version. (Grand Rapids: Zondervan, 1983), p. 393.

9. 1 John 1–3. New International Version, p. 94.

10. Heather Couper and Nigel Henbest, *Big Bang* (New York: DK Publishing, 1997), p. 10.

11. Fritjof Capra, *The Tao of Physics* (New York: Bantam, 1984), p. 209.

12. Ibid., pp. 201–2.

VINESH SAXENA—RELIGION, FUNDAMENTAL QUESTIONS, AND HUMAN SOCIETY

1. "Welcome to the Vinesh Saxena Family Foundation," Vinesh Saxena Family Foundation, www.vsffoundation.ca.

MABEL ARANHA—BEYOND RELIGION

1. Wilkie Au, *By Way of the Heart: Toward a Holistic Christian Spirituality* (Mahwah, N.J.: Paulist, 1991), p. 3.

GLOSSARY

A

Abraham: considered as father of the people of Israel, in the religious traditions of Judaism, Christianity, and Islam.

Ad bellum: regarding the justification of war, as in *jus ad bellum*, Latin for "rules of going to war."

Ahimsa: a rule of conduct to do no harm (avoiding violence) in the religious traditions of Hinduism, Buddhism, and especially Jainism.

Al Qaeda (al-Qaeda): a militant Islamist group founded in the late 1980s.

Al-Ghafur: one of many Islamic names of God, meaning "the all-forgiving."

Al-Haqq: one of many Islamic names of God, meaning "the truth, the real."

Anti-Semitism: having a prejudice or hostility towards Jewish people.

Apartheid: a system of legal racial segregation, derived and associated with its practice in South Africa from 1948–1994, but used for other examples of legalized segregation.

Asceticism: a lifestyle in which one abstains from worldly concerns to instead pursue religious or spiritual goals; often associated with monastic life.

Atheism: non-belief in the existence of deities (gods).

Axial Age: term coined by German philosopher Karl Jaspers to describe the period between 800 and 200 B.C.E., which saw the appearance of a large number of great religious figures throughout the world (including authors of the Upanishads, the Buddha, Elijah, Isaiah, Jeremiah, Mahavir, Confucius, Lao Tzu, Homer, Socrates, and Zarathustra).

B

Bible: sacred scripture for Christianity, containing both the Old and New Testaments. *See also* Hebrew Bible.

Buddha: born as Siddartha Gautama, this spiritual leader lived in India during the sixth and fifth centuries B.C.E. and was the founder of Buddhism. "Buddha" means "enlightened one."

C

Casuistry: used in legal and ethical discussions, this refers to case-based reasoning (compared to principle- or rule-based reasoning).

Celibacy: a lifestyle of abstaining from all sexual activity.

Chastity: a condition of observing moral norms and guidelines that designate proper sexual activity in a given culture, civilization, or religious tradition.

Clash of civilizations, theory of: developed by the political scientist Samuel P. Huntington in the early 1990s, this theory posits that peoples' cultural and religious identities will be the primary source of conflict in the new world order.

Cloning: a biological process of producing genetically identical organisms.

Colonialism: largely occurring from the fifteenth to twentieth centuries C.E., this process refers to one people's extending sovereignty over another people's territory, where the colonizing power establishes unequal relations between it and the indigenous population.

Communitarianism: a philosophical position that argues that individuals are shaped by the culture and values of their communities, and that individual rights must be balanced with community interests as a whole.

D

Diaspora: a scattering or dispersion, or movement or migration of a people, often associated with the exile of the Jewish people outside of the land of Israel.

E

Ecclesiology: the theological study of church, especially in Christianity, regarding the church's doctrine, role in salvation and relationship to Christ.

Empiricism: a theory of knowledge that argues that what we know comes through evidence based on sense perceptions.

Enlightenment, The: a philosophical era, largely occurring in Europe, spanning the seventeenth and eighteenth centuries C.E., known for its intellectual, scientific, and cultural life based on valuing reason as the source of knowledge, legitimacy, and authority.

Ethics: a branch of philosophy that concerns morality.

Evangelism: teaching or preaching of one's beliefs to others who do not hold those beliefs, often associated with the preaching of the Christian faith.

F

Faith: a strong belief or trust in a supernatural power, or a person, concept, or thing.

Fanaticism: uncritical belief, especially zealous belief, in a religious or political cause.

Feminism: a set of philosophical, political, cultural, and economic positions and movements that aim to establish greater rights and legal protection for women.

Fundamentalism: strict adherence to key, sometimes narrowly-defined, principles and beliefs, especially within religious groups.

G

Globalization: a process where local and regional economies, political systems, societies, and cultures become integrated with global networks of communication, trade, and transportation.

Golden Rule: an ethical code or moral dictate, derived from numerous historical civilizations, which generally requires that one treat others as one would wish to be treated oneself.

Good Samaritan: a Christian parable, from the Gospel of Luke (10:25-37) in the New Testament, which is told to encourage moral behavior of treating strangers, even those whom are despised, with charity and mercy.

H

Hebrew Bible: the sacred scriptures of Judaism, including the Torah, the Prophets, and the Writings (Tanakh), but not identical to the Old Testament. *See also* Bible.

Hermeneutics: the study, art, or practice of interpretation, especially of written texts.

Holocaust: the systematic murder (genocide) of six million Jews and millions of other religious and political opponents throughout Europe by the Nazi government of Germany during World War II.

Humanism: a philosophical approach that centers on human values and concerns, sometimes criticized for positing a universal human nature.

I

Ideology: a comprehensive vision of understanding the world and achieving express goals, sometimes criticized for being doctrinaire and dominating in a political culture or system.

Intelligent design: a recent argument that states that existence is explained by an intelligent cause as opposed to chance or theories of natural selection.

Interfaith/intrafaith dialogue: cooperative and positive collaboration and discussion either among different religious traditions (i.e. interfaith) or within a single religious tradition (i.e. intrafaith).

Islamophobia: prejudice against or fear of Islam and Muslims.

J

Jihad: the concept of "struggle" in Islam, which describes Muslims' struggle against both inner forces that prevent God-realization and outer barriers to establishing the divine order.

Just war: a doctrine of military ethics, notably derived from Roman Catholic theology, which specifies criteria for determining the justice of going to war and justice in war.

K

Karma: the concept of "action", it describes for Hinduism, Buddhism, and Jainism individual actions and their effects on this life and other lives to come.

Koran (Qur'an): sacred scripture of Islam.

Kyoto Declaration of 1970: a statement from the World Conference on Religion and Peace held in Kyoto, Japan, which specified responsibilities of the world's religions to promoting global peace.

Kyoto Protocol: an international agreement, adopted in 1997 in Kyoto, Japan, which committed signatory nation-states to reduce causes of global warming. Over 180 nation-states have signed and ratified the Protocol (as of 2009).

L

Liberalism: generally used to describe an Englightenment philosophy that advocates on behalf of individual liberty, liberal democracy, capitalism, free trade, and the separation of church and state.

M

Manichean: used to describe a general struggle between good (that which is spiritual) and evil (that which is material).

Materialism: a philosophical theory that understands matter as the only real substance, in contrast to theories of idealism or spiritualism.

Messianism: a religious belief in a messiah, or savior or redeemer.

Modernity: the era of post-traditional, post-medieval social organization, beyond feudal institutions toward capitalism, industrialization, secularization, and the rise of the nation-state.

Monotheism: belief in one god (for example, Judaism, Christianity, Islam).

Muhammad (Mohammed): founder of Islam.

N

Nag Hammadi: city in Egypt where fourth century C.E. papyrus writings were found in 1945, which included non-canonical Gnostic gospels, such as the Gospel of Thomas.

Natural law: those principles or "laws" that are arguably set by nature and are thus universally applicable and are understood by the use of reason in analyzing human behavior. Natural law may be contrasted with positive law, or those laws that are man-made.

Neocolonialism: a critique in the post–World War II world of new and continued dependence of former colonies, which are now sovereign nation-states, upon former colonial powers and the global capitalist system.

O

Orthodox Judaism: a strain in Judaism that observes strict interpretation and adherence to laws and ethical principles as found in Talmudic texts.

P

Pacifism: a philosophical (and practical) opposition to war and violence.

Pluralism: generally understood to recognize and value the diversity of persons and religious traditions, according each its due rights and social and cultural space.

Polygamy: a form of marriage in which a person has more than one spouse.

Polytheism: belief in more than one god.

Q

Qur'an (Koran): sacred scripture of Islam.

R

Rights: legal, social, or moral principles that specify what is allowed or owed to persons or groups.

S

Sacred: realm of the supernatural, beyond everyday perceptions; that which is holy.

Self-determination: international legal principle that extends the right of sovereignty to nation-states, to be free from external interference.

September 11 attacks: a series of suicide attacks by members of al-Qaeda upon the United States on September 11, 2001. The two most serious attacks took place in New York City (destruction of the World Trade Center) and near Washington, D.C. (partial destruction of the Pentagon in Virginia).

Spirituality: personal response to those parts of life that are considered sacred.

T

Taliban: a Sunni Islamist political movement that formally governed Afghanistan from 1996–2001. It now acts as a political insurgency in the region.

Terrorism: a systematic use of terror in order to coerce persons or groups.

Theology: the study of God, especially of religious faith and practice.

U

Upanishads: together with the Vedas, these constitute sacred scriptures of Hinduism.

V

Vedas: a set of four canonical texts that constitute the oldest of sacred scriptures of Hinduism.

Y

Yin-yang: a concept of Chinese philosophy, reflecting how polar or contradictory forces exist and interact in the natural world.

Z

Zionism: a nationalist Jewish movement, founded by Theodor Herzl in the late nineteenth century C.E., that advocates self-determination for the Jewish people and the establishment of a sovereign Jewish nation-state.

INDEX

9/11, 3-4, 5, 7, 9-12, 161-167, 178,
    252, 275, 298, 310, 322, 323.
    See also September 11 attacks

A

Abraham, 16, 21-22, 58-60, 64, 71,
    205, 274
Abrahamic tradition, 16, 184, 198,
    275
Absolutism, 68, 254
Ad bellum norms, 28-31
Adultery, 156, 209
Afghanistan, 31, 33, 59, 150, 194,
    197, 204, 210, 278-279, 284
Africa, 10, 33, 61, 73, 118, 138-139,
    142, 169, 178, 194, 228, 231,
    267, 274, 278-279, 285-286,
    296, 312, 314
Afterlife, 191
Agriculture, 178-180, 183
Ahimsa, 68, 77
AIDS, 286, 303, 312, 314
Al Jazeera, 289-290
Al Qaeda, 49, 94, 242
Al-Ghafur, 69
Al-Haqq, 64
America, 30-32, 59-62, 66-67,
    103, 105, 107, 119, 138-139,
    149-151, 162-163, 185, 191,

194-197, 227, 243, 246, 248-
    249, 274-278
Analects (Confucius), 76, 84, 108
Anti-Semitism, 5, 61
Apartheid, 142, 228, 231
Arab/s, 7, 10, 18-20, 57-58, 60-61,
    65, 68, 90, 94, 194, 196, 278,
    281, 290
Asceticism, 11, 145, 147
Atheism, 7, 48, 226
Axial Age, 203-204

B

Babri Mosque, 275
Baghdad Religious Accord, 231
Baha'i, 76-79, 115-117, 206, 210,
    280, 321
Bahá'u'lláh, 76, 78, 115-116
Balfour Declaration, 61
Bangladesh, 94, 250
Basham, A.L., 99, 237-238
Belief, 4-6, 10, 21-22, 27-29, 31,
    34, 40, 43-44, 48, 51, 76-77,
    89-93, 95-96, 106-107, 111-
    112, 114, 116, 119, 122, 124,
    126, 136, 139-140, 142, 167,
    177, 179, 191-192, 206-211,
    215-217, 219, 297, 333-336
Benedict XVI, Pope, 228

Bhagavadgita, 1, 23-26, 67, 76-77,
    100, 249, 303-309
Bhakti, 262-264, 306,
Bible, 66, 84, 121,131-132, 184, 205,
    209, 216, 218, 220, 228, 245,
    248, 275, 282, 312
Bill of Rights, U.S., 138
bin Laden, Osama, 63, 210, 275, 278
Blind men and the elephant, parable
    of, 200-202
Buddha, 33, 37, 39, 66, 79, 84-85,
    115, 146, 199-201, 204, 235-
    239, 296-297, 315
Buddhism, xi, 5, 7, 33, 59, 83, 85, 87,
    101, 145-148, 151, 189, 206,
    234-240, 242, 248, 260, 273,
    287, 296, 315-316, 321-322
Bush, George W., 30, 151, 175

C

CaoDai, 192-193, 315-317
Capital punishment, 38, 134, 156
Capitalism, ix, 11, 61, 151, 242,
    312-313
Caste system, 100, 146-148, 160,
    186, 262-263
Casuistry, 29, 168
Catholicism, 68, 275
Celibacy, 148, 157

Chastity, 156

Checks and balances, 47, 80

Children, 15, 31, 39-40, 60, 62, 66, 77, 85, 109, 120-135, 139, 151, 154-155, 157, 163, 184, 210, 220, 263, 267-270, 272, 274, 279, 281, 285, 289, 294, 306, 314, 319-320, 324, 326-327, 329

China, xi, 10, 91, 94, 103-108, 150, 152, 169, 273

Christ. *See* Jesus Christ

Christian Zionists, 282

Christian/Christianity, xi, 3, 5-9, 11, 14, 16, 19, 20, 22, 27-28, 30-33, 51, 56-68, 70-71, 79, 83-85, 87, 91, 94, 96, 103, 111, 116, 119-124, 129, 132, 139, 142, 145-151, 161-165, 167, 171, 179, 182, 189, 191, 198, 205-208, 210, 216-220, 222-228, 232, 241-250, 252-253, 255, 265, 271, 272, 274-283, 285, 287-290, 292, 297, 300, 310-316, 323, 325

Civil laws, 119, 124

Civil Rights, 38, 74, 141-142, 169, 226, 231

Civil unions, 126, 129-130, 133

Clash of civilizations, theory of, 90, 241

Cloning, 128

Colonial/ism, 33, 48, 58, 60-61, 137-138, 149-151, 194-196, 222, 227, 242, 282-283, 292

Common ground, 41, 65, 164, 218, 312, 314, 318, 320

Common law unions, 121

Communism, 10, 33, 44, 242, 313

Communitarianism, 114, 179-180

Community, 14-16, 18-20, 37-39, 41, 47-48, 64, 69, 95, 105-106, 108, 111, 113-114, 118, 120, 126, 131, 134, 137-138, 139-140, 142, 161, 164, 171, 178-180, 182-187, 205, 208, 210-211, 216-219, 225-226, 230-233, 246-248, 254, 260, 262-263   269-270, 2828, 286, 288-293, 295, 306, 311, 313, 318

Compassion, 18-20, 29, 35, 40, 66, 76, 85, 87-88, 135, 143, 163, 176-177, 203-205, 207, 219, 237, 260, 265, 270-271, 299, 307, 314, 317, 319-320, 324-325, 327

Conflict, xi, 1, 10-11, 13-20, 22, 26, 39, 43, 48-49, 51, 60-63, 65, 67, 69, 70-79, 86, 99, 107, 112, 116, 125-126, 136, 148, 150, 152, 161, 167, 169, 200, 206-210, 215, 221-222, 225-226, 228-229, 235, 243, 251-255, 261, 267, 269, 274, 285, 287, 296-297, 300, 307, 315, 318-319, 325-326

Confucian/Confucianism, xi, 6, 8, 70-71, 77-79, 84, 91, 97, 102-114, 145-150, 185, 189, 206, 274, 278, 315

Conscience, 111-112, 138, 140, 260, 265-266, 303

Constitution, U.S., 91, 138, 141, 160, 290

Conversion, 150, 218, 228, 290, 311, 313

Corpus Juris Canonici, 27

Covenant on Civil and Political Rights, 140

D

Dalai Lama, 6-7, 9, 234, 240, 245, 285

Dalits, 139-140

Daoism (Taoism), xi, 145-146, 189, 206, 274, 315, 321

De Jure Belli ac Pacis (Grotius), 27

Declaration of Human Rights, United Nations (U.N.), 86, 92, 102, 110, 115-117, 136, 138-141

Democracy, 4-11, 89-93, 113, 122, 141, 173, 186, 197, 208, 266, 277

Dewey, John, 104-109

Dharma (*dhamma*), 26, 40, 87, 100, 153, 155, 236, 260, 296, 304-306, 309, 319

Dialogue, xi, 4, 9, 11, 14, 16, 18, 22-24, 57-58, 60-61, 65, 67, 79, 95, 161-166, 169, 192, 211, 213-255, 275-277, 299, 302, 314, 317, 320

Diaspora, 56, 241

Dissent, 8, 54, 136, 138, 150, 207, 226

Diversity, ix, xi, 16, 77, 96, 115, 123-124, 134, 163, 189, 191, 207, 209, 215-216, 218, 265, 269, 288, 300, 311-312, 314, 320

Divorce, 57, 120, 124, 131, 145, 148, 192, 283

Domination, 140, 194, 211, 225-227

Drugs, 268, 287, 328

Duties, 27, 29, 84, 87, 111-114, 117, 139, 146, 153-155, 157, 216

E

Eastern Orthodoxy, 6

Ecclesiology/ies, 3, 8, 10-11

Eck, Diana, 192-193

Economics, x, 3, 8, 15, 29, 44-46, 50-51, 72, 78, 103-104, 107-110, 113, 137-138, 140, 142, 148, 150, 159, 171, 182-187, 216, 227-228, 261-262, 266-267, 303, 306, 308, 313

Education, 44-45, 49, 86, 92, 103-109, 114, 117, 129, 138, 141, 145, 147-148, 150, 157, 162, 184, 196, 208, 209, 216, 255, 260, 263, 269, 312, 318-320

Egypt, 60, 149, 194, 204, 206, 242, 278-279

Empiricism, 200-201

Enlightenment, The, x, 11, 108, 116, 222-229, 246

Environment, xi, 45, 59, 105, 123, 171, 182, 184-186, 230, 266, 268, 313

Equal marriage, 118-119

Ethics, 5, 28, 32, 72, 87, 101, 108, 110, 113, 127, 132-134, 136-137, 182-187, 221, 247-248, 255, 268

European Union, 6, 281

Evangelism, 216, 219

Evil, x-xi, 9, 15, 21, 24, 26, 33-34, 55, 62, 73, 84, 101, 142, 145, 196, 207, 211, 220, 222-223, 225,

231, 236, 268-269, 271-272, 274, 298, 305, 316
Evolution, theory of, 242, 309
Executions, 93-94
Exploitation, 44, 153, 184, 187, 225, 227, 266-267, 269, 324, 326
Extremism, 15, 60, 63, 67, 117, 275

F

Faith, 4-10, 19, 33, 35, 43, 55, 56, 67, 116, 118-119, 121, 123, 133, 136, 139-140, 162-165, 167, 183, 185, 191-193, 208-210, 217-220, 224-225, 227-228, 230-233, 241, 244, 248, 252-255, 261, 263, 284-285, 287-291, 296, 303-304, 306-307, 309, 310, 315, 317, 321, 333
Families, 31, 45, 83, 120, 126, 129, 131, 135, 148, 169, 207, 223, 281
Fanaticism, x, 4, 8-9, 46, 57, 76, 116-117, 200
Farmers, 178, 262, 268
Female deities, 153
Feminine, the, 145, 228, 310-311, 319-320
Feminism, 150-151, 195, 281
Force, ix-xii, 1, 15, 28-31, 39, 47-49, 55-56, 62, 75, 77, 79-80, 231, 252, 272
Forgiveness, 69, 90, 210, 228, 272, 319-320
Freedom, xii, 25, 34-35, 43, 47, 75, 84, 86, 96, 104, 112-114, 120, 122-124, 131, 134, 138-142, 148, 150, 156, 191, 207-209, 211, 254, 290, 318, 329
Freedom, religious, 84, 120, 123, 138, 140-142, 208-209, 211
Fundamentalism (fundamentalist), x, 15, 62-63, 66-68, 90, 119, 131, 145, 149-151, 175, 184, 194, 241-250, 253, 257, 259, 270, 274-277, 280-282, 306, 312, 322

G

Gandhi, Mahatma, 23-26, 37, 43, 67, 73, 142, 169, 199, 204, 243, 249, 297-299, 302

Garden of Forgiveness, 69
Gays, 93, 118, 123-124, 130, 132, 134
Gender, xi, 58, 126, 140, 151, 167-169, 186, 209, 266
Globalization, ix, 8, 11, 19, 221, 259, 261, 269
God, 4, 15-17, 21, 27, 32-34, 39-40, 46-47, 49, 53, 57-58, 62, 64, 68-69, 73, 76-78, 83, 85, 95, 111, 115, 117, 122, 133, 139, 140, 146-149, 156, 167, 174-177, 179, 181, 184, 192, 198-199, 201, 203-206, 208-209, 211, 216-220, 223-227, 232, 237, 239, 245, 247, 252, 254, 259-260, 263-266, 273-276, 279-280, 294, 297, 299-300, 306-307, 312-316, 318-322
Golden Rule, 8, 63, 70-75, 84-87, 135, 203-204, 315-316, 319-320
Good and evil, 9, 21, 24, 145, 225, 236, 305
Good Samaritan, 76, 87
Government, 6, 8, 28, 43, 45, 50, 57, 59, 61-62, 68, 72, 89-93, 103, 106-107, 113, 117, 118, 120, 124, 127, 138-139, 142, 150, 162, 164, 183-187, 208, 211, 216, 226, 228, 230, 247, 267, 269, 278-279, 281, 285, 311-319

H

Hamas, 17, 57
Hanh, Thich Nhat, 73
Hare Krishna movement, 321
Hebrew Bible, 205, 218
Hermeneutics, 30-32, 49, 225, 244, 249
Hezbollah, 279
Hinduism, xi, 7, 59, 72, 76, 83, 101, 143, 145-146, 148, 150, 153, 189, 198, 206, 234-240, 242, 248-249, 273, 276-277, 280-281, 284, 286-287, 289, 291, 294-295, 296-297, 300, 302, 315, 319, 321-322
Holocaust, 33, 56-57, 60, 66, 223, 225
Holy Land, 13, 17, 19-20, 282

Human nature, 8, 32, 220, 271
Human rights, xi, 6, 18, 27, 29-30, 61-62, 78-79, 81, 83-88, 89-94, 97-101, 102-114-142, 171, 182, 208-209, 216, 231, 267
Humanism, 105, 108, 110

I

Identity, 10, 14-16, 17, 20, 62, 66, 71, 85, 122, 127-129, 154, 159, 161, 163, 219, 221, 224, 252, 254, 281, 319
Ideology, ix, 48-50, 59, 63, 102, 110, 140, 161, 192, 194, 224-226, 228, 266, 278, 297-298
India, 26, 33, 35, 37-38, 39-41, 48, 52, 60, 73-74, 92, 98-101, 139-142, 147, 149-150, 152-153, 169, 174-176, 192, 194, 199, 200-201, 208, 234-240, 259, 262, 278, 281, 286, 289-293, 297, 301, 304, 308, 319
Indic tradition, 249, 260
Injustice, 28, 54, 78, 107, 158, 160, 183-184, 224-225, 228, 242, 266, 268, 272, 304-306
Innocence, 31, 244
Intelligent design, 175-176
Interfaith dialogue, 163, 241, 243, 245-246, 250
Interracial marriage, 122
Intolerance, 4, 46, 142, 191, 211, 216, 317
Intrafaith dialogue, 245, 248
Iran, 48, 50, 57, 67, 92-94, 119, 134, 150, 195-197, 273, 278-279, 282-283
Iranian Revolution, ix, 275, 278
Iraq, 10, 30-31, 33, 59, 61, 103, 164, 173, 194, 196-197, 204, 222, 227, 231, 247, 277-279, 284-285
Islam, xi, 3, 5-8, 10-11, 19, 22, 33, 43, 45-51, 53-55, 59, 64-66, 68-69, 72, 83-84, 87-91, 93-94, 96, 116, 145-151, 171, 189, 196, 198, 204, 206-211, 242, 248, 250, 265, 268, 270, 272, 274-279, 280-282, 286-290, 292, 295, 297, 312, 315, 321-322. *See also* Muslims

Islamophobia, 3, 194-197, 275-276
Israel, 15, 17-20, 56-58, 60-63,
    66-68, 163, 217, 220, 223,
    231-232, 242-243, 267, 279,
    281-282

J
Jainism, 9, 33, 35, 37, 84, 101, 145-
    146, 148, 206, 296, 321
Jesus Christ, 96, 121-122, 139, 215,
    224, 271, 309
Jewish-Christian dialogue, 61
Jewish-Muslim relations,60, 281
Jews. See Judaism
Jihad, 5, 40, 46-49, 55, 278, 286
John Paul II, Pope, 13, 31, 185
John XXIII, Pope, 29
Judaism, xi, 6-8, 14, 17-18, 21, 33,
    56, 58-62, 65-66, 83-84, 116,
    145-151, 162, 185, 189, 198,
    204, 206, 216, 223, 242, 248,
    250, 274-275, 277-278, 280-
    282, 297, 315-316, 321-322
Just war (*justum bellum*), 1, 27-32,
    40, 67, 76, 78-79, 98, 100,
    167-169, 227, 247
Justice, xii, 11, 14, 29, 32, 43, 54, 60,
    63-64, 66, 68-69, 76-79, 88,
    100, 112, 116-117, 141, 143,
    150, 156, 173-174, 182-187,
    192, 211, 216, 219, 222-224,
    226, 228-229, 242, 254, 260-
    261, 264-266, 269-272, 283,
    292, 302, 304-305, 310, 314-
    315, 320

K
Karma, 35, 146, 305
King,Martin Luther, Jr., 31, 73, 231
Koran. *See* Qur'an
Kyoto Declaration of 1970, 222
Kyoto Protocol, 230

L
Lebanon, 33, 57-58, 60, 62, 64-65,
    69, 89, 163, 279, 285
Liberalism, 4, 7-8, 10, 67, 247
Love, 4, 6, 14, 19, 21-22, 28-32, 35,
    50, 58, 61, 72-73, 76-79, 84-85,
    87-88, 90, 116, 120, 131, 134,

139, 157, 165, 179-180, 192,
    204-205, 207, 210, 211, 215,
    217-220, 222-224, 226, 228,
    243-244, 250, 254-255, 259-
    261, 263, 297, 299, 305, 307,
    313-314, 315-320, 324-329

M
Mahabharata, 24-26, 84, 99-100, 304
Mahavira, 33, 37, 39-41, 199, 309
Mahdiism, 279
Maithuna, 36, 38
Mandela, Nelson, 44, 169
Manichean worldview, 15-16
Marriage, 81, 94, 118-135, 145, 147-
    151, 155-158, 196, 209, 231,
    243, 269, 288
Marxism, 150, 199
Mary, Mother of Jesus, 312, 319
Mary Magdalene, 310-314
Materialism, 41, 48, 78, 151, 199,
    315
Media, ix, 13, 27-28, 45, 49, 51, 59,
    65, 162, 166, 175-176, 187,
    211, 274-275, 284-295
Meditation, 5, 7, 37, 165, 304-305,
    319, 325-329
Mencius, 70-71, 106, 108, 112
Messianism, 277, 279
Metaphysics, 28, 110-112
Middle East, 1, 10, 16, 22, 50, 56-59,
    61, 63-65, 75, 90, 94, 109,
    164-165, 194, 217, 233, 243,
    267, 284, 303, 312, 322
Mindfulness, 73, 319
Missionaries, 39, 59-60, 106, 150,
    292
Modernity, ix-x, 11, 27-28, 31, 50,
    61-62, 174, 242, 281
Modernization, 50, 103-107, 145,
    149-150, 259
Monasticism, 145
Monotheism, xi, 68, 201
Morality, 38, 45, 49, 70, 72, 87-88,
    106, 129, 136-137, 152-154,
    160, 192, 265, 269, 323
Mormon/ism, 122, 206, 321
Muhammad, 31, 39
Muhammad (Mohammed), 10,
    22, 47, 49, 84, 90, 96, 115,

150-151, 204, 207, 265, 271,
    275, 293
Muslim-Christian relations, 60, 282
Muslim-Jewish relations, 57, 60, 282
Muslims. *See also* Islam
Mysticism, 5

N
Nag Hammadi, 311
Nationalism, 45, 50, 150, 242
Natural Law, 27-29, 32, 111, 133,
    305, 309, 318
Neocolonialism, 150-151
Neoconservatism, 150, 194-195, 197
New Testament, 77-78, 147, 149,
    151, 216-217, 224, 243, 249
Nonviolence, xi, 24-26, 38, 41, 68,
    73-74, 77, 101, 204, 227, 298,
    302, 319
Nuclear war, 168, 303

O
Old Testament, 121, 139, 223, 282
Oppression, 14, 54, 79, 93, 141, 150,
    195-196, 210, 225, 227, 266,
    269
Orthodox Judaism, 149, 242
Osama bin Laden. See bin Laden,
    Osama.

P
Pacificism, 1, 9, 31, 98, 167
Palestinians, 17-19, 57-58, 61-63,
    66-68, 71, 243, 267, 279, 281
Parliament of the World's Religions,
    89, 116, 118, 122, 173, 222,
    234, 246, 251, 281, 286
People's Republic of China, 104
Pius XII, Pope, 275-276
Pluralism, x-xi, 31, 90, 151, 161-
    163, 191-193, 199-202, 213,
    222, 226, 248, 250, 253, 286,
    310-313
Politics, 3-4, 10, 31, 57, 108, 141,
    151, 153, 173, 185, 187, 194,
    208, 251-252, 255, 276
Polygamy, 121-122, 148, 156-157,
    195-196
Polytheism, 198, 201

Pope Benedict XVI. *See* Benedict XVI, Pope.
Pope John Paul II. *See* John Paul II, Pope.
Pope Pius XII. *See* Pius XII, Pope.
Postmodern/ism, 27, 65-66
Poverty, 44, 48-49, 61, 77-78, 132, 151, 182, 185-186, 261, 267, 289, 305, 313, 319
Pragmatism, 104, 111

Q

Qur'an, 22, 46-48, 50, 53-55, 76-79, 146, 207, 209, 272, 279, 283

R

Religious freedom, 84, 120, 123, 130, 138, 140-142, 208-209, 211
Rights,xi, 6, 18, 20, 27, 29-30, 38, 47, 54-55, 61-62, 74, 78-79, 81, 83-94, 97-99, 101-142, 148-151, 156-160, 169, 171, 173, 182, 184, 191, 194-197, 208-209, 211, 216, 226, 230-231, 247, 266-267, 290, 292, 312
Rituals, 147, 152-154, 158, 164, 192, 261-262, 296
Roman Catholic Church, 29, 122, 134, 139, 178, 185, 206, 248, 281, 310

S

Sacred, 38, 40, 46, 54, 62, 65, 66, 99, 116, 121, 132, 134, 147, 151, 165, 206, 223-226, 231-233, 242, 247, 253, 262-263, 291, 310-311, 313, 324-325
Salvation, 26, 191-192, 199, 219, 231, 253-254, 268, 298, 306-307
Same-sex marriage, 81, 118, 120-127, 129-134, 243
Science, 5, 10-11, 48, 71, 104, 122, 128, 131, 173-177, 185, 246-247, 259-260, 262, 268, 283, 301, 303, 316
Secularization, ix-x, 11, 149, 227, 276, 278
Self-determination, 61, 71, 109, 137-138

Separation of church and state, 3, 6, 10, 141
September 11 attacks, x-xi, 3, 17, 31-33, 46, 57, 59, 69, 83, 98, 117, 134, 162-164, 173, 178, 194, 207, 211, 215, 222, 232, 241, 259, 273-282, 284, 289-290, 303
Sexuality, 118-119, 129. *See also* AIDS
Shiism (Shiite, Shi'ite), 50, 189, 206, 279, 285
Spirituality,xi-xii, 5, 7, 95, 118, 163, 165, 179, 251-255, 257, 260-261, 265-266, 269-271, 303, 306-307, 310, 312-314, 324-325
Sufism, 278-279, 286
Sunni, 189, 206

T

Taliban, 33, 49, 150, 194-195, 197, 272, 278
Talmud, 17, 84
Taoism. *See* Daoism.
Technology, 36-37, 49, 104, 127, 129, 132, 183, 185-186, 247, 259-260, 303, 319
Terrorism, 10, 43-44, 46, 50-52, 59, 61, 63, 69, 75, 78, 90-91, 93, 98, 194, 211, 298, 303, 313
Theology, 3, 7, 9-11, 39, 49, 58, 68, 111, 167, 192, 206, 208, 220, 245, 248-249, 278, 287, 300, 311
Theory of evolution, 242, 309
Tolerance, 4, 8, 46, 50, 89, 111-112, 116, 141, 191-192, 207, 209-211, 215-216, 232, 236, 243, 250, 253, 260-261, 265-266, 270-271, 289, 294, 325
Torah, 17, 21-22, 66, 71, 204, 243, 283
Torture, 4-5, 8, 11, 30, 43, 62, 83, 91, 222, 226, 245, 268-269
Transhumanism, 132

U

UNESCO, 44, 305
United Nations, 61, 79, 86, 91, 93, 102-103, 126, 134, 136-139,

142, 173, 184-186, 269, 281, 305
United States, 30, 59, 62-65, 67-68, 81, 91, 103-104, 117, 126, 138-142, 149, 151, 161-166, 169, 173, 175, 185, 194, 197, 224, 227, 230-231, 242-243, 245, 250, 268, 273-276, 278-279, 281, 286-287, 289, 310, 312
Universal Declaration of Human Rights (UDHR), 86, 92, 102, 110, 115-117, 136, 138-141
Universality, 29, 139, 279
Upanishads, 72, 238, 281, 283

V

Vedas, 98, 152, 155-156, 236-239, 261, 281, 283, 296, 304, 306, 309
Virtues, 31, 76, 78, 97, 153, 177, 252, 300

W

War, xi, 1, 3-4, 7-8, 10, 24-33, 37, 40, 43, 46, 49, 55, 57-60, 62-64, 67, 70, 75-79, 83, 89, 91, 97-101, 103, 108, 138, 151, 162, 164, 167-170, 173, 194-197, 207, 210, 218, 225, 227, 233, 243, 247, 249, 254, 267-270, 274-276, 278-279, 281, 285, 296-297, 303-306, 308, 312-314, 318
Women, 25, 57, 61-62, 79, 84, 90-91, 93-95, 116, 126, 128, 133, 136, 139, 143-171, 179, 180, 183-184, 194-197, 206, 222, 224, 227-228, 242, 250, 260, 263, 281, 287, 289, 297, 306, 310-314, 319-320

Y

Yin-yang, 146
Yoga, 25-26, 305, 308

Z

Zionism, 56, 60, 62, 242, 282
Zoroastrianism, 84